Handbook for British and Irish Archaeology

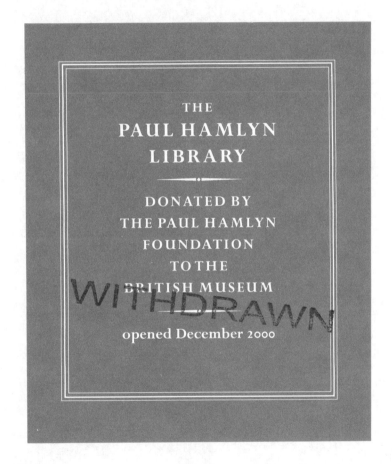

Handbook for British and Irish Archaeology
Sources and Resources

COMPILED BY

Cherry Lavell

Edinburgh University Press

In loving memory of Dorothy Lavell, 1892–1986, best of mothers

© Cherry Lavell, 1997

Edinburgh University Press
22 George Square, Edinburgh

Typeset in Sabon
by Bibliocraft, Dundee, and
printed and bound in Great Britain

A CIP record for this book is available from the British Library

ISBN 0 7486 0764 1

'Archaeologists themselves, whether practical or academic, can only claim detailed knowledge of very small parts of the subject: most of the time they are in the same position as the interested layman.' (Catherine Hills, in J Hunter and I Ralston, eds, *Archaeological resource management in the United Kingdom*, 1993, pp 215–16)

'Information in hand, however imperfectly presented, is more important to the user than the promise of an ideally compiled work which may never be completed.' (Sir Frank Francis, 1901–1988, Director and Principal Librarian of the British Museum 1959–68)

'One gets such wholesale returns of conjecture for a trifling investment of fact.' (Mark Twain, *Life on the Mississippi*, 1883)

'If you are troubled with a pride of accuracy, and would have it completely taken out of you, print a catalogue.' (Benjamin Franklin Stevens, 1833–1902, bookman and antiquary)

Contents

Acknowledgements

My first acknowledgement must be to the Leverhulme Trust, who provided a small grant towards travel and postal expenses in the first two years of this project, allowing me to visit libraries and informants in Cardiff, Edinburgh, Belfast and Dublin and to distribute a questionnaire to over 400 organisations. Next I must thank all who completed the questionnaires, especially those who did so cheerfully and without reminders!

Beyond that, many people have been kind enough to contribute their knowledge towards this book, some of them well beyond the call of duty. I must specially single out those who extended overnight hospitality as well as allowing me the privilege of rummaging in their personal libraries – Ann Hamlin, Barry and Nuala Raftery, and Anna and Graham Ritchie. Siobhán de hÓir and Richard Haworth were most generous with their expertise in the libraries in their charge (the Royal Society of Antiquaries of Ireland and the Freeman Library, Trinity College Dublin respectively), while Belinda Barratt in the UCL Institute of Archaeology has been an adviser and good friend for three decades. In my weekly visits to the Society of Antiquaries of London Bernard Nurse has been quietly supportive and Ortrun Peyn has cheerfully tolerated my frequent interruptions.

A book as wide-ranging as this must depend on the advice of many specialists. All those listed below have helped me, those starred having really put themselves out through a belief in this book. My grateful thanks to all of them; I hope I have not let them down. Or left anyone out.

*Dr Joan Alcock, Fionna and Patrick Ashmore, *Professor Richard Bailey, David Baker, *Patrick Begg, *Dr C S Briggs, S R Bryant, Matthew Canti, Jon Cannon, Joanna Clark, *Dr Henry Cleere, Dr Juliet Clutton-Brock, Michael Coulter, Angélique Day, Dr Ben Ferrari, D Eveleigh, *Keith Falconer, Dr David Fraser, *Dr Andrew Fitzpatrick, Claire Foley, *Dr Margaret Gelling, Felicity Gilmour, Allan Hall, Barrie Hartwell, *Dr David Hill, Dr Robin Holgate, Malcolm Holmes, Aideen Ireland, Claire Johnston, Belinda Jupp, *J R Kenyon, Caroline Kerkham, *Dr Ann Lynch, Dr F G McCormac, *Brian Malaws, Professor Gwyn Meirion-Jones, Dr R K Morris (Warwick Univ), *Chris Musson, Stuart Needham, Beverley Nenk, Professor Michael O'Connell, *Dr Miles Oglethorpe, *Dr Sebastian Payne, Professor Susan Pearce, John Powell, Jim Reynolds, Val Rigby, Dr Seamus Ross, Dr Michael Ryan, Paul Spoerry, Geraldine Stout, Richard Suggett, P D Sweetman, Hazel Symons, Christopher Taylor, *Simon

Taylor, *Professor Charles Thomas, Richard Warner, Leslie Webster, Dr David Weir, H Wyatt, and *John Wymer. David Lee, erstwhile special librarian and current freelance indexer and bibliographer, most generously read a very large portion of the whole book and made many pertinent comments. Bill Swainson very kindly designed a possible layout for the printed page to help me visualise the final product. I am grateful to the staff at the Press and to my indexer, Susanne Atkin, for their valuable contributions to this work. Finally, I remember with gratitude Ronnie Lightbown's cheering words of encouragement in this task whenever we chanced to meet by the local Tube station!

Added in proof

British archaeological bibliography has been retitled *British and Irish archaeological bibliography* (ISSN 1367-4765) with effect from April 1997. It is available on Internet at http://britac3.britac.ac.uk/cba/cba/bab.html

The National Museum of Scotland will be moving to new premises as the Royal Museum of Scotland in Chambers Street, Edinburgh EH1 1JF, in late 1997 or during 1998. This will affect other organisations (Council for Scottish Archaeology, Society of Antiquaries of Scotland) previously accommodated at the museum buildings in Queen Street, as well as the museum collections themselves.

Introduction

The main aim of this book is to indicate at least some of the rich resources available in Britain and Ireland, many of them grossly underused despite the fact that archaeologists rely heavily for their own studies on previous workers' results, both published and unpublished. The need for such a work was first articulated twenty years ago when a high-powered, cross-sectional seminar identified a wide-ranging sourcebook as a prime need for our discipline.[1] However, nobody leapt to the task, and pressure of my normal work meant that this compilation had to be set aside for my retirement.

By now, so much material is available that I can only provide a 'first-resort' guide to it, whether in books or from specialist organisations. I have tried to provide a springboard to almost any aspect of the subject and to cover a whole spectrum of needs and capabilities. Since it has been necessary to stay firmly within these shores it would be splendid if some of our Continental colleagues could follow suit to provide us with a key to their own riches.

As David Lee has said, 'Users require from the bibliographies they consult answers to very different questions, from the briefly specific to the very fully descriptive.'[2] A user of this book could be a sixth-former just beginning to develop an interest in archaeology, a reference librarian helping a reader to find 'the most authoritative book on Hadrian's Wall' or a work on tree-ring dating of traditional houses, or a reader wanting to unpick an acronym such as MARS or HS. I also envisage that some users will be specialists suddenly confronted with the need to get to grips with some previously unexplored area of the subject. As Richard Gem once rightly said, 'the archaeologist . . . willy nilly is cast in the role of historical jack of all trades'.[3] This book attempts to satisfy at least some of the needs that any of those readers might have. If it does not offer a source directly, it should at least suggest clues to other possible sources.

Hints on how best to use this book are given later in this introduction, but in broad outline there are six principal sections, each with subsections. Within each section or subsection the chosen references are arranged as simply as possible, alphabetically by author (because all library users are accustomed to dealing with the alphabet, whereas few, in my experience, are happy with a complex classification). Another reason for avoiding a heavily subdivided subject classification is that serendipity often plays a significant part in research: it is browsing that can provide the really interesting nourishment.

Because knowledge overlaps itself and refuses to be tightly categorised, the best point of entry to this work will usually be the index, which is as full as possible (authors and subjects) to aid rapid retrieval. But if you prefer to browse in a patch which relates broadly to your interest you are almost certain to find references worth following up.

Principles of selection in a work like this are always difficult to establish; every time one makes a rule, some compelling reason for breaking it emerges. And if one includes x, then y and z clamour to be added. Compilers of bibliographies tend to run the risk of the charge that they have, like poor Nennius, [4] heaped together all that they found. I would resist that charge, if only because each title included has been carefully considered in the context of the whole, and many were discarded at a late stage. Even so, this work can only be one person's selection, with the priority being always the presentation of reference works, sourcebooks, catalogues and corpora, books with good bibliographies which assist a move to the next stage of research, and good regional surveys providing a context for more localised research. A few titles with negative appraisals are included, simply because they tend to be found in libraries, and rather than omit them altogether it seems more helpful to suggest why some other work might be preferred. To any author who might feel unfairly slighted, I apologise for my ignorance or oversight.

With a few exceptions, only books have been selected for the bibliographic sections, despite the fact that the discipline's cutting edge is mostly in the specialist journals. The work would rapidly have become impossibly large without this restriction. Obviously a very short article in a periodical can sometimes answer an enquiry better than a very large book: but anyone who wants to keep at the forefront of the subject should be reading *British archaeological bibliography* anyway. Nonetheless, a few journal articles were added when really needed. (Periodical articles were well covered in A C King's *British and Irish archaeology*, listed in Section 1.3, a book which I have ransacked as a check on my own efforts.)

One depressing aspect of the research for this book was the surprising gaps in so many library collections; despite librarians' best efforts, their ever-reducing budgets, the high cost of books and the constriction of shelf space are all having a severe effect on scholarship. No amount of Internet publishing or Web-surfing is going to solve this problem in the foreseeable future.

In the section on organisations, 4.2, efforts were made to seek out those which could offer advice or publications. They cover a very wide spread of topics, reflecting the multifarious nature of archaeology itself: architecture, geology, history, conservation, historic gardens, natural sciences, as well as the obvious national archaeological institutions and societies. Excluded from Section 4.2 are museums, county and local archaeological societies, and archaeological units; partly because their inclusion would have unbalanced the book, but also because it would be pointless to duplicate the regularly revised listings of *Museums yearbook, Archaeology Ireland, Current archaeology,* and now the CBA's *British archaeological yearbook.* However, I have listed the county and regional archaeologists for the first local contact points. (As this book was nearing completion, severe cuts in many branches of archaeological work were just taking hold and it is impossible to forecast the consequences for many organisations, including those of most national importance.)

Most of the 'organisation' entries in Section 4.2 were compiled using questionnaires returned by the organisations themselves, but when repeated applications failed to elicit responses, entries have been collected from various other sources and denoted by the obelus symbol '†'. Compiling directories and bibliographies is like shooting a rapidly moving target: new interest groups emerge, others fizzle out, society officers are replaced, new books clamour for attention and new editions of old ones appear. Moreover there have been wholesale alterations in telephone numbers on both sides of the Irish Sea. Despite my best efforts you may find that you draw a blank with post or telephone (see if the CBA can help: tel. 01904 671417). For these reasons no responsibility can be taken for misinformation in this work.

How to Use This Book

If you want to join a society, or locate an organisation with the expertise to answer your enquiry, look in Section 4.2, Organisations, which is arranged alphabetically (ignoring 'A', 'The' and connecting prepositions). Other parts of Section 4 list universities, county archaeological services, grant sources, regular conferences, national park archaeologists and the like. If you are looking for general bibliographies to get you started, Section 1 should help. Suggestions for finding unpublished sources are in Section 2 (and Section 6.17 lists the local history manuals which help with documentary research). Principal periodicals and directories to them are given in Section 3. (Incidentally, I have used 'periodicals' and 'journals' virtually interchangeably in this work, with apologies to librarians who make a distinction between them.)

Photographic sources, both for aerial photographs and other kinds, are in Section 5. Finally, Section 6 is a very substantial bibliography dealing with a wide range of sources, from dictionaries and atlases through works on archaeological periods to vernacular architecture, maritime and wetlands archaeology. Excavation reports are normally listed only for 'classic' sites, i.e. those that open up a whole new topic (e.g. Star Carr, Danebury) or cause reassessment of an older report (e.g. Maiden Castle). For a selection of good introductory texts, see Section 6.2.

Where the amount of material warranted it, Wales, Scotland, Ireland, the Isle of Man and the Channel Islands have been given separate subsections within each major division. Ireland has been taken as a single unit, except in administrative matters where the different systems of Northern Ireland and the Republic necessitated a separation.

New Internet sites seem to spring up every week and I have been extremely selective in listing them (p. 8).

For those beginning in archaeology, working through the *Shire archaeology* series (not all listed here) will provide a very good grounding. In Ireland the equivalent series comes from Town House and Country House.

REFERENCES AND ANNOTATIONS

A very high proportion of the works have been seen by myself, though in some cases I have had to rely on informants, on secondary sources or on library catalogues (which are as liable to error as any of us). The order of information given for books is: author or editor, title (and sub-title if any), place of publication, publisher (with series title if any), year, pagination, glossary, bibliography, index, ISBN. Works are in hardback (hb) unless annotated pb (for paperback). For articles in periodicals the information given is: author, title of paper, periodical, volume, year, page run. Illustrations have not been noted, since it is a rare archaeology book that has none at all. Short descriptions of most books are given except where the full title is completely transparent, and I have tried to indicate with stars the most useful works,

from one star signifying 'very useful' to three for 'essential' works. Where periodicals have been cited using abbreviated titles the full form should be readily reconstructable from the context.

As with any work compiled over a long period it has not been easy to maintain a constant standard, particularly with the annotations; indeed I have not striven for a 'foolish consistency', but said what seemed necessary. Some works are deliberately entered in more than one section, and ample use has been made of cross-references.

Finally: there should be something for everyone here, including those who like to find errors . . . After all, archaeology is 'A subject where you are guaranteed to be torn to shreds by someone whatever you do.'[5]

Cherry Lavell
London, summer 1996

1 *Problems of information handling in archaeology: report of a seminar.* Brit Lib Res Devel Dept rep, 5329, 1977.

2 David Lee in P Lea & A Day (eds), *Printed reference material and related sources of information.* Lib Ass, 3 edn 1990, p 318

3 Richard Gem, reviewing Fascicule 29 of *Typologie des sources du moyen âge occidental* in *Medieval archaeology*, 25, 1981, p 243

4 Nennius is the supposed compiler of a hotchpotch of manuscripts known as the *Historia Brittonum* or History of the Britons, probably assembled in the second half of the tenth century AD: numerous references, but see (e.g.) David Dumville, *Histories and pseudo-histories of the Insular middle ages* (1990), I, p 176.

5 Paul Bahn, *Bluff your way in archaeology*, Ravette, 1989, p 38.

Abbreviations

Abbreviations Commonly Used in British and Irish Archaeology

This list will allow the 'decoding' of abbreviations which may be encountered in archaeological literature.

AAI Area of Archaeological Importance
AAS Atomic absorption spectrophotometry
ACAO Association of County Archaeological Officers (obsolete, *see now* ALGAO)
ACO Association of Conservation Officers
ADAO Association of District Archaeological Officers (obsolete, *see now* ALGAO)
ADAS Agricultural Development and Advisory Service (of MAFF)
ADMIS Archaeology Division Management Information System
AEA Association of Environmental Archaeologists
AIA Association for Industrial Archaeology
AIM Association of Independent Museums
ALGAO Association of Local Government Archaeology Officers
ALS Afforestable Land Survey (Scotland)
AMAC Ancient Monuments Advisory Committee (English Heritage)
AML Ancient Monuments Laboratory (English Heritage)
AMS Accelerator mass spectrometry
AONB Area of Outstanding Natural Beauty
AP Air photograph
ARIA Association of Regional and Islands Archaeologists (Scotland)
ARTEMIS Application for ReTriEval and Mapping Information System
AS Anglo-Saxon
ASSI Area of Special Scientific Interest (N Ireland)

BA Bronze Age
BALH British Association for Local History
BAR British Archaeological Reports
BARBS British Archaeological Reports British Series
BAR Int Ser British Archaeological Reports International Series
BGS British Geological Survey
BM British Museum
BPF British Property Federation
BPN Building Preservation Notice
BSAC British Sub-Aqua Club

CAD Computer aided design

CAS Central Archaeological Service (of English Heritage)

CBA Council for British Archaeology

CC County Council

CCC Council for the Care of Churches

CEU Central Excavation Unit (retitled as CAS – *see above*)

CIA Council for Independent Archaeology

CIDOC Comité International pour la Documentation, Conseil International des Musées (ICOM)

CPRE Council for the Protection of Rural England

CPRW Campaign for the Protection of Rural Wales

CRM Cultural resource management

CSA Council for Scottish Archaeology

CTICH Computers in Teaching Initiative, Centre for History, Archaeology and Art History

CUCAP Cambridge University Committee on Aerial Photography

DC District Council

DfE Department for Education

DGLA Department of Greater London Archaeology (now subsumed within MOLAS)

DMV Deserted medieval village

DANI Department of Agriculture Northern Ireland

DNH Department of National Heritage

DoE Department of the Environment

DOENI Department of the Environment for Northern Ireland

DTp Department of Transport

DTP Desktop publishing

DUA Department of Urban Archaeology (now subsumed within MOLAS)

EC European Community

EDM Electronic distance measurer

EDX Energy dispersive x-ray

EH English Heritage (Historic Buildings and Monuments Commission for England)

EIA/EIS Environmental Impact Assessment/Statement

EPMA Electron-probe microanalysis

ERT Electronic resistivity tomography

ESA Environmentally Sensitive Area

ES.HMB Environment Service Historic Monuments and Buildings (N Ireland)

EU European Union

FA Forestry Authority

FASA Fund for Applied Science in Archaeology

FC Forestry Commission

FE Forestry Enterprise

FSG Fortress Study Group

FWAG Farming and Wildlife Advisory Group

GIS Geographical Information Systems

GLAAS Greater London Archaeology Advisory Service

GMPCA Groupement des méthodes pluridisciplinaires contribuant à l'Archéologie (previously Groupe des méthodes physiques et chimiques de l'archéologie)

GPS Global Positioning System (i.e. for satellite-assisted survey work)

GUARD Glasgow University Archaeological Research Division

HBC Historic Buildings Council

HMBB Historic Monuments and Buildings Branch (N Ireland: now Environment and Heritage Service: Historic Monuments and Buildings)

HBMCE Historic Buildings and Monuments Commission for England (the now rarely used original and official name for English Heritage)

HS Historic Scotland

HMSO Her Majesty's Stationery Office

IA Iron Age *or* Institute of Archaeology *or* Industrial Archaeology

IAPA Irish Association of Professional Archaeologists

ICARUS Interactive Computerised Aerial Reconnaissance User System

ICCROM International Centre for the Study of the Preservation and the Restoration of Cultural Property

ICOM International Council of Museums (*and see* CIDOC *above*)

ICOMOS International Council on Monuments and Sites

ICPS Inductively coupled plasma spectrometry

IFA Institute of Field Archaeologists

IIC International Institute for Conservation of Historic and Artistic Works

IIS Institute of Irish Studies (The Queen's University Belfast)

IPCRA Irish Professional Conservators' and Restorers' Association

IUPPS *see* UISPP

LARF London Archaeological Research Facility

LBC Listed Building Consent

MA Museums Association

MAFF Ministry of Agriculture, Fisheries and Food

MAP Management of archaeological projects (English Heritage scheme)
MARS Monuments at Risk Programme
MBC Metropolitan Borough Council
MBR Monuments and Buildings Record (N Ireland)
MDA Museum Documentation Association
MDR Manorial Documents Register
Meso Mesolithic
MGC Museums and Galleries Commission
MNR Marine Nature Reserve
MoD Ministry of Defence
MOLAS Museum of London Archaeology Service
MOLRS Medieval or later settlement project (Scotland)
MPBW Ministry of Public Building and Works (obsolete; previously MoW, Ministry of Works; subsequently Department of the Environment)
MPP Monuments Protection Programme
MSC Manpower Services Commission
MSRG Medieval Settlement Research Group

NAR National Archaeological Record
NAS Nautical Archaeology Society
NBR National Buildings Record
NCC Nature Conservancy Council (see now English Nature, Scottish Natural Heritage)
NCSS National Council for Social Service
Neo Neolithic
NERC Natural Environment Research Council
NFU National Farmers' Union
NHMF National Heritage Memorial Fund
NI Northern Ireland
NLAR National Library of Air Photographs
NMM National Maritime Museum
NMR National Monuments Record (sc England)
NMRS National Monuments Record of Scotland
NMRW National Monuments Record for Wales
NMS National Museums of Scotland
NMW National Museum of Wales
NNR National Nature Reserve
NPA National Parks Authority
NPPG National Planning Policy Guidance (Scotland)
NRA National Rivers Authority or National Register of Archives
NT National Trust
NTS National Trust for Scotland
NVQs National Vocational Qualifications (see also SVQs)

OAL Office of Arts and Libraries
OPW Office of Public Works (Republic of Ireland)

OS Ordnance Survey
OSL Optically stimulated luminescence
OST Office of Science and Technology
OU Open University
OUCA Oxford University Committee for Archaeology

PACT European Study Group on Physical, Chemical and Mathematical Techniques applied to Archaeology
Pal Palaeolithic
PAN Planning Advice Note (Scotland)
PPG Planning Policy Guidance (DoE)
PRO Public Record Office
PRONI Public Record Office Northern Ireland
PSA Property Services Agency

RAI Royal Archaeological Institute
RB Romano-British
RCAHMS Royal Commission on the Ancient and Historical Monuments of Scotland
RCAHMW Royal Commission on Ancient and Historical Monuments in Wales
RCF Redundant Churches Fund
RCHME Royal Commission on the Historical Monuments of England
RIAS Royal Incorporation of Architects in Scotland
RIBA Royal Institute of British Architects
RILEM (International Union of Testing and Research Laboratories for Materials and Structures)

SAAPC Scottish Archaeological Air Photographs Committee
SAM Scheduled Ancient Monument
SCAUM Standing Conference of Archaeological Unit Managers (formerly SCUM, Standing Conference of Unit Managers)
SBAC Science-based Archaeological Committee of the Science and Engineering Research Council (defunct from 1995)
SCLH Standing Conference on Local History (obsolete, see now BALH)
SCOLA Standing Conference on London Archaeology
SDA Scottish Development Agency
SEEC Scottish Environmental Education Council
SEM Scanning electron microscope
SERC Science and Engineering Research Council
SHBT Scottish Historic Building Trust
SMC Scheduled Monument Consent or Scottish Museums Council
SMR Sites and Monuments Record/Register

SNH Scottish Natural Heritage
SOEnD Scottish Office Environment Department
SPAB Society for the Protection of Ancient Buildings
SRO Scottish Record Office
SSCR Scottish Society for Conservation and Restoration
SSSI Site of Special Scientific Interest
SUAT Scottish Urban Archaeological Trust
SVQs Scottish Vocational Qualifications
SWCL Scottish Wildlife and Countryside Link
SWT Scottish Wildlife Trust

TAG Theoretical Archaeology Group
TIDES Thames Interdisciplinary Environmental Study
TLD Thermoluminescence dating
TLTP Teaching and Learning Technology Programme
TRAC Theoretical Roman Archaeology Conference
TVAC Thames Valley Archaeological Services

UAHS Ulster Architectural Heritage Society
UCL University College London
UDC Urban Development Corporation
UISPP Union International des Sciences préhistorique et protohistorique/ International Union of Prehistoric and Protohistoric Sciences
UKIC UK Institute for Conservation of Historic and Artistic Works (Archaeology Section)
UNESCO United Nations Educational, Scientific and Cultural Organisation

WARP Wetland Archaeology Research Project
WO Welsh Office

XRF X-ray fluorescence

YAT York Archaeological Trust

ref(s) reference(s)
repr reprint
rev revised
s l sine loco [without place – of publication]
suppl supplement
vol(s) volume(s)

ISBN International Standard Book Number
ISSN International Standard Serial Number

Bibliographical abbreviations used in this work

bibl bibliography
ed edited by
enl enlarged
in inches
incl including
MSS manuscripts
n d no date
n p no publisher
o p out of print
orig originally
p or pp page(s)
pt(s) part(s)

Internet

Internet resources for archaeology

Users are advised to refer to Sara Champion's excellent survey in *British archaeological yearbook 1995* (CBA, 1995, pp 250–60), in which she describes the services available at that date. She has very kindly supplied most of the following information, valid at June 1997; in case of difficulty she may be reached by e-mail, stc@soton.ac.uk.

1. VIRTUAL LIBRARIES AND RESOURCE GUIDES
(with many links to other sites)

ArchNet, the virtual library for archaeology worldwide: http://www.lib.uconn.edu/ArchNet/ArchNet.html

Archaeological Resource Guide for Europe, the virtual library for European archaeology: http://www.bham.ac.uk/ARGE/

UK archaeology on the Internet: http://www.ccc.nottingham.ac.uk/~aczkdc/ukarch/ukindex.html

British archaeology on the Internet: http://www.dur.ac.uk/Archaeology/BritArch/

Irish archaeology: http://www.xs4all.nl/~tbreen/ireland.html

2. ORGANISATIONS

Council for British Archaeology: http://britac3.britac.ac.uk/cba/
also Internet e-mail – archaeology@compuserve.com

Council for Scottish Archaeology: http://www.gla.ac.uk/Acad/Archaeology/scotland/csa.html

English Heritage: http://www.eng-h.gov.uk

Historic Scotland: http://www/electricscotland.com/historic.index.html

Cadw: http://www.castlewales.com/cadw.html

The Heritage Council (Ireland) Archaeology Division: http://homepages.iol.ie/~sec/Archaeology

The Discovery Programme (Ireland): http://ireland.iol.ie/~discovry/

RCHME: http://www.rchme.gov.uk/

RCAHMS: http://www.open.gov.uk/scotoff/heritage.htm

3. SOCIETIES

Society for the Promotion of Roman Studies: http://www.sas.ac.uk/icls/Roman/

Society for Post-Medieval Archaeology: http://britac3.britac.ac.uk/cba/spma/index.html

4. JOURNALS AND MAGAZINES

British Archaeology: http://britac3.britac.ac.uk/cba/ba/ba.html

Current Archaeology: http://www.cix.co.uk/~archaeology

assemblage (Sheffield University postgraduate journal): http://www.shef.ac.uk/~assem/

Archaeology Ireland: http://slarti.ucd.ie/pilots/archaeology

Trowel (UCD student journal): http://www/ucd.ie/ucdpubls.html
(NB not updated since March 1996, but existing material is of interest)

Internet Archaeology: http://intarch.ac.uk

Antiquity: http://intarch.ac.uk/antiquity/index.html

5. DISCUSSION LISTS

britarch covers British archaeology in general: to subscribe send e-mail message to mailbase@mailbase.ac.uk (inserting your own name): join britarch firstname lastname

arch-theory: to subscribe send e-mail message to mailbase@mailbase.ac.uk (inserting your own name): join arch-theory firstname lastname

6. ARCHAEOLOGICAL BOOKSHOP
Oxbow Books: http://www.oxbowbooks.com

7. LIBRARIES
(all UK on-line academic library catalogues and some others, including world-wide): http://www.niss.ac.uk/reference/index.html

More Internet addresses will be found at appropriate points in this book.

SECTION 1

Finding out 1

Guides to published sources

This section lists some guides to general information which may be of use to archaeologists; more specifically archaeological writings are listed in Section 1.3 below.

One general aid of possible use to archaeologists is the citation index, now found in three main branches of study: sciences, arts and humanities, and social sciences. This type of index works on the principle that the reader can look up one relevant reference and find listed under it the details of other publications which have cited it. These fresh references can then be used to find yet others, so that in the end the reader finds a whole constellation of potentially useful references. The printed volumes are very unwieldy to use but there are online versions (SCISEARCH, ARTS and HUMANITIES SEARCH & SOCIAL SCISEARCH).

Britain and the wider world

*Bell, Barbara L, *An annotated guide to current national bibliographies*. Cambridge: Chadwyck-Healey, 1986, xxvi, 407 p. 0 85964 123 6.
Explains precise nature of each national bibliography (e.g. *Irish Publishing Record*) – how organised, how current and so on.

Besterman, Theodore, *A world bibliography of bibliographies* . . . Totowa, NJ: Rowman and Littlefield, 4 rev edn in 5 vols, 1971. *Continued by*:
Toomey, Alice F, *A world bibliography of bibliographies, 1964–1974* . . . *a decennial supplement to Besterman* . . . Totowa, NJ: Rowman and Littlefield, 1977, 2 vols.
These two massive works cover separately published (ie non-serial) bibliographies only and have only limited uses now.

Bibliographic index: a cumulative bibliography of bibliographies (0006–1255). 1937–. New York: H W Wilson, 3/yr.
Subject list of bibliographies containing 50 or more citations, whether separately, in monographs or in periodicals. Available also online (Wilsonline, BRS, OCLC), 1984–. Attempts

wide coverage, and contains a few items on UK archaeology.

British books in print, see under *Whitaker's* below.

British Library catalogue on CD-ROM (quarterly updates).

BRITISH LIBRARY DOCUMENT SUPPLY CENTRE (Boston Spa, W Yorks).
Produces many finding aids and only a few can be indicated here: they are increasingly being made available on CD-ROM.
Index of conference proceedings (0959–4096; monthly, with annual cumulation; microfiche 1964–88, CD-ROM and online (BLAISE) versions also available.) Earliest record 1787; picks up many archaeological conferences.
Current serials received (annually).
Keyword index to serial titles (quarterly on microfiche, access to over 450K serials).

British Museum/British Library subject catalogues: several different, multi-volume series cover the period 1881 to 1990, with years from 1975 available on fiche. The indexing, especially over so long a period, is of variable quality.
The most recent issue is *British Library general subject catalogue 1986 to 1990.* London: Saur, 1991–2, 42 vols (or 261 fiche).

****British national bibliography* (ISSN 0007–1544) 1950–. Weekly, with quarterly and annual cumulations. Also available on microfiche and CD-ROM covering materials from 1950. (The 1994 software for the CD-ROM includes many new search features and allows networking through college library departments into student reference areas and to lecturers' own workstations for reference purposes.)
The official national record of all new UK publications, and first issues of serial titles, received by the Legal Deposit (copyright) Office of the British Library. Whitaker's list (below) tends to be faster.

The CD-ROM directory. Published annually in print and twice yearly on CD-ROM. London: TFPL (Task Force Pro Libra). Includes (at 1996) half a dozen archaeological titles.

Cox, John, *Keyguide to information sources in online and CD-ROM database searching.* London: Mansell, 1991, xxiv, 247 p, index. 0 7201 2093 4.

An integrated, worldwide guide to the literature, reference aids and key organisational sources of information on this topic.

Hall, James L (ed), *Online bibliographic databases: a directory and sourcebook.* London: Aslib, 1986 (or any later edition).
Included here for reference, although a new edition is badly needed. Gives an alphabetical list with details of start date, coverage, amplitude, yearly accrual, service suppliers (eg DIALOG), indications of the access charges. Shows search templates for several different services including QUESTEL. Bibliography of selected references dealing with online databases.

Lea, Peter W and Day, Alan (eds), *Printed reference material and related sources of information.* London: Lib Ass, 3 edn 1990, xxv, 589 p. 0 85365 749 1 pb.
Contains chapters on dictionaries, encyclopaedias, periodicals, maps/ atlases/ gazetteers, local history and so on. The UDC classification makes it very hard to use and the selection of archaeological (at least) items is idiosyncratic.

Leistner, Otto, *International bibliography of Festschriften from the beginnings until 1979.* Osnabrück: Biblio Verlag, 2 rev edn, 1984, 3 vols, subject index. 3 7648 1275 3.
Contains basic information, eg person honoured, editors, publishers, but no volume contents; and subject index not good.
See also Rounds, D on Festschriften for topics in antiquity, in Section 1.3.

Sheehy, E P (rev and ed Robert Balay), *Guide to reference books, covering materials for 1985–1990.* Supplement to the tenth edition. Chicago / London: Amer Lib Ass, 1992, x, 613 p. 0 8389 0588 9.
Sheehy's classic reference work is brought up to date. This is 'the American Walford' so has a strong US bias. (Prefer Walford, next entry)

Walford's guide to reference material, various editors. London: Lib Ass, 3 vols, revised every few years.
Vol 1, *Science and technology,* eds M Mullay and P Schlicke, 6 edn, 1993.
Vol 2, *Social and historical sciences, philosophy and religion,* eds Alan Day and Joan Harvey, 6 edn 1994 (contains the archaeological material, but the classification scatter makes it extremely

hard to use and the principles of selection are impossible to glean).

Vol 3, *Generalia, language and literature, the arts*, eds A Chalcraft et al, 6 edn 1995. (Includes CD-ROMS, online etc.)

Whitaker's books in print (ISSN 0953–0398). Formerly *British books in print*. London: Whitaker and Sons, monthly fiche.

The most useful and accessible source for checking what books are available, giving very basic information for each. Libraries and many bookshops have it.

Wales

Bibliotheca Celtica. A register of publications relating to Wales and the Celtic peoples and languages. Aberystwyth: National Library of Wales, 1910–27/8; new series 1929–48; 3rd series 1953–84.

Appeared about every 4 years, until that covering 1984. Then became *The Bibliography of Wales* (see next item). Classified order (e.g. History Auxiliaries – archaeology, diplomatic, archives, numismatics, inscriptions, heraldry, biography) and author index only. Most of the archaeology will be found under *topography*.

The bibliography of Wales, including the subject index to Welsh periodicals (0968–0748). Biennial. 1, 1985/6–. National Library of Wales, Aberystwyth.

Covers books and articles, with alphabetical subject sequence and author index. Currently runs about four years behind the material it treats.

Huws, Gwilym and Roberts, D Hywel E (comp), *Wales* (World Bibliographical Series, 122). Oxford: Clio Press, 1991, xv, 247 p, index. 1 85109 118 1.

Selective and annotated. Rather sparse for archaeology, but has short section on inventories and archaeological guides; medieval archaeology; industrial archaeology; Roman occupation to AD 1282, etc.

Scotland

Bibliography of Scotland (0143–571X). 1976–. Annual. National Library of Scotland, Edinburgh. Printed version to 1987; from 1988 available online on JANET/NISS, with annual printout on microfiche. CD-ROM forthcoming.

Contains entries for books, parts of books and major periodical articles, of Scottish interest, plus all relevant theses received by the National Library.

Grant, E, *Scotland* (World Bibliographical Series, 34). Oxford: Clio, 1982, 224 p. 0 903450 64 X.

See also entries for Mitchell and Hancock (respectively) in Section 1.3.

Ireland

Baumgarten, Rolf, *Bibliography of Irish linguistics and literature, 1942–71.* Dublin Inst for Advanced Stud, 1986, xxiii, 776 p, indexes. 0 901282 81 2.

Includes prehistoric and cultural history (pp 656–90). A follow-up volume was expected.

***Eager, Alan R, *A guide to Irish bibliographical material: a bibliography of Irish bibliographies and sources of information.* London: Lib Ass, 2 rev and enl edn, 1980, 560 p. 0 85365 931 1.

Archaeology and antiquities are on pp 269-74; seems rather random selection in comparison to what an archaeologist would have done, but the guide is very rich in topographical references.

Elmes, R, on Irish topographic prints, see Section 2.2, Guides to manuscript (etc) sources.

**Hayes, Richard J (ed), *Sources for the history of Irish civilisation: articles in Irish periodicals.* 9 vols. Boston, Mass: G K Hall, 1970 (no ISBNs).

Massive reference work indispensable for any kind of Irish research. It covers 'all the articles, poems and reviews ... in the periodicals published in Ireland, which contained material likely to be of value for research ...'; bear in mind therefore that the work excludes relevant material originating outside Ireland. Items are entered under Persons (vols 1–5), Subjects (6–8), Places and Dates (9).

See also Hayes in Section 2.2, Guides to manuscript (etc) sources.

****Irish publishing record* (0579–4056), compiled by (from 1990) National Library of Ireland, Dublin, 1967–, annual.

The official Irish national bibliography, covering Northern Ireland as well as the Republic, for books, pamphlets, the first number of new periodicals, etc. Classified order; includes list of publishers and their addresses. Is compiled from databases of six libraries and runs a couple

of years behind the material treated, but is an
excellent and reliable source.

**Kenney, James F, *The sources for the early
history of Ireland: an introduction and guide*. 1,
Ecclesiastical [a second planned volume, Secular, never appeared]. New York: Columbia UP,
1929. (Various reprints, then: Dublin: Four
Courts Press, 2 edn 1993, 815 p, 1 85182
115 5.)
Written sources only, pre-Viking to 12th century.

***Northern Ireland bibliography* (0959–8812).
Title varies: began as *Northern Ireland local
history*, 1, 1970–. Then *Northern Ireland local
studies*, 1, 1981–17, 1986. Then *Local studies*,
18, 1987–26, 1989. Then *Northern Ireland
bibliography*, 27, 1990– (qrly). Cumulative
index to nos 1–23, 1981–88.
A joint publication of the five Public Library
services in Northern Ireland, edited by the
Library Service of NE Education and Library
Board, c/o Area Reference Library, Demesne
Avenue, Ballymena, Antrim BT43 7BG. Contains list of publications, list of journals and
newspapers, name index.

Shannon, Michael Owen (comp), *Irish Republic*
(World Bibliographical Series, **69**). Oxford:
Clio Press, 1986, 404 p, index. 1 85109 014 2.
Gives only four pages of archaeology as such, so
more use for background.

—, *Northern Ireland* (World Bibliographical
Series, **129**). Oxford: Clio Press, 1991. 1
85109 032 0.
Similar to previous entry.

1.2
County Bibliographies and some
pre-twentieth century sources

A mass of potential material is available under this
heading, so the works listed here can only point
the way generally. To quote the foreword to a
recent reissue of a British Museum catalogue, 'No
library would be complete without the classic
reference works of previous generations. They laid
the foundations upon which later scholars built.'
(M J Cuddeford in the Anglia reprint of the BM
Guide to Anglo-Saxon antiquities). Hence the old
county histories, in particular, should not be
scorned out of hand: they can turn up very
interesting material, but the two works by Currie
and Lewis and by Simmons (below) should be
consulted for guidance.

***Currie, C R J and Lewis, C P (eds), *English
county histories: a guide. A tribute to C R
Elrington*. Stroud: Alan Sutton, 1994, xii, 483
p, footnote refs, index. 0 7509 0289 2.
In this historiographical survey each contribu-
tor treats one county. As the first qualitative
guide to the wealth of printed historical material available it should be consulted before
embarking on any county or regional study.
See also the next two entries.

Humphreys, Arthur L, *A handbook to county
bibliography, being a bibliography of bibliographies relating to the counties and towns of
Great Britain and Ireland*. Folkestone: Dawson,
1974 reprint of 1917 original, 501 p, indexes.
Lists 6000 bibliographies, of which the author
says 'I have searched the Transactions of
County Antiquarian Societies, and unearthed
a large amount of valuable bibliographical
work buried therein. Until our public libraries
catalogue, as they should do, each of the various
items in these collections, they must remain
almost an unexplored field.'

**Simmons, Jack (ed), *English county histories:
first series*. Wakefield: EP Publishing, 1978, viii,
246 p, chapter refs, index. 0 7158 1309 9.
This was the only volume to appear, in the
event: contributors assess the county historians
who published between 1677 and 1781. These
were: Robert Thoroton (Notts); Sir Robert
Atkyns (Glos); William Borlase (Cornwall
and Scilly); John Hutchins (Dorset); Joseph

Nicolson and Richard Burn (Cumberland and Westmorland); Edward Hasted (Kent); Sir Richard Worsley (Isle of Wight); and James Wright (Rutland).

Two old works which can turn up interesting material are:
Anderson, John P, *The book of British topography: a classified catalogue of the topographical works in the library of the British Museum relating to Great Britain and Ireland.* London: 1881, reprinted complete in 1966 by Theatrum Orbis Terrarum of Amsterdam, xvi, 472 p, indexes.
This catalogue of monographs contains a general section divided by subject (eg castles, halls) then come English counties, divided into town sections. (For London there is a subject breakdown.) Wales, Scotland and Ireland follow. There are relatively few annotations but it is a careful piece of work; index of place-names and (exiguously) subjects, but no author index.

Upcott, William, *A bibliographical account of the principal works relating to English topography.* First published 1818, 1576 p, index; reprinted in four-page-up photographic reduction in 1978 by EP Publishing, 400 p.
This describes all the major county and local histories extant at the time, gives their contents and lists their illustrations.

———

There are dozens, if not scores, of county and regional bibliographies so they cannot be individually noted here, but your local librarian will know what is available for your area of interest. The quality varies enormously and for the older works it would be wise to make an initial check for a mention in Currie and Lewis (above). Sussex has a regular *History and archaeology bibliography* (1985 to date), for instance. Depending on date, volumes of the *Victoria county history* (VCH) may also prove useful (e.g. Frank Sainsbury's bibliographic supplement to VCH Essex, 1987). Some authors have diligently harvested references to their own particular subject interest from the 19th century *Gentleman's magazine* (e.g. Arthur Jones for Hertfordshire over the period 1731–1800). Local directories can sometimes turn up something useful, for urban archaeology at least: an example might be Peter Atkins's compilation of the directories of London 1677–1977 (Mansell, 1990, 736 p. 0 7201 2063 2).
Some county bibliographies have been entered

on computer, e.g. East Yorkshire Bibliography (held at Hull University and available through JANET). Some of these efforts were made under the Manpower Services Scheme and related projects; since the amount of experienced professional (as opposed to inexperienced amateur) input varied from place to place, it is advisable to run your own quality check or take good advice.

———

19th century sources

PERIODICALS
The Antiquary. 1880–1915.
Very uneven quality, but can turn up useful material.

The Archaeological review. 1888–90. London. Edited by G L Gomme. Subtitled 'a journal of historic and pre-historic antiquities', with items on ancient field systems, the Picts, a review of Pitt Rivers's first two Cranborne Chase volumes, and the like. It reports the formation of the Congress of Archaeological Societies which existed for many years from 1888 and eventually (1944) was transformed into the CBA. The folklore side of this journal took over and the name changed to *Folklore*.

The Builder. 1842–1966 (title then changed to *Building*, March 1966). London.
The Victorian era's foremost illustrated architectural journal also recorded discoveries made during the course of 19th century development works, and occasionally gave an archaeological item not noted elsewhere. There were yearly or half yearly indexes, of very variable quality; several attempts to make the material more accessible are listed in Kamen's 1981 bibliography – *see entry in Section 1.4 below*. The illustrations from the first 40 years have now been indexed by Ruth Richardson and Robert Thorne: *The Builder illustrations index 1843–1883.* London: Builder Group and Hutton + Rostron in assoc with Inst Hist Res, 1994, xiii, 832 p, multiple indexes. 0 907101 06 2. (Note that the publishers plan a CD-ROM of 12,000 images derived from the illustrations indexed.)

The Gentleman's magazine. 1731–1907. (There is a Kraus reprint.) Particularly after 1824 this periodical contained many antiquarian and topographical items, e.g. Charles Roach Smith's 'Antiquarian Notes'. G L Gomme published various organised extracts from it in his *Gentleman's magazine library*: eg the references to Romano-British remains (1867); the ecclesiological material from 1731–1868 (1894); and the references to English topography in 30 county volumes (1883–1905).

The Reliquary. First series, vols 1–26, 1860–86. This set has been indexed in recent times by P Riden, who published it as *Derbys Record Soc occas pap*, 2, 1979, with author arrangement of 'every article of any substance' and an index to persons and places; alas, no subject index.
The journal merged with *The Illustrated archaeologist* (1893–4) in 1895, adopting the new title *The Reliquary and illustrated archaeologist*, New Series, vols I–XV, 1895–1909. These later volumes dealt mainly with Anglo-Saxon and Norman architecture but contain much else besides.

Walford's antiquarian magazine and bibliographer. 1882–7. This 'chronicles the meetings of learned societies in town and in country', so the grains of wheat have to be searched for among the mix of news, reviews and letters.

BOOKS AND OTHER REFERENCE WORKS
Akerman, J Y, *An archaeological index to remains of antiquities of the Celtic, Romano-British and Anglo-Saxon periods*. London: J R Smith, 1847.
A valiant effort for its time, classifying sepulchral remains of Britain in the three periods named in the title, plus other items such as extracts from the Notitia Dignitatum. Illustrations collected at the end act as a broad key to the contents.

CONGRESS OF ARCHAEOLOGICAL SOCIETIES 'in union with the Society of Antiquaries of London' was instrumental in producing the 225-year bibliography compiled by G L Gomme (*see entry in Section 1.3 below. The CAS's Year's work in archaeology is treated in Section 1.5 below.*)

Cox, E G, *Reference guide to the literature of travel . . . Vol 3, Great Britain*. Seattle: Washington Univ Press, 1949, x, 732 p.
The travellers and tourists of past centuries often made useful records of what they saw on their journeys. *See also Fussell and Moir (respectively) below.*

EIGHTEENTH CENTURY SHORT TITLE CATALOGUE 1990. Microfiche edition, 'ESTC 1990' consists of about 250 fiches in two ring binders. It gives some 305,000 detailed records of items printed in Britain, N America and the British colonies, and in English language anywhere in the world, 1701–1800.
Author/title sequence, with indexes by date of publication, place of publication, by genre (five of), etc.

Fussell, G E, *Exploration of England: a select bibliography of travel and topography, 1570–1815*. London: Mitre Press, 1935, 56 p. (Not seen)

Gomme, G L, see his index in Section 1.3.

Moir, Esther, *The discovery of Britain: the English tourists 1540–1840*. London: Routledge and Kegan Paul, 1964, xvi, 183 p, bibl, index.

Royal Society of London. *Catalogue of scientific papers (1800–1863)*. London: Eyre and Spottiswoode for HMSO, 1867 (with supplement to 1925).
Subject indexes were done for the whole of the 19th century journal literature, classified by branch (eg Physics). It was 'intended to serve as an index to the Titles and Dates of Scientific Papers contained in the Transactions of Societies, Journals and other Periodical Works'.

Worcestre, William, *edited from the unique Corpus Christi College Cambridge 201*, by J H Harvey. Oxford: Clarendon, 1969, xxiv, 456 p.
William Worcestre, b.1415, was the first English antiquary and made journeys 1478–80 during which he recorded many observations, perhaps most usefully on medieval architecture. (Latin text complete, with page-by-page English translation.)

Wales

WELSH TOURISTS
Coxe, William, *An historical tour through Monmouthshire, illustrated with views by Sir Richard Colt Hoare . . .* London: 1801, 450 p, refs, index.
Coxe, a seasoned historian, offers some useful records.

Fenton, Richard, *A historical tour through Pembrokeshire*. Brecknock: Davies and Co, 1903 (reprinted Dyfed County Council Cultural Services Dept, 1994, 388 p, index. 0 86075 091 4.
Originally published in 1811, contains useful

records of topographical and other features noted on a journey. This edition includes R and J Fenton's own notes towards a second edition that they intended.

Fisher, John (ed), *Tours in Wales (1804–1813)* by Richard Fenton. London: Cambrian Archaeol Ass, 1917, xvi, 371 p, index.
Includes many comments on antiquities seen, and a certain amount of 'opening' of ancient monuments was done . . .

Enquire locally for other early material concerning Welsh counties: eg for Glamorgan, see the *Glamorgan county history* in several volumes.

Scotland

Is reportedly not well supplied for county bibliographies as such, but apart from the title listed below see entries for Humphreys and Anderson, respectively, at the head of this section; and for Terry in Section 1.3.

Mitchell, Arthur, *Lists of travels and tours in Scotland, 1296 to 1900.* Edinburgh: 1902. (Not seen)

Ireland

Consult Eager in Section 1.1 above for a list of numerous 19th century county bibliographies; see also Humphreys at the head of this section. Numerous newer county bibliographies for Ireland, often originating as librarianship theses, are discoverable by local enquiry. Several such compilations exist only in typescript deposited locally. However, a major contribution to Irish research comes from the collective county works from Geography Publications listed below, which contain substantial bibliographies as well as excellent surveys.

Heaney, Henry, *Tourists in Ireland, 1800–1859: an annotated bibliography.* (Typescript, 1967, deposited in Linen Hall Library, Belfast.)
Tourist diaries often contained information useful to archaeologists.

Cork: O'Flanagan, Patrick, and Buttimer, C G (eds), *Cork history and society: interdisciplinary essays on the history of an Irish county.* Dublin: Geography Publications, 1993, xxiv, 999 p, bibl, index. 0 906602 22 X.

Donegal: Nolan, William, Ronayne, L and Dunlevy, Mairead (eds), *Donegal history and*

society. Dublin: Geography Publications, 1995 (1996?), 920 p, bibl, index. (Not seen)

Dublin: O'Sullivan, Peter (ed), *Newcastle Lyons: a parish of the Pale.* Dublin: Geography Publications, 1986, 163 p. 0 906602 03 3 [sic: ISBN repeats that of Tipperary below].

— Aalen, F H A and Whelan, Kevin (eds), *Dublin City and County: from prehistory to present. Studies in honour of J H Andrews.* Dublin: Geography Publications, 1992, xiv, 450 p, bibl, indexes. 0 906602 19 X.

Kilkenny: Nolan, William and Whelan, Kevin, *Kilkenny: history and society. Interdisciplinary essays on the history of an Irish county.* Dublin: Geography Publications, 1990, xx, 715 p, bibl, index. 0 906602 13 0.

Tipperary: Nolan, William (ed, with T G McGrath), *Tipperary: history and society: interdisciplinary essays on the history of an Irish county.* Dublin: Geography Publications, 1985, 493 p, bibl, index. 0 906602 03 3.

Waterford: Nolan, William and Power, T P (eds), with Des Cowman, *Waterford history and society: interdisciplinary essays on the history of an Irish county.* Dublin: Geography Publications, 1992, xxiv, 784 p, bibl. 0 906602 20 3.

Wexford: Whelan, Kevin (ed) with W Nolan, *Wexford: history and society. Interdisciplinary essays on the history of an Irish county.* Dublin: Geography Publications, 1987, xvi, 564 p, bibl, index. 0 906602 06 8.

Wicklow: Hannigan, Ken and Nolan, William (eds), *Wicklow history and society: interdisciplinary essays on the history of an Irish county.* Dublin: Geography Publications, 1994, xxii, 1005 p, bibl, index. 0 906602 30 0.

1.3
Guides to Literature
– archaeology

These are books giving one-off guides to multi-period and general archaeological works. King is probably the most useful work currently, with Butcher and Garwood invaluable in its own field. Mullins is useful within its 30-year timespan. For bibliographies confined to a particular archaeological period, turn to Section 6, Select Bibliography, under the period sought. For a means of updating the information in this section, see Section 1.5 on indexing and abstracting services.

Britain and NW Europe

Bakka, Liv, *Norsk arkeologisk bibliografi 1957–76* published as *Universitets Oldsaksamling Årbok*, 1977/8, 192 p. 82 7181 008 1.
Classified and author-indexed guide to Norwegian archaeological publications.

BIBLIOGRAPHIES SUR L'ÉPOQUE ROMAINE, BTA 9–22 (*Bibliographies thématiques en archéologie*, 0989–5892). Montagnac: Edns monique mergoil, 1991, 2 907303 03 1.
Intended to be of European application, but coverage outside France is poor and there are many small errors. Each bibliography deals with a particular category, whether French Département or type of site or find, and is followed by a geographical index. Gives a list of periodicals scanned to produce the bibliographies.

Bonser, Wilfrid, extended and edited by Troy, J, *A prehistoric bibliography*. Oxford: Blackwell, 1976, xvi, 425 p. 0 631 17090 1.
Has to be used with care because the death of the original compiler in mid-work led to misunderstandings and many typographical errors, but this work can sometimes turn up useful references sheerly on account of the large number of British and Irish journals it covered.

Bonser's other works, on Romano-British and Anglo-Saxon/Celtic bibliography respectively, are listed in Sections 6.11.4 and 6.11.5 respectively.

***Butcher, Sarnia and Garwood, Paul (comp),

Rescue excavation 1938 to 1972. A report for the Backlog Working Party of the Ancient Monuments Advisory Committee of English Heritage. London: Engl Heritage, 1994, 82 p, refs. 1 85074 482 3.
Essential for the researcher, despite its unfortunate lack of index. Lists about 1,000 sites excavated over the period, noting any resultant publication and/or the location of the excavation archive. Does not cover 'research' excavations even though they may have included public funding elements.

CBA North-West is reportedly compiling an archaeological bibliography for its area.

Day, Alan E, *Archaeology: a reference handbook*. London: Bingley, 1978, 319 p, index. 0 208 01672 4.
The deficiencies of the index make this descriptive guide very difficult to consult, and its age now also tells against it; but as casual reading it contains some interesting items, eg on the history of individual societies.

Duncan, G S, bibliography of glass, see Section 6.15 Archaeology of industrial processes.

Fowler, P J, 'Tradition and objectives in British field archaeology, 1953–78', in *Archaeol J*, 137, 1980, pp 1–21.
Contains a list (as well as severe castigation) of nearly all the 'implications' reports (ie surveys of archaeological implications of expected building developments) produced over a quarter-century for individual towns or areas.

Gerlach, G and Hachmann, R, *Verzeichnis vor- und frühgeschichtlicher Bibliographien* [Catalogue of prehistoric and early historic bibliographies]. *Beiheft zum Bericht der römisch-germanischen Kommission*, 50, 1969 (1971), 269 p.
Intended to provide a complete list of European printed bibliographies (excluding Greece), but in fact not very complete and rather superficial, though it may give some useful pointers.

Gomme, G L, *Index of archaeological papers 1665–1890*. London: Congress of Archaeol Socs, 1907. Reprinted 1965 within a series from Burt Franklin of New York, 2 vols, xi, 910 p.
Admirable attempt to provide an author listing of all archaeological papers from transactions of learned societies in Great Britain and Ireland over more than two centuries. The promised

classified subject index never materialised. Continuation, in one form or another, was provided in an annual publication under Congress of Archaeological Societies auspices: see in Section 1.5, Abstracting and indexing services.

Hachmann, Rolf (ed), *Ausgewählte Bibliographie zur Vorgeschichte von Mitteleuropa* [Select bibliography on the prehistory of Central Europe]. Stuttgart: Franz Steiner/RGK des DAI, 1984, lxiii, 390 p. 3 515 04088 9.
Somewhat out of our area but could be useful for (eg) Bronze Age/Iron Age studies.

Halkon, Peter, Corbishley, Mike and Binns, Gareth (eds), *The archaeology resource book 1992*, from the CBA and English Heritage, contained selected book titles for teachers among a host of other material. It has now been replaced, though not superseded as far as book titles go, by the CBA's *British archaeological yearbook* (1995).

Heizer, R F, Hester, T R and Graves, C, *Archaeology: a bibliographical guide to the basic literature.* New York/London: Garland, 1980, xi, 434 p, author index. 0 8240 9826 9.
Primarily New World in scope, this work also attempts 'reasonable coverage' of the Old. It deals with the work of the archaeologist, the nature and purpose of archaeology, history of archaeology, archaeology as profession, sources of primary data (bibliographies and atlases etc). 4,818 entries.

Kamen, Ruth see entry under Architecture in Section 1.4 Guides to literature (ancillary subjects).

***King, A C (comp), *British and Irish archaeology: a bibliographical guide.* Manchester: Manchester Univ Press, 1994, 324 p, author index. 0 7190 1875 7.
An useful compilation, selected mainly from publications of 1960–90, which would have been much improved by the addition of a subject index; a rather complex classification makes it difficult to use, and it is inevitably selective at nearly 7,780 items for the three decades. Accuracy of citations is high.

Makjanic, R and Roseff, R (comp), *British Archaeological Reports complete catalogue 1974–1994.* Oxford: Tempvs Reparatvm, 1994, iii, 48 p, indexes. 1 871314 04 6 pb.
Useful list, in serial order, of the titles of 237 British and 591 International Series reports,

with indexes by author, subject, geographical location and period. (The subject indexes leave something to be desired, but at least they tried.)

*Mullins, E L C (comp), *A guide to the historical and archaeological publications of societies in England and Wales 1901–1933* compiled for the Institute of Historical Research. London: Athlone Press, 1968, xiii, 850 p, indexes. [o] 485 11094 6.
Over 400 local and national journals were analysed for this great and under-used work. Essentially it lists contents pages in volume order, but a subject index compiled from the article titles (only) somewhat eases access to the desired information; there is also an author index. Each journal listing is preceded by a small snapshot of that society's history and coverage. For journals in neighbouring disciplines the listings are necessarily confined to those having archaeological or historical interest.

***OXBOW BOOK NEWS: new books on archaeological, ancient and medieval history (0269–2147). Oxbow Books, Park End Place, Oxford OX1 1HN, tel 01865 241249, fax 01865 794449. (For Internet see p. 8 above.)
No apology is offered for including this bookshop's indispensable quarterly catalogue of new titles, presented in sensibly classified order, with its informative (sometimes pungent) annotations. A particularly useful feature is the list of titles-in-series which may otherwise not be easy to discover. An index would be a great help.

Rounds, Dorothy, *Articles on antiquity in Festschriften: the ancient Near East, the Old Testament, Greece, Rome, Roman Law, Byzantium: an index.* Cambridge (Mass): Harvard UP, 1962, 560 p.
Invaluable for the early period of Festschriften, those elusive volumes which, though sometimes disappointing, can contain papers which have achieved classic status. *See also Leistner in Section 1.1 above.*

Shire Publications, *Thirty years of Shire publications: a bibliography for collectors 1962–91.* Princes Risborough: Shire, 1992, 96 p, refs, index. 0 7478 0170 3 pb.
Complete catalogue of Shire books including various series: Archaeology, Albums, Garden History, 'Discovering' etc, with index of titles.

Solon, M L (comp), *Ceramic literature: an*

analytical index to the works published in all languages on the history and the technology of the ceramic art . . . London: Charles Griffin, 1910, xviii, 660 p.
Still useful 80 years later.

*Woodhead, Peter, *Keyguide to information sources in archaeology*. London: Mansell, 1985, xiv, 219 p, index. 0 7201 1745 3.
Offers a rapid survey of the history and scope of archaeology, a list of sources of information (arranged by continent), and a highly selected list of relevant organisations world-wide. Its treatment of British material is necessarily very shallow (and it omits two of the principal organisations!), but it provides a useful conspectus of the state of archaeology in 1985, and is quite good on printed serial bibliographies.

The Year's work in archaeology, see under Congress of Archaeological Societies in Section 1.5 Indexing and abstracting services.

Scotland

Mitchell, (Sir) Arthur and Cash, C G, *A contribution to a bibliography of Scottish topography*. Edinburgh: Scot Hist Soc, 2 vols, 1917.
Regional and local histories, descriptions and other relevant works, ordered alphabetically by regions/counties and by towns/parishes within counties.
CONTINUED BY Hancock, P D, *A bibliography of works relating to Scotland, 1916–1950*. Edinburgh: EUP, 1959–60, 2 vols (similarly arranged).
Thenceforward, National Library of Scotland maintains a running catalogue (*see Section 1.1*).

Ritchie, J N G, 'Rescue and salvage excavation in Scotland 1960–1975', in the short-lived *Scottish material culture: a bibliography*, 1976.

Terry, Charles Sanford (ed), *A catalogue of the publications of Scottish historical and kindred clubs and societies with a subject index, 1780–1908*. Glasgow: MacLehose, 1909, xiii, 253 p.
CONTINUED BY Matheson, Cyril (ed), [same title, but covering period 1908–27]. Aberdeen: Milne and Hutchinson, 1928, viii, 232 p, index.
Both these volumes list the works under the individual societies (eg Soc Antiq Scotl, Hawick, Spalding, Orkney, Perth etc, with the subject index as alternative access).

SCOTLOC (from the Scottish Library Association) is a computer database of books and pamphlets published by local history organisations and libraries. It also includes Scottish Central Film and Video Library material. User-friendly, and revised annually; mainly bought by public library services and other interested institutions. Scottish Library Association, Motherwell Business Centre, Coursington Road, Motherwell ML1 1PW, tel. 01698 252526.

Ireland

Belier, A-C, 'Archéologie celtique en Irlande 1930–79', in *Etudes celtiques*, 19, 1982, pp 327–41.
Classified list from 6th century BC to arrival of Patrick.

Bradley, John, *A bibliography of Irish archaeology 1980–82*. Belfast: Ulster Archaeol Soc, 1983.
Gives a list of Irish journals consulted, classified list of items (371) and author index. A brave start which somebody ought to have continued!

Lynn, Chris, 'A bibliography of northern linear earthworks', *Emania*, 6, 1989, pp 18–21.
Annotated references.

Megaw, Basil and continuers, bibliographies in *Ulster j archaeol*, from 1937 to 1950.

1.4
Guides to Literature
– ancillary subjects

This section lists non-serial bibliographies and other guides to published literature in archaeology's neighbouring subjects – anthropology and ethnology, art and architecture, geography and earth sciences, history, science and medicine, and miscellaneous (archery, folk life). Relevant entries for Scotland and Ireland then follow. For serial bibliographies and abstracting/indexing services, see Section 1.5.

Anthropology and ethnology

Annotated bibliographies for anthropologists are available in several disk formats and xeroxed hard copy, 1992 onwards. Apply to Cheryl Claassen (ed), ABA, Rt 3, Box 150, Boone, NC 28607, USA (e-mail: claassencp@appstate.bitnet). (Described in *Archaeol comput newsl*, 30, March 1992, p 18; is centred on USA materials and may have only marginal interest in Britain.)

Annual review of anthropology (0084-6570). 1972–. Palo Alto. Contains useful round-up articles giving the current state of a topic, sometimes with archaeological interest this side of the Atlantic. Previous title *Biennial review of anthropology* (1959–71) from Stanford Univ Press.

Smith, Margo L and Damien, Y M (eds, for Library-Anthropology Resource Group), *Anthropological bibliographies: a selected guide*. South Salem, NY: Redgrave Publg, 1981, 307 p, index. 0 913178 63 2.
From the British viewpoint this appears a rather random selection of books containing bibliographies.

See also the European Ethnological Research Centre noted in Section 4.2 Organisations (Scotland).

Art and architecture

British Architectural Library: 500-fiche main catalogue (to 1984); computer catalogue thereafter, accessible as Architecture Database on DIALOG. *See also* Architectural periodicals index *listed in Section 1.5.*

Kamen, Ruth, *British and Irish architectural history: a bibliography and guide to sources of information.* London: Architectural Press, 1981, vi, 249 p, index. 0 85139 077 3.
Parts are now out of date, but it is excellently laid out and indexed.

Richardson and Thorne, see entry incorporated in that for The Builder *in Section 1.2 above.*

Russell, Terence M, *The built environment: a subject index 1800–1960.* Aldershot: Gregg, 1989, 4 vols. 0 576 40006 8.
Contains over 70,000 entries; relevant volumes are:
> 1, architectural history including gardens and landscape design, domestic architecture, ecclesiastical and sacred architecture; 3, decorative art and industrial design; 4, working class housing, municipal services, etc.

Geography and earth sciences

Dolphin, Philippa, Grant, Eric and Lewis, Edward, *The London region: an annotated geographical bibliography.* London: Mansell, 1981, xiv, 379 p, indexes. 0 7201 1598 1.
Contains general bibliographies, atlases, physical environment, historical patterns of growth and development, transport etc.

Goddard, S, *A guide to information sources in the geographical sciences.* London: Croom Helm, 1983, 273 p, bibl. 0 7099 1150 5.
Includes historical geography, pp 43–55.

Wood, David N, Hardy, J E and Harvey, A P (eds), *Information sources in the earth sciences.* London/New York: Bowker-Saur, 2 edn 1989, xvi, 518 p, index. 0 408 01406 7.
Detailed bibliographic essays by 19 contributors. International in scope: could be useful on geophysics, minerals, soil science; and it has a list of computerised information services.

History

*Altschul, Michael, *Anglo-Norman England 1066-1154.* Cambridge: CUP for Conference on British Studies, 1969, xii, 83 p, author index. 0 521 07582 3.
Covers general works followed by more specialised topics: fine arts, agricultural history, military history including castles, science and technology, etc.

Beresford, M W and Finberg, H P R, *English medieval boroughs: a handlist*. Newton Abbot: David and Charles, 1973, 200 p, bibl, index. o 7153 5997 5.
Lists 609 boroughs in county order with their significant dates.

Bibliography of British history 1485–1789. Oxford: OUP, 3 vols, 1933–51.
The main source for historical writings on the post-medieval period over these two decades. *See also (respectively) Brown and Christie, Graves, and Hanham (all below).*

Brown, Lucy M and Christie, Ian R, *Bibliography of British history 1789–1851*. Oxford: Clarendon/OUP, 1977, xxxi, 759 p, index. o 19 822390 0.
Selective listing of 5,000 titles, most of them with further titles appended which greatly increase the total number.

Bruce, Anthony P C, *A bibliography of British military history from the Roman invasions to the Restoration*. München: Saur, 1981, x, 349 p, author index. 3 598 10359 X.
Selects the principal British (and Irish) printed sources, offering over 3,000 entries with cross-references. Includes a section on fortifications, castles, weaponry, and lists relevant periodicals; but will need supplementing from more recent sources.

Chaloner, W H and Richardson, R C (comp), *Bibliography of British economic and social history* [from 1066]. Manchester: Manchester UP, 2 edn 1984, xiv, 208 p, author index. o 7190 0888 3.
Unannotated; separate sections for Wales, Scotland and Ireland.

Cheney, C R (ed), *Handbook of dates for students of English history*. London: Roy Hist Ass, 1961, xviii, 164 p, index.
Covers reckonings of time; rulers of England; Popes; saints' days and festivals used in dating; legal chronology; the Roman calendar; Easter days AD 500–2000 and so on.

CONFERENCE ON BRITISH STUDIES BIBLIOGRAPHICAL HANDBOOKS see *(eg) Altschul above, Wilkinson below.*

***Creaton, Heather (ed) with Tony Trowles, *Bibliography of printed works on London history to 1939*. London: Lib Ass Publg, 1994, xxxiii, 809 p, indexes. 1 85604 074 7.
From the Centre for Metropolitan History:

classified arrangement and 200-page index. Unfortunately excludes writings on London's archaeology, which were then being compiled elsewhere for the abortive database 'Bibliography of the Archaeology of Greater London' (BAGL).

**Dewe, Michael (ed), *Local studies collections: a manual*. Vol. 2. Aldershot: Gower, 1991, ix, 375 p. o 566 03631 2.
A good source for local historians: contains chapters by different specialists including Bernard Nurse on prints, drawings and watercolours; R Abbott on maps and plans; I Jamieson on institutions and societies in local studies.

Fryde, E B et al (eds), *Handbook of British chronology (Roy Hist Soc guides and handbooks*, 2), 3 edn 1986, xxxix, 605 p. o 86193 106 8.
Mostly concerned with identifying rulers and officers of state; covers England, Scotland, Wales, Channel Isles, plus Ireland to 1922. Could be useful up to 1066 for archaeologists.

Graves, Edgar B (ed), *A bibliography of English history to 1485*. Oxford: Clarendon, 1975, xxiv, 1103 p, index.
Revision of Gross's classic 1900 work, containing over 7,000 entries (many of them composite); mainly restricted to England with a few fundamental works on pre-Conquest Wales and Ireland. Reckoned to be particularly helpful to beginners; reasonable coverage of archaeology, and helpfully classified and indexed.

Hall, A T (comp), *Local history handlist: a select bibliography and guide to sources*. London: Hist Ass (= *Helps for students of history*, 69), 5 edn 1982, x, 170p. o 85278 251 9.
Includes works on the Roman period onwards, with special topics like agriculture, industry/trade, architecture, buildings, warfare; contains Welsh material but no Scottish.

Hanham, H J (comp and ed), *Bibliography of British history 1851–1914*. (In series) Oxford: Clarendon, 1976, xxvii, 1606 p, index. o 19 822389 7.

Henige, guide to serial bibliographies, see entry at head of Section 1.5.

Jones, Philip Henry (comp), *A bibliography of the history of Wales compiled for the Law Committee of the University of Wales Board of*

Celtic Studies. Cardiff: Univ Wales Press, 3 edn 1989, 80 p + 21 microfiches. 0 7083 1037 0
A FAMULUS catalogue on fiche only; the printed element consists essentially of the guide to the classification. Sequences in author (5 fiches), classified (5 fiches), and title (KWIC) index (11 fiches). No prehistoric or Roman material.

***Martin, G H and McIntyre, S, *A bibliography of British and Irish municipal history: volume 1,* general works. Leicester: Leicester Univ Press, 1972, lviii, 806 p, index. 0 7185 1093 3.
Massive, extremely useful guide to the printed sources (over 6,000 works for the period up to 1966), with analytical scheme covering bibliographies and guides to libraries, records and archives, general printed records, general history, the urban community; Wales, Scotland and Ireland separately treated.

Mullett, Michael (comp), *Sources for the history of English nonconformity 1660–1830.* London: Brit Rec Ass (= *Archives and the user,* 8), 1991, 116 p. 0 900222 09 3.
Useful for chapels research; works listed by denomination. No subject index.

Mullins, E L C, *Texts and calendars II: an analytical guide to serial publications 1957–1982. Roy Hist Soc guides and handbooks,* 12, 1983, xi, 323 p, subject index. 0 86193 100 9.
Lists publications, by issuing society, with brief indication of contents; includes EPNS and RCHME as well as guides to parish registers, lay subsidy rolls, cartularies etc. Is a sequel to similarly-titled edition from Roy Hist Soc 1958 (corrected reprint 1978) covering material up to March 1957.

Patten, John, *English towns 1500–1700.* Folkestone: Dawson, 1978, 348 p, bibl, index. 0 7129 0793 9.
Entered here for its excellent bibliography and notes: mainly provincial towns.

Read, Conyers (ed), *Bibliography of British history: Tudor period, 1485–1603.* Oxford: Clarendon, 2 edn 1959, xxviii, 624 p, index. Could be useful for its local history section.

Sutcliffe, Anthony, 'What to read on urban history', in *Local historian,* 16, 1984, pp 67–72.

Victoria history of the counties of England ('VCH'). The *General introduction* (1970) and its *Supplement* (1990) list the counties which have been completed, are in progress, are dormant, or not yet begun. They also list contents of the volumes published so far, with an index of titles of articles (essentially the places treated) and another of authors.

West, John, on Town records and Village records (respectively), see Section 6.17 Placenames . . .

Wilkinson, Bertie, *The High Middle Ages in England 1154–1377.* Cambridge: CUP for Conference on British Studies, 1978, ix, 130 p, index. 0 521 21732 6.
Contains sections on political, social, economic, cultural and religious history, for scholars and advanced students.

Writings on British history: a bibliography of books and articles on the history of Great Britain from about 450 AD to 1939, published during the years 19xx to 19xx. London: Univ London Inst Hist Research.
The series runs: 1901–33 (published 1968–70); 1934–45; thence every three years or so up to 1973/4, after which the *Annual bibliography of the Royal Historical Society* should be used (*see entry in Section 1.5 below*). The book titles were extracted from BNB, the *British national bibliography,* rather than being individually examined, though about 400 periodicals were systematically searched and a few other references added. Subject and name indexes.

Science and medicine

Conrad, Lawrence I et al (eds), *The Western medical tradition 800 BC to AD 1800.* Cambridge: CUP, 1995, xiii, 556 p, bibl, index. 0 521 38135 5.
Includes a few Roman references, but the serial publication *Current work in the history of medicine* will be more generally useful (*see entry in Section 1.5*).

Davis, Elisabeth B, *Guide to information sources in the botanical sciences.* Littleton, Colorado: Libraries Unlimited, 1987, ix, 175 p, refs, index. 0 87287 489 7.
Includes a chapter on historical materials (mainly herbals, plant hunters, etc).

Wyatt, H V (ed), *Information sources in the life sciences.* East Grinstead: Bowker-Saur, 4 edn due 1996, c 250 p. 1 85739 070 9.
Includes a chapter on abstracting and indexing

services and bibliographies: what is available and method of use.

Miscellaneous

ARCHERY

Lake, Fred and Wright, Hal, *Bibliography of archery*. Manchester: Simon Archery Foundation Univ Manchester, 1974, xvii, 501 p, indexes. o 9503199 o 2.
Indexes 5,000 articles, books, films, MSS, theses etc, covering material on earliest times to the present day. Gives library locations.

FOLK LIFE

Wilfrid Bonser compiled two bibliographies for the Folklore Society, covering the 80 years up to 1957 and then from 1958–67, which appeared as *Publications of the Folklore Society*, respectively 121 (1961) and 130 (1969). There followed *An index to the journal Folklore, [vols] 79–103 (1968–91)*, comp Steve Roud and Jacqueline Simpson (Enfield: Hisarlik Press, 1994. 1 874312 16 8).

Steinfirst, Susan, *Folklore and folklife: a guide to English-language reference sources*. New York/London: Garland (= *Garland Folklore Bibliographies*, 16), 1992, 2 vols, xxi, 1208 p. o 8153 0068 9.
Volume 1 (not available to compiler) contains a guide to bibliographies, dictionaries, guides, handbooks etc.

Thomas, Northcote W, *Bibliography of anthropology and folk-lore 1906*. Published for Joint Committee of the Royal Anthropological Institute and the Folklore Society, 1907, lxxii p, indexes.
Also 2nd annual issue 1907 (1908), lxxiv p, indexes.
Contained some archaeology and was reasonably classified by country.

International bibliography of folklore and folk life not available to compiler.

Scotland

Whyte, I D and K A, *Sources for Scottish historical geography: an introductory guide*. Norwich: Geo Abstracts (= *Hist geogr res ser*, 6), 1981, ii, 47 p. o 96094 066 7 pb.
Narrative bibliography.

Ireland

ETHNOGRAPHY AND FOLKWAYS

O Danachair, Caoimhín, *A bibliography of Irish ethnology and folk tradition*. Dublin/Cork: Mercier Press, 1978, 95 p, index. o 85342 490 x pb.
Classified entries with author index.

Ulster Folk Life (0082–7347, 1955–, annual) has bibliographical material, including vernacular architecture.

HISTORY

Cullen, Clara and Henchy, Monica (ed Jacqueline Hill), *Writings on Irish history: 1984 incorporating addenda from 1973–83*. Dublin: Irish Committee of Historical Sciences, 1986, 98 p. o 9502097 1 6 pb.
This bibliography was hived off from bibliographies produced 1936–78 in the periodical *Irish historical studies*. There then followed a microfiche issue, *Writings on Irish history 1979–83*. The present volumes follow from that. An author index was added in the volume for 1985 (published 1987). It seems so far to run about three or four years behind the material covered (ISSN 0791–9824).

Edwards, R W Dudley and O'Dowd, Mary, *Sources for early modern Irish history, 1534–1641*. Cambridge: CUP, 1985, x, 222 p, refs, index. o 521 25020 x.

Foster, Roy F, *Modern Ireland 1600–1972*. London: Penguin, 1989, 688 p, bibl, index. o 14 013250 3.
Includes a bibliographic essay for the period covered.

GEOGRAPHY

Irish geography: journal of the Geographical Society of Ireland (0075–0778, 1934–. 2/yr) has annual lists of recent geographical literature, including historical geography, relating to Ireland.

LOCAL STUDIES

Nolan, W, *Tracing the past: sources for local studies in the Republic of Ireland*. Dublin: Geography Publns, 1982, x, 159 p, bibl. No ISBN, pb.
An excellent starter manual.

1.5
Indexing and Abstracting Services

This section contains:
  General guides to services
  Archaeology and closely related subjects
  (British and Irish; overseas)
  Other subjects: printed services; some online
  services; some CD-ROM services

General guides to services

**Henige, David (comp), *Serial bibliographies and abstracts in history: an annotated guide.* Westport (Conn): Greenwood Press, (= *Bibliographies and indexes in world history*, 2), 1986. 0 313 25070 7.
A very useful annotated bibliography, whose compiler was astonished to find that historians do not use systematic bibliographies, their nonchalance being further demonstrated by the lack of a work like his! He lists about 875 titles (excluding books since these are not at the cutting edge). He warns that databases offer a beguiling illusion: 'the keyword concept is too devoid of context for truly successful searching'; hence databases are no substitute for the manual searching of printed bibliographies.

The index and abstract directory: an international guide to services and serials coverage. Birmingham, Alabama: EBSCO Publishing, 2 edn 1990. 0 913956 50 3.
Attempts to include every periodical covered by the indexing and abstracting services, but coverage and accuracy are poor for archaeology.

Inventory of abstracting and indexing services (comp J Stephens). London: Brit Lib Board (= *LIR*, 21), 1983, 228 p. 0 7123 3030 5 pb.
Alphabetical list, indexes by subject etc, and by database host. Contains 387 titles, whether printed or other. Gives scope, start date, publishing details etc for each service. A new edition is needed.

Scientific abstracting and indexing periodicals in the British Library: a guide to SRIS holdings and their use, comp Rodney Burton et al. London: Science Ref Info Service, 4 edn 1991, 64 p. 0 7123 0780 X.

Archaeology and closely related subjects

BRITISH AND IRISH
The most important in this context are *British archaeological abstracts* and *British archaeological bibliography*, both listed below. However, for the forty years 1940–80 the much more detailed *Archaeological bibliography for Great Britain and Ireland* should be used for preference.

Annual bibliography of British and Irish history. (ISBNs only). 1976–. London: Royal Historical Society/OUP.
Appears before the end of the year following the material treated, and covers the period from Roman Britain onwards, extracting material from over 200 journals; aims to list all relevant books and articles published in the UK. Indexed by author, place, personal name and subject.

Annual bulletin of historical literature: publications of the year 19 . . . (0066–3832). 1911–. London: Historical Association.
Critical selection of the year's publications, tends to run two or three years behind the material analysed. Ceased including prehistory after issue for 1974.

Anthropological index to current periodicals in the library of the Museum of Mankind, incorporating the library of the Royal Anthropological Institute, covering archaeology, ethnomusicology, physical anthropology, ethnography, linguistics, cultural anthropology and human biology (0003–5467). 1963–. Qrly. London: Royal Anthropological Institute of Great Britain and Ireland, Museum of Mankind, London.
Covers some 8,000 items per year, and the grand total now exceeds 100,000 items; but lists titles only (no abstracts) of articles, and the coverage is really only useful to archaeologists seeking cross-disciplinary materials. Currently two years behind even its cover date. (Card index in author sequence available for 1963–91, housed in Museum of Mankind Library, 6 Burlington Gardens, London W1X 2EX; microfiche edn from Mindata Ltd, Bathwick Hill, Bath BA1 6LA.)

***Archaeological bibliography for Great Britain and Ireland* (from 1940/46 to 1948/9 was titled *Archaeological bulletin for the British Isles*). 1946–80.

Annual (occasionally biennial). London: Council for British Archaeology.

For the forty years of its life this was the most comprehensive and detailed archaeological index anywhere in the world, allowing the reader to trace reports on single sites, on specific artefact types, by specific authors, or to survey everything reported for a particular county. Publication was abandoned for economic reasons, since when readers have had to rely on the much less detailed indexing of *British archaeological abstracts* and its successor *British archaeological bibliography* (see below). For a fuller description of the *Archaeological bibliography* see Lavell, C, 'Forty years of information collection by the Council for British Archaeology', in R Martlew (ed), *Information systems in archaeology* (Gloucester, 1984), pp 111–14.

Archaeological site index to radiocarbon dates for Great Britain and Ireland (no ISSN/ISBN). 1971–82. C Lavell (ed). London: CBA.

This work consisted of an initial or 'main' index (1971) and four looseleaf supplements issued at irregular intervals thereafter, to 1982. The aim was to collect all radiocarbon dates issued for British and Irish archaeological sites, whether published in the official journal *Radiocarbon* or (much more frequently) in county or local journals. As the flow of radiocarbon determinations increased, compilation of the index slowed and finally ceased for lack of resources. In recent years progress was made in computerising both the CBA printed index and subsequently issued dates up to about 1986, but once again the project has ground to a halt for lack of resources.

Architectural publications index: periodicals indexed and books catalogued by the British Architectural Library (1359–740X). Qrly with annual cumulations. London: RIBA Publications for British Architectural Library.

Originally an index of selected articles in some 450 periodicals, international in scope, on architectural and related topics, covering both current and historical practice. Computerised since 1978 as 'Architectural database', containing a very large number of records updated monthly and including books added to the library from 1984 onwards; available on DIALOG. Continues the *Comprehensive index to architectural periodicals* (1956–72); the RIBA *Annual review of periodical articles* (1966–73);

and the *Architectural periodicals index* (1973–94). (*See also Avery Index under overseas services below.*)

****British archaeological abstracts*. (0007–0270). 1968–91. 2/yr. London: CBA (now removed to York).

Once described as 'the Rolls Royce in how to find out', this publication consisted of selective summaries of books and articles drawn from the entire range of periodicals dealing with archaeology and cognate subjects in Britain and Ireland. For the first fifteen years coverage was selective, material being chosen for abstracting when it added to or altered the picture already held of archaeology in these islands. From 1983, because of the cessation of the original *Archaeological bibliography* (see above), Abstracts was no longer selective but attempted full coverage of all except minor or ephemeral publications. The annual index contained an average of 5/6 entries per individual item abstracted. From 1992 it was replaced by *British archaeological bibliography* (see next entry).

****British archaeological bibliography* (0964–7104). 1992–. 2/yr. London: British Archaeological Bibliography.

Founded as a fully computerised service on the cessation of *British archaeological abstracts* (above), it includes more of the minor and 'ephemeral' publications. It incorporates the 'London Archaeological Abstracts' (see entry below), and also reproduces Parliamentary references to archaeology and historic buildings from the POLIS (Parliamentary On-line Service) service. Books, however, currently figure far less than they did in its predecessor service, though an attempt is being made to remedy this by supplying book reviews on the Internet (details from CBA). '*BAB*' is funded by a consortium formed by the principal archaeological organisations in the UK. (See note on p xii)

British geological literature: a bibliography and index of geology (and related topics) of the British Isles and related sea areas (0140–7813). 1964–, new series 1972–. Qrly. (various publishers, currently Bibliographic Press Ltd, Worthing).

Coin hoards from Roman Britain. 1979–. Irreg. London: British Museum occasional papers series.

Lists all coin hoards known to have been recovered during the period.

*CONGRESS OF ARCHAEOLOGICAL SOCIETIES IN UNION WITH THE SOCIETY OF ANTIQUARIES OF LONDON. *The year's work in archaeology*, subsequently *Reports of the Earthworks Committee*. 1905–38.
This (mostly annual) publication was the precursor of the *Archaeological bibliography* (see above), listing publications and discoveries of the year. Subject indexing is rather exiguous but this publication is unjustly neglected, considering its wealth of references. *See also Gomme in Section 1.3 for references from AD 1665 to 1890.*

Current titles in speleology. 1969–. Brit Cave Res Ass.
Classified arrangement with county cross-references.

Current work in the history of medicine (0011–3999). 1954–. Qrly. London: Wellcome Institute for the History of Medicine.
Index of periodical articles with broad classification and subject index; contains a section for 'archaeology-numismatics-anthropology' so includes material on palaeopathology, drug jars etc. Author index now computerised.

Geographical abstracts: human geography (0953–9611). 1966–. 6/yr. (Various earlier subtitles, eg *Social and historical geography*). Norwich/London: Geo Abstracts/Elsevier Science Publishers.
Covers a little field archaeology, though its main use to archaeologists would be as human geographical background. Annual indexes were formerly rather crudely computed from titles; from 1993 there is a subject index with keyword strings (not very easy to use) in each issue. Also available as GEOBASE online via DIALOG and on CD-ROM (1980–).

Geographical abstracts: physical geography (0954–0504). 1989–. 12/yr. (Same publisher as preceding entry).
Covers Quaternary, sedimentology, remote sensing, etc.

History of technology index, comp H V Wyatt.
Two printed cumulations were issued from the Science Museum Library in 1991 and 1992, but the index is now, temporarily, available only on the library computer catalogue of the joint libraries of the Science Museum and Imperial College in S Kensington. This can be consulted on the Internet – http://www.nmsi.ac.uk/library/Welcome.html.

* *International medieval bibliography: bibliography for the study of the European Middle Ages* (0020–7950). 1967–. 2/yr. University of Leeds School of History.
Covers the period AD 450–1500, and has recently added maritime studies. Titles of books and articles are presented in classified order with a rather thin subject index. Appears about a year after the material covered.

'London Archaeological Abstracts', comp by London Archaeological Research Facility, c/o Institute of Archaeology, University College London.
Incorporated within *British archaeological bibliography* (see entry above).

Maritime bibliography, issued annually with the journal *Mariner's mirror* (0025–3359).

Museum abstracts (0267–8594). 1985–. 12/yr. Edinburgh: Scottish Museums Council.
Includes some archaeology; covers a high proportion of 'ephemeral' material (newspapers and magazines), but no books, and there is no index.

NUMISMATICS. Clayton, Peter, 'Bibliography of articles on numismatics from non-numismatic journals', in *Numis chron* for 1969, 1971, 1973, 1975, 1977.

**'Scottish archaeological bibliography'. Formerly incorporated (most years) in *Discovery and excavation Scotland* (Council for Scottish Archaeology). Compiled by A C Grieve and D V Clarke, then by Colleen Batey; discontinued, unfortunately, after 1989.
This was the principal means of access to Scottish books and articles, Palaeolithic to modern. Appeared in 1975–6 as a separate, duplicated typescript entitled *Scottish material culture*, which included methodological and other studies relevant to, though not specially treating, Scottish studies. A full index for 1946–77 material in '*DES*' was compiled but lacked funds for publication.

Society of Antiquaries of London (comp Ortrun Peyn), *Bibliography of periodical literature: accessions to the Library of the Society of Antiquaries of London* (0961–1940). Annual. London: Society of Antiquaries of London.

As the compiler herself says, 'coverage of most subjects is inevitably highly selective' owing to the sheer quantity and multifariousness of material entering the Society's library. Entries are classified under the main headings: Archaeology (general and by period/culture); European archaeology [including Britain]; Archaeology of the Near East, Africa, Asia, the Americas, Australia and Oceania; other subjects (archives, history of art and architecture, manuscripts, museology and so on). Formerly incorporated within *Antiquaries journal*.

Urban history (formerly *Urban history yearbook*) (0963–9268) contains annual classified bibliography of historical references with some archaeology.

OVERSEAS SERVICES

L'année épigraphique: revue des publications epigraphiques relative à l'antiquité romaine (0066–2348). 1888–. Paris: Presses Universitaires de France.
Britannia is faster and better for British material, so this is best used for non-UK material.

Anthropological literature: an index of periodical articles and essays (0190–3373). 1979–. Qrly. Cambridge, Mass: Tozzer Library, Harvard Univ. Vols 6–10 (1984–8) appeared only in fiche; vol 11 reverted to printed format and added a subject index. Limited appeal for British/Irish archaeologists.

Archäologische Bibliographie: Beilage zum Jahrbuch des Deutschen Archäologischen Instituts (0341–8308). 1913–. Berlin: de Gruyter. Mediterranean world only, little of British relevance and not easy to use; from 1994 available on DYABOLA.

Archéologie (0003–8210). Brussels: originally CNRS Belgique, 1938–88; resumed 1990 from Stichting Archeologisch Patrimonium and Instituut voor het Archeologisch Patrimonium, with subtitle 'Flanders Archeological Bulletin', ie no longer covers all Belgium). In abeyance since 1990.
Mixture of informal abstracts and annotations, current news, excavations: no subject index, but keywords in English and based on *Brit archaeol abstr* usage, plus site index. Cumulative site index 1938–77 (1980).

Art and archaeology technical abstracts (0004–2994). 1955– (2/yr). From 1984 produced at The Getty Conservation Institute, Marina del Rey, Calif, USA.
Original title: *Abstracts of the technical literature on archaeology and fine arts*, known familiarly as *IIC abstracts* (International Institute for Conservation of Historic and Artistic Works, London). Before that, R J Gettens and B M Usilton had produced a ten-year collection of *Abstracts of technical studies in art and archaeology 1943–52* (1955). Cumulative indexes to vols 1–10 (1955–73, publ 1974) and 11–25 (1974–88, publ 1994).
Essentially for the conservator: covers 1,200 journals and abstracts all material of conservation interest, including technical examination, analysis, restoration, etc, from world-wide sources. Some issues contain special subject bibliographies, eg on natural patinas, amber provenance, ivory, stained glass, medieval textiles, multilingual dictionaries of conservation interest. 'AATA' is also available online through BCIN, the bibliographic database of the Conservation Information Network (Canada).

Ausgrabungen und Funde: Archäologische Berichte und Informationen (0004–8127). 1956–. 6/yr. Akademie-Verlag Berlin, previously Zentralinstitut für Alte Geschichte und Archäologie.
Good subject index to vols 1–25, 1956–80; last issue of each year contains Neue Schriften (classified bibliography).

Avery index to architectural periodicals (0196–0008). Boston (Mass): G K Hall, 2 edn 1973 (15 vols) and subsequent supplements; now CD-ROM (annually) and online via DIALOG.
Dictionary catalogue listing material from 1934 onwards. Currently 4 vols/yr, subjects A–Z, including materials on British archaeology and architectural history; not very easy to use but can reward the browser.

Bibliographie zur alteuropäischen Religionsgeschichte. Berlin: de Gruyter, 3 vols 1967, 1974, 1985.
Emphasis on pagan religions.

Bibliographie zur Archäologie der norddeutschen Küstenländer. 1980–. (Not traced after 1984.) Neumünster: Wachholtz.
Classified and subject-indexed materials from the N German coastal area.

Bibliographie zur Archäozoölogie und Geschichte der Haustiere (0232–4865). 1971–91. Berlin: Zentralinst für Alte Geschichte und Archäologie.
Gave wide coverage of archaeological domestic animal material, effectively back to 1955. See now the running bibliography in *ArchaeoZoologia* (0299-3600).

Bibliographie normande, in *Annales de Normandie* (0003–4134). 1951–.
Classified sequence with name and place-name indexes, slight annotations.

Bibliographie zur schweizerischen Kunst und Denkmalpflege (1012–3970). Ceased. Zürich: Institut für Denkmalpflege ETHZ.
Treated art, together with art-historical aspects of above-ground monuments.

Bibliography of archaeozoology (privately published at Bellach and Basel by Hans Rudolf Stampfli and Jörg Schibler); regular disk supplements to the 6-fiche initial publication are promised.

Bibliography of the history of art/Bibliographie d'histoire de l'art (BHA). (1150–1588). 1991–. Qrly with cumulative index. Williamstown, Mass: Getty Art History Information Program *and* Vandoeuvre-lès-Nancy: INIST Diffusion.
Massive compilation of some 24,000 citations a year covering over 3,000 periodicals and monographs. Also available online through DIALOG and QUESTEL. Arranged by country, topic and period, and heavily indexed. Replaces two former publications, *Répertoire d'art et d'archéologie* and *RILA, Répertoire international de la littérature de l'art* (both ceased 1989).

Bulletin signalétique see now FRANCIS (below).

Cahiers de civilisation médiévales (0007-9731). 1958–. Qrly with annual bibliographic supplement (0240–8678). Poitiers: Centre d'Études Supérieures de Civilisation Médiévale.
The bibliographic supplement has dictionary-type subject headings.

Council for Old World Archaeology, *COWA surveys and bibliographies.* Entered here purely for identification; several numbers were produced for the British Isles (Area I, numbers 1 to 4), the bibliographic items being extracted by various hands from the CBA's *Archaeological bibliography* series. The COWA operation, which was based at the Peabody Museum,

Harvard University, closed down in about 1971.

Fasti archaeologici: annual bulletin of classical archaeology (0390–6833). 1948–. Florence: Licosa-Libreria Commissionaria (for International Association for Classical Archaeology).
Appears at least three years after the material treated; contains some 19,000 entries in six main sections (eg 5: The Roman West).

FRANCIS, Bulletin signalétique, Préhistoire et protohistoire 525 (1157-3759). 1947–. Qrly plus annual cumulative index. Vandoeuvre-lès-Nancy: INIST/Getty Art History Information Program.
The FRANCIS prefix was added in 1991. In French; is best on French and adjacent Continental material, coverage for Britain being patchy. Available online through Télésystèmes QUESTEL. A complementary volume, *Art et archéologie* 526 (1157-3767), deals with the Near East, Asia, America.

Germania: Anzeiger der römisch-germanischen Kommission des Deutschen Archäologischen Instituts (0016–8874). 1917–. Berlin: de Gruyter.
Includes regular list of additions to the RGK Library.

Historical abstracts (0018–2435). 1955–. Irreg. Santa Barbara, Calif: ABC-Clio Press.
Contains a little archaeology, some of it from UK and Irish publications.

International bibliography of historical sciences (0074–2015). 1926–. Annual. Munich: Saur for Int Committee Hist Sciences.
Books and articles; includes some prehistory, but basis of selection not clear to this reader.

Journal of glass studies (0075–4250). 1959–. Corning, NY: Corning Museum of Glass.
Contains annual checklist of books and articles on glass.

Kommentierte Bibliographie zur Archäologie der Kelten (0724–4274). 1978–. Irreg. Comp H Lorenz. Vorgeschichtliches Seminar der Philipps-Univ Marburg-am-Lahn.
Annotated items with site and subject indexes.

Nordic archaeological abstracts (0105–6492). 1974 (1975)–. Annual. Stavanger: Historisk Museum.
Set up on the model of *British archaeological abstracts* but with a two, three or four-year

timelag on the material treated. Covers all archaeological periods in Norway, Sweden, Denmark, Finland, Greenland, Iceland; thoroughly indexed. Computerised, and printed cumulative site and author index available for 1974–88.

Note that J P Lamm published a complete list of all Nordic archaeological bibliographies issued up to 1976 in *Fornvännen*, 71, 1976, pp 205–6.

Numismatic literature (0029–6031). 1947.– 2/yr. New York, NY: American Numismatic Society.
Nearly 1,000 periodicals are scanned to produce international coin abstracts; delay is 1–2 years. Coverage of coin reports within British excavation (etc) reports has often been patchy. Subject and author indexes.

Polish archaeological abstracts (0137–4885). 1972–. Annual. Wrocław: Polish Academy of Sciences.
The first archaeological abstracts to copy the British model; published in English, though the translations leave something to be desired. Covers Polish books and articles only, with considerable timelag.

Recently published articles (0145–5311). 1976–. 3/yr. American Historical Association, Washington DC.
Almost entirely historical, difficult to use; not recommended for British/Irish archaeological work.

Répertoire d'art et d'archéologie, see Bibliography of the history of art (above).

Résumés d'archéologie suisse: époque romaine (1010–8459). 1981–. Annual. Lausanne: Institut d'Archéologie et d'Histoire Ancienne, Lausanne University.
AND
Résumés zur Archäologie der Schweiz: Paläolithikum–LaTènezeit (1010–3368). 1984–. Annual. Schweizerische Gesellschaft für Ur- und Frühgeschichte, Basel.
Both these abstracts publications (modelled on *Brit archaeol abstr*) cover Swiss material only.

Revue archéologique de l'ouest (0767–709X). 1984–. Annual. Rennes: CNRS.
Each issue contains a 'Chronique bibliographique' of recent publications; titles on the prehistory and historic archaeology of (in rotation) Brittany, Normandy, the Loire, arranged by period.

RILA see Bibliography of the history of art (above).

Siedlungsforschung: Archäologie–Geschichte–Geographie (0175–0046). 1983–. Bonn: Seminar für Historische Geographie der Univ Bonn.
Focuses on German-speaking Central Europe: contains a bibliography on settlement in each issue, arranged on a basic classification with author index but no subject index.

Swedish archaeological bibliography (ISBNs only). 1939–75. Stockholm: Statens Historiska Museum.
These were five-yearly volumes containing topic surveys of recent trends. They ceased at the inception of *Nordic archaeological abstracts* (see above), but classical archaeology continues to be treated in the quinquennial series *Swedish archaeology* from Almqvist and Wiksell for Svenska Arkeologiska Samfundet.

Technology and culture: the international quarterly of the Society for the History of Technology (0040–165X). 1960–. Qrly. Chicago: Society for the History of Technology.
One issue each year contains current bibliography arranged by topic. Cumulative index to vols 1–10.

Other subjects

PRINTED SERVICES

British humanities index (0007–0815). 1962–. Qrly with annual cumulation. Bowker-Saur.
After 1992 is very marginal to archaeology, and the arrangement is unhelpful.

Current technology index (formerly *British technology index* to 1980). (0260–6593). Bimonthly with annual cumulation. London: Bowker-Saur. Also online via DIALOG.

Forest products abstracts (0140–4784). 1978–. Bimonthly. Wallingford: Commonwealth Agricultural Bureaux.
Occasionally treats vernacular architecture and other timber uses.

Forestry abstracts (0005–7538). Wallingford: CAB.
For woodland management practice etc.

The Times index. 1785–. Monthly. Reading: Research Publications International.
Printed indexes and microfilms. Useful for tracking archaeological press reports (etc) in the entire *Times* stable of publications.

Many specialist journals also have regular biblio-
graphies.

SOME ONLINE SERVICES

Note that BIDS (Bath Information and Data Services) offers a range of online databases accessible via JANET to members of subscribing institutions. Also, this is a fast-moving field, with many online producers progressively moving to CD-ROM issue, so it is best to check the latest situation. It is also advisable to check on any charges for access! The name of the provider is given for each.

Architecture database. 1978–. British Architectural Library.

Arts and Humanities Search. 1980–, with access to over 1,100 journals world-wide. Institute for Scientific Information (ISI).

Biosis Previews. 1969–. All aspects of life sciences. Also on CD-ROM.

CAB Abstracts. 1972–. Commonwealth Agricultural Bureaux material. Also on CD-ROM.

CA Search. 1967–. Chemistry (same content as printed *Chemical Abstracts*). Chemical Abstracts Service.

GEOBASE. 1980–. Geography, geology, ecology. Elsevier Science BV.

GEOREF. 1785– (for N American material); 1933– (for worldwide material). Geology, geophysics, hydrology, palaeontology. American Geological Institute.

MEDLINE. 1964–. Medical sciences (same content as *Index Medicus*). Also available from 1985 as CD-ROM. US National Library of Medicine.

MLA International Bibliography. 1963–. Literature, languages, linguistics, folklore. Also on CD-ROM. Modern Languages Association.

SciSearch®. 1974–. General science, corresponds to *Science Citation Index*. Available on CD-ROM from 1986. Institute for Scientific Information (ISI).

Social Sciences Index. 1983–. Social and behavioural sciences with some other topics. H W Wilson Co.

Social SciSearch. Institute for Scientific Information (ISI).

SOME CD-ROM SERVICES

(Some of these are available as WinSPIRS, Windows SilverPlatter Information Retrieval System).

Art Index. 1984–. Includes archaeology and museums. H W Wilson Co.

ASLIB Index to Theses, with abstracts. 1970–. Lists higher degrees in British universities. Learned Information (Europe).

Avery Index to Architectural Periodicals on CD-ROM. 1977–. G K Hall and Co.

Bodleian Library Catalogue of pre-1920 books. OUP Electronic Publishing.

British Borehole Catalogue. Current. Over 700,000 boreholes and wells registered with British Geological Society. Geo Information International.

British Library General Catalogue of Printed Books to 1975 on CD-ROM. Saztec Europe Ltd.

British National Bibliography. 1950–. Lists monographs published in the UK. British Library.

Dissertation Abstracts. 1861–. Indexes theses, mainly USA PhD and MPhil, but including some from Europe and elsewhere. CD Plus Technologies.

Historical Abstracts on Disc. 1991–. World history, 1450–present. ABC-CLIO Inc.

ICONDA. 1976–. Indexes the literature of building worldwide. SilverPlatter Information Ltd.

Life Sciences Collection (including ecology). 1982–. SilverPlatter Information Ltd.

MEDLINE. As for online service (above).

MLA International Bibliography. 1963–. Also online, above.

Science Citation index. 1980–. Institute for Scientific Information (ISI).

URBADISC. 1980–. Architecture, environment, local government, urban studies etc. European material. London Research Centre.

1.6
Listings of Theses

Listings for archaeological theses are shown first, followed by those for other subjects.

Archaeology

Although general lists of theses such as the *Aslib index* have been published for a very long time, it is always hard to be sure of locating those on archaeological topics because the indexes to those lists tend to be poor, often failing to reognise what is an archaeological topic. Moreover there has been little success in producing regular listings of archaeological theses, despite the valuable information they usually contain. The CBA and the (London) Institute of Archaeology collaborated for some years (to 1977) on a duplicated list of 'Archaeological theses in progress', but lack of resources saw an end to it. The informal publication *Current research in archaeology*, which was issued from various universities in turn during the late 1970s, began listing completed theses one university at a time (see below), but soon discontinued publication altogether. Efforts since then have been intermittent, to say the least, but some of them are listed below. In addition, *British archaeological bibliography* has started to provide abstracts of theses notified to it.

The following universities are known to have produced individual lists:

Cambridge: *Doctoral research in Cambridge (1922–1987)* (ed Sarah Taylor) appeared as *Archaeol research from Cambridge occas pap*, 1, 1989, listing the theses in three chronological periods, 1922–50, 1950–70, and 1970–87, with commentaries by J G D Clark, C F W Higham and I Hodder respectively.

Durham: undergraduate and higher degree theses were listed in *Current research in archaeology*, 2, 1977.

Leicester: a list of theses submitted for the Museums Association Diploma is held by the Dept of Museum Studies at Leicester University.

London: theses from the Roman Department of the Institute of Archaeology, London were listed in *Current research in archaeology*, 1, 1976. From 1995, thesis abstracts are provided

in *Papers of the Institute of Archaeology* (0965–9315), which also lists MPhil and PhD topics in progress.

Oxford: theses from the Institute of Archaeology, Oxford were listed in *Current research in archaeology*, 3, 1978

Wales: Welsh studies are carried in *Studia Celtica*.

Ireland: *Trowel* (0791–1017), the journal of the Archaeological Society of University College Dublin, is undertaking regular listings of all the Irish university theses, and these now also appear on a 'Web' site (see p. 8 above). Previously, the Association of Young Irish Archaeologists (Dept of Archaeology, UCD) produced thesis lists, at least for 1976, 1977, 1983 . . .) and some of these were consolidated into *Trowel*'s fourth issue (1993).

Regional collections
(There may well be later references than those given below.)

East Anglia   *East Anglian Studies: theses completed* (comp and ed Janice Henney with Victor Morgan). Norwich: Centre for E Anglian Studies, 1982, x, 99 p.

East Midlands   University of Nottingham theses on E Midlands subjects were logged in *Midland history*, 4.1, 1977.

E Yorkshire and Humberside   A checklist for this area made by Brian Dyson was published by the University of Hull Centre for Regional and Local History in 1986.

North-West England   Northwest theses and dissertations 1950–78 were logged by U Lawler as *Occas pap* 8, 1981, of the Centre for NW Regional Studies, Univ Lancaster.

Surrey   Lists of theses in history and archaeology relating to Surrey are regularly listed in *Surrey archaeol collect*: eg vols 75 (1984), 78 (1987) and 81 (1991–2).

Topics related to archaeology

Agrarian history
Morgan, Raine, *Dissertations on British agrarian history: a select list of theses awarded higher degrees in Britain and foreign universities [1876–1978]*. Reading: Univ Reading, 1981, xxv, 170 p. (*Inst Agric Hist bibliographies in*

agricultural history, 2). Continuation lists are included from time to time in *Agric hist rev*.

Architectural history

The Society of Architectural Historians of Great Britain maintains a register of research in progress, with occasional printed copies; currently c. 3,000 entries with cross-references. Number 6 covered the years 1981–93 and contained more postgraduate work than had previous numbers. Apply to the Secretary, SAHGB (address given in Section 4.2 Organisations).

Classical studies

Annual list in *Bulletin of the Institute of Classical Studies*.

History

Annual lists appear from the University of London's Institute of Historical Research: *Historical research for higher degrees in the United Kingdom* (1986–) which includes theses in progress and completed. There have been two retrospective cumulations done respectively by Phyllis M Jacobs in 1976 (for 1901–70) and Joyce M Horn in 1984 (for 1971–80). *See also Schürer and Anderson in Section 2.3 Databases*.

Urban history (formerly *Urban history yearbook*) has occasional review articles on theses but no list of work in progress.

For **Wales**, periodical lists appear in *Welsh historical review*.

For **Scotland**, theses received by the National Library of Scotland are listed in the *Bibliography of Scotland (see Section 1.1 Guides to Literature – general)*.

For **Ireland**, alternate issues of *Irish historical studies* contain lists of research for historical degrees.

General lists of theses and/or current research

Some universities publish lists of their own theses, which may be more up to date than the ASLIB compilation.

Aslib index to theses accepted for higher degrees by the universities of Great Britain and Ireland and the Council for National Academic Awards (1950–). Archaeology is treated as a subhead of history, and since the subject index is based mainly on specific words in titles it frequently fails to reveal relevant material (eg 'gentry houses' are found under 'houses' but would not be picked up by a search under 'architecture' or 'vernacular' or 'social history'). The publication contains a list of universities which deposit thesis copies (with various entry dates to the scheme). There is now a CD-ROM version of this publication (from Expert Information Ltd of Hinksey Hill, Oxfordshire).

For the period before 1950 see:

Bilboul, Roger R, *Retrospective index to theses of Great Britain and Ireland 1716–1950: vol 1, social sciences and humanities*. Oxford: ABC-Clio Press, 1975, ix, 393 p. Covers some 13,000 theses by subject and author up to the start of the Aslib series.

British reports, translations and theses. British Library, monthly with quarterly cumulations on fiche.

Comprehensive dissertation index 1861–1972 ('CDI'). Within the 37 volumes (or 800 fiche) archaeology is filed in the Social Sciences volume (17) and given as a separate heading in the contents list. Indexing is by keywords from titles, so searching will be unreliable.

Current research in Britain ('CRIB'). London: Brit Lib Board, 9 ed 1994 (or any later edn). Very useful if you can work out in which of the several volumes (Humanities; Social Sciences; Biological Sciences; Physical Sciences) the topic sought will lie. It is also fairly comprehensive, including (besides universities and polytechnics) colleges, other further education institutions, and some bodies like the CBA not normally thought of as research institutions. The indexing, as for the Aslib volume, tends to be naive, being based on keywords suggested by authors.

1.7
Library Directories and Specialist Libraries

Wales, Scotland and **Ireland** are treated in separate sections below.

Public libraries often have union catalogues of periodicals showing which titles are held in which library branches for a particular borough or district, and for how long they are kept. The six national **copyright deposit libraries** are the British Library, the Bodleian Library of Oxford University, the University of Cambridge Library, the National Library of Wales in Aberystwyth, the National Library of Scotland in Edinburgh, and the library of Trinity College Dublin.

The conditions and/or hours of access for libraries can change, so always telephone before planning a visit. Many university library catalogues are available over Telnet and/or JANET (the Joint Academic NETwork), but bear in mind that their computer cataloguing may only have started a decade or so ago, and that many libraries still rely on card catalogues for their older materials.

Library directories

(see also Section 2.1 Record offices . . .)

Alston, R C, *Handlist of library catalogues and lists of books and manuscripts in the British Library Department of Manuscripts*. London: *Occas pap Bibliogr Soc*, 6, 1991. Includes large numbers of titles not previously brought together in one volume.

*Aslib directory of information sources in the United Kingdom (eds K W Reynard and J M E Reynard). London: Aslib, 8 edn 1994, 1286 p, subject index. 0 85142 321 3.
Regularly revised, but relies largely on questionnaire response, and with only 90 entries under 'archaeology' this work may disappoint.

*Bloomfield, Barry (ed), *A directory of rare books and special collections in the United Kingdom and the Republic of Ireland*. Lib Ass, 2 edn due 1996. 1 85604 063 1 [The previous edition edited by Moelwyn Williams has very lengthy descriptions of the individual library collections.]

Bryon, Rita V and Bryon, Terence N (eds),

Maritime information: a guide to libraries and sources of information in the United Kingdom. London: Witherby for Maritime Info Ass, 3 edn 1993, vi, 222 p, index. 1 85609 069 8 pb.
Lists c 500 institutions, giving notes on their holdings.

Dale, Peter (ed), *Guide to libraries in Western Europe: national, international and government libraries*. Boston Spa: Brit Lib, 1991, iv, 169 p. 0 7123 0785 0.

—, *Guide to library and information units in government departments and other organisations*. London: British Lib, 32 edn 1996, 190p. 0 7123 0828 8 pb.
Does not claim to be exhaustive on any topic, but is including more archaeological libraries as they come to notice at each revision. Now includes e-mail and Internet addresses.

Dewe, Michael (ed), *A manual of local studies librarianship*. Aldershot: Gower, 1987, xv, 419 p, bibl, index.
A useful article is D Paul and M Dewe, 'Local studies collections in academic libraries', pp 52–69.

***Guy, Susanna (comp), *English local studies handbook. A guide to resources for each county including libraries, record offices, societies, journals and museums*. Exeter: Univ Exeter Press, 1992, xiv, 343 p. 0 85989 369 3 pb.
An excellent compilation with many uses for archaeologists, eg maps showing the pre-1974 and post 1974 counties, and lists of local societies and their journals.

*Harrold, Ann (ed), *Libraries in the United Kingdom and the Republic of Ireland 1996*. London: Lib Ass, 22 edn 1995, 278 p, indexes. 1 85604 147 6 limp cloth (or any current edition: revised annually).
A very basic listing, without descriptions of collections, of public libraries, academic institutions, selected government, national and special libraries. Rather scanty for Ireland; use the directory listed below under Ireland for preference.

—, *Academic libraries in the United Kingdom and the Republic of Ireland, 1994*. London: Lib Ass Publishing, 1994, viii, 148 p, indexes. 1 85604 114 X. Included here for completeness, though archaeology (and history) are not indexed and therefore hard to locate.

**Kimura, A and Howes, K A (eds), *Libraries*

directory 1993–95. Cambridge: James Clarke, 1994, v, 310 p. 0 2276 7928 8 (Formerly *Libraries Yearbook*).

Includes Irish public and special libraries; gives useful indications of collection size and character for each. The best of the library guides, though not easy to navigate through, with its somewhat basic index.

LRCC (Univ London Library Resources Coordinating Committee) has produced various subject guides to libraries in London: *Archaeology, Art history, Classical studies, Geography and map collections, Geology, History* have all been treated.

***McBurney, Valerie et al, *Guide to libraries in London*. London: Brit Lib, 1995, iv, 368 p, bibl, index. 0 7123 0821 0.

Covers public, academic and 'special' libraries in 33 London boroughs. To be updated every couple of years.

Mace, Angela, *The Royal Institute of British Architects: a guide to its archive and history*. London: Mansell, 1986, xliv, 378 p, partial index. 0 7201 1773 9.

Walton, Mary (comp), 'The Hunter collection in the Sheffield Central Library', *Trans Hunter Archaeol Soc*, 13, 1985, pp 47–64 (followed on pp 65–6 by C M Short's guide to the Hunter Society archives).

Listed here as an example of the kind of description of a local collection that is worth looking out for in your own area.

Libraries in England of particular use to archaeologists

Most of these libraries can take brief telephone enquiries; more detailed questions should be put by post or in person. Their catalogues may be available over Telnet, NISS or other systems. Times of opening vary so check first by telephone. You should also check if you want older materials which might be in distant stores. To take **London** first:

Society of Antiquaries of London, Burlington House, Piccadilly, London W1V 0HS (tel 0171 734 0193 or 0171 437 9954, fax 0171 287 6967, e-mail soc.antiq.lond@bbcnc.org.uk). The principal library covering archaeology and antiquities, with some 200,000 books and a large collection of prints and drawings,

photographs etc (card-indexed). Non-Fellows of the Society, if members of the Royal Archaeological Institute or the British Archaeological Association, may use the library; other readers need a letter of introduction from a Fellow or tutor, or should arrange beforehand with the Librarian or General Secretary. (Closed for several weeks in summer.)

University College London, Gower Street, London WC1E 6BT, tel 0171 387 7050 (switchboard), fax 0171 380 7373, e-mail library@ucl.ac.uk. Much of the library catalogue is automated and available online (telnet lib.ucl.ac.uk), though the card catalogue may need to be consulted for older, little-used material. Items in store requested before 2 pm are available at 10 am next day.

UCL Institute of Archaeology, 31–34 Gordon Square, London WC1H 0PY, tel 0171 380 7485. (This library is treated in some detail as the most comprehensive collection of archaeological material in both UCL and the University of London.) It contains c. 40,000 books and as many periodical volumes, plus 23,000 pamphlets and well over 900 current periodical titles. It has recently added materials on medieval archaeology, and there are emphases on museums, conservation and materials science topics. Also includes the Tylecote collection of archaeometallurgical works and the Margaret Wood collection of English architectural history. The library's catalogue is increasingly appearing on computer; being prepared for computerisation are the Institute's valuable guardbook indexes to publications on archaeological sites. Pre-1975 issues of all but seven periodical titles are in store within the building; if ordered before 10 am are available within 30 minutes, similarly if ordered before 2 pm. PhD theses are in UCL store but appear on the computer catalogue by author, title and keyword. Undergraduate and MA/MSc theses are mostly in the Institute of Archaeology, on microfiche to c. 1989, later ones in store across the road.

Other sections of UCL within easy reach of the Institute of Archaeology are:

The *Science Library* (D M S Watson Building, UCL, tel 0171 380 7789) contains extremely useful collections on anthropology, botany, geography, geology, history of science, medical archaeology, statistics and computer science, and zoology.

The *Main Library* (tel 0171 380 7793 for enquiry desk) contains strong collections of Scandinavian studies, history, and Classical archaeology; also fine art and the history of art.

The *Environmental Studies Library* in the Bartlett School of Architecture and Planning (Wates House, 22 Gordon Street, London WC1H 0QB, tel 0171 387 7050 ext 4900) is a good source for building history, conservation areas and town planning information.

Institute of Classical Studies Library (includes the Joint Library of the Hellenic and Roman Societies), Senate House, Malet St, London WC1E 7HU (tel 0171 323 9574, fax 0171 323 9575). ICS is a postgraduate institution, part of the University of London School of Advanced Study. A guide to contents and services is available. Guardbook catalogue to 1991, thereafter computerised. Borrowing rights for members of Roman Society and Hellenic Society; others should enquire about access for reference. Maintains as a database the annual section from *Britannia*, 'Roman Britain in 19..'; also has a copy of DYABOLA (see Section 2.3 Databases). Publishes *Bulletin* (annual); series of *Supplements* (irreg); *Guide to audiovisual resources for the classics* (1995): a catalogue of its Roman slide collection, searchable by computer, slides available for hire to members only; lists of classical meetings in London etc.

Other libraries in London which may be useful: listed by name of library

British Architectural Library, housed at the Royal Institute of British Architects, 66 Portland Place, London W1N 4AD (tel 0171 580 5533, fax 0171 631 1802). Extremely important for architectural history: drawings, photographs, slides, manuscripts and archives from early 17th century, travel journals and the like. Manuscripts relating to 19th century excavations at Fountains Abbey and at Newton St Loe are held. There is a 500-fiche main catalogue up to 1984, computer catalogue thereafter. The *Architecture Database* (books and journals) is available on DIALOG. The very important Drawings Collection is housed at 21 Portman Square, London W1H 9HF (same telephone as main library). Not being publicly funded, the library now charges a quite substantial fee for

consultation. For a guide to the library see under Mace p33 above; several information leaflets can be sent for

British Library Reference Division, Great Russell Street, London WC1B 3DG (Reading Room Enquiries 0171 412 7676). Too well known to need description here; as a copyright library it is entitled to receive a copy of every book published in the UK and the Republic of Ireland, and also contains large collections of maps, topographical views and Ordnance Survey material. The move to new, high-technology premises next to St Pancras Station is currently projected for some time in 1997. Two other British Library reading rooms in London are for **Life Sciences** (9 Kean Street, London WC2 4AT, tel 0171 412 7288) – a calm oasis off Aldwych – and for **Science and Technology** (25 Southampton Buildings, London WC2A 1AW, tel 0171 412 7494) – the extremely busy former Patent Office Library which can be useful for the history of technology. The **British Library Document Supply Service**, Wetherby, Boston Spa, W Yorks LS23 7BQ (tel 01937 546000) is the main source of lending and photocopy material.

Civic Trust, 17 Carlton House Terrace, London SW1Y 5AW (tel 0171 930 0914). Considerable stock of books, pamphlets and periodicals on many aspects of the environment including architecture, topography, planning, etc. Available for reference by appointment only.

Greater London Record Office and History Library, 40 Northampton Road, London EC1R 0HB (tel 0171 332 3820, fax 0171 833 9136). London history and topography, prints and maps etc, open to the general public Tues-Fri for reference purposes.

Guildhall Library, The Guildhall, Aldermanbury, London EC2P 2EJ, tel 0171 332 1868/1870 (Printed Books); 0171 332 1839 (Prints, maps and drawings). Mainly historical records relating to London's past: the Printed Books section concentrates on the 'Square Mile' of the City of London, but has quite good cover of Greater London. The Manuscripts section (tel 0171 332 1863) contains City of London records; archives of the Diocese of London; St Paul's Cathedral; City wards and parishes; livery companies. Numerous publications include *A guide to archives and manuscripts at Guildhall Library* and *London buildings and sites: a guide* for *researchers in Guildhall Library* (1976); bookshop selling own and many other publications. *See also entry in Section 2.1 Record offices.*

Lambeth Palace Library, Lambeth Palace Road, London SE1 7JU (tel 0171 928 6222). The main source for the history of the Church of England, also ecclesiastical history and topography, and strong local collections (Kent, Surrey, Sussex, etc). Available for public use (letter of introduction needed). Appealing for funds to computerise its catalogue.

Linnean Society, Burlington House, Piccadilly, London W1V 0LQ (tel 0171 434 4479). The Library contains over 90,000 books and journals on biology, available to non-members via British Library Document Supply Service at Boston Spa.

London Library, 14 St James's Square, London SW1Y 4LG (tel 0171 930 7705, fax 0171 930 0436 – book enquiries, 0171 930 8803). The famous subscription library. Several catalogues were published up to 1953, then microform catalogue and subject index 1984–9. Computer catalogue from 1984 on. Good archaeological collection and close relationship with Society of Antiquaries.

National Art Library, Victoria and Albert Museum, Cromwell Road, London SW7 2RL (0171 938 8315, fax 0171 938 8461). Intended for reference only when other sources have been tried. Readers register on arrival; identification is asked for but there is no charge for using the library, and a 5-visit pass is issued for limited research purposes. Full season ticket facilities (eg for research projects) require the production of passport photographs. Library open 10.00–5.00 Tuesday to Saturday.

Public Record Office *see entry in Section 2.1 Record Offices.*

Royal Armouries Library, Tower of London, London EC3N 4AB (tel 0171 480 6358, fax 0171 481 2922). Accessible to public, but 24 hours' notice advisable to obviate need to pay heavy Tower admission fee. Includes arms and armour; history of fortifications; photographic reference archive; brass rubbings.

Royal Geographical Society, 1 Kensington Gore, London SW7 2AR (tel 0171 589 5466, fax 0171 584 4447; e-mail rgs@uk.ac.bbk.ge). (Members only.) Geography, topography, cartography, map room etc, with extensive series of geographical periodicals.

Royal Institute of British Architects *see British Architectural Library above.*

Royal Institution of Chartered Surveyors, 12 Great George Street, London SW1P 3AE (tel 0171 222 7000, fax 0171 222 9430). Includes architecture, fine arts etc as well as all aspects of land measurement and management. Reference library by appointment only.

Wellcome Institute for the History of Medicine, Library, 183 Euston Road, London NW1 2BE (tel 0171 611 8888). Its library database and catalogue (WILDCat) are available via JANET (uk.ac.ucl.wihm) or Internet wihm.ucl.ac.uk

LIBRARIES OUTSIDE LONDON
A small selection only, listed by name of library:

England
Ashmolean Library, Oxford: Beaumont Street, Oxford OX1 2PH, (tel 01865 278088, fax 01865 278018). Supports the important archaeological collections of the Museum.

Bodleian Library, Oxford: Broad Street, Oxford OX1 3BG, (tel 01865 277000, fax 01865 277182). One of the six copyright deposit libraries.

Borthwick Institute of Historical Research Library, St Anthony's Hall, Peasholme Green, York YO1 2PW (tel 01904 642315). Extensive archives, substantial research library, many ecclesiastical materials including architecture, centre for Yorkshire local history etc. Printed guides to the deposited archives are available. Access by appointment only.

British Geological Survey Keyworth Library, Keyworth, Notts NG12 5GG (tel 0115 936 3100, fax 0115 936 3200). Large collection of books, maps, journals photographs, archives; open to members of the public for reference purposes. Also libraries in Edinburgh (0131 667 1000) and the London Information Office in the Natural History Museum Earth Galleries, Exhibition Road, London SW7 2DE (tel 0171 589 4090, fax 0171 584 8270).

Haddon Library, University of Cambridge, Faculty of Archaeology and Anthropology, Downing Street, Cambridge CB2 3DZ (tel 01223 333505/6; e-mail asb12@cam.ac.uk OR eth1@ula.cam.ac.uk). Has an annually

updated guide.
Open access, if reader can show a library card from another university or produce other evidence of bona fide interest.

Leeds Metropolitan University Library, Brunswick Terrace, Leeds LS2 8BU (tel 0113 283 2600 ext 3356). Good architectural history, conservation and environmental collection, including historic gardens.

Leeds University Library, Leeds LS2 9JT (tel 0113 233 5501, e-mail library@library.novell. leeds.ac.uk). The Brotherton Collection here consists of rare books and MSS, especially of 17th and 18th century England. Good archaeological collection.

Royal Commission on the Historical Monuments of England (Swindon), *see entry in Section 4.2 Organisations.*

Sheffield University, St George's Library, Mappin Street, Sheffield S1 4DT (tel 0114 282 5041, fax 0114 279 6406, e-mail t.clarke@sheffield. · ac.uk). Includes the Society of Glass Technology collection of journals and printed materials.

Surrey Archaeological Society, Castle Arch, Guildford, Surrey GU1 3SX (tel 01483 32454). Included here as an example of the kind of library some county archaeological societies can provide (appointment needed).

(York) Institute of Advanced Architectural Studies, The King's Manor, York YO1 2EP, tel 01904 433969. Excellent book collection including planning, architecture, cities, transport, conservation of historic gardens; slide collection, architectural theses.

York Minster Library, Dean's Park, York YO1 2JD (tel 01904 625308). The strength of this collection is in church architecture, particularly on the practical side of maintenance; reasonable collection of county materials. In manuscripts section are a few antiquarian notes which can be useful for understanding obliterated features in ecclesiastical buildings. Also Yorkshire local history.

Yorkshire Archaeological Society, Claremont, 23 Clarendon Road, Leeds LS2 9NZ (tel 0113 245 7910). Another exemplar of the well stocked and catalogued county archaeological society library. This one is available to non-members by appointment.

Wales

Directory of information sources in Wales (ed D M Hooper). Cardiff: Welsh Development Agency/ Information Services Group Wales, 1989, iii, 83 p. 0 950340 67 7.
Gives 160 entries for public, academic and special libraries etc; indicates subject coverage, access, etc.

The main libraries for archaeological purposes are:

National Library of Wales, Penglais, Aberystwyth SY23 3BU (tel 01970 623816, fax 01970 615709, e-mail nlw@uk.ac.aberystwyth). Founded 1907 as the central repository for public and private archives in Wales: holds large collection of prints, drawings and maps, and has been a copyright deposit library since 1911. Includes archives of Welsh churches. Computer catalogue of own holdings. Produces the biennial *Bibliography of Wales.* Persons over 18 may apply for a ticket.

National Museum of Wales, Cathays Park, Cardiff CF1 3NP (tel 01222 397951 ext 234, fax 01222 373219). Library contains large collection relating to the archaeology and industrial archaeology of Wales in particular; also houses the libraries of the Cambrian Archaeological Association and the Cardiff Naturalists' Society. Important manuscript collections include the John Ward archive of excavations etc.

Royal Commission on the Ancient and Historical Monuments of Wales, Crown Buildings, Plas Crug, Aberystwyth SY23 1NJ (tel 01970 621233). For the very extensive Welsh National Monuments Record collection of photographs, drawings, etc, see entry in Section 4.2 Organisations.

Scotland

LIBRARY DIRECTORIES/CONTENTS
Cox, Michael (ed), *Exploring Scottish history: a directory of resource centres for Scottish local and national history in Scotland.* [s l: Edinburgh?]: Scottish Library Ass and Scottish Local History Forum, 1992, 161 p. 0 900649 79 8 pb. Gives considerable detail for individual libraries and archive collections, but provision of a subject index would have much enhanced its usefulness.

Dunsire, Gordon and Osborne, B D, *Scottish library and information resources*. Motherwell: Scottish Lib Ass, 8 edn 1995, 178 p, subject and name indexes. Contains little archaeology, so mostly to be used for adjacent topics.

Hill, Paulette M, *Historic buildings and monuments in Scotland: a listing of guidebooks and reference works held in Scottish Office Library, Brandon Street*. Edinburgh: Scott Off Lib, 1992 (duplicated, no ISBN).
This library (now with Historic Scotland in Longmore House, Salisbury Place) keeps all editions and revisions of Scottish guides for the sake of recording changing interpretations.

PRINCIPAL SCOTTISH LIBRARIES FOR ARCHAEOLOGICAL PURPOSES

National Library of Scotland, George IV Bridge, Edinburgh EH1 1EW (tel 0131 226 4531, fax 0131 220 6662). Founded 1682, copyright library since 1710. Reference only, for research not easily done elsewhere. Publication *Microform research collections in the National Library of Scotland* (1989). The **Map Library** is at 33 Salisbury Place, Edinburgh EH9 1SL [ie near Historic Scotland]; tel 0131 226 4531 ext 3413, fax 0131 668 3472.

National Monuments Record for Scotland, see under Royal Commission on the Ancient and Historical Monuments of Scotland in Section 4.2 Organisations.

National Museum of Scotland Library, Queen Street, Edinburgh EH2 1JD (tel 0131 225 7534 ext 369/375, fax 0131 557 9498). Excellent Scottish archaeological collection, and contains papers of the Society of Antiquaries of Scotland.

Edinburgh City Libraries, Scottish Library, Central Public Library, George IV Bridge, Edinburgh EH1 1EG (tel 0131 225 5584, fax 0131 225 8783). Stronger on Scottish life than on archaeology; prior consultation advised.

Glasgow, Mitchell Library, North Street, Glasgow G3 7DN (tel 0141 305 2937, fax 0141 305 2815). Contains the Glasgow Collection.

Historic Scotland library, Longmore House, Salisbury Place, Edinburgh EH9 1SH (tel 0131 668 8651). Staff collection relating to historic buildings and monuments in care. The photograph library, open for public use, contains transparencies and prints of monuments in state care (tel 0131 668 8647).

St Andrews University Library, North Street, St Andrews, Fife KY16 9TR (tel 01334 476161, fax 01334 477323). For maritime studies including maritime archaeology.

Scottish Natural History library, Foremount House, Kilbarchan, Renfrewshire PA10 2EZ. Extensive collection of books and journals on Scottish environment, botany, geology, geography, agriculture, archaeology and wildlife, etc. Bibliographic service. The library is intended, when complete, to be transferred to National Library of Scotland.

Ireland

Directory of libraries and information services in Ireland. [Dublin]: Lib Ass of Ireland and Lib Ass (Northern Ireland Branch), 4 edn 1993, 205 p, indexes. 0 946037 20 4 (LAI), 0 906066 08 5 (LANIB).
(See also Kimura and Howes, listed above in the main UK sub-section; and note that Ann Walsh at Trinity College Dublin Library keeps a record of local research centres in Ireland.)

PRINCIPAL IRISH LIBRARIES FOR ARCHAEOLOGICAL PURPOSES

[Belfast] Linen Hall Library, 17 Donegall Square North, Belfast BT1 5GD (tel 01232 321707, fax 01232 438586) is well-known for its collection of Irish and local studies, including many old and rare books, but with no particular archaeological emphasis. Founded 1788.

Belfast Public Library, Royal Avenue, Belfast BT1 1EA (tel 01232 243233, fax 332819). Has a good Irish and Local Studies Department and includes the antiquarian archives of F J Bigger.

Gilbert Library, 138–142 Pearse Street, Dublin 2 (tel Dublin 677 7662). For Dublin and local Irish collections.

Maritime Institute of Ireland, Museum and Library, Haigh Terrace, Dun Laoghaire, Co Dublin (tel Dublin 280 0969, fax 284 4602). Open in summer months only. Contains several thousand volumes on maritime subjects.

National Library of Ireland, Kildare Street, Dublin 1 (tel Dublin 661 8811, fax 676 6690). The Republic's copyright library and its main bibliographic centre. Printed books, manuscripts, maps, prints, drawings, exhibitions etc. Phone for opening hours.

Royal Irish Academy, 19 Dawson Street, Dublin 2 (tel Dublin 676 2570/676 4222, librarian 668 0499, fax 676 2346). A letter of introduction from a Member of the RIA, a faculty member or another library is needed, and a charge is made for using the library. Closed for first 2–3 weeks in August.

Royal Society of Antiquaries of Ireland, 63 Merrion Square, Dublin 2 (tel Dublin 676 1749). Non-Fellows may use the library by appointment; afternoons only.

Trinity College Dublin, College Street, Dublin 2 (tel Dublin 677 2941, fax 671 9003). Apply in writing in advance. There is no department of archaeology in the College, though the library does have some relevant materials, mainly for the medieval course. Is one of the six copyright libraries.

University College Dublin, Belfield, Dublin 4 (tel Dublin 706 7583, fax 283 7667). Archaeology is taught in UCD and the library collections reflect that; a charge is made to non-university members.

Isle of Man

Manx National Heritage, Manx Museum, Kingswood Grove, Douglas, IoM IM1 3LY (tel 01624 675522, fax 01624 661899). Open to public for reference only; small reference stock on archaeology etc. Produced *Bibliography of the literature of the Isle of Man* (2 vols, 1933 and 1939).

Channel Islands

Jersey States Library, Halkett Place, St Helier JE2 4WH, CI (tel 01534 59991, fax 69444). Includes archaeology, especially that of the Bailiwick of Jersey.

La Société Guernesiaise, Candie Gardens, St Peter Port, Guernsey, CI (tel 01481 63410). Small library of books on local topics; holds comprehensive index to the society's *Report and transactions*.

And finally, for when libraries fail:
Sheppard's book dealers in the British Isles. A directory of antiquarian and secondhand book dealers in the UK, the Channel Islands, Isle of Man and the Republic of Ireland. London: Europa, any recent edition (0950–0715).
Arranged by area and subject-indexed.

1.8
Excavation Roundups

This section indicates where to find good collections of summary results of recent excavations and other discoveries. The fullest source, for the period 1961–76 only, was that published by the Ministry of Public Building and Works (later Department of the Environment). The publication's first title was *Excavations annual report* (running from 1961–7) and then *Archaeological excavations: a brief summary of prehistoric, Roman and medieval sites throughout the country excavated in advance of destruction* (1968–76). It listed both grant-aided and direct Government excavations, by broad chronological period and county. A consolidated index for the whole series never materialised in the form originally envisaged, but see under Butcher below. After 1976 these reports appeared in appropriate period journals, eg *Britannia, Medieval archaeology, Post-medieval archaeology*. Note too that several county journals run similar roundups for their own areas.

One-off reports

***Butcher, Sarnia and Garwood, Paul (comp), *Rescue excavation 1938 to 1972: a report for the Backlog Working Party of the Ancient Monuments Advisory Committee of English Heritage*. London: English Heritage, 1994, 82 p. 1 85074 482 3 pb.
Contains a straight alphabetical list of sites excavated in advance of destruction, using Government funds, during what Barry Cunliffe terms in his preface 'the Heroic Age of rescue archaeology in Britain'. (Excavators received a minimum of support at that time and few were able to complete their reports.) For each site listed, excavator names and references to any resultant reports are given, with an indication of archaeological periods examined. An invaluable record, with a list of sites by county, but unfortunately no index of excavators.

**Hamlin, Ann and Lynn, Chris, *Pieces of the past: archaeological excavations by the Dept of the Environment for Northern Ireland 1970–86*. Belfast: HMSO for DoENI, 1988, xxi, 109 p. 0 337 08216 2 pb.
Useful summaries of the excavations, including

brief statistics. Three triennial roundups entitled *Finding and minding* appeared covering the years 1983 to 1992; future reports from Historic Monuments and Buildings will be subsumed within those of the Environment and Heritage Service.

Serial publications

Archaeological excavations, see note at head of this section.

Archaeology in Britain (CBA) which ran from 1972 to 1992 carried brief excavation reports, following on from the 'Summaries of excavations' published in the *CBA Calendar of Excavations* every January from 1967 to 1984. Nothing has yet taken its place in the shape of a comprehensive annual roundup.

Archaeology in Wales (0306–7629, from CBA Wales, formerly CBA Group 2) carries excavation and fieldwork summaries and (more recently) full-scale articles as well.

Britannia (0068–113X) from the Society for the Promotion of Roman Studies has run a near-comprehensive annual section 'Roman Britain in 19XX' since 1970.

Discovery and excavation in Scotland (0419–411X) from CSA (formerly CBA Group 1) has been a mine of Scottish excavation and field survey information ever since 1946, and until 1989 carried an excellent bibliography of Scottish material culture in addition. 'The indispensable tool of anyone interested in Scotland's archaeology [and] the exemplar throughout the United Kingdom for such publications' (Sir Hector Monro).

Discovery Programme reports: Vol 1, Project results 1992 and *Vol* 2, Project results 1993. Dublin: Roy Ir Acad, 1993 and 1994 respectively (and continuing).
These reports detail the results of the four important projects running under the Discovery Programme: Western Forts, Tara, Ballyhoura Hills, North Munster.

Excavations annual report, see note at head of this sub-section.

Excavations 19XX: summary accounts of archaeological excavations in Ireland (0790–7745). From 1985 used this title, with predecessors from 1970 (Assoc of Young Irish Archaeologists and then Irish Association of Professional Archaeologists) published in various forms including two numbers in the *Journal of Irish archaeology* (vols 4 and 5). Invaluable short summaries of virtually all Irish excavations, north and south of the border. Is now available on Internet at http://slarti.ucd.ie/pilots/archaeology/

Medieval archaeology (0076–6097) has run 'Medieval Britain in 19XX' since its inception in 1956.

Medieval Settlement Research Group annual report (0959–2474) includes a list of works published during the year.

Post-medieval archaeology (0079–4236) similarly offers post-medieval research summaries since its inception in 1967.

Proc Prehist Soc (0079–497X) ran excavation roundups for only a short period, 1982–85 (vols 48–51).

Whitaker's almanac, perhaps surprisingly, contains several pages on the most significant archaeological discoveries of the year.

SECTION 2

Finding out 2

Guides to unpublished sources

2.1
Record offices and other Repositories of Manuscripts and other Unpublished Materials

This section lists directories to record offices and other repositories, and also suggests some introductory books and aids to the use of unpublished sources. The most useful directory will probably be Foster and Sheppard, with Guy and the Royal Commission having less detail. Guides to actual contents of the repositories will be found in the next section, 2.2.

Advisory organisations, England and Wales

Addresses, where not given below, are listed in Section 4.2 Organisations.

Association of County Archivists

Manorial Documents Register (part of Royal Commission on Historical Manuscripts): the central point for information on the nature and location of manorial records; indexed by parish and arranged alphabetically by manor within county. Computerisation intended.

National Council on Archives, c/o Hon Sec, N Kingsley, Birmingham City Archives, Central Library, Chamberlain Square, Birmingham B3 3HQ, tel 0121 235 4219.

National Register of Archives

Royal Commission on Historical Manuscripts

Society of Archivists

Journals

Archives, Journal of the British Records Association (0003–9535). 1949–.
Journal of the Society of Archivists (0037–9816). 1955–.

Directories of record offices and other repositories

The Aslib directory of literary and historical collections in the United Kingdom (ed Keith Reynard). London: Aslib, 1993, 287 p, index. 0 85142 309 4 pb.

Based on questionnaire returns from the various collections; many local studies collections included.

Forbes, Heather, *Local authority archive services 1992: a survey commissioned by the Royal Commission on Historical Manuscripts and the National Council on Archives. Brit Lib Res and Devel rep*, **6090**, 1993, vii, 34 p. 0 11 887540 X pb.
Provides a picture of record offices on the eve of local government reorganisation, and records progress since the 1985 survey.

***Foster, Janet and Sheppard, Julia, *British archives*. London: Macmillan, 3 edn, 1995, lxiv, 627 p, indexes.
Valuable guide arranged alphabetically by town, with indexes by repository, collection and subject. Long list of useful publications.

*Gibson, J S W and Peskett, Pamela, *Record offices: how to find them*. Birmingham: Fed of Family History Societies, 6 edn, 1993, 60 p, maps, index.
Basic guide to locations.

***Guy, Susanna (comp), *English local studies handbook. A guide to resources for each county including libraries, record offices, societies, journals and museums*. Exeter: Univ Exeter Press, 1992, xiv, 343 p. 0 85989 369 3 pb.
Indispensable collection of data arranged by county; although the emphasis is on local history there is plenty of archaeology (local societies, lists of periodicals, museums, etc). A true 'vade mecum'.

Public Record Office: current guide. London/ Kew: PRO, 1991. 17 fiches in looseleaf plastic binder with printed introduction treating the PRO, access to records, their arrangement; scope of the Current Guide and how to use it; contents and arrangement of the separate parts.

**Royal Commission on Historical Manuscripts, *Record repositories in Great Britain: a geographical directory*. London: HMSO, 9 edn 1991 (or any later). 0 11 440243 4 pb.
Gives details of 256 repositories and other institutions able to help locate specific classes of records; for each, notes the address, telephone, custodian, opening hours, facilities, published guides to holdings, etc.

—, *Surveys of historical manuscripts in the United Kingdom: a select bibliography*. London: HMSO, 2 edn 1994, 24 p. 0 11 887544 2 pb.

Classified list: includes ecclesiastical, local/ topographical/ cartographic etc.

Silverthorne, Elizabeth (ed), *London local archives: a directory of local authority record offices and libraries*. London: Guildhall Library and Greater London Archives Network, 3 edn 1994, 44 p. 0 900422 38 6 hb, 0 9510665 3 6 pb.
Basic information for each repository: address, hours, facilities, area covered.

Wallis, H, guide to map sources, see Section 6.1 Reference (under Maps).

Introductory books and study aids

See also Section 6.17 Place-names and local history

Emmison, F G, *Archives and local history*. Chichester: Phillimore, 2 edn 1974, xvi, 112 p, index. 0 85033 091 2.

—, *How to read local archives 1500–1700*. London: Historical Association (= *Helps for students of history*, **H82**), 1967.
Is a 'guide to the last of the pre-italic hand-writings'.

Historical Association Short Guides to Records: numerous booklets with 'SG' prefix, dealing with such topics as building plans, railway and canal maps, fire insurance plans, manorial court rolls and books (all 1993; many more in preparation including OS maps, prints and engravings, etc). The first 24 guides in the series were collected into a single volume, *Short guides to records* (ed Lionel Munby, 1993, 120 p, 0 85278 347 7); they cover topics like estate maps and surveys, enclosure awards, tithe maps, rate books, probate inventories, and so on.

Iredale, David, *Enjoying archives: what they are, where to find them, how to use them*. Chichester: Phillimore, 1985, 214 p. 0 85033 561 2.

Martin, C Trice (comp), *The record interpreter: a collection of abbreviations, Latin words and names used in English historical manuscripts and records*. London: 2 edn 1910, latest reprint Phillimore 1994, xv, 464 p. 0 85033 465 9.
The standard 'decoder' for manuscripts.

Schürer and Anderson's guide to historical datafiles, see Section 2.3 Databases.

Scotland

Advisory organisation: Scottish Records Association

Journal: *Scottish archives: journal of the Scottish Records Association* (1353–1964). 1995–.

Directory

Cox, Michael (ed), *Exploring Scottish history: a directory of resource centres for Scottish local and national history in Scotland.* [s l]: Scot Lib Ass and Scot Local Hist Forum, 1992, 161 p. (No subject index). 0 900649 79 8 pb.
Gives considerable detail for individual archive collections (and libraries).

Ireland

Repositories and organisations concerned with records
Addresses, where not given below, are listed in Section 4.2 Organisations.

Irish Architectural Archive
[Irish] National Archive
Irish Society for Archives, Cumann Carlannaiochta Éireann, c/o Ms Jane Maxwell (Sec), Manuscripts Department, The Library, Trinity College, Dublin 2. Publishes *Irish archives* annually.
Maritime Institute of Ireland
Public Record Office Northern Ireland (PRONI)

Directories

Connolly, S J, *The public record: sources for local studies in the Public Record Office of Ireland.* Dublin: PROI, 1982, 48 p.

***Helferty, Seamus and Refaussé, Raymond, *Directory of Irish archives.* Dublin: Ir Acad Press, 2 edn 1993, 154 p. 0 7165 2507 0 hb, 0 7165 2508 9 pb.
Lists some 200 repositories with basic details including published or in-house guides, names of main collections; county and subject indexes.

2.2
Guides to Specific Sources of Manuscripts, Topographical Material, Prints, Drawings, Maps etc

---

The following are just a few of the many guides to specific collections. Bear in mind that most museums, whether local or national, hold valuable collections of papers, which may include excavation archives; they are not individually listed here. See also Section 6.1 Reference works (under Maps).

Britain (general)

Abbey, J R, *Scenery of Great Britain and Ireland in aquatint and lithograph, 1770–1860, from the library of J R Abbey: a bibliographic catalogue.* London: Curwen Press, 1952, reprinted Dawson 1972, further reprinted San Francisco: Alan Wofsy Fine Arts, 1991, xx, 399 p, index. 1 55660 130 1.

Barley, M W with contributions by P D A Harvey and J E Poole, *A guide to British topographical collections.* London: CBA, 1974, 159 p, bibl, indexes. 0 900312 24 6.
Describes briefly those collections of drawings, prints and photographs to be found in public repositories, and also in a few private collections, in Britain. Now needs to be used with care, according to B Nurse (see below). The author's notes were deposited in the Society of Antiquaries' Library (Ms.89b).

Brayley, E W and Britton, J, *The beauties of England and Wales, or delineations, topographical, historical and descriptive, of all the counties, collected from authentic sources and actual survey.* 18 vols in 25. London: 1801–18.
Contains 684 engraved plates in all; but must be used with care, because as B Nurse (below) says, like all engravings they can 'depart from verity'.

British Library, *Index of manuscripts in the British Library.* Cambridge: Chadwyck-Healey, 10 vols 1984–6. 0 85964 140 6 (set)
Entries for persons and places, but not subjects, for collections registered up to 1950.

British Museum, *Catalogue of manuscript maps, see Section 6.1 Reference works (under Maps).*

Chadwyck-Healey National inventory of documentary sources ('NIDS').

Commercial venture producing subject-indexed microfiche copies of catalogues (etc) from archive offices, libraries and other repositories in the UK. Available at British Library, National Library of Wales, National Library of Scotland, Bodleian Library Oxford, Leicestershire Museums Service and several university libraries. Index on CD-ROM with user manual, 1994.

Gray, Irvine, *Report on the manuscript collections of the Society of Antiquaries of London, twelfth to twentieth centuries.* Limited typescript edition, RCHMSS for Soc Antiquaries, 1985.

A select summary list (with relatively little archaeological material) issued as a temporary measure; full catalogue of the Society's important MS collections is forthcoming. (The Society has manuscripts of the Revd Bryan Faussett, William Stukeley, Cunnington/Colt Hoare, the Albert Way archive, Elliot Curwen, St John Hope, Wheeler, and many others.)

Griffiths, Antony and Williams, Reginald, *The Department of Prints and Drawings in the British Museum . . . user's guide.* London: Brit Mus Publ, 1987, viii, 189 p, index. 0 7141 1634 3.

A 26-page general introduction and other descriptive material is followed by 'Topics' in alphabetical order (eg antiquities, merchants' marks, industrial imagery). Also a list of periodicals held in the Department.

Guildhall Library (London), *Selected prints and drawings from the collection in the [Guildhall] Library: Part 1* (The Library, 1964)
   Part 2, Metropolitan boroughs (1965)
   Part 2, Environs of the metropolis and the Home Counties (1969)

Nurse, Bernard, 'Prints, drawings and watercolours', in M Dewe (ed), *Local studies collections: a manual*, vol 2 (Gower, 1991), pp 329–51.

Includes a useful survey of the kinds of material that can be found in collections (pp 332–5), but is mainly advice for librarians in charge of such material. The main collections are of course British Library/British Museum (with four separate indexes and repositories), the Bodleian Library (Dept of Western MSS), the Society of Antiquaries of London, RIBA, the Victoria and Albert Museum Prints and Drawings.

Payne, Ann, *Views of the past: topographical drawings in the British Library.* London: Brit Lib, 1987, 80 p. 0 7123 0130 5.

A selection illustrating the range of material held, eg antiquarian, military, travellers' views.

Public Record Office, *Maps and plans in the Public Record Office: 1, British Isles, c. 1410–1860.* London: PRO, 1967, xv, 648 p, index. 0 11 440109 8.

Regional arrangement, alphabetically by place-name within that. Said to describe only a small portion of those available; indeed the PRO holds a wealth of material valuable to the archaeologist – drawings and photographs as well as maps and plans.

RIBA, *Catalogue of the drawings collections of the Royal Institute of British Architects.* Aldershot: Gregg, 1972–89, 20 vols.

For 'polite' architecture; the catalogue is arranged by architect's name A-Z. There is a cumulative index (ed James Bettley) – Aldershot: Gregg, 1989, 602 p. 0 576 40004 1.

Russell, R, *Guide to British topographical prints.* Newton Abbot: David and Charles, 1979, 224 p, bibl, index. 0 7153 7810 4.

Chapters treat: the various print-making processes; books illustrated with prints; painters, draughtsmen and engravers.

Smith, Alfred Russell, *Catalogue of 10,000 tracts and 50,000 prints and drawings illustrating the topography and antiquities of England and Wales, Scotland and Ireland, collected by W Upcott and J R Smith.* London, 1878.

B Nurse (above) notes this as 'still one of the largest published collections'.

Somers Cocks, J V, *Devon topographical prints 1660–1870: a catalogue and guide.* Exeter: Devon Library Services, 1977, 0 86114 001 X.

Example of a county list: contains 3,500 items in parish and town order, with list of sources, very selective subject index, etc.

Wales

[Davies, Robert (comp)], *Estate maps of Wales 1600–1836: the holdings of the National Library of Wales with specific reference to an exhibition held in 1982.* Aberystwyth: Nat Lib Wales, 1982, 51 p. 0 907158 06 4.

Includes an index of surveyors and cartographers, but no topographical index.

National Museum of Wales (Cardiff): Papers of John Ward (1856–1922), the Keeper of the Department of Archaeology there from 1912. The Ward Papers relate to his work and interests at (notably) Gelligaer and the St Nicholas megalithic tomb, but also to Caerwent, Cardiff district, Cwmbrwyn Roman site, Merthyr Mawr Warren and many other sites. (Entered here as an illustration of the type of archives that may be found in museums.)

Scotland

Adams, Ian H (comp), *Descriptive list of plans in the Scottish Record Office.* Edinburgh: HMSO, 4 vols 1966–88, indexes of persons and subjects.
This work can help guide the discovery of pre-enclosure settlement patterns, pre-turnpike routes, arrangements of infield/outfield and the like.

Dunbar, J G, 'Source materials for Scottish architectural history', in *Art libraries journal*, 4.3, 1979, pp 17–26.
Short guide to the main printed and documentary sources.

Fenton, Alexander et al, *The Scottish ethnological archive.* Edinburgh: Nat Museums of Scotland *Information series*, 2, 1988, 24 p. 0 948636 41 6 pb.
Is an alphabetical list of archive subjects, with some illustrations. *See also entry in Section 4.2 Organisations.*

RCAHMS, *National Monuments Record of Scotland Jubilee 1941–1991: a guide to the collections.* Edinburgh: HMSO, 1991, 77 p, index. 0 11 494125 4 pb.
Introduces these very rich collections; treats the growth of NMRS; memorabilia; designs of houses and gardens; industrial surveys, excavation records, air photographs etc.

Smith, Alfred Russell, Catalogue, *see under Britain above.*

Ireland

Abbey, J R, on scenery illustrations, see under Britain above.

Connolly, S J, *The public record: sources for local studies in the Public Record Office of Ireland.* Dublin: PROI, 1982, 48 p.

Elmes, Rosalind, *Catalogue of Irish topographical prints and original drawings. New edition revised and enlarged by Michael Hewson.* Dublin: Malton Press for Nat Lib Ireland Society, 1975, 256 p, indexes. 0 7165 2276 4. Over 2,100 entries: indispensable for any study of the historic period. There is a 3-reel microform collection of the prints listed in Part I ('Prints and drawings in the National Library of Ireland'), so this volume forms an index to the microform.

Griffin, David J and Lincoln, Simon, *Drawings from the Irish Architectural Archive.* Dublin: Ir Archit Archive, 1993, 79 p. 0 9515536 6 6 pb.

Hayes, Richard J (ed), *Manuscript sources for the history of Irish civilisation.* 11 vols. Boston, Mass: G K Hall, 1965.
—, *First supplement (1965–1975).* 3 vols. Boston, Mass: G K Hall, 1979.
Like his guide to articles in Irish periodicals, this massive compilation is an essential tool for the scholar. Vols 1–4 of the main work treat Persons; 5–6 Subjects; 7–8 Places; 9–10 Dates; and 11 Collections covered. The supplement consists of Vol 1, Persons; 2, Subjects and places; 3, Dates and Manuscripts. Note that the National Library also has a card catalogue which carries this work on beyond 1975.

Hewson, M see Elmes above.

Lohan, Rena, *Guide to the archives of the Office of Public Works.* Dublin: OPW, 1994, 307 p, select bibl, index. 0 7076 0465 6.
The archives contain a broad range of documents covering two centuries, especially all branches of historical work.

McCutcheon Archive (industrial materials for N Ireland): is described in *Ulster local studies,* 15.1, 1993.

Prochaska, A, *Irish history from 1700: a guide to the sources in the Public Record Office.* London: Brit Records Ass (= *Archives and the user,* 6), 1986, 96 pp, index. 0 900222 07 7.
Governmental sources.

Smith, Alfred Russell, Catalogue, *see under Britain above.*

2.3
Databases

This section begins by listing two directories of well-established and publicly available databases on a wide range of subjects, plus one restricted to historical data. The remainder of the section deals with archaeologically-related databases. It is NOT concerned with major archaeological/architectural databases like those of RCHME or English Heritage. Instead it tries to identify some of the smaller collations of information, whether computerised or not, that might be overlooked. Questionnaire responses produced relatively little to add to the compiler's pre-existing collection, and there must be many more sources which people are prepared to share. This sample does at least give an idea of the kinds of information that people have troubled to computerise, and perhaps another compiler will be inspired to take up the search.

Bearing in mind that both hardware and software change so rapidly that it can be difficult to transfer data from one system to another indefinitely, the British Academy Arts and Humanities Data Service has been set up to advise on the preservation of electronic resources for the future. It includes the **Archaeology Data Service**, which will aim at the long-term provision, preservation and integration of data generated in the course of archaeological research. It is based at York University under the charge of Julian Richards, initially for three years in the late 1990s, and is in the care of the University of York, the CBA and a consortium of UK universities.

Directories

ECO *directory of environmental databases in the UK 1995/6* (eds Monica Barlow and John Britton). Bristol: ECO Environmental Information Trust, 1995, 357 p. 1 874666 01 6 pb.
No archaeology, but some architectural material.

Gale directory of databases: Vol. 1, Online databases (ed K L Nolan). New York: Gale Research, 1995 (or any current edition). ISSN 1066-8934.
Regularly revised.

Schürer, K and Anderson S J (eds), *A guide to*

historical datafiles held in machine-readable form. London: Assoc for History and Computing, 1992. 0 9515352 1 8 pb.
Well-indexed British Academy-funded report on questionnaire survey, covering as many databases as could be discovered in England plus a few from Wales and Scotland; also some for Europe and the rest of the world. Sample contents: castles of England and Wales 1050–1990 (from Cathcart King); underground sites, Neo onwards, in the southeast; Anglo-Saxon charters; medieval religious houses (from Hadcock and Knowles); Irish Ordnance Survey memoirs, etc. Individual items record purpose, content, sources used, hardware and software involved, etc.

Subject groups (not all available on computer networks)

Agricultural history
At Rural History Centre, University of Reading: computerisation (and JANET access) under way for over 30,000 bibliographical references. Contact Dr Raine Morgan.

A certain amount of material on the early history of agriculture can also be found in the Commonwealth Agricultural Bureaux CD-ROM of *CAB Abstracts*.

Ancient cultures and religions
At CREDO – Centre de Recherche sur la Documentation dans les Sciences de l'Antiquité (Villeneuve d'Ascq, Univ de Lille III). The 7-volume guide to the database includes an introduction, user manual, four volumes of thesauri, list of periodicals extracted.

Anglo-Saxon beads
The non-glass beads from two AS cemeteries at Mucking form a database available on disc provided with Ancient Monuments Lab Report 52/95.

Anglo-Saxon illuminated manuscripts, iconographic subjects
Computerised index in charge of Thomas Ohlgren, Dept of English, Purdue University, West Lafayette, Indiana 47907 (*see also his publication listed in Section 6.11.5 Migration and Early Medieval, Anglo-Saxon sub-section*).

Anglo-Saxon pottery stamps archive, see entry in Section 4.2 Organisations.

Archaeobotany

1. At University of York Environmental Archaeology Unit; 'ABCD', Archaeobotanical computer database for records of plant macrofossil remains (including wood and charcoal) from Great Britain and Ireland. Contact Allan Hall, 01904 433851. (*See also Philippa Tomlinson's computerised bibliography entered in Section 6.10 Science-based archaeology, sub-section Biological and environmental examination.*)

2. Plant remains archive at Herbarium, Reading University, being the collection by Percival and Helbaek from excavations of 1920s and 1930s, many classic British sites plus material from Scotland and Ireland. Contact Wendy Carruthers (Sawmills House, Pont y Clun, Llantrisant, Mid Glamorgan CF7 8LP, tel 01443 223462).

Archaeological book news

See CBA entry on the Internet page after the Introduction to this volume.

Archaeozoology, see entry in Section 6.10 Science-based archaeology, sub-section Biological and environmental examination; see also under Stampfli in same section.

Architectural database (bibliography)

Books and journals, from British Architectural Library, available on DIALOG.

Architectural mouldings

Warwick Mouldings Archive (Dr Richard K Morris, History of Art, Warwick University, Coventry CV4 7AL, tel 01203 523005, fax 01203 523006). Primary field record of c. 4,000 drawings of stone moulding profiles, especially ecclesiastical, 12th to 16th century, for England and Wales, indexed alphabetically by place. See R K Morris, 'Development of Later Gothic mouldings in England c. 1250–1400', Parts I and II, *Architectural history*, 21, 1978, pp 18–57; 22, 1979, pp 1–48; and 'An English glossary of medieval mouldings . . . c. 1040–1240', *Archit hist*, 35, 1992, pp 1–17.

Buildings of England on CD-ROM

Access to the 46 volumes of the Pevsner series available from OUP Electronic Publishing.

Church plans index

From RAI: initially for English medieval churches, eventually all British churches and other religious buildings. Computer program in use for cataloguing plans of churches (Michael Good).

Classical studies

DYABOLA: bibliographic database of the subject catalogue of the library of the German Archaeological Institute at Rome. Covers material from 1956. Enquire at Institute of Classical Studies Library, London, about consultation there.

Durham City

Database of archaeological and topographical documentary findings together with research on 900 buildings. Is essentially for planning purposes, and only bona fide researchers should apply. Contact: Martin Roberts, Historic Buildings Office, City of Durham Council (tel 0191 386 6111 ext 332).

Geophysics

At English Heritage, database of geophysical surveys.

Gower database

A retrieval system for archaeological material and historical sources, compiled from desk and aerial survey in a 22-field format. Foxpro or Quattro for Windows. Various refinements, eg data output on to map background. Apply to H Middleton-Jones, Willow Bank Cottage, Sandy Lane, Parkmill, Swansea SA3 2ER.

Historic parks and gardens

IOAAS Landscapes and Gardens (Kings Manor, York YO1 2EP) – Inventory of historic parks and gardens

Compatible with that is the English Heritage Gardens and Landscape team's database on garden archaeology projects: simple and easily accessible, giving site, assessment, field study, techniques used, features identified and detailed reports (both published and unpublished).

Implement petrology index (CBA)

Held at RCHME Swindon (details in NMR *Guide to the Archive*: 7,800 implements thin-sectioned; data computerised, printouts can be ordered at nominal charge). Contact NMR Archive at Swindon.

Ironworking sites

For details of database see Historical Metallurgy Society entry in Section 4.2 Organisations.

London in the 1690s

At Centre for Metropolitan History, University of London Institute of Historical Research.

Contact Craig Spence. e-mail metrolon@uk.ac.ulcc.clusi

Also:

Medieval London's interaction with its hinterland, c. 1250–1400, obtainable via ESRC Data Archive.

Bibliography of printed works on London to 1939 (also available in printed version: see Creaton entry under History in Section 1.4 Guides to literature: ancillary subjects).

Medieval villages
Records of former Deserted Medieval Villages Research Group now computerised at RCHME (Swindon).

National Museums of Scotland databases and 'Wealth of a Nation'
Contact John Burnett, Head of Library and Documentation Services, Royal Museum of Scotland, Chambers Street, Edinburgh EH1 1JF (tel 0131 225 7534). *See also SCRAN entry in Section 4.9 Museum catalogues.*

National Trust
Its Cirencester office holds an SMR for NT properties. Contact Dr David Thackray, National Trust, 33 Sheep Street, Cirencester GL7 1QW (tel 01285 651818).

Place-names
Database being developed at University of Nottingham, as project 'The survey of the language of English place-names', five years from 1992.

Potterne Midden Site (Bronze Age)
Wessex Archaeology material, reached via Dr Paul Reilly, reillyp@winvmd.vnet.ibm.com

Roman Bath
At University of Bath, contact Dr A Bowyer, School of Mechanical Engineering, e-mail: a.bowyer@uk.ac.bath

Roman Britain in 19..
Available from 1970 records onwards on program Archaeological Data Manager at Institute of Classical Studies: 1921–69 material to be added in due course. Search by site or subject area.

Romanesque sculpture in Britain and Ireland
Corpus in preparation as database at British Academy (Dr Seamus Ross).

Roman pottery
Database of Italian terra sigillata potters' stamps: in care of P Kenrick at Oxford Institute of Archaeology; see *J Roman pottery stud*, 6, 1993, pp 27–35.

Scottish Church Heritage Inventory
Contact Council for Scottish Archaeology.

Shipwreck register
(Classical): at University of Bristol Dept of Classics, c/o Dr A J Parker
(British coasts): contact Dr Ben Ferrari at NMR Swindon.
A separate register is held by Richard Larn, Shipwreck and Heritage Centre, Charlestown, St Austell, Cornwall PL25 3NN (tel 01726 73104)

Stone axes
Irish Stone Axe Project, contact G Cooney at University College Dublin.
See also Implement Petrology Index above.

Stone crosses
T D Kendrick archive: consultable at British Museum Dept of Medieval and Later Antiquities; consists of card index and some unique archival photographs etc, mainly up to 1940 with some later additions. Complements the material in the next entry.
Pre-Norman Sculpture Archive: Professor Rosemary Cramp and Dr Derek Craig, University of Durham Dept of Archaeology (tel 0191 374 7626).

Tithe files
R J Kain's socio-economic survey of land use and the agricultural economy at 1836 is available on CD-ROM from Adam Matthew Publications, 8 Oxford Street, Marlborough, Wilts SN8 1AP (tel 01672 511921).

Tree rings
It is hoped that a European information point for tree ring databases can be set up: contact Jennifer Hillam, Sheffield University (tel 0114 282 5107) who is collecting information. UK laboratories currently operating are in Belfast, Edinburgh, London (MOLAS), Nottingham and Sheffield.

The journal *Vernacular architecture* contains regular tree ring date lists (indexed).

Underwater archaeology
Scottish Trust for Underwater Archaeology has a database of archaeological resources in Scottish waters.

SECTION 3

Periodicals

3.1
Principal Archaeological Journals and Magazines

These journals all have multi-period concerns and fairly general appeal, except perhaps where noted below as 'academic level'. This list does not include the period-orientated journals like *Britannia* and *Medieval archaeology* which will be found listed under the appropriate period in Section 6. All are annual productions except where otherwise stated.

Antiquity (0003–598X). 4/yr. Published by Antiquity Publications Ltd at Oxford University Press. Academic-level journal but reasonably accessible to the general reader who has some archaeological knowledge. Also noted, even famous, for its characteristic editorials.

Archaeologia Cambrensis (0306–6924) is the national journal for Wales, published by the Cambrian Archaeological Association. Academic level. Address: CAA (Publications), c/o RCAHMW, Crown Building, Plas Crug, Aberystwyth, Dyfed SY23 1NJ.

Archaeological journal (0066–5983). From the Royal Archaeological Institute, one of the oldest of our national societies. Academic level. Address: RAI, c/o Society of Antiquaries, Burlington House, Piccadilly, London W1V 0HS.

Archaeology Ireland (0790–982X). 4/yr. Wordwell Ltd, PO Box 69, Bray, Co Wicklow, Republic of Ireland. Arguably the best and liveliest of all those produced in these islands, and reasonably priced in addition. It ably reflects the fizzing excitement found in Ireland's archaeology today.

British archaeology (1357–4442). 10/yr. Formerly *British archaeological news* (0269–1906, to end 1994). (Not to be confused with the defunct periodical of the same name, details of which are given at the end of this section.)
The official magazine for members of the Council for British Archaeology, containing items of interest from all over the UK and illustrated with colour cover and black-and-white photographs. Every other issue is accompanied by a *Briefing* (1354–702X) which gives details of excavations requiring volunteer help, forthcoming conferences, new books and the

49

like. Annual index. Currently tends to disappoint: despite the title it includes much non-British material, and contains only a fraction of the news previously carried.

Current archaeology (0011–3212). 5 or 6/yr; edited by Andrew and Wendy Selkirk, 9 Nassington Road, London NW3 2TX. Established in 1966, this is the longest-lived of the 'popular' magazines; it tends to concentrate on excavations, nicely illustrated in colour, though also contains other archaeological news and gossip, and editorials which often arouse controversy.

Discovery and excavation in Scotland (0419–411X). Council for Scottish Archaeology, c/o National Museum of Scotland, Queen Street, Edinburgh EH2 1JD. The indispensable record for Scotland, giving brief reports on field and other discoveries and excavations; formerly contained an excellent annual bibliography of Scottish material culture.

Heritage today (1356–0824). 4/yr. Issued to members of English Heritage; contains quite substantial pieces on EH properties plus news items.

Historic Scotland (no ISSN). 4/yr. Issued to Friends of Historic Scotland; contains news items and short articles.

History today (0018–2753). Monthly magazine from History Today Ltd, 83–84 Berwick Street, London W1V 3PJ. Attractively produced, illustrated in colour and written by acknowledged experts; often contains articles of archaeological interest.

Journal of the British Archaeological Association (0068–1288). One of the oldest national societies, publishing at academic level. BAA Membership Sec, John Jenkins, 75 Budmouth Avenue, Preston, Weymouth, Dorset DT3 6QJ.

Journal of the Royal Society of Antiquaries of Ireland (0035–9106). Academic-level journal from the Republic, with a long and distinguished history, published from 63 Merrion Square, Dublin 2.

Landscape history (0143–3768). Academic-level journal which traces the long history of development of our landscape from earliest times. Society for Landscape Studies, c/o Carenza Lewis, RCHME National Monuments Record Centre, Kemble Drive, Swindon SN2 2GZ.

Minerva, the international review of ancient art and archaeology (0957–7718). 6/yr. Began publication in 1990; a highly professional and attractive magazine of international scope, whose origin in the world of antiquities dealing means that it carries advertisements and auction reports which may not appeal to readers who prefer their archaeology market-free. Address: Aurora Publications Ltd, 7 Davies Street, London W1Y 1LL.

Proceedings of the Prehistoric Society (0079–497X). Heavyweight (in both senses) academic journal of worldwide scope. Membership details from the Society, c/o Institute of Archaeology, 31–34 Gordon Square, London WC1H 0PY.

Proceedings of the Royal Irish Academy (0035–8991). Several parts per year, not all archaeological; one of the two principal academic level journals from the Republic. Address: Royal Irish Academy, 19 Dawson Street, Dublin 2.

Proceedings of the Society of Antiquaries of Scotland (0081–1564). Scotland's premier academic journal, with a wide readership in Scotland and beyond. The Society is at the National Museum of Scotland, Queen Street, Edinburgh EH1 2JD.

Scottish archaeological news (0958–2002). 3/yr. The newsletter of members of the Council for Scottish Archaeology.

Scottish archaeological review (0262–3489). Academic level journal published from the Department of Archaeology, University of Glasgow, but apparently inactive at the time of writing.

Ulster journal of archaeology (0082–7355). One of the handsomest of the academic journals; details from Dept of Archaeology and Palaeoecology, School of Geosciences, The Queen's University, Belfast BT7 1NN.

Select list of defunct titles

Apart from the relatively long-lived *Archaeological News Letter*, and the still-going *Current archaeology*, popular archaeological magazines seem always to have had trouble establishing themselves. Consequently they offer something of a bibliographer's nightmare, but the following notes may help sort out any references found in the literature.

Archaeology in Britain (0308–8486). Ceased 1994: formerly annual roundup, A5 size, compiled for many years by the Council for British Archaeology and containing short reports of excavation and survey work from around the UK. Illustrated with black-and-white photographs and occasional line drawings; was quite the best way of getting an all-round picture of new discoveries, and is much missed.

The old-style *British archaeology* (0952–7877, not to be confused with the current one produced by the CBA from 1995) originated as *British archaeological monthly* (independently published) which ran for four numbers during 1987 before dropping the 'monthly' from the title. *British archaeology* then ran from issue 5 (1988) to issue 14 (1989). It was, in its turn, acquired by *Yesterday's world* which ran for a few numbers in 1990–91 before itself being absorbed into *Minerva*, which still exists (see above).

Ago ran for only 10 issues, 1970–71.

Archaeological news letter ('ANL') was a highly respected magazine which ran from 1948 to 1965 and should be found in archaeological libraries as it remains the only source of published information on some sites.

Archaeology today ran (monthly) only from 1987–88, replacing *Popular archaeology* which ran 1979–86.

Medieval world (0963–2751) ceased publication after only a few numbers.

Scottish archaeological forum. A widely respected academic level journal, usually with a single theme, which ran for a dozen years, 1970–81.

3.2
Directories and Lists of Journals

This section contains:
International periodical directories
British, Welsh, Scottish and Irish periodical directories
Guides to title abbreviations
Archaeological journals
Journal lists in related subjects

International periodical directories

The principal international reference aids for periodicals in all disciplines, which usually include full titles, publishers, ISSNs, frequency, etc, are:

ISDS International Serials Data System. The organisation which assigns ISSNs (International Standard Serial Numbers) to journals produces a quarterly CD-ROM, now including over half a million serials from 200 countries.

The serials directory: an international reference book. Birmingham, Alabama: EBSCO Publishing, 3 vols, biennial.
Like all international compilations, this one has its omissions and errors, but sometimes outdoes its main competitor, Ulrich (below) which most UK libraries have.

Ulrich's international periodicals directory (including irregular serials and annuals). New Providence, NJ: R R Bowker, 5 vols, any current edn.
Gives information on over 116,000 serials under 668 subject heads, and continues to improve its coverage, including its archaeological content and indexing. Three times a year comes *Ulrich's update* (0000–1074) giving new titles. Also available online via several hosts, and on CD-ROM.

British periodical directories

Boston Spa serials: a CD-ROM of BLDSC's holdings of serials; over 500,000 individual titles, including newspapers and irregulars.

British union catalogue of periodicals 'BUCOP'. A brave attempt over the period 1955–80 to show the actual holdings of a good number of libraries, but scarcely usable now.

SBL, Serials in the British Library (0260–0005). 1981–.

Lists titles newly received from contributing libraries, with annual and interim printed supplements. Also 33 fiche issued 1988 to cover 1976–86 material (57,000 titles). From 1987, a quarterly printed version with annual cumulation.

Walford, A J with Harvey, J M, *Walford's guide to current British periodicals in the humanities and social sciences.* London: Lib Ass, 1985, 480 p, bibl, index. 0 85365 676 2.

Gives a useful analysis of each title; Dewey Classification, with archaeology mainly in 930.26, regionally arranged, but with some odd slips.

Willings' press guide: a comprehensive index and handbook of the press of the UK . . . and Irish Republic. East Grinstead: Reed Information Service (annual).

Most libraries have this and it now contains many of the archaeological societies and other small, relatively obscure journals. Arranged alphabetically by title, with subject index.

Wolff, Michael et al, *The Waterloo directory of Victorian periodicals 1824–1900; phase 1.* [Waterloo, Ontario]: Wilfrid Laurier Univ Press for Univ Waterloo, [1977].

A single alphabetical sequence of newspaper and periodical titles published in England, Scotland, Ireland and Wales during the period. This was then expanded in *Phase II* (by John S North, publ North Waterloo Academic Press in Ontario) to list separately for **Scotland** (1989) and **Ireland** (1986) the periodicals from 1800–1900.

Welsh periodical directories

Subject index to Welsh periodicals see Section 1.1 Guides to literature.

Scottish periodical directories

Current periodicals in the National Library of Scotland (consult most recent edition).

Edinburgh University Library has a union list of current serials (cumulated bi-annually) which includes the main and departmental libraries of the University together with holdings of a number of other important research libraries in Edinburgh.

Glasgow University also has a list of serials received.

See also under Wolff at end of main British sequence above.

Irish periodical directories

McAllister, Kate (ed), *Irish periodicals first published before 1901: a union list of Northern Ireland library holdings.* Omagh: Library Local Studies Panel, 1995, 95 p. 0 9516510 1 3 pb, plastic comb-bound.

Indicates which libraries hold runs of these titles.

SHIRL, Serial Holdings in Irish Libraries. Dublin: The Library Council. Microfiche giving details of runs of periodicals (etc) held in the principal public, specialist and academic libraries. Like all such massive cooperative compilations it is also liable to gaps and inaccuracies.

For a general introduction to the Irish historical journals see David Dickson, 'Historical journals in Ireland: the last hundred years' in B Hayley and E McKay (eds), *Three hundred years of Irish periodicals* (Dublin, 1987), pp 87–101.

See also Wolff under British above, and also Hayes in Section 1.1 Guides to literature for a compilation of Irish journal articles.

Guides to title abbreviations

The most useful for archaeology will be Tulok, Von Müller or Wellington below.

Alkire, L G (comp), *Periodical title abbreviations: Vol 1. By abbreviation.* New York (etc): Gale Research, 10 ed 1996 (or later ed). 0 8103 5653 8.

(Two other volumes in different orders are earlier editions.)

Useful in that if the researchers find six different abbreviations for the same title, all will be entered. Even so, some familiar UK acronyms are missing.

Leistner, Otto, *International title abbreviations of periodicals, newspapers, important handbooks, dictionaries, laws etc* [title also given in German]. Osnabruck: Biblio Verlag, 1981, 2 vols, 1265 p. 3 7648 1266 4.

(Later edition, if any, not traced.)

Tulok, M (comp), 'Abbreviations of periodicals and series of archaeology and auxiliary

sciences', in *Acta Academiae Scientarum Hungaricae*, **36**, 1984, pp 333–84.
Emphasis on Hungary and neighbouring countries; list given in two orders, abbreviations, and full titles.

Von Müller, O (et al), 'Sigelschlüssel der archäologischen Literatur (SAL)', in *Acta praehistorica et archaeologica*, **9–10, 1978–9, pp 167–383.
Includes international periodicals, series, monograph series, and dictionaries of European and Near/Middle Eastern archaeology. Two orders, by abbreviation (usually acronym or near-acronym) and by full title (with all known abbreviations).

Wellington, Jean S, *Dictionary of bibliographic abbreviations found in the scholarship of classical studies and related disciplines*. Westport (Conn): Greenwood Press, 1983, xv, 393 p, refs. 0 313 23523 6.
Part I gives the abbreviations (eg 'DAI', 'JbNum') and Part II provides bibliographic descriptions for each title. Claims double the number given in *Sigelschlüssel* (see previous entry).

Archaeological journals

Unfortunately there is no complete published list of archaeological journals for Britain and Ireland, although the team on *British archaeological bibliography* could probably help with identifications. For specific locations or areas of England, the very useful *English local studies handbook* (comp Susanna Guy, Exeter, 1992) lists local history and archaeology journals under each county heading.

Journal lists in related subjects

See also Section *1.5 Indexing and abstracting services*.

Classics
A list is badly needed to replace Joyce Southern's survey in the 1960s.

Geology
Current serials received by the Library of the Geological Society London (1992 or later edition). Computer database; list of holdings planned.

History
Boehm, E H (et al, eds), *Historical periodicals directory: an annotated world list of historical and related serial publications*. Santa Barbara/Oxford: ABC-CLIO, 1981–6, 5 vols.
Lists all current titles and those ceasing since 1960, alphabetically within country of publication. Western Europe in volume 2 treats archaeology to some extent.

Natural History
The Natural History Museum Library maintains an informal list of natural history periodicals (contact: Audrey Meenan).

3.3
Journals with Running Bibliographies

In this section are listed some of the journals that include, either occasionally or regularly, bibliographies of relevant new publications (mostly or entirely from journals). This does not attempt to be an exhaustive list of such journals. Archaeological periodicals (and those with an archaeological component) from Britain and Ireland are listed first, followed by those from the adjacent Continent and the USA. Finally come periodicals in disciplines useful to archaeology, again divided between British/Irish and other. Bear in mind that financial or other difficulties may cause a bibliographic service to cease with little or no warning.

Archaeological: British and Irish

Anglo-Saxon England
Antiquaries journal (latterly with separate bibliographic supplements)
Association for Environmental Archaeology (newsletter)
British Brick Society information (newsletter)
British numismatic journal
Discovery and excavation Scotland
Fortress
Garden History Society (newsletter)
Historical metallurgy
International journal of nautical archaeology and underwater exploration
Journal of Roman studies
Journal of Roman pottery studies
Medieval ceramics
Medieval and later pottery in Wales
Medieval Settlement Research Group annual report
Post-medieval archaeology
(and many county journals treating their own area)

Archaeological: Adjacent Continental (plus USA)

Archeologické Rozhledy (Prague) [ironworking bibliography]
ArchaeoZoologia (Grenoble)
Association international pour l'étude de la mosaïque antique (AIEMA) (Paris)
Bulletin de la Société Française (Paris)

Cahiers archéologique de Picardie (Amiens)
Cahiers de civilisation médiéval (bibliographic supplement) (Poitiers)
Etudes celtiques (Paris)
Fornvännen (Stockholm)
Helinium (Wetteren) [for Netherlands, Belgium, Luxembourg]
Madrider Mitteilungen (Heidelberg)
Medieval Scandinavia (Odense) [ran 1968–88]
Mesolithic miscellany (Madison, Wisconsin)
Revue archéologique de l'est et du centre-est (Dijon)
Revue archéologique de l'ouest (Rennes)
Revue d'études anciennes (Paris)
Revue du nord (Lille)
Siedlungsforschung: Archäologie–Geschichte–Geographie (Bonn)
Zeitschrift für Archäologie des Mittelalters (Köln)

Related disciplines: British and Irish

Agricultural history review
Archives
Costume
Economic history review
English historical review
Furniture history
Historical research (formerly Bulletin of historical research)
Irish historical studies
Journal of ecclesiastical history
Journal of the Society of Archivists
Journal of transport history
Nomina
Northern history
Scottish geographical review
Scottish historical review
Southern history
Urban history
Welsh history review

Related disciplines: Adjacent Continental and USA

Journal of glass studies (Corning, NY)
Old English newsletter (Binghamton, NY)
Speculum (Cambridge, Mass)
Technology and culture (Chicago)

3.4
Archaeological Periodicals with Cumulative Indexes

This list is intended to help readers conducting retrospective searches through the principal periodicals of 'national' scope: it indicates which titles have produced merged indexes for runs of issues (as distinct from an index per volume). Information is given in the order: current title, ISSN, total span of years covered by cumulative indexes. (Some periodicals have gaps in the cumulative indexing sequence; moreover, while some have excellent indexes, the quality of most depend on the availability of both adequate funds and suitably qualified indexers.)

(A similar list for county journals, also prepared, proved too long to publish.)

Agricultural history review (0002–1490). 1953–87

Anglo-Saxon England (0263–6751). 1972–91

Antiquaries journal (0003–5815). 1921–80 (also, ceased: *Proceedings of the Society of Antiquaries of London*, 2nd series 1859–1920)

Antiquity: a periodical review of archaeology (0003–598X). 1927–91

Archaeologia: or, miscellaneous tracts relating to antiquity (0261–3409). 1770–1966

Archaeologia Cambrensis: journal of the Cambrian Archaeological Association (0306–6924). 1846–1960. (Note that Lily Chitty's full index to vols 1–54 is available in typed form in a few institutions.)

Archaeological journal (0066–5983). 1844–1968

Archaeological review from Cambridge (0261–4332). 1981–91

Archaeology in Britain (0308–8456). 1976–80

Archaeology in Wales (0306–7629). 1961–80

Archaeometry (0003–813X). 1958–86

Architectural history (0066–6222X). 1958–82

Association for Studies in the Conservation of Historic Buildings/ Transactions (0142–5803). 1973–82

Britannia: a journal of Romano-British and kindred studies (0068–113X). 1970–94

Current archaeology (0011–3212). 1967–date, available on disk in .dbf format.

Discovery and excavation Scotland (0419–411X). Typescript for 1946–77 awaiting publication funds

Garden History Society (0307–1243). 1966–86

Industrial archaeology review (0309–0728). 1976–87

Irish historical studies (0021–1214). 1938–67

Journal of the British Archaeological Association (0068–1288). 1846–1919 and 1967–90

Journal of Roman studies (0075–4358). 1911–70

Journal of the Royal Society of Antiquaries of Ireland (0035–9106). 1849–1930

Lithics, the newsletter of the Lithic Studies Society (0262–7817). 1979–89

Medieval archaeology: journal of the Society for Medieval Archaeology (0076–6097). 1957–91

Post-medieval archaeology: journal of the Society for Post-Medieval Archaeology (0779–4326). 1967–76

Proceedings of the Prehistoric Society (0079–497X). (Previous title: *Proceedings of the Prehistoric Society of East Anglia*) 1935–84

Proceedings of the Royal Irish Academy: Section C: Archaeology, Celtic studies, history, linguistics, literature. (0035–8991). 1836–1970

Proceedings of the Society of Antiquaries of Scotland (0081–1564). 1851–1974

Sylloge of coins of the British Isles (ISBNs only). 1958–91

Ulster journal of archaeology (0082–7355). 3 ser, 1938–82

Vernacular architecture (0305–5477). 1970–88

Also: *List and index of the publications of the Royal Historical Society 1871–1924 and of the Camden Society 1840–97* (ed Hubert Hall), RHS, 1925

3.5
Irish Archaeological Periodicals

This list is intended to raise awareness, on the British side of the Irish Sea, of the value of many of these publications; also some of them have had rather complex name changes. *See also the union lists for Ireland noted in Section 3.2.*

Principal Irish archaeological (and historical) journals and monograph series
This is a highly selected list taken from a near-complete collection of nearly 100 relevant titles made by the compiler of this work. (‡ signifies defunct journals, which may still yield useful information not easily gleaned otherwise.)

The sequence of elements is: Title, ISSN (if any), start year, frequency, publishing body, indexes where present. As elsewhere in this book, three stars signify the most essential publications.

Nineteenth century 'penny journals' and the like

These publications, running for short periods in the 19th century, included notes and news of antiquarian and archaeological interest, among other more literary productions. The best British parallel might be the *Illustrated London News*. So far as is known nobody has gone through them to index all the archaeological information they contain.

‡ *The Dublin penny journal*, 1831–6. Dublin: John S Folds and later publishers. Four volumes of weekly parts issued, then New Series 1–3, 1903/2–1904/5. George Petrie was co-editor. Indexes at least partly usable.

‡ *The Dublin Saturday magazine*, 1865–7. Dublin.

‡ *The Irish literary gazette*, 1857–8. Dublin/Cork/Belfast. Only occasional archaeological interest.

‡ *The Irish penny journal*, 1832–5 and 1840–1. Dublin: James Duffy. George Petrie was editor.

‡ *The Irish penny magazine*, 1833–42?. Dublin: T and J Coldwell.

Also of this period was a journal recording gravestones and the like:
‡ *Association for the Preservation of Memorials of the Dead in Ireland*. 1888–1920. Dublin: Pon-

sonby and Gibbs. Then *Journal of the Irish Memorials Association* (1921–38?).

Current journals (selected)

Ainm (Bulletin of the Ulster Place-Name Society) (0953–461X). Irregular, title varies, several series: originally *Bulletin* (duplicated typescript), 1952–7; Ser 2, (*Ainm*), 1–4, 1978–1981/2; Ser 3, 1, 1986–. Belfast: Queen's University Dept of Celtic.

Archaeological research publications (Northern Ireland) (1952–5; now replaced by *Northern Ireland archaeological monographs*, which see below).

****Archaeology Ireland* (0790–892X). 1987–. 4/yr. Bray: Wordwell. A truly valuable addition to the Irish archaeological scene; lively articles, good illustrations, news items, debate, and perhaps best of all, (mainly) reliable directories to Irish organisations. Indispensable for anyone interested in Irish (or indeed any) archaeology. Also contains occasional articles discussing Irish county/local archaeological periodicals. Available on Internet at http://slarti.ucd/pilots/archaeology

***Emania (0951–1822). 1986–. 2/yr. Belfast: Navan Research Group, The Queen's University of Belfast. Devoted to the study of the important site of Emain Macha and related or contemporary monuments.

****Excavations 19.. summary accounts of archaeological excavations in Ireland* (0790–7745). 1985–. Annual. Bray: Wordwell for Org of Irish Archaeologists. Annual round-up of excavations.

**Irish Archaeological Research Forum (no ISSN)*. 1974–78. Belfast: Dept of Archaeology, Queen's University of Belfast. Good while it lasted!

****Irish Archaeological Wetland Unit/transactions* (0791–8186). 1993–. Dublin: IAWU, Dept of Archaeology, University College Dublin. Monograph series.

Irish geography, journal of the Geographical Society of Ireland (0075–0778). 1944–. 2/yr. Dublin: Dept Geography, Univ College Dublin. Previous title *Bulletin of the Geographical Society* (to 1945 or 1946). Includes section on recent Irish geographical literature, including historical geography.

Irish heritage series (small popular booklets from Eason's).

Irish historical studies, joint journal of the Irish Historical Society and the Ulster Society for Irish Historical Studies (0021–1214). 1938–. 2/yr. Dublin: Dublin Univ Press (imprint varies). Contains regular bibliographic articles. Index to vols 1–15 in *Ir hist stud suppl*, 1, 1968, pp 8–70.

Irish roots (0791–6329). 1993–. 4/yr. Cork: Belgrave Publications.
General-level magazine treating all aspects of Ireland's past, with a regular archaeological column.

**Journal of the Cork Historical and Archaeological Society* (0010–8731). 1892–. Currently annual. Cork: the Society. Some rather inadequate indexes have been provided for most of the journal's run.

**Journal of the County Kildare Archaeological Society* (ISBNs only). 1891–. Annual. Naas: the Society. No indexes to date.

**Journal of the County Louth Archaeological and Historical Society* (0070–1327). 1969–. Annual. Dundalk: the Society. (Continues *County Louth archaeological journal* (1904–68). Contains regular contents-lists for related Irish periodical publications. Index to vols 1–13 (1904–57) in vol 14 (1957–60), pp 232–78.

**Journal of the Galway Archaeological and Historical Society* (0332–415X).
1900–. Irreg. Galway: the Society. Index to vols 1–7 (1900–12) publ 1913.

***Journal of Irish archaeology* (0268–537X). 1983–. Irreg. Subs: Prof J Waddell, Univ Coll Galway. Editor: c/o Irish Antiquities Division, National Museum of Ireland.

Journal of the Kerry Archaeological and Historical Society (0085–2503). 1968–. Tralee. Irreg, and now supplemented by *Kerry magazine* (0791–2846).

****Journal of the Royal Society of Antiquaries of Ireland* (0035–9106). (1849–). Annual. Dublin: the Society, 63 Merrion Square, Dublin 2. The Society, which publishes many important excavations and artefact studies, has a complex past, beginning as The Kilkenny Archaeological Society (1849), then with various titles and series numbers until the present one. Despite all the changes the Journal has appeared continu-ously since 1849. Indexes: 1849–89; 1890–1910; 1911–1930.

****Medieval Dublin excavations 1962–1981*: (irregular monograph series). Series A, *Building and topography*; Series B, *Artefacts*; Series C, *Environmental evidence*. Dublin: Roy Ir Academy for Nat Mus Ireland/RIA

Museum Ireland: the journal of the Irish Museums Association (0961–9690). 1991–. Annual. Belfast. (Replaces *IMA annual proceedings*.)

****Northern Ireland archaeological monographs* (two issued); then *Northern Ireland monographs*. Continuation of *Archaeological research publications (Northern Ireland)*, noted above.

***North Munster antiquarian journal* (0332–0820). 1936–. Irreg. Limerick: Thomond Archaeological Society. (Various former titles.) Excellent for reviews. General index (1992) to vols 1–30, 1936–1988 (also includes reprinted index to vols 1897–1908 of *Journal of the Limerick Field Club* and 1909–19 of *Journal of the North Munster Archaeological Society*).

Peritia, journal of the Medieval Academy of Ireland, (0332–1592). 1982–. Cork: The Academy. Important journal but few archaeological articles.

****Proceedings of the Royal Irish Academy, (Section C, Archaeology, Celtic studies, history, linguistics and literature)* (0035–8991). 1836–. Dublin: the Academy. Several (varying) parts per annual volume. (The RIA has a complete list of contents, by volume/part no.) Many important excavations and museum studies appear in this periodical. Indexes to RIA series were published as follows: 1786–1906 in 1912; 1907–32 in 1934; 1932–53; 1953–70. Also a *Transactions* series (1787–1906).

Riocht na Midhe, Records of Meath (0461–5050). 1955–. Meath Archaeological and Historical Society, Drogheda. Index to vols 1–8 (1955–89).

****Royal Irish Academy monographs in archaeology* (two issued so far).

***Trowel* (0791–1017). 1988–. Dublin: Department of Archaeology, University College Dublin. An undergraduate production of very high quality; recent issues list archaeological theses completed at Irish universities. Now available on Internet.

****Ulster journal of archaeology* (0082–7355). Belfast: Ulster Archaeological Society. Usually annually. The Journal has had two interruptions in its publication: it appeared 1853–62; 1894–1911; and 1938– (3rd series, continuing). Excellent content and fine production.

SECTION 4

Organisations, Institutions and Societies

These directories provide details of organisations that might be relevant to archaeological studies. Most of them list the organisations in a standardised database-style format, and their completeness may depend on return of questionnaires. No single directory will, alas, provide within its covers everything an archaeologist could possibly want. For directories to museums see Section 4.8; and to record offices, Section 2.1.

Archaeological, and closely related, organisations

Directories of archaeological societies or organisations are provided annually in two magazines: *Current archaeology* (0011–3212) for the UK and *Archaeology Ireland* (0790–982x) for the Irish Republic and Northern Ireland. The CBA's new publication *British archaeological yearbook 1995–96* (300 p) also lists substantial numbers of societies, organisations, museums and universities dealing with archaeology; but beware of typographical errors, changed addresses, etc.

Conservation sourcebook. London: HMSO for Conservation Unit, Museums and Galleries Commission, new edn 1991, 122 pp. 0 11 290493 9 pb.
Extremely useful, though some information is now out of date; lists a wide range of bodies in the fields of conservation, heritage, arts and crafts, giving the aims and backgrounds of each, their publications, technical services offered, grants and awards.

Directory of archaeological heritage management. Paris: ICOMOS, 2 edn 1990.
Covers 120 countries with 363 entries, covering relevant state and independent organisations; lists name, address, function, type of organisation, and main fields of work.

Directory of finds study and special interest groups. Birmingham: IFA Finds Group, 1992.
Includes nearly 80 groups from AML to WARP, with index by subject/material and by period of interest.

Directory of natural history and related societies in Britain and Ireland (comp and ed A Meenan).

London: Brit Mus Natural History, 1983, 407 p, subject and geographical indexes.

Gives full data for some 750 societies, including archaeological societies where these have a strong natural history component. In need of revision now, but meanwhile A Meenan at the Natural History Museum may be able to provide an up-to-date address for a particular society.

Guide to museums and visitor centres [in Ireland]. Annual supplement to *Archaeology Ireland,* very full and useful.

Historical, archaeological and kindred societies in the United Kingdom: a list. Hulverstone Manor, IoW: Pinhorns, 1986.

Although now badly out of date, this work is regularly updated by additions and amendments printed in the magazine *Local history.*

Institute of Field Archaeologists directory of members. Birmingham: IFA (available to members only).

Includes a list of the organisations that currently employ IFA members, together with much other useful information, advertisements for consultancies and the like.

Other organisations

These directories may help readers to find organisations in other disciplines than archaeology.

Centres and bureaux: a directory of concentrations of effort, information and expertise. Beckenham: CBD Research Ltd, any current edition.

Councils, committees and boards: a handbook of advisory, consultative, executive and similar bodies in British public life. Beckenham: CBD Research Ltd, any current edition.

Current British directories: a guide to directories published in the British Isles. Beckenham: CBD Research Ltd, any current edition.

A listing of listings!

Directory of British associations and associations in Ireland. Beckenham: CBD Research Ltd, current year.

Includes an archaeology section, rather oddly ordered but giving a reasonable selection of national and county societies, including those that deal with industrial archaeology, nautical, or historic buildings. (Not very strong on Irish

material: prefer *Ireland: a directory* listed below.)

Directory for the environment: organisations, campaigns and initiatives in the British Isles (comp Monica Frisch). London: Greenprint (Merlin Press), 4 edn 1994, 294 p, index.

Includes about 40 archaeological organisations.

Directory of European professional and learned societies (ed R W Adams). Beckenham: CBD Research, 4 edn 1989 (or later).

Includes about 30 associations in or related to archaeology; not very easy to use.

Environmental information: a guide to sources (ed Nigel Lees et al). Boston Spa: British Library, 1992.

Covers a range of disciplines and 'green' issues, but little use for archaeology.

Ireland: a directory. Dublin: Institute of Public Administration (annual). Very full listing of all kinds of organisations, government and other, including the main archaeological ones; well indexed.

Register of learned and professional societies 1992. London: Foundation for Science and Technology, 1992, 220 p, index. 1 872387 03 9 pb.

Reference work listing nearly 400 societies dealing with science, technology, humanities and the arts. Useful as far as it goes, but very incomplete, and lists only a handful of archaeological bodies.

Who's who in the environment: England. (Edited and updated by Kate Aldous and Rachel Adatia with Kim Milton.) London: Environment Council, 3 edn 1995, 399 p, index. 0 903158 52 3 pb. Also available on disk, updated twice yearly (apply to Environment Council, 21 Elizabeth Street, London SW1W 9RP for details).

Contains some organisations of possible use to archaeologists, eg British Cave Research Association, British Lichen Society, etc. The next three directories are in the same format.

Who's who in the environment: Northern Ireland (comp Timely Designs). London: Environment Council, 1994, 100 p. 0 903158 41 8 pb.

Who's who in the environment: Scotland (comp Environment Council). Perth: Scottish Natural Heritage, 2 edn 1993, 116 p. 1 85397 019 0 pb.

Who's who in the environment: Wales (eds Kate

Aldous and Rachel Adatia for Environment Council). London: Environment Council, 1995, 89 p (+91 p in Welsh). 0 903158 47 7 pb.

Windrow and Green's militaria directory and sourcebook (ed Martin Windrow). London: Windrow and Green, 1996, 128 p, indexes. 1 85915 086 1 pb.

Lists about 3,000 contacts of all aspects of militaria: historical societies, re-enactment societies, retailers of uniforms, wargamers, manufacturers, military hardware etc.

World guide to scientific associations and learned societies (ed Michael Sachs). Munich/London etc: K G Saur, 6 edn 1994.

More useful than one might hope for an international collection: contains some 17,000 associations for all areas of academic study, culture and technology.

World of learning. London: Europa Publications, annually.

Lists not only learned societies, professional associations, research institutes, libraries and archives, museums and art galleries, universities and colleges, but also includes the names of many scholars, eg a complete list of Fellows of the British Academy (by subject).

Yearbook of international organisations (ed Union of International Associations). München: K G Saur, any recent edition.

Gives very full information on each organisation.

4.2
National Societies, Special Interest Groups, Environmental Associations and Professional Bodies

The data in this chapter come mainly from questionnaires completed by the organisations themselves, supplemented from other sources where necessary. Organisations from which no response was received are marked by an obelus – †. Accuracy cannot be guaranteed, although every effort has been made to ensure it (for instance by many telephone calls): small voluntary associations rarely have a headquarters, and any address listed here may well go out of date when officers change.

Organisations in this list are not necessarily able to supply advice on a particular topic; their listing here is for identification purposes and to forestall inappropriate enquiries. Some are 'marginal' to archaeology but possibly even more useful for that. All enquiries to organisations should be as specific as possible and should be accompanied by SAE (stamped addressed envelope). Where society officers have supplied a home telephone number, please do not call them at unreasonable times. Where individual (or institutional) membership is available for a society or group, current rates may be obtained from the address given. Unless otherwise stated, the main source of funds for these organisations is the membership subscription.

Organisations are entered alphabetically, whether national or specialised in coverage; English (and a few European) organisations form the first group, followed by Welsh, Scottish and Irish (Northern Ireland and Republic) organisations in turn. In alphabetising, connecting words like 'if' and 'for' are ignored: hence the 'Association of Railway Preservation Societies' precedes the 'Association for Roman Archaeology'. County and local archaeological societies are not entered, since other directories such as those of the CBA or *Current Archaeology* (for Ireland, *Archaeology Ireland*) already cover them very well.

Data are entered in the following order: NAme; ADdress; TeLephone; Founding Date; SOurce of funds (if other than members' subscriptions); AIms; Collections and/or Library scope; ENquiry services and conditions of use; HouRs of consultation; PuBlications; ACtivities.

England, and Britain generally

NA: **Academia Europaea**
AD: 31 Old Burlington Street, London WIX ILB
TL: 0171 734 5402 (Dr Craig Sinclair, Executive Secretary)
FD: 1988
SO: Various governments and foundations
AI: Is a self-governing association of individual European scholars, covering the whole range of disciplines. Members all belong to their respective national academies, and are elected on the criterion of personal distinction in scholarship and research. There are over 1,100 members from 29 countries.
PB: Yearbooks, AGM reports, study group reports. Quarterly journal *European review* (published by Wiley).
AC: Annual plenary conferences; study groups consider various problems of pan-European concern.

NA: **Advisory Board for Redundant Churches**
AD: Fielden House, Little College Street, London SWIP 3SH
TL: 0171 222 9603/4
FD: 1969
SO: Church of England
AI: Is a statutory body established by the Pastoral Measure 1968 to give information and advice to Church Commissioners on the historic and architectural qualities of redundant and near-redundant Anglican churches.
PB: Annual report.

Advisory Committee on Historic Wreck Sites *see under Dept of National Heritage.*

NA: **Aerial Archaeology Research Group**
AD: c/o Secretary, Dr G Barrett, Geography Dept, University of Wolverhampton, Dudley Campus, Castle View, Dudley DY1 3HR
TL: 01902 321000, fax 01902 323379
FD: 1980
AI: To advance the education of the public in archaeology (including man-made landscape and the built environment) through the promotion of high standards of research, application and communication in the fields of air photography and other methods of remote sensing. All archaeological periods covered. Main area of operation is UK and Republic of Ireland, but there is a growing membership in other European countries.
CL: None held, but advice can be provided on archives of aerial photography, research methods including interpretation and mapping, and recent developments in aerial survey and photography. Database of members and their research interests.
EN: Post or telephone only
HR: 9am–5pm
PB: Newsletter *AARGnews* (2/yr); non-members may subscribe for a fee.
AC: Annual conference open to members and non-members; additional meetings, exhibitions, courses and training schemes; promotion of exchange of information about aerial archaeology.

Agricultural History *see British Agricultural History Society.*

NA: **Airfield Research Group**
AD: c/o Peter W Homer (Hon Gen Sec), 12 Trident Close, Sutton Coldfield, West Midlands B76 ILF
TL: 0121 351 3035
FD: c. 1990
AI: The dissemination of material on the history, architecture, development, current status and use of military and civil airfields, and the provision of assistance to other aeronautical, archaeological and heritage bodies on airfield matters.
CL: Archive in course of preparation (to include airfield histories, detailed plans and layouts, architectural data on special-purpose and standard military buildings).
EN: Postal only
PB: *Airfield review* (3/yr).
AC: Local group meetings, occasional sales stands and site visits; specialists available to deal with enquiries, normally without charge other than photocopy and postage costs.

NA: **Ancient Metallurgy Research Group**
AD: c/o Dr G McDonnell, Dept of Archaeological Sciences, Bradford University, Bradford BD7 IDP
TL: 01274 383535 or 383531, fax 01274 381590
FD: 1991
SO: University-based
AI: AMRG conducts national and international research programmes on the technology and archaeological interpretation of early mining, metal production and artefact fabrication (Bronze Age to present). It provides archaeometallurgical support for excavations, having

access to a range of analytical facilities, and will undertake consultancy work.

CL: Ironworking slag reference collection; other collections being formed.

EN: Postal, telephone, personal visit, JANET

HR: 8am–6pm

PB: Activities reported within departmental annual report.

NA: **Ancient Monuments Society**

AD: St Ann's Vestry Hall, 2 Church Entry, London EC4V 5HB

TL: 0171 236 3934, fax 0171 329 3677 (Matthew Saunders, Secretary)

FD: 1924

AI: The study and conservation of ancient monuments and historic buildings. (The Society is one of the national amenity societies statutorily consulted over listed building applications, and it administers the Joint Committee of National Amenity Societies.) Works in partnership with the Friends of Friendless Churches (which see below).

PB: Annual *Transactions*; newsletter (3/yr); occasional publications on special topics.

(Early) Anglo-Saxon Pottery Group *see now Medieval Pottery Research Group.*

NA: **Anglo-Saxon Pottery Stamps Archive**

AD: c/o Diana Briscoe, 19 Sandwell Mansions, West End Lane, London NW6 1XL

TL: 0171 794 6300

SO: Private funds and donations

AI: To provide a research archive of casts of pottery stamps.

CL: Over 20,000 stamp impressions are available for study.

EN: Postal or personal visit (appointment needed).

NA: **Antique Metalware Society**

AD: c/o Mrs Jennifer Hornsby (Sec), 97 Corn Street, Witney, Oxon OX8 7DL

TL: 01865 61441

FD: 1991 (as Society)

AI: To study artefacts made of non-precious metals and their alloys, their manufacture and history with a view to increasing the knowledge and appreciation of them.

EN: Postal or telephone

HR: Any reasonable hours

PB: *Base thoughts* (annual); newsletter (2/yr).

AC: Meetings in spring and autumn.

NA: **Antiquities Dealers' Association**

AD: c/o Susan Hadida (Secretary), Faustus Fine Art, Duke's Court, 32 Duke Street, London SW1Y 6DF

TL: 0171 930 1864, fax 0171 938 1628

FD: 1982

AI: Is a Corporate Member of the Museums Association; is represented on Art Trade Liaison Committee; is in liaison with CBA. Code of Conduct binds members to ensure that to the best of their knowledge all objects sold are genuine and as described. Membership subject to vetting.

PB: Annual directory.

AC: Holds regular antiquities fairs.

NA: **Archaeological Indexers' Panel**

AD: c/o L and R Adkins, Longstone Lodge, Aller, Langport, Som TA10 0QT

TL: 01458 250075, fax 01458 250858, e-mail 101331.2065@compuserve.com Internet http://ourworld.compuserve.com/homepages/Adkins_Archaeology

FD: 1987

SO: Voluntary

AI: To promote the practice of good archaeological indexing and to provide a corps of experienced archaeological indexers who can be recommended to publishers and others wishing to commission indexes.

EN: Postal or telephone

HR: Any reasonable hours

PB: Series of fact sheets directed to authors, publishers, editors, etc; related publication *Trial trench* (occasional newsletter edited by C Lavell for the Society of Indexers' Archaeological Special Interest Group).

NA: **Archaeological Leather Group**

AD: c/o Esther Cameron (Sec), Institute of Archaeology, 36 Beaumont Street, Oxford OX1 2PG

TL: 01865 278253 (direct line)

FD: 1985, refounded 1994

AI: To promote the study of leather and leather objects from archaeological contexts by leather scientists, conservators and artefact specialists.

EN: Postal preferred

PB: Newsletter (2/yr); *Guidelines for the care of waterlogged archaeological leather* (1996: obtain from Glynis Edwards, Ancient Monuments Lab, English Heritage).

AC: Two meetings a year.

NA: **Archaeological Site Photographers' Association**

AD: c/o Eric Houlder, 31 Fairview, Carleton, Pontefract WF8 3NT

TL: 01977 702995 (evenings)

FD: 1991

AI: To bring together archaeological photographers and to provide a forum for excellence in site photography.

PB: Newsletter (2/yr).

AC: Conferences, seminar (exhibitions proposed).

NA: **Archaeology Abroad Service**

AD: 31–34 Gordon Square, London WC1H 0PY

TL: no telephone, fax 0171 383 2572, e-mail arch.abroad@ucl.ac.uk

FD: 1971

AI: To provide regular listings of excavations taking place overseas and needing volunteer workers; list of scholarships available.

PB: *Archaeology abroad* (3/yr)

NA: **The Archaeology Centre, Bagshot**

AD: 4–10 London Road, Bagshot, Surrey GU19 5HN

TL: 01276 451181 (Geoffrey Cole)

FD: 1988

SO: Surrey Heath Archaeological and Heritage Trust

AI: To assist people from all walks of life to discover archaeology, to create employment and to give opportunities for developing archaeological knowledge.

EN: Postal or telephone

HR: Normal office hours

PB: Newsletters (4/yr each) for SHAHT, British Archaeology Students, and Young Archaeologists' Club (SE England branch).

AC: Training excavations; organises events for National Archaeology Day; has plans, if funds become available, to develop numerous archaeological projects for young people and adults.

NA: **Architectural Heritage Fund**

AD: 27 John Adam Street, London WC2N 6HX

TL: 0171 925 0199, fax 0171 930 0295

FD: 1976

SO: Central and local government, various other types of organisation

AI: To promote the permanent preservation for the benefit of the public generally of buildings, monuments or other edifices or structures . . . of particular beauty or historical, architectural or constructional interest in all parts of the UK. (Effectively a national revolving fund with the ability to make loans and grants to charitable

organisations (only) undertaking the repair and rehabilitation of historic buildings where a change of ownership or use is involved.)

EN: Postal enquiries re conditions of loan/grant

PB: Newsletter (2/yr); *How to rescue a ruin by setting up a Buildings Preservation Trust* (1989 but o/p). Editorial responsibility for APT's *Guidance notes for Building Preservation Trusts*.

AC: Active member and supporter of UK Association of Building Preservation Trusts. Has a support group Friends of the Architectural Heritage Fund. Provides limited grants for feasibility studies.

NA: **Architectural Salvage Index**

AD: c/o Hutton + Rostron, Netley House, Gomshall, Guildford, Surrey GU5 9QA

TL: 01483 203221, fax 01483 202911

FD: 1977

SO: Registration fees

AI: To act as an agency to put those in need of reusable building materials and items of architectural value directly in contact with those who wish to dispose of such materials. (The organisation does not encourage the demolition or stripping of buildings.) National scope, and any chronological period.

CL: Database of salvaged items and of suppliers of architectural salvage. Enquirers can register items available for sale, or their requirements for item(s). 'Expert system' being developed, incorporating advice on works to historic buildings.

EN: Postal and telephone/fax only; online service under development (for access via modem)

HR: Mon-Fri 9am–1pm; 2pm–5.30pm

PB: None, but printouts supplied in response to particular requests for information; charges vary.

NA: **Arkwright Society**

AD: Cromford Mill, Mill Lane, Derby DE4 3RQ

TL: 01629 823256/825776 (Dr Christopher Charlton, Director)

FD: 1971

AI: To promote the conservation of buildings and machinery of industrial archaeological and/or historical interest; international scope.

CL: (No reading room space as yet)

EN: Postal, telephone or personal visit (by appointment only)

HR: Normal office hours. The site (Arkwright's Mill under restoration) is open every day, though the office may not be staffed.

PB: Newsletter (occasional: about 2/yr).

AC: Meetings and exhibitions.

ARMA see *Roman Military Equipment Conference.*

NA: **Arms and Armour Society**

AD: c/o Secretary, Edmund Greenwood, Field House, Upper Dicker, Hailsham, E Sussex BN27 3PY

TL: 01323 844278, fax same

FD: 1951

SO: Members' subscriptions

AI: To assist in the study, collection and preservation of arms and armour from earliest times to present day; international in scope.

EN: Postal, telephone or personal visit (appointment necessary)

HR: Any reasonable hours

PB: *Journal* (2/yr) (includes useful review of literature); newsletter (4/yr).

AC: Meetings, occasional visits, use of Education Centre at Tower Armouries.

NA: **Association of Archaeological Illustrators and Surveyors**

AD: c/o Michael Fossick (Hon Sec), Dept of History and Archaeology, University of Exeter, Queen's Building, Exeter, Devon EX4 4QH

FD: 1978

AI: To develop and promote an increased understanding and professional application of archaeological illustration and surveying techniques. Mainly UK and Ireland but with some overseas members.

EN: Postal only

PB: Annual journal *Graphic archaeology*; Newsletter (3/yr); annual report for Conference; Technical Papers (list available).

AC: Annual conference; maintains a travelling exhibition about the Association; occasional day schools on technical aspects of illustration/surveying; reciprocal arrangements with likeminded bodies; information sheets on courses/training available to non-members (send SAE + £1 for information pack).

NA: **Association of Conservation Officers**

AD: PO Box 301, Brighton, Sussex BN2 1BQ

IN: Dr Richard Morrice

FD: 1982

AI: To promote good practice in the conservation of historic buildings through planning authorities in the United Kingdom. Effectively covers Saxon period onwards.

EN: Postal only

PB: Annual report; *Context* (4/yr); newsletter (4/yr).

AC: Annual school, branch conferences and schools, exhibitions; its members, working in local authorities, can provide specialist advice on building restoration, adaptation etc.

Association of County Archaeological Officers see now *Association of Local Government Archaeologists.*

NA: **Association of County Archivists**

AD: c/o Rachel Watson, County Archivist Northamptonshire, Wootton Hall Park, Northampton NN4 9BQ

TL: 01604 762129, fax 01604 767562

FD: 1980

AI: To represent county archive services on important or urgent issues; to provide a forum for exchange of views and information; to produce policy statements and guidelines.

AC: Biennial conference and seminar.

NA: **Association of County Councils** (*merging in April 1997 with Association of District Councils*)

AD: Eaton House, 66a Eaton Square, London SW1W 9BH

TL: 0171 201 1500, fax 0171 235 8458

AI: Represents [at 1996] the interests of 47 county councils in England and Wales, which have responsibility for numerous environmental matters.

Association of District Archaeological Officers see now *Association of Local Government Archaeologists.*

NA: **Association of District Councils** (*merging in April 1997 with Assocation of County Councils*)

AD: Chapter House, 26 Chapter Street, London SW1P 4ND

TL: 0171 233 6868, fax 9171 233 6551

AI: Represents [at 1996] over 300 non-metropolitan DCs in England and Wales whose responsibilities include local planning and development control, local buildings and conservation areas, museums etc.

NA: **Association for Environmental Archaeology**

AD: c/o Allan Hall, Environmental Archaeology Unit, The Walled Garden, University of York, Heslerton, Yorks YO1 5DD (Membership Sec: Dr Rebecca Nicholson, Dept of Archaeological Sciences, Bradford University, Bradford BD7 1DP)

TL: 01904 433851, fax 01904 433850; e-mail biol8@york.ac.uk
FD: 1979
AI: To study the human use of, and effects on, the environment in the past.
PB: Journal *Circaea* (2/year); newsletter (4/yr, includes recent references).
AC: Annual conference (published); day meeting in spring.

NA: **Association of Garden Trusts**
AD: Oaklea, Smalls Hill Road, Leigh, Reigate, Surrey RH2 8PF
TL: 01306 611268, fax same
FD: 1993
AI: As an educational charity, aims to promote and coordinate the work of County Gardens Trusts (24 in England, 9 in Wales) in connection with historic gardens.
CL: Photographic library (apply to individual Trusts) of gardens and parks open to public.
EN: Postal
PB: None centrally; some by individual County Gardens Trusts.
AC: Provides training on aspects of national recording of gardens. Is in liaison with IoAAS: Landscapes and Gardens (York).

NA: **Association for History and Computing – UK Branch**
AD: c/o Matthew Woollard (Sec), Faculty of Humanities, University of the West of England, Bristol, St Matthias Campus, Oldbury Court Road, Bristol BS16 2JP
TL: 0117 965 5384 ext 4487; e-mail mge-wool@uwe.ac.uk
FD: 1987
AI: To promote and develop interest in the use of computers in all types of historical study at every level, in both teaching and research.
EN: Postal, telephone and e-mail
HR: Normal office hours
PB: *History and computing* (journal, 3/yr); *Guide to historical datafiles held in machine-readable form* (1992); research publication series to begin in 1996.
AC: Annual conference.

NA: **Association for the History of Glass Ltd**
AD: c/o Hon Ed *Glass news*, Dr John Shepherd, Museum of London (Early Collection), London Wall, London EC2Y 5HN
TL: 0171 600 3699
FD: 1977
SO: No regular income

AI: To promote the study of all aspects of glass (Britain, all periods; is the British section of the Association Internationale pour l'Histoire du Verre).
EN: Postal only
PB: *Bibliography of medieval glass vessels from British sites AD 1200–1500* (1994); newsletter.
AC: Annual conferences/meetings.

Association of Independent Museums *see Section 4.8 Museum Directories.*

NA: **Association for Industrial Archaeology**
AD: Hon Sec, c/o The Wharfage, Ironbridge, Telford, Shropshire TF8 7AW
TL: 01952 432751, fax 01952 432204
FD: 1973
AI: To promote the study, preservation and presentation of Britain's industrial heritage, and to encourage better standards of recording, research, conservation and publication.
CL: Books and journals housed at the Ironbridge Gorge Museum Trust library at Longware House, Coalbrookdale, Telford TF8 7AW.
EN: Postal (referral service)
PB: *IA news* (4/yr); *Industrial archaeology review* (journal, 2/yr); newsletter (4/yr); handbook *Recording the industrial heritage.*
AC: Affiliation scheme for local IA societies; responsible for IRIS, Index Record for Industrial Sites (see under IRIS below); conferences, education/training, research; awards for high standards in fieldwork and recording, and President's Award annually to a site achieving a high standard of interpretation and display.

NA: **Association Internationale pour la Peinture Murale Antique**
AD: c/o Sec, Prof Sandro De Maria, Dipartimento di Archeologia, Università degli Studi, Piazza San Giovanni in Monte 2, I-40124 Bologna, Italy
PB: Bibliographical bulletin from 1992, *Apelles, bull de l'Association Internationale pour la Peinture Antique.*

NA: **Association of Learned and Professional Society Publishers**
AD: c/o Professor Bernard Donovan, 48 Kelsey Lane, Beckenham, Kent BR3 3NE
TL: 0181 658 0459, fax 0181 663 3583
FD: 1972
AI: To encourage communication and cooperation between learned and professional societies and institutions of all sizes in matters concerning publishing.

PB: *Learned publishing* (4/yr).
AC: Discussion meetings, seminars, participation in exhibitions; fostering of close relations with other bodies involved in publishing, including electronic publishing.

NA: **Association of Local Government Archaeological Officers** (*formed from merger in 1996 of Association of County Archaeological Officers and Association of District Archaeological Officers*)
AD: c/o Hon Sec, Stewart Bryant, Planning and Estates Dept, Herts County Council, County Hall, Hertford SG13 8DN
TL: 01992 555244/5, fax 01992 555648
FD: 1996 (originally 1974 for ACAO, 1991 for ADAO)
AI: To advise on matters of archaeological planning, conservation and research; to further the cause of archaeology generally.
PB: *Model briefs and specifications for archaeological assessments and field evaluations.*
AC: Formal meetings, working groups etc.

NA: **Association of Metropolitan Authorities**
AD: 35 Great Smith Street, London SW1P 3BJ
TL: 0171 222 8100, fax 0171 222 0878
FD: 1974
AI: To promote and protect the interests of its member authorities and the communities they serve.

NA: **Association of Preservation Trusts**
AD: 27 John Adam Street, London WC2N 6HX
TL: 0171 930 1629, fax 0171 930 0295
FD: 1988
SO: Has close links with Architectural Heritage Fund (which see)
AI: To encourage and assist building preservation trusts' objectives, namely to preserve, for the benefit of the people of the UK, buildings and structures of particular beauty or of historic, architectural or constructional interest, ancient monuments and associated land.
PB: *Guidance notes for Building Preservation Trusts.*
AC: Has nine areas with their own coordinators and committees, meeting together regularly.

NA: **Association of Professional Archaeological Consultants**
AD: c/o Oxford Archaeological Associates Ltd, Lawrence House, 2 Polstead Road, Oxford OX2 6TN
TL: 01865 310209, fax 01865 311187
FD: 1993

AI: To provide a forum for the practice of archaeological consultancy.
EN: Postal
HR: Normal office hours
PB: (Bulletin planned)

NA: **Association of Railway Preservation Societies Ltd**
AD: c/o General Administrator, Raymond Williams, 16 Woodbrook, Charing, Ashford, Kent TN27 0DN
TL: 01233 712130
FD: 1959
AI: To help and coordinate the activities of the various groups pioneering railway preservation in Great Britain and Ireland.
EN: Postal or telephone
HR: Reasonable office hours, but postal enquiry with SAE preferred.
PB: *Guide to steam trains in Britain and Ireland; ARPS journal*; yearbook, *Railways restored* (per Ian Allen Ltd); etc.
AC: Meetings and seminars, awards and competitions, advisory services, representations to government departments and industry, etc.

NA: **Association for Roman Archaeology**
AD: c/o Bryn Walters (Director/Administrator), 27 Broadway, Rodbourne Cheney, Swindon SN2 3BN
TL: 01793 534008
FD: 1995 (reformed from former Friends of Roman Research Trust)
AI: To promote the advancement of the education of the public in the history and archaeology of the Roman period.
PB: Bulletin (2/yr).
AC: Offers privileged entry to most Roman sites and collections in Britain; guided tours.

NA: **Association for Studies in the Conservation of Historic Buildings**
AD: 31–34 Gordon Square, London WC1H 0PY
FD: 1968
AI: To provide a forum for advancing studies in the conservation of historic buildings (from the earliest built structures to the present day).
EN: Postal only
PB: Annual *Transactions*; Newsletter (4/yr).
AC: Meetings, lectures and discussions, visits to buildings and places of interest.

NA: **Association for the Study and Preservation of Roman Mosaics (ASPROM)**
AD: c/o S R Cosh, 38 Oaklea, Ash Vale, Aldershot, Hants GU12 5HP

TL: 01252 316018

FD: 1979 (was previously British Branch of the Association International pour l'Etude de la Mosaïque Antique)

AI: To advance education of the group by fostering the study and preservation of Roman mosaics and related material.

PB: *Mosaic* (annually); newsletters (2/yr).

AC: Two meetings/yr.

NA: **The Battlefields Trust**

AD: c/o Michael Rayner (Coordinator), Meadow Cottage, 33 High Green, Brooke, Norwich NR15 1HR

TL: 01508 558145

FD: 1992

AI: To work for better preservation, interpretation and presentation of battlefields, as educational and heritage resources; worldwide scope.

EN: Postal or telephone

HR: 8.00am–8.00pm, 7 days/week

PB: Newsletter (4/yr).

AC: Annual conference, field days, study days.

NA: **Bead Society of Great Britain**

AD: c/o Secretary, Dr Carole Morris, 1 Casburn Lane, Burwell, Cambs CB5 0ED

TL: 01638 742024, fax same

FD: 1989

AI: For the appreciation, private or professional, of beads, ancient and modern, of all types, their techniques of manufacture and their application.

EN: Postal only

PB: Newsletter (5/yr).

AC: Annual bead fair; AGM/visit/workshop; other lectures/workshops.

NA: **Bead Study Trust**

AD: c/o Mrs M E Hutchinson, 29 Elliscombe Road, London SE7 7PF

TL: 0181 858 2649

FD: 1980

AI: To promote bead research for all periods (archaeological, ethnographical and anthropological aspects only) internationally.

CL: The Trust is based on the Beck Collection of beads held at the University Museum of Archaeology and Anthropology, Cambridge, which will also hold the Trust's library when formed.

EN: Postal only

PB: Newsletter (2/yr, with running bibliography); catalogues of the Beck Collection in preparation.

AC: Guido Scholarships are to be offered for the study of beads abroad.

NA: **British Academy (for the Promotion of Historical, Philosophical and Philological Studies)**

AD: 20–21 Cornwall Terrace, London NW1 4QP

TL: 0171 487 5966, fax 0171 224 3807, e-mail basec@britac.ac.uk; Internet http://britac3. britac.ac.uk

FD: 1901

SO: Public funds, with some private

AI: The promotion of advanced scholarship in the humanities. (Fellows are elected on the basis of distinction in their field.) The Academy is one of the main sources of funding for archaeological fieldwork, both in the UK and abroad, by British archaeologists: eg it supports the British Schools and Institutes of Archaeology abroad and offers post-graduate studentships in the humanities. Also collaborates with NERC and other organisations in FASA, the Funding of Applied Science in Archaeology. Supports many large-scale projects such as Corpus of Anglo-Saxon Stone Sculpture; Sylloge of Coins of the British Isles; Corpus of Romanesque Sculpture in Britain and Ireland; Corpus Signorum Imperii Romani; Corpus Vitrearum Medii Aevi; English Place-Name Society, etc.

EN: Postal and telephone, relating only to activities outlined in the Academy's Guide

HR: 9.30am–5.30pm

PB: Annual report; *Guide to awards*; *Research grants in archaeology newsletter*; *Proceedings*; lectures etc.

AC: Some lectures/seminars open to public; scholarly exchanges overseas, etc.

NA: **British Agricultural History Society**

AD: c/o Rural History Centre, University of Reading, PO Box 229, Whiteknights, Reading RG6 6AG

TL: 01734 318660, fax 01734 751264

FD: 1953

AI: To encourage the study of the history of agriculture in all its aspects, and of the countryside in Britain and overseas.

CL: Has access to Museum of English Rural Life's large collection of artefacts and historical records, photographic collection (1 million images), paintings, prints etc.

EN: Postal or telephone only

HR: Normal office hours

PB: *Agricultural history review* (2/yr).

AC: Annual conference, spring and autumn meetings.

NA: **British Archaeological Association**
AD: c/o Hon Sec, Dr W Filmer-Sankey, Victorian Society, 1 Priory Gardens, London W4 1TT; Membership Sec John Jenkins, 75 Budmouth Avenue, Preston, Weymouth, Dorset DT3 6QJ
TL: (Membership Sec) 01305 833447
FD: 1844
AI: To promote and further the study of archaeology and the preservation of our national antiquities, to encourage research into art, architecture and antiquities of Roman to post-medieval date, and to publish material in furtherance of its activities.
CL: Members are allowed to use the library of the Society of Antiquaries of London.
PB: Annual *Journal*; series on the medieval art and architecture of cathedrals.
AC: Annual conference; lectures; biennial essay prize; for Brick Section see under British Brick Society below.

British Archaeological Awards *see section 4.6 Grants and awards.*

NA: **British Archaeologists' and Developers' Liaison Group**
AD: Joint Secretaries, c/o British Property Federation, 35 Catherine Place, London SW1E 6DJ
TL: 0171 828 0111
FD: 1985
SO: Jointly sponsored by BPF and SCAUM
AI: To encourage close cooperation between developers and archaeologists, and to establish good working practice through a voluntary code of conduct and model forms of contract.
PB: *BADLG code of practice* (1991; for archaeologists and developers).

British Archaeological Trust *see RESCUE.*

British Archaeology Students *see under The Archaeology Centre, Bagshot.*

NA: **British Association for the Advancement of Science**
AD: 23 Savile Row, London W1X 1AB
TL: 0171 973 3500, fax 0171 973 3051
FD: 1831
SO: Charitable and members' donations
AI: To promote the public understanding of science
EN: Postal, telephone or personal visit
HR: 9.30am–5.00pm
PB: Annual report; *Science and public affairs;*

Science awareness newsletter; *Scope*; wide-ranging surveys, including archaeological evidence, of various regions were produced in connection with annual conferences (1949–72); teachers' packs.
AC: Annual meeting; regional meetings; national week of science and technology; BAYS (network of science clubs); database of science speakers; local branches.

NA: **British Association for Local History**
AD: c/o Michael Cowan, 24 Lower Street, Harnham, Salisbury, Wilts SP2 8EY
TL: 01722 320115 Internet http://indigo.stile.le.ac.uk/~bon/LOCAL_HIST/frontpage.html
FD: 1982 (formed from previous Standing Conference on Local History)
AI: To promote local history for the complementary purposes of academic study and leisure activity.
EN: Postal or telephone only
HR: no restriction
PB: Annual report; *The local historian* (4/yr; also concise index to vols 1–21); many booklets on various aspects of local history research.
AC: Conferences, specialist visits, schools consultation group, insurance for societies (some 400 societies in membership).

NA: **British Association of Nature Conservationists**
AD: c/o The Wildlife Trust for Northampton, Lings House, Billing Lings, Northampton NN3 8BE
TL: 01604 405285
FD: 1979
AI: To advance nature conservation in the UK by providing a forum for discussion on all aspects of nature conservation, promoting better understanding of nature conservation principles in planning of rural and urban environments (etc).
EN: Postal, phone
HR: 9.00am–5.00pm
PB: *Ecos* (4/yr); occasional publications.
AC: Regular conferences and liaison with bodies having similar objectives.

NA: **British Association of Numismatic Societies**
AD: c/o Mr P H Mernick, at Bush, Boake, Allen Ltd, Blackhorse Lane, London E17 5QP
TL: 0181 523 6431
AI: To coordinate the activities of local numismatic clubs.
PB: Occasional publications.
AC: Congresses.

NA: **British Aviation Archaeological Council**
AD: c/o R J Collis, 8 Holly Road, Oulton Broad, Lowestoft, Norfolk NR32 3NH
TL: 01502 585421
FD: 1978
AI: To establish and maintain ethical standards, to provide a forum for discussion, to provide advice for member groups and to promote the preservation of aircraft relics and relevant historical documents.
EN: Postal
HR: Normal office hours
PB: Newsletter *Wrecksearch* (4/yr).
AC: Two national meetings annually.

NA: **British Brick Society**
AD: c/o Brick Development Association, Woodside House, Winkfield, Windsor, Berks SL4 2DX (for general enquiries about the society, Michael Hammett (Hon Sec), 9 Bailey Close, High Wycombe, Bucks HP13 6QA, tel 01494 520299)
TL: 01344 885651 ext 108, fax 01344 890129
FD: 1972
AI: To promote all aspects of the study of bricks and brickwork, of all periods, and not restricted to the UK. (The British Archaeological Association's Brick Section is an affiliate.)
CL: The Society's Bibliographer maintains a library collection (for use of members) and a bibliography on bricks, brick-making and architectural usage of brick.
EN: For technical information, write to Enquiries Secretary, Dr R Firman, 12 Elm Avenue, Beeston, Nottingham NG9 1BU
PB: Newsletter (3 or 4/yr) with articles on relevant topics (complete sets are maintained in copyright libraries and that of the Society of Antiquaries of London, and an index is available).
AC: The Society is mainly a corresponding one but does promote two or three visits a year to sites of interest.

NA: **British Cave Research Association** (*see also* *Cave Burial Research Project*)
AD: c/o Mr Ellis, 20 Woodland Avenue, Westonzoyland, Bridgwater, Som TA7 0LQ
TL: 01278 691539
AI: To coordinate all aspects of the discovery, exploration, description and conservation of caves and similar natural features and their environment.
EN: Postal
PB: Transactions *Cave and karst science*; magazine *Caves and caving*; occasional publications.

AC: Range from research investigations (research fund available for small grants) to purely sporting activities.

British Dovecote Society. *This society ceased operating in 1994 but its former Secretary, A Whitworth, maintains an interest as Secretary of the Yorkshire Dovecote Society at Linden, 10 The Carrs, Sleights, Whitby, YO21 1RR (tel 01947 810819); he has also published a comprehensive bibliography of dovecotes.*

NA: **British Geological Survey**
AD: Kingsley Dunham Centre, Keyworth, Nottingham NG12 5GG
TL: 0115 936 3100, fax 0115 936 3200 (also London Information Office at Geological Museum, 0171 589 4090)
FD: 1835
SO: Component body of NERC
AI: To carry out geoscience mapping of the UK landmass and offshore area; to provide the National Geoscience Information Service.
CL: Books, scientific journals, maps, geological specimens, borehole records.
EN: Postal, telephone, fax and e-mail, or by visit to Library/Records Centre. A fee may be charged if enquiries require an in-depth response.
HR: Normal office hours
PB: Maps, memoirs, technical reports; catalogue available.
AC: The Survey is equipped for geophysical and remote-sensing applications in archaeology.

NA: **British Numismatic Society**
AD: c/o Hon Sec, J D Bateson, Hunterian Museum, University of Glasgow, Hillhead Street, Glasgow G12 8QQ
TL: 0141 330 4221, fax 0141 307 8059
FD: 1903
AI: To encourage the study of British coinage in all its forms from the introduction of coinage into Britain in 1st century BC down to modern times.
PB: *British numismatic journal* (annual); Special Publications series.
AC: Monthly meetings Jan-June and Sept-Nov at the Warburg Institute in London.

NA: **British Records Association**
AD: 18 Padbury Court, London E2 7EH
TL: 0171 729 1415
FD: 1932
AI: To coordinate and promote the work of archivists, historians and owners in the pre-

servation and use of records. Includes the finding of new homes for historical documents in danger of destruction.

EN: Postal, telephone

HR: Normal office hours

PB: *Archives* (2/yr); newsletter (2/yr); occasional series *Archives and the user*.

AC: Courses, annual conference.

NA: **British Record Society**

AD: College of Arms, Queen Victoria Street, London EC4V 4BT

TL: 0171 236 9612

FD: 1889

SO: Subscriptions to Index Series

AI: Concerned with the publishing of indexes to historical records, especially probate.

EN: Postal, telephone

HR: Normal office hours

British Sub-Aqua Club: *Enquiries about archaeological diving are best directed to the Nautical Archaeology Society's Portsmouth training centre – see under Nautical Archaeology Society below.*

NA: **British Tourist Authority** (*see also English Tourist Board*)

AD: Thames Tower, Black's Road, Hammersmith, London W6 9EL

TL: 0181 846 9000, fax 0181 563 0302

AI: To advise government and public bodies on matters concerning inward tourism.

PB: Annual report; *English heritage monitor* (with English Tourist Board: annual tables of statistics of visitor numbers etc).

NA: **British Trust for Conservation Volunteers**

AD: 36 St Mary's Street, Wallingford, Oxfordshire OX10 0EU

TL: 01491 839766, fax 01491 839646

AI: To support the activities of volunteers in practical steps to improve their environment.

CL: Slides and prints on practical conservation work, available to organisations only (no fee).

EN: Postal, phone, personal visit

HR: Normal office hours

PB: *The conserver* (newspaper, 4/yr); brochures and leaflets.

AC: Network of 90 local offices (England, Wales and Northern Ireland).

NA: **British Waterways Archive**

AD: The Archivist, British Waterways, Llanthony Warehouse, Gloucester Docks, GL1 2EJ

TL: 01452 318041

FD: 1963

CL: Database index by keyword; engineering drawings, photographs (13,000 b/w), etc.

EN: Postal or personal visit (by appointment)

HR: Normal office hours

Building Conservation Trust *see UPKEEP.*

NA: **Building Research Establishment – Heritage Support Service**

AD: Garston, Watford, Herts WD2 7JR

TL: 01923 664850, fax 01923 664786

FD: 1993

SO: Central Government plus consultancy fees/ commissions

AI: To offer to building conservators comprehensive information, often based on long-term research, to assist in assessing the most appropriate methods or techniques for particular problems of timber, stone, fire prevention, decay, materials, etc.

CL: Collection of stone samples (fee may be charged to view).

EN: Postal, telephone, personal visit (appointment needed)

HR: Normal office hours

NA: **Buildings at Risk Trust**

AD: Number One Greenhill, Wirksworth, Derbys DE4 4EN

TL: 01629 826292, fax 01629 826390 (Alan Bemrose, Sec)

FD: 1992 (as successor to British Historic Buildings Trust founded 1981)

SO: DNH grants and own revolving fund activities

AI: To secure the preservation of historic buildings throughout the UK by acquisition, repair, restoration and conversion.

EN: Postal

AC: Seminars, conferences, advisory service, preparation of feasibility studies and business plans.

NA: **Buildings of England Office**

AD: Penguin Books, 27 Wright's Lane, London W8 5TZ

TL: 0171 416 3000, fax 0171 416 3099

CL: Pevsner's original notebooks are with RCHME at Swindon; at the Society of Antiquaries is the card index from which Michael Good compiled material for a CD-ROM *Compendium of Pevsner's Buildings of England on compact disk* incorporating 46 volumes of Pevsner (details from OUP Electronic Publishing, Walton Street, Oxford OX2 6DP).

NA: **Butser Ancient Farm**
AD: Nexus House, Gravel Hill, Waterlooville, Hants PO8 0QE
TL: 01705 598838, fax same
FD: 1972
SO: Mainly self-supporting
AI: To conduct research into Romano-Celtic methods of farming and building by means of an open-air 'laboratory' where controlled experiments can be undertaken and demonstrated to the public in a full-scale educational resource centre.
CL: Site at Bascombe Copse open to the public 1 March–30 November annually.
EN: Postal, telephone, personal visit
HR: 10.00am–5.00pm in summer, 10.00am–4.00pm in winter
PB: Guide book, leaflets, information packs.
AC: Group tours, practical domestic skills of Iron Age/Roman period, school visits, residential archaeological courses, workshops, events and lectures. Support group: Friends of Butser Ancient Farm.

NA: **Caerdroia**
AD: c/o Jeff Saward, 53 Thundersley Grove, Thundersley, Benfleet, Essex SS7 3EB
TL: 01268 751915
FD: 1980
AI: To study the history, development and distribution of mazes and labyrinths. Computer database of relevant material under development.
CL: Extensive archive on subject area, from books to ephemera; photo library of ancient and modern mazes from around the world.
EN: Postal, telephone or personal visit (by appointment)
HR: All reasonable times
PB: Annual journal *Caerdroia*, books, booklets and pamphlets, reprint service for own journal. List available on request.
AC: Occasional conferences.

NA: **Cambridge Music-Archaeological Survey**
AD: c/o Archaeologia Musica, PO Box 92, Cambridge CB4 1PU
TL: 01223 351069
FD: 1979
AI: Post-excavation research, survey and conservation: music- and sound-related finds of all periods.
EN: Postal, telephone and fax (from archaeologists and conservators only)
HR: (24-hr answering service)

AC: Related to CMAS is Archaeologia Musica, engaged in the commercial reproduction, distribution and broadcasting of ancient musics.

Cambridge University Committee for Aerial Photography *see Section 5.2 Sources for air photographs.*

NA: **Castle Studies Group**
AD: c/o Dr Robert A Higham (Hon Sec), Dept of History and Archaeology, Queen's Building, Queen's Drive, Exeter, Devon EX4 4QH
TL: 01392 264349
FD: 1987
AI: To pursue and promote research into the medieval castles of Great Britain and Ireland, and to communicate results of that research through newsletters, conferences and other means.
EN: Postal (to Hon Sec, other committee members, or to Newsletter contributors)
PB: *Newsletter* (annual).
AC: AGM and conference; joint conferences with other bodies.

NA: **The Cathedrals Fabric Commission for England** (formerly Cathedrals Advisory Commission for England)
AD: Fielden House, 10 Little College Street, London SW1P 3SH
TL: 0171 222 3793, fax 0171 222 3794
FD: 1991
SO: Statutory body of the General Synod of the Church of England
AI: To further the care and conservation of cathedral churches of the Church of England in accordance with the provision of the *Care of cathedrals measure 1990* and with particular reference to their architecture, archaeology, history and art.
CL: Library with collections relating to churches and their contents, mainly in England; open for consultation by prior arrangement with the Librarian.
EN: Postal only
HR: 9.30am–5.30pm Monday to Friday
PB: Annual report; list of other publications available for SAE; video *Looking after your church* (1991).
AC: There is a Fabric Advisory Committee for each Anglican cathedral in England.

NA: **Cave Burial Research Project**
AD: c/o J A Gilks, 6 Old Bank Fold, Almondbury Bank, Huddersfield HD5 8HF
TL: 01484 532175

FD: 1983
SO: Privately funded
AI: To collect and preserve material relating to early cave excavations; to record finds etc in a modern way and publish them. To make others aware of what has been found and what is being destroyed.
CL: Library of relevant books and offprints; small (but growing) photographic library; individual site files; drawings of artefacts (Neo–EBA) found in caves; enlargements of cave drawings.
EN: Postal, telephone or personal visit (by prior appointment)
HR: 10.00am–12.00pm; 2.00pm–4.30pm
PB: Offprints of articles published in relevant journals available on request.
AC: Survey work and excavation.

NA: **Census of Medieval Tiles in Britain**
AD: c/o Dr E C Norton, Centre for Medieval Studies, The King's Manor, York YO1 2EP
TL: 01904 433911, fax 01904 433918
FD: 1960s
SO: Various grant-giving bodies
AI: To promote the study and recording of medieval floor tiles in Britain, and to sponsor county surveys.
CL: Some archive material of notes and drawings held.
EN: Postal only
AC: Conferences. Note that John Bradley at UC Dublin is collecting relevant Irish material.

NA: **Central Archaeology Service (English Heritage)**
AD: Fort Cumberland, Fort Cumberland Road, Eastney, Portsmouth PO4 9LD
TL: 01705 817472, fax 01705 838060

Centre for the Conservation of Historic Parks and Gardens, *see now Institute of Advanced Architectural Studies: Landscapes and Gardens.*

NA: **Centre for Environmental Change and Quaternary Research**
AD: Dept of Geography and Geology, Cheltenham and Gloucester College of Higher Education, Francis Close Hall, Swindon Road, Cheltenham GL50 4AZ
TL: 01242 543494, fax 532997, e-mail fchambers@chelt.ac.uk
FD: 1995
AI: To study environmental change through pollen analysis, particle size analysis, chemical analysis (phosphate and elemental), analysis of diatoms, non-marine mollusca, peat macro-

fossils, tephrochronology, magnetic susceptibility; luminescence dating laboratory from 1997.
EN: Postal, phone

NA: **Centre for Environmental Interpretation**
AD: Manchester Metropolitan University, St Augustine's, Lower Chatham Street, Manchester M15 6BY (*see also under Scotland for Scottish branch*)
TL: 0161 247 1067, fax 0161 236 7383
FD: 1980
AI: To promote and develop good practice in environmental interpretation in the fields of recreation, conservation, tourism and heritage. The Centre is a national charitable unit which provides consultancy, advice and information; projects; and training.
CL: Specialist reference library holding material related to the presentation of sites to visitors.
EN: Not stated
HR: Not stated
PB: *Environmental interpretation* (3/yr); occasional publications; directory of training courses nationwide (list on request).

NA: **Centre for Metropolitan History**
AD: University of London School of Advanced Study, Institute of Historical Research, Room 351, Senate House, University of London, Malet Street, London WC1E 7HU
TL: 0171 636 0272, fax 0171 436 2183
FD: 1987
SO: Corporation of London, ESRC, English Heritage, Leverhulme Trust etc
AI: To promote the study of the character and development of Greater London from its beginnings to the present day, and to set the history of London in the wider context of other metropolises.
CL: Various databases under compilation: medieval London and its hinterland; research in progress on London's history.
EN: Postal, telephone, personal visit, JANET
HR: 9.30am–5.30pm
PB: Annual report, Newsletter (annual), seminar lists, *Bibliography of London history to 1939*, other publications (list on request).
AC: Seminars and conferences.

NA: **Ceramic Petrology Group**
AD: British Museum Dept of Scientific Research, London WC1B 3DG; or c/o Hon Sec, Susan Pringle, 212 Ferme Park Road, London N8 9BN
FD: 1988
AI: To promote the investigation of ceramic

materials, particularly by petrographic methods; to develop skills, techniques and understanding of members; worldwide and all periods.

EN: Postal only

PB: Newsletter (3/yr).

AC: Two specialist one-day workshops/lecture meetings yearly.

NA: **The Chapels Society**

AD: c/o Christine van Melzen (Hon Sec), Rookery Farmhouse, Laxfield, Woodbridge, Suffolk IP13 8JA

TL: 01986 798308

FD: 1988

AI: To further interest in English non-conformist buildings, both architecturally and historically.

EN: Postal and telephone

HR: Reasonable hours

PB: Newsletter (twice yearly), occasional papers.

AC: Day and residential meetings throughout the country.

NA: **The Church and Conservation Project**

AD: Arthur Rank Centre, National Agricultural Centre, Stoneleigh Park, Warks CV8 2LZ

TL: 01203 696969 ext 364

FD: 1987

SO: Arthur Rank Fund and English Nature

AI: To enhance wildlife in its habitat in all kinds of churchyards and burial grounds through conservation management; to create an atmosphere of benefit to grieving visitors; to encourage the educational use of churchyards and burial grounds . . . ; to enhance the amenity value of these places.

EN: Postal and telephone

HR: Normal office hours

PB: Seminar and conference reports, leaflets, slide-tape pack etc for churchyard managers.

AC: Living Churchyard Project (flora and fauna, eg bats, lichens etc); liaison with Council for the Care of Churches; some involvement with archaeologists (eg early earthworks).

Church archaeology see Society for Church Archaeology.

NA: **The Churches Conservation Trust** (formerly Redundant Churches Fund)

AD: 89 Fleet Street, London EC4Y 1DH

TL: 0171 936 2285, fax 0171 936 2284

FD: 1994 (under new title: 1969 as RCF)

SO: Church Commissioners and Dept of National Heritage

AI: To preserve surplus Church of England churches of architectural, historical and archaeological merit, together with their fittings.

EN: Postal, telephone

PB: Annual report; *Churches in retirement: a gazetteer* (1990 but under revision); guidebook for each of the 300 churches in care; county guides in preparation.

AC: Advice on conservation (not restoration) of redundant churches, with indication of where a church's records are kept. Five field officers, regionally disposed, and four caseworkers.

NA: **The Church Monuments Society**

AD: c/o The Royal Armouries, HM Tower of London, London EC3N 4AB

FD: 1979

AI: To promote the study, care and conservation of funerary monuments of historical, artistic and educational importance and related art of all periods.

EN: Postal, to Hon Sec, Dr John Lord, 13 Wragby Road, Lincoln LN2 5SH (01522 512912)

PB: *Church monuments* (annual jnl); Newsletter (2/yr).

AC: Seminars, visits, advice to those needing expert help and funds for restoration.

NA: **Civic Trust**

AD: 17 Carlton House Terrace, London SW1Y 5AW

TL: 0171 930 0914, fax 0171 321 0180

FD: 1957

SO: Some government support, but mainly funded by sponsorship, covenants, donations and members' subscriptions

AI: To improve and regenerate the environment in the places where people live and work. Nationwide network of nearly 1,000 local amenity societies (see also National Council of Civic Trust Societies below).

CL: Reference library (appointment needed) and information service.

EN: Postal, telephone

HR: normal office hours

PB: *Urban focus* (4/yr); guide to Civic Trust Awards; 'Treasures' series (county heritage). List available for SAE.

AC: Awards, training, workshops, exhibitions, regeneration projects, Environment Week, project advice etc, speaker service (directory £5).

NA: **Common Ground**

AD: Seven Dials Warehouse, 44 Earlham Street, London WC2H 9LA

TL: 0171 379 3109, fax 0171 836 5741

FD: 1983

SO: Various trusts and government agencies

AI: To promote the importance of our common cultural heritage, everyday nature and buildings, popular history and local places, by assisting local people to set up their own projects.

EN: Postal, telephone or personal visit

HR: Mon-Fri 9.00am–5.00pm

PB: *Holding your ground: an action guide to local conservation*; *Parish maps*; *Local distinctiveness*, etc (list available for SAE).

AC: Exhibitions, sculpture in landscape, lectures, compiling an informal directory of archaeologists willing to help local people understand the local distinctiveness of fields.

NA: **Confederation of British Industry**

AD: Centre Point, 103 New Oxford Street, London WC1A 1DU

TL: 0171 379 7400, fax 0171 240 1578

PB: *CBI Archaeological investigations code of practice for mineral operators* (rev 1991).

NA: **Conference on Training in Architectural Conservation (COTAC)**

AD: Room 328, 429 Oxford Street, London W1R 2HD

TL: 0171 973 3615, fax 0171 973 3656

FD: c. 1960

SO: English Heritage, DNH, members' subscriptions

AI: To promote building conservation training of appropriate kinds.

EN: Postal, telephone

PB: Newsletter (3 or 4/yr); *COTAC past, present and future*; course list throughout UK.

AC: Annual international conference (eg with Interbuild in 1995).

NA: **Conservation Unit of the Museums and Galleries Commission** *see also parent body under M below.*

AD: 16 Queen Anne's Gate, London SW1H 9AA

TL: 0171 233 4200, fax 0171 233 3686, e-mail rnet (gbr-cu@immedia.ca)

FD: 1987

SO: Department of National Heritage and outside sponsors

AI: To set, raise and promote standards of conservation and collection care for the moveable heritage throughout the UK, in both public and private sectors.

CL: Register of over 740 conservation and restoration workshops throughout the country, consultable for a small fee (tel 0171 233 3683, free to member museums of AMCs). Library of conservation literature available to conservators and students (appointment required). Information and advice on relevant training courses, sources of funding, and conservation as a career. Cooperates with Conservation Information Network (bibliographic file of over 120,000 citations now available on Internet).

EN: Postal, telephone, JANET

HR: 9.00am–5.00pm

PB: *Conservation sourcebook*; newsletter (occas); *Training in conservation*; *How to choose a conservator or restorer.*

AC: Grants programme designed to improve conservators' skills; internships for recent graduates and others.

NA: **Construction History Society**

AD: c/o Chartered Institute of Building, 'Englemere', Kings Ride, Ascot, Berks SL5 8BJ

TL: 01344 23355, fax 01344 23467

FD: 1981

AI: To encourage research in the history of construction (mainly UK; emphasis on 18th century onwards).

CL: No collections or library, but through members can often help researchers with information.

EN: Postal only

HR: Normal office hours

PB: Annual journal *Construction history*; newsletter (4/yr).

AC: Annual lecture, annual seminar, visits to buildings and artefact collections.

NA: **COSQUEC, Council for Occupational Standards and Qualifications in Environmental Conservation**

AD: The Red House, Pillows Green, Staunton, Glos GL19 3NU

TL: 01452 840825, fax 01452 840824

FD: 1989

SO: Registered charity

AI: To promote education and training in environmental conservation and related subjects, in particular by establishing, maintaining, supervising and controlling occupational standards and qualifications.

PB: Newsletter (2/yr); materials on NVQ/SVQ implementation, etc.

AC: Has developed National Vocational Qualifications (NVQs) in England, Wales and Northern Ireland, and Scottish Vocational Qualifications (SVQs) in Scotland, covering archaeology, landscapes and ecosystems; building conservation standards to follow.

NA: **Costume Society**
AD: c/o Membership Sec, Ms Pat Poppy, 21 Oak Road, Woolston, Southampton SO19 9BQ
FD: 1965
AI: To promote the study of costume and its history, and help in the preservation of significant examples of historic and contemporary costume, including the study of documentary, literary and pictorial sources.
PB: *Costume* (annual jnl); various special publications (list available for SAE from Cara Lancaster, 42 Sydney Street, London SW3 6PS).
AC: Annual symposium, visits (including to museum stores), lectures, study days, etc.

COTAC *see Conference on Training in Architectural Conservation above.*

NA: **Council for British Archaeology**
AD: Bowes Morrell House, 111 Walmgate, York YO1 2UA
TL: 01904 671417, fax 01904 671384; e-mail archaeology@compuserve.com
or URL http://britac3.britac.ac.uk/cba
FD: 1944
SO: Grant-aid from British Academy, members' subscriptions
AI: To advance the study and safeguarding of Britain's historic environment, to improve public awareness of Britain's past, and to represent and coordinate archaeological opinion. The CBA has a network of 12 regional groups and also works in close liaison with the Council for Scottish Archaeology (see below under Scotland).
CL: No reference facilities but can answer a wide range of questions or refer enquirers to an authoritative source.
EN: Postal or telephone
HR: Normal office hours
PB: Annual report; magazine *British archaeology* (10/yr); series of over 80 CBA *research reports* and of several *Practical handbooks in archaeology*; fact sheets on various topics; *British archaeological yearbook 1995*; many other occasional publications (list available for SAE).
AC: Conferences, meetings, annual Beatrice de Cardi Lecture, specialist committees concerned with research on various topics; support for *British archaeological bibliography*; educational programme.

NA: **Council for the Care of Churches** (formerly Council for Places of Worship)
AD: Fielden House, Little College Street, London SW1P 3SH
TL: 0171 222 3793, fax 0171 222 3794
FD: 1921
SO: Permanent commission of General Synod of Church of England; also grants from charitable bodies
AI: Has a wide range of responsibilities relating to the care of churches in use for worship; advice is given through a range of specialist sub-committees.
CL: Substantial library (appointment required)
EN: Postal, telephone and personal visit (by appointment)
HR: Normal office hours
PB: *Churchscape* (annual journal); *How to look after your church*; *A guide to church inspection and repair*; and many more, list available for SAE.
AC: Can offer grants to parish churches for the conservation of internal furnishings such as organs, clocks, bells, wallpaintings etc; technical advice on application to the Conservation Officer.

NA: **Council for Independent Archaeology**
AD: c/o Mike Rumbold, 3 West Street, Weedon Bec, Northampton NN7 4QU
TL: 01327 340855
FD: 1989
AI: To provide a forum to explore how amateur archaeologists and local archaeological societies can contribute more effectively to archaeology in Britain and Ireland.
EN: Postal or telephone
HR: Any reasonable hours
PB: Newsletter (4/yr), occasional reports.
AC: Meetings, exhibitions, biennial congress; maintains register of experts (c/o Kevan Fadden, 7 Lea Road, Ampthill, Bedford MK45 2PR).

NA: **Council for National Parks**
AD: 246 Lavender Hill, London SW11 1LJ
TL: 0171 924 4077, fax 0171 924 5761
FD: 1936
SO: 40 member organisations plus Friends of National Parks
AI: Campaigns for the continued protection of the National Parks of England and Wales and

for promoting their quiet enjoyment by everyone.

EN: Cannot be dealt with

PB: Newsletter (3/yr); annual report; list available for SAE.

AC: Most of the National Parks have a staff archaeologist: see separate list in Section 4.5 National Park Archaeology.

Council for Occupational Standards . . . *see COSQUEC above.*

NA: **Council for the Prevention of Art Theft (COPAT)**

AD: (Registered address) 17 Whitcomb Street, London WC2H 7PL

TL: 0181 244 8445 (evenings) or (day) 0171 351 5694 (Mrs Chita Clarke)

FD: 1992

AI: To promote crime prevention in the fields of art, antiques, antiquities and architecture; to promote the clarification and harmonisation of international laws relating to the sale and ownership of stolen items, and the regulation of the architectural salvage industry.

EN: Postal or telephone

HR: Office hours

PB: Annual report; leaflet.

AC: Advice given on receipt of written enquiry.

NA: **Council for the Protection of Rural England (CPRE)**

AD: Warwick House, 25 Buckingham Palace Road, London SW1W 0PP

TL: 0171 976 6433, fax 0171 976 6373

FD: 1926

SO: Members' subscriptions and donations, corporate and trust sponsorship

AI: To promote and encourage the improvement and protection of the English countryside and its towns and villages; stimulate public awareness and enjoyment of the countryside; act as a centre of advice and information on matters affecting the planning, improvement and protection of the countryside; and undertake and commission research to allow a better understanding of the issues affecting the countryside, including archaeological features and historic landscapes.

CL: Information on countryside planning and on other organisations dealing with specific aspects of conservation.

EN: Postal and telephone only

HR: Mon-Fri 9.30am–5.30pm

PB: Annual report; *Countryside campaigner* (3/yr); *Campaigners' guide to local plans*; *Responding to planning applications*; list available for SAE.

AC: County branch activities.

NA: **Country Landowners' Association**

AD: 16 Belgrave Square, London SW1X 8PQ

TL: 0171 235 0511, fax 0171 235 4696

FD: 1907

AI: Voluntary association which seeks to promote and safeguard the legitimate interests of owners of agricultural and other rural land, so far as is consistent with the interests of the nation. It makes political representations, advises members, and publicises matters of concern to them.

PB: *Country landowner* (12/yr); advisory handbooks; list available for SAE.

AC: 17 local branches in England. Administers two charities.

NA: **Countryside Commission**

AD: John Dower House, Crescent Place, Cheltenham, Glos GL50 3RA

TL: 01242 521381, fax 01242 584270

FD: 1968

SO: DoE

AI: Is the statutory agency advising government on countryside conservation and recreation in England. Among other things, operates the Countryside Stewardship scheme using government funds to encourage landowners and farmers to protect and enhance valued landscapes (in 1992 extended to cover historic landscapes).

PB: Newsletter (6/yr); occasional bibliographies; list available for SAE.

NA: **Countryside Education Trust**

AD: Beaulieu, Brockenhurst, Hants SO42 7YG

TL: 01590 612401, fax 01590 612624

FD: 1975

AI: To provide facilities and services which make the countryside accessible, educational and enjoyable for all; to encourage concern for the environment; to be involved in practical conservation of the natural environment and its sites of historic significance. (Mostly for children, but also adults).

PB: *Facet* (3/yr).

AC: Runs two field studies centres, day and residential; Friends' organisation.

NA: **The Dark Ages Society**

AD: c/o Roseanna Day (Hon Sec), 20 Highwood Close, Shaw, Newbury, Berks RG14 2EJ

TL: 01635 32447 (pm only)

FD: c. 1975

AI: To promote interest in late 9th century England by demonstrations of 'reconstructed' Saxon and Viking life; members are encouraged to undertake individual studies to this end.

PB: Newsletter (4/yr).

AC: Displays (own society's and on request) of late Saxon-Viking life.

NA: **Dartmoor Tinworking Research Group**

AD: c/o Dr Tom Greeves (Director), 39 Bannawell Street, Tavistock, Devon PL19 0DN

TL: 01822 617004

FD: 1991

AI: To promote the study and interpretation of Dartmoor tinworking of all periods.

PB: Newsletter (2/yr).

AC: Regular survey training weekends, walks, conferences.

NA: **The Defence of Britain Project**

AD: c/o Jim Earle (Project Coordinator), Imperial War Museum, Duxford Airfield, Cambridge CB2 4QR

TL: 01223 830280, fax same

FD: 1994

SO: Government and other sources (project coordinated by CBA)

AI: To gather, within five years, as complete a record as possible of 20th-century military sites and structures in the UK.

EN: Postal, telephone

HR: Normal office hours

PB: Newsletter (4/yr) *Defence lines*; CBA handbook *Twentieth century defences in Britain*.

AC: Volunteers required to assist with the survey of physical remains and the recording of oral evidence.

Defence Ministry see *Ministry of Defence*.

NA: **Department of the Environment**

AD: 2 Marsham Street, London SW1P 3EB

TL: 0171 276 3000 (library 0171 276 4401), fax 0171 276 0818

FD: 1970

SO: Is Government Department

AI: The Department's responsibilities include planning, local government, housing and construction, conservation of the built and natural heritage, water resources, and many other matters. It maintains the Building Research Establishment (see separate entry above), and Inspectorates for Planning and Pollution respectively.

CL: The Library is open to researchers, by appointment, 10.00am–4.30pm for material not readily available elsewhere.

PB: Wide range of publications.

AC: Has ten regional offices.

NA: **Department of National Heritage**

AD: 2–4 Cockspur Street, London SW1Y 5DH

TL: 0171 211 6367/8/9, fax 0171 211 6382

FD: 1992

SO: Is Government department

AI: To preserve the heritage of the past, to help create the culture of today and add to the heritage for future generations, and to broaden opportunities for people to enjoy the benefits of their heritage and culture. Includes Heritage and Tourism Group and Historic Royal Palaces Agency as well as Millennium Fund and National Lottery. Has assumed responsibility for aspects of government policy formerly spread over six departments.

PB: *A guide to the Department and its sponsored bodies*.

AC: Sponsors English Heritage, RCHME, national museums and galleries, Royal Armouries, Royal Parks, National Heritage Memorial Fund, British Library, Royal Fine Art Commission, Architectural Heritage fund, the tourism authorities. Responsible for issue of export licences for archaeological items; also houses the Advisory Committee on Historic Wreck sites.

Deserted Medieval Village Research Group see now *Medieval Settlement Research Group*.

Early Anglo-Saxon Pottery Group see *Medieval Pottery Research Group*.

NA: **Early Mines Research Group**

AD: c/o Simon Timberlake, 98 Victoria Road, Cambridge CB4 3DU

TL: 01223 329737

FD: 1988

SO: Grants towards excavation costs from the National Museum of Wales (and other bodies)

AI: To perform research, fieldwork and archaeological excavation on early mine sites in Britain, principally prehistoric metalliferous mines in (mid-) Wales.

CL: Collection of stone mining tools and of metal ores, excavation archive.

EN: Postal, telephone or personal visit

HR: Any reasonable hours

PB: Papers published in established journals, plus *Early mining in the British Isles* (eds Crew and Crew 1990).

AC: Papers at meetings; excavations; assisting contacts with people working in similar fields. No membership as such.

NA: **Earthwatch Europe**
AD: Belsyre Court, 57 Woodstock Road, Oxford OX2 6HJ
TL: 01865 311600, fax 01865 311383
FD: 1971
SO: Public funding
AI: To improve human understanding of the planet, the diversity of its inhabitants, and the processes that affect the quality of life on earth; provides both funds and workforce.
CL: Extensive library on fieldwork.
EN: Postal or telephone (contact Valda Uden)
HR: 10.00am–4.00pm
PB: *Earthwatch* (6/yr); leaflets; teachers' packs.
AC: Membership events; sponsorship of research expeditions; information to members wishing to join excavations and other projects.

NA: **Ecclesiastical Architects' and Surveyors' Association**
AD: c/o David S Clark, Scan House, 29 Radnor Cliff, Folkestone, Kent CT20 2JJ
FD: 1872
AI: To act as a forum for architects and surveyors engaged on ecclesiastical work, both historic and modern, throughout the British Isles.
EN: Postal only
PB: Various titles (available from RIBA Bookshop).

NA: **Ecclesiological Society**
AD: St Andrew-by-the-Wardrobe, Queen Victoria Street, London EC4V 5DE
IN: K V Richardson, Hon Asst Sec (Correspondence)
FD: 1839
AI: To study the arts, the architecture and the liturgy of the Christian Church; to seek to preserve churches which the Society thinks are worthy of retention; and to promote seemly church building today.
CL: Library for members only
EN: Members only
PB: Monographs, eg *An introduction to church archaeology*; newsletter; backlist of publications available for SAE.
AC: Lectures and visits

NA: **English Heritage**
AD: 23 Savile Row, London W1X 1AB
TL: 0171 973 3000, fax 0171 973 3001
FD: 1984
SO: Central government
AI: To secure the preservation of the best of England's prehistoric and historic sites, monuments and buildings; to raise awareness of this shared heritage and increase commitment to its preservation; to promote people's enjoyment and understanding of this country's past through its material remains. English Heritage is the Government's adviser on all matters concerning the conservation of the historic environment; and is the main source of public funding for rescue archaeology, conservation areas and repairs to historic buildings and ancient monuments.
CL: Archaeological and social history artefacts (either displayed on their site, or in reserve collections not easily accessible to the public); database and catalogues in preparation, apply to EH Collections Registrar at the address above. Architectural study collection (at two sites outside Central London); photographic library.
EN: Postal, telephone or personal visit (by appointment)
HR: 9.00am–5.00pm
PB: Annual report and numerous publications, including series of substantial excavation reports; guides to properties in care; annual *Guide to English Heritage properties*; continual supply of advisory leaflets; teaching materials; *Conservation bulletin* (3/yr); etc, catalogue on request.
AC: English Heritage has three main directorates: **Conservation** (listing, archaeology, grants, Central Archaeology Service, cathedrals, monuments protection, Ancient Monuments Laboratory, etc); **Historic Properties** (collections, gardens and landscape, marketing, membership, design and interpretation, publications, education, etc); and **Major Projects** (Stonehenge, professional services, historic property restoration, etc). Specialist advisory committees/panels for, respectively, Ancient Monuments; Battlefields; Cathedrals and Churches; Hadrian's Wall; Historic Buildings and Areas; Historic Parks and Gardens; Industrial Archaeology; London; Museums and Collections; Science and Conservation. Disburses large amounts of money in grants annually. Individuals joining English Heritage receive a range of benefits. *See also Central Archaeology Service.*

NA: **English Historic Towns Forum**

AD: The Huntingdon Centre, The Paragon, Bath
BA1 5NA
TL: 01225 469157, fax 01225 334454
FD: 1987
SO: Is a local government association running on members' subscriptions
AI: To promote and reconcile prosperity and conservation in historic towns, eg through better management of historic areas, and management of tourism to avoid environmental damage.
PB: Newsletter (4/yr); various publications on traffic, visitors, etc.

NA: **English Nature** (formerly part of Nature Conservancy Council)
AD: Northminster House, Peterborough PE1 1UA
TL: 01733 455000, fax 01733 68834
FD: 1991
SO: Government
AI: As the statutory advisor to Government on nature conservation in England, promotes the conservation of England's wildlife and natural features.
PB: *English Nature* magazine; annual report and other publications (catalogue free on request).
AC: Selection and management of National Nature Reserves, Sites of Special Scientific Interest, etc; provision of advice; support and conduct of relevant research; grants for nature conservation.

NA: **English Place-Name Society**
AD: Dept of English, The University, Nottingham NG7 2RD
TL: 0115 951 5919, fax 0115 951 5924
FD: 1923
SO: British Academy and subscriptions
AI: To survey the place-names of England and publish the results county by county.
EN: Postal, telephone, e-mail
HR: Normal office hours
PB: Annual volumes, one of more of which deal with the place-names of a single county; see entry in Section 6.17 Place-names and local history. Also annual *Journal*.

NA: **English Tourist Board** (*see also British Tourist Authority*)
AD: Thames Tower, Blacks Road, Hammersmith, London W6 9EL
TL: 0181 846 9000, fax 0181 563 0302
AI: To stimulate and coordinate the development and marketing of tourism in England.
PB: *English heritage monitor* (annual statistical review, jointly with British Tourist Authority, of numbers of visitors to listed and historic buildings, numbers of listed buildings by county, etc).

NA: **The Environment Council** (*formerly CoEnCo*)
AD: 21 Elizabeth Street, London SW1W 9RP
TL: 0171 824 8411, fax 0171 730 9941
FD: 1969 (as CoEnCo: 1988 as EC)
SO: Donations, subscriptions, grants, and sponsorship for specific projects
AI: To conserve the environment by helping people to work together to resolve environmental problems, taken to include the presence of artefacts of historic and/or architectural value.
EN: Referral service
PB: *habitat* and newsletter (both 10/yr); *Who's who in the environment* (printed separately for England, Scotland, Wales, Northern Ireland, and regularly revised, also on computer disk for England); guides to sources of environmental information.
AC: Meetings and seminars; Environmental Information Forum; *Business and environment programme handbook*; environmental dispute resolution; Friends' organisation.

NA: **Ermine Street Guard**
AD: Oakland Farm, Dog Lane, Witcombe, Gloucester GL3 4UG
TL: 01452 862235, fax same
FD: 1972
SO: Display fees, sales of postcards etc
AI: To conduct research into the Roman Imperial Army and to reconstruct and display Roman armour and equipment of (principally) the latter half of the first century AD.
EN: Postal, telephone, personal visit
HR: All reasonable hours
PB: *Exercitus* (annual newsletter); *The Ermine Street Guard handbook*.
AC: Puts on public displays (normally April to September) including legionary drill, aspects of Roman military training, the firing of artillery weapons, exhibition tent; two members of the Guard are fully equipped as Roman cavalrymen.
Compiler's note: this was the first of the 'Roman reconstruction' societies: various newer 'units' have been formed, eg Legio IX Hispana, Leg VI Victrix, Leg XIII Gemina; and see Roman Army Research Group of London.

NA: †**Europa Nostra/International Castles Institute also known as Europa Nostra/IBI**
AD: Lange Voorhout 35, 2514 EC, The Hague, Netherlands
TL: +(31) 70 356 0333, fax +(31) 70 361 7865
FD: 1963
SO: Members' subscriptions, grants, donations, Council of Europe etc
AI: To awaken the pride of European people in their common inheritance of architectural and natural beauty ... and to call for action to preserve them (etc). (Europa Nostra is an international federation of some 200 non-governmental associations concerned with heritage and conservation.)
PB: Annual report; *Europa Nostra magazine* (2/yr).
AC: Studies, conferences, seminars, Historic Towns Forum, exhibitions, annual general assembly, awards scheme.

NA: **European Association of Archaeologists**
AD: Hon Sec, Dr H F Cleere OBE, Acres Rise, Lower Platts, Ticehurst, Wadhurst, E Sussex TN5 7DD; secretariat rotates, currently c/o MOLAS, Walker House, 87 Queen Victoria Street, London EC4V 4AB
TL: (Hon Sec) 01580 200752, fax same
FD: 1994
AI: To promote the development of archaeological research and the exchange of archaeological information; to promote the management and interpretation of Europe's archaeological heritage; to promote proper ethical and scientific standards (etc).
PB: *Journal of European archaeology* (2/yr).
AC: Meetings: eg Santiago de Compostela 1995, Riga 1996; information service planned.

NA: **European Environmental Bureau**
AD: rue de la Victoire 22–26, 1060 Brussels, Belgium
TL: +(32) 2 539 0037/0921
FD: 1974
AI: Is a federation of the chief non-governmental environmental associations in the European Community (eg UK's Environment Council), with its focus on ecology. To promote the protection and conservation of the environment; to use education to increase public awareness, etc.
PB: Several for members.
AC: Links with other organisations, eg Europa Nostra; wetlands etc; seminars, workshops, lobbying. Runs Maison européenne de l'Environnement.

NA: **European Forum of Heritage Associations**
AD: (General secretariat) via Cà Magno, 35133 Padua, Italy
TL: +(39) 49 60 45 26
FD: 1990
AI: To create a network for the non-professional world, particularly for archaeology, to heighten public awareness of a common history with regional diversity; has 30 member organisations from 14 countries.
PB: Newsletter.
AC: Exchange visits, information exchange, summer camps for fieldwork and conservation.

NA: **European Heritage Centre (Fundacio Centre Europeu del Patrimoni)**
AD: Pg de Gràcia, 35, 2on, 08007 Barcelona, Spain
TL: +(34) 3 3 373 73 63, fax +(34) 3 3 373 74 63
FD: 1991
SO: Various activities
AI: The promotion and comprehensive management of heritage in its economic, social and cultural aspects and with a European perspective.
EN: Postal, telephone or personal visit
HR: 9.00am–2.00pm, 4.00pm–6.00pm
AC: Training programmes, study projects, heritage management.

NA: **European Science Foundation**
AD: 1 quai Lezay-Marnésia, F 67080 Strasbourg Cedex, France
TL: +(33) 88 76 71 00, fax +(33) 88 37 05 32
FD: 1974
AI: Acts as coordinator for the main European academic and research councils which support basic science research at national level; stress on interdisciplinary character.
PB: *ESF communications*; *ESF report*.
AC: Interests include humanities; social sciences; Palaeolithic occupation of Europe (project 1993–6); European palaeoclimate and man since glaciation (1988–); origins of the modern state in 13th–18th century Europe; GIS, etc.

NA: **Experimental Earthworks Committee**
AD: c/o Gillian Swanton (Sec), North Farm, West Overton, Marlborough, Wilts SN8 1QE
TL: 01672 861229, fax 01672 861689
FD: 1959
SO: No core funding: grants are applied for to aid specific schemes

AI: To administer two experimental sites in southern England (Overton Down in Wiltshire and Morden in Dorset) and make comparison with other sites in southern England; to investigate by experiment, over several decades and using interdisciplinary skills, the denudation and burial of archaeological structures.

CL: Archive of experimental results under active management

EN: Postal, telephone, personal visit (by appointment)

PB: Numerous reports in journals; CBA research report on the first 32 years (published 1996).

AC: Intermittent sectioning of the earthworks.

NA: †Experimental Firing and Ceramic Technology Group

AD: c/o Ann Woods, School of Archaeological Studies, University of Leicester, Leicester LE1 7RH

TL: 0116 252 2618 (Dept Sec 0116 252 2611)

FD: 1982

AI: To conduct research on the manufacture, use and firing of ceramic materials.

NA: Farming and Wildlife Advisory Group

AD: National Agricultural Centre, Stoneleigh, Kenilworth, Warks CV8 2RX

TL: 01203 696699, fax 01203 696760

FD: 1969

SO: MAFF/DoE (33%); remainder raised from other sources

AI: To unite wildlife and landscape conservation with farming and forestry, recognising the importance of historic sites for landscape value and habitat opportunities.

EN: Postal, telephone and personal visit

HR: 9.00am–5.00pm

PB: Various leaflets of advice for farmers, including *Handbook for environmentally responsible farming*.

AC: Royal Show and other national and local shows; regional groups in England, Wales and Scotland.

NA: Finds Research Group AD 700–1700

AD: (Membership Sec), Katey Banks, City Museum and Art Gallery, Bethesda Street, Hanley, Stoke-on-Trent, Staffs ST1 3DW

TL: 01782 202173, fax 01782 205033

FD: 1983

AI: To promote the study of finds dating principally from AD 700–1700 by holding meetings to discuss, view and identify such finds, and to

encourage research on them; to endeavour to coordinate finds terminology.

EN: Postal, telephone

HR: Normal office hours

PB: *Datasheets* (irregular) on specific find types; newsletter (2/yr).

AC: Two meetings/yr (AGM in London).

Folk life *see Society for Folklife Studies.*

NA: The Folly Fellowship

AD: c/o Andrew Plumridge (Sec), Woodstock House, Winterhill Way, Burpham, Surrey GU4 7JX; or Membership Secretary, M Cousins, 21 Beacon Road, Ware, Herts SG12 7HY, tel 01920 487587

TL: (Secretary) 01635 42864, fax 01635 552366 (work); 01483 65634 (home)

FD: 1988

AI: To preserve and promote the enjoyment and awareness of follies, grottoes and garden buildings; to advise and/or assist folly owners and builders (etc: 12 objects in all).

EN: Postal, telephone or personal visit by bona fide enquirers

HR: Not specific

PB: *Follies: the international magazine for follies, grottoes and garden buildings* (4/yr).

AC: Annual garden party, regional meetings. exhibition, annual award (substantial) for the best measured drawing of a folly or garden building. The Fellowship tries to maintain a balance between academic studies and the humorous side of follies.

Forestry Authority/Commission *see entries under Wales and Scotland below.*

NA: Fortress Study Group

AD: c/o Hon Sec (D W Quarmby), Blackwater Forge House, Blackwater, Newport, Isle of Wight PO30 3BJ

TL: 01983 526207

FD: 1975

AI: To advance the education of the public in the study of all aspects of fortifications and their armaments, especially works constructed to mount or resist artillery.

CL: Library (members only); database of 20th century fortifications (in conjunction with RCHME).

EN: Postal only

PB: *Fort* (annual journal); newsletter (3/yr).

AC: Annual weekend conference; annual overseas visit; occasional cooperation with other bodies. Can offer advice on the restoration of forts, particularly relating to detailed fittings.

NA: **Foundation for Science and Technology** (formerly London Science Centre)
AD: 78 Buckingham Gate, London SW1E 6PE
TL: 0171 222 1222, fax 0171 222 1225
FD: 1981
AI: To assist learned societies through acting as a focus for sharing experience and knowledge on administrative, legal, charity and other issues of common concern.
EN: Postal plus e-mail 100575.3510@compuserve.com
HR: Normal office hours
PB: Newsletter (6/yr); *Register of learned and professional societies* (1992).
AC: Seminars.

NA: **The Fountain Society**
AD: 16 Gayfere Street, London SW1P 3HP
TL: 0171 222 6037/2917, fax 0171 799 2900
FD: 1985
AI: To conserve our heritage of fountains from the past and to develop new ones.
PB: Reports and other literature.
AC: To compile a national register of fountains; to promote relevant research; to make surveys and prepare maps and plans etc relating to fountains, waterfalls or cascades; to arrange meetings, lectures, visits, exhibitions.

NA: **Friends of Friendless Churches**
AD: St Ann's Vestry Hall, 2 Church Entry, London EC4V 5HB
IN: Matthew Saunders
TL: 0171 236 3934, fax 0171 329 3677
FD: 1957
AI: To save churches and chapels of architectural and historical interest, threatened with collapse, demolition or conversion to unsuitable use. (Works in partnership with Ancient Monuments Society, whose address it shares.)
EN: Postal
PB: Annual report.

NA: **Garden History Society**
AD: 77 Cowcross Street, London EC1M 6BP; (Membership Secretary) Mrs Anne Richards, 5 The Knoll, Hereford HR1 1RU
TL: (London) 0171 608 2409; (Hereford) 01432 354479
FD: 1965
AI: To be a central organisation for everyone interested in the history of gardens, parks and landscape architecture; are statutory consultees on development proposals related to designed landscapes.
EN: Postal or telephone
PB: *Garden history* (2/yr); newsletter; *Guide to researching historic gardens in Scotland* (1996); list available for SAE.
AC: UK weekends, overseas tours, day visits, research register, symposia (all for members only).

For gardens see also entries for Association of Garden Trusts; Folly Fellowship; Historic Gardens Foundation; Tradescant Trust; (for Wales) Welsh Historic Gardens Trust; (for N Ireland) Northern Ireland Heritage Gardens Committee.

NA: **Geological Society**
AD: Burlington House, Piccadilly, London W1V 0JU
TL: 0171 434 9944 (Library 0171 734 5673), fax 0171 439 8975
FD: 1807
AI: To promote, as both a learned society and a professional body, all aspects of the geological sciences.
CL: Library not open to public
EN: Postal only
PB: *J Geological Society* and other journals.
AC: Courses open to public. **NB: The Geologists' Association** caters for amateur geologists at the same address, phone 0171 434 9298; it publishes guides and acts as a clearing house for gravestone information.

Geological Survey *see British Geological Survey.*

NA: **Georgian Group**
AD: 6 Fitzroy Square, London W1P 6DX
TL: 0171 387 1720, fax 0171 387 1721 (enquiries to Dana Arnold, Education Sec)
FD: 1937
SO: Dept of National Heritage and members' subscriptions
AI: (abridged) To save Georgian buildings (ie 1700–1837, together with interesting pre-and neo-Georgian buildings), monuments, parks and gardens from destruction or disfigurement, and to stimulate public knowledge of these things.
EN: Postal and telephone enquiries can be dealt with to a limited extent
HR: 9.45am–4.30pm
PB: *Georgian Group journal*; series of advisory leaflets on correct materials and furnishings for Georgian houses; series of Town Reports; other publications (list available for SAE).

AC: Members' meetings, symposia, visits, lectures; Cleary Fund for grants towards restoration of Georgian buildings.

NA: †The Glass Circle (formerly The Circle of Glass Collectors)
AD: c/o Glaziers' Hall, 9 Montague Close, London Bridge, London SE1 9DD
TL: 0171 403 3300
FD: 1937
PB: *The glass circle* (annual).

NA: Heritage Co-ordination Group
AD: The Lady Wise (Hon Sec), Lynn Cottage, Hemyock, Devon EX15 3RU
TL: 01823 680645
FD: 1980
AI: Is an informal association of national bodies concerned with the preservation of the manmade cultural heritage; aims to encourage communication between existing amenity and heritage preservation organisations, to co-ordinate activities when mutually advantageous and needed, to encourage awareness of the need for trained voluntary help.
EN: Postal (for SAE) or telephone
HR: 9.00am–5.00pm
AC: Annual and regional conferences, with displays; conferences on 'disaster' and security precautions.

NA: Hillfort Study Group
AD: c/o Hon Sec, Dr Gary Lock, Institute of Archaeology, 36 Beaumont Street, Oxford OX1 2PG
TL: 01865 278240
FD: 1965
AI: To act as a forum for scholars with an interest in hillforts.
EN: Postal or telephone
PB: *British hillforts: an index* (*see* Hogg entry in Section 6.11.3 Iron Age).
AC: Spring and autumn meetings, some in field.

NA: The Historical Association
AD: 59a Kennington Park Road, London SE11 4JH
TL: 0171 735 3901, fax 0171 582 4989 (enquiries to Development Officer)
FD: 1906
AI: To further the study and teaching of history at all levels. (There is no involvement with archaeology as such, though some Roman and Anglo-Saxon teaching publications are available.)
CL: No library or formal information service, but own publications and archives may be seen.

EN: Postal, telephone, personal visit, JANET
HR: 9.30am–5.30pm
PB: *History* (journal, 3/yr); *The Historian* (qrly); series of *Helps for students of history* and *Short guides to records*; *Annual bulletin of historical literature*; and many books and booklets on various aspects of teaching history (list available for large SAE).
AC: Conferences, day schools, local lectures.

NA: The Historical Metallurgy Society Ltd (formerly Historical Metallurgy Group)
AD: (official) 1 Carlton House Terrace, London SW1Y 5DB; enquiries to Mr Peter Hutchinson (Hon Gen Sec), 22 Easterfield Drive, Southgate, Swansea SA3 2DB
TL: 01792 233223
FD: 1963 (as HMG); 1979 (as HMS)
SO: Members' subscriptions, plus publication grant from Inst of Materials
AI: The study, investigation, description and presentation of the historical and archaeological evidence of the extraction and working of metals, etc.
CL: The Society owns certain relevant books and documents, placed in the care of the Ironbridge Gorge Museum Library. In addition a database of ironworking sites in Britain is being compiled (c. 1,500 records): apply to Chris Salter, Dept of Materials, University of Oxford, Parks Road, Oxford OX1 3PH (via JANET: salter@vax. oxford.ac.uk). Similar database on non-ferrous metalworking sites under consideration.
EN: Postal enquiries dealt with by volunteers
PB: *Historical metallurgy* (2/yr); conference proceedings; *Datasheets* for identifying archaeological metal residues (available for £1 from David Starley at English Heritage's Ancient Monuments Laboratory); occasional reprints of scarce historical texts; list available for SAE from Peak District Mining Museum, Matlock Bath, Derbys DE4 3PS.
AC: Two conferences yearly, sometimes jointly with other societies.

Historic Buildings Council for England *ceased in April 1984.*

Historic Buildings and Monuments Commission for England *see English Heritage.*

NA: The Historic Chapels Trust
AD: 29 Thurloe Street, London SW7 2LQ
TL: 0171 584 6072, fax 0171 225 0607
FD: 1993

SO: Dept of National Heritage, English Heritage, private sources

AI: To take into care redundant chapels, and other places of non-Anglican worship in England, of outstanding architectural and historic interest; their contents, burial grounds and curtilages included.

EN: Postal and telephone; personal visits only by arrangement

HR: 9.30am–5.00pm

PB: Leaflets.

NA: **Historic Churches Preservation Trust**

AD: Fulham Palace, London SW6 6EA

TL: 0171 736 3054 (Mr R H C Heptinstall, Sec)

FD: 1953

SO: Donations

AI: To provide financial assistance to help in the repair of churches (of all denominations) in current and regular use for worship in England and Wales.

EN: Postal, telephone or personal visit

HR: 09.00am–4.00pm

PB: *Historic churches review.*

AC: There are 25 affiliated County Historic Church Trusts.

NA: **Historic Farm Buildings Group**

AD: c/o Roy Brigden (Sec), Museum of English Rural Life, University of Reading, Whiteknights, Reading RG6 2AG

TL: 01734 318663, fax 01734 751264

FD: 1985

AI: To promote research into, and to appreciate, historic farm buildings.

EN: Postal, telephone and personal visit

HR: 9.00am–5.00pm

PB: *Journal* (annual); newsletter (2/yr); series of information sheets; occasional conference proceedings.

AC: Annual weekend conference and other occasional meetings.

NA: **Historic Gardens Foundation**

AD: 34 River Court, Upper Ground, London SE1 9PE

TL: 0171 633 9165, fax 0171 401 7072 (Gillian Mawrey, Director)

FD: 1995

SO: Various sources including Council for Europe

AI: To promote historic gardens and provide links between all those whose work is connected with this subject, including garden archaeologists.

EN: Postal, telephone

HR: 10.00am–10.00pm

PB: *European gardens* (2/yr).

AC: Conferences; liaison with National Trust, Europa Nostra, ICOMOS etc.

NA: **Historic Houses Association**

AD: 2 Chester Street, London SW1X 7BB

TL: 0171 259 5688, fax 0171 259 5590

FD: 1973

AI: To work for a fiscal, political and economic climate in which private owners can maintain Britain's historic houses (with associated contents, gardens and designed landscapes) for the benefit of the nation.

EN: Postal or telephone

HR: 9.30am–5.00pm

PB: Annual reports; *Planning procedures and listed building controls*; *Conversion of a listed building*; and many others (list available for SAE).

AC: Seminars, AGM and trade exhibition, regional meetings; Friends of the Historic Houses Association.

Historic Parks and Gardens/Conservation *see Institute of Advanced Architectural Studies: Landscapes and Gardens.*

NA: **Historic Royal Palaces Agency**

AD: Hampton Court Palace, East Molesey, Surrey KT8 9AU

TL: 0181 781 9750

FD: 1989

SO: Dept of National Heritage, visitor income

AI: To care for the historic royal palaces.

CL: Archaeological archives and reports are held for HM Tower of London and Hampton Court Palace.

EN: Postal, telephone or personal visit

HR: Office hours

AC: Six palaces are open to the public.

NA: **ICAHM, International Committee on Archaeological Heritage Management**

AD: Service de l'habitation et du développement urbain, Ville de Montréal – 5e étage, 303 rue Notre-Dame Est, Montréal, Québec, Canada H2Y 3Y8 (Paul Blouin, Coordinator) [As the Secretariat moves periodically, it is advisable to check its current address with ICOMOS in Paris: see ICOMOS UK entry below.]

TL: +(1) 514 872 7531

FD: 1986

SO: Is a committee of ICOMOS

AI: To act as a forum where the exchange of ideas

promotes the better handling of the protection of the archaeological heritage across the world.

PB: *Charter for the Protection and Management of the Archaeological Heritage* (ratified at ICOMOS General Assembly, Lausanne 1990); *Directory of archaeological heritage management* (1990: new edn promised).

AC: International symposia, eg 1988: *Archaeology and society* – large-scale rescue operations, their possibilities and problems, 1989.

ICAZ *see International Council for Archaeozoology.*

NA: **ICOMOS UK (International Council on Museums and Sites, UK branch)**

AD: 10 Barley Mow Passage, Chiswick, London W4 4PH (Sec Dr Philip Whitbourn)

TL: 0181 994 6477, fax 0181 747 8464

FD: 1965

SO: Dept of National Heritage, benefactors and members

AI: To initiate, undertake and disseminate information about conservation research projects not covered by other organisations. Specialist committees deal with topics such as historic gardens and landscapes; cultural tourism; recording; wood; education. ICOMOS UK also advises the UK government on the selection, nomination and protection of World Heritage Sites. (The parent body ICOMOS in Paris is an international non-governmental body composed of specialists professionally concerned with conservation, from over 60 member nations. It sets standards in conservation philosophy and techniques throughout the world.)

EN: Postal and telephone

HR: Normal office hours

PB: Newsletter (4/yr); *Cathedral damage by visitors; Recording before repairs* (with Butterworth); *Managing UK World Heritage sites* (1992); and many others (list available for SAE).

AC: Occasional conferences and seminars; scholarships. The library at the ICOMOS Documentation Centre in Paris (49-51 rue de la Fédération 75015 Paris) is open to members and non-members.

NA: **ICOM UK (International Council of Museums – UK)**

AD: c/o Mrs Nell Hoare (Hon Sec), Textile Conservation Centre, Apt 22, Hampton Court Palace, East Molesey, Surrey KT8 9AO

TL: 0181 977 4943, fax 0181 977 9081

FD: 1973

AI: To further the educational purpose of museums and encourage cooperation and collaboration internationally.

EN: Postal or telephone only

HR: Normal office hours

PB: Newsletter (3/yr)

AC: Occasional meetings.

NA: **Inland Waterways Association**

AD: 114 Regent's Park Road, London NW1 8UQ

TL: 0171 586 2510/2556, fax 0171 722 7213

FD: 1946

AI: To campaign for the restoration, retention and development of inland waterways in the British Isles and for their fullest commercial and recreational use.

EN: Postal, telephone or personal

HR: 8.30am–12.30pm, 1.30pm–4.30pm

PB: *Waterways* (3/yr); many publications and guides (list available for SAE).

AC: Liaison with government and with other waterways organisations; local committees; financial support for restoration of derelict waterways; festivals, rallies, youth activities etc.

NA: **Inland Waterways Protection Society**

AD: c/o Dr W M Whalley (Hon Sec), 18 Wentworth Drive, Bramhall, Stockport, Cheshire SK7 2LQ, or: Mr A J Findlow, 36 Prestbury Road, Macclesfield, Cheshire SK10 1AU

TL: 0161 439 7588 (Dr Whalley); 01625 420770 (Mr Findlow)

FD: 1958

SO: Various grants (English Heritage, English partnerships, Mersey Basin Campaign etc)

AI: To campaign for the restoration, preservation and development of inland waterways of Great Britain.

CL: Historical and archaeological archive with photographs, site records and reports, oral history material, etc; database of own minutes and associated historical material.

EN: Postal, telephone, personal visit; e-mail to Don Baines, iclenv@wg.icl.co.uk

HR: Daytime and evenings

PB: Journal (3/yr); newsletter; interpretive leaflets; forthcoming research paper on Bugsworth Basin.

AC: Working parties; project work centred on restoration of Bugsworth Basin (NW Derbys).

INQUA *see International Union for Quaternary Research.*

NA: **Institute of Advanced Architectural Studies: Landscapes and Gardens (***formerly Centre for*

the Conservation of Historic Parks and Gardens)
AD: University of York, The King's Manor, York YOI 2EP
TL: 01904 433966, fax 01904 433949
FD: 1982
SO: University of York plus consultancies
AI: To promote the study and conservation of historic parks and gardens by acting as a forum for information, and by providing guidance and education.
CL: Library etc open to bona fide members of the public, by appointment
EN: Postal or telephone
HR: 9.00am–5.00pm
PB: Various.
AC: Short courses run via the Institute: advice and guidance; consultancy services; survey and database inventory of historic parks and gardens under way for England and Wales.

Institute of Agricultural History *see now Rural History Centre.*

Institute for Conservation (IIC) *see UK Institute for Conservation . . .*

NA: **Institute of Field Archaeologists**
AD: University of Manchester, Oxford Road, Manchester M13 9PL (contact Kitty Sisson, Asst Secretary)
TL: 0161 275 2304, fax same
FD: 1982
AI: To advance the practice of field archaeology and allied disciplines by promoting professional standards and ethics for the conservation, management and study of the archaeological resource.
PB: Journal *The field archaeologist*; newsletter; series of *Technical papers*; series of *Occasional papers*; Code of Conduct; *Archaeological resource management in the UK: an introduction*; *Directory of finds study and special interest groups*; other publications, leaflets etc (list available for SAE).
AC: Annual conference; special interest groups for Finds, Buildings, Maritime Affairs, Cultural Resource Management.

NA: **Institute of Historical Research**
AD: Senate House, University of London London WC1E 7HU
TL: 0171 636 0272, fax 0171 436 2183, e-mail ihr@sas.ac.uk; Internet http://ihr.sas.ac.uk:8080
FD: 1921

SO: University of London
AI: Is the University of London's centre for postgraduate studies in history and an important resource and meeting place for history scholars from all over the world. Includes the Centre for Metropolitan History (which see) and the Victoria County History.
CL: Substantial library open to members and on a more limited basis to Friends of IHR (who pay a subscription of £20/yr).
AC: Training of postgraduate students, seminars, summer schools etc.

NA: **The International Committee for the Conservation of the Industrial Heritage (TICCIH)**
AD: c/o Stuart B Smith (Hon Sec), 'Chygarth', 5 Beacon Terrace, Camborne, Cornwall TR14 7BU
TL: 01209 612142, fax same
FD: 1973
SO: Each country contributes to central funds (via AIA in UK)
AI: To act as a clearing house in the promotion of international cooperation in the preservation, conservation, investigation, documentation, research and presentation of our industrial heritage.
EN: Postal, telephone
PB: Bulletin (4/yr) to national correspondents.
AC: Triennial conference; intermediate conferences on specific subjects.

International Council for Museums of Archaeology and History *see brief entry in Section 4.8 Museum directories.*

NA: **International Council for Archaeozoology (ICAZ)**
AD: c/o Prof Dr A T Clason, Biologisch-Archaeologisch Instituut, Poststraat 6, 9712-ER Groningen, Netherlands (UK contact: Dr Sebastian Payne, English Heritage, tel 0171 973 3378; e-mail s.payne@eng-h.gov.uk)
AI: To develop and stimulate archaeozoological research, to strengthen cooperation between archaeozoologists and with archaeologists and other scientists working in archaeology.
PB: *ArchaeoZoologica* (periodical, irreg.); newsletter.
AC: Conferences from time to time.

NA: **International Institute for Conservation of Historic and Artistic Works ('IIC')** *(see also Archaeology section under UK below)*
AD: 6 Buckingham Street, London WC2N 6BA
TL: 0171 839 5975, fax 0171 976 1564

FD: 1950
SO: Subscriptions and sales of publications
AI: To coordinate and improve the knowledge, methods and working standards needed to protect, preserve and maintain the condition and integrity of historic or significant objects and structures.
PB: *Studies in conservation* (4/yr); *Art and archaeology technical abstracts* (jointly with Getty Conservation Institute); *IIC bulletin* (6/yr, members only); various conference proceedings.
AC: Conferences, autonomous regional groups in various countries; can refer enquirers to appropriate information source.

NA: **International Institute of Maritime Studies** (*due to open Sept 1997*)
AD: Fort Tourgis, Alderney, CI (for up-to-date information write to Mensun Bound at Oxford University MARE, 4 Butts Road, Horspath, Oxford OX33 1RH)
SO: International consortium of universities forming an educational trust, plus income from fees and leasing of facilities
AI: To offer taught MSc postgraduate courses within the three related disciplines of archaeology, marine biology and physical oceanography. Also to be available year-round as a study centre with the most up-to-date laboratory and research equipment.
AC: Archaeology in the following sub-disciplines: maritime, wetlands, lakes and rivers, ship development, small craft, wood science and construction, ship contents and weaponry; plus oceanography and marine biology.
Note: although teaching institutions are mostly not entered in this section, an exception has been made for IIMS because it is new and information about it may not be easy to find.

NA: **International Union for Quaternary Research (INQUA)**
AD: c/o Sec General, Prof Sylvia Haldorsen, Agricultural University of Norway, Dept of Soil and Water Sciences, Geology and Water Section, PO Box 5028, N-1432 Aas, Norway
TL: +(47) 64 94 82 52, fax +(47) 64 94 74 85
e-mail sylvi.haldorsen@ijvf.nlh.no
Internet http://www.INQUA.NLH.NO
FD: 1928
SO: National Research Councils and Academies of Sciences
AI: To coordinate research on the Quaternary throughout the world.

EN: Postal, telephone, e-mail
PB: *Quaternary international* (journal, 2/yr); newsletter (2/yr); numerous field guides produced for 1977 INQUA conference in Britain and Ireland.
AC: International conferences, commissions, working groups etc. Affiliated to IUSPP etc. Congress in 1999 will be in Durban (SA) and include many archaeological site visits.

Interpret Britain *see* **Society for Interpreting Britain's Heritage.**

NA: **IRIS, Index Record for Industrial Sites**
AD: c/o Project Assistant, Lancaster University Archaeological Unit, Storey Institute, Meeting House Lane, Lancaster LA1 1TH
TL: 01524 848666
FD: 1993
SO: Association for Industrial Archaeology
AI: To register, on SMR-compatible forms, the existence and nature of industrial archaeological features in order that they may acquire protection under PPG16 guidelines.
CL: Records are passed to local SMRs.
EN: Postal or telephone, to Project Assistant (as above)
HR: Normal office hours
PB: *Recording the industrial heritage*; IRIS record forms.
AC: Encouragement of local groups.

NA: **The Ironbridge Institute**
AD: Ironbridge Gorge Museum, Ironbridge, Telford, Shropshire TF8 7AW
TL: 01952 432751, fax 01952 432204
FD: 1980
SO: Self-funding post-graduate institute of University of Birmingham, jointly managed with Ironbridge Museum
AI: To provide advanced training programmes and carry out research in heritage management and industrial archaeology.
EN: Postal or telephone
HR: Mon-Fri 9.00am–5.00pm
PB: Research reports.
AC: Postgraduate training courses, research, short courses, consultancies.

The Joint Centre for Heritage Conservation and Management is a collaboration, for the purpose of continuous professional development, between Bournemouth University School of Conservation Sciences, the Weald and Downland Open Air Museum, the Centre for the Conservation of the Built Environment (Bursledon,

Southampton), the Lime Centre, Morestead (Winchester), Fort Brockhurst (English Heritage) and the Interface Analysis Centre (Univ Bristol) to bring together a wide range of facilities and staff specialising in archaeology, building conservation, and site/museum/collection management. It runs short conferences and courses, specialist research and consultancy services. Apply to Una Lyons, School of Conservation Sciences, Bournemouth University, Fern Barrow, Poole, Dorset BH12 5BB, 01202 595273, fax 01202 595255.

The **Joint Committee of the National Amenity Societies** coordinates the strategic activities of those societies. It consists of representatives of the Ancient Monuments Society, the Civic Trust, the Council for British Archaeology, the Garden History Society, the Georgian Group, the Society for the Protection of Ancient Buildings, the Twentieth Century Society and the Victorian Society; numerous other bodies have observer status. Its secretariat is at the Ancient Monuments Society (which see).

NA: **Joint Nature Conservation Committee** (*formerly part of the Nature Conservancy Council*)
AD: Monkstone House, City Road, Peterborough PE1 1JY
TL: 01733 62626, fax 01733 555948
FD: 1991
SO: Statutory Government body
AI: Was established under the Environmental Protection Act 1990 by English Nature, Scottish Natural Heritage and Countryside Council for Wales. Its responsibilities are to identify and promote strategic nature conservation issues across Great Britain, to set common scientific standards and to advise government on nature conservation. Also works at international level.
EN: Postal (charges for supply of information sometimes apply)
PB: *Coasts and seas of the United Kingdom* (series of 17 directories containing a wealth of environmental data to assist all concerned with using and managing the coastal zone; contact Caroline Robson, Coastal Directories Coordinator, 01733 866829, or Rob Keddie, contracted archaeologist). Other publications (list available for SAE).

Joint Nautical Archaeology Policy Committee *apply to Nautical Archaeology Society.*

NA: **The Landmark Trust**

AD: Shottesbrooke, Maidenhead, Berks SL6 3SW (contact Julia Abel Smith, Information Officer)
TL: 01628 825925, fax 01628 825417
FD: 1965
SO: The Manifold Trust
AI: To rescue buildings in distress and bring them back to useful life as holiday lets.
CL: Photographic library
EN: Postal and telephone only
HR: 9.00am–5.00pm
PB: *The Landmark handbook* (annual); newsletter (2/yr).

NA: **Landscape Conservation Forum**
AD: c/o Julien Parsons (Sec LCF), City Museum, Weston Park, Sheffield S10 2TP
TL: 0114 276 8588, fax 0114 275 0957
FD: 1987
AI: To involve ecologists, archaeologists, planners and all those with an interest in integrated approaches to landscapes, to: promote greater understanding between professionals; establish joint approaches to case work; create a unified input to conservation management; promote integration of heritage conservation into interpretation and education.
EN: Postal, telephone
HR: 9.30am–4.30pm Mon-Fri
PB: Beswick and Rotherham (eds), *Ancient woodlands: their archaeology and ecology . . .* (1993); other occasional publications.
AC: Annual seminars, occasional conferences.

Landscape History *see Society for Landscape Studies.*

NA: **The Landscape Research Group Ltd**
AD: c/o School of Design, University of Plymouth, Earl Richards Road N, Exeter EX2 6AS (Lyn Roberts, Membership Secretary)
TL: 01392 475027, fax 01392 475012
FD: 1967
AI: To promote education and research into the landscape over a wide range of academic disciplines, with emphasis on architectural and aesthetic aspects.
EN: Referral service available
PB: *Landscape research* (3/yr); newsletter; conference reports (list available for SAE).
AC: Conferences and events.

Later Prehistoric Ceramics Research Group (*ceased*)

Leather *see Archaeological Leather Group.*

NA: **The Linnaean Society of London**

AD: Burlington House, Piccadilly, London W1V 0LQ

TL: 0171 434 4479, fax 0171 287 9364, e-mail john@linnaean.demon.co.uk

FD: 1788

AI: To promote all aspects of pure biology and related disciplines.

CL: Library of c. 90,000 volumes and MSS; database of members' interests.

EN: Postal

PB: Various natural history journals and occasional publications.

AC: Lectures open to public on request; grants, fellowships etc.

NA: **The Lithic Studies Society**

AD: c/o J S C Lewis (Hon Sec), MOLAS, Walker Ho, 87 Q Victoria St, London EC4V 4AB

FD: 1979

AI: To advance the international study of lithic industries (prehistoric and historic periods, and mainly Britain and Europe) in the broadest possible context.

EN: Postal only

PB: *Lithics* (annual); series of *Occasional papers*; joint publications with other bodies.

AC: Meetings, seminars, conferences, field trips and excursions.

London Science Centre *see now Foundation for Science and Technology.*

NA: **McDonald Institute for Archaeological Research**

AD: Downing Street, Cambridge CB2 3DZ

TL: 01223 333538, fax 01223 333536

FD: 1990

SO: (private foundation)

AI: To perform fieldwork and research in certain areas of archaeology, with special facilities for archaeological science.

CL: Not available to unofficial visitors

EN: Postal only (intending researchers can submit a project proposal for consideration)

PB: *Cambridge archaeological journal* (2/yr; subscription enquiries to Cambridge Univ Press).

NA: **Manchester Ancient Textile Unit**

AD: Dept of Archaeology, University of Manchester, Oxford Road, Manchester M13 9PL

TL: 0161 275 3019, fax 0161 275 3016

FD: 1989

SO: University of Manchester

AI: (abbreviated) To conduct research into all aspects of the study of ancient textiles from archaeological sites in Europe and the Mediterranean world.

CL: Specialist archaeological-textile library

EN: Postal, telephone, personal visit

HR: Mon-Fri 9.00am-5.00pm

PB: Annual reports.

AC: Symposia, academic exchanges/visits.

NA: **The Manorial Society of Great Britain**

AD: 104 Kennington Road, London SE11 6RE (also offices in USA and Australia)

TL: 0171 735 6633, fax 0171 582 7022

FD: 1906

AI: Is an association of Lords of the Manor which aims to promote (among other objects): the study of English history and traditions; the preservation of manorial records and their transfer where possible to local record offices; awareness of the Lord's privileges and responsibilities in the local community.

PB: *Domesday, 900 years of England's Norman heritage* (with the Public Record Office); bulletin (2/yr); etc.

AC: Historical exhibitions (eg Domesday in 1986); annual conference; social functions.

NA: **Manx National Heritage** (includes National Museum, National Trust, National Art Collections, National Archive and Reference Library)

AD: Manx Museum and National Trust, Douglas, Isle of Man IM1 3LY

TL: 01624 675522, fax 01624 661899

FD: 1886

SO: Is a statutory body established by Tynwald

AI: To carry out the functions of the Ancient Monuments Inspectorate and maintain the Sites and Monuments Records. The Manx National Trust acquires and preserves significant buildings and AONBs for public use and recreation and the conservation of wild life.

CL: Museum contents, national archive and reference library, sites and monuments records, art collection .

EN: Postal, telephone, personal visit

HR: Mon-Sat 9.00am-5.00pm

AC: Various, throughout year.

NA: **MARE (Marine Archaeological Research and Excavation)**

AD: c/o Mensun Bound (Director of Archaeology, Oxford University MARE), 4 Butts Road, Horspath, Oxford OX33 1RH

TL: 01865 872896, fax 01865 278855

FD: 1984

AI: Conducts surveys and excavations on maritime sites of all periods and from all parts of the world.

EN: Postal, telephone, personal visit

HR: 9.00am–7.00pm including weekends

PB: (Editing of *International maritime archaeology series*); books on ship excavation.

AC: Fieldwork, teaching, conferences, museum exhibits.

NA: **Maritime Trust** (*absorbed the Cutty Sark Society*)

AD: 2 Greenwich Church Street, London SE10 9BG

TL: 0181 858 2698, fax 0181 858 6976

FD: 1969

AI: To restore and display historic ships and to collect relevant historical information.

CL: Several vessels including *Cutty Sark*, *Gipsy Moth* etc, and three traditional Cornish fishing boats.

EN: Postal only, and limited to enquiries about Trust vessels only

PB: Annual report; newsletter (for Friends of the Trust); leaflets etc.

AC: Lectures, visits, trips abroad (all organised by Friends of the Trust); occasional grants to like-minded organisations.

NA: **MARS Project**

AD: School of Conservation Sciences, Bournemouth University, Talbot Campus, Fern Barrow, Wallisdown, Poole, Dorset BH12 5BB

TL: 01202 595430

FD: 1994

SO: English Heritage

AI: Over 3 years, to make appraisal of the condition and survival of archaeological sites throughout England, as the first systematic quantification of the archaeological resource and physical changes to it. The project is in association with RCHME.

NA: **The Mary Rose Trust**

AD: College Road, HM Naval Base, Portsmouth PO1 3LX

TL: 01705 750521, fax 01705 870588, e-mail maryrose@cix.compulink.co.uk

FD: 1979

SO: Admission fees

AI: To promote and develop interest, research and knowledge relating to the Mary Rose and all matters relating to underwater cultural heritage, for the education and benefit of the nation.

CL: Excavation and documentary archives for the

Mary Rose site; the hull, associated artefacts and environmental material. Associated computer database. (Note that a Code of Practice relates to access to these materials.) The Trust's Virtual Maritime Museum is on Internet at http://www.synergy.net/homeport.html

EN: Postal only

HR: For normal exhibition times check with Trust

PB: List available from Mary Rose Trading Ltd, No 5 Boathouse, HM Naval Base, Portsmouth; schools particularly catered for.

AC: Full-time exhibition; various academic, educational and general interest events.

Medieval Archaeology *see Society for Medieval Archaeology.*

NA: **Medieval Dress and Textile Society**

AD: c/o Frances Pritchard (Membership Sec), Whitworth Art Gallery, University of Manchester, Oxford Road, Manchester M15 6ER

TL: 0161 273 4865, fax 0161 274 4543

FD: c. 1991

AI: To encourage the study and conservation of dress and textiles of the period c. AD 400–1540.

PB: Newsletter (3/yr).

AC: Three meetings a year.

NA: **Medieval Pottery Research Group**

AD: (Hon Sec MPRG) c/o Dept of Medieval and Later Antiquities, British Museum, Great Russell Street, London WC1B 3DG

FD: 1975

AI: To bring together people interested in pottery vessels made, traded and used in Britain and Europe, 5th to 16th centuries AD.

EN: Postal only

PB: *Medieval ceramics* (annual; includes running bibliography); newsletter (3/yr).

AC: Annual conferences and occasional regional meetings. There are several regional groups: London area, S Central England, SE Midlands, E Midlands, W Midlands, Wales, SW England, each with its own secretary.

NA: **Medieval Settlement Research Group**

AD: c/o Dr Robin Glasscock (Hon Treasurer), Dept of Geography, University of Cambridge, Downing Place, Cambridge CB2 3EN

FD: 1986 (amalgamation of two well-founded Research Groups, on Moated Sites and Medieval Villages respectively)

AI: To increase public awareness of medieval rural settlements (mainly but not exclusively of 5th to 16th centuries), to offer advice and information to researchers, to encourage the preservation of medieval settlement sites wherever possible (etc).

CL: Database of village and moat sites held at National Monuments Record, RCHME. Wharram Percy site data will be lodged in Hull Museum.

PB: Annual report (contains research reports); *Index to MSRG records by county* (1993).

AC: Meetings and conferences.

Medieval tiles *see Census of Medieval Tiles.*

NA: **Men of the Stones**
AD: c/o D Mackenzie-Ross (Hon Sec), 25 Cromarty Road, Stamford, Lincs PE9 2TO
TL: 01780 53527
FD: 1947
AI: To stimulate public interest in architecture and good buildings of all periods; to encourage the use of stone and other natural and local building materials; and to encourage the related constructional arts and crafts.
CL: (Library for members' use only)
PB: *Yearbook and directory.*
AC: Annual meeting open to the public; advice on stone repairs etc.

Millennium Project (in its early planning stages at the time of writing) is a joint venture by CBA, Society of Antiquaries, Earthwatch Europe: the hope is for a network of small projects addressing several shared themes to celebrate the Millennium. Contact CBA for progress.

NA: **Ministry of Defence Conservation Office**
AD: Defence Lands Service (Conservation), Room B2/3, Government Buildings, Leatherhead Road, Chessington, Surrey KT9 2LU
TL: 0181 391 3028/9, fax 0181 391 3257
FD: 1973
SO: Government
AI: To preserve and enhance the conservation interest on the Defence estate and military training areas (including 200 SSSIs).
PB: *Sanctuary* (annual).
AC: Local groups (about 200).

Moated Sites Research Group *see now Medieval Settlement Research Group.*

NA: **Monumental Brass Society**
AD: Lowe Hill House, Stratford St Mary, Suffolk CO7 6JX
FD: 1887
AI: (abridged) To encourage the appreciation and preservation of monumental brasses, and in-

dents of lost brasses and incised slabs; to record lost and stolen brasses and those remaining in private hands.
EN: Postal only
PB: *Transactions* (annual); bulletin (3/yr).
AC: Meetings, annual excursion, annual conference, advice and assistance to churches on the care and preservation of brasses.

NA: **Museum Documentation Association**
AD: Jupiter House, Station Road, Cambridge CB1 2JD
TL: 01223 315760, fax 01223 362521, e-mail mda@mdocassn.demon.co.uk Internet http://www.open.gov.uk/mdocassn/index.htm
FD: 1977
SO: Museums and Galleries Commission, DoE-NI, Scottish Office Education Dept, Council of Museums in Wales, National Museums of Wales
AI: To encourage, enable and empower museums to create, capture, manage, access and use information in order to advance the management and use of collections, and to expand curatorial, public and scholarly access to their collections.
CL: Extensive documentation and IT-related library containing both UK and overseas materials; also maintain a software survey on database.
EN: Postal, telephone, personal visit (by appointment) or e-mail
HR: 9.00am–5.00pm
PB: Extensive catalogue available for large SAE.
AC: Some 200 events annually, ranging from local sessions to national workshops and international conferences. Object name thesaurus under discussion.

NA: **Museums and Galleries Commission** (*see also Conservation Unit above*)
AD: 16 Queen Anne's Gate, London SW1H 9AA
TL: 0171 233 4200, fax 0171 233 3686, e-mail rnet(gbr-cu@immedia.ca)
FD: 1931, reconstituted 1981
SO: Dept of National Heritage
AI: To advise government (including DEdNI, ScottEd and Welsh Office) on museum affairs; to safeguard and promote the interests of museums and galleries throughout the UK.
CL: Library of UK museum and gallery literature (available for reference use only, by appointment).
PB: *MGC guidelines on the care of archaeological*

collections (1992); newsletter; list available for SAE.

AC: Various grant schemes; and provides regular funding for the Area Museum Councils and the Museum Documentation Association.

NA: **Museums Association**
AD: 42 Clerkenwell Close, London EC1R OPA
TL: 0171 608 2933, fax 0171 250 1929
FD: 1889
SO: Membership and other income
AI: To inform, represent and develop museums and galleries in the UK.
EN: Enquiries cannot be dealt with
PB: *Museums Yearbook*; *Museums Journal* (monthly); list of museum-related books available for SAE.
AC: Seminars and conferences.

NA: **Museum Training Institute**
AD: 1st floor, Glyde House, Glyde Gate, Bradford BD5 0UP
TL: 01274 391056/391087/391092, fax 01274 394890
FD: 1989
SO: Dept of National Heritage
AI: To approve, promote and provide education and training for museums, galleries and heritage organisations in the UK.
EN: Postal or telephone (information provided on training course, not individual career guidance)
PB: List available for SAE.

Music-Archaeological Survey *see Cambridge Music-Archaeological Survey.*

National Archaeology Day *enquiries to CBA or to Archaeology Centre Bagshot.*

NA: †**National Association of Mining History Organisations**
AD: c/o Dr R Burt, Peak District Mining Museum, Matlock Bath, DE4 3NR
TL: 01629 583834
FD: 1979
AI: To promote knowledge of the development of mining history.
PB: *NAMHO Yearbook*; *Mining history handbook* (1991); *Bibliography of British metalliferous mining history*; codes of practice.
AC: Conferences, meetings, research.

NA: **National Council of Civic Trust Societies**
AD: 31 Berry Hill Road, Cirencester, Glos GL7 2HE
TL: 01285 653132

FD: 1991
AI: Represents the c. 1,000 local amenity societies in England and works on problems referred by them.

NA: **National Council for Metal Detecting**
AD: c/o Gerald Costello (Gen Sec), Room 9/11 Breedon House, Edlestone Road, Crewe, Cheshire CW2 7EA
(This entry is purely for reference, since attempts over the years to persuade NCMD into a mutually beneficial relationship with archaeologists have not succeeded. However, many individual metal-detector users and/or their clubs are working very well with local archaeologists and museum staff.)

NA: **National Heritage: the Museums Action Movement**
AD: 9a North Street, London SW4 0HN
TL: 0171 720 6789, fax 0171 978 1815
FD: 1971
AI: To support and encourage museums and museum visitors; to organise the Museum of the Year Award.
PB: *Museum news* (3/yr to members only).

NA: **National Heritage Memorial Fund**
AD: 10 St James's Street, London SW1A 1EF
TL: 0171 930 0963, fax 0171 930 0968
FD: 1980
SO: Statutory body of Government
AI: Was established by Parliament to give financial assistance towards acquiring, maintaining and preserving for the nation exceptional parts of our heritage – land, buildings, works of art, manuscripts and other historical artefacts. With the establishment of the National Lottery, the Fund also acquired a new role, the Heritage Lottery Fund, to help the creation and preservation of buildings, and to increase the public's enjoyment of or access to the heritage.
EN: Postal, telephone, personal visit (occasionally, depending on subject)
HR: 9.30am–5.30pm
PB: Annual report; grants information leaflet; guides to the Heritage Memorial Fund and the Heritage Lottery Fund.

NA: **National Heritage Select Committee of the House of Commons**
AD: House of Commons, London SW1A 0AA
TL: 0171 219 3000
FD: 1992
SO: Government

AI: To examine the expenditure, administration and policy of the Dept of National Heritage.
EN: Postal and telephone only
HR: 10.00am–6.00pm
PB: Various House of Commons papers etc.
AC: Public sessions of oral evidence on current topic of inquiry.

National Heritage *see also Department of National Heritage.*

NA: **National Historic Ships Committee**
AD: c/o National Maritime Museum, Greenwich, London SE10 9NF
FD: 1994
AI: To work towards and establish a national policy on historic ships and to establish the means to give it effect.

NA: **National Inventory of War Memorials**
AD: c/o Mrs Catherine Moriarty (Research Co-ordinator), Imperial War Museum, Lambeth Road, London SE1 6HZ
TL: 0171 416 5353, fax 0171 416 5379
FD: 1989
SO: Leverhulme Trust
AI: To record every war memorial in the British Isles.
CL: Survey records, associated photographs etc; database maintained.
EN: Postal, telephone or personal visit (by appointment)
HR: 9.00am–4.30pm Mon-Fri
PB: Annual reports.
AC: Conference 1993, exhibition 1994.

National Monuments Record *see Royal Commission on the Historical Monuments of England.*

NA: **National Register of Archives**
AD: Royal Commission on Historical Manuscripts, Quality House, Quality Court, London WC2A 1HP
TL: 0171 242 1198, fax 0171 831 3550, e-mail nra@hmc.gov.uk   Internet http://www.hmc.gov.uk   Telnet \public.hmc.gov.uk
FD: 1945 (parent org 1869)
SO: Government
AI: To provide an index to the location of manuscript sources for British history outside the public records.
CL: Has assembled some 38,000 unpublished catalogues of MS collections with a computerised index of businesses, persons, locations and subjects.

EN: Can accept specific and limited enquiries by post, fax and e-mail
HR: Search Room 9.30am–5.00pm Mon-Fri
PB: *The National Register of Archives* (celebratory volume published as *Historical research special suppl*, 13, 1995).

NA: **The National Trust for Places of Historic Interest or Natural Beauty**
AD: (Archaeology section): Dr David Thackray (Chief Archaeological Adviser), 33 Sheep Street, Cirencester, Glos GL7 1QW. (Head office: 36 Queen Anne's Gate, London SW1H 9AS, tel 0171 222 9251)
TL: 01285 651818, fax 01285 657935
FD: 1980 (NT founded 1895)
SO: Members' subscriptions, donations, and many other sources
AI: (for archaeology) As the largest private owner of archaeological sites, structures and landscapes in the UK, the Trust is undertaking a comprehensive survey and study of all its properties in order to establish an inventory of all sites, landscapes, structures (including vernacular and other historic buildings), maritime sites and structures, etc, in order to provide effective conservation and protection. It works closely with other organisations in this field.
CL: Sites and monuments database under compilation.
EN: Postal, telephone and personal visit (by appointment)
HR: Mon-Fri 9.00am–5.00pm
PB: Numerous in-house archive survey reports etc; leaflet *The National Trust and archaeology* (1995).
AC: Held a national conference on archaeology in the National Trust ('Figures in the Landscape', 1995); does educational work with children (National Curriculum work) and adults (Lifelong Learning Project).

Natural Environment Research Council *see NERC below.*

Natural History societies: *there is no full and up-to-date published directory, but Audrey Meenan, at the Natural History Museum's Dept of Library and Information Services, Cromwell Road, London SW7 5BD, 0171 938 8743, fax 0171 938 9290, may be able to help with addresses. Her e-mail address is a.meenan@uk.ac.nhm.*

NA: **Nautical Archaeology Society**

AD: c/o Rosemary Taylor, at 19 College Road, HM Naval Base, Portsmouth PO1 3LJ

TL: 01705 818419

FD: 1981

AI: To further research in all aspects of nautical archaeology; to improve techniques; to bring together all those interested in nautical and underwater archaeology.

PB: *International journal of nautical archaeology and underwater exploration* (4/yr); newsletter (4/yr); pamphlet *Nautical archaeology: getting involved.*

AC: Training scheme for nautical archaeologists; reconstruction and testing of replica craft, etc.

NA: Neolithic Studies Group

AD: c/o Professor Timothy Darvill, School of Conservation Sciences, Bournemouth University, Fern Barrow, Poole BH12 5BB

TL: 01202 595178, fax 01202 595478

FD: 1984

AI: To provide a forum for interchange of views between archaeologists interested in the Neolithic period in Northern Europe, especially the British Isles.

EN: Postal only

AC: Spring and autumn meetings.

NA: NERC, Natural Environment Research Council

AD: Polaris House, North Star Avenue, Swindon, Wilts SN2 1EU

TL: 01793 411796, fax 01793 411756, e-mail dga@wpo.nerc.ac.uk (David Gale, Awards and Training Section)

FD: 1978 (original date of SBAC foundation under SERC)

SO: Central Government

AI: Science-based archaeology was formerly overseen by SBAC (the Science-Based Archaeology Committee of NERC); it is now the responsibility of the SBA Strategy Group which advises NERC's Council, through its Earth Sciences and Technology Board, on the general strategic development of SBA. The remit of SBA is to advance the understanding and subsequent conservation of the archaeological record through the development, or novel application, of scientific techniques. The aim is to encourage basic research and training in science-based archaeology, to support higher education institutions and persons based therein to pursue methodological innovation and development, and to assist in the formulation of thematic programme proposals.

EN: From persons based in higher education institutions only: postal, telephone, JANET, e-mail

HR: Normal office hours

PB: *Science-based archaeology newsletter* (2/yr; no. 9, November 1995 contains full details of facilities available through NERC).

AC: Sponsors occasional one-day meetings of the SBA community (usually by invitation); deals with applications for research grants, studentships and fellowships through one of its Research Grant and Training Awards Committees (normally Earth Sciences RGTAC or Terrestrial Sciences RGTAC) under the non-thematic funding mode; runs a thematic programme (Ancient Biomolecules Initiative) with SBA projects; collaborates with the British Academy over grants from the Fund for Applied Science in Archaeology (FASA); and provides support for AMS radiocarbon dating through the Oxford University Radiocarbon Accelerator Unit via NERC Scientific Services.

NA: The Newcomen Society

AD: The Science Museum, London SW7 2DD

TL: 0171 589 1793, fax same

FD: 1920 (incorp 1961)

AI: To promote, encourage and co-ordinate the study of the history of engineering, industry and technology (internationally) by means of meetings, publications, correspondence etc.

CL: Archive material belonging to the Society is accessible through the Science Museum Library.

EN: Postal, telephone, personal visit (by arrangement)

HR: 9.00am–4.30pm

PB: *Transactions* (annually); members' bulletin (3/yr); 'extra publications'.

AC: Lectures, 5-day residential summer meeting, 3-day residential visits, one-day visits and conferences.

NA: †North Atlantic Biocultural Organization

AD: Bioarchaeological Laboratory, Anthropology Department, Hunter College CUNY, 695 Park Avenue, New York NY 10021, USA

TL: e-mail thmh@cunyvm; Internet thmh@cunyvm.cuny.edu

AI: Is a multidisciplinary and international association of scholars concerned with this region.

North European Symposium for Archaeological Textiles *details available from Manchester Ancient Textile Unit.*

NA: Offa's Dyke Association

AD: c/o Correspondence Secretary, West Street, Knighton, Powys LD7 1EN

TL: 01547 528753

FD: 1969

SO: Members' subscriptions plus local authority grant

AI: To promote the conservation, improvement and better knowledge of the Welsh Border region and to encourage action by official bodies responsible for the Offa's Dyke Path.

CL: Tourist information centre with exhibition

EN: Postal, telephone or personal visit

HR: Check before visiting: generally, Easter to end Sept, open 7 days/wk; in winter, limited opening at weekends

PB: Newsletter (3/yr); list of accommodation addresses.

AC: Volunteer path wardens.

NA: **Office for Humanities Communication**

AD: Oxford University Computing Service, 13 Banbury Road, Oxford OX2 6NN (Christine Mullings, Research Offr, is at Bath: tel 01225 866962)

TL: 01865 273221 (Admin); e-mail ohc@oucs.ox.ac.uk

FD: (1980s)

SO: British Library and others

AI: Is a national centre concerned with disseminating information on scholarly activities involving the use of new technologies, and with promoting an awareness of current concerns among scholars, libraries, learned societies and publishers.

EN: Postal or telephone

HR: Normal office hours

PB: *Computers and texts* (3/yr, free in UK).

AC: Conferences (eg 'Networking and the European Cultural Heritage'), seminars, workshops, meetings, research projects.

NA: **The Ordnance Society**

AD: c/o Membership Secretary, Rudi Roth, 12 Farrow Close, Great Moulton, Norwich NR15 2HR

FD: 1986

AI: To promote, encourage and co-ordinate the study of all aspects of the history of ordnance and artillery (from AD 1300 on).

EN: Postal or telephone only

HR: Any reasonable times

PB: *Journal* (annual); newsletter (qrly).

AC: Visits, lectures, conferences.

NA: **Ordnance Survey**

AD: Romsey Road, Southampton SO16 4GU

TL: 01703 792000, fax 01703 792404

FD: 1791

SO: Government

AI: National survey and mapping authority (is Government agency).

CL: Large technical library of books, archives, OS maps past and present, slides, videos. (Librarian: Miss P A Poppy, 01703 792334; monthly library accession list.)

EN: Postal, telephone or personal visit (bona fide users only, and appointment needed)

HR: 9.00am–4.30pm

PB: Professional and technical papers, maps including archaeological and historical; atlases, guides; *The future history of our landscape* (1994: contains user responses to suggestion that maps might no longer be printed conventionally, but only on demand).

NA: **Osteoarchaeological Research Group**

AD: c/o Heather Gill-Robinson, Dept of Archaeology, University of York, The King's Manor, York YO1 2EP

TL: 01904 433931

FD: 1993

AI: To provide a forum for discussion and exchange of information on osteoarchaeological topics, both human and animal.

EN: Postal (SAE required)

PB: Newsletter *Organ* (4/yr).

AC: Meetings, usually thematic.

NA: **Palaeopathology Association (British Section)**

AD: c/o Dr Charlotte Roberts, Dept Archaeol Sciences, University of Bradford, Bradford BD7 1DP

TL: 01274 383538, fax 01274 385190

FD: late 1970s

AI: To promote the study of palaeopathology (ancient disease) and to advocate integration of generated data into the rest of the archaeological site to understand human behaviour.

EN: Postal, telephone, personal visit or e-mail (c.a.roberts@uk.ac.bradford)

PB: Newsletter (includes current bibliography on palaeopathology).

AC: Occasional meetings.

NA: **Palmerston Forts Society**

AD: c/o D Moore (Treasurer), 17 Northcroft Road, Gosport, Hants PO12 3DR

TL: 01705 586575

FD: 1984

SO: Members' fees and local government grant

AI: To educate the public in the history of Victorian fortifications worldwide (including later uses).

CL: Archive of books, maps, plans, MSS, military treatises, relevant Victorian military equipment; computerised gazetteer of Victorian fortifications.

EN: Postal, telephone, personal visit

HR: Evenings after 6.00pm

PB: *Journal* (3/yr, members only); information sheets; *Handbook of military terms*; *Arming the forts* (etc: list available for SAE).

AC: Monthly meetings, study visits, research, publishing, work parties, historical interpretation, re-enactment of Victorian artillery drills by uniformed section.

NA: **Peak District Mines Historical Society Ltd**

AD: Peak District Mining Museum, The Pavilion, Matlock Bath, Derbys DE4 3NR

TL: 01629 534775

FD: 1959

SO: Membership subscriptions plus entrance fees of small show mine

AI: (Initially) preservation and recording of Peak District metal mining remains; now widened to include all UK and other economic minerals like coal.

CL: Large collection of artefacts in Peak District Mining Museum (run by Society); access to good collection of mining journals, books, surveys etc in Local Studies Dept, Derbyshire CC at Matlock HQ; database of personal names, places, mines (c. 250,000 entries: for specific enquiries only, and printouts chargeable).

EN: Postal, sometimes telephone

HR: 8.00am–midnight

PB: Bulletin (2/yr); newsletter (4/yr); occasional monographs.

AC: Symposia (often in conjunction with other societies, eg Historical Metallurgy Society).

NA: **Pewter Society**

AD: Hunter's Lodge, Paddock Close, St Mary's Platt, Sevenoaks, Kent TN15 8NN

TL: 01732 883314

FD: 1918

AI: Location and preservation of and research on old pewter.

CL: 'Probably the best library on pewter in UK'

EN: Postal, telephone, personal visit (perhaps), computer network

HR: Any reasonable hours

PB: *Pewter journal* (2/yr); newsletter (2/yr).

AC: Four meetings per year; involvement with museum exhibitions.

NA: **Pillbox Study Group**

AD: c/o 3 Chelwood Drive, Taunton, Som TA1 4JA (John Hellis)

TL: 01823 283596

FD: 1992

AI: Research into and recording of small-scale defences in UK including Home Guard, ROC and Regular Army.

EN: Postal, telephone, Internet j.hellis@bbcnc.org.uk

HR: 9.00am–7.00pm

PB: Newsletter *Loopholes*.

AC: Events organised locally. Passes information to Defence of Britain database.

NA: **Prehistoric Ceramics Research Group**

AD: c/o Lorraine Mepham, Wessex Archaeology, Portway House, Old Sarum Park, Salisbury SP4 6EB

TL: 01722 326867, fax 01722 337562

FD: 1984/5

AI: To work towards full training for pottery workers and towards standardisation of terms for pottery.

CL: (Hoping to assemble a reference collection in due course)

EN: Postal or telephone

HR: Normal office hours

PB: *Occasional papers* series (eg *Guidelines for publication*); collections gazetteer and bibliography in preparation.

AC: Spring and autumn conferences, opportunities for ceramics handling.

NA: **The Prehistoric Society**

AD: c/o UCL Institute of Archaeology, 31–34 Gordon Square, London WC1H 0PY

FD: 1935

AI: To advance education and promote interest in prehistory in all its branches, and to promote the conservation of the archaeological heritage.

EN: Postal only

PB: *Proceedings* (annually); newsletter (2 or 3/yr).

AC: Winter lectures in London, Newcastle, Sheffield; conferences; study tours in UK and overseas; annual awards to support research and to assist Third World prehistorians to attend international conferences.

NA: **Public Record Office**

AD: Ruskin Avenue, Kew, Richmond, Surrey TW9 4DU

TL: 0181 876 3444, 0181 878 8905, fax 0181 878 7231

FD: 1838

SO: Executive agency of government

AI: To preserve, house and make available to researchers the national archives of England and the United Kingdom.

CL: Records of central government since 1066; holds a wealth of archaeology-related documents (maps, plans, drawings, sketches, photographs) for both field monuments and standing buildings.

EN: Personal callers only; simple application procedure, identification needed

HR: 9.30am–5.00pm

PB: Numerous *Guides* to the collections, including 19,000-frame microfiche. HMSO Sectional List 24 deals with British national archives. Leaflet available *Maps and archaeology*.

AC: Exhibitions.

NA: **Public Monuments and Sculpture Association**

AD: c/o Jo Darke, 72 Lissenden Mansions, Lissenden Gardens, London NW5 1PR

TL: 0171 485 0566, fax 0171 267 1742

FD: 1991

AI: The protection of public monuments and sculpture, from Eleanor Crosses to present day, and their promotion for greater public enjoyment.

CL: None, but its corporate members (eg RCHME) have archival material.

EN: Postal, telephone, personal visit (within reason)

HR: 9.30am–5.30pm

PB: Newsletter *Circumspice* (4/yr).

AC: Conferences, events, monument walks; National Recording Project (for central database fed by numerous Regional Archives Centres); bibliography; contacts with groups in Eire and other countries.

NA: **The Quaternary Research Association**

AD: c/o Dr P Coxon, Secretary QRA, Dept of Geography, Trinity College, Dublin 2, Ireland

TL: Dublin 772941 ext 1213, fax Dublin 772694

FD: 1964

AI: To foster communication between archaeologists, botanists, civil engineers, geographers, geologists, soil scientists, zoologists and others interested in research on the Quaternary.

EN: Postal, telephone, e-mail (pcoxon@vax1.tcd.e)

HR: Normal office hours

PB: *Quaternary newsletter*; *Quaternary circular*; *Journal of quaternary science*; *Quaternary proceedings*; *Field guides* (0261–3611).

AC: Field meetings, discussion meetings, workshops.

See also International Union for Quaternary Research; and (under Ireland below) Irish Association for Quaternary Studies.

NA: **Quern Study Group**

AD: enquiries to Lisa Brown, 222 High Street, Batheaston BA1 7QZ

NA: **Railway Heritage Trust**

AD: Melton House, 65/67 Clarendon Road, Watford, Herts WD1 1DP

TL: 01923 240250, fax 01923 207079

FD: 1985

SO: Independent company supported by Railtrack plc and BR

AI: To assist in the conservation of listed buildings and structures which form part of the operational railway; to assist in the transfer of non-operational listed buildings and structures to local trusts or other interested parties; to provide advice to amenity and preservation groups and trusts.

EN: Postal, telephone

HR: Normal office hours

AC: Referral service.

Redundant Churches Fund *see now Churches Conservation Trust.*

NA: **Regia Anglorum**

AD: c/o J Siddorn, 9 Durleigh Close, Headley Park, Bristol BS13 7NQ

TL: 0117 964 6818, fax same

Internet homepage http://www/ftech.net/~/regia.htm

FD: 1980

SO: Fees and expenses from clients

AI: The accurate recreation of the life and times of the folk of the islands of Britain in the century before the Norman Conquest.

EN: Postal, telephone, personal visit (by appointment)

HR: 9.30am–6.00pm

PB: Newsletter (6–8/yr), various research publications, *Clamavi* (5/yr), annual Handbook.

AC: 'Living History Exhibitions', military displays, teaching of relevant craft activities, 3 wooden-hulled ship reconstructions, provision of film extras etc, speakers and exhibits for schools, 38 local groups, etc.

NA: **Rei Cretariae Romanae Fautores (RCRF)**
AD: (in UK) c/o Philip Kenrick (Hon Treas RCRF), Charity Farmhouse, Netherton Road, Appleton, Abingdon OX13 5JX. International Secretary: Frau Dr K Roth-Rubi, Postfach 222, 3000 Bern 11, Switzerland
FD: 1957
AI: To establish contact between scholars of different countries specialising in Hellenistic to late Roman pottery.
EN: Postal or telephone
PB: *Acta* (approx biennial); *Communicationes* (occas newsletter with annual bibliography of Roman pottery studies); *Acta supplementa* (irreg).
AC: Biennial congresses in different countries, generally in September: 1998 provisionally at Ephesos.

NA: **Relief Patterned Tiles Research Group**
AD: c/o Dr John Leveson Gower, Surrey Archaeol Soc, Castle Arch, Guildford, Surrey GU1 3SX
TL: (for urgencies only) 01934 842945, fax 01934 843130
AI: The study of Roman relief-patterned tiles.
CL: Corpus of 1:1 drawings of all known patterns.
EN: Postal, telephone, visits by arrangement
PB: (Corpus intended for publication in *J Roman pot stud*, with subsequent addenda.)

NA: **Rescue, the British Archaeological Trust**
AD: 15a Bull Plain, Hertford, Herts SG14 1DX
TL: 01992 553377
FD: 1971
SO: Members' subscriptions, donations, legacies
AI: To promote and foster the discovery, excavation, preservation, recording and study of archaeology in Great Britain and to promote public knowledge, understanding and appreciation of archaeology.
EN: Postal and telephone only
HR: 9.30am–5.00pm Mon and Fri; Weds 9.30am–1.00pm (also answerphone)
PB: *Rescue News* (3/yr); *Rescuing the historic environment*; *Archaeology and legislation in Britain*; etc (list available for SAE).
AC: Meetings, conferences, technical assistance, advice.

NA: **Research Laboratory for Archaeology and the History of Art**
AD: 6 Keble Road, Oxford OX1 3QJ
TL: 01865 273939, fax 01865 273932
FD: 1955
SO: University of Oxford, SERC/NERC
AI: Application of scientific methods to archaeology and art history.
EN: Postal only
PB: *Archaeometry* (2/yr).

NA: **Roman Army Research Group of London**
AD: c/o Nicholas Fuentes (Chairman), 7 Coalecroft Road, London SW15 6LW
TL: 0181 788 0015
FD: 1969
AI: To explore the various problems relating to Roman military equipment, and to attempt to solve them through practical research.
EN: Postal, telephone, personal visit
HR: Any reasonable hours
PB: Fact sheets.
AC: Field trials of reconstruction equipment, lectures and displays at museums, schools etc in London area.

NA: **Roman Building Trust**
AD: c/o Dr Rook (Director), 23 Mill Lane, Welwyn, Herts AL6 9EU
TL: 01438 715300
FD: 1993
SO: Charitable donations
AI: Research on building technology of the Roman Empire.
EN: Postal, telephone or personal visit
HR: Any reasonable hours

NA: **Roman Finds Group**
AD: c/o Angela Wardle (Mem'ship Sec), 1 Stebbing Farm, Fishers Green, Stevenage, Herts SG1 2JB
FD: 1988
AI: To act as a forum for the study of small Roman artefacts and the contribution they make to understanding the Roman world.
PB: Newsletter (c 2/yr).
AC: Two meetings a year in various places.

NA: **Roman Military Equipment Conference**
AD: c/o Dr M C Bishop, Braemar, Kirkgate, Chirnside, Duns TD11 3XL
TL: 01890 818197, e-mail mcbishop@arma.demon.co.uk
FD: 1983
AI: To conduct and publish research into Roman military equipment.
EN: Postal or e-mail
PB: *Journal of Roman military equipment studies*; newsletter *Arma*.
AC: Conference (ROMEC) every 2 years; running bibliography of relevant published articles.

Roman Mosaics *see Association for the Study and Preservation of Roman Mosaics.*

Roman Pottery Study Group *see Study Group for Roman Pottery.*

NA: **Roman Research Trust**
AD: c/o Hon Sec, E P Johnson, 63 Wenhill Heights, Calne, Wilts SN11 0JZ
FD: 1990
SO: Bequest of Mrs Audrey Barrie Brown
AI: To advance the education of the public in the science of archaeology by promoting the research and excavation of archaeological sites, in particular in the county of Wiltshire and its neighbouring counties to the west.
CL: Important collection of books, slides and photographs of Roman mosaics, donated by Dr David Smith FSA and housed at Devizes Museum.
EN: Postal
PB: Annual report.
AC: Award of grants from the Audrey Barrie Brown Memorial Fund (*see entry in Section 4.6 Grants and awards*). Former 'Friends of Roman Research Trust' now re-formed as Association for Roman Archaeology (which see).

NA: **Roman Roads 'Group'**
AD: c/o K Jermy, 5 Far Sandfield, Churchdown, Gloucester GL3 2JS
TL: 01452 855338
FD: 1982
AI: To disseminate and exchange information on Roman roads in Britain and how to trace them.
EN: Postal, telephone or personal visit (by appointment)

'Roman Society' *see Society for the Promotion of Roman Studies.*

NA: **Royal Anthropological Institute**
AD: 50 Fitzroy Street, London W1P 5HS
TL: 0171 387 0455, fax 0171 383 4235
FD: 1843
AI: To promote the study of anthropology.
EN: Postal only
PB: *Man* (qrly); *Anthropology today* (6/yr); *Anthropological index* (4/yr); occasional papers.
AC: Lectures, seminars, grants/fellowships etc.

NA: **The Royal Archaeological Institute**
AD: c/o Society of Antiquaries, Burlington House, Piccadilly, London W1V 0HS
FD: 1844
AI: To encourage an interest in all aspects of British and Irish antiquities of all periods and including architectural conservation.
CL: No collections, but members are able to read in the library of the Society of Antiquaries of London.
EN: Postal only
PB: *Archaeological journal*; occasional publications; newsletter.
AC: Lectures, one-day excursions, annual 5-day residential meetings in summer, seminars, awards and research grants, etc.

NA: **Royal Commission on Historical Manuscripts**
AD: Quality House, Quality Court, Chancery Lane, London WC2A 1HP
TL: 0171 242 1198
FD: 1869
SO: Government (Dept of National Heritage)
AI: To investigate and advise on all matters concerning historical records throughout the UK (except public records, for which see Public Record Office) and to promote and assist the preservation and study of these records.
CL: Maintains the National Register of Archives (*see separate entry under National*) as a central collection point for unpublished information on manuscript sources.
EN: Personal visit only (no reader's ticket necessary); it may be possible to answer limited and specific enquiries by post.
HR: 9.30am–5.00pm
PB: Numerous publications including *Record repositories in Great Britain* (regularly revised).

NA: **Royal Commission on the Historical Monuments of England/National Monuments Record**
AD: Kemble Drive, Swindon, Wilts SN2 2GZ (London office at 55 Blandford Street, London W1H 3AF; other regional offices at Cambridge, Exeter, Keele, Newcastle and York)
TL: 01793 414700, fax 01793 414707; general enquiries Jon Cannon (Information Officer) 01793 414617; National Monuments Record enquiries 01793 414600, fax 01793 414606. Internet http://www.rchme.gov.uk
London office: 0171 208 8200 (fax 0171 224 5333) for general customer services and NMR; *see also separate entry for Survey of London*
FD: 1908
SO: Government
AI: To compile, manage and promote the national record of archaeological sites and historic buildings in England, and make it publicly accessible.

CL: Reference library of over 32,000 books and journals, plus:
- *Buildings Section of the NMR* containing 3 million historic buildings records and photographs (75,000 photographs of London buildings held in London office)
- *Archaeological Section of the NMR* containing data on most known archaeological sites and landscapes in England, with a newer Maritime Section which covers the 12-mile coastal limits (underwater sites and wrecks). Includes the *Excavation Index* of over 38,000 records covering all archaeological (and geophysical etc) interventions conducted in England. Provides archaeological information to Ordnance survey for mapping purposes.
- *Air Photographs Section of the NMR* providing total aerial photographic cover of England, some as early as 1903.

The relational database MONARCH (MONuments and ARCHitecture) contains 800,000 (and rising) detailed records on archaeological sites, historic buildings and shipwrecks, and gives rapid on-screen access to the entire content of the NMR. It matches records of sites and monuments with other activities (excavations, surveys, photographic and other archives). The main public search room is in Swindon, with a smaller one in London linked by computer to the Swindon office and giving access to the MONARCH database.
- Also maintains, with the British Academy, the *Corpus Vitrearum Medii Aevi* project for the systematic recording of stained glass.

EN: Postal, or personal visit
HR: Public search rooms open Mon-Thur 9.30am–5.30pm, Fri 9.30am–5.00pm; some Saturday opening under review; London search room open Mon-Fri 10.00am–5.30pm
PB: *The National Monuments Record: a guide to the archive*; newsletter (3/yr); *Guidance to local authorities on archaeological and architectural record systems* (1995); and a large number of other publications (list available for SAE).

NA: **Royal Historical Society**
AD: University College London, Gower Street, London WC1E 6BT
TL: 0171 387 7532, fax same
FD: 1868
AI: To further historical work and publication.
CL: Library (not open to public) has pre-1850 publications on English history and antiquities;

record societies series (England and Wales); archives of own and Camden Society papers.
EN: Postal only
PB: *Transactions* (annual); *Camden series*; *Studies in history*; *Annual bibliography of British and Irish history* (1975–); *Bibliography of British history* (6 vols covering medieval period to 1914); guides and handbooks.
AC: Conferences; lectures (open to public on request); grants and scholarships.

NA: **Royal Institute of British Architects**
AD: 66 Portland Place, London W1N 4AD
TL: 0171 580 5533, fax 0171 255 1541
FD: 1834
SO: Members' subscriptions plus activities of subsidiary companies such as RIBA Publications
AI: The general advancement of civil architecture and the acquisition of knowledge of related arts and sciences.
CL: Maintains the British Architectural Library (see separate entry under LIBRARIES in Section 1); some material useful to archaeologists.
HR: Leaflet available giving hours and charges
PB: *RIBA Journal* (monthly); many other publications (list available from RIBA Publications Ltd, 39 Moreland Street, London EC1V 8BB).
AC: Lectures, exhibitions, bookshop.

NA: **Royal Institution of Chartered Surveyors, Building Conservation Committee**
AD: Building Surveyors Division, 12 Great George Street, London SW1P 3AE
TL: 0171 222 7000, fax 0171 222 9430
FD: 1988 (parent institution 1868)
AI: To co-ordinate the activities of the Building Conservation Group, to determine policy, to liaise with relevant government departments and other conservation organisations etc.
PB: *Building Conservation Newsletter* (3/yr); various *Guidance Notes*.
AC: Post-graduate diploma course in building conservation; maintains register of chartered surveyors with relevant experience in building conservation.
See also Scottish branch of RICS, entered below under Scotland.

NA: **Royal Numismatic Society**
AD: c/o British Museum Coins and Medals Dept, London WC1B 3DG
TL: 0171 323 8288
FD: 1836
AI: To promote the study of numismatics.

CL: Library service to members
EN: Postal only
PB: *Numismatic chronicle* (annual); *Coin hoards of Roman Britain* (irreg).
AC: Lectures open to public on request; grants, fellowships, scholarships.

NA: **Royal Photographic Society Archaeology and Heritage Group**
AD: c/o J Spence (Sec), 87 Blackbrook Lane, Bickley, Kent BR1 2LS
TL: 0181 402 1306
FD: 1972
AI: The photography of archaeology and items of heritage; all periods.
EN: Postal, telephone
HR: Any time
PB: *Heritage photography* (approx annually); newsletter (3/yr).
AC: Monthly meetings, annual exhibition.

NA: **The Royal Society**
AD: 6 Carlton House Terrace, London SW1Y 5AG
TL: 0171 839 5561, fax 0171 930 2170
FD: 1660
SO: Government, investments, bequests, Fellows' subscriptions etc
AI: To encourage scientific research and its application; to represent and support the scientific community (etc).
CL: Important library and archive collection from 1660 onwards; photographic collection; access to online databases.
EN: Postal and telephone, personal visit (by appointment)
HR: 9.00am–5.00pm
PB: *Philosophical transactions*; *Proceedings*; *Yearbook*; *Notes and records*; etc.
AC: Meetings, exhibitions, colloquia, grants and awards, Committee on the Public Understanding of Science (COPUS, which offers small grants to assist with public understanding of science matters, etc).

NA: **Royal Town Planning Institute**
AD: 26 Portland Place, London W1N 4BE
TL: 0171 636 9107, fax 0171 323 1582
FD: 1914
AI: To advance the science and art of all aspects of town planning for the benefit of the public.
EN: Free referral service to general public
AC: 14 regional branches including N Ireland.

NA: **Rural History Centre** (*incorporating the Museum of English Rural Life and the Institute of Agricultural History*)

AD: University of Reading, Whiteknights, PO Box 229, Reading RG6 6AG
TL: 01734 318664, fax 01734 751264
FD: 1951 (MERL); 1968 (IAH)
SO: University of Reading
AI: Is a national centre for the study of the history of farming, food and the countryside.
CL: Museum of English Rural Life (Keeper of Study Collections 01734 318663); library of some 35,000 books on all aspects of the history of agriculture etc but with bias to ethnography and history; a million photographs, paintings, prints and engravings; bibliographical index of some 50 000 references; photographic collection (01734 318668/318665) from mid-19th century.
EN: Postal, telephone and personal visit; JANET pending completion of Rural History Database (enquiries to Raine Morgan, 01734 318670)
HR: Mon-Fri 9.30am–5.00pm
PB: Researcher's guide; museum guide; *Research series*; *Bibliography of Roman agriculture*; *Bibliography of farm tools, implements and machines in Britain*.
AC: Occasional temporary exhibitions.

NA: **SAVE Britain's Heritage**
AD: 68 Battersea High Street, London SW11 3HX
TL: 0171 228 3336, fax 0171 223 2714
FD: 1975
SO: Various private and public sources, sales of publications
AI: To conserve historic buildings by encouraging restoration and finding continuing uses; to prevent demolition and radical alteration of historic buildings and conservation areas.
CL: Photographic library for historic buildings.
EN: Postal only
PB: *Newsletter* (annual); case studies and other publications (list available for SAE).

Science-Based Archaeology Committee has ceased to exist as such: see entry under NERC above.

NA: **SEARCH** (*see also Scottish section for organisation with same title*)
AD: c/o Hilary Tidswell, Barnfield, Danes Crescent, Staveley, Kendal, Cumbria, LA8 9QJ
TL: 01539 821740
FD: 1981
AI: To promote for the benefit of the public the study and practice of the science of archaeology in the District of South Lakeland and neighbourhood.
EN: Postal preferred

PB: Newsletter (4/yr).
AC: Excavations (eg Kentmere), fieldwalking with National Trust, field trips.

Severn Estuary Levels Research Committee *see under Wales below.*

Shell Better Britain *see Section 4.6 Grants and awards.*

NA: **Shipwreck and Heritage Centre**
AD: Ropewalk House, Charlestown, St Austell, Cornwall PL25 3NN
TL: 01726 73104, fax (marked ATTN SHIP-WRECK and MARINE) 01726 69878
FD: 1976
SO: Admission fees only
AI: To provide the public with an informative, interesting and educational centre exhibiting shipwreck in the context of artefacts, photographs and general information; Roman period to present day.
CL: Comprehensive shipwreck library including many rare works; Board of Trade and Lloyds publications; database of shipwrecks, in process of publication by Lloyds.
EN: Postal, telephone, personal visit
HR: Centre open 1 Mar to 10 Nov annually, 10.00am–5.00pm (later in high season); telephone enquiries normal office hours
PB: 20 publications on SW coast and other shipwrecks; *Shipwreck index* (for Lloyds) in 8 or 9 volumes; etc.
AC: Special exhibitions, tours; welcomes input into practical diving, search and research projects.

NA: **Society of Antiquaries of London**
AD: Burlington House, Piccadilly, London W1V 0HS
TL: 0171 734 0193 and 0171 437 9954, fax 0171 287 6967, e-mail socantiq.lond@bbcnc.org.uk
FD: 1707 (incorporated by Royal Charter 1751)
SO: Fellows' subscriptions and investments
AI: The encouragement, advancement and furtherance of the study and knowledge of antiquities and history of this and other countries.
CL: Library of some 200,000 books on archaeology, architectural history, etc, including periodicals, broadsides, brass rubbings, seal casts, manuscripts; the prints and drawings collection includes many topographical drawings. The Library is open to Fellows and to members of both the Royal Archaeological Institute and the British Archaeological Association. Other re-searchers may apply to use the library (for reference purposes only and for a limited period), on the recommendation of a Fellow or university tutor, or by arrangement with the Librarian or General Secretary. Card catalogue up to July 1988; computer catalogue for material acquired since then. Searches can also be made on the British Library's online bibliographical information service, for which a charge will be levied.
EN: Postal, telephone, personal visit (by appointment)
HR: 10.00am–5.00pm; premises are sometimes closed for part of the summer
PB: *Antiquaries journal* (1 or 2/yr); *Archaeologia* (occasional); series of *Research reports* and *Occasional papers*, irregular.
AC: Lectures (non-Fellows may attend by invitation); occasional conferences; various research (etc) grants available.

NA: **Society of Archer-Antiquaries**
AD: c/o Hon Sec, D Elmy, 61 Lambert Road, Bridlington, Yorks YO16 5RD
TL: 01262 601604
FD: 1956
AI: To research and publish all aspects of the history of archery.
CL: Small select library and display room.
EN: Postal and telephone
HR: evenings only
PB: *Journal of the Society of Archer-Antiquaries* (annual); newsletter (2/yr).
AC: Two meetings a year, AGM, antiquarian shoot in August.

NA: **Society of Architectural Historians of Great Britain**
AD: c/o Sally Jeffery, Hon Sec, 23B Home Park Road, London SW19 7HP
FD: 1956
AI: The encouragement of the study of architectural history.
EN: The Society is unable to answer outside enquiries.
PB: *Architectural history* (annual); newsletter (3/yr); research register (approx every 5 years); occasional monographs.
AC: Annual residential conference; symposia; foreign study tours; annual lecture by a distinguished scholar; awards.

NA: **Society of Archivists**
AD: Information House, 20–24 Old Street, EC1V 9AP

TL: 0171 253 5087, fax 0171 253 3942 (Executive Sec)

FD: 1947

AI: Is the professional body in the UK and Republic of Ireland for the promotion of the care and preservation of archives, the better administration of archive repositories, the training of its members, together with research and publication.

PB: *Journal* (2/yr) and other publications.

AC: Regional groups (11), special interest groups, conferences, seminars, training days.

NA: **Society for Church Archaeology**

AD: c/o CBA, Bowes Morrell House, 111 Walmgate, York YO1 2UA

TL: 01904 671417

FD: 1996

AI: To complement existing organisations and to improve the position of church archaeology, involving itself in such issues as redundancy and the proper archaeological scrutiny of church repairs and building projects.

PB: *Church archaeology* (annual).

AC: Annual conference and regional meetings.

NA: **Society for Clay Pipe Research**

AD: c/o R Jackson, 4 Portishead Lodge, Beach Road West, Portishead, Bristol BS20 9HJ

TL: –

FD: 1984

AI: To encourage and stimulate research on clay tobacco pipes (world-wide, late 16th century to present day).

EN: Postal, or via S Atkin, e-mail 100744.2367@compuserve.com

PB: Newsletter (4/yr); *Clay pipe research* (irreg).

AC: Annual conference.

NA: **Society for Folk Life Studies**

AD: c/o David Eveleigh, Blaise Castle House Museum, Henbury, Bristol BS10 7QS

TL: 0117 950 6789

FD: 1961

AI: To promote the study of the traditional ways of life and work of the people of the UK, Ireland and Isle of Man, and to provide a forum for those engaged with the subject.

EN: Postal only

PB: *Folklife: a journal of ethnological studies* (annual).

AC: Annual conference.

NA: **Society for the Interpretation of Britain's Heritage**

AD: c/o Lesley Hehir, 12 The Grove, Benton, Newcastle NE12 9PE

TL: 0191 266 5804 (evenings)

FD: 1975

AI: To promote high standards of interpretation in Britain. Also collaborates with Centre for Environmental Interpretation (see above).

PB: *Interpretation journal* (3/yr); *Directory of consultants in heritage interpretation.*

AC: Conferences, training workshops, exhibitions, 'Interpret Britain' award scheme.

NA: **Society of Jewellery Historians**

AD: c/o Susan Coelho (Sec), Dept of Prehistoric and Romano-British Antiquities, British Museum, London WC1B 3DG

TL: (no tel), fax 0171 323 8588

FD: 1977

AI: To advance public education by promoting (whether by formal meetings, lectures, publications or otherwise) the study and the making known of the history and development of the craft and craftspeople connected with the manufacture, design and processes concerning jewellery.

EN: Postal

PB: *Jewellery studies* (occasional); *Gem and jewellery news* (4/yr, jointly with the Gemmological Assoc and Gem Testing Lab of Great Britain).

AC: Lectures, symposia and seminars, museum private views, etc.

NA: **Society for Landscape Studies**

AD: c/o Carenza Lewis, RCHME, National Monuments Record Centre, Kemble Drive, Swindon, Wilts SN2 2GZ

TL: 01793 414787 (direct line)

FD: 1979

AI: To promote interdisciplinary discussion between geomorphologists, palynologists, archaeologists, historical geographers, architectural historians and place-name scholars, in order to study the interaction of people and their environment as reflected in landscape today.

EN: Postal, telephone

HR: Normal office hours

PB: *Landscape history* (annual); newsletter (2/yr).

AC: Two conferences a year.

NA: **The Society for Medieval Archaeology**

AD: c/o Dr Paul Stamper (Hon Sec), 'Devonia', Forton Heath, Shrewsbury SY4 1EY

TL: 01743 254009, fax 01743 254047
FD: 1957
AI: To further the study of British history since the Roman period (mainly by means of material evidence, and including NW Europe).
EN: Postal, telephone, personal visit (by appointment)
HR: 9.00am–5.00pm
PB: *Medieval archaeology* (annual); newsletter; monograph series (occasional).
AC: Occasional conferences.

NA: **Society of Museum Archaeologists**
AD: c/o Dave Allen (Hon Sec), Museum of the Iron Age, 6 Church Close, Andover, Hants SP10 1DP
TL: 01264 366283, fax 01264 339152
FD: 1976
AI: (abridged) To promote museum involvement in all aspects of archaeology; to promote greater public understanding of the archaeological past; to develop a coherent philosophy of the role of archaeologists in museums.
EN: Postal or telephone
HR: Mon-Fri 9.00am–5.00pm
PB: *The museum archaeologist* (annual); *Selection, retention and dispersal of archaeological material* (first in a series of guidelines on museum practice); newsletter.
AC: Annual conferences, seminars and training events etc.

NA: **Society for Name Studies in Britain and Ireland** (formerly the Council for Name Studies in Great Britain and Ireland)
AD: c/o Miss J Scherr (Hon Sec), Queen's Building Library, University of Bristol, University Walk, Bristol BS8 1TR
TL: (no tel), e-mail j.scherr@bristol.ac.uk
FD: 1991 (1962 under original name)
AI: To promote the study of proper names, primarily the place- and personal names of Britain and Ireland, and to provide a source of authoritative advice on all matters concerning such names. (Emphasis on the period before AD 1500.)
EN: Postal (or telephone, evenings only 0117 973 9053)
PB: *Nomina* (annual journal); newsletter (occas).
AC: Spring conference; occasional day conferences. Works closely with archaeologists and refers enquiries to leading national experts.

NA: **Society for Nautical Research**

AD: c/o National Maritime Museum, Greenwich, London SE10 9NF
FD: 1910
AI: To further all aspects of nautical research; the preservation of *HMS Victory*.
EN: Postal or computer network udylo10@ uk.ac.kcl.cc.bay
PB: *Mariner's mirror* (4/yr); newsletter.
AC: Meetings, lectures, seminars, conferences, essay competition.

NA: **Society for Post-Medieval Archaeology**
AD: c/o David Gaimster, Dept of Medieval and Later Antiquities, British Museum, London WC1B 3DG
TL: 0171 323 8734, fax 0171 323 8496
FD: 1967
AI: To promote the study of archaeological evidence of British and colonial history of the post-medieval period before industrialisation.
EN: Postal
PB: *Post-medieval archaeology* (annual); newsletter.
AC: Two conferences a year.

NA: **Society for the Promotion of Roman Studies**
AD: Senate House, Malet St, London WC1E 7HU
TL: 0171 323 9583; Joint Library 0171 323 9574, fax 0171 323 9575; e-mail romansoc@sas.ac.uk
FD: 1911
AI: To further the study of Roman history, archaeology, literature and art down to about AD 700.
CL: Library of over 83,000 volumes and over 520 current periodicals, maintained jointly with the Hellenic Society and in conjunction with the University of London's Institute of Classical Studies, which houses a lending collection of over 6,500 slides with computerised catalogue (1995). Computer access to library of DAI (German Archaeological Institute) at Rome.
EN: Postal
PB: *Britannia* (annual: for Roman Britain); *Journal of Roman studies* (annual: for the wider Roman world); two monograph series.
AC: Public lectures in London and around Britain; biennial conference; grants for excavations; grants for schools to help teaching about the Roman world.

NA: **The Society for the Protection of Ancient Buildings (SPAB)**
AD: 37 Spital Square, London E1 6DY
TL: 0171 377 1644, fax 0171 247 5296

FD: 1877

AI: To promote the conservative repair of old buildings [is one of the several organisations statutorily concerned with planning applications concerning listed buildings].

CL: Extensive archives (available to researchers by prior appointment only) covering cases considered by the Society since 1877; many early cases were churches, and the records mostly concern structural condition.

EN: Postal or telephone only, to Archivist

HR: 10.00am–4.00pm

PB: Newsletter (4/yr); *Repair of ancient buildings*; list of properties for sale and in need of repair (4/yr); technical pamphlets and information sheets on repair and conservation of historic structures; list available for SAE.

AC: Training courses, lectures, visits; technical advice; separate Windmill and Watermill Section with its own activities.

NA: **Soil Survey and Land Research Centre** (formerly Soil Survey of England and Wales)

AD: Cranfield University, Silsoe Campus, Silsoe, Bedfordshire MK45 4DT

TL: 01525 863000, fax 01525 863253

FD: 1987 (1939 under former name)

SO: Is university unit undertaking consultancies etc

AI: To provide professional research, development and consultancy service in all aspects of land management, land use planning, and land policy development; among other services, provides monitoring of soil quality and conducts environmental impact assessments.

PB: Soil maps and related books: list available for SAE.

AC: Three local branches – Exeter, Shardlow and York.

NA: **Southern Rivers Palaeolithic Project** (to 1994; succeeded by **English Rivers Palaeolithic Survey**, to run 1994–7)

AD: Wessex Archaeology, Portway House, Old Sarum Park, Salisbury, Wilts SP4 6EB

TL: 01722 326867, fax 01722 337562

SO: English Heritage

AI: To assess the Lower and Middle Palaeolithic resource, in the context of contemporary Quaternary deposits, for the purposes of its better management and protection and the furtherance of academic knowledge.

EN: Postal, telephone or personal visit (by appointment)

HR: 9.30am–4.30pm

PB: Three volumes of results (gazetteer and maps) from the Southern Rivers Project have been deposited with county archaeological officers, English Heritage, British Geological Survey, British Museum, RCHME, English Nature, University of Southampton (Dept Archaeology) and Society of Antiquaries. Also *The English Palaeolithic reviewed* (1996).

NA: **Standing Conference of Archaeological Unit Managers (SCAUM)**

AD: Postal enquiries c/o Society of Antiquaries of London, Burlington House, Piccadilly, London WIV OHS (Hon Sec John Walker, Greater Manchester Archaeological Unit, Oxford Road, Manchester M13 9PL)

TL: 0161 275 2314, fax 0161 275 2315

FD: 1975

AI: To provide a forum for establishing professional opinion on current matters of concern; to foster the adoption of best practice in employment, fieldwork and publication; to promote the preservation of the archaeological resource.

PB: *Health and safety in field archaeology* (1991); co-sponsors of BDLG Code of Conduct; and other publications or co-publications.

NA: **Standing Committee of University Professors and Heads of Archaeology**

AD: c/o Professor Anthony Harding (Chair), Dept of Archaeology, University of Durham, South Road, Durham DH1 3LE

TL: 0191 374 3622

NA: **The Study Group for Roman Pottery**

AD: c/o Lindsay Rollo (Sec), Edgson House, The Lane, Etton, Peterborough PE6 7DD

TL: 01733 253284

FD: 1971

AI: To further the study of pottery of the Roman period in Britain.

PB: *Journal of Roman pottery studies* (annual); newsletter (3/yr).

AC: Annual and regional conferences.

NA: **Subterranea Britannica**

AD: c/o M and B Tadd (Jt Secretaries), 65 Trindles Road, South Nutfield, Redhill, Surrey RH1 4JL

TL: 01737 823456

FD: 1974

AI: To provide information on all types of man-made man-used underground structures; comparative study of individual sites with others in Britain and Europe is encouraged; responsibility and concern for the safety of persons, property and wildlife are promoted, both in those conducting investigations underground and in owners of mineral rights, occupiers and local authorities etc.

EN: Postal, telephone, personal visit (by appointment)

HR: Office hours

PB: *Subterranea Britannica* (annual); newsletter.

AC: Spring and autumn conferences; annual study weekend; opportunities to join international conferences which include visits to underground sites; association with Société Française d'Etude des Souterrains and with Arbeitskreis für Erdstallforschung.

NA: **Survey of London**

AD: RCHME, 55 Blandford Street, London W1H 3AF

TL: 0171 208 8242, fax 0171 208 8240

FD: 1894

SO: RCHME

AI: To record London's building fabric, undertaking detailed surveys of individual buildings of outstanding architectural significance, and comprehensive parish surveys.

CL: Library (appointment needed); enquire for details as some material is at RCHME Swindon, and early materials at Greater London Record Office.

EN: Postal, telephone, personal visit (by appointment)

HR: 10.00am–5.00pm (search room open Mon-Weds 10.00am–5.30pm, extended Thurs till 7.00pm, Fri closes 5.00pm)

PB: Some 40 volumes of the *Survey* have been completed so far; *London survey'd* (H Hobhouse 1995); list available for SAE.

NA: **Sutton Hoo Research Project/Sutton Hoo Research Trust**

AD: Dept of Archaeology, University of York, The King's Manor, York YO1 2EP

TL: 01904 433901, fax 01904 433902

FD: Project period 1983–96

SO: Society of Antiquaries, British Museum, other grant-aiding bodies

AI: To research the Anglo-Saxon burial ground at Sutton Hoo by excavation and post-excavation study.

CL: All finds and archives destined for British Museum in 1997

EN: Postal or telephone

PB: *Bulletin of the Sutton Hoo Research Committee* (1–8, 1983–93) available as compen-

dium volume from Boydell Press, Woodbridge, Suffolk.

Textiles *see Manchester Ancient Textile Unit, also Medieval Dress and Textile Society.*

NA: †**Thames Archaeology Survey**

AD: c/o Mike Webber, Early London Dept, Museum of London, London Wall, London EC2Y 5HN

NA: **Tiles and Architectural Ceramics Society**

AD: c/o Myra Brown (TACS Sec), Decorative Art Dept, Liverpool Museum, Liverpool L3 8EN

TL: 0151 478 4264

FD: 1981

AI: The study and protection of tiles and architectural ceramics.

CL: Small TACS archive with mainly visual material on tiles, held at Stoke-on-Trent City Museum and Art Gallery, open for consultation (members only by prior arrangement). A database on tiles and architectural ceramics in Europe and the Middle East is under development at Leeds Metropolitan University (contact H van Lemmen for further information).

EN: Postal only

PB: *Journal* (biennial); *Glazed expressions* (magazine, 2/yr); newsletter (4/yr); *Bibliography* (1988); other publications (list available from TACS Publications Secretary, City Museum and Art Gallery, Hanley, Stoke-on-Trent ST1 3DW, for SAE).

AC: Visits with tour notes; exhibitions.

Tiles *see also Census of Medieval Tiles.*

NA: **The Tool and Trades History Society**

AD: 60 Swanley Lane, Swanley, Kent BR8 7JG

TL: 01322 662271

FD: 1983

AI: To advance the education of the general public in the history and development of hand tools and their use and of the people and trades that used them.

CL: Small library for members' use only

EN: Postal, telephone and personal visit (by appointment only)

HR: Weekday afternoons, except Wednesdays

PB: *Journal* (15- to 18-month intervals); newsletter (4/yr); occasional publications.

AC: National meetings, annual 3-day conference, exhibitions, regional group meetings, museum visits, etc.

NA: **Town and Country Planning Association**

AD: 17 Carlton House Terrace, London SW1Y 5AS

TL: 0171 930 8903/4/5, fax 0171 930 3280

FD: 1899

AI: To improve the environment through effective planning, public participation and sustainable development.

PB: *Town and country planning* magazine (11/yr); other publications (list available).

AC: Scottish section. Referral service.

NA: **Tradescant Trust**

AD: Museum of Garden History, Lambeth Palace Road, London SE1 7LB

TL: 0171 261 1891 (answerphone 0171 373 4030), fax 0171 401 8869

FD: 1971

SO: Voluntary contributions

AI: To preserve the historic church of St Mary-at-Lambeth as a museum of garden history.

CL: The Museum presents an outline of the history of gardens and has a replica seventeenth-century garden adjacent.

EN: Postal

HR: Normal museum hours

AC: Maintains a bibliography of gardens and is a resource for finding out about gardens of various styles including those abroad. Day courses and events, lectures.

NA: **The Trevithick Society**

AD: c/o Hon Sec, Dr John Ferguson, 15 Abbey Meadow, Lelant, St Ives, Cornwall TR26 2LL

TL: 01736 753310

FD: c. 1972

AI: The study of the history of technology in Cornwall and the preservation of buildings, machinery and sites connected with mining, engineering, china clay workings, transport, and any other industry with Cornish associations.

EN: Postal

PB: *Journal* (annual); newsletter (4/yr).

AC: Lectures, visits, Levant beam engine restoration/maintenance group, liaison with other preservation bodies.

NA: **The Trevithick Trust**

AD: 'Chygarth', 5 Beacon Terrace, Camborne, Cornwall TR14 7BU

TL: 01209 612142

FD: 1993

SO: National Trust, local authorities

AI: To preserve and interpret industrial sites as part of the landscape.

CL: Management agreement with Trevithick Society; Pool engines (Nat Trust); Porthcurno Museum; Geevor tin mine; submarine telegraphy museum.

EN: Postal, telephone

HR: Normal museum hours

AC: Identifying, managing and conserving the industrial archaeology of Cornwall.

NA: **The Twentieth Century Society** (previously The Thirties Society)

AD: 70 Cowcross Street, London EC1M 6BP

TL: 0171 250 3857, fax 0171 250 3022

FD: 1979 (as Thirties Soc)

AI: To protect British architecture and design after 1914 (also advises local authorities on planning applications affecting this period).

EN: Postal and telephone; personal visits by appointment occasionally possible

PB: *Thirties Society journal* (nos 1–7, irregular); from 1994, *Twentieth Century Society journal*; newsletter (3/yr); reports; walk and tour notes (list available for SAE).

AC: Lectures, visits, conservation advice.

NA: **UK Institute for the Conservation of Historic and Artistic Works (Archaeology Section)**

AD: 6 Whitehorse Mews, Westminster Bridge Road, London SE1 7QD

TL: 0171 620 3371

FD: 1976

AI: To serve the needs of those actively engaged in, or interested in, the conservation of archaeological objects.

PB: Section in UKIC's *Conservation news* (3/yr); *Guidelines for the preparation of excavation archives for long-term storage* (1990, OP); conservation guidelines series (etc: list available for SAE).

AC: Annual conference, occasional workshops, training courses, study visits.

See also International Institute for Conservation . . .

NA: **United Kingdom Fortifications Club**

AD: c/o Peter Cobb, 4 Mablethorpe Road, Portsmouth PO6 3LJ

TL: 01705 387794

FD: 1972

AI: To pursue the study of fortifications and compile records of them.

CL: Archives of fort plans, photographs, slides, literature and data on fortified sites.

EN: Postal, telephone, personal visit

HR: 6.00pm–11.30pm Mon-Sat, 6.30pm–9.45pm Sun
PB: Newsletter (2/yr); numerous booklets, eg *Plymouth papers*; *Solent papers*; plans of forts etc (list available for SAE).
AC: Members' study tours, seminars etc.

NA: **Upkeep, the trust for training and education in building maintenance (formerly The Building Conservation Trust)**
AD: Apt 39, Hampton Court Palace, East Molesey, Surrey KT8 9BS
TL: 0181 943 2277, fax 0181 943 9552
FD: 1979
SO: Grants, donations and fees
AI: To encourage better maintenance of buildings, particularly ordinary houses, and to promote the use of proper materials and techniques.
CL: Technical library open 9.30am–5.00pm Mon-Fri (appointment needed).
EN: Postal and telephone
HR: Office hours
PB: Teachers' guides, worksheets, slide sets with text.
AC: Permanent exhibition 'Care of buildings' at Hampton Court Palace showing why maintenance problems occur and how they may be avoided or corrected; school and college visits encouraged; seminars; training courses on care and maintenance.

NA: **Vernacular Architecture Group**
AD: c/o Bob Meeson (VAG Sec), 16 Falna Crescent, Coton Green, Tamworth, Staffs B79 8JS
TL: 01827 69434
FD: 1952
AI: To further the study of lesser traditional buildings.
CL: Library of offprints available by postal loan to members only.
EN: Postal only
PB: *Vernacular architecture* (annual); newsletter (3/yr); quinquennial bibliography (three available, fourth in preparation); index of tree-ring dated buildings.
AC: Spring 4-day conference, various places; winter 2-day conference in London.

VESARP, Viking and Early Settlement Archaeological Research Project *see entry in Scottish section below.*

Victoria County History *see note under Institute of Historical Research.*

NA: **The Victorian Society**
AD: 1 Priory Gardens, London W4 1TT
TL: 0181 994 1019, fax 0181 995 4895
FD: 1958
SO: Members' subscriptions, legacies, DoE grant, investment income
AI: To study and protect the architecture and decorative arts of the Victorian and Edwardian periods. Is one of the societies statutorily consulted over planning applications involving listed buildings.
CL: Photographic library
EN: Postal or telephone
HR: Office hours
PB: Series *Care for Victorian houses*; *Public prospects: historic urban parks under threat*; other publications (list available for SAE).
AC: Lectures; three-week Anglo-American Summer School on Victorian architecture; regional groups; administers Linley Sambourne House Museum in London W4.

NA: **The Viking Society for Northern Research**
AD: c/o Dept of Scandinavian Studies, University College London, Gower Street, London WC1E 6BT
TL: 0171 387 7050
FD: 1892
AI: To promote research in the Scandinavian North, its literature and antiquities.
CL: The Society's library forms part of UCL Library, in which members of the Society have full borrowing rights.
EN: Postal, telephone and personal visit (by appointment)
HR: Office hours
PB: *Sagabook* (annually); a text series.
AC: Meetings, awards.

NA: **The Vivat Trust**
AD: 61 Pall Mall, London SW1Y 5JA
TL: 0171 930 2212, fax 0171 930 2295
FD: 1981
SO: EH, DNH, public companies, charitable trusts
AI: To save, for the future benefit of the nation, buildings of historic or architectural significance that have fallen through the net of other organisations set up for their preservation.
EN: Postal, telephone, personal visit
HR: 9.00am–5.00pm
PB: Annual report; property leaflets, etc.
AC: Open days at restored properties, seminars, restoration projects.

NA: **Wealden Iron Research Group**
AD: c/o Shiela Broomfield, 8 Woodview Crescent, Hildenborough, Tonbridge, Kent TN11 9HD
TL: 01732 838698
FD: 1968
AI: To foster research into the extractive industry of the Weald of Kent and Surrey and above all to publish its researches.
PB: Bulletin, Newsletter etc.
AC: Two meetings/yr, field research, documentary research.

NA: **Wellcome Institute for the History of Medicine** – Library
AD: 183 Euston Road, London NW1 2BE
TL: 0171 611 8582 (Library enquiries), fax 0171 611 8369
FD: 1897
SO: Wellcome Trust
AI: To provide resources for research and teaching in the history of medicine and allied sciences.
CL: Iconographic collections (videodisc for part); photographic library; bibliographic services, etc.
EN: Postal, telephone, personal visit (by appointment), JANET for part of collections accessible on-line (uk.ac.ucl.wihm + 0000 0511 3700 03)
HR: 9.45am–5.15pm Mon, Weds, Fri; 9.45am–7.15pm Tues, Thurs; 9.45am–1.00pm Sat (advisable to phone before visit)
PB: *Current work in the history of medicine* (regular bibliographic bulletin); other publications of less archaeological interest.
AC: Exhibitions, seminars, symposia, lectures.

NA: **West Midlands Pottery Research Group**
AD: c/o Derek Hurst, County Archaeological Service, Hereford-Worcester County Council, Tolladine Road, Worcester WR4 9NB
TL: 01905 611086
FD: 1983
SO: Meeting fees
AI: To provide a forum for pottery/ceramic researchers working on the sub-Roman to post-medieval period in the region (Glos, Herefs, Shrops, Staffs, Warks, W Midl, Worcs).
EN: Postal, telephone, personal visit (by appt)
HR: Normal office hours
PB: Newsletter (2/yr).
AC: Meetings.

NA: **Wetland Archaeology Research Project (WARP)**
AD: Dept of History and Archaeology, University of Exeter, Exeter EX4 4QH
TL: 01392 264347
FD: 1986
AI: To support and encourage wetland research throughout the world.
EN: Postal
PB: *NewsWarp* (2/yr); series of occasional papers (irregular).
AC: Conferences (usually in association with English Heritage or other body).

NA: **WHAM! Women, heritage and museums**
AD: c/o Margaret Brooks (Treas), Keeper of the Sound Archive, Imperial War Museum, Lambeth Road, London SE1 6HZ
TL: 0171 416 5360
FD: 1984
AI: (abridged) To promote positive images of women through museum collections, exhibitions and activities; to encourage informed museum practice in collection and display; to provide a wider forum for exchange of ideas and information on women's heritage; to campaign for equal employment in museums and related fields (etc).
PB: Newsletter (4/yr); *Resources list* (on all museum subjects) obtainable from Marie Turner, 75 Cambridge Road, Teddington, Middx.

NA: **Wildlife and Countryside Link**
AD: 246 Lavender Hill, London SW11 1LJ
TL: 0171 924 2355, fax 0171 924 5761
FD: 1993 (1980 as Wildlife Link)
SO: Part-funded by government; plus institutional members
AI: Was formed from a merger of Wildlife Link and the Countryside Link Group, to coordinate views of non-governmental organisations on both wildlife and countryside, and to conduct liaison with government bodies. Collaborates with Links in Wales, Scotland and Northern Ireland.
PB: List available for SAE.

NA: **Young Archaeologists' Club**
AD: c/o Council for British Archaeology, Bowes Morrell House, 111 Walmgate, York YO1 2UA
TL: 01904 671417, fax 01904 671384 (Juliet Mather, Club Coordinator)
FD: 1972 (as Young Rescue), 1976 (as YAC)
SO: Parent body and members' subscriptions
AI: To act as the junior section of the CBA for anyone between the ages of 9 and 16.
EN: Postal or telephone only

HR: Normal office hours
PB: *Young archaeologist* (4/yr).
AC: Branch activities (17 branches currently), annual Archaeology Days, field study holidays, Young Archaeologist of the Year Award, etc.

Wales

(*For* **National Parks** *see section 4.5 National Park Archaeologists*)

NA: **Ancient Monuments Board for Wales**
AD: Brunel House, 2 Fitzalan Road, Cardiff CF2 1UY
TL: 01222 500224, fax 01222 500300
FD: 1913
SO: Welsh Office
AI: To advise the Secretary of State for Wales on the exercise of his functions under the Ancient Monuments and Archaeological Areas Act 1979, including scheduling and other matters related to the protection and presentation of ancient monuments. The Board consists of nine members appointed by the Secretary of State.
PB: Annual Report (as House of Commons Paper).

NA: **Cadw, Welsh Historic Monuments**
AD: Crown Building, Cathays Park, Cardiff CF1 3NQ
TL: 01222 500200, fax 01222 826375
FD: 1984 (as Executive Agency)
SO: Is an executive agency within the Welsh Office
AI: Is responsible for carrying out the statutory responsibilities of the Secretary of State for Wales for the preservation, protection and maintenance of ancient monuments, historic buildings, conservation areas and historic wrecks throughout the Principality; also sponsors RCAHMW, grant-aids the four Welsh Archaeological Trusts, and provides the secretariat for the Ancient Monuments Board for Wales and the Historic Buildings Council for Wales (see separate entries for both).
CL: No library, and enquirers should address themselves to RCAMW at Aberystwyth (*see below under Royal*) where the more extensive National Monuments Record is kept. Guidance leaflets are available on the scope of Cadw's work, on the legislation affecting ancient monuments and listed buildings, etc.
EN: Postal and telephone, personal callers by appointment; usually no charge
HR: Mon-Fri 8.30am–5.00pm

PB: Guides to monuments, pamphlets, themed booklets; lists of repair grants offered (two volumes, 1985–93 and 1993–5); information pack and newsletter (4/yr); teachers' packs; cartoon booklets. Some material is produced in Welsh and English. Lists of scheduled ancient monuments and of listed historic buildings. Publications list available for SAE.
AC: Field Monument Wardens keep a check on the condition of ancient monuments. Cadw can provide advice on ancient monuments and historic buildings through its professional archaeologists, architectural historians and conservation architects, and may offer grants for repair, etc. Speakers on relevant topics can be provided. Membership of 'Heritage in Wales' provides a season ticket for all Welsh sites in care, and reduced rates for entry to properties in the care of English Heritage and Historic Scotland.

NA: **Cambrian Archaeological Association**
AD: c/o General Secretary, Dr J M Hughes, The Laurels, Westfield Road, Newport NP9 4ND
TL: 01633 262449
FD: 1846
AI: To examine, preserve and illustrate the ancient monuments and remains of the history, language, manners, customs, arts and industries of Wales and the Marches, and to educate the public in such matters. Its interests extend to other Celtic lands (Cornwall, Brittany, Ireland, Scotland, Isle of Man).
CL: Library maintained at the National Museum of Wales in Cardiff.
EN: Postal or telephone only
PB: *Archaeologia Cambrensis* (annually); occasional monographs (list available for SAE); newsletter (annually).
AC: Annual field meetings; biennial Easter conference; grants and awards for research; annual competition for young amateurs; etc.

NA: **Cambrian Caving Council**
AD: c/o Hon Sec, F S Baguley, White Lion House, Ynys Uchaf, Ystradgynlais, Swansea SA9 1RW
TL: 01639 849519
FD: 1969
SO: Subscriptions, and Schools Council for Wales
AI: (abridged) To encourage the exchange of information; to maintain friendly relations with . . . similar bodies; to encourage the recording of information on sites of spelaeological interest; to encourage conservation.
EN: Postal or telephone

HR: Any reasonable hours

PB: Annual journal; monthly newsletter; other reports (list available for SAE).

AC: Is the national association for caving in the Principality.

NA: **Campaign for the Protection of Rural Wales/ Ymgyrch Diogelu Cymru Wledig (CPRW/ YDCW)** (former titles Council for the Preservation of Rural Wales to 1962, then Council for the Protection of Rural Wales to 1991)

AD: Ty Gwyn, 31 High Street, Welshpool, Powys SY21 7JP

TL: 01938 552525/556212, fax 01938 552741; e-mail cprw@mcr1.geonet.de

FD: 1928

AI: To protect and enhance the scenery and amenity of the countryside, towns and villages of Wales, while encouraging sustainable development.

EN: Postal and telephone only

HR: Mon-Fri 9.00am–5.00pm

PB: *Rural Wales* (3/yr); annual report; other reports; teachers' packs etc.

AC: Monitoring of, and making representations on, local planning matters through its local branches, or nationally to Welsh Office and central government.

NA: **Capel, The Chapels Heritage Society**

AD: c/o Miss S G Beckley (Hon Sec), West Glamorgan Archive Service, County Hall, Oystermouth Road, Swansea SA1 3SN

TL: 01792 471589

FD: 1986

AI: To preserve the nonconformist heritage of Wales.

EN: Postal or telephone only

HR: Normal office hours Mon-Fri

PB: Newsletter (3/yr), information leaflets.

AC: Meetings (2/yr); provides advice to Cadw and to planning authorities about listed chapels.

NA: **Cathedrals and Churches Commission**

AD: Representative Body of the Church in Wales, 39 Cathedral Road, Cardiff CF9 9XF

TL: 01222 231638

FD: 1996

AI: To give advice on the care, conservation, repair and development of the Anglican cathedrals and churches throughout Wales.

NA: **Civic Trust for Wales**

AD: Fourth Floor, Empire House, Mount Stewart Square, Cardiff CF1 6DD

TL: 01222 484606, fax 01222 482086

FD: 1964

SO: Members' subscriptions, donations, and Cadw

AI: To promote high quality in town and country planning and to protect the built heritage. (Affiliated to The Civic Trust.)

EN: Postal, telephone or personal visit (by appointment)

HR: Mornings preferred

PB: *About Wales* (4/yr); and others, list available for SAE.

AC: Conferences, discussions.

NA: **The Council of Museums in Wales**

AD: 32 Park Place, Cardiff CF1 3BA

TL: 01222 225432/228238, fax 01222 668516

FD: 1969

SO: Part-funded by the Welsh Office

AI: (abridged) To foster the preservation and presentation of Welsh heritage; to assist museums in Wales in various ways and to develop a national framework of museum provision in Wales.

EN: Postal, telephone, personal visit

HR: 10.00am–4.00pm

PB: Annual reports.

AC: Study/training meetings (open to non-members if room); exhibitions; database on all aspects of museology; conservation services and advice on the continuing care of artefacts (to archaeologists and others); grants.

The Council for National Parks in Wales *is now based in London at the Council for National Parks.*

NA: **Countryside Council for Cyngor Cefn Gwlad Cymru** (replacing the Nature Conservancy Council and the Countryside Commission in Wales)

AD: Plas Penrhos, Ffordd Penrhos, Bangor, Gwynedd LL57 2LQ

TL: 01248 370444, fax 01248 355782 or 370688

FD: 1991

SO: Welsh Office

AI: As the Government's statutory adviser on wildlife and countryside conservation matters in Wales, the Council is the executive authority for the conservation of habitats and wildlife. Through partners it promotes the protection of landscape, opportunities for enjoyment, and the support of those who live and work in, and manage, the countryside. It enables these partners to pursue countryside management projects through grant aid.

EN: Postal, telephone or personal visit

HR: 8.30am–5.00pm

PB: Newsletter (3/yr); occasional publications (list available for SAE); educational resources.

AC: Has occasionally grant-aided the purchase of land containing archaeological sites; is compiling a list of historic environment features.

NA: **Early Medieval Wales Archaeology Research Group**

AD: c/o Dr Nancy Edwards, School of History and Welsh History, University College of North Wales, Bangor LL57 2DG

TL: 01248 382154, fax 01248 382759

FD: 1984

AI: To promote and communicate research on the archaeology of Wales c AD 400–1100.

EN: Postal only

PB: *Early medieval settlements in Wales c. 400–1100* (1988).

AC: Annual day school; field weekends; occasional conferences.

NA: **Forestry Authority, Wales National Office**

AD: North Road, Aberystwyth SY23 2EF. (Regional offices in Ruthin, Llandrindod Wells and Abergavenny.)

TL: 01970 625866, fax 01970 626177

FD: 1992 (as separate arm of Forestry Commission)

SO: Central government

AI: To implement Government forestry policy.

CL: (Library in Edinburgh head office)

EN: Postal, telephone or personal visit (by appointment)

HR: 8.30am–5.00pm

PB: *Guidelines on forestry and archaeology.*

NA: **Groundwork Cymru Wales**

AD: Fedw Hir, Lwydcoed, Aberdare CF44 0DX

TL: 01685 883880, fax 01685 879990

FD: 1987

SO: Welsh Office, local authorities etc

AI: To bring together local authorities, the private sector and local communities for environmental improvement.

EN: Postal, telephone or personal visit

HR: Normal office hours

PB: Newsletters and other, locally-produced, leaflets and books on topics including heritage interest.

AC: Offer professional help with landscape design, advice on sources of funding etc.

NA: **Historic Buildings Council for Wales**

AD: Brunel House, 2 Fitzalan Road, Cardiff CF2 1UY

TL: 01222 500244 fax 01222 500300

FD: 1981 (originally constituted 1953)

SO: Welsh Office

AI: Statutory body set up to advise the Secretary of State for Wales on matters relating to historic buildings (consists of chairman and six members appointed by the Secretary of State).

PB: Annual report (as House of Commons Paper).

AC: Provides grants towards repair or acquisition of outstanding buildings and towards works which have a significant impact on conservation areas; advises on policy for historic buildings.

National Monuments Record for Wales *see under Royal Commission below.*

Offa's Dyke Association *see under England above.*

Pembrokeshire Coast National Park Authority – no archaeologist but included here for its responsibility for building conservation – The County Office, St Thomas Green, Haverfordwest Pembs SA61 1QZ, tel 01437 764591, fax 01437 769045, e-mail compuserve 100070.1366

NA: **Royal Commission on the Ancient and Historical Monuments of Wales**

AD: Crown Building, Plas Crug, Aberystwyth, SY23 1NJ

TL: (General enquiries) 01970 621233; (Nat Monuments Record) 01970 621200; fax 01970 627701

FD: 1908

SO: The Commission is a non-departmental public body funded by the Welsh Office (and sponsored by Cadw)

AI: To survey, record, publish and maintain a database of ancient, historical and maritime sites, structures and landscapes of Wales. It is reponsible for the National Monuments Record of Wales (which is open daily for public reference), for the supply of archaeological information to the Ordnance Survey for mapping purposes, for the coordination of archaeological aerial photography in Wales, and for the sponsorship of the regional Sites and Monuments Records.

CL: Is the public place of deposit and national collection of records, photographs (ground and aerial), surveys, drawings, maps and databases, complemented by research library. Collections include c. one million photographs, 70,000 drawings, and 30,000 large-scale Ordnance

Survey maps. Site information is in process of computerisation and it is intended to provide an Extended National Database for Wales (EN-DEX), amalgamating site records from the NMR, SMRs, Cadw and other interested bodies. The NMR is now being extended to include maritime sites.

EN: Postal, telephone, fax and personal visit (appointment helpful but not essential)

HR: Mon-Fri 9.30am–4.00pm (reduced service 1.00–2.00pm)

PB: Annual reports; county inventories; thematic studies.

The Royal Institution of South Wales: *this institution's collections are now with Swansea Museum.*

NA: **Severn Estuary Levels Research Committee**

AD: c/o Nigel Nayling, Glamorgan-Gwent Archaeological Trust Ltd, Ferryside Warehouse, Bath Lane, Swansea SA1 1RD

TL: 01792 655208

FD: 1989

AI: To act as an umbrella organisation or forum assisting and fostering archaeological explorations on both sides of the Severn Estuary.

EN: Postal only

PB: Annual reports from 1991; list available for SAE.

AC: Annual meetings; field visits.

NA: **Wales Tourist Board**

AD: Brunel House, 2 Fitzalan Road, Cardiff CF1 1UY

TL: 01222 499909, fax 01222 485031

PB: Annual report; *Tourism Wales* (4/yr); research reports and papers, guides, brochures (list available on request).

NA: **Wales Wildlife and Countryside Link**

AD: Bryn Aderyn, The Bank, Newtown, Powys SY16 2AB

TL: 01686 629194, fax 01686 622339

FD: 1989

AI: Is an umbrella organisation for voluntary bodies whose primary aims are the conservation, protection and quiet enjoyment of the countryside.

EN: Postal

HR: Normal office hours

PB: Newsletter (6/yr); some educational resources.

AC: Meetings, conferences, displays of material.

NA: **Welsh Archaeological Institute**

AD: Old Custom House Building, 41 Dockview Road, Barry, S Glam CF62 5JP (Karl James Langford)

TL: Office 01446 749747; mobile 0589 192233

FD: 1988 (as Glamorgan-Gwent Young Archaeologists' Society)

AI: To advance education in archaeology in Wales.

CL: Small book collection and excavated artefacts.

EN: Postal or telephone

HR: Normal office hours

PB: Newsletter (4/yr); annual report; site reports.

AC: Excavations when possible (eg a Cowbridge site); guided walks to historical and archaeological sites; lectures; leaflets and educational packages; contract work (managed by professional archaeologist).

NA: **Welsh Historic Gardens Trust/Ymddiriedolaeth Gerddi Hanesyddol Cymru**

AD: c/o Hon Sec, Col R Gilbertson, Coed-y-Ffynnon, Lampeter Velfrey, Narberth, Dyfed SA67 8UJ

TL: 01834 283396, fax same

FD: 1989

SO: Countryside Council for Wales, and members' subscriptions

AI: To encourage the appreciation of the garden and landscape heritage of Wales; to assist in compiling the Registers of (1) Historic Landscape, (2) Parks and Gardens in Wales; to develop a strategy for the restoration and conservation of threatened sites and to assist in that work.

CL: Archive of transparencies

EN: Postal, telephone or personal visit (by appointment)

HR: Any reasonable time

PB: Annual journal; newsletter (4/yr); occasional bulletins.

AC: Meetings of the 10 'old-county' branches; collaboration with other conservation organisations; provision of expert advice; practical work in summer; gazetteer of lesser gardens.

NA: **Welsh Institute of Maritime Archaeology and History at the University of Bangor**

AD: c/o Dept of History, Univ Wales Bangor, Gwynedd LL57 2DG

TL: 01248 351151

Function currently limited to providing teaching the maritime element in the undergraduate degree in History.

NA: **Welsh Mills Society/Cymdeithas Melinau Cymru**
AD: c/o Welsh Folk Museum, St Fagans, Cardiff CF5 6XB
TL: 01222 569441, fax 01222 578413
FD: 1984
AI: To study, record, interpret and publicise the wind and water mills of Wales; to advise on their preservation and uses; to encourage working millers.
EN: Postal, telephone
PB: Newsletter (4/yr); *Melin* (annual journal); leaflets on mills.
AC: Conferences, meetings, research, information.

NA: **Welsh Mines Society**
AD: c/o David Bick, Pound House, Newent, Glos GL18 1PS
TL: 01531 820650
FD: 1979
AI: To bring together those interested in any aspect of Welsh mines, including their history and preservation.
EN: Postal
PB: Newsletter (2/yr).
AC: Meetings, research, information, two field meetings/yr.

NA: **The Welsh Office**
AD: Cathays Park, Cardiff, CF1 3NQ
TL: 01222 825111, fax 01222 823036
FD: 1965
SO: Government
AI: Has overall responsibility for (among other things) the town and country planning system in Wales; countryside and conservation; protection of the environment etc.
CL: Extensive collection of air and other photos available without hire charge
EN: Postal, telephone
HR: Normal office hours
PB: Educational resources.
AC: Grant schemes.

NA: **West Wales Maritime Heritage Society**
AD: 44 West Haven, Cosheston, Pembroke Dock, Pembs SA72 4UL (David James, Hon Sec)
TL: 01646 683764 (evenings)
FD: 1984
AI: To bring together maritime interests in the region and to foster active participation in nautical skills such as boat-building (including historical replicas).
CL: Small library

EN: Postal, telephone or personal visit (by appointment)
PB: Newsletter (4/yr); *The secret waterways* (booklet on historic remains in Pembroke–Haverfordwest area).
AC: Lectures, displays and publications, involvement of Sea Cadets etc, two large workshops for boat restoration (steam and sail), etc.

WELSH ARCHAEOLOGICAL TRUSTS

Clwyd-Powys Archaeological Trust 7a Church Street, Welshpool SY21 7DL. Tel 01938 553670, fax 01938 552179

Dyfed Archaeological Trust Ltd The Shire Hall, Carmarthen Street, Llandeilo SA19 6AF. Tel 01558 823121, fax 01558 823133

Glamorgan-Gwent Archaeological Trust Ltd Ferryside Warehouse, Bath Lane, Swansea SA1 1RD. Tel 01792 655208, fax 474469

Gwynedd Archaeological Trust Ltd Fordd y Garth, Bangor LL57 2SE Tel 01248 352535

Scotland

NA: **Ancient Monuments Board for Scotland**
AD: Longmore House, Salisbury Place, Edinburgh EH9 1SH
TL: 0131 668 8600, fax 0131 668 8765
FD: 1953
SO: Central government
AI: To advise the Secretary of State for Scotland on the exercise of his responsibilities under the Ancient Monuments and Archaeological Areas Act 1979.
EN: Postal, telephone or personal visit (by appointment)
HR: 08.30am–5.00pm Mon-Fri
PB: Annual reports.
AC: The Board (whose secretariat is provided by Historic Scotland) meets four times a year, makes an annual tour to some part of Scotland and issues lists of historic buildings and monuments recommended for scheduling.

NA: **Archaeological Diving Unit**
AD: Scottish Institute of Maritime Studies, University of St Andrews, Fife KY16 9AJ
TL: 01334 462919 (mobile 0860 320679), fax 01334 462921
FD: 1986
SO: Dept of National Heritage
AI: To provide a link between UK Government

departments and all those interested in archaeological discoveries underwater; primary duties are to the Protection of Wrecks Act.

CL: Holds documentary information on sites designated under the Protection of Wrecks Act 1973, together with information on sites that are or may be candidates for designation. It is hoped to establish a video archive of sites visited by the ADU.

EN: Postal, telephone, personal visit, computer access

HR: 9.00am–5.00pm

PB: *Guidelines on acceptable standards in underwater archaeology* (1988); *Guide to historic wrecks designated under the Protection of Wrecks Act 1973* (1994) (available on request); ADU leaflet; other publications by staff members in conjunction with other authors/societies.

AC: Can offer lectures, and give advice on a wide range of topics including: site and object identification and dating; site protection and care; legislation; applications to carry out licensed work on protected wrecks; Development Control and Environmental Assessment; work specifications and archaeological contractor's standards; archaeological and conservation methods; diving regulations and safety in underwater archaeology; involvement in training and archaeology underwater; research and fieldwork in the UK and abroad; publication and presentation of results.

NA: **Architectural Heritage Society of Scotland** (formerly the Scottish Georgian Society)

AD: The Glasite Meeting House, 33 Barony Street, Edinburgh EH3 6NX

TL: 0131 557 0019, fax 0131 557 0049

FD: 1957 (present name from 1984)

SO: Government grant and members' subscriptions

AI: The study and protection of good examples of Scottish architecture of all periods.

CL: (Very small library of amenity society publications)

EN: Postal, telephone, personal visit (telephone first)

HR: 9.00am–5.00pm Mon-Fri

PB: *Architectural heritage* (annual); newsletter (2/yr).

AC: Inspects applications to demolish or alter listed buildings or buildings in conservation areas, and if needed makes representations at public inquiries; holds talks, lectures and conferences and arranges visits and tours.

NA: **Artefact Research Unit**

AD: Archaeology Department, National Museums of Scotland, Queen Street, Edinburgh EH2 1JD

TL: 0131 225 7534, fax 0131 557 9498

FD: 1979

SO: National Museums of Scotland

AI: Research on artefacts.

CL: Apart from the museum collections the ARU holds collections of lithic raw materials exploited during prehistory (Scotland and beyond), and also collections of modern knapped material.

EN: Postal, telephone or personal visit

HR: 9.00am-12.30pm; 2.00pm–5.00pm Mon-Fri

NA: **Association of Certificated Field Archaeologists** (Glasgow University)

AD: c/o Dept of Adult Education, 59 Oakfield Avenue, Glasgow G12 8LW

TL: (Secretary) 0141 330 4394

FD: 1987

AI: To promote all aspects of archaeological field survey in Scotland and elsewhere; to cooperate with other authorities/organisations having similar objects (members are holders of the University of Glasgow Certificate in Field Archaeology).

CL: (Records of field surveys undertaken)

EN: Postal and telephone only

HR: From 10.00am

AC: Field surveys and excavations when requested; visits; no public meetings, exhibitions or events.

NA: **Association for the Protection of Rural Scotland**

AD: Gladstone's Land, 3rd Floor, 483 Lawnmarket, Edinburgh EH1 2NT

TL: 0131 225 7012/7013, fax 0131 225 6592

FD: 1926

AI: To stimulate and guide public opinion on the need for action to protect the countryside from undesirable developments.

CL: Building a slide library.

EN: Postal, telephone or visit (preferably by appointment – Mrs Elizabeth Garland)

HR: 9.30am–5.00pm

PB: Annual report, newsletters, occasional publications; photographic slides.

AC: Offers talks on the work of the Association and gives advice on all matters relating to preservation of rural scenery and amenities, etc.

NA: **Association of Regional and Island Archaeologists**
AD: c/o Peter Yeoman, Fife Dept of Economic Development and Planning, Fife House, North Street, Glenrothes, Fife KY7 5LT
TL: 01592 416153
FD: 1990
AI: To coordinate and represent views of regional and island archaeologists to government and to national archaeological and environmental organisations.

Borders Heritage is a 5-year project to research and publish a new historical record of the Borders; Scottish address Borders Council, Dept of Planning and Development, Newtown St Boswells, Melrose, Roxburghshire, TD6 0SA.

NA: **British Geological Survey – Scottish Office** (formerly Institute of Geological Sciences)
AD: Murchison House, West Mains Road, Edinburgh EH9 3LA
TL: 0131 667 1000, fax 0131 668 2683
FD: 1835
SO: NERC
AI: Is the principal Government body for the systematic acquisition and interpretation of geological and related data; publishes geological maps of the UK and provides geological advice to Government departments and other bodies. It is the national repository for borehole and mine-plan data.
CL: Library with considerable collection.
EN: Postal, telephone
HR: 9.00am–4.30pm (4.00pm Friday)
PB: Annual report, maps, memoirs, research reports etc.

NA: **British Waterways** – Scottish Region
AD: Canal House, 1 Applecross Street, Glasgow G4 9SP
TL: 0141 332 6936
FD: 1962
SO: Statutory undertaking
AI: The efficient management of inland waterways for increased benefit to the nation.
EN: Postal, telephone
PB: Leaflets and information sheets.
AC: Speaker service on all aspects of canals past and present.

NA: †**Cairdean nan Taighean Tugha/Friends of Thatched Houses**
AD: c/o J. Souness, 40 Marchmont Crescent, Edinburgh EH9 1HG
TL: 0131 668 1480
FD: 1985
AI: To help retain, by practical means and research, the few remaining traditional thatched buildings in Scotland
CL: Photographic collection
PB: Newsletter (annually).
AC: Local branches

NA: **Centre for Environmental Interpretation (Edinburgh)**
AD: c/o James Carter, University of Edinburgh, 20 Chambers Street, Edinburgh EH1 1JZ
TL: 0131 650 8017, fax 0131 650 6517
FD: (1982 for UK)
SO: Scottish National Heritage
AI: To develop the concept of interpretation as the art of explaining the meaning and significance of sites to visitors.
AC: Training courses on various aspects of interpretation from guided walks to copywriting for leaflets, exhibitions etc.

NA: **Church of Scotland Advisory Committee on Artistic Matters**
AD: 121 George Street, Edinburgh EH2 4YN
TL: 0131 225 5722 ext 359, fax 0131 220 3113
FD: 1934
SO: Church of Scotland
AI: To ensure that all repairs, alterations and renovations to churches in Scotland are carried out in sympathy with the architectural merit and aesthetic quality of the buildings.
CL: Is assembling a collection of building records, photographs etc for Church of Scotland churches.
EN: Postal, telephone, visit (by appointment)
HR: 9.00am–5.00pm
PB: Annual report; *Care for your church* (1984).
AC: Advice on alterations and installation of stained glass, crosses, memorials, etc, is given free to congregations. Maintains list of approved craftspeople and artists.

NA: **The Cockburn Association** [The Edinburgh Civic Trust]
AD: Trunk's Close, 55 High Street, Edinburgh EH1 1SR
TL: 0131 557 8636, fax 0131 557 9387
FD: 1875
AI: To preserve and enhance the amenity of the City of Edinburgh and its neighbourhood.
EN: Postal, telephone or personal visit
HR: 9.00am–5.00pm Mon-Fri
PB: Annual report; newsletter.
AC: Range of relevant activities for members.

Conservation Bureau *see Historic Scotland Conservation Centre (below).*

NA: **Convention of Scottish Local Authorities (COSLA)**
AD: Rosebery House, 9 Haymarket Terrace, Edinburgh EH12 5XZ
TL: 0131 474 9274, fax 0131 474 9292
FD: 1975
AI: To represent and promote the interests of Scottish local government (32 member councils).

NA: **Council for Scottish Archaeology**
AD: c/o National Museums of Scotland, Queen Street, Edinburgh EH2 1JD (Director: Patrick Begg)
TL: 0131 225 7534 ext 386, e-mail CSA@dial. pipex.com also CSA@bbcnc.org.uk
FD: 1944 (as CBA Scotland)
SO: Scottish Office grant, members' subscriptions, local authority grants, charitable trusts, donations
AI: To promote informed opinion on the study and conservation of Scotland's archaeological heritage.
CL: Inventory of Scottish Church Heritage (database: see its own entry below); archive of own publications.
EN: Postal and telephone only
HR: 10.00am–4.00pm Mon-Fri
PB: *Discovery and excavation in Scotland* (annual); newsletter (3/yr); *How to record graveyards*; Adopt-a-Monument scheme leaflet; fieldwalking action pack; other publications (list available for SAE).
AC: Summer school; training weekends; Young Archaeologists (Jane Fletcher, Asst Dir); speaker service (expenses, donation if possible).

Countryside Commission for Scotland *see Scottish Natural Heritage.*

NA: **CTICH (Computers in Teaching Initiative Centre for History, Archaeology and Art History)**
AD: University of Glasgow, 1 University Gardens, Glasgow G12 8QQ
TL: 0141 330 4942, e-mail ctich@glasgow.ac.uk
Internet   http://www.arts.gla.ac.uk/www/ CTICH
FD: 1989
SO: Higher Education Funding Council
AI: To promote and coordinate the use of computers in the teaching of history and archaeology throughout higher education by encouraging the spread of computer-based teaching and the exchange of good software, teaching materials, datasets and pedagogical methods.
PB: *Craft* (newsletter); guide to software; computer bulletin board.

NA: **The Environment Centre**
AD: Drummond High School, Cochran Terrace, Edinburgh EH7 4QP
TL: 0131 557 2135
FD: 1983 (subsumed 1993 within Lothian Regional Council Education Dept)
SO: Lothian Regional Council
AI: To promote innovatory approaches to environmental education, and to support the Education Dept with research on information, provision of training etc [is not so far involved in archaeology].
CL: Maintains IDEAS database (environmental information); photographic slides library.
EN: SAE required for enquiries to database
PB: List available.
AC: Speaker service.

NA: **European Ethnological Research Centre** (*see also Scottish Ethnological Archive*)
AD: c/o Alexander Fenton, National Museums of Scotland, Queen Street, Edinburgh EH2 1JD
TL: 0131 225 7534 ext 302
FD: 1989
SO: Core funding from National Museums of Scotland
AI: (main) Compilation of multi-volume Compendium of Scottish Ethnology.
CL: Collaborates with NMS's Scottish Ethnological Archive; maintains database of farm diaries.
EN: Postal only
HR: 9.00am–5.00pm Mon-Fri
PB: *Review of Scottish culture* (annual journal); Flashback series; Sources in Local History series.

NA: **Farming and Wildlife Advisory Group Scotland**
AD: Rural Centre, Ingliston, Newbridge, Midlothian EH28 8NZ
TL: 0131 335 3999, fax 0131 333 2926
FD: 1971
SO: Members' subscriptions and government
AI: To promote, by bringing together relevant organisations and government bodies, the development of an attractive living countryside

including the conservation and enhancement of wildlife habitats and landscape (etc).
EN: Postal, telephone
HR: 9.00am–5.00pm
PB: Newsletter (3/yr); advisory leaflets and publications (list available for SAE).
AC: Speaker service.

NA: **Forestry Commission**
AD: 231 Corstorphine Road, Edinburgh EH12 7AT (Tim Yarnell, Archaeologist)
TL: 0131 334 0303, fax 0131 334 4473
FD: 1919
SO: Is Govt department
AI: To promote the interests of forestry . . . with a reasonable balance between forestry and conservation; the archaeologist is charged with the management of important archaeological features of all periods.
CL: Data at local level, mostly extracted from SMRs; some of the FC visitor centres hold small collections of material on woodland and agricultural history.
EN: Postal only

NA: **Glasgow West Conservation Trust**
AD: 30 Cranworth Street, Glasgow G12 8AG
TL: 0141 339 0092, fax same
FD: 1990
SO: Glasgow District Council and other sources
AI: The conservation of the built heritage of Glasgow's West End; the promotion of research, the improvement of standards of repair and restoration of historic structures and planned landscapes.
CL: Technical and trade literature on conservation; photographs etc of West End (public may consult by arrangement).
EN: Postal, telephone, personal visit
HR: 09.00am–5.00pm Mon-Fri
PB: Annual report; newsletter (4/yr); *Glasgow West conservation manual* (5 of 15 sections complete so far: 1, Principles/practice; 2, Law and finance; 3, Domestic decorative glass; 4, Stonework; 5, Ironwork).
AC: Empowered to offer conservation grants for approved schemes; conservation masterclasses (Jan–Mar) in partnership with National Trust for Scotland; autumn lecture series (socio-cultural, Sept-Dec) in partnership with Univ Glasgow.

NA: **Historic Buildings Council for Scotland**
AD: Longmore House, Salisbury Place, Edinburgh EH9 1SH

TL: 0131 668 8799, fax 0131 668 8788
FD: 1953
SO: Central government
AI: The Council (whose Secretariat is provided by Historic Scotland) advises the Secretary of State for Scotland on the exercise of his responsibilities under the 1953 Ancient Monuments Act. It meets four times a year, makes an annual tour and lays its Annual Report before Parliament.

NA: **Historic Scotland** (formerly Historic Buildings and Monuments Scotland)
AD: Longmore House, Salisbury Place, Edinburgh EH9 1SH
TL: 0131 668 8600, fax 0131 668 8730
FD: 1984
SO: Exchequer, plus visitors
AI: To safeguard the nation's built heritage and to promote its understanding and enjoyment, making the best use of resources available. (Historic Scotland is an executive agency within the Scottish Office Development Department responsible for administering the laws concerning the protection and management of ancient monuments and historic buildings, and now also of historic wrecks.)
CL: Database of scheduled monuments
EN: Postal, telephone or personal visit
HR: 08.30am–5.00pm Mon-Fri
PB: Annual report; Corporate Plan 1995; *List of ancient monuments in Scotland* (1995); *Memorandum of guidance on listed buildings and conservation areas* (1993); *Scotland's listed buildings: a guide to their protection* (3 rev ed 1993); *Archaeological information and advice in Scotland* (leaflet on sources of information); numerous guide handbooks and leaflets, advice leaflets etc (list available for SAE). *Historic Scotland* (Quarterly supporters' magazine).
AC: Events at properties in its care; exhibitions; speakers available; see also its separate division Scottish Conservation Bureau (below). Provides secretariat for Ancient Monuments Board and Historic Buildings Council (see their separate entries).

NA: **Historic Scotland Conservation Centre Stenhouse**
AD: 3 Stenhouse Mill Lane, Edinburgh EH11 3LR
TL: 0131 443 5635, fax 0131 455 8260
FD: 1980
SO: Historic Scotland
AI: To provide information and advice on conservation (objects and buildings) in Scotland.
CL: Relevant books, videos, periodicals, slide and

photograph collection; databases of conservation suppliers, health and safety information, careers in conservation.

EN: Postal, telephone, personal visit

HR: 9.00am–5.00pm

PB: *Scottish conservation directory*; *Training in conservation*; *Working in conservation*; leaflet; annual report incorporated within that for Historic Scotland.

AC: Administers grants for conservators; maintains register of Scottish conservators; arranges courses for conservators.

NA: **Institute of Field Archaeologists (Scottish Group)**

AD: c/o Dr W L Finlayson, Centre for Field Archaeology, Old High School, 12 Infirmary Street, Edinburgh EH1 1LT

TL: 0131 650 8197

FD: 1985

AI: (As for English IFA) together with examination of implications under Scottish law and practice of any new developments.

EN: Postal

PB: Newsletter (2/yr).

AC: Winter programme of meetings, occasional workshops.

Institute of Maritime Studies *see Archaeological Diving Unit.*

NA: **Inventory of the Scottish Church Heritage**

AD: Accessible by visiting RCAHMS or by writing to Council for Scottish Archaeology (with details of requirements); or by special arrangement with Mr Bruce Hunter at the Graham Hunter Foundation, Restenneth Library, Forfar DD8 2SZ

FD: 1990

SO: Grants

AI: To provide a basic level of information on churches and places and Christian worship in Scotland from the origins of Christianity to the present day, and to be maintained as a current database.

CL: Over 10,000 sites inventoried on dBase IV (v.1.1) .

EN: see above

NA: **Kilmartin House Trust**

AD: Kilmartin, Argyll PA31 8RQ

TL: 015465 10278, fax 015465 10330

SO: Private charitable trust

AI: Is a new centre for archaeological and landscape interpretation, with education programmes for children. Museum to open spring 1997, study centre to follow.

NA: **Landscape Institute Scotland**

AD: 5 Coates Crescent, Edinburgh EH3 7AL

TL: 0131 226 3939

FD: 1929

AI: Is a professional institute representing landscape architects, scientists and managers; seeks to cooperate with other environmental organisations and professions.

EN: Postal

PB: *Landscape Scotland quarterly.*

AC: Members' symposia, conferences, etc.

NA: **Macaulay Land Use Research Institute (MLURI)**

AD: Craigiebuckler, Aberdeen AB15 8QH

TL: 01224 318611, fax 01224 311556

FD: 1987

SO: Scottish Office

AI: Is an independent institute mainly concerned with understanding how land can be used to achieve a range of different objectives.

CL: Books on historical agriculture and pre-1900 land use; geological and land use maps and surveys.

EN: Appointment essential

HR: 8.45am–12.45pm, 1.45–5.15pm Mon-Fri

PB: Annual report; scientific papers; soil, land classification and climatic maps; list available on request.

NA: **Medieval Archaeology Research Group**

AD: c/o Mark Collard (President), Edinburgh City Archaeology, 10 Broughton Market, Old Broughton, Edinburgh EH3 6NU

TL: 0131 558 1040

FD: 1987

AI: To encourage research into the medieval settlement of Scotland.

EN: Postal only

PB: Newsletter (occasional).

AC: Members' forum, annually.

Medieval History *see Scottish Medievalists.*

NA: **John Muir Trust Ltd**

AD: 13 Wellington Place, Leith, Edinburgh EH6 7JD

TL: 0131 554 9101

FD: 1983

SO: Benefactions, bequests, subscriptions etc

AI: To acquire, and manage sensitively, key wild areas.

PB: Newsletter.

AC: Volunteers active in conservation work; archaeological surveys are conducted to assist in management plans of land acquired.

NA: **National Committee on Carved Stones in Scotland**
AD: c/o Society of Antiquaries of Scotland, National Museum of Scotland, Queen Street, Edinburgh EH2 1JD (Chair: John Higgitt, Dept of Fine Art, Edinburgh Univ, 19 George Square, Edinburgh EH8 9LD)
FD: c. 1993
AI: To increase awareness of the importance of Scotland's carved stones and of the threats that face them, and to act as a forum for coordinating programmes for recording and protecting these stones.
EN: Postal
PB: Leaflet 'Principles of recording and preservation'.
AC: To suggest sources of advice on preservation and recording.

NA: **National Register of Archives (Scotland)**
AD: West Register House, Charlotte Square, Edinburgh EH2 4DF
TL: 0131 535 1403
FD: 1945
SO: Government
AI: To provide a source for discovering archives in private ownership.
CL: Nearly 4,000 reports on collections of papers; index to titles of these; and summaries published in the annual reports of the Keeper of Records of Scotland.
EN: Postal, telephone, personal visit
HR: 9.00am–4.45pm Mon-Fri
PB: List available on request.
AC: Advice to private owners of historic papers, and assistance to researchers wishing to gain access to these papers.

NA: **National Trust for Scotland**
AD: 5 Charlotte Square, Edinburgh EH2 4DU (Archaeologist: Robin Turner, The Old Granary, Western Mill Street, Perth PH1 5QP, tel 01738 636711, fax 01738 643143)
TL: (HQ) 0131 226 5922, fax 0131 243 9302
FD: 1931
AI: To promote the permanent preservation, for the benefit of the nation, of lands and buildings in Scotland of historic or national interest or natural beauty.
CL: Sites and monuments record based on NMRS and regional SMRs.

EN: Postal, telephone, personal visit (by appointment)
HR: 9.00am–5.00pm
PB: Annual report; *Guide to properties*; *Heritage Scotland* (4/yr); guides to individual properties.
AC: Archaeological projects include work with volunteers and amateurs; conservation projects include rehabilitation of small vernacular houses.

NA: **Northern Studies Centre**
AD: c/o Mrs Angela Williamson, 8 Rose Street, Thurso KW14 7HH
TL: 01847 894161
FD: 1989
AI: To promote the study of the distinctive culture, history, environment and development of the area.
CL: Records of published work on geology, birds, archaeology, history, etc.
PB: Newsletter (occas); summaries of research work etc.
AC: Lectures, guided walks (which may include archaeological sites) etc.

NA: **Ordnance Survey (Scottish Region)**
AD: Grayfield House, 5 Bankhead Avenue, Edinburgh EH11 4AE
TL: 0131 442 2590 (Marketing 0131 442 3985), fax 0131 453 3021
FD: 1791
SO: Government
AI: To maintain OS mapping and services covering Scotland.
EN: Enquiries may be made direct or via OS Southampton
HR: Normal office hours
PB: Annual report (Southampton); etc (list available for SAE).
AC: Speaker service.

NA: **Pictish Arts Society**
AD: School of Scottish Studies, 27 George Square, Edinburgh EH8 9LD
TL: 0131 332 0277 (Hon Sec, evenings)
FD: 1988
AI: To preserve, study and promote Pictish art and culture and other Dark Age studies.
CL: Archive of relevant publications, photos and drawings being built up for use of artists, scholars and thinkers worldwide.
EN: Postal, telephone, personal visit (appointment essential)
PB: *Pictish Arts Society journal* (3/yr); *A Pictish*

panorama (ed Eric Nicoll, 1996); Perthshire field guide; etc.

AC: Monthly meetings Sept-April; annual conference and craft exhibition; field trips.

NA: **Royal Commission on the Ancient and Historical Monuments of Scotland**

AD: John Sinclair House, 16 Bernard Terrace, Edinburgh EH8 9NX

TL: 0131 662 1456, fax 0131 662 1477; e-mail rcahms.jsh@gtnet.gov.uk Internet URL http://www.open.gov.uk/scotoff/heritage.htm

FD: 1908

SO: Scottish Office

AI: Is a non-departmental public body which records and interprets the man-made environment of Scotland's past, promotes its greater appreciation through a National Monuments Record, and enhances its understanding by selective publication.

CL: Is the main repository for excavation and field survey archives and architectural archives for Scotland (including *Buildings of Scotland* series archives); computer database containing National Archaeological Record (printouts available for nominal charge).

EN: Postal, telephone, personal visit

HR: 9.30am–4.30pm Mon-Thu, 9.30am–4.00pm Fri

PB: Annual review; *Guide to the collections NMRS 1941–1991*; long series of county *Inventories* and other publications on ancient monuments and historic buildings; leaflets and guidebooks etc (list available for SAE).

AC: Occasional seminars.

NA: **Royal Incorporation of Architects in Scotland**

AD: 15 Rutland Square, Edinburgh EH1 2BE

TL: 0131 229 7545, fax 0131 228 2188

FD: 1916

AI: Is the professional body representing the interests of all chartered architects practising in Scotland; has links with the Association for the Protection of Rural Scotland and with the Saltire Society.

PB: Pocket guide series *Illustrated architectural guides to Scotland*; professional journals etc; catalogue available.

AC: Speaker service, gallery, bookshops, local branches.

NA: **Royal Institution of Chartered Surveyors in Scotland**

AD: 9 Manor Place, Edinburgh EH3 7DN

TL: 0131 225 7078, fax 0131 226 3599

FD: 1897

AI: As a professional body, aims to represent the interests of chartered surveyors and to maintain high standards among its members.

PB: List available.

AC: Normal activities for professional association.

NA: **Royal Scottish Geographical Society**

AD: Graham Hills Building, 40 George Street, University of Strathclyde, Glasgow G1 1QE

TL: 0141 552 3330, fax 0141 552 3331

FD: 1884

AI: To further the science of geography, stimulate research and disseminate knowledge about it.

CL: Library (held within the University of Strathclyde) open to public.

EN: Postal, telephone, personal visit

HR: 9.00am–5.00pm Mon-Thur, 9.00am–4.00pm Fri

PB: *Scottish geographical magazine* (3/yr); newsletter; symposia proceedings.

AC: Lectures, symposia, tours, eleven local branches etc.

NA: **Royal Town Planning Institute** – Scotland

AD: 15 Rutland Square, Edinburgh EH1 2BE

TL: 0131 228 5477, fax 0131 228 6477

FD: 1914

AI: As professional body, to promote the professional practice of town and country planning.

PB: *Scottish planner* (c. 6/yr).

AC: Conferences, seminars, support for environmental education projects etc.

NA: **Saltire Society**

AD: 9 Fountain Close, 22 High Street, Edinburgh EH1 1TF

TL: 0131 556 1836, fax 0131 557 1675

FD: 1936

AI: To encourage everything that might improve the quality of life in Scotland and restore the country to its proper place as a creative force in European civilisation.

PB: Newsletter etc; list on request.

AC: Awards for restoration projects etc; historical tours; exhibitions.

NA: **Scottish Archaeological Forum**

AD: c/o John Atkinson (President), Dept of Archaeology, University of Glasgow, G12 8QQ

TL: 0141 330 4917

FD: c. 1970

PB: Series *Scottish archaeological forum*

(1970–81), and occasional publications thereafter.

AC: Conferences, workshops.

NA: †Scottish Archaeological Link
AD: c/o Council for Scottish Archaeology

NA: Scottish Burgh Survey
AD: c/o Dr Pat Torrie, Centre for Scottish Urban History, University of Edinburgh, 17 Buccleuch Place, Edinburgh EH8 9LN
TL: 0131 650 4030
FD: 1978 in original form
SO: Historic Scotland (from 1994) via CSUH
AI: To study the history and archaeology of Scotland's historic burghs and to alert planners, curators and developers to areas of archaeological importance, publishing burgh surveys for public use.
PB: *Historic Kirkcaldy* (1995) is the first of a long series due for publication by Historic Scotland with Scottish Cultural Press. Previously 56 burgh surveys were informally produced between 1978 and 1990; the new series (distributed by Oxbow Books) is considerably extended and deepened.

NA: Scottish Churches Architectural Heritage Trust
AD: 15 North Bank Street, The Mound, Edinburgh EH1 2LP
TL: 0131 225 8644
FD: 1978
SO: Donations and legacies
AI: To offer building repair grants to Scottish churches in regular use for public worship (all denominations).
EN: Postal only
PB: Annual report.

NA: The Scottish Civic Trust
AD: 24 George Square, Glasgow G2 1EF
TL: 0141 221 1466, fax 0141 248 6952
FD: 1967
SO: Central and local government, business and charitable sources
AI: (abridged) The encouragement and promotion of high quality in the built environment; the promotion of new uses for redundant buildings of distinction through 'Buildings at Risk' service; the encouragement of public concern for quality in planning and design (etc).
CL: General 'built environment' references including complete, up-to-date lists of buildings of architectural and historic interest, but no pre-medieval archaeology.

EN: Postal, telephone, personal visit (occasionally)
HR: 9.00am–1.00pm, 2.00pm–5.00pm Mon-Fri
PB: Annual report, newsletter (3/yr), Buildings at Risk bulletin (list available for SAE).
AC: Annual conference, exhibition material, lectures, European Heritage Day coordination, network of local civic amenity societies etc.

Scottish Crannog Research Project *see Scottish Trust for Underwater Archaeology*.

NA: Scottish Ethnological Archive *see also European Ethnological Research Centre*
AD: c/o Dorothy I Kidd (Curator), National Museums of Scotland, Queen Street, Edinburgh EH2 1JD
TL: 0131 225 7534 ext 347, fax 0131 557 9498
FD: 1959
SO: Scottish Office
AI: To record, document and preserve evidence of the social and economic history of the Scottish people through the two-dimensional historical record.
CL: Two main assemblages: the Miss Dickie Collection and the Alasdair Alpin MacGregor Collection (both containing good photographs of Pictish and Early Christian stones etc); bibliographies, maps, diaries, 'ephemera' etc; also some comparative material from outside Scotland; some 700 loose-leaf binders in all. Also taped reminiscences.
EN: Postal, telephone and personal visit (appointment preferred)
HR: 9.00am–5.00pm Mon-Fri
PB: *The Scottish Ethnological Archive* (1988) (description and topic list).
AC: Supplies materials for relevant exhibitions within the NMS and outside it.

The Scottish Field School of Archaeology: *apply to Council for Scottish Archaeology for current information.*

Scottish Georgian Society *see now Architectural Heritage Society of Scotland.*

NA: Scottish Historic Buildings Trust
AD: Saltcoats, Gullane, E Lothian EH31 2AG
TL: 01620 842757, fax same
FD: 1985
SO: Scottish Office
AI: The acquisition and repair of buildings of architectural or historic interest throughout Scotland (in practice, post-conquest).

CL: Relevant books, journals etc; reports and surveys on buildings owned by the Trust.

EN: Postal, telephone and personal visit (appointment essential)

HR: 9.30am–7.30pm

PB: Annual report; newsletter (2/yr).

AC: The trust is unable to grant-aid investigations, research or publications connected with buildings that are not in its ownership, but can give advice on technical aspects of the restoration and conservation of buildings. Occasional Open Days at properties undergoing restoration.

Scottish Industrial Archaeology Survey *is now situated within RCAHMS (see above under Royal Commission).*

NA: **Scottish Industrial Heritage Society**

AD: c/o E T Watt (Secretary), 129 Fotheringay Road, Glasgow G41 4LG

TL: 0141 423 1782

FD: 1984

AI: To promote the study of and interest in the history and development of industry in Scotland, and to secure the preservation and recording of plant, machinery and other relevant remains.

PB: Annual report; *50 Industrial archaeology sites in Scotland* (new edn in preparation); newsletter (3/yr).

AC: Speaker service for adult groups within 50 miles of Glasgow (travel expenses charged).

NA: **Scottish Inland Waterways Association**

AD: c/o G A Hunter OBE OStJ KLJ (Secretary), 139 Old Dalkeith Road, Edinburgh EH16 4SZ

TL: 0131 664 1070

FD: 1968

SO: Subscriptions from canal societies in Scotland

AI: To promote the restoration, use and development of inland waterways in Scotland for all commercial and recreational purposes.

EN: Postal, telephone

AC: Coordinates and assists local canal societies.

Scottish Institute of Maritime Studies *see Archaeological Diving Unit.*

NA: **Scottish Local History Forum**

AD: c/o Elaine Greig (Hon Sec), Huntly House Museum, 142 Canongate, Edinburgh EH8 8DD

TL: 0131 529 4012, fax 0131 557 3346

FD: 1983

AI: To bring people together to promote and share the study of local history in Scotland; to act as a catalyst for action at both local and national levels and to help with the establishment of groups and societies throughout the country.

EN: Postal and telephone only

PB: *Scottish Local History* (3/yr); *A sense of place*; *Exploring Scottish history* (directory of resource centres); resources for school teachers, etc.

AC: AGM/outing, exhibitions, 2 conferences/yr; a few small grants for local history publications.

NA: **The Scottish Medievalists** (*formerly Conference of Scottish Medievalists*)

AD: c/o Dr John Rogers (Hon Sec), 23 Wallacebrae Drive, Danestone, Aberdeen AB22 8YA

TL: 01224 823906

FD: 1959

AI: To further the study of the medieval and Renaissance history of Scotland, including art history, archaeology and place-names.

EN: Postal or telephone

AC: Annual thematic conference.

NA: **Scottish Museum Archaeologists**

AD: c/o Convenor, Dr Robin Hanley, Inverness Museum, Castle Wynd, Inverness IV2 3ED

TL: 01463 237114

FD: 1988

AI: To act as the collective voice for museum archaeologists in Scotland.

AC: Meetings in Edinburgh and elsewhere; working groups on various topics; workshops; commissioned surveys on metal detecting and museums, and on archaeological collections in Scotland, etc. Collaborates with English SMA.

NA: **Scottish Museums Council**

AD: County House, 20–22 Torphichen Street, Edinburgh EH3 8JB

TL: 0131 229 7465, fax 0131 229 2728

FD: 1964

SO: Scottish Office

AI: To improve the quality of museum and gallery provision in Scotland.

EN: Postal, telephone and personal visit

HR: 2.00pm–4.00pm

PB: *Scottish museum news* (2/yr); *Museum abstracts* (12/yr); numerous other publications, bibliographies and reading lists (list on request).

AC: Conservation, advisory work, grant-aid, training seminar programme.

Scottish National Trust *see National Trust for Scotland.*

NA: **Scottish Natural Heritage** (*replaced two former bodies, Nature Conservancy Council for Scotland and Countryside Commission for Scotland*)
AD: Battleby, Redgorton, Perth PH1 3EW
TL: 01738 627921, fax 01738 630583
FD: 1992
SO: Government
AI: Is a statutory body established to secure the conservation and enhancement of, and to foster understanding and facilitate enjoyment of, the natural heritage of Scotland, in a sustainable manner.
EN: Postal, telephone or personal visit (appointment preferred)
HR: 8.30am–5.00pm Mon-Thurs, 8.30am–4.30pm Fri
PB: Annual report; *Who's who in the environment* – Scotland (1993); *Inventory of gardens and designed landscapes in Scotland* (1987–9); list available.

NA: **Scottish Natural History Library**
AD: c/o Dr John Gibson (Chairman and Hon Librarian), Foremount House, Kilbarchan, Renfrewshire PA10 2EZ
TL: 01505 702419
FD: 1974
AI: To collect in one library everything ever published on the natural history of Scotland (including archaeology), for eventual transfer when complete to the National Library of Scotland.
CL: Over 100,000 books and periodicals: the largest separate collection of Scottish natural history books and journals in the world.
EN: Reference only
PB: Annual report; *Scottish naturalist* (3/yr); lists of relevant bibliographies, natural history organisations etc.

NA: **Scottish Office Environment Department**
AD: New St Andrews House, Edinburgh EH1 3TG
TL: 0131 244 4042, fax 0131 244 4822
SO: Is Government Dept
AI: Its numerous responsibilities include the central administration of the town and country planning system, countryside conservation, and the sponsorship of Historic Scotland and RCAHMS.
PB: *Archaeology and planning* (NPP Guideline 5); *Archaeology* – the planning process and scheduled monument procedures (Planning Advice Note 42); etc (list available from Scottish Office Library, Publications Sales, Room 1/44 at address above).

NA: **Scottish Place-Name Society (SPNS)**
AD: School of Scottish Studies, University of Edinburgh, 27 George Square, Edinburgh EH8 9LD (subscriptions to Dr Carole Hough, Hon Treas, Dept of English, University of Glasgow, 12 University Gardens, Glasgow G12 8QQ)
TL: 0141 339 8855
FD: 1996
AI: To further the study of Scottish place-names.
CL: Database being planned
EN: Postal only
PB: Newsletter (annual).
AC: Annual symposium; promoting the publication of a series of analytical volumes on Scottish place-names.

NA: **Scottish Place-Name Survey**
AD: c/o Mr Ian A Fraser, School of Scottish Studies, University of Edinburgh, 27 George Square, Edinburgh EH8 9LD
TL: 0131 650 4162
CL: Archive of early spellings; collection of oral Gaelic material.

NA: **Scottish Railway Preservation Society**
AD: Bo'ness Station, Union Street, Bo'ness, W Lothian EH51 9AQ
TL: 01506 822298
FD: 1961
AI: To preserve, restore and display to the public the equipment and relics of railways in Scotland.
CL: Scottish Railway Exhibition
EN: Postal only
HR: (Volunteers and answerphone)
PB: *Blastpipe* (4/yr); guide books.
AC: Speaker service (no fee).

NA: **Scottish Record Office**
AD: HM General Register House, 2 Princes Street, Edinburgh EH1 3YY
TL: 0131 535 1314, fax 0131 535 1360
FD: 1286 (in present building 1774)
SO: Government
AI: To select, preserve and make available the national archives of Scotland to the highest standards; to promote the growth and maintenance of proper archive provision throughout the country; and to lead the development of archival practice in Scotland.
CL: National archives of Scotland; substantial

deposits of private papers; large collection of plans; maintains National Register of Archives (Scotland) (see separate entry under 'National' above); (computer database of holdings under development).

EN: Postal, telephone, personal visit (note: two different search rooms)

HR: 9.00am–4.45pm Mon-Fri

PB: Annual report; various printed texts and calendars of major national records; information leaflets; school packs; etc.

AC: Exhibitions, occasional talks, training schools on Scottish archives, evening classes on Scottish handwriting, visits for schools and other groups.

NA: **Scottish Records Association**

AD: c/o Scottish Record Office, HM General Register House, Princes Street, Edinburgh EH1 3YY

TL: 0131 535 1314, fax 0131 535 1360

FD: 1977

AI: To encourage the preservation and use of public records in Scotland.

EN: Postal, telephone

HR: As for Scottish Record Office

PB: *Scottish archives* (new journal from 1995); datasheets on various record office holdings, etc.

AC: Discussion forums etc.

NA: **†Scottish Record Society**

AD: c/o Dept of Scottish History, University of Glasgow, Glasgow G12 8QQ

TL: 0141 339 8855 ext 5682, fax 0141 330 4808

FD: 1897

AI: To publish calendars, indexes of public records and private muniments relative to Scotland for the use of historians and genealogists.

PB: Calendars and indexes.

AC: (No research undertaken for private individuals)

NA: **Scottish Society for Conservation and Restoration**

AD: Administrator, SSCR, Glasite Meeting House, 33 Barony Street, Edinburgh EH3 6NX

TL: 0131 556 8417, fax 0131 557 5977

FD: c. 1975

AI: To promote the conservation and restoration of Scotland's historic and artistic artefacts, seeking to maintain and improve standards of practice.

EN: Postal only

PB: *SSCR journal* (4/yr); bulletins on special

topics; conference proceedings; other publications.

AC: One-or two-day meetings, lectures, visits with a conservation content.

Scottish Society for Industrial Archaeology *see Scottish Industrial Heritage Society.*

NA: **Scottish Society for Northern Studies** (*originated as Scottish branch of the Viking Society for Northern Research*)

AD: c/o School of Scottish Studies, University of Edinburgh, 27 George Square, Edinburgh EH8 9LD

TL: 0131 650 4162

FD: 1964/5

AI: To provide a Scottish meeting ground for papers and informal discussion on subjects in various fields concerned with Scandinavian and related cultures.

EN: Postal, telephone

HR: Normal office hours

PB: *Northern studies* (annual); conference proceedings; list available for SAE.

AC: Conferences and symposia.

NA: **Scottish Tourist Board**

AD: 23 Ravelston Terrace, Edinburgh EH4 3EU

TL: 0131 332 2433, fax 0131 343 1513

NA: **Scottish Trust for Underwater Archaeology**

AD: University of Edinburgh Department of Archaeology, Infirmary Street, Edinburgh EH1 1LT

TL: 0131 650 2368, fax 0131 650 2369, e-mail ndixon@hsyl.ssc.ed.ac.uk

FD: 1988

SO: Research grants, donations, subscriptions

AI: To promote the research, recording and protection of Scotland's underwater heritage; to raise awareness through training, lectures, exhibitions and publications.

EN: Postal, telephone, personal visit (sometimes)

HR: 11.00am–4.00pm Mon-Fri during Oct–Dec, and on irregular days for rest of year

PB: Annual report; newsletter.

AC: Training courses ranging from one day to several weeks' duration; autumn/winter seminar series; occasional exhibitions in conjunction with museums; survey and excavation; contract and consultancy services; advice on all aspects of underwater archaeology including legislation, Health and Safety Executive regulations; work performed in both marine and freshwater environments; special interest in submerged settlements and pre-16th century ships and boats. Replica crannog in Loch Tay.

NA: **The Scottish Urban Archaeological Trust Ltd**
AD: 55 South Methven St, Perth PH1 5NX
TL: 01738 622393, fax 01738 631626
FD: 1982
SO: Project funding by Historic Scotland plus some local authorities and developers
AI: To understand the origins and development of urban centres in Scotland through excavation and research.
CL: Excavation archives for historic burghs (pending transfer to NMRS and SMRs); database.
EN: (Within reason!) Postal, telephone, personal visit (by appointment)
HR: 8.30am–12.30pm, 1.30–4.30pm
PB: Annual report; excavation monograph(s); articles in journals; booklets.
AC: Exhibitions, participation in conferences; speaker services (expenses charged and voluntary donations welcome).

NA: **Scottish Vernacular Buildings Working Group**
AD: c/o Secretary, Margaret King, Arbroath Museum, Signal Tower, Ladyloan, Arbroath DD11 1PU
TL: 01241 875598
FD: 1972
AI: To record, study and promote traditional buildings in the Scottish countryside, especially those with little or no statutory protection.
EN: Postal, telephone
HR: Normal museum hours
PB: *Vernacular building* (annual); *Highland vernacular building* (1993).
AC: Annual conference, normally in spring, and one-day autumn meeting.

Scottish Vocational Qualifications (SVQs) *see COSQUEC entry under England above.*

NA: **Scottish Wildlife and Countryside Link**
AD: PO Box 64, Perth PH2 0TF
TL: 01738 630804, fax 01738 643290
FD: 1987
SO: WWF-UK, Scottish Office, Scottish Natural Heritage, members' subscriptions
AI: To provide a forum for liaison for the main Scottish voluntary environmental bodies (including archaeological organisations), and to help coordinate action on issues of mutual concern.

EN: (Within limits!) Postal or telephone
HR: 9.00am–4.00pm Mon-Fri
AC: Members' meetings; seminars (sometimes open to public); annual conference.

SCRAN 2000 *see entry in Section 4.9 Museum catalogues.*

NA: **†SEARCH, Sheffield Environmental and Archaeological Research Campaign in the Hebrides**
AD: c/o Professor Keith Branigan, Department of Archaeology and Prehistory, University of Sheffield, Northgate House, West Street, Sheffield S1 4ET
PB: Five-volume series planned, 1995–.

NA: **Society of Antiquaries of Scotland**
AD: National Museum of Scotland, Queen Street, Edinburgh EH2 1JD
TL: 0131 225 7534
FD: 1780
AI: 'The study of the antiquities and history of Scotland, more particularly by means of archaeological research' (from 1783 Charter).
CL: Some of the Society's archive and MSS material is held in the National Museums of Scotland Library in Queen Street (open Mon-Fri 10.00am–12.30pm, 2.00pm–5.00pm except Friday, when closes 4.30pm: tel. 0131 225 7534 ext 369)
EN: Postal, telephone (24-hour answerphone) or personal visit (by appointment only)
HR: 9.00am–5.00pm (but part-time staff only)
PB: *Proceedings* (annual); monograph series; newsletter (2/yr).
AC: Meetings and lectures (some open to public); Rhind Lecture series; conferences; seminars.

Society of Scottish Medievalists *see Scottish Medievalists.*

NA: **Soutra Hospital Archaeoethnopharmacological Research Project (SHARP)**
AD: Dr Brian Moffatt, 5 Fala Village, Pathhead, Midlothian EH37 5SY
TL: 01875 833248
SO: Grants and members' subscriptions
AI: To explore the medical practices of a medieval monastic hospital.
CL: Mobile exhibitions
PB: *SHARP practice reports* (irregular).
AC: Open days on excavation: Easter weekend, last weekend in August, and all August afternoons except Mondays.

NA: **Tayside and Fife Archaeological Committee**

AD: c/o John Sherriff (Sec), 21 Burleigh Crescent, Inverkeithing, Fife KY11 1DQ
FD: c.1976
SO: Self-funding
AI: To promote archaeology, in all its forms, within Tayside and Fife and to act as liaison between amateur and professional.
EN: Postal only
PB: *Journal* (1995–).
AC: Annual conference; promotion of classes in fieldwalking.

Thatched houses (Friends of) *see Cairdean nan Taighean Tugha*.

NA: **UNIVED Technologies Ltd**
AD: 16 Buccleuch Place, Edinburgh EH8 9LN
TL: 0131 650 8390, fax 0131 650 6532, e-mail brian.verph@ed.ac.uk
FD: 1981
SO: University of Edinburgh
AI: Is contact for all Univ Edinburgh departments offering consultancies.
(Included here for identification purposes only.)

NA: **VESARP, Viking and Early Settlement Archaeological Research Project**
AD: c/o Professor C D Morris, Dept of Archaeology, University of Glasgow, Glasgow G12 8QQ
TL: 0141 330 5690/6058, fax 0141 307 8044
FD: 1978
SO: Grants from Historic Scotland, British Academy etc
AI: To investigate by fieldwork and excavation the nature of Viking settlement and economy and its relationship to pre-existing native settlements, primarily in North Britain.
EN: Postal, telephone, personal visit (by appointment only), JANET
PB: (Various monographs and articles)
AC: Excavation, survey, post-excavation, publication.

NA: **Whithorn Trust**
AD: 45/47 George St, Whithorn DG8 8NS
TL: 01988 500508
FD: 1986
SO: Historic Scotland, local authorities, archaeological trusts, donations
AI: Archaeological research in the town of Whithorn and its interpretation to the interested public.
CL: Whithorn Priory site with ruins, crypts, carved stone monuments.
EN: Postal, telephone or personal visit

HR: 10.00am–3.00pm Mon-Fri
PB: Annual *Whithorn lectures*; leaflets; interim reports of annual excavations; final report of 6-year excavation.
AC: Exhibitions regularly updated; lectures.

Ireland

Northern Ireland and the Republic are merged for convenience in this list. Much of the information comes from questionnaires filled in by the organisation concerned; in some cases (eg where no reply was received) information has been assembled from other sources. Government departments and statutory bodies may have only address and telephone shown; other details are provided where they seem helpful. Local archaeological/historical societies in Ireland are far too numerous to list here, and if your local library or museum cannot help, you are advised to consult the annual directory given in the magazine *Archaeology Ireland*.

NA: **Association of Local Authorities of Northern Ireland**
AD: 123 York Street, Belfast BT15 1AB
TL: 01232 249286, fax 01232 326645
FD: 1973
SO: Voluntary organisation
AI: To represent the interests of District Councils in the province.

NA: **Association of Young Irish Archaeologists**
AD: (rotates between universities of Belfast, Cork, Dublin and Galway; last known is c/o Dept of Archaeology and Palaeoecology, School of Geosciences, The Queen's University, Belfast BT7 1NN)
FD: 1968
AI: To provide a forum for communication between students of archaeology at universities in the Republic of Ireland and Northern Ireland.
AC: Annual conference, essentially for young professional archaeologists.
(*NB do not confuse with Irish Young Archaeologists' Club for children: see below.*)

Ballyhoura Hills Project *see Discovery Programme*.

NA: **Belfast Civic Trust**
AD: 28 Bedford Street, Belfast BT2 7FE
TL: 01232 238437
FD: 1982
AI: To promote high standards of planning and architecture, to educate the public in the

geography, history, natural history and architecture of the Belfast area, and to secure the preservation, protection, development and improvement of features of historic or public interest in the Belfast area.
PB: Magazine (2/yr); urban trail leaflets.

NA: **Belfast Naturalists' Field Club**
AD: c/o Richard S J Clarke (Hon Sec), 78 Kings Road, Belfast BT5 6JN
TL: 01232 797155
FD: 1863
AI: To make a practical study of the natural sciences and archaeology in Ireland.
PB: Annual report.
AC: Field trips, winter lectures, exhibitions etc.

NA: **Bord Fáilte Éireann** (Irish Tourist Board)
AD: Baggot Street Bridge, Dublin 2
TL: +(353) 1 602 4000, 1 661 6500
PB: *Ireland of the welcomes* (magazine containing occasional archaeological articles).

NA: **An Bord Pleanála** (Irish Planning Board)
AD: Floor 3, Blocks 6 and 7, Irish Life Centre, Lower Abbey Street, Dublin 1
TL: +(353) 1 872 8011
FD: 1976
AI: Is the statutory corporation responsible for planning appeals.

NA: **Conservation Volunteers Ireland**
AD: PO Box 3836, Dublin
TL: +(353) 1 668 1844
AI: To create awareness of and provide practical opportunities for people to protect and advance Ireland's natural and cultural heritage.
AC: Various projects, from one day to much longer.

NA: **Conservation Volunteers Northern Ireland**
AD: Dendron Lodge, Clandeboye Estate, Bangor, Co Down BT19 1RN
TL: 01247 853778, fax 01247 853776
FD: 1983
AI: Like the British Trust for Conservation Volunteers (BTCV), of which it is part, brings together volunteers to carry out practical conservation projects.
CL: Slides available (without charge to affiliated groups) on all aspects of practical conservation work.
AC: Six regional offices; speaker service etc.

NA: **Council for Nature Conservation and the Countryside**

AD: Environment and Heritage Service, 5–33 Hill Street, Belfast BT1 2LA
TL: 01232 235000
FD: 1989
SO: Is statutory body
AI: To advise DOE(NI) on nature conservation issues.
PB: Annual report; occasional policy statements, eg on peatland conservation.

NA: **Council for the Protection of Irish Heritage Objects**
AD: c/o J G Lefroy (Chairman), Carriglas Manor, Longford, Co Longford
TL: (Chairman) +(353) 43 45165, fax +(353) 43 41026; Secretary +(353) 44 66344, fax +(353) 44 66245
FD: 1995
SO: Victims of Irish heritage object thefts
AI: To combat the theft damage or vandalism to Irish heritage objects (eg fine arts, antiques, architectural 'salvage', statuary/monuments) in private or voluntary hands. (Possibly extending to official hands in future.)
EN: Postal or fax preferred; also telephone, or personal visit by appointment
HR: 8.30am–8.30pm 'be merciful'
AC: Meetings for members, especially to help in the recovery of property and the conviction of criminals; liaison with police forces of British Isles; campaigning for changes in the law and procedures to enable the forces of law to operate more justly and effectively.

NA: **Department of Agriculture for Northern Ireland (DANI)**
AD: Dundonald House, Upper Newtownards Road, Belfast BT4 3SB
TL: 01232 524512, fax 01232 482245
AI: Administers the Government's agricultural, horticultural, fisheries, forestry, arterial drainage, inland navigation and rural development policies; endeavours to balance the need for economic growth with conservation and enhancement of the countryside (etc).
PB: Annual report, various other publications (list available).

NA: **The Discovery Programme Ltd**
AD: 13–15 Hatch Street, Dublin 2
TL: +(353) 1 661 3111 ext 3144
FD: 1991
SO: Company limited by guarantee (since Jan 1996); funding from National Lottery through the Heritage Council.

AI: To enhance understanding of Ireland's past through an integrated programme of archaeological and related research and to disseminate the results of such research. Four projects have been established, addressing issues in North Munster, the Ballyhoura Hills, the Western Stone Forts and Tara.

PB: *The Discovery Programme: strategies and questions; Discovery Programme reports 1, 2 and 3*; guidebook on Tara; etc.

NA: **Dublin Historic Settlement Group**
AD: c/o Professor Anngret Simms, Dept of Geography, University College Dublin, Belfield, Dublin 4
FD: 1975
AI: To provide a cross-disciplinary forum for archaeologists, historians and geographers.

NA: **Dublin Institute for Advanced Studies**
AD: 10 Burlington Road, Dublin 4
TL: +(353) 1 668 0748, fax 668 0561
SO: University College Dublin

NA: **ENFO, The Environmental Information Service**
AD: 17 St Andrew Street, Dublin 2
TL: +(353) 1 679 3144, fax +(353) 1 679 5204
FD: 1990
SO: DoE, Republic of Ireland
AI: To help protect and enhance the environment by promoting a wider understanding and fuller awareness of the world around us, to promote the concept of individual responsibility for protection of the environment (etc); to this end provides convenient public access to wide-ranging and authoritative information on the environment.
CL: Environmental reference library for general public use: access to international databases.
EN: Postal, telephone and personal visit
HR: 10.00am–5.00pm Mon-Sat
PB: Series of Briefing Sheets (eg Medieval Dublin; Georgian Dublin).
AC: Exhibitions with environmental themes (eg 'Disappearing landscapes – aerial archaeology in Ireland'; 'Peat').

NA: **Environment and Heritage Service: Historic Monuments and Buildings**
AD: 5–33 Hill Street, Belfast BT1 2LA
TL: 01232 235000, fax 01232 310288
FD: 1950 (as Archaeological Survey NI); accessible to public from 1992: agency status from 1.4.96
SO: UK government

AI: To protect, record and conserve monuments and buildings in Northern Ireland, and to enhance public awareness by publicity, publications and education; to list buildings of special architectural or historic interest and to schedule a selection of historic monuments; to issue excavation licences; and to maintain the Monuments and Buildings Record (now including maritime sites and historic wrecks).
CL: Monuments and Buildings Record covering some 14,000 archaeological sites and monuments, industrial sites, historic buildings, historic gardens, many thousands of photographs and drawings, slides etc, plus extensive library.
EN: Postal, telephone or personal visit
HR: 9.30am–1.00pm, 2.00pm–4.30pm
PB: *Finding and minding* (triennial reports up to 1992); archaeological monographs; State Care and Scheduled Historic Monuments to 1995, lists of historic monuments; slide packs; leaflets, etc (list available for SAE).

NA: **Federation of Local History Societies [Ireland]**
AD: c/o Rothe House, Kilkenny
TL: Kilkenny 22893
PB: *Local history review* (annual).

NA: **Federation for Ulster Local Studies**
AD: 8 Fitzwilliam Street, Belfast BT9 6AW
TL: 01232 235254, fax same
FD: 1975
SO: Central Community Relations Unit
AI: To promote the study and recording of the history, antiquities and folk-life of Ulster; to encourage the provision of the necessary services to this end; to develop communication and cooperation among voluntary associations and other institutions. The Federation covers the old province of Ulster, ie the modern state of Northern Ireland plus the neighbouring counties of Donegal, Cavan and Monaghan.
EN: Postal, telephone or personal visit
HR: 9.30am–5.00pm
PB: *Ulster Local Studies* (2/yr); newsletter (2/yr); occasional publications; information sheets (eg on grant sources); teachers' resource packs.
AC: AGM, autumn seminar, training courses; insurance cover scheme. Has some 70 local societies and associated institutional members.

NA: **Forest Service [Irish Republic]**
AD: Dept of Agriculture, Food and Forestry, Leeson Lane, Dublin 2
TL: +(353) 1 678 9011, fax +(353) 1 607 2902/12

PB: *Forestry and archaeology guidelines* (1992).

NA: **Forest Service, Dept of Agriculture for Northern Ireland**
AD: Dundonald House, Upper Newtownards Road, Belfast BT4 3SB
TL: 01232 520100
AI: Is responsible for all aspects of forestry.

NA: **Friends of Medieval Dublin**
AD: c/o Dept of Medieval History, Arts-Commerce Building, University College, Belfield, Dublin 4
TL: +(353) 1 706 8100 (Dr H B Clarke, Chairman), fax +(353) 1 283 7022 (combined Departments of History)
FD: 1976
AI: Founded as an interdisciplinary working group of experts with the aim of 1. promoting studies of medieval Dublin, 2. diffusing knowledge of medieval Dublin, 3. offering advice to decision-making bodies as to the best way of promoting medieval Dublin in the modern city.
EN: Postal, telephone, personal visit
AC: Occasional lectures and seminars; preparation of a map of County Dublin in the medieval period; regular liaison with Dublinia visitor centre (interprets the period 1170–1540) at St Michael's Hill, Dublin 8; adjacent to Dublinia in Synod Lodge is a 'small foundling research facility'.

NA: **Geographical Society of Ireland**
AD: c/o Dr Jacinta Prunty, Dept of Geography, University College, Belfield, Dublin 4
TL: +(353) 1 706 8174
FD: 1934
AI: To stimulate interest in the study of geography.
PB: *Irish geography*
AC: Meetings, excursions.

NA: **Geological Survey of Ireland**
AD: Beggars Bush, Haddington Road, Dublin 4
TL: +(353) 1 660 9511, fax +(353) 1 668 1782

NA: **Geological Survey of Northern Ireland**
AD: 20 College Gardens, Belfast BT9 6BS
TL: 01232 666595, fax 01232 662835
FD: 1947
SO: NI Dept of Economic Development
AI: To provide the main N Ireland centre for earth science information and expertise (work relates directly to mineral, energy and groundwater resources, land use, geological hazards and the protection of the environment).

CL: Geology field documents sometimes include archaeological information; also borehole data; 1:50 000 scale geological maps, geological memoirs, etc.
EN: Postal, telephone, personal visit and e-mail d.reay@bgs.ac.uk
HR: 9.00am–5.00pm
PB: (None specific to archaeology)

NA: **Group for the Study of Irish Historic Settlement**
AD: c/o Michael O'Hanrahan, 12 Oak Road, Dukes Meadow, Kilkenny
TL: Kilkenny 21667
FD: 1969
AI: (abridged) To produce and circulate useful information concerning Irish historic settlement; to promote and coordinate studies of particular aspects of settlement; (etc).
PB: Bulletin.

NA: **HEARTH**
AD: 185 Stranmillis Road, Belfast BT9 5DU
TL: 01232 381263, fax 01232 682528
FD: 1972/1978
SO: Grants etc
AI: Is a housing association (from 1978) managed jointly by UAHS and the National Trust to restore historic buildings at risk, to provide either rental housing or property for sale using the sister organisation, Hearth Revolving Fund (from 1972).

NA: **The Heritage Council (An Chomhairle Oidhreachta)**
AD: Rothe House, Kilkenny
TL: +(353) 56 70777
FD: 1995 (in present form)
SO: Statutory body
AI: To propose policies and priorities to identify, protect, preserve and enhance awareness of Ireland's heritage in archaeology, architecture, flora and fauna, landscape, heritage gardens and inland waterways. The Council has special responsibility for buildings of architectural or historic importance in public ownership. It will ensure the coordination of all activities in the heritage field and decide on the distribution of funds allocated to it for heritage works.
EN: Postal or telephone
PB: Annual reports.
AC: Arranges meetings with various organisations in relation to heritage matters; assists funding of publications; has advisory commit-

tees on wildlife, archaeology, architecture and waterways.

NA: **Historic Buildings Council for Northern Ireland**
AD: 5–33 Hill Street, Belfast BT1 2LA
TL: 01232 235000, fax 01232 310288
FD: 1973
SO: Government
AI: To provide advice to DOE(NI) on the listing of buildings of special architectural or historic value, and on the designation of conservation areas.
PB: Annual and triennial reports.

Historic Monuments and Buildings, Northern Ireland *see Environment and Heritage Service.*

NA: **Historic Monuments Council**
AD: 5–33 Hill Street, Belfast BT1 2LA
TL: 01232 235000, fax 01232 310288
FD: 1971
SO: Government
AI: To advise DOE(NI) on the exercise of its powers under the Historic Monuments Act (NI) 1971.
PB: Annual report.

NA: **Inland Waterways Association of Ireland**
AD: c/o Stone Cottage, Claremont Road, Killiney, Co Dublin (permanent referral address)
TL: +(353) 1 285 2258
FD: 1954
AI: To promote the development, use and maintenance of Ireland's navigable rivers and canals.
PB: Newsletter (4/yr); guide books etc.
AC: Campaigns against threatened closures and focuses interest and activity on the restoration of closed navigations. Boat rallies etc.

NA: **Inland Waterways Northern Ireland**
AD: c/o Jim Davis, 61 Victoria Rise, Carrickfergus, BT38 7UR
TL: 01960 366207
FD: 1992
AI: To promote the preservation of N Ireland's inland water heritage and the development of a linked and fully working system as a recreational resource for all.
PB: Annual report; newsletter (4/yr).

NA: **The Institute for the Conservation of Historic and Artistic Works in Ireland**
AD: 73 Merrion Square, Dublin 2 (Registered address)
TL: +(353) 1 661 5133, fax +(353) 1 661 5372 (Maighréad McParland, Hon Sec)

FD: 1991
AI: To promote for the benefit of Ireland the preservation and conservation of historic and artistic works therein.
EN: Postal, telephone
HR: 10.00am–6.00pm
AC: Organising lectures and courses. The Institute is currently under development towards becoming a full professional (accrediting) institution. *See also Irish Professional Conservers' and Restorers' Association below.*

NA: **Institute of Irish Studies**
AD: 8 Fitzwilliam Street, Belfast BT9 6AW
TL: 01232 245133 ext 3388, e-mail a.day@ qub.ac.uk
FD: 1965
SO: The Queen's University of Belfast
AI: To encourage interest and to promote and coordinate research in those fields of study which have a particular Irish interest [archaeology being one of the main foci].
CL: Full text database transcriptions of the OS Memoirs of Ulster parishes of the 1830s (38 to 40 printed volumes prepared in association with the Royal Irish Academy, Dublin).
PB: Numerous, eg volumes of place-name studies (list available for SAE).
AC: Is a teaching institution with courses in archaeology, geography, history etc for BA, MA and Diploma courses etc. Houses, on behalf of Environment and Heritage Service: Historic Monuments and Buildings (see above), the Maritime Archaeology Project (Colin Breen, Fellow: e-mail c.breen@uk.ac.qub). This is a computerised database of all underwater archaeological sites (wrecks, harbour works, submerged settlements, estuarine sites) in N Ireland coastal waters.

IQUA *see Irish Association for Quaternary Studies.*

NA: **Irish Archaeological Wetland Unit**
AD: c/o Dept of Archaeology, University College Dublin, Belfield, Dublin 4 (Director: Aonghus Moloney)
TL: +(353) 1 706 8728, mobile tel 088 544259, fax +(353) 1 706 1184
FD: 1990
SO: Office of Public Works (accommodation provided by UCD)
AI: To survey, investigate and publish all archaeological material found in the midland raised

bogs of Ireland, especially those being exploited industrially.

CL: No collections or library, but computer database on wetland sites, not currently accessible.

EN: Postal, telephone, personal visit (appointment only, from Nov to May)

HR: 9.30am–5.30pm Mon-Fri, Nov-May

PB: *Transactions* series (ISSN 0791–8186: list available).

NA: **Irish Architectural Archive**

AD: 73 Merrion Square, Dublin 2

TL: +(353) 1 676 3430

FD: 1976

SO: Dept of Arts, Culture and the Gaeltacht; Dept of the Environment; Office of Public Works

AI: Primarily, to record historic buildings throughout Ireland, to collect records of all types relating to Ireland's architectural heritage, and to make these freely available to the public.

CL: Photographs (c. 250,000), architectural drawings (c. 50,000), books (c. 10,000), news cuttings etc; computer database of biographical information on c. 2,000 architects; information on conservation and restoration of old buildings.

EN: Postal, telephone, personal visit, computer network

HR: 10.00am–1.00pm, 2.30pm–5.00pm Tues-Fri

PB: List available.

AC: Can produce, on commission, architectural reports and photographic surveys.

NA: **Irish Association of Professional Archaeologists**

AD: c/o Declan Hurl (Sec), at Environment Agency, Historic Monuments and Buildings, 5–33 Hill Street, Belfast BT1 2LA

TL: 01232 235000

FD: 1973

AI: To promote contact, collaboration and co-operation between professional archaeologists in Ireland, to express corporate professional opinions on archaeological matters throughout the country, to improve archaeological standards, to establish contact with similar associations and to promote by discussion and action the solution of practical and academic problems of archaeology in Ireland.

PB: Newsletter (2/yr).

AC: Two meetings a year.

NA: **Irish Association for Quaternary Studies (IQUA)**

AD: c/o Kevin Barton (Hon Sec IQUA), Applied Geophysics Unit, University College Galway

TL: Galway 524411, fax Galway 525700

FD: (mid-1970s)

AI: To encourage the study of the Quaternary period in Ireland, drawing on many specialities (archaeology, botany, climatology, geology, geography, soil science and zoology).

EN: Postal

PB: Newsletter (2/yr); field guides (list available from Catherine Delaney, Coastal Resources Centre, Dept of Geography, UC Cork).

AC: Field excursions, annual symposium, annual evening lecture by distinguished academic visiting Ireland, etc.

NA: **Irish Georgian Society**

AD: 74 Merrion Square, Dublin 2

TL: +(353) 1 676 7053, fax +(353) 1 662 0290

FD: 1958

AI: To encourage an interest in and preservation of distinguished examples of architecture in Ireland, north and south, and to provide comment on planning applications.

EN: Postal, telephone, personal visit

HR: 9.30am–5.00pm

PB: Bulletin; newsletter (annual); *A bibliography of Irish architectural history* (1988); *Restoring your old building*, etc.

AC: Provides grants to save buildings; lectures, tours, conferences.

NA: **Irish Heritage Education Network**

AD: c/o Denise Ferran, Education Department, Ulster Museum, Belfast BT9 5AB

TL: 01232 381251 ext 225

AI: To promote heritage education in Ireland through museums, galleries, etc, and to provide a forum for contact and support between workers in education and in museums . . . to monitor and influence education policy, and encourage the use of museums by all sections of the community.

Irish museums, both Northern and Republic, are listed regularly in Archaeology Ireland *supplements.*

NA: **Irish Museums Association**

AD: c/o National Archives, Bishop Street, Dublin 8

TL: +(353) 1 478 3711, fax +(353) 1 478 3650

FD: 1970s

AI: To further the work of museums throughout

Ireland; promote professional standards; provide support for members; and encourage exchange of ideas through seminars, workshops and training courses.

EN: Postal, telephone, personal visit
HR: 9.00am–5.30pm Mon-Fri
PB: *Museum Ireland* (annual); newsletter; directory *Support and funding for museums* (1990).
AC: Seminars, meetings, lectures, outreach training programme, acts as host to the Gulbenkian/ Norwich Union Awards for Museums and Galleries in Ireland.

NA: **Irish Peatland Conservation Council**
AD: Capel Chambers, 119 Capel Street, Dublin 1
TL: +(353) 1 872 2397/2384
FD: 1982
SO: Voluntary charitable organisation
AI: To campaign for preservation of a representative sample of Irish bogs; to identify and monitor peatland sites of conservation value; to make the public aware of the need for peatland conservation; to raise funds to purchase threatened bogs and for educational programmes.

NA: **Irish Planning Institute (Institiúid Pleanála na hÉireann)**
AD: 8 Merrion Square, Dublin 2
TL: +(353) 1 676 2310, fax +(353) 1 661 0948
FD: 1975
AI: (abridged) Is the professional body representing most professional planners involved in environmental planning; aims to raise standards (etc), to encourage environmental awareness in the community (etc).

NA: **Irish Professional Conservation and Restorers' Association**
AD: c/o Alison Muir (Sec), Ulster Museum, Belfast BT9 5AB
TL: 01232 381251
FD: 1982
AI: To promote the practice of conservation and restoration to internationally accepted standards in public and private bodies.
EN: Postal or telephone
HR: Normal office hours
PB: Newsletter (occas); *Irish conservation directory* (2 ed 1995?); guidelines for various aspects in preparation.
AC: AGM, spring plenary meeting, occasional events and exhibitions.

Irish Society for Archives *see entry in Section 2.1 Record Offices.*

Irish Stone Axe Project (established 1990): c/o Gabriel Cooney, Dept of Archaeology, University College Dublin, Dublin 4 (database on petrology, morphology, context and history of each axe).

Irish Tourist Board *see Bord Fáilte.*

NA: **Irish Underwater Archaeological Research Team (IUART)**
AD: c/o Graham Clines, 25 Cairnmore Park, Lisburn, BT28 2DT
TL: 01846 677847
FD: 1989
AI: To act as advisory agency to State and other bodies.
AC: Training for sports divers and archaeologists, using a programme adapted from the international 4-stage course structure. Involved with research and independent projects.

NA: **Irish Young Archaeologists' Club**
AD: c/o Bernard Guinan, Dublinia, St Michael's Hill, Dublin 8
TL: +(353) 1 679 4611, fax +(353) 1 679 7116
AI: For all young people between 9 and 18 who wish to know more about archaeology.
PB: Magazine (2/yr).

NA: **Joint Committee on the Industrial Heritage (Northern Ireland)**
AD: 5–33 Hill Street, Belfast BT1 2LT
TL: 01232 235000
FD: 1992 (in present form)

NA: **The Maritime Institute of Ireland / Foras Muirí na h-Éireann**
AD: National Maritime Centre and Museum, Haigh Terrace, Dún Laoghaire, Co Dublin
TL: +(353) 1 280 0969
FD: 1941
SO: Members' fees, gate charges and donations
AI: To promote awareness of the vital importance to the Irish people of shipping, ports, fishing and offshore resources.
CL: Over 3,000 maritime titles; historical documents and charts; modern publications and press cuttings; museum displays. Open to non-members by special arrangement.
EN: Postal or personal visit
HR: 2.30pm–5.30pm Tues-Sat May-Sept (and October weekends)
PB: *Maritime Journal of Ireland*; newsletter (4/yr).
AC: Meetings, lectures and film shows in winter months (public welcome); summer visits to

places of maritime interest. Underwater Heritage Committee.

NA: **The Medieval Trust**
AD: St Michael's Hill, Christ Church, Dublin 8
TL: +(353) 1 679 4611, fax +(353) 1 679 7116
FD: 1990
SO: National and European sources
AI: To research and present to the public the history of medieval Dublin.
CL: (DVBLINIA Interpretation Centre)
AC: Profits arising from DVBLINIA operation will assist continued research in the Centre for Medieval Studies (based in Synod Lodge behind DVBLINIA building, St Michael's Hill, Dublin 8).

NA: **National Archives**
AD: Bishop Street, Dublin 8
TL: +(353) 1 478 3711, fax +(353) 1 478 3650
FD: 1702 (State Paper Office); 1867 (Public Record Office); 1988 (National Archives)
SO: Dept of Arts, Culture and the Gaeltacht
AI: The collection, preservation and production of departmental records, private records, Church of Ireland records, etc.
CL: Those particularly relevant to archaeology include the map collection (private and estate maps predating 1820s OS mapping); OS records from 1820s; OPW records from c. 1800; papers relating to the establishment of the Royal Irish Academy, National Museum of Ireland, funding of Treasure Trove payment, and finding of antiquities; records of private antiquarian collections and of 18th century visits to monuments; national exhibitions; and modern departmental records dealing with development of National Museum etc; excavations etc.
EN: Postal, telephone or personal visit
HR: (Reading room) 10.00am–5.00pm Mon–Fri
PB: Various reports.
AC: Visits, seminars, meetings etc.

National Committee for Archaeology see *Royal Irish Academy.*

National Heritage Council (1988–95) *see now* **Heritage Council.**

National Library of Ireland *see Section 1.7 Libraries.*

National Parks: *no Irish park has an archaeologist.*

National Trust for Ireland *see (An) Taisce.*

NA: **National Trust (Northern Ireland)**

AD: Rowallane House, Saintfield, Ballynahinch, Co Down BT24 7LH
TL: 01238 510721
FD: 1895
SO: Members' subscriptions, DOE(NI), and other sources
AI: (as for UK National Trust)

NA: **Navan Research Group**
AD: c/o Dept of Archaeology and Palaeoecology, School of Geosciences, The Queen's University, Belfast BT7 1NN
TL: 01232 245133
FD: 1986
PB: *Emania* (irreg)
AC: Is one of three bodies involved in management of the Navan area monuments.

NA: **Northern Ireland Environment Link**
AD: 47A Botanic Avenue, Belfast BT7 1JL
TL: 01232 314944, fax 311558
FD: 1990
SO: DOE(NI), World Wildlife Fund, members' subscriptions (institutional and individual)
AI: To act as forum for voluntary organisations concerned with conservation of the countryside, wildlife and environment (including archaeological organisations).
CL: Library and photocopying service
PB: Annual report; fact sheets (6/yr) to members; poster-calendar of events (including archaeological talks and field trips).

NA: **Northern Ireland Heritage Gardens Committee**
AD: PO Box 252, Belfast BT9 6GY
TL: 01232 668817 (Belinda Jupp, Hon Sec: home number)
FD: 1980
SO: No finance
AI: To foster recognition and conservation of historic gardens and plant heritage in Northern Ireland, to promote and facilitate research, and to raise public awareness.
PB: *Northern gardens* (1982); *Heritage gardens inventory* (1992).
AC: Speaker service (fee charged); conferences.

NA: **Northern Ireland Museums Council**
AD: 185 Stranmillis Road, Belfast BT9 5DU (Aidan Walsh, Director)
TL: 01232 661023, fax 01232 661715
FD: 1993
SO: Dept of Education N Ireland
AI: To provide grant-aid, advice, information and training for museums in N Ireland.

CL: Small library of museological literature
EN: Postal, telephone or personal visit
HR: Office hours
PB: Annual report; training publications.

NA: **Northern Ireland Tourist Board**
AD: St Anne's Court, 59 North Street, Belfast BT1
INB
TL: 01232 231221
PB: *Industrial Heritage of Northern Ireland* (map and county list of sites).

North Munster Project *see Discovery Programme.*

NA: **Office of Public Works, National Monuments and Historic Properties Service**
AD: 51 St Stephen's Green, Dublin 2
TL: +(353) 1 661 3111, fax +(353) 1 661 0747
FD: 1831
SO: Government
AI: To preserve, conserve and present National Monuments; to perform systematic survey of all monuments; to advise on planning matters; to issue excavation and underwater survey licences; and to implement the National Monuments legislation.
CL: SMR files on paper (complete for country) accessible by appointment.
EN: Postal, telephone or personal visit
HR: Normal office hours
PB: Annual reports; detailed *Survey of County Louth*; *Inventories* (brief data) published or approaching completion for counties Louth, Monaghan, Meath, West Cork, Carlow, W Galway, E and S Cork, Cavan, Laois, Wexford; excavation reports in journals and periodicals; *Guide to the archives of the Office of Public Works* (1994).
AC: Heritage Card (season ticket) available for visits to OPW sites.

NA: **Ordnance Survey of Ireland (OSI) Archaeological Branch** [Republic]
AD: Phoenix Park, Dublin 8
TL: +(353) 1 820 6100, fax +(353) 1 820 4156 (Eamon Cody and/or Paul Walsh, Archaeologists)
FD: 1824 (for OS Ireland); 1947 (for Archaeological Branch)
SO: Government
AI: To play an advisory role over the archaeological content of OS maps; to make a survey of the megalithic monuments of Ireland.
CL: Archive (plans and photographs) of megalithic monuments (research fee may apply);

aerial photographs (vertical, at various map scales, and colour obliques of selected sites).
EN: Postal, telephone or personal visit
HR: 9.15am–4.15pm Mon-Fri
PB: *Survey of the megalithic tombs of Ireland* (vols 1–5, 1961–89).
AC: Also has a Placenames Branch (from 1955) engaged in publishing continuing series of bilingual lists by county.

NA: **Ordnance Survey of Northern Ireland (OSNI)**
AD: Colby House, Stranmillis Court, Belfast BT9 5BJ
TL: 01232 255755
FD: 1920 (for Northern Ireland OS)
SO: Parliamentary vote
AI: To maintain a topographical information archive for Northern Ireland and to meet the needs of customers for information from this archive.
CL: Maps, street-plans, atlases, aerial photographs, remotely-sensed images; cartographic data in alphameric, graphical and digital format; superseded editions of maps.
EN: Postal, telephone or personal visit
HR: 9.15am–4.30pm Mon-Fri
PB: Annual report; map catalogues; over 16,000 map sheets.
AC: Services include special surveys, aerial photography, cartographic and reprographic services, technical assistance to customers, etc; developing Northern Ireland Geographical Information Service (NIGIS); operation of Northern Ireland Remote Sensing Centre.
See also Institute of Irish Studies, relevant to transcribing of 19th century OS information on N Ireland into database and print.

NA: **Organisation of Irish Archaeologists**
AD: c/o Eoin Halpin, 71 Carmel Street, Belfast BT7 1QF
TL: 01232 233631
FD: 1984
AI: To represent and support all those engaged in professional archaeology in Ireland and to promote the development of and interest in our archaeological heritage.
EN: Postal or telephone
PB: *Excavations 19..* (annual synopses); newsletter.
AC: National Archaeology Day for the public; meetings, seminars and workshops; advice to members (through involvement of other professions) on contracts, tendering, site safety etc.

NA: **Public Record Office Northern Ireland (PRONI)**
AD: 66 Balmoral Avenue, Belfast BT9 6NY (Director Dr A P W Malcomson)
TL: 01232 661621, fax 665718
FD: 1923
SO: Government
AI: To receive and safeguard public records; also to acquire private papers of historic, economic or social interest.
CL: A 20-page guide indicates the main categories of document, from c. AD 1600 onwards, with some material from 14th/16th centuries; maps, plans, surveys etc form a strong component of the collection.
EN: Personal visit (reader's ticket valid 1 yr issued on satisfactory completion of application form and proof of identity)
HR: 9.15am–4.45pm Mon-Fri (check in advance for two-week annual closure in late Nov/early Dec)
PB: No single printed guide to records, but acquisitions are indexed by personal names, places and subjects. Extensive card indexes in process of computerisation.
AC: Video recording explains procedures and search aids.

NA: **Railway Preservation Society of Ireland**
AD: Castleview Road, Whitehead, Co Antrim BT38 9NA
TL: 01960 353567, fax 01232 662013 (Paul McCann, Sec)
FD: 1964
AI: To preserve and operate vintage locomotives and rolling-stock on the main lines of the Irish railway network.
PB: Annual journal; newsletter (5/yr).
AC: Speaker service on railway history.

NA: **Royal Irish Academy**
AD: 19 Dawson Street, Dublin 2
TL: +(353) 1 676 4222, fax +(353) 1 676 2346
FD: 1785
SO: Government grant-in-aid and other sources
AI: Is the principal learned society of the country, with c. 240 members elected for their academic distinction. National Committee for Archaeology is one of its responsibilities.
CL: Library +(353) 1 676 4222 ext 219 or 220, open to Members of the Academy or to readers recommended by Members (fee payable); many historic documents and manuscripts as well as a large collection of books and periodicals.
EN: Postal

PB: *Proceedings* (several/yr); *The Royal Irish Academy: a bicentennial history* (1985); many other publications on archaeology, Celtic studies, history and literature.
AC: Advises OPW on annual archaeological research grants.

NA: **Royal Society of Antiquaries of Ireland**
AD: 63 Merrion Square, Dublin 2
TL: +(353) 1 676 1749 (Mrs Siobhán de hÓir)
FD: 1849 (as Kilkenny Archaeol Soc; numerous name changes since then)
AI: Is a voluntary body concerned with the preservation of the Irish cultural heritage, particularly in the fields of archaeology, history and the arts.
CL: Substantial library open to members (and others by arrangement)
EN: Postal, telephone, personal visit
HR: (afternoons only)
PB: *Journal* (annually); other publications from time to time.
AC: Lectures, field excursions; organises Sheppard Trusts fund competitions for children.

NA: **Royal Town Planning Institute – N Ireland branch**
AD: (enquire of RTPI London, 0171 636 9107, for current contact)
AI: (as for main RTPI entry under England)

Society for Name Studies in Britain and Ireland *see entry under England/Britain above.*

NA: **An Taisce – The National Trust for Ireland**
AD: The Tailors' Hall, Back Lane, Dublin 8 (Valerie Bond, Administrator)
TL: +(353) 1 454 1786, fax +(353) 1 453 3255
FD: 1948
AI: An Taisce is concerned with the conservation of the best of Ireland's heritage and with development which sits well in the environment and enhances it; and is consulted on various planning matters.
EN: Postal, telephone or personal visit (but resources limited and contributions towards running costs welcomed)
HR: 9.30am–5.00pm
PB: *Living heritage* (magazine); guides, books and pamphlets (list available).
AC: Local branches run various activities.

Tara Project *see Discovery Programme.*

NA: **Teagasc, Agriculture and Food Development Authority**
AD: 19 Sandymount Avenue, Dublin 4

TL: +(353) 1 668 8188, fax +(353) 1 668 8023
FD: 1988

NA: **Ulster Archaeological Society**
AD: c/o Dept of Archaeology and Palaeoecology, School of Geosciences, The Queen's University of Belfast, Belfast BT7 1NN
TL: 01232 245133 ext 3447, fax 01232 321280 (Dr F McCormick)
FD: 1942
AI: To advance the education of the public in archaeology and history particularly in regard to Ulster (ie the nine historic counties) and to publish an annual Journal.
EN: Postal or telephone
HR: 10.00am–4.00pm
PB: *Ulster journal of archaeology* (annually); newsletter.
AC: Lectures, field trips.

NA: **Ulster Architectural Heritage Society**
AD: 185 Stranmillis Road, Belfast BT9 5DU
TL: 01232 660809, fax 01232 661715 (Miss Joan Kinch, Sec)
FD: 1967
AI: To promote the appreciation and enjoyment of good architecture of all periods – from the prehistoric to the contemporary – in the nine counties of Ulster; to encourage the preservation and restoration of buildings of merit or importance; and to increase public awareness of the beauty, history and character of local neighbourhoods. (Also maintains database of buildings at risk.)
EN: Postal, telephone or personal visit
HR: 9.00am–1.00pm Mon-Fri
PB: Many (eg *Directory of traditional building skills*, 1994 – list available for SAE).
AC: Lectures and outings, conferences and courses, meetings.

NA: **Ulster Society for the Preservation of the Countryside**
AD: Peskett Centre, 2a Windsor Road, Belfast BT9 7FQ (A G Kennedy, Hon Sec)
TL: 01232 381304
FD: 1937
AI: The preservation of the Ulster countryside.
EN: Postal, telephone or personal visit
HR: 10.00am–1.00pm Mon-Fri (occasional variations)
PB: *Caring for the countryside.*
AC: Monitoring of planning applications, developments etc, and action where necessary.

Western Stone Forts Project *see Discovery Programme.*

4.3
Local Government Archaeologists

This list, necessarily simplified for reasons of length from a very complex (and changing) situation, is intended to provide, for each county or area, at least a contact point for archaeological advice related to planning and/or development control matters. Frequently that address will include the county (or other area) **Sites and Monuments Record (SMR)**, which plays an important part in the planning process. Where there are District Archaeological Officers the county contact should be able to refer enquirers onwards. Consult the CBA's *British archaeological yearbook* (current year) for a much fuller list of 'archaeological curators' and SMRs, including those for Districts; it also contains a brief explanation of the respective roles of 'curators' and 'contractors' in archaeological work. The Association of Local Government Archaeologists is the voice for county and district archaeologists in England and Wales, while the Association of Regional and Island Archaeologists is that for Scotland. Addresses for both are in Section 4.2 Organisations.

In **Northern Ireland** there are no county archaeologists: all the functions are performed by Environment and Heritage Service: Historic Monuments and Buildings, 5–33 Hill Street, Belfast BT1 2LA, tel 01232 235000.

NB: Local government reorganisation into unitary authorities early in 1996 has meant changes in arrangements for archaeology; the titles and addresses listed here are believed correct at the time of writing (mid-1996), but some arrangements are still rather fluid. For that reason no responsibility can be taken for wrong information.

National Park Archaeologists are separately listed, Section 4.5.

For what is now rapidly becoming historic interest, readers may wish to consult Paul Spoerry (comp), *The structure and funding of British archaeology: the RESCUE questionnaire 1990–91* (Hertford, RESCUE, 1992) which offered results of a survey of 109 organisations at that time.

Thanks are due to Stewart Bryant of ALGAO and Peter Yeoman of ARIA for their help in understanding such a complex and unsettled situation.

England

(**Avon:** the former county is now split between Bristol City, Bath and NE Somerset, N Somerset, and S Glos; see separate entries below.)

Bath and North-East Somerset: Archaeologist, Historic Conservation, Trimbridge House, Trim Street, Bath BA1 2DP, tel 01225 477537

Bedfordshire: Heritage and Environment Group, Dept of Envir/Econ Devel, County Hall, Cauldwell Street, Bedford, Beds MK42 9AP, tel 01234 228074, fax 01234 228232

Berkshire: Principal Archaeologist, Babtie Shaw and Morton, Public Service Division, Shinfield Park, Reading, Berks RG2 9XG, tel 01734 234938, fax 01734 310268

Bristol: City Archaeologist, Planning, Transport and Development Services, Bristol City Council, Brunel House, St George's Road, Bristol BS1 5UY, tel 0117 922 3044

Buckinghamshire: County Archaeologist, Bucks County Museum, Technical Centre, Tring Road, Aylesbury, Bucks HP22 5PJ, tel and fax 01296 696012

Cambridgeshire: Archaeology Section, Libraries and Heritage Service, Cambs County Council, Babbage House, Shire Hall, Cambridge CB3 0AP, tel 01223 317312

Cheshire: Principal Archaeologist, Cheshire County Council, Environmental Planning Service, Commerce House, Hunter Street, Chester, Cheshire CH1 2QP, tel 01244 603160, fax 01244 603802

Cleveland see now **Tees Archaeology**.

Cornwall: County Archaeological Officer, Cornwall Committee for Archaeology, Old County Hall, Station Road, Truro, Cornwall TR1 3EX, tel 01872 323603

Cumbria: County Archaeologist, Economy and Environment, County Offices, Kendal, Cumbria LA9 4RQ, tel 01539 814378, fax 01539 726276

Derbyshire: Archaeologist, Planning and Highways Dept, County Offices, Matlock, Derbys DE4 3AG, tel 01629 580000 ext 7125, fax 01629 580119

Devon: County Archaeologist, Engineering and Planning Dept, Devon County Council, County Hall, Exeter, Devon EX2 4QQ, tel 01392 382626, fax 01392 382135

Dorset: Archaeological Officer, Planning Dept, County Hall, Dorchester, Dorset DT1 1XJ, tel 01305 224277, fax 01305 224482

Durham: County Archaeology Officer, Antiquities Dept, The Bowes Museum, Barnard Castle, Co Durham, DL12 8NP, tel 01833 690107, fax 01833 637163

East Sussex *see under* **Sussex**

Essex: County Archaeologist, Essex County Council, Planning Dept, County Hall, Chelmsford, Essex CM1 1LX, tel 01245 492437, fax 01245 258353

Gloucestershire: County Archaeological Officer, Planning Dept, Shire Hall, Gloucester GL1 2TN, tel 01452 425683, fax 01452 425356

—South Gloucestershire: Archaeology Officer, Environment and Conservation, Civic Centre, High Street, Kingswood, S Glos BS15 2TR, tel 01454 863649

Greater London: Greater London Archaeology Advisory Service, English Heritage, 23 Savile Row, London W1X 1AB, tel (for SMR) 0171 973 3731

Greater Manchester: County Archaeological Officer, Greater Manchester Archaeological Unit, University of Manchester, Oxford Road, Manchester M13 9PL, tel 0161 275 2314, fax 0161 275 2315

Hampshire: Senior Archaeologist, Environment Dept, The Castle, Winchester, Hants SO23 8UE tel 01962 846735, fax 01962 846776

Hereford and Worcester: Archaeological Officer, Hereford and Worcester County Council, Tolladine Road, Worcester WR4 9NB, tel 01905 611086, fax 01905 29054

Hertfordshire: County Archaeologist, Environment Dept, County Hall, Hertford, Herts SG13 8DN, tel 01992 555244, fax 01992 555251

Humberside: the former county is now split between Humber and North-East Lincolnshire (under Lincolnshire below).

Humber Archaeology Partnership, The Old School, Northumberland Avenue, Hull HU2 0LN, tel 01482 217466

Isle of Wight: County Archaeological Officer, County Archaeological Centre, 61 Clatterford Road, Carisbrooke, Newport, Isle of Wight PO30 1NZ, tel 01983 529963, fax 01983 823810

Kent: County Archaeological Officer, County Planning Dept, Kent County Council, Springfield, Kent ME14 2LX, tel 01622 696055, fax 01622 687620

Lancashire: Archaeologist, Lancashire County Planning, PO Box 160, East Cliff County Offices, Preston, Lancs PR1 3EX, tel 01772 261550 (Lancs SMR Officer at same address, tel 01772 261551.)

Leicestershire: Archaeological Survey Officer, Archaeological Survey Team, Leics County Council, Jewry Wall Museum, St Nicholas Circle, Leicester LE1 7BY, tel 0116 247 3023, fax 0116 251 2257

Lincolnshire: County Archaeological Officer, City and County Museum, 12 Friar's Lane, Lincoln LN2 5AL, tel 01522 575292, fax 01522 552811

—North East Lincolnshire: NE Lincs Archaeology Unit, Thrunscoe Centre, Highgate, Cleethorpes, DN35 8NX, tel 01472 323586 or 323590, fax 01472 323555

London *see* **Greater London**

Merseyside: County SMR, Liverpool Museum, William Brown Street, Liverpool L3 8EN, tel 0151 478 4258, fax 0151 478 4390

Norfolk: County Archaeological Officer, Field Archaeology, Union House, Gressenhall, Dereham, Norfolk NR20 4DR, tel 01362 861187/ 860528, fax 01362 860951

Northampton: County Archaeologist, Northamptonshire Heritage, PO Box 287, 27 Guildhall Road, Northampton NN1 1BD, tel 01604 237242, fax 01604 236696

North Yorkshire *see under* **Yorkshire**

Northumberland: County Archaeological Officer, Planning Dept, Northumberland County Council, County Hall, Morpeth, Northumberland NE61 2EF, tel 01670 534058, fax 01670 534069

Nottinghamshire: County Archaeologist, Heritage Team, 6 Wilford Lane, West Bridgford, Nottingham NG2 7QX, tel 0115 977 2116/2129

Oxfordshire: County Archaeological Officer, Dept of Leisure and Arts, Central Library, Westgate, Oxford OX1 1DY, tel 01865 810115 (SMR 810825), fax 01865 810187

Shropshire: County Archaeological Officer, Environment Dept (Historic Conservation), Shropshire County Council, Shire Hall, Abbey Foregate, Shrewsbury SY2 6ND, tel 01743 252563, fax 01743 252505

Somerset: County Archaeological Officer, Architectural and Historic Heritage, Environment Dept, Somerset County Council, County Hall, Taunton TA1 4DY, tel 01823 255426, fax 01823 332773/334346

—North Somerset: Archaeologist, Environment Group, N Somerset Council, The Town Hall, Weston super Mare, Som BS23 1UJ, tel (temporary) 0117 987 5171, fax 0117 987 5168 *and see Bath and NE Somerset under Bath above.*

South Yorkshire *see under* **Yorkshire**

Staffordshire: Archaeological Officer, Planning and Economic Development Dept, County Buildings, Martin Street, Stafford ST16 2LE, tel 01785 277283, fax 01785 223316

Suffolk: Principal Archaeological Officer, Planning Dept, Suffolk County Council, St Edmund House, County Hall, Ipswich IP4 1LZ, tel 01473 265202, fax 01473 288221

Surrey: Principal Archaeologist, County Planning Dept, Surrey County Council, Kingston on Thames, Surrey KT1 2DT, tel 0181 541 9402, fax 0181 541 9447

Sussex: East: Archaeological Adviser, Planning Dept, E Sussex County Council, Southover House, Southover Road, Lewes, E Sussex BN7 1YA, tel 01273 481608, fax 01273 479040

—West: County Archaeological Officer, Planning Dept, W Sussex County Council, County Hall, Tower Street, Chichester, W Sussex PO19 1RL, tel 01243 752058, fax 01243 752062

Tees Archaeology (formerly Cleveland Archaeology): Sir William Gray House, Clarence Road, Hartlepool TS24 8BT, tel 01429 523455

Tyne and Wear: Archaeologist (if continuing), Environment Design Team, Planning Dept, Newcastle City Council, Civic Centre, Newcastle upon Tyne NE1 8PH, tel 0191 232 8520 ext 5626

Also Archaeology Unit, Jesmond Cemetery Gates, Jesmond Road, Newcastle upon Tyne NE2 1NJ, tel 0191 281 6117

Warwickshire: County Field Archaeologist, Field Archaeology Office, The Butts, Warwick CV34 4SS, tel 01926 412276, fax 01926 412974

West Midlands: Archaeologist, West Midlands Joint Data Team, PO Box 1777, Clarendon House, Solihull, W Midlands B91 3RZ, tel 0121 704 6550 or 0121 704 6930, fax 0121 704 6554

West Sussex *see under* **Sussex**

West Yorkshire *see under* **Yorkshire**

Wiltshire: County Archaeologist, Library and Museums Service, Wiltshire County Council, Bythesea Road, Trowbridge, Wilts BA14 8BG, tel 01225 713733, fax 01225 713993

Worcestershire *see* **Hereford and Worcester**

Yorkshire: North: County Archaeological Officer, Planning Dept, County Hall, Northallerton, N Yorks DL7 8AQ, tel 01609 780780 ext 2330

—South: (S Yorks Archaeology Service wound up): SMR is at Sheffield City Museum, Weston Park, Sheffield S10 2TP, tel 0114 276 8588

—West: County Archaeological Officer, W Yorkshire Archaeology Service, 14 St John's North, Wakefield, W Yorks WF1 3QA, tel 01924 306791, fax 01924 306810

Isle of Man: Manx National Heritage, Manx Museum and National Trust, Douglas, Isle of Man, tel 01624 675522, fax 01624 661899

Wales

Clwyd: archaeology in the former county authority is now split as follows:

—Denbighshire County Council, County Archaeologist, Directorate of Planning and Economic Development, Council Offices, Station Road, Ruthin LL15 1YN, tel 01824 706194

—Wrexham County Borough Council: Wrexham Archaeology Service, Wrexham Museum, Council Buildings, Wrexham LL11 1RB, tel 01978 358916, fax 01978 353882 (temporary accommodation)

The four Welsh Archaeological Trusts are:
Clwyd-Powys Archaeological Trust, 7a Church

Street, Welshpool, Powys SY21 7DL, tel 01938 553670, fax 01938 552179

Dyfed: Dyfed Archaeological Trust, The Shire Hall, Carmarthen Street, Llandeilo, Pembs SA19 6AF, tel 01558 823121, fax 01558 823133

Glamorgan and Gwent: Glamorgan-Gwent Archaeological Trust Ltd, Ferryside Warehouse, Bath Lane, Swansea SA1 1RD, tel 01792 655208, fax 01792 474469

Gwynedd: Gwynedd Archaeological Trust, Ffordd y Garth, Bangor, Gwynedd LL57 2SE, tel 01248 352535, fax 01248 370925

Powys *see* **Clwyd-Powys**

Conway and **Flintshire** are unprovided for at the time of writing.

Scotland

A number of fundamental changes were made early in 1996 to the administrative arrangements for the former Scottish Regions; the situation presented below is that obtaining in mid-1996. The Association of Regional and Island Archaeologists (address in Section 4.2 Organisations) should be able to confirm any subsequent modifications.

Aberdeenshire: Aberdeenshire Archaeology Service, Woodhill House, Westburn Road, Aberdeen AB9 2LU, tel 01224 664723 (also covers Morayshire)

Borders: Archaeologist, Dept of Planning and Development, Newtown St Boswells, Melrose, Roxburghshire TD6 0SA, tel 01835 824000, fax 01835 822145

Dumfries and Galloway: Council Archaeologist, Environment and Infrastructure, Dumfries and Galloway Council, 4 Market Street, Castle Douglas, DG7 1BE, tel 01556 502351, fax 01556 503478

City of Edinburgh: Archaeology Officer, 10 Broughton Market, Old Broughton, Edinburgh EH3 6NU, tel 0131 558 1040

Fife: Archaeologist, Dept of Economic Development and Planning, Fife House, North Street, Glenrothes, Fife KY7 5LT, tel 01592 416153, fax 01592 611862

Highland: Archaeology Service, The Old School, High Street, Clachnaharry, Inverness IV3 6RB, tel 01463 711176, fax 01463 711188

Lothian: No cover at present for East, Mid or West Lothian

Orkney: Island Archaeologist, Orkney Heritage Society, The Janitor's House, Old Academy, Back Road, Stromness, Orkney, tel 01856 850285

Shetland: Shetland Amenity Trust, 22–24 North Road, Lerwick, Shetland ZE1 0NQ, tel 01595 4688, fax 3956

Stirling: Archaeologist, Dept of Economic Development and Planning, Stirling Council, Viewforth, Stirling FK8 2ET, tel 01786 442752, fax 01786 443003
(now covering Stirling, probably Clackmannan, but not Falkirk area).

(former Strathclyde Region): Archaeologist, West of Scotland Archaeology Service, House 3, Charing Cross Complex, 20 India Street, Glasgow G2 4PF, tel 0141 227 2242/3669, fax 0141 227 3644

(former Tayside): No cover at present for Perthshire, Dundee City or Angus.

May possibly employ an archaeologist:

Western Isles: Western Isles Council Museum, Nan Eilean, Old Town Hall, Stornoway, Harris, Western Isles, tel 01851 3773

4.4
Sites and Monuments Records:
Descriptive Literature

Note that staff of the National Monuments Record for England have produced articles for each of the English county journals detailing the scope and extent of the Record representing that county. In contrast, the publications noted below deal with the more general level.

Association of County Archaeological Officers, *Sites and monuments records: policies for access and charging.* ACAO, 2 ed 1993, 19 p.
Because archaeological information is now perceived to have potential monetary value, this paper offers advice to local authorities on what constitutes 'public information'; discusses public access and whether it is right to charge for it; and suggests how to reckon any such charges.

Avery, Michael and Rose, Petra, 'GIS, Irish grid references and the Northern Ireland Sites and Monuments Record', *Ulster journal of archaeology*, 56, 1993, pp 163–78.
Describes the creation of a GIS database from data in the various components of the SMR, Irish Grid References being calculated for all the sites currently on the County Series 6-inch maps.

Dept of National Heritage, *Local government reorganisation: guidance to local authorities on conservation of the historic environment.* Letter ref HSD 56/2/1 of 8 Aug 1995, explaining the responsibilities of local authorities in the new situation. *See also under Royal Commission (1995) below.*

Hansen, H J, 'European archaeological databases: problems and prospects', in Jens Andresen et al (eds), *Computing the past: computer applications and quantitative methods in archaeology,* CAA92 (Aarhus 1993), pp 229–37.

Larsen, C U (ed), *Sites and monuments: national archaeological records.* Copenhagen: Nat Mus Denmark, 1992, 250 p, bibl. 87 89364 02 3.
A Europe-wide survey includes six papers on British and Irish national records.

Royal Commission on the Historical Monuments of England, *Inventories of monuments and historic buildings in Europe.* London: RCHME, 1992, 175 p. 1 873592 08 6 pb.
Papers from a European colloquium in Oxford, 1988, cover the relationship between inventories and protective legislation, the use of thesauri and computerised databases, the conflict between finite resources and an infinite task, and ways of involving the public more deeply in appreciation of their heritage.

—, *Recording England's past: a data standard for the extended National Archaeological Record.* London: RCHME/ACAO, 1993, 116 p. 1 873592 18 3 pb.
Gives minute instructions for completing each data field of the Record, which incorporates the NMR at Swindon plus the individual county SMRs.

—, *Recording England's past: a review of national and local SMRs in England.* London: RCHME, 1993, 54 p, refs. 1 873592 17 5 pb.
Surveyed the current state of the official archaeological record.

—, *Local Government Act 1992: Guidance from RCHME for new authorities on the role of Sites and Monuments Records.* RCHME: NMRC 1/95, 1995, 6 pp.

4.5
National Park Archaeology

England and Wales

The parent body is the **Council for National Parks** in London: see its entry in Section 4.2 Organisations.

Brecon Beacons (Archaeologist Peter Dorling): 7 Glamorgan Street, Brecon, Powys LD3 7DP, tel 01874 624437

Dartmoor (Archaeologist Debbie Griffiths): Haytor Road, Bovey Tracey, Devon TQ13 9JQ, tel 01626 832093

Exmoor (Archaeologist Veryan Heal): Exmoor House, Dulverton, Som TA22 9HL, tel 01398 323665

Lake District (Archaeologist John Hodgson): Murley Moss, Oxenholme Road, Kendal, Cumbria LA9 7RL, tel 01539 724555 ext 215

Northumberland (Archaeologist Paul Frodsham): Eastburn, South Park, Hexham, Northumberland NE46 1BS, tel 01434 605555

North York Moors (Archaeologist Graham Lee): Old Vicarage, Bondgate, Helmsley, York YO6 5BP, tel 01439 770657

Peak National Park Archaeology Service (Archaeologist K Smith): Aldern House, Baslow Road, Bakewell, Derbys DE45 1AE, tel 01629 816206, fax 01629 816310

Snowdonia (Archaeologist Peter Crew): (main office) Penrhyndeudraeth, Gwynedd LL48 6LS; P Crew is at Snowdonia National Park Study Centre, Plas Tan y Bwlch, Maentwrog, Blaenau Ffestiniog, Gwynedd LL41 3YU, tel 01766 590324

Yorkshire Dales (Archaeologists Robert White and Phil Brown): Yorebridge House, Bainbridge, Leyburn, N Yorks DL8 3BP, tel 01969 650456

National Parks so far without archaeologists are: **Broads Authority, Pembrokeshire Coast, New Forest.**

Ireland

None has an archaeologist at the time of writing, but the park visitor centres usually include information about archaeological monuments.

Burren National Park (Co Clare)
Connemara National Park (Co Galway)
Glenveagh National Park, Church Hill, Letterkenny, Co Donegal, tel +(353) 74 37088
Killarney National Park, Muckross House, Killarney, tel +(353) 64 31440
Wexford National Heritage Park, Ferrycarrig, Co Wexford, tel +(353) 53 41733
Wicklow Mountains National Park, Glendalough, Co Wicklow, tel +(353) 404 45338

Relevant publications

National Parks Review Panel, *Fit for the future.* Cheltenham: Countryside Commission, 1991, 0 861702 91 3.
The part of this review that affects archaeological matters was reproduced in *Brit Archaeol News*, 6.3, 1991, p 29: six recommendations were made, designed to improve the status and management of archaeological monuments in the National Parks. The review also calls for higher priority to be given to the protection and sensitive management of the architectural heritage of the Parks.

White, R F and Iles, R (eds), *Archaeology in National Parks.* [Skipton?]: National Parks Staff Association, 1991.
Papers from a 1989 workshop at the Yorkshire Dales NP office, illustrating among other things the problems of balancing the need to conserve against the need for greater public access.

4.6
Grant-making Bodies and Competitive Awards

These are listed under:
>   General advice and directories
>   Specifically archaeological grant-awarding bodies
>   Advanced scholarships and research grants
>   Competitive or other awards and prizes.

Grants and awards specific to Wales, Scotland and Ireland are listed at the end. Only bare details can be entered here; moreover some charities rotate their objects of concern around a fairly broad field. Accordingly, always check the current year's conditions and requirements.

General advice and directories (entered alphabetically by title)

The arts funding guide (ed Anne Marie Doulton). London: Directory of Social Change, 3 edn 1994, 348 p. (Or any later edn).
Describes fundraising methods, funding sources (eg Dept of National Heritage, Museums and Galleries Commission, etc); local authority funding, grant-making trusts; gives some interesting case studies including two for museums; training courses and addresses.

Central Government grants guide (ed Anne Marie Doulton). London: Directory of Social Change, 3 edn 1995/6, 272 p. (Or any later edn).
A guide to the grants, loans and payments for services available to voluntary bodies.

The **Charity Commission** (St Albans House, 57–60 Haymarket, London SW1 4QX; tel 0171 210 4556) maintains a database of charities by category (most useful to search would be the preservation categories named below):
>   buildings; churches of historical interest not used for worship; named buildings of cultural or historical interest; objects and places of local interest; local history and other historical records.

The database can be consulted without charge, between 10am and 4pm, keying in one's own enquiry; or postal enquiry can be made for a small charge per charity retrieved.

Complete fundraising handbook (Sam Clarke). London: Directory of Social Change, 2 edn 1993 (or any later edn).

***The **Council for British Archaeology** aims to supply up-to-date advice on all sources of funds: consult its *Yearbook* or apply direct to the CBA, Bowes Morrell House, 111 Walmgate, York YO1 2UA, tel 01904 671417.

****Directory of grant-making trusts.* Tonbridge: Charities Aid Foundation, (current year). The principal source, well-thumbed in every library; indexed by subject and geographical area; lists for each trust the name of correspondent, finances, objects, policy etc.

Directory of public sources of grants for the repair and conversion of historic buildings (English Heritage, rev edn 1990, looseleaf).
(A revised edn is under consideration at the time of writing.)

Environmental grants: a guide to grants for the environment from government companies and charitable trusts (Stephen Woollett). London: Directory of Social Change, 2 edn 1993.
Content excellent, but there is no index by subject.

The grants disk is intended to be a comprehensive guide to public sector grants for heritage organisations. (Check current machine requirements.) Heritage Development, c/o IMS Publications, 35 Aylesbury Street, Milton Keynes MK2 2BR.

Grants from Europe: how to get money and influence policy (Ann Davison). London: Directory of Social Change for NCVO, 2 edn 1993 (or any later edn).

****Handbook of grants: a guide to sources of public funding for museums, galleries, heritage and visual arts organisations* (Graeme Farnell). Milton Keynes: Mus Devel Co, 1990, looseleaf binder. 1 87311 400 1.
Includes a section 'How to apply for grants and get them.'

Grant-giving bodies with archaeological interests

GOVERNMENT FUNDED BODIES
British Academy: Fund for the Application of Science to Archaeology (FASA). Offers grants for small research projects in science-based archaeology. Closing date 31 December annually. Applied Science in Archaeology application forms

available from British Academy (FAO Miss E Ollard), 20–21 Cornwall Terrace, London NW1 4QP, tel 0171 487 5966. Preliminary advice may be obtained from Sebastian Payne, FASA Coordinator, English Heritage, 23 Savile Row, London WIX IAB.

Cadw)
English Heritage) all have advice leaflets giving
current position
Historic Scotland)

Council for British Archaeology: offers grants for publication, making awards three times a year through its Publications Committee. Applications must concern publications making a substantial contribution to national or regional problems; the funding of reports of excavations financed by government agencies is excluded. Details from CBA (address earlier in this section).

Department of National Heritage (Heritage Grant Fund: for voluntary organisations in England whose work relates to historic buildings, monuments, gardens, industrial and underwater archaeology). Identifying and recording preferred, or promoting a high standard of conservation (etc). Mainly for national organisations, but also local projects if exemplars of good practice with wider application. Matching funding is required. Information and application forms from Graham Bond or Luella Barker, DNH, 3rd floor, 2–4 Cockspur Street, London SW1Y 5DH (tel 0171 211 6367/8).

European Union Funding for Architectural Heritage is a five-year Community action programme, named Raphael, which aims to conserve, safeguard and develop the European cultural heritage. For instance, applications for assistance in 1996 could relate to: improving access to European museums; increasing public cultural awareness; preservation and enhancement of the European baroque (or 'baroque period') heritage and archaeological heritage; training and mobility of professional conservers in the cultural heritage field. Details from Joe Gallagher at English Heritage (0171 973 3000).

National Heritage Memorial Fund: to give financial assistance towards the cost of acquiring, maintaining or preserving land, buildings, works of art and other objects of outstanding interest which are also of importance to the national heritage. Also administers the Heritage Lottery Fund. Is advised by English Heritage on specific applications. Grants or loans. Leaflet available

from NHMF, 10 St James's Street, London SW1A IEF, tel 0171 930 0963, fax 0171 930 0968.

OTHER BODIES WITH ARCHAEOLOGICAL INTERESTS

British Archaeological Research Trust, managed by the CBA (address earlier in this section). For research and development projects intended to advance archaeological knowledge and develop new techniques of investigation. These grants are designed to initiate projects and attract further grant aid, and will not be given for topping-up existing projects. Applications to CBA Finance Officer by 30 June in any year.

Brown: Audrey Barrie Brown Memorial Fund, for research and education in Romano-British archaeology, especially in Wiltshire and the West, but anyone working in Britain may apply: Hon Sec, E P Johnson, 63 Wenhill Heights, Calne, Wilts SN11 0JZ. Completed application forms must be received by 15 April or 15 November in any year.

Buxton: Dennis Buxton Trust, a small trust for archaeology and conservation (among other social projects). Only registered charities (not individuals) may apply and there is a preference for small, local projects in Essex, Norfolk, East London or Northern Ireland. Secretary, Dennis Buxton Trust, Messrs Smith and Williamson, 1 Riding House Street, London W1A 3AS.

Challenge funding, a joint CBA/English Heritage scheme to encourage voluntary effort in making original contributions to the study and care of the historic environment in Britain. Awards are for equipment, materials or scientific analyses, not salaries, and are normally up to £500. Apply to CBA.

Charterhouse Charitable Trust, 1 Paternoster Row, St Paul's, London EC4M 7DH, 0171 248 4000. To registered charities only, no grants to individuals, and no start-up finance.

Cole Charitable Trust, Dr J L Cole, 128 Tamworth Road, Sutton Coldfield B75 6DH. Makes grants to registered charities only, mainly to local organisations in the Birmingham area for (preferably one-off) community projects including archaeology.

Cook: Ernest Cook Trust, Fairford Park, Fairford, Glos GL7 4JH, tel 01285 713273. For charitable activites of educational nature in the countryside, promoting its conservation, etc.

Corfield: Holbeche Corfield Charitable Settle-

ment, c/o C H Corfield-Moore, Greenoaks, Bradford Road, Sherborne, Dorset DT9 6BW. To registered charities only, mainly museums and environmental projects.

Countryside Trust, John Dower House, Crescent Place, Cheltenham, Glos GL50 3RA. Grants towards costs of fund-raising campaigns for local (rather than national) practical conservation projects.

Earthwatch Europe *see Section 4.2 Organisations*.

Essex Heritage Trust, c/o Mrs G Walsh, Cressing Temple, Witham Road, Braintree, Essex CM7 8PD, tel 01376 584903. For preservation of Essex land, buildings, objects or records; includes publications and restoration projects. To bodies or individuals; usually one-off start-up financing. Three application dates annually.

Fairbairn: Esmee Fairbairn Charitable Trust, 5 Storey's Gate, London SW1H 9JH, tel 0171 799 2679. For registered charities, not individuals; for encouragement of the arts and heritage, including conservation of historic buildings, museums etc.

Fitch: Marc Fitch Fund, mainly for publication of archaeological and related works; apply to the Fund c/o Roy Stephens, 7 Murray Court, Banbury Road, Oxford OX2 6LQ.

Getty: J Paul Getty Jr General Charitable Trust, 149 Harley Street, London W1N 2DH, tel 0171 486 1859. Historic landscapes and gardens are among the projects which have received grants; also conservation in the broadest sense, including training in conservation skills.

Goldsmiths' Company's Charities, c/o The Clerk, Goldsmiths' Company, Goldsmiths' Hall, Foster Lane, London EC2V 6BN, tel 0171 606 7010. To registered charities in London; many restrictions, but archaeology is among its objects.

Gulbenkian: Calouste Gulbenkian (Lisbon) Foundation, UK Branch, to registered charities only, for specific significant development projects including arts, education, etc. Apply for advice leaflet to the Foundation at 98 Portland Place, London W1N 4ET, tel 0171 636 5313.

Howard: John and Ruth Howard Charitable Trust, for the advancement of public education in archaeology; may assist with publication of archaeological excavations, archaeological activities or exhibitions for the public, and preservation of buildings etc. Apply to Mr A S Atchison, Messrs

Vickers and Co, Midland Bank Chambers, 111 High Road, London NW10 2TB.

Kiln: Robert Kiln Charitable Trust: general charitable purposes with preference for archaeology, environmental conservation, etc. Grants (up to £1,000) are made to organisations, not to individuals, with an emphasis on the Hertfordshire-Bedfordshire region. Apply to Mrs M A Archer, Sec RKCT, 15A Bull Plain, Hertford SG14 1DX.

Knott: Sir James Knott 1990 Trust, c/o Secretary at 16–18 Hood Street, Newcastle upon Tyne NE1 6JQ. To registered charities in Northumberland, Durham, Tyne and Wear only, for community benefit including archaeological purposes.

Manifold Charitable Trust, c/o Miss C C Gilbertson, 21 Dean's Yard, London SW1P 3RA. To registered charities only, mainly for preservation of historic buildings and the countryside, but most funds already committed in advance.

Medieval Settlement Research Group: makes small grants annually for projects relating to medieval settlement, normally for field survey, documentary research and/or preparation of reports for publication. Apply to Dr R Glasscock, MSRG, Dept of Geography, University of Cambridge, Downing Place, Cambridge CB2 3EN.

Morland: S C and M E Morland's Charitable Trust, c/o M E Morland, 88 Roman Way, Glastonbury, Somerset. To registered charities only, archaeological purposes included.

Nathan: Peter Nathan Charitable Trust, c/o Dr P W Nathan, 85 Ladbroke Road, London W11 3PJ. Single grants for specific projects including archaeology.

The Pilgrim Trust, to charitable bodies only, for a wide variety of projects under the general headings of Preservation (buildings, works of art, countryside) and Art and Learning (includes archaeology). Details from: Secretary, The Pilgrim Trust, Fielden House, Little College Street, London SW1P 3SH.

Prehistoric Society Research Fund: research grants (to members only) for various types of project, preferably small-scale. Also Conference Fund (two awards annually) to foster international cooperation among prehistorians. Apply to Prehistoric Society, Institute of Archaeology, 31–34 Gordon Square, London WC1H 0PY. (*See also under Awards and prizes below*.)

Royal Archaeological Institute: small cash grants for archaeological fieldwork and survey, some aspects of excavation and post-excavation research, architectural recording and analysis, artefact and art-historical research. Maximum of three years for any one project. Applications from amateurs are especially welcome, and small projects favoured (normally within the British Isles). Forms and details from RAI Assistant Secretary, c/o Society of Antiquaries, Burlington House, Piccadilly, London WIV OHS: applications by 1 December each year.

Scouloudi Foundation (formerly the Twenty Seven Foundation). Provides sponsorship of historical research in Institute of Historical Research, plus some other awards. Details from Secretary, The Scouloudi Foundation Awards Committee, Institute of Historical Research, Senate House, University of London, London WC1E 7HU.

Shell Better Britain Campaign, for the encouragement of various local group environmental projects; apply to SBBC, Victoria Works, 21 Graham Street, Hockley, Birmingham B1 3JR, tel 0121 212 9221.

Society of Antiquaries of London, for various research funds related to the Society's objects (eg Tessa and Mortimer Wheeler Memorial Fund; Hugh Chapman Memorial Research Fund; William Lambarde Memorial Fund; Joan Pye Awards): details from General Secretary, Society of Antiquaries of London, Burlington House, Piccadilly, London WIV OHS.

Society for Medieval Archaeology, three funds available: Sudreys Fund for assistance with travel costs relating to Viking studies; Eric Fletcher Fund for 'personal projects', especially relating to research into medieval life, but study tours or conference attendance are also assisted; Research Fund for personal research (eg for scientific dating or architectural study). Apply to Hon Sec, Society for Medieval Archaeology, 'Devonia', Forton Heath, Shrewsbury SY4 IEY.

Society for the Promotion of Roman Studies: grants towards projects (normally post-doctoral) in the history, archaeology, literature or art of Italy and the Roman Empire. Applications and two references to Secretary, SPRS, Senate House, Malet Street, London WC1E 7HU, before 15 January each year.

Sumner: Sir John Sumner's Trust Section 'A', c/o The Secretary, 8th Floor, Union Chambers, 63

Temple Row, Birmingham B2 5LT. Donations to charitable organisations including archaeological.

Tebbutt Research Fund: in tribute to the life and work of the late C F Tebbutt, OBE, FSA; small grants (up to £200 in total) available for research into any aspect of the Wealden iron industry; apply to Shiela Broomfield, Wealden Iron Research Group, 8 Woodview Crescent, Hildenborough, Tonbridge, Kent TN11 9HD, tel 01732 838698.

Twenty Seven Foundation *see now* **Scouloudi Foundation.**

Advanced scholarships, research grants etc.

Directory:
***The Grants Register 1993–1995** [or current edn], ed Lisa Williams (Macmillan, biennial). 'Primarily intended for students at or above the graduate level and for all who require further professional or advanced vocational training', ie scholarships, fellowships, research grants, grants-in-aid for attending conferences etc.

British Academy for the Promotion of Historical, Philosophical and Philological Studies. P W H Brown, Secretary, 20–21 Cornwall Terrace, London NW1 4QP. For research projects of established (ie postdoctoral level) UK-resident scholars; personal research grants and major research projects; also conference grants and subventions for publication. Apply for booklets to help decide your eligibility. The Humanities Research Board has responsibility for most of the award-making in the humanities; various types of research grant, attendance at conferences abroad etc, publication grants, (some) support for learned journals; postgraduate studentships. *See also FASA entry under British Academy earlier in this section.*

Churchill: Winston Churchill Memorial Trust. For Travelling Fellowships; includes archaeology from time to time (eg 1994: 'The British heritage: the conservation and restoration of historic buildings, their contents and gardens.'). The aim is to allow the Fellow to search overseas for knowledge to be applied for the benefit of the holder's work and the community. Send large (22cm x 11) SAE for current schedule to the Winston Churchill Memorial Trust, 15 Queen's Gate Terrace, London SW7 5PR.

Cramp: The Rosemary Cramp Fund: makes grants

to individuals and organisations for projects with emphasis on innovation, especially for Northern Britain AD 400–1100. Excavations are normally excluded. Application forms from Rosemary Cramp Fund, Dept of Archaeology, South Road, Durham DH1 3LE; closing date 31 October each year.

Guido Scholarships from the Bead Study Trust, for the study of beads abroad. Details from Mrs M E Hutchinson, 29 Elliscombe Road, London SE7 7PF.

Leverhulme Trust offers research fellowships and grants to individuals, and research grants to institutions for innovative or technically experimental research (not excavation); details from The Secretary, Research Awards Advisory Committee, The Leverhulme Trust, 15–19 New Fetter Lane, London EC4A 1NR, tel 0171 822 6938.

Natural Environment Research Council: *see Section 4.2 Organisations.*

Royal Society, for scientific research (normally post-doctoral), also grants for scientific publications of societies and institutions; details from 6 Carlton House Terrace, London SW1Y 5AG, tel 0171 839 5561.

Competitive (or other) awards and prizes

Anglia Water 'Caring for the Environment' award, to help voluntary or charitable educational organisations to develop environmental projects; details from Director of Quality, Conservation Awards, Anglian Water Services Ltd, Compass House, Chivers Way, Histon, Cambs CB4 4ZY.

Association for Industrial Archaeology Fieldwork Award. To encourage recording of physical remains to high archaeological standards; open to both amateur and professional workers. There is also an Initiative Award for innovative projects (eg local societies) and a student category. Apply to Victoria Beauchamp, c/o Division of Adult Continuing Education, University of Sheffield, 196–198 West Street, Sheffield S1 4ET.

Alan Ball Local History Awards, up to five trophies awarded annually to local authorities in the UK, with the aim of encouraging the publication of high quality local history material. Apply to Library Services Trust, 7 Ridgmount Street, London WC1E 7AE (tel 0171 580 8290).

British Academy: Derek Allen Prize; awarded annually for outstanding published work in (by turns) musicology, numismatics and Celtic studies. Grahame Clark Medal: awarded biennially for distinguished achievement in prehistoric archaeology.

British Archaeological Association: Reginald Taylor and Lord Fletcher Essay Prize, £300, not restricted to BAA members. (List of previous winners, from the original foundation in 1934 to date, given in *J Brit Archaeol Ass*, 147, 1994.)

British Archaeological Awards: biennially, various categories (eg best archaeological discovery made and reported promptly by a non-archaeologist; best archaeological book; Young Archaeologist of the Year, etc); supported by the main national archaeological bodies. Watch for announcements or apply to Juliet Mather, British Archaeological Awards, CBA, Bowes Morrell House, 111 Walmgate, York YO1 2UA.

British Gas Grassroots Action Scheme, Awards Administration, 2 Portland Road, Holland Park, London W11 4LA, tel 0171 221 7883. (Situation beyond 1996 not clear at time of writing.)

Dorset Archaeological Awards: biennial, to recognise outstanding archaeological work in the county. Details from Hon Sec, Dorset Archaeology Committee, Dorset County Museum, High Street West, Dorchester, DT1 1XA.

Essex Amenity Awards: organised biennially by Essex County Council to stimulate public awareness and interest in our surroundings. The 1995/6 awards are in four categories, the winner of each receiving up to £200: historic buildings and historic areas; countryside projects; history and archaeology; school projects. Individual or corporate efforts; especially welcomed are practical and physical projects, though entries may also be written, drawn or photographic. Apply for details and current closing date to Natalie Drewett, Historic Buildings and Design Section, Planning Dept, Essex County Council, County Hall, Chelmsford CM1 1LF, tel 01245 437644.

Europa Nostra Awards, about forty awards made annually to projects which make a distinguished contribution to the conservation and enhancement of Europe's architectural and natural heritage (eg several won by the National Trust). Apply by 1 June each year to Europa Nostra Awards, 35 Lange Voorhout, 2514EC The Hague, Netherlands. Also a Restoration Fund which can make donations towards restoration of endangered monuments in private ownership; public attention must be drawn to the need for conservation care. Apply by 31 December to same address.

Gulbenkian Awards for Museums and Galleries, various categories annually; apply c/o Museums Association, 42 Clerkenwell Close, London EC1R 0PA.

Nautical Archaeology Society Essay competition; apply for details to the NAS address given in Section 4.2 Organisations.

Prehistoric Society: the Bob Smith Award and the Leslie Grinsell Award; and, for the best paper published in the *Proceedings*, the R M Baguley Award.

Reginald Taylor and Lord Fletcher Essay Prize *see above under British Archaeological Association.*

Riley: Derrick Riley Fund for Studies in Aerial Archaeology: bursaries available, maximum value £500, preference given to younger applicants. Application form obtainable from Prof K Branigan, Dept of Archaeology and Prehistory, Univ Sheffield, Northgate House, West Street, Sheffield S1 4ET.

Royal Institution of Chartered Surveyors Awards: annually, for outstanding work in the preservation of the natural and built environment. Apply to Awards Officer, Corporate Communications Dept, RICS, 12 Great George Street, London SW1P 3AD, tel 0171 222 7000.

Society for the Interpretation of Britain's Heritage: Interpret Britain Awards. Open to any organisation or individual interpreting a theme, a place, a site, a collection or a facility for the benefit of the general public. Innovation is looked for, whether in large or small schemes. Apply to John Iddon, Awards Organiser, Interpret Britain Awards, St Mary's University College, Strawberry Hill, Twickenham TW1 4SX, tel 0181 892 0051.

Wales

Wales funding handbook 1995/96. Caerphilly: Wales Council for Voluntary Action. Covers general voluntary work, ie is not specifically environmental or archaeological. Tel 01222 869224.

Cambrian Archaeological Association: two funds available. The Research Fund exists for the encouragement of research in Wales and the Marches, and may be used for travel, fieldwork, excavation and associated scientific services, his-

torical research, and assistance with preparation of drawings for publication, photocopying etc. Closing date 1 December for following year. The Benefactors Fund makes small grants (in the region of £25 to £50) to persons under the age of 25 to help with the cost of books, fees, subscriptions, etc. Apply to General Secretary, Dr J M Hughes, The Laurels, Westfield Road, Newport, Gwent NP4 4ND.

Scotland

It is important as a first step to consult the Council for Scottish Archaeology's Development Officer (address in Section 4.2 Organisations) for advice and for up-to-date information from their database. Then try these two guides:

Directory of Scottish grant-making trusts. Edinburgh: Scottish Council for Voluntary Organisations (18–19 Claremont Crescent, Edinburgh EH7 4QD, tel 0131 556 3882). 1994/5 or any later edn.

The Scottish grants guide (ed Lucy Stubbs). London: Directory of Social Change, 1995, c. 180 p. 1 873860 82 X (not available to compiler).

As a rough guide, the main sources of archaeologically-oriented grants in Scotland are:

Glenfiddich Living Scotland Awards, c/o Tait and McLay Advertising, 9 Royal Crescent, Glasgow G3 7SP (tel 0141 332 0193 for application form and details).

Robertson Awards (for CSA members only) for the best examples of interpretation literature (leaflets, guidebooks, trails etc).

The **Scottish Civic Trust** produces, for Historic Scotland, a leaflet *Sources of financial help for Scotland's historic buildings.*

The **Scottish Local History Forum** has a few small grants available to aid local history publications; address in Section 4.2 Organisations.

Society of Antiquaries of Scotland:
Full details, and application forms where appropriate, of all these are available from Fionna Ashmore, Director SAS, National Museums of Scotland, Queen Street, Edinburgh EH2 1JD.
   Grants: towards all aspects of archaeological and historical research in Scotland. Annual allocations.
      Regional Buchan Lectures: grants to local archaeological, antiquarian or similar societies to

help fund a lecture, symposium or conference, the aim being to encourage lectures in parts of Scotland not at present served by the Society's meetings.

Awards:

The Gunning Jubilee Gift – to help experts to visit museums and collections for the purposes of special investigation and research. Open to non-Fellows. Applications by 5 Jan of relevant year.

The Chalmers-Jervise Prize – £150 offered every other year for the best essay (to publication standard) on the archaeology or history of Scotland before AD 1100. Open to non-Fellows.

The Dorothy Marshall Medal was instituted 1995 to recognise (triennially) the contribution made to archaeology by an individual amateur.

Bursaries: up to £300, awarded competitively, to enable young Fellows of the Society to read papers on Scottish themes at international conferences.

Ireland

For the latest information on grant sources apply to the Federation for Ulster Local Studies (8 Fitzwilliam Street, Belfast BT9 6AW) or to the Royal Society of Antiquaries of Ireland (63 Merrion Square, Dublin 2). Otherwise, use:

The Irish funding handbook (Leonie Baldwin). London: Directory of Social Change and others, 3 edn 1994, 178 p.

Few of the the following grant-making bodies have history, still less archaeology, as a primary concern, but applications may qualify under a cultural or community heading:

The **Blackburn Trust**, c/o Cleaver, Fulton and Rankin (Solrs), 50 Bedford Street, Belfast BT2 7FW, tel 01232 243141 (not to individuals, and there are restrictions on the type of organisation eligible).

Interpret Ireland Awards, Secretary, John Iddon, Awards Organiser, St Mary's University College, Strawberry Hill, Twickenham TW1 4SX, tel 0181 240 2078, fax 0181 240 4255. Open to any organisation or individual interpreting a theme, a place, a site, a collection or a facility for the benefit of the general public: innovation is looked for, whether in large or small schemes.

Mitchell: Esmé Mitchell Trust, Northern Bank Executor and Trustee Co Ltd, PO Box 800, Donegall Square West, Belfast BT1 7EB. Tel 01232 245277 (not to individuals: general charitable purposes especially cultural/artistic objects; certain heritage bodies are eligible).

Sheppard Trusts Competition for schoolchildren: apply to The Royal Society of Antiquaries of Ireland, 63 Merrion Square, Dublin 2.

The **Ulster Local History Trust Fund**, PO Box 900, Belfast BT9 6BL.

Some projects might find it worth applying to:

International Fund for Ireland, PO Box 2000, Belfast BT4 3SA. Tel. 01232 768832

The Irish-American Partnership, 32 Lower Baggot Street, Dublin 2. Tel. Dublin 676 3683.

Ireland Funds, 20–22 College Green, Dublin 2. Tel. Dublin 679 2743.

For Northern Ireland see also **Dennis Buxton Trust** *under 'Other bodies ... ' earlier in this section.*

4.7
Universities teaching Archaeology in the UK and the Republic of Ireland

This is a bare list of relevant universities; much fuller details (courses, staff numbers and interests) will be found in the CBA's *British archaeological yearbook*, which you should consult if contemplating a university course (whether full-time or extramurally). Note that some teach archaeology only as part of or incidental to a subject such as history.

Aberystwyth: Department of History and Welsh History, University of Wales Aberystwyth, Penglais, Aberystwyth SY23 3DY. Tel 01970 622662, fax 01970 622676

Bangor: School of History and Welsh History, University of Wales Bangor, Bangor LL57 2DG Tel 01248 382144, fax 01248 382759

Belfast: Dept of Archaeology and Palaeoecology, School of Geosciences, The Queen's University, Elmwood Avenue, Belfast BT7 1NN. Tel 01232 245133 (Dept: ext. 3186), fax 01232 321280

Birmingham: Department of Ancient History and Archaeology, University of Birmingham, Edgbaston, PO Box 363, Birmingham B15 2TT. Tel 0121 414 5497, fax 0121 414 3595

Bournemouth: School of Conservation Sciences, Bournemouth University, Talbot Campus, Fern Barrow, Wallisdown, Poole, Dorset BH12 5BB. Tel 01202 595178, fax 01202 595255

Bradford: Department of Archaeological Sciences, University of Bradford, Bradford, W Yorks BD7 1DP. Tel 01274 383531/2, fax 01274 385190

Bristol: Department of Archaeology, University of Bristol, 11 Woodlands Road, Bristol BS8 1TB. Tel and fax 0117 928 8877

Cambridge: Department of Archaeology, University of Cambridge, Downing Street, Cambridge CB2 3DZ. Tel 01223 333529, fax 01223 333503
see also McDonald Institute, same address, in Section 4.2 Organisations

Cardiff: School of History and Archaeology, University of Wales Cardiff, PO Box 909, Cardiff CF1 3XU. Tel 01222 874821, fax 01222 371921

Carmarthen (Trinity College): Department of Archaeology, Carmarthen, SA31 3EP. Tel 01267 237971, fax 01267 230933

Cork: Department of Archaeology, University College Cork, Cork, Republic of Ireland. Tel 0035321 276871

Dublin, UCD: Department of Archaeology, University College Dublin, Belfield, Dublin 4, Republic of Ireland. Tel 003531 706 8314, fax 003531 706 1184

Dublin, TCD: Department of Medieval History, Trinity College, Dublin 2. Tel 003531 677 2941, fax 003531 677 2694

Durham: Department of Archaeology, University of Durham, South Road, Durham DH1 3LE. Tel 0191 374 3622, fax 0191 374 3619

East Anglia: Department of History, University of East Anglia, Norwich NR4 7TJ. Tel 01603 593521, fax 01603 593519

Edinburgh: Department of Archaeology, University of Edinburgh, Old High School, Infirmary Street, Edinburgh EH1 1LT. Tel 0131 650 2501, fax 0131 662 4094
see also Centre for Field Archaeol in Section 4.2 Organisations (Scotland)

Exeter: Department of History and Archaeology, University of Exeter, Queen's Building, The Queen's Drive, Exeter EX4 4QH. Tel 01392 264287, fax 01392 264377

Galway: Department of Archaeology, University College Galway, Galway, Republic of Ireland. Tel 00353 91 524411

Glasgow: Department of Archaeology, University of Glasgow, 10 The Square, Glasgow G12 8QQ. Tel 0141 330 5690, fax 0141 307 8044
see also CTICH, Computers in Teaching Initiative in Section 4.2 Organisations (Scotland)

Lampeter: Department of Archaeology, University of Wales Lampeter, Lampeter, Ceredigion SA48 7ED. Tel 01570 424732, fax 01570 423669

Leicester: School of Archaeological Studies, University of Leicester, Leicester LE1 7RH. Tel 0116 252 2611/2609, fax 0116 252 5005
Dept of Museum Studies, 105 Princess Road East, Leicester LE1 7LG, tel 0116 252 3964, fax 0116 252 3960

Liverpool: Department of Archaeology, University of Liverpool, PO Box 147, Liverpool L69

3BX. Tel 0151 794 2467, fax 0151 794 2226 (Prof Slater)

London (Birkbeck College): Department of History, Birkbeck College, University of London, Malet Street, London WC1E 7HX. Tel 0171 631 6266/6299, fax 0171 631 6552

London (UCL): Institute of Archaeology, University College London, 31–34 Gordon Square, London WC1H 0PY. Tel 0171 380 7495, fax 0171 383 2572

London (East London): Department of Environmental Sciences, University of East London, Stratford Campus, Romford Road, Stratford, London E15 4LZ. Tel 0181 590 7722 ext 4327, fax 0181 849 3499

Manchester: Department of the History of Art and Archaeology, University of Manchester, Oxford Road, Manchester M13 9PL. Tel 0161 275 3016, fax same

Newcastle upon Tyne: Department of Archaeology, University of Newcastle upon Tyne, Newcastle upon Tyne NE1 7RU. Tel 0191 222 7844, fax 0191 261 1182

Newport [formerly **Gwent** College of Higher Education]: Department of History and Archaeology, Caerleon Campus, University of Wales Newport, PO Box 179, Newport NP6 1YG. Tel 01633 432112/430088, fax 01633 432006

Nottingham: Department of Archaeology, University of Nottingham, Nottingham NG7 2RD Tel 0115 951 4820, fax 0115 951 4824

Oxford: Institute of Archaeology, 36 Beaumont Street, Oxford OX1 2PG. Tel 01865 278240, fax 01865 278254.
See also Research Laboratory for Archaeology and the History of Art, Section 4.2 Organisations

Plymouth: Faculty of Science, Department of Marine Studies, Division of Ocean Studies, University of Plymouth, Drake Circus, Plymouth PL4 8AA. Tel 01752 233427, fax 01752 232406

Reading: Department of Archaeology, University of Reading, Whiteknights, PO Box 218, Reading RG6 2AA. Tel 01734 318132, fax 01734 316718

St Andrews: School of History and International Relations, Scottish Institute of Maritime Studies, St Andrews, Fife KY16 9AJ. Tel 01334 462916, fax 01334 462921

Sheffield: Department of Archaeology and Prehistory, Northgate House, West Street, Sheffield S1 4ET. Tel 0114 282 5030, fax 0114 272 2563

Southampton: Department of Archaeology, University of Southampton, Highfield, Southampton SO17 1BJ. Tel 01703 592247, fax 01703 593032

Swansea: *(Archaeology taught only as component of MA in Ancient History)* Department of Classics and Ancient History, University of Wales Swansea, Singleton Park, Swansea SA2 8PP. Tel 01792 295187, fax 01792 295739

York: Department of Archaeology, University of York, The King's Manor, York YO1 2EP. Tel 01904 433901, fax 01904 433902
At same address are the **Centre for Medieval Studies** *and the* **Institute for Advanced Architectural Studies**

Other institutions

International Institute of Maritime Studies (Alderney) *see Section 4.2 Organisations*

Ironbridge Institute *see Section 4.2 Organisations*

Winchester: Department of History and Archaeology, King Alfred's College of Higher Education, Winchester, Hampshire SO22 4NR. Tel 01962 827423, fax 01962 842280

See also summer schools listed in Section 6.9 The excavator's training . . .

4.8
Museum Directories and general Museology

This section contains:
Organisations
Principal museological journals
Directories of museums
Works about museums.
Section 4.9, Museum catalogues, gives more details about individual museums and their contents.

Internet: the **Virtual Library Museums Page** is at http://www.comlab.ox.ac.uk/archive/other/museums.html
The **Museum Documentation Association**'s home page is at http://www.comlab.ox.ac.uk/archive/other/museums/mda/

Organisations

Where no address is given below, look in Section 4.2 Organisations.

Association of Independent Museums, c/o Weald and Downland Open Air Museum, Singleton, Chichester, W Sussex PO18 0EU, tel 01243 811348, fax 01243 822475.
Hon Sec Andrew Patterson (not himself based at Singleton): the Association deals with areas of decision and policy and is run by its members, who are those museums not directly administered by central or local government.

Committee of Area Museum Councils, 141 Cheltenham Road, Cirencester, Glos GL7 2JF, tel 01285 640428. The AMCs are 10 regional councils which support and promote the work of museums in the regions.

European Society of Museum Archaeologists (in process of setting up at time of writing; G M R Davis at Colchester Museum, 01206 282931, may be able to help with enquiries). For other European organisations enquire of CBA.

Group for Education in Museums (GEM), c/o John Yorath, 1 Annsworthy Avenue, Thornton Heath, Surrey CR7 8QD, tel 0181 653 6432, fax 0181 653 5594. The Group promotes the educational use of museums and galleries for all ages, from pre-school to retirement; it produces a newsletter, bibliography, and other publications such as conference proceedings.

ICOM, International Council of Museums, Maison de l'UNESCO, 1 rue Miollis, F75732 Paris Cedex 15, tel +(33) 1-47-34-05-00
ICOM UK
ICOMOS (UK), International Council on Museums and Sites
International Council for Museums of Archaeology and History (ICMAH): Hon Sec at 1995 is M Perissière, Conservateur, Esplanade Dwight Eisenhower, BP 6261, F14066 Caen, France; but David Devenish at Wisbech and Fenland Museum, 01945 583817, may be able to help with enquiries.
Irish Museums Association
Museum Documentation Association
Museum Professionals Group, c/o Salisbury Museum, The King's House, 65 The Close, Salisbury SP1 2EN
Museums Association
Museums and Galleries Commission
Museum Training Institute
Northern Ireland Museums Council
Scottish Museum Archaeologists
Scottish Museums Council
Society of Museum Archaeologists

Principal journals

Museological review (1354–5825). 1994–. 2/yr. Students of the Leicester University Department of Museum Studies. The first number includes a review of a decade (1983–93) of PhD research in the Department.
Museum archaeologist (ISBNs only). 1978–.
Museum international (1350–0775). 1993–. (Formerly *Museum,* 1948–92). UNESCO, Paris
Museum Ireland, Journal of the Irish Museums Association (0961–9690). 1991–.
Museum management and curatorship (0260–4779). 1982–. 4/yr. (Formerly *International journal of museum management and curatorship.*)
Museums journal (0027–416X). 1901–. 12/yr. Museums Association: the principal channel for museum discussions and news.

Directories

Dale, Peter (ed), *Directory of museums and special collections in the United Kingdom.* London: Aslib, 1993, 309 p. 0 85142 308 6.
Lists over 1,000 institutions, but is poorly indexed.

**Hudson, Kenneth and Nicholls, Ann, *The Cambridge guide to the museums of Britain and Ireland*. Cambridge: CUP, 1989, o 521 38902 3 pb (or any later edn).
County order with indexes of subjects and museum names.

The museum directory (ed Maggie Heath). Milton Keynes: The Museum Development Co, 1994, 420 p, indexes.
A products and services directory for museum professionals, not a directory of 'where to find' museums themselves, for which the *Museums yearbook* (below) should be used.

Museum Documentation Association, *UK Museums e-mail directory* (printed form: contact Tony Gill at MDA, 01223 315760).

Museums and galleries in Great Britain and Ireland. East Grinstead: Reed Information Services. Annual.
The guide that is most commonly found on bookstalls and in public libraries, but is far less comprehensive than one might hope. County order with indexes by subject, town name and museum name.

***Museums yearbook, including a directory of museums and galleries of the British Isles* (0307-7675). London: Museums Association. Annual.
Since computerisation this invaluable guide gives more information on collections and events, as well as listing related organisations. Lists museums and their departments and main staff, gives guidelines and codes of conduct for museum staff and authorities, and provides a list of Mus Assoc members plus a directory of products and services.

Ostler, Timothy (comp), *The building museums guide*. London: Interbuild Publications for Building Museums Project, 1993, xxvii, 148 p, indexes. o 9500404 1 x pb.
Pocket guide to over 100 museums which deal with architecture, building, building materials, and 'people who make buildings happen'.

**Woodhead, Peter and Stansfield, Geoffrey, *Keyguide to information sources in museum studies*. London: Mansell/Fitzroy Dearborn, 2 edn 1994, xiv, 224 p, bibl, index. o 7201 2151 5.
Lists the main sources, with a selective list of organisations world-wide.

Works about museums

Biddle, M, 'Can we expect museums to cope? Curatorship and the archaeological explosion', in D Gaimster (ed), *Museum archaeology in Europe* (Oxford: Oxbow, 1994), pp 166–71.
Important conference paper discussing the plight of museums as excavators continue to remove material from the ground and want curatorial care for it.

Bourn, J, *Management of the collections of the English national museums and galleries: report by the Comptroller and Auditor-General*. London: House of Commons, 1988, 17 p. o 10 239948 1 pb.
Official inquiry revealed the unsatisfactory state of collections management in most of our national museums, and reported a 3-year funding settlement to assist museum finances and help with building and maintenance needs. *See also National Audit Office below*.

British Museum Research Register 1991–3 (or current triennium). London: Trustees of the British Museum, 1994, 69 p. (ISSN 1354-8514). *See also Wallace below*

Dept of National Heritage see under National Audit Office below.

Eckstein, Jeremy (ed), 'Museums and galleries', in *Cultural trends 1993*, 19, pp 1–44. (Policy Studies Institute).
Independent review of statistics: finance, admissions figures, work of MGC and AMCs, Museum Training Institute, improvement funds, etc. Includes Wales, Scotland, Northern Ireland.

***Exploring Museums* (series). London: HMSO for Museums and Galleries Commission. Regional books published between 1989 and 1992, the regions being: London, Home Counties, NE England, NW England and the Isle of Man, SW England, Wales, S England and the Channel Isles, Scotland, and Ireland.

Greenfield, Jeanette, *The return of cultural treasures*. Cambridge: CUP, 1989, xviii, 361 p, bibl, index. o 521 33319 9.
Discusses the vexed issue of items being returned to their homelands, with reference to the approaches taken in different countries.

Knell, S, bibliog of museum studies, see Section 4.9 Museum catalogues.

***Museum Documentation Association, *Computers in museums 1994–95*. MDA, 1994, 72 p. Discusses what are databases, how to choose software and personal computer, glossary, list of software by museums using it, and by museums using which software.

Museums and Galleries Commission, on standards in the museum care of archaeological collections, see Section 4.9 Museum catalogues.

National Audit Office, *Department of National Heritage/National museums and galleries: quality of service to the public: report by the Comptroller and Auditor General.* London: HMSO (= [HC] 841), 1993, 43 p. 0 10 022243 9 pb.
Gives qualified approval to the work of the five national museums, and suggests that all others follow their marketing approach. *See also under Bourn above.*

Owen, Janet (ed), on accessible archaeological archives, see Section 6.9 The excavator's training . . . (under Post-excavation processes).

Pearce, Susan, on archaeological curatorship, see Section 4.9 Museum catalogues.

'Thesaurus' is a subscription database at Didier Ciambra, Thesaurus Group Ltd, 76 Gloucester Place, London WIH 4DQ (tel 0171 487 3401, fax 0171 487 4211), which lists full details of all catalogued lots offered for sale. Museums can by this means search for their stolen items or follow leads to fill out their collections. Over 500 catalogues for UK auction houses are immediately loaded, totalling some 3 million items/yr. It can be searched daily against individual user profiles and subscribers notified of interesting items.

Vergo, Peter (ed), *The new museology.* London: Reaktion Books, 1989 (repr 1993), viii, 230 p, bibl, index. 0 948462 04 3 hb, 0 948462 03 5 pb.
Essays on topics which authors felt needed to be addressed.

Wallace, Janet, 'The central archives of the British Museum', in *Archives,* 19, 1990, pp 213–23 (a general description of what is held).

Wales

Jenkins, Geraint, *Getting yesterday right: interpreting the heritage of Wales.* Cardiff: Univ Wales Press, 1992, [xii], 179 p, short bibl. 0 7083 1151 2
Includes selective inventories of castles and of museum and heritage sites, and discusses farming, rural industry, industrial heritage, maritime, buildings, in the context of urging historical integrity against cheapening of the heritage.

Scotland

Scottish museum news (0266–6898). 2/yr.

***Alexander, Wilma and Castell, Lesley (comp), *Scottish museums and galleries: the guide.* [Aberdeen]: Aberdeen Univ Press/Scot Mus Council, 1990, 110 p, index. 0 08 037974 5.

Ambrose, Timothy M (ed), *Presenting Scotland's story.* Edinburgh: HMSO for Scot Mus Council, 1989, 95 p. 0 11 493498 3 pb.
Illustrated papers from ten contributors involved in either public or private sector heritage organisations.

MOSAICS and **SCRAN** *see entries under Scotland in Section 4.9 Museum catalogues.*

Ireland

Archaeology Ireland (0790–982x) issues an annual supplement listing Irish museums and visitor centres.

Popplewell, Sean (ed), *The Irish museums guide.* Dublin: Ward River Press/Ir Mus Trust, 1983, 207 p. 0 907085 55 5.

Wood, Helen, *Survey of museums in Ireland.* Dublin: Ir Mus Ass, 1994. 0 952299 50 X.
A statistical survey of museum trends.

4.9
Museum Catalogues and related Works

This section contains:
  Bibliographic works
  General works relating to museum catalo-
    guing
  Some specific catalogues and reference works
    (by topic; ie general works which may not
    be appropriate in the Period bibliographies
    of Section 6)
  Museum catalogues (listed by town)
  Wales, Scotland, Ireland (separately).
Note that the Leicester University Dept of Mu-
seum Studies maintains a documentation centre
on museum archives: computerisation in pro-
gress.

*See also Section 4.8 for museum directories and
general museological information, including relevant principal journals.*

Bibliographic works

*Bassett, D A, 'Museum publications: a descrip-
tive and bibliographic guide', in J M A Thompson et al (eds), *Manual of curatorship*.
Butterworth/Heinemann, 2 edn 1992, pp
590–622.
Contains a mass of useful information on
primary, secondary and tertiary publications,
ie from museum pamphlets through to abstracting services and guides to museological literature. All museum topics, not just archaeology.

Bosdet, Mary and Durbin, Gail (comp), *GEM
museum education bibliography 1978–88*. [sl]:
Group for Education in Museums, 1989. 1
872164 02 1.

International museological bibliography. Paris:
UNESCO-ICOM Docum Centre, 1967–85 (annual, with indexes; on CD-ROM from 1986).

*Knell, S (comp and ed), *A bibliography of
museum studies*. Aldershot: Scolar Press, 11
edn 1994, viii, 248 p, index. 1 85928 061 7.
Wide-ranging collection of references, in classified arrangement with author index and list of
museum-related periodicals.

*Museum abstracts, see Section 1.5 Indexing and
abstracting services.*

Roulstone, Michael (ed), *The bibliography of
museum and art gallery publications and
audio-visual aids in Great Britain and Ireland
1979/80*. Cambridge: Chadwyck-Healey, 1980,
unpag (c. 450 p), author and subject indexes.
Seemingly the only attempt to produce a
comprehensive list of museum publications
and slides (etc); a brave shot, but patchy in
coverage and now very much out of date.
Bassett (above) gives a much more recent,
though more selective view.

Sotheby catalogues on microfilm: University Microfilms International in association with
Sotheby Parke-Bernet. Sales held between
1733 and 1990 are annotated with prices and
buyers. 538 reels or 7,000 fiche available from
UMI, 60 High Street, Godstone, Reigate, Surrey
(tel 01883 744123).

General works relating to museum
cataloguing

Archaeological Object Thesaurus Working
Group: c/o Neil Beagrie (Chair), National
Monuments Record Centre, RCHME Swindon
(tel 01793 414700). Aims to develop a shared
thesaurus to benefit archaeological specialists of
all kinds, whether in museums, SMRs, NMRs,
English Heritage or archaeological units.

Beagrie, Neil, 'Museum collections, national archaeological indexes and research: information
resources, access and potential', in G T Denford
(ed), *Museum archaeology – what's new?* (=
Mus archaeol, 21 for 1994), pp 28–34.
Presents NMR figures on numbers of excavations 1940–80 and discusses future access to
and potential of the archaeological materials
held by museums.

British Museum Object Name Working Party (c/o
Collections Data Management Section). Formal
thesaurus of object names compiled for in-
house use; possible plans for wider dissemination (contact Tanya Szrajber of CDMS, British
Museum, London WC1B 3DG).

Blackaby, J R, Greeno, P and The Nomenclature
Committee, *The revised nomenclature for museum cataloguing: a revised and expanded
version of Robert G Chenhall's system for
classifying man-made objects*. Nashville: Amer
Ass for State and Local Hist, 1988, approx 520
pp (section-numbered). 0 910050 93 7.
American materials but a useful approach.

Bradley, Susan, *A guide to the storage, exhibition and handling of antiquities, ethnographia and pictorial art. Brit Mus occas pap*, **66**, 1990. o 86159 066 x pb.
Contains articles by contributors on various aspects, eg organic materials, ceramics and glass, etc.

CIDOC directory of thesauri for object names – English/Français. 1994. Obtain from Art and Architecture Thesaurus, 62 Stratton Road, Williamstown, MA 01267, USA. (Assembled from a dozen countries and no strong archaeological emphasis.)

Fahy, Anne and Sudbury, Wendy, *Information: the hidden resource. Museums and the Internet. Proceeedings of the 7th International Conference of the Museums Documentation Association . . . Edinburgh 6–7 November.* Cambridge: Mus Doc Ass, 1995, 424 p, index. o 905963 96 2 pb.

Grant, Alice, on SPECTRUM, see under Museum Documentation Association below.

Hertfordshire Curators' Group, *Hertfordshire simple name list: a thesaurus of terms for use in cataloguing general social history collections . . .* [Hertford?]: Standing Committee for Museums in Hertfordshire, c. 1984, 177 leaves in ring binder. o 901354 30 9.

Holm, Stuart A, *Guidelines for constructing a museum object name thesaurus.* Cambridge: Mus Docum Ass, 1993. o 905963 87 3.

—, *Facts and artefacts: how to document a museum collection.* Cambridge: Mus Docum Ass, 1991, 36 p. o 905963 79 2 pb.

Merriman, Nick, *Beyond the glass case: the past, the heritage and the public in Britain.* Leicester: Leicester Univ Press, 1991, xii, 188 p, bibl, index. o 7185 1349 5.
On why people go, or do not go, to museums.

Museum Documentation Association: *The MDA data standard.* Cambridge: MDA, rev edn 1991, large ring-binder. o 905963 74 1.
The introduction is followed by sections illustrating fields in the data standard for registering museum collections (160 fields in the full standard); terminal standards; character set; application guidelines; field table; data dictionary; and bibliography.
NB: MODES (Museum Object Data Entry System) ceased development in August 1995.

—, *SPECTRUM: the UK Museum Documentation Standard* (comp and ed Alice Grant). Cambridge: MDA, 1994, large looseleaf binder, various pagings, bibl, glossary, indexes. o 905963 92 X.
SPECTRUM (= Standard Procedures for Collections Recording Used in Museums) sets out 20 procedures for museum recording (whether manually or by computer) of inventory control, conservation, reproduction, indemnity management and so on.

—, *Thesauri for museum documentation: proceedings of a workshop held at the Science Museum, London.* Cambridge: *Mus Docum Ass occas pap*, **18**, 1992, 106 p, bibl. o 905963 86 5 ring-bound.

See also 'Computers in museums 1994–5' listed under Museum Documentation Association in Section 4.8 Museum directories.

Museums and Galleries Commission: Standards in the museum care of archaeological collections. London: MGC, 1992, 59 p. o 948630 15 9 pb, spiral binding.
The message of this volume is that preservation of museum materials is not a passive activity but requires active work. The first part deals with collection management, the second with collection protection, and there are technical appendices.

Owen, J (ed), on transfer of archaeological archives to museums, see Section 6.9 The excavator's training . . . (under Post-excavation processes).

Pearce, Susan, 'Museum archaeology' in J Hunter and I Ralston (eds), Archaeological resource management in the UK (1993), pp 232–42.
Discusses the management of collections and the presentation of this material in a wide range of display and interpretive projects.

—, *Archaeological curatorship.* Leicester: Leicester Univ Press, 1990, xvi, 223 p, bibl, index. o 7185 1298 7.
Comprehensive and authoritative survey from the Professor of Museum Studies at Leicester University.

Roberts, D A (ed), Terminology for museums: proceedings of an international conference held in Cambridge, England, 21–24 September 1988. Cambridge: Mus Docum Ass/Getty Grant Program, 1990, xiv, 625 p. o 905963 62 8.

Important and wide-ranging consideration of an extremely difficult problem (or set of problems), including papers on applications in sites and monuments records, and the 'Getty' thesaurus (*for which see entry in Section 6.1 General reference works (under Dictionaries)*).

SHIC Working Party, *Social History and Industrial Classification (SHIC): a subject classification for museum collections.* Cambridge: Mus Docum Ass for SHIC Working Party, 2 (rev) edn 1993, xxiv + c 100 pp looseleaf. (Index also available from 1996.) 0 905963 91 1.
Slightly reworked since the first edition, but still no real concessions to archaeological needs (see this compiler's critique in *Mus archaeol*, 11, 1986, pp 85–7). Machine-readable version under consideration.

**Society of Museum Archaeologists often publishes conference proceedings, some listed below. Most are edited by Edmund Southworth (latterly, G T Denford) and printed in the *Museum archaeologist* journal, for instance:
Selection, retention and dispersal of archaeological collections: guidelines for use in England, Wales and Northern Ireland. 1993, 48 p. 1 871855 05 5 pb.
Still begging! Fund raising for archaeology. = *Mus archaeol*, 15, 1991, 28 p. (1988 conference: includes a survey of English Heritage storage grants.)
What's mine is yours! Museum collecting policies. = *Mus archaeol*, 16, 1991. (1989 conference: includes a paper on the relevant laws in Scotland.)
Taking stock: access to archaeological collections. = *Mus archaeol*, 20, 1995. (1993 conference: includes papers on a survey of Scottish archaeological collections, local government reform in Scotland and in Wales, etc.)
Museum archaeology – what's new? = *Mus archaeol*, 21, 1996. (1994 conference)

Stone, Peter G and Molyneaux, B L, *The presented past: heritage, museums and education.* London/New York: Routledge/English Heritage, 1994, 520 p, chapter bibls, index. 0 415 09602 2.
Includes papers on the redisplay of the Keiller Museum in Avebury, and on the teaching of the past in English formal curricula; the remainder deal with overseas practice.

***Thompson, John M A et al (eds), *Manual of curatorship: a guide to museum practice.* Lon-

don: Butterworth/Heinemann, 2 edn 1992, xvii, 756 p, bibls, index. 0 7506 0351 8.
The curator's bible: includes important papers on archaeological collections by Ian Longworth and John Cherry, and on museum libraries by John Kenyon.

*Walker, Kristen, *Guidelines for the preparation of excavation archives for long term storage.* London: UKIC, 1990, 29 p. 1 871656 06 0 pb.

Some subject-specific catalogues and reference works

Beads: *Bead Study Trust Newsletter* lists recently published work on beads

Bronzes (prehistoric): *in Royal Ontario Museum, see under Hayes and Pryor (respectively) in Section 6.11.2 Neolithic-Bronze Age.*

Coins: *Sylloge of Coins of the British Isles (SCBI)* is a series of catalogues published by OUP for the British Academy: 20-year cumulative indexes are produced.

The National Museums of Scotland have a coins catalogue of some 23,000 entries, completion due 1996.

Footwear: Thornton, J H (ed), *Textbook of footwear manufacture* (includes glossary etc). London: Butterworth, 3 edn 1964 (repr 1971).

The national collection and register for 'foundation deposit' shoes is held at Northampton Museum.

Leather: Walsall Leather Museum, *Leather bibliography.* 1993, 18p. Classified list of references.

Medical ceramics: Crellin, J K, *Medical ceramics: a catalogue of the English and Dutch collections in the Museum of the Wellcome Institute for the History of Medicine.* London: WIHM, 1969, 304 p.

Medical glassware: Crellin, J and Scott, J R, *Glass and British pharmacy 1600–1900: a survey and guide to the Wellcome Collection of British Glass.* London: Wellcome Institute for the History of Medicine, 1972, 72 p, bibl, index. pb.
Illustrated catalogue based on study of over 1,200 pieces of pharmaceutical glassware.

Pottery: Romano-British Reference Collection being assembled at the British Museum: contact

Val Rigby (0171 636 1555). This resource will have colour charts and colour photographs of fabrics for basic identifications by pottery workers, together with a users' manual etc (due late 1996/7).

Medieval and later pottery: the National Reference Collection for medieval pottery (fabrics and kiln samples etc) is held at the British Museum (contact Beverley Nenk, 0171 323 8286). The BM also holds very substantial collections of post-medieval British and Continental wares, including many complete pots (contact David Gaimster, 0171 323 8734). The Welsh reference collection is at the National Museum of Wales, and the National Reference Collection of post-medieval wares (concentrating on the Potteries) is held at Stoke-on-Trent City Museum and Art Gallery.

Lambeth Stoneware Pottery Archives, Lambeth Archives Dept, Minet Library, 52 Knatchbull Road, London SE5 9QY (tel 0171 926 6076). Relates to the famous post-medieval potteries here.

Textiles: Walton, Penelope and Eastwood, Gillian, *A brief guide to the cataloguing of archaeological textiles.* London: Inst Archaeol Publ, 4 edn 1988, 24 p, glossary. 0 905853 20 2 pb.

Treen: Pinto, Edward H, *Treen and other wooden bygones: an encyclopaedia and social history.* London: Bell and Sons, 1969, x, 458 p, refs, glossary, index. 0 7135 1533 3 (Reprinted 1979).
Considers wooden artefacts under 28 functional divisions. A classic work.

Museum catalogues

These are of widely disparate publication dates, some being much more up to date than others. These publications are probably under-used in any event: the interpretations may have changed since publication, and the detail much increased, but the basic data remain.

NATIONAL COLLECTIONS

British Museum: several catalogues from 1920s onwards, for instance:
Stone Age (1902); Bronze Age (2 edn 1920); Early Iron Age (1925, reprinted Anglia 1994); Later prehistoric antiquities of the British Isles (1953); Roman Britain (3 edn 1964); Anglo-Saxon antiquities (1923, reprinted Anglia 1993); Medieval and later objects (1924).

Subsequent BM catalogues are much more detailed, for instance:
Kinnes, I A and Longworth, I H (et al), *Catalogue of the excavated prehistoric and Romano-British material in the Greenwell Collection.* London: Brit Mus Publications, 1985, 154 p, bibl, glossary, indexes. 0 7141 1371 9
Covers the material collected by Canon William Greenwell (1820–1918) in his extensive excavations on the Yorkshire Wolds; Neolithic to RB, especially BA. Addenda to the catalogue appear in *Yorkshire archaeol j*, 60, 1988, pp 173–4.

Smith, Reginald, *The Sturge Collection: an illustrated selection of flints from Britain bequeathed in 1919 by William Allen Sturge.* London: British Mus, 1931, xiii, 136 p.
Good drawings by C O Waterhouse, photographs less good. Sturge collected at Icklingham and elsewhere, and also bought collections from Canon Greenwell, Allen Brown, Greenhill, Worthington Smith and others.

See also more specialised catalogues from the British Museum in their appropriate period sections: D M Bailey for Roman lamps and W H Manning for RB ironwork, both in Section 6.11.4 Romano-British; D M Wilson for Anglo-Saxon ornamental metalwork, in Section 6.11.5 Migration and early medieval; G Egan for lead cloth seals etc, in Section 6.11.7 Post-medieval.

REGIONAL COLLECTIONS, LISTED BY TOWN

There may well be many more of these discoverable locally; the following can only be a sample.

Bristol
Britton, F, *English Delftware in the Bristol collection.* London: Philip Wilson for Sotheby, 1982, 335 p, bibl, index. 0 85667 152 5.
Catalogues 800 pieces.

Grinsell, L V, *Guide catalogue to the south western British prehistoric collections.* Bristol: City Museum, 1968, 70 p, refs. Pb.

Hebditch, Max, *Guide catalogue to the Roman collections from south western Britain.* Bristol: City Museum, 1970, 48 p, refs. Pb.

Devizes
See Annable and Simpson in Section 6.11.2 Neolithic-Bronze Age.

Cunnington, W (revised E H Goddard), *Catalogue of antiquities in the Museum . . . at Devizes: part 1, the Stourhead collection* (originally 1896); *part 2, Miscellaneous* (1911, 1934). Devizes: Wilts Archaeol Natur Hist Soc, 1934.

Liverpool

Nicholson, Susan M, *Catalogue of the prehistoric metalwork in Merseyside County Museums (formerly Liverpool Museum)*. Univ Liverpool Dept Prehist Archaeol work notes 2, 1980, 148 p, bibl, indexes. 0 906367 02 6 pb. Includes material from Britain and Ireland, with a note on Joseph Mayer (1803–86), founder of the collection.

London: (Note: Guildhall Museum and London Museum merged to form the Museum of London in 1975.)

Catalogue of the collection of London antiquities in the Guildhall Museum. London: Corp of the City of London, 2 edn, 1908, 411 p, 100 pls.
A few Stone Age pieces, Late Celtic, Roman, Anglo-Saxon and 'Danish', medieval and later.

The London Museum also produced a series of catalogues between 1927 and 1940, covering (respectively) Roman, Saxon, Viking, medieval London; also costumes.

Museum of London series 'Medieval finds from excavations in London': see entries in Section 6.11.6, Medieval, under J Clark (horse equipment), J Cowgill (knives and scabbards), E Crowfoot (textiles), G Egan and F Pritchard (dress accessories), and F Grew and M de Neergard (shoes and pattens).

Murdoch, Tessa (comp), *Treasures and trinkets: jewellery in London from pre-Roman times to the 1930s*. Museum of London, 1991, 208 p, bibl, index. 0 904818 48 9 pb.

Merseyside *see Liverpool above.*

Newcastle University *see L Allason-Jones and W H Manning respectively in Section 6.11.4 Romano-British; and R Cramp and R Miket on Anglo-Saxon and Viking material in Section 6.11.5 Migration and early medieval.*

Oxford, Ashmolean Museum *see D Hinton and A MacGregor (respectively) in Section 6.11.5 Migration and early medieval.*

See also MacGregor, Arthur (ed), *Antiquities*

from Europe and the Near East in the collection of The Lord McAlpine of West Green. Oxford: Ashmolean Museum, 1987, 142 p, refs, indexes. 0 907849 70 9.
These mostly unprovenanced objects, from a collection of 'unashamedly antiquarian character' (including many from Britain), nonetheless provide useful information.

Salisbury *see C N Moore and M J Rowlands in Section 6.11.2 Neolithic–Bronze Age; and P and E Saunders on harness pendants etc, B Spencer on pilgrim badges, both in Section 6.11.6 Medieval.*

Sheffield

Howarth, E, *Catalogue of the Bateman collection of antiquities in the Sheffield Public Museum*. London, 1899.

York

Allason-Jones, Lindsay, *Roman jet in the Yorkshire Museum*. York: Yorkshire Mus, 1996, 55 p, bibl. 0 905807 17 0 pb.
Introduction and catalogue: ornaments and partly-worked pieces of shale, cannel coal etc as well as jet.

Wales

see H N Savory in Section 6.11.2 Neolithic-Bronze Age, and Section 6.11.3 Iron Age.

Exploring museums: Wales, see Section 4.8 Museum directories.

Grimes, W F, *The prehistory of Wales*. Cardiff: Nat Mus Wales, 2 edn 1951, xvii, 288 p, bibl, indexes.
Catalogue of the NMW collections to 1937, mainly superseded by the Savory volumes noted above, but listed here for the quality of the writing (Grimes's fine drawings suffered from over-reduction).

Lee, John Edward, *Isca Silurum, or, an illustrated catalogue of the Museum of Antiquities at Caerleon*. London: Longman, 1862, xii, 148 p. (plus supplement issued as *Monmouthshire and Caerleon Antiquarian Assoc*, 15, 1868)
Mostly RB material.

Lynch, Frances (comp), *Museum of Welsh antiquities, Bangor: catalogue of archaeological material*. Bangor: Univ College N Wales, 1986. No ISBN, pb.
Covers Neolithic to medieval material.

Stevens, Christine (ed), *Classification of objects in*

the Welsh Folk Museum collection. Cardiff: Nat Mus Wales, 1982. 0 85485 047 3 pb.

Scotland

Ambrose, T on museum presentation, see Section 4.8 Museum directories.

Bell, A S (ed), *The Scottish antiquarian tradition: essays to mark the bicentenary of the Society of Antiquaries of Scotland and its museum, 1780–1980.* Edinburgh: John Donald, 1981, 286 p, refs, index. 0 85976 080 4.
Numerous contributed papers on Scottish museums, the development of archaeology in Scotland, and a bibliography of Scottish numismatics.

Calder, J (ed), on the wealth of a nation in the National Museums of Scotland, see Section 6.4 Regional surveys.

Catalogue of the National Museum of Antiquities of Scotland. Edinburgh: Soc Antiq Scotl, new and enl edn 1892, 380 p.
Covers all periods; drawings of good 1890s standard; but the National Museums collections have more than doubled in the last century.

Coutts, Herbert, *Tayside before history: a guide-catalogue of the collection of antiquities in Dundee Museum. Dundee Museum and Art Gallery publ,* 1, 1971
Illustrated with line drawings and photographs; short bibl.

Exploring museums: Scotland, see Section 4.8 Museum directories.

MOSAICS (Museums of Scotland Advanced Interactive Computer System). This is a project designed for the galleries of the new Museum of Scotland building (1998) which will offer a full cultural history of Scotland as represented in the National Museum of Scotland, including topics such as 'The Enlightenment' as well as artefactual material.

Saville, Alan, 'Artefact research in the National Museums of Scotland', in Gaimster D (ed), *Museum archaeology in Europe (Oxbow monogr 39, 1994),* pp 155–66.

SCRAN 2000, the Scottish Cultural Resources Access Network, is a Millennium Commission-supported project incorporating digital resources for presenting Scottish human history.

The organisations concerned as partners are Scottish Museums Council, National Museums of Scotland and RCAHMS.

Ireland

Armstrong, E C R, *Guide to the collection of Irish antiquities: catalogue of Irish gold ornaments in the collection of the Royal Irish Academy.* Dublin: HMSO, 1920.

Belfast Museum, *Descriptive catalogue of the collection of antiquities, etc, illustrative of Irish history, exhibited . . . at the 22nd meeting of the British Association, 1852.* Belfast: 1852. (Not confined to Belfast Museum's own holdings.)

Coffey, G, *Guide to the Celtic antiquities of the Christian period preserved in the National Museum.* Dublin: 2 edn 1910.

Eogan, George, 'Irish antiquities of the Bronze Age, Iron Age and Early Christian period in the National Museum of Denmark', in *Proc Roy Ir Acad C,* 91.6, 1991, pp 133–76, bibl.
Catalogues 134 objects of stone and metal.

Herity, Michael, 'Early finds of Irish antiquities', *Antiq J,* 59, 1969, pp 1–21.

—, 'Irish antiquarian finds and collections of the early 19th century', *J Roy Soc Antiq Ir,* 99, 1969, pp 21–37.

Tempest, H G, 'Catalogue of the collection of antiquities of the Co Louth Archaeological Society 1961', *J Co Louth Archaeol Soc,* 14.4, 1960, pp 214–31.

Wallace, P F (forthcoming), *Guide to the National Museum of Ireland.*

Wilde, Sir W R W, *A descriptive catalogue of the antiquities, etc, in the Museum of the Royal Irish Academy.* 2 vols. Dublin: Hodges and Smith, 1857–61.
Indispensable classic! with some illustrations, well drawn but small and lacking scales; discursive text.

—, *A descriptive catalogue of the antiquities of gold in the Museum of the Royal Irish Academy.* Dublin: 1862

4.10
Recurrent Conferences and Congresses

The principal official finding list for the published results of this kind of meeting is the British Library's *Index of conference proceedings received* (0959–4906, monthly with annual cumulations; quarterly CD-ROM and 25-year cumulation, 1964–88, on fiche; online via BLAISE). It usually includes such archaeological conferences as achieve publication. The following list endeavours to include all recurrent archaeological conferences (or those with an archaeological component), whether published or not. They are listed by official title, inverted to bring topic first, with cross-references where needed. The usual frequency is annual, except where otherwise noted. Most are peripatetic with organisers liable to change from one conference to the next. So-called 'conferences' which are really study tours are not included.

Ancient Mosaics *see under* Mosaics below
Anglo-Norman Studies *see* Battle Conference
Archaeometry [and Archaeological Prospection], International Symposia on
Archaeozoology, International Council on (tri-or quadrennial)
Archaeological Illustrators and Surveyors, Association of
Atlantic Colloquia (irreg. 1961–80)
Battle Conference on Anglo-Norman Studies
Boat and Ship Archaeology, International Symposia on (triennial)
British Archaeological Science (biennial)
British Association for the Advancement of Science
Burnt Mound Conferences (1988, 1990)
Celtic Studies, International Congress of (irreg.)
Château Gaillard [international castles conference]
Coinage and Monetary History, Oxford Symposia on
Computer Applications [and Quantitative Methods] in Archaeology (title varies)
Conservation *see* IICHAW *and* UKIC
Dyes in History and Archaeology, Assoc of Researchers into
Environmental Archaeologists, Symposia of the Association of
Flint Symposia, International (quadrennial)
(Glass History) Congrès de l'Association Inter-

nationale pour l'Histoire du Verre (biennial or triennial)
Heritage Coordination
Historical Metallurgy Society
IICHAW, International Institute for Conservation of Historic and Artistic Works, International Congress
Industrial Archaeology, Association for
Insular Art, International Conference on (irreg.)
IUPPS/UISPP, International Union of Prehistoric and Protohistoric Sciences (irreg.)
Limeskongressen (Congress of Roman Frontier Studies) (every 2 or 4 years)
Medieval Archaeology, Society for
Medieval Art and Architecture (British Archaeological Association)
Medieval Congress (Kalamazoo, Michigan)
Metallurgy in Numismatics (Royal Numismatic Soc, irreg.)
[Mills], International Molinological Society, Symposia (frequency not known)
Mosaics, International Colloquia on Ancient (Assoc Internationale pour l'Etude de la Mosaïque Antique) (irreg.)
Museum Archaeologists, Society of
Museum Documentation Association
Museums Association
Music Archaeology, Study Group on (irreg.)
Palaeopathology Association, European Meetings of the
Post-Medieval Archaeology, Society for
Prehistoric Society
Radiocarbon, International Conference on
Rei Cretariae Romanae Fautorum (biennial)
Roman Archaeology Conference (SPRS/J Roman Archaeol/Brit Acad, biennial)
Roman Frontier Studies *see* Limeskongressen
Roman Military Equipment Conference
Roman Pottery *see* Rei Cretariae . . .
Rural Landscape, Permanent European Conference for the Study of the
Scientific Methods, Nordic Conference on the Application of
Scottish Archaeological Forum (published from 1970–81)
Textiles, North European Symposium for Archaeological (NESAT) (triennial)
Theoretical Archaeology Group (TAG)
Theoretical Roman Archaeology Conference (TRAC)
UISPP *see* IUPPS
UKIC (UK Institute for Conservation)
Underwater Archaeology Conference (USA, irreg.)

Viking Congress (irreg.)

Waterfront Archaeology in Northern European Towns (irreg.)

Wetlands (irreg.)

World Archaeological Congress (quadrennial with biennial intercongresses)

World Congress on Heritage Presentation and Interpretation (tri- or quadrennial)

4.11
Lecture Series from various Organisations

Allen Brown Memorial Lectures (published in *Anglo-Norman studies* from 1991)

Caerleon (Annual) Lectures (published individually by National Museum of Wales)

CBA Presidential Addresses (triennially in *CBA annual reports*)

Dalrymple Lectures (sometimes published as monograph)

de Cardi (Beatrice) Annual Lectures (mostly published in *CBA annual reports*)

Deerhurst Lectures (annual, published by Oxbow)

Gerald Dunning Lectures (annual, published in the periodical *Medieval ceramics*)

Groam House Lecture Series (published by Groam House Museum Trust, Rosemarkie)

Tom Hassall Lectures (published in *Oxoniensia*)

Jarrow Lectures (published individually in Jarrow: checklist up to 1987 published by Charles Thomas in *Glasgow archaeol j*, 14, 1987, pp 75–6; collected volume published by Variorum in 1994 under the title *Bede and his world*)

Hunter Marshall Lectures (sometimes published as monograph)

O'Donnell Lectures (published in various places for Board of Celtic Studies)

Oxbow Lectures (annual, published by Oxbow Books, Oxford)

Rhind Lectures (annual, published by Society of Antiquaries of Scotland)

Rolt Memorial Lectures (eg 1994 in *Industrial archaeology review*)

Wessex Lectures (annual, published by Wessex Archaeology)

Mortimer Wheeler Lectures (annual, published in *Proc British Academy* but not always on British or Irish topics)

Whithorn Lectures (annual, published by Whithorn Trust)

SECTION 5

Photographic Sources

Sources for Photographs (non-air)

Here is a selection of sources of archaeological (and architectural) photographs. Bear in mind that while some of these organisations are very well set up for supplying copies of photographs or slides for research purposes, others have very slender resources indeed. A preliminary enquiry is always advisable, and for visits appointments should always be made.

Directories

British Association of Picture Libraries and Agencies (BAPLA), 18 Vine Hill, London EC1R 5DX, tel 0171 713 0780. Produces an annual members' directory of a large number of picture libraries, with subject index and quick reference charts, but even so not very easy to use.

British Photographers' Liaison Committee, *The ABC of UK photographic copyright*. London: BPLC, 1994, 36 p. 0 9514671 1 5.
Includes amendments made after the 1988 Copyright Act.

Eakins, Rosemary (ed), *Picture sources UK*. London: Macdonald, 1985, 474 p, subject and collection indexes. 0 356 10078 2.
A large volume, but over a decade old now; archaeology is filed among natural history and anthropology, and the air photo section is well out of date. The local history/geography section may be useful.

Evans, Hilary and Evans, Mary (comp), *Picture researcher's handbook: an international guide to picture sources and how to use them*. London: Blueprint (Chapman and Hall), 5 edn 1992, xvii, 516 p, subject and source indexes. 0 948905 75 1.
Rather more up to date than Eakins (above), but not an easy volume to use, especially as the index is rather poor (for instance omitting Ireland, although Irish sources are listed); and Great Britain forms only a small part of the whole volume. Nonetheless, this work contains much useful information, and if an address fails to work the authors offer to help find the new one. *See also Mary Evans Picture Library listed below under Selected collections.*

McKeown, Roy, *National directory of slide*

collections. [London]: Brit Lib Board (= *Brit Lib info guide*, 12), 1990, 310 p, indexes. 0 7123 3208 1.

Mainly non-commercial collections, and less complete than one might hope.

Wall, John (comp), *Directory of British photographic collections.* London: Heinemann for Roy Photogr Soc, 1977, 226 p, indexes. 0 434 92226 9.

Showing its age by now, and depended on questionnaire responses; it recorded 1,580 collections, ordered by subject. Difficult to use and the BAPLA guide (above) will be more help now.

Willetts, Susan J (comp), *Resources guide to audiovisual material for the classics.* London: Inst Classical Stud, 1995, 72 p. 0 9527347 0 2 pb. Lists the material with sources and suppliers.

Selected collections

Many museums have good photographic collections, and no attempt is made to give a full list here. Remember that the three Royal Commissions (addresses given in Section 5.2 Sources for air photographs) have large collections of ground-level subjects in addition to their air photographs.

Lesley and Roy Adkins Picture Library, Longstone Lodge, Aller, Langport, Som TA10 0QT, tel 01458 250075, fax 01458 250858; many thousands of 35mm transparencies (catalogue available). Material on sites in England, Scotland, Wales, France, Germany, Italy, Luxembourg, Spain and Greece.

Architectural Association Slide Library, 34–36 Bedford Square, London WC1B 3ES, tel 0171 636 0974. Dating from end 19th century, this claims to be the largest architectural slide library in Europe with about 80,000 35mm slides for hire; includes a reasonable number of Anglo-Saxon and medieval buildings, only a few prehistoric and RB sites. Catalogue and guide, but personal search is recommended.

Beamish Photographic Archive, North of England Open Air Museum, Beamish, Co Durham DH9 0RG, tel 01207 231811. Has over 12,000 negatives on the development of industry and social history of N England.

British Architectural Library, 66 Portland Street, London W1N 4AD, tel 0171 0171 580 5533. Has a very rich and wide-ranging photographic collection, 30,000 colour and 345,000 b/w, from earliest buildings onwards. Appointment essential.

British Waterways Archive, Llanthony Warehouse, Gloucester Docks, GL1 2EJ, tel 01452 318000. The national collection of canal and inland navigation materials, with a collection of 10,000 negatives.

Council for the Care of Churches, Fielden House, Little College Street, London SW1P 3SH, tel 0171 222 3793. The slide library, unavailable at time of writing, documents churches, fixtures, floors etc; mostly colour, with a classified list. Phone to check current availability.

Country Life Magazine Photographic Library. Derived from the magazine's weekly features on stately homes, from late 19th century onwards. Some 5,000 houses, including many now lost, are represented. The original glass plate negatives (up to the 1950s) have now been moved to RCHME at Swindon and also transferred to film kept at Country Life (from which prints can be made). Other b/w pictures in addition, many never published. Appointment needed: Country Life, King's Reach Tower, Stamford Street, London SE1 9LS, tel 0171 261 7058.

East Anglia, University of, School of World Art Studies and Museology, UEA, Norwich NR4 7TJ, tel 01603 592820. Strong collection of (Western) medieval architecture. Limited access for bona fide research, by appointment only.

English Heritage Photograph Library, 23 Savile Row, London W1X 1AB, tel 0171 973 3338. Photographs of sites in care: large format colour transparencies etc, 25,000 colour, 250,000 b/w.

English Heritage Parks and Gardens, address in previous entry, tel 0171 973 3243 (Inspector). Has an extensive slide collection: is not really set up to answer outside enquiries, but serious researchers may make appointment to visit.

Mary Evans Picture Library, 59 Tranquil Vale, London SE3 0BS, tel 0171 318 0034. Commercial library with a wide range of photographs and other illustrations.

Fortean Picture Library, Janet Bord, Henblas, Mwrog Street, Ruthin, Denbighs LL15 1LG, tel 01824 707278, fax 01824 705324. The Bords' atmospherically-illustrated books are well known on the less academic ('mysteries') side of archaeology, and the library contains an enormous number of archaeological site photographs.

Francis Frith Collection, Birmingham Public Libraries Local Studies Collection, 6th floor, Central Library, Chamberlain Square, Birmingham B3 3HQ (tel 0121 235 4549/20); negatives and a microfiche set of prints. Also at Charlton Road, Andover, Hants SP10 3LE, tel 01264 53113. The collection contains over 330,000 topographical (mostly British) subjects covering the period 1886–1970. Microfilm copies available in many county libraries.

Hellenic and Roman Societies Slide Collection, Senate House, Malet Street, London WC1E 7HU, tel 0171 323 9574, fax 0171 323 9575. Slides, slide sets with lecture notes, filmstrips available for hire; over 3,000 slides on Roman topics including Roman Britain. Catalogue(s) and/or computer printouts on selected topics available. *See also Willetts under Directories at the head of this section.*

Historic Scotland, Longmore House, Salisbury Place, Edinburgh EH9 1SE, tel 0131 668 8647. Photos of monuments and historic sites in care. Written application needed.

Institute of Advanced Architectural Studies, The King's Manor, York YO1 2EP, tel 01904 433969, fax 01904 433949. Covers the history of architecture, especially in Britain, medieval to early 20th century. 3,000 b/w photos.

Manx Museum and National Trust, Kingswood Grove, Douglas, IoM, tel 01624 675522, fax 01624 661899. Photos of topography and archaeology of the island.

National Art Slide Library, (Roy McKeown) De Montfort University, The Gateway, Leicester LE1 9BH, tel 0116 257 7148, fax 0116 257 0307. Postal slide loan service (charge made), telephone enquiries Mon–Fri 9.00am–1.00pm; answer phone other times, and personal visits not yet possible. The collection is strongest in fine and decorative arts but is extending. Leaflet available: revision of printed catalogue under way and computer database in preparation.

National Library of Wales, (Dept of Prints, Drawings and Maps), Aberystwyth SY23 3BU, tel 01970 623816, fax 01970 615709. Large collection of photos.

National Monuments Record Wales (*see entry in 4.2 Organisations*): c. 1 million photographs.

Newcastle University: The Department of Archaeology's Museum of Antiquities, The Quadrangle, Newcastle upon Tyne NE1 7RU, tel 0191 222 7846. Photos of Northumbrian sites (including air photos) and the Hadrian's Wall archive. 5,000 colour, 8,000 b/w; enquiries welcomed.

Office of Public Works, Dublin: Archive of photographs, many as glass plate negatives, offering the earliest objective visual records of many monuments, and of some of the people who visited them. A selection is published in John Scarry (comp), *Monuments in the past: photographs 1870–1936*. Dublin: Stationery Office, 1991, 83 p, index.

Mick Sharp: Eithinog Waun, Penisa'rwaun, Caernarfon, Gwynedd LL55 3PW, tel and fax 01286 872425. One of our best-known photographers, with an extensive library of fine quality archaeological and landscape history photographs, plus a special collection of grave memorials. 4,000 colour, 2,000 b/w. (No lecture slides.) Phone or write with specific requests.

J C D Smith, Old Arch, Four Forks, Spaxton, Bridgwater, Som TA5 1AA, tel 01278 671404. Covers medieval wood carvings (misericords etc), British architecture and landscape. 100 colour, 3,000 b/w. Visit by arrangement.

Society of Antiquaries of London. Photographs, mostly on architectural subjects; card-indexed by county. Also some microfilms. An under-used resource is a large collection (c. 20,000) of glass lantern slides, some in poor condition, including some rare subjects (eg made for Society lectures); card-indexed.

Surrey County Council: Photographic collection of Surrey historic buildings (mainly), Planning Dept, County Hall, Kingston on Thames, KT1 2DT, tel 0181 541 9419.

Tann, Professor Jennifer: School of Continuing Studies, Univ of Birmingham, B15 2TT, tel 0121 414 5609. Informal photographic collection on industrial and working class housing of 18th/19th centuries; b/w prints and negatives, colour transparencies, subject indexes, copy prints, postal enquiries preferred.

Ulster Folk and Transport Museum: Cultra, Holywood, Co Down BT18 0EU, tel 01232

428428, fax 01232 428728. Apply to Ken Anderson, Photographic Department, for details of the William A Green Collection (c. 1905–mid 1930s) which contains many archaeological sites, accessible via a topographical card index. Copies of the archaeological photographs are being made for Environment Service/Historic Buildings and Monuments in Belfast. Many other related subjects are represented in the Museum's photographic collections.

Ulster Museum: Botanic Gardens, Belfast BT9 5AB, tel 01232 381251. The Local History Department has a fine collection of relevant materials including 19th century photographs.

Victoria and Albert Museum, Cromwell Road, London SW7 2RL, tel 0171 938 8352/8354, fax 0171 938 9353. Holds 30,000 colour, 400,000 b/w photographs relating to the museum's collections.

York Archaeological Trust: Cromwell House, 11–13 Ogleforth, York YO1 2JG, tel 01904 663044 (Chris Daniell). Has over 80,000 colour or b/w photographs of York archaeology and architecture; appointment needed. Enquire about charges for prints etc.

British Universities Film and Video Council (BUFVC), 55 Greek Street, London W1V 5LR, tel 0171 734 3687, fax 0171 287 3914. Encourages the production and use of films and videos, and offers a forum for exchange of information.

5.2
Sources for Air Photographs

This section has been greatly improved by Chris Musson, though any remaining faults are mine. It lists the main institutions which hold collections of photographs taken from the air, and also some of the books which use selections from that material to illustrate aspects of the past in Britain and Ireland. Such books give a good idea of the kinds of photographs one might look for in the national and regional collections. Many fliers around the country regularly take photographs, some of them depositing the results in private collections but most of them contributing to the readily accessible regional or national records. Techniques are developing constantly: for instance all three Royal Commissions on Historical Monuments are adding to their collections copies of thermal infra-red linescan images taken by the RAF. Copies of Luftwaffe sorties from World War II are also available for England and Scotland.

This section is divided thus:
England
Wales
Scotland
Northern Ireland
Republic of Ireland

For a **directory** of all kinds of air photographs (not just archaeological) available in the UK, see:
***National Association of Aerial Photographic Libraries, *NAPLIB directory of aerial photographic collections in the United Kingdom, 1993.* London: ASLIB/NAPLIB, 1993, iv, 68 p. o 85142 304 3 pb.
A key work listing over 200 sources with key symbols for photo type, angle of view, coverage, etc. Includes picture libraries, resource centres and other organisations (eg planning authorities) with holdings of air photographs.

England

The largest and most comprehensive source for archaeological air photographs for England is the **National Monuments Record** of the RCHME at Swindon (see under Air Photographs Section of NMR, below). **Cambridge University Committee for Aerial Photography** (CUCAP) is another invaluable source, of international scope. Of the commercial groups, **Aerofilms Ltd** of Boreham Wood is among the best known and longest established. The *NAPLIB Directory* (see above) will be found useful for locating other sources. Many planning authorities hold collections of air photographs for their own areas, though few were taken with archaeological requirements in mind: councils for Norfolk, Devon and West Yorkshire, in particular, have good archaeological collections.

Immense advances in the interpretation and indexing of air photographs are continually being made: eg image processing and enhancement, transcription and mapping from air photographs, computerised retrieval systems, disc storage of images and the like. Developments are often recorded in *AARGnews* (below) and in *Archaeological computing newsletter* (Institute of Archaeology, 36 Beaumont Street, Oxford OX1 2PG).

PERIODICALS

AARGnews: newsletter of the Aerial Archaeology Research Group (0960–2852, 2/yr). Edited by Rog Palmer, 21 Grunhild Way, Cambridge CB1 4QZ.

Aerial archaeology. 1977–84 (irreg, and now in abeyance). Aerial Archaeology Foundation (later: Aerial Archaeology Publications).
Was for several years the principal journal for publishing the results of archaeological aerial reconnaissance in Britain and beyond, as well as discussions of related technical matters.

archaeoLOG: newsletter of the Archaeological Group of the Royal Photographic Society of Great Britain. 1978–. 3/yr. This group also produces *Heritage photography*, approximately annually, for its members. (Details of the Group are in Section 4.2 Organisations.)

ORGANISATIONS

Cambridge University Committee for Aerial Photography (CUCAP), Mond Building, Free School Lane, Cambridge CB2 3RF, tel 01223 334578, fax 01223 334400. Curator D R Wilson. Founded 1949: flies regularly for coverage of many disciplines. Special attention was paid to archaeological features (both upstanding and crop/soilmarks) in the period 1945–80; since about 1980 CUCAP has concentrated on vertical photography for survey and other purposes, much of it valuable for the detection and mapping of archaeological features. As well as

Britain and Ireland, CUCAP covers parts of Denmark, Netherlands and N France. Descriptive folder available; location and subject indexes are maintained for the c. 415,000 photographs held for all disciplines. Visits by appointment. *See books under St Joseph and Wilson (respectively) below.*

Air Photographs Section of the National Monuments Record, RCHME National Monuments Record Centre, Kemble Drive, Swindon, Wilts SN2 2GZ, tel 01793 414710, fax 01793 414606. Head of Air Photography, Robert Bewley. Over 3 million archaeological air photographs are now held at Swindon, giving virtually complete cover for England, from the early days of flying to the present time; apply for descriptive leaflet and current charges. (Basic access is free: copies etc are charged for.) A computerised retrieval system allows enquirers to be told what photographs are available for a given area; orders can be placed by post, fax, telephone or personal visit. Conventional prints or colour laser reproductions are available.

National Parks in England and Wales. An air photographic survey to monitor recent changes in the landscape was done by Aerial Photography Unit, ADAS, Brooklands Avenue, Cambridge CB2 2BL, tel 01223 455780. Scale approx 1:20,000: stereoscopic viewing possible, colour or b/w prints available.

Many other organisations hold air photo collections: eg National Coal Board, British Gas, water companies, Soil Survey, Forestry Commission, John Innes Institute, planning authorities, various universities (eg Keele, Wolverhampton), Meridian Air Maps, Hunting Aerofilms, Fairey Aviation, etc, as well as bodies with specifically archaeological interests such as Medieval Settlement Research Group or Yorks Archaeological Society. Use the NAPLIB Directory to locate those of interest.

BOOKS

Beresford and St Joseph on medieval England from the air, see Section 6.11.6 Medieval.

Brown on castles from the air, see Section 6.11.6 Medieval.

Burton, Neil, *English heritage from the air.* London: Sidgwick and Jackson, 1989, 192 p, site-index. 0 283 99605 6 hb, 0 283 99899 7 pb. Colour photos from Skyscan with descriptive text.

Crawford, O G S and Keiller, Alex, *Wessex from the air*. Oxford: Clarendon, 1928, vii, 264 p, refs, index.
Seminal study of earthwork sites in Wessex, mostly no longer upstanding.

Croft, Robert and Aston, Michael, *Somerset from the air*. [Taunton]: Somerset Co Co, 1994, 122 p. 0 86183 215 9 pb.

Frere and St Joseph on Roman Britain from the air, see Section 6.11.4 Romano-British.

Griffith, Frances, *Devon's past: an aerial view*. Exeter: Devon Books, 1988, 128 p. 0 86114 833 9 pb.

Hudson on industrial history from the air, see Section 6.15 Archaeology of industrial processes.

Kennedy, D L (ed), *Into the sun: essays in air photography in honour of Derrick Riley*. Sheffield: Sheffield Academic Press/J R Collis Publications, 1989, x, 211 p, bibls, index. 0 906090 36 9 pb.
Wide-ranging set of papers in tribute to a renowned air archaeologist.

Léva, Charles (ed), *Aerial photography and geophysical prospection in archaeology, 2. Proceedings of the Second International Symposium, Brussels, 8.xi.1986*. Brussels: CIRA–ICL, 1990, 277 p. 90 800477 1 6.
A collection of papers by contributors from Britain and Europe.

Maxwell, G S (ed), *The impact of aerial reconnaissance on archaeology*. CBA res rep, **49**, 1983, ix, 150 p, bibl, index. 0 906780 24 1 pb.
Seventeen papers from an important conference (Nottingham 1980).

Oosthuizen, Susan, *Cambridgeshire from the air*. Stroud: Alan Sutton, forthcoming 1996, 128 p. 0 7509 1064 X.
From prehistory to the present day.

Palmer on Danebury environs, see Section 6.11.3 Iron Age.

Platt on medieval Britain from the air, see Section 6.11.6 Medieval.

*RCHME, *A matter of time: an archaeological survey of the river gravels of England*. London: HMSO, 1960, 64 p, bibl, pb.
Classic work which forcefully brought to attention the rich potential of these soils for revealing hitherto unknown settlements.

Riley, Derrick, *Air photography and archaeology*. London: Duckworth, 1987, 151 p, bibl, index. 0 7156 2101 7.
Explains the historical background to the discipline, how sites show up, interpretation and mapping etc.

*St Joseph, J K S, *The uses of air photography*. London: John Baker, 2 ed 1977, 196 p, refs, index. 0 212 97016 X.
A sample of the multidisciplinary work of the Cambridge University Committee for Aerial Photography: archaeology, geology, soil science, biology, cartography are all disciplines which benefited from this kind of evidence.

Simpson on castles from the air, see Section 6.11.6 Medieval.

Start, David, *Lincolnshire from the air*. Sleaford: Heritage Lincolnshire, 1993, 127 p. 0 948639 10 5.
Colour and monochrome photographs, principally by Christopher Cruickshank, with accompanying text; all periods.

Wade-Martins, P (ed), *Norfolk from the air*. [Norwich?]: Norfolk Museums Service, 1987, 168 p. 0 903101 55 6 hb, 0 903101 56 4 pb.
Finely reproduced colour and monochrome photographs, principally by Derek A Edwards, of all periods, with commentary.

Watson, Michael and Musson, Chris, *Shropshire from the air: man and the landscape*. Shrewsbury: Shropshire Books, 1993, 119 p, short bibl. 0 903802 57 0 pb.
Photographs, many in colour, with descriptive text.

*Whimster, Rowan, *The emerging past: air photography and the buried landscape*. London: RCHME, 1989, x, 101 p, bibl. 0 96072369 X pb.
Describes methods of photographic interpretation, cartographic transcription and morphological analysis which in the 1980s helped to establish a framework of standard principles and techniques for analysing air photo information, and hence to further the conservation of below-ground sites.

Wilson, D R (ed), *Aerial reconnaissance for archaeology*. CBA res rep, **12**, 1975, 158 p, refs. 0 900312 29 7 pb.
Largely of historic interest now, but seminal at the time.

***—, *Air photo interpretation for archaeologists*.

London: Batsford, 1982, 212 p, bibl, glossary, index. 0 7134 1085 x hb, 0 7134 1086 8 pb.
The most authoritative introduction to the practice and techniques of aerial photography.

As well as the work of individual fliers recorded in book form in this section, see also the celebration of Jim Pickering's work in Current archaeology *13.1, November 1995; his collection of 62,000+ photographs reflects assiduous reconnaissance over many years, and most have been copied for RCHME's holdings.*

Wales

ORGANISATIONS

RCAHM Wales, Crown Building, Plas Crug, Aberystwyth, SY23 1NJ, tel 01970 621200, fax 01970 627701. Holds the principal collection, approaching one million images, of archaeological air photographs for Wales. Includes RAF and OS vertical photography.

Welsh Office, Central Register of Air Photography for Wales, Rm G-003, Crown Offices, Cathays Park, Cardiff CF1 3NQ, tel 01222 823819, fax 01222 825466.
The Register, as the most comprehensive source of air photographic information for Wales, aims to index all vertical cover by the RAF, OS, and other air survey organisations. Contact prints and enlargements from original RAF and pre-1971 OS air film obtainable on prepayment; there is extensive colour cover from 1983, plus oblique and infra-red photographs of the Welsh coastline.

The regional **Archaeological Trusts** in Wales also hold collections of oblique aerial photographs for their own areas. In particular enquire of the Clwyd-Powys Archaeological Trust and the Dyfed Archaeological Trust; smaller collections are held (respectively) by the Glamorgan-Gwent Archaeological Trust and the Gwynedd Archaeological Trust. Addresses for all four are in Section 4.2 Organisations (under Wales).

BOOKS FOR WALES

Aerofilms (intro Jan Morris), *Wales from the air.* London: Barrie and Jenkins, [n d but 1990], 160 p.
Virtually a picture a page, mostly in colour.

James, Terrence and Simpson, D, *Ancient West Wales from the air.* Carmarthen: Carm Antiq Soc, 1980, 33 p. 0 906972 00 0 pb.

Photos with extended captions: hillforts to castles.

*Musson, Chris, *Wales from the air: patterns of past and present.* Aberystwyth: RCAHM Wales, [1994], 160 p, bibl, site-index. 1 871184 14 2 pb.
Photographs, many in colour, with accompanying introduction and regional summaries.

Scotland

ORGANISATONS

Aberdeen Archaeological Surveys issues lists of sorties flown and observations recorded. Address c/o Aberdeenshire Archaeologist, Woodhill House, Westburn Road, Aberdeen AB9 2LU

RCAHM Scotland, John Sinclair House, 16 Bernard Terrace, Edinburgh EH8 9NX, tel 0131 662 1456, fax 0131 662 1477 and 1499. Is the principal repository for air photographs of Scottish archaeological sites, and issues annual lists of sites recorded during the year. Holds negatives of the All Scotland Survey (Scottish Office 1988–9) and the Luftwaffe sorties (obtained from archives in the USA).

Many Scottish sites are illustrated in the books noted above under England, eg Maxwell, Frere and St Joseph.

BOOKS FOR SCOTLAND

Shepherd, Ian A G and Greig, Moira K, *Grampian's past: its archaeology from the air.* Aberdeen: Grampian Regional Council (Economic Devel and Planning Dept), 1996, 80 p, index. 0 946449 06 6.
Colour plates and extended captions illustrate the wide range of sites available from the air.

Northern Ireland

ORGANISATIONS

The Environment and Heritage Service: Historic Monuments and Buildings, 5–33 Hill Street, Belfast BT1 2LA, tel 01232 235000, fax 01232 310288. The main repository of archaeological air photographs in the North. Holdings include nearly 500 photos of archaeological interest from the St Joseph sorties (1951–73).

The Institute of Irish Studies, 8 Fitzwilliam St, Belfast BT9 6AW, tel 01232 245133 ext 3386, holds the Newman collection of geographical air photos.

PUBLICATIONS

Chart, D A, 'Air photography in northern Ireland', *Antiquity*, 4, 1930, pp 453–9.
A pioneering article.

Common, Robert (ed), *Northern Ireland from the air*. Belfast: Dept Geogr Queen's Univ Belfast, 1964.
A photographic atlas with commentary and line drawings, folding map.

Williams, Brian, 'Aerial archaeology in Northern Ireland', *AARGnews*, 4, 1992, pp 8–11.
A 60-year retrospective and a look at future aims.

Republic of Ireland

(With thanks to Geraldine Stout who offered useful information.)

ORGANISATIONS

The **BRUFF Aerial Photographic Survey** (for OPW and UC Cork Dept Archaeol) was commissioned to assess the potential of medium-altitude vertical stereos for discovering sites in the Lough Gur region. See M G Doody, *Tipperary hist j* for 1993, pp 173–80.

The **Geological Survey of Ireland** holds nearly 6,500 vertical air photographs taken 1973–7 on the nominal scale of 1:30,000 and covering all 26 counties of the Republic. The **Ordnance Survey** also holds vertical cover, some of it in colour at 1:5,000 taken in 1992. The OPW archaeologists make extensive use of both these sources, together with commercial vertical photography by **Irish Air Surveys** (Balgriffin House, Balgriffin, Co Dublin, tel Dublin 846 0668). Irish Air Surveys relies for its photography on **BKS Ltd** of 47 Ballycairn Road, Coleraine, Co Londonderry, BT51 3HZ (tel 01265 52311).

The **Cambridge University Committee for Aerial Photography** collection includes photographs taken in the Republic: index held in **National Museum of Ireland**, applications for copies to CUCAP, Mond Building, Free School Lane, Cambridge CB2 3RF.

The **Geography Dept of the University of Wolverhampton** (Dudley Campus, Castle View, Dudley DY1 3HR, tel 01902 321000, fax 01902 323379) has a collection of air photographs for certain areas of the Republic's archaeological and historic landscapes of all periods; active programme since 1989, and travelling display available. Contact Dr Gillian Barrett.

The **Irish Tourist Board** (Bord Fáilte Éireann, Baggot Street Bridge, Dublin 2) also has a collection.

Private flier: Mr Leo Swann, 746 Howth Road, Dublin 5 has one of the largest private collections of oblique aerial photographs in the Republic, concentrating on early ecclesiastical sites.

BOOKS

***Kiely, Benedict, *The Aerofilms book of Ireland from the air*. London: Weidenfeld and Nicolson, 1985, 160 p. (1990 pb 0 297 83084 8).
Excellent photographs, mainly in colour, of natural, prehistoric, urban and industrial features (one photograph revealed a previously unknown hillfort).

Mould, Daphne D C Pochin, *Ireland from the air*. Newton Abbot: David and Charles, 1972, 112 p, index. 0 7153 5758 1.
The photographs would be better reproduced today.

Norman, E R and St Joseph, J K S, *The early development of Irish society: the evidence of aerial photography*. Cambridge: CUP, 1969, xi, 126 p, bibl.

SECTION 6

Select Archaeological Bibliography

This section contains four parts:
Dictionaries, thesauri and glossaries
Encyclopaedias and chronologies
Atlases: world and European; England (sometimes including Wales); Wales; Scotland; Ireland.
Maps and gazetteers: England; Wales; Scotland; Ireland

'The true potential of the archaeological reference book has not yet been realized' (Ian Shaw reviewing archaeological dictionaries and encyclopaedias in *Antiquity*, 64, 1990, p 161). Nonetheless, here are some of the most useful.

Dictionaries, Thesauri and Glossaries

Dictionaries covering two languages are marked **BL**, those covering more than two, **ML**. See also entries in Section 4.9 Museum catalogues, for the Archaeological Object Thesaurus Working Group and the British Museum Object Name Working Party. A useful listing of multilingual dictionaries is:
Asher, Catherine G, *Multi-lingual specialized dictionaries of use to conservators. Art archaeol techn abstr suppl*, 16.2, 1979, pp 326–60.

BRITAIN: GENERAL

Adams, I H, *Agrarian landscape terms: a glossary for historical geography. Institute of British Geographers' special publication* 9, 1976, xii, 314 p.
see also Coleman and Wood below.

***Adkins, Lesley and Adkins, Roy A, *The handbook of British archaeology*. London: Macmillan Papermac, 1983, 319 p, bibl, index. 0 333 34843 5 (previously published by David and Charles in hardback as *A thesaurus of British archaeology*).
Regrettably out of print but an extremely useful, even indispensable compendium of terms and explanations.
See also their dictionary of Roman religion in Section 6.11.4 Romano-British.

Alcock, N W and others, glossary for timber-framed buildings, see Section 6.18 Vernacular architecture.

BL Apelt, Mary L, *German-English dictionary: art history/archaeology*. Berlin: Erich Schmidt Verlag 1982, 275 p. 3 503 1619 8 limp cloth.
Better on art historical and architectural terms than on archaeology: eg 'postholes' will not be found here, nor 'Grubenhäuser', but no competitor dictionary has emerged yet.

Art and architecture thesaurus, see below under Getty.

***Bahn, Paul, *Collins dictionary of archaeology*. Glasgow: HarperCollins, 1992, 654 p. 0 00 434158 9 pb.
World-wide in scope, and sometimes curiously slanted (eg moated sites are not actually peculiar to SE Asia!), but much the best and most up-to-date available. Reasonably priced and indispensable for the student, or anyone faced with a new archaeological problem. The illustrations are clear but without scales. Good cross-referencing.

**—, *Bluff your way in archaeology*. Horsham: Ravette Books, 1989, 62 p, glossary. 1 85304 102 5 pb.
Not at all the frivolity it sounds, though the jokes are good ones: there is much wisdom and truth here.

Bray, Warwick and Trump, David, *The Penguin dictionary of archaeology*. Harmondsworth: Penguin, 2 edn 1982, 283 p. 0 14 051116 4 pb.
After a decade and a half this looks old-fashioned, but is well cross-referenced and the illustrations are reasonable (though also, like the Bahn dictionary, without scales). The Bahn will be better for most purposes.

BL Brézillon, M N, 'La dénomination des objets de pierre taillé: matériaux pour un vocabulaire des préhistoriens de langue française', in *Gallia préhistoire suppl* 1977(4), pp 7–423.
French terminology for flaked lithics.

[British Architectural Library], *Architectural keywords*. London: Royal Institute of British Architecture Publications, 1982, 256 p. 0 900630 80 9 limp cloth. Also a 1991 *Supplement*.
Contains 3,000 alphabetical keywords and 7,000 cross-references. More useful is the RCHME/EH thesaurus (below).

Burnham, Dorothy K, *Warp and weft: a textile terminology*. Toronto: Royal Ontario Museum, 1981, xiv, 216 p, bibl. 0 88854 256 9.

ML Cameron, F, 'Dictionary of Roman pottery terms', in *J Roman pottery studies*, 1, 1986, pp 58–79.
Gives the commoner current terms in English with French, Italian, Spanish, German, and Dutch equivalents.

Champion, Sara, *A dictionary of terms and techniques in archaeology*. Oxford: Phaidon, 1980, 144 p, bibl. 0 7148 2177 9 hb, 0 7148 1999 9 pb.
For scientific aspects, not names of cultures or artefacts. A little out of date now but good and clear.

Chesshyre, D H B and Woodcock, Thomas (eds), *Dictionary of British arms: medieval ordinary. Volume I, A – Bend*. London: Society of Antiquaries, 1992, lxvi, 530 p, bibl, indexes. 0 85431 258 7.
Also known as 'The Papworth Project'. Useful to those needing to identify coats of arms on medieval artefacts. Contains index of names, abbreviations, terminology. The first of four volumes of the Ordinary. Volume 2 covering Bend – Chevronny is edited by Thomas Woodcock et al, publisher as above, 1996, xciv, 677 p, refs, names index.

CIDOC, *Directory of thesauri for object names, see entry in Section 4.9 Museum catalogues.*

Cocke, Thomas and others, *Recording a church: an illustrated glossary, see entry in Section 6.9 under 'Drawing'.*

Coleman, Stephen and Wood, John, *Historic landscape and archaeology: glossary of terms*. Bedford: Beds County Planning Dept Conservation Section, rev edn 1988, 60 p. 0 907041 25 6 pb.
Defines terms from *abbey* to *yeoman* and provides tables of historic measures and monetary units; useful for those engaged in text-assisted archaeological research. *See also Adams above.*

Colvin's biographical dictionary of British architects, see Section 6.11.7 Post-medieval.

Curl, James Stevens, *Classical architecture: an introduction to its vocabulary and essentials, with a select glossary of terms*. London: Batsford, 1992, 231 p, select bibl, index. 0 7134 6772 X.
From Graeco-Roman times through the Renaissance and Neoclassical to modern times. Well illustrated.

—, *English architecture: an illustrated glossary.* Newton Abbot: David and Charles, rev edn 1986, 192 p, bibl. 0 7153 8887 8.

ML *Dictionarium museologicum* (ed I Éri and B Végh). Budapest: ICOM (CIDOC Working Group on Terminology), 1986, lv, 774 p. 9 635711743.
Terms are given in 20 languages (English, French, Spanish, Russian, German, Bulgarian, Czech, Danish, Esperanto, Finnish, Hungarian, Italian, Dutch, Norwegian, Polish, Portuguese, Romanian, SerboCroat, Slovak, and Swedish) with about 1,800–2,000 technical terms for each language. Main sequence is by English term, with indexes for each language. Definitions are not given.

DICTIONARY OF ART see below under Turner.

Dictionary of National Biography. OUP, 1885–.
The standard reference tool for notable people, presumably including archaeologists, with 37,000-plus entries and cumulative indexes. Another 1,086 persons were added in *The Dictionary of National Biography: missing persons* (ed C S Nicholls, OUP, 1993), which includes persons who lived before AD 1500. A *New DNB* in preparation will revise and expand to 50,000 entries.

Eden, P, Dictionary of surveyors, see below under Maps.

Fairholt, F W, *A glossary of costume in England.* EP Publishing reprint, 1976, of the glossary part of H A Dillon's 1885 revised (3rd) edn.
Concise illustrated encyclopaedia with sources quoted for each entry; many interesting details.

ML Fénelon, Paul, *Dictionnaire d'histoire et de géographie agraires.* Paris: Conseil International de la langue française, 2 edn (rev and enlarged) 1991, 801 p. 2 85319 210 5.
Multilingual dictionary giving French–English–German–Spanish–Italian equivalents, with long or short definition as needed. Illustrations are few and inadequate.

Fisher, J L, *A medieval farming glossary of Latin and English words taken mainly from Essex records.* London: NCSS for SCLH, 1968, 41 p. [o] 7199 0752 7 pb.

Getty Art History Information Program (dir Toni Petersen), *Art and architecture thesaurus* ('AAT'). New York/Oxford: OUP, 2 edn 1994, 5 vols. 0 19 508884 0.

The principal authority for terminology in these subjects; some archaeological terms are naturally included. Also available electronically for single or network use, and there are guides to usage etc; however the American terminology is giving rise to some difficulties in the UK. *See also next item.*

Getty Art History Information Program, *Art and architecture thesaurus: the authority reference tool edition.* New York/ Oxford, OUP, 1993. 0 19 508144 7.
This is a software tool for giving 'immediate and intuitive access to any AHIP authority resource' (from OUP catalogue). It is intended to make it easy to navigate around the AAT levels, allowing cutting and pasting of terms into a word processor or database record.

Green, Miranda J, *Dictionary of Celtic myth and legend.* London: Thames and Hudson, 1992, 240 p, bibl. 0 500 01516 3.
Illustrated; but not universally well received.

Hamer, Frank and Janet, *The potter's dictionary of materials and techniques.* London: A and C Black, 3 edn 1991, x, 385 p, bibl. 0 7136 3337 9.

Hammond, N G L and Scullard, H H (eds), *Oxford classical dictionary.* Oxford: Clarendon, 2 edn 1970, xxii, 1176 p. 0 19 869117 3.

Hertfordshire Curators' Group, see Section 4.9 Museum catalogues.

Illustrated dictionary of archaeology. London: Trewin Copplestone, 1977.
If come across, not recommended.

Lavell, Cherry (comp), *British archaeological thesaurus for use with British archaeological abstracts and other publications in British archaeology. CBA practical handbooks in archaeology,* 4, 1989, 69 p, refs. 0 906780 77 2 pb.
Intended for use when compiling, or using, indexes to monographs and serials, including runs of abstracts, ie gives assistance with choice of cross-references and alternative terms.

Leroi-Gourhan, André (ed), *Dictionnaire de la préhistoire.* Paris: Presses Universitaires de France, 1988, viii, 1222 p. 2 13 041459 1.
Worldwide in scope; gives short paragraph definitions for items like 'flottation' or 'fluorescence X' and some illustrations. Numerous British contributors.

Lewis, S, *Topographical dictionary of England.*

London: S Lewis, 5 edn 1845, 4 vols plus atlas). (In fact there were 7 edns between 1831 and 1848/9).
A classic 19th-century work giving descriptions of many places; the same author also treated Wales, Scotland and Ireland (separately noted below).

ML Mack, Roy, *Dictionary for veterinary sciences and biosciences*. Berlin/ Hamburg: Paul Parey Scientific, 1988. 3 489 50516 6.
German–English and English–German, with trilingual appendix of Latin terms, bibliography of multi- and bilingual dictionaries and relevant guides. European scope.

BL Marois, Roger, *English-French, French-English vocabulary of prehistoric archaeology*. Montréal: Presses Univ Québec, 1972, 42 + 43 p. 0 7770 0043 1 pb.
A straight translation of terms, without definitions or illustrations, for flaked lithic tools.

Mignon, Molly Raymond, *Dictionary of concepts in archaeology*. London: Greenwood Press (= *Sources for the social sciences and humanities*, 13), 1993, xii, 364 p, bibl, indexes.
Includes many terms used in modern theoretical archaeology.

Milward, Rosemary, *A glossary of household and farming terms from 16th-century probate inventories*. Derbyshire Record Society occas pap, 1, 2 rev edn, 1982, 52 p. 0 9505940 1 6 pb.

Moore, David, *A handbook of military terms used in connection with fortifications of the Victorian era*. Fareham: Palmerston Forts Soc, 2 edn 1993, 66 p. No ISBN, pb.

BL Owen, L R, *Prähistorisches Wörterbuch: Fachwörterbuch zur Ur- und Frühgeschichte, Deutsch–Englisch/ English–German*. [Dictionary of prehistoric archaeology.] *Archaeologica venatoria* (Tübingen), 11, 1991, 176 p, bibl. 3 921618 32 0.
Contains over 2,200 terms, especially for Europe and N America, from Palaeolithic to Iron Age in scope. Much the best German-English dictionary currently available.

Pevsner, Nikolaus, Fleming, J and Honour, Hugh, *A dictionary of architecture*. London: Allen Lane, rev and enlarged edn 1975, 554 p. 0 7139 0733 9.
Includes Greek, Meso-American etc.

***Royal Commission on the Historical Monuments of England/English Heritage, *Thesaurus of monument types: a standard for use in archaeological and architectural records* (dir Neil Beagrie). Swindon: RCHME/EH, 1995, xxviii, 322 looseleaf pp in binder. 1 873592 20 5.
Replaces the earlier edition which covered archaeological terms only. Fully formalised thesaurus for words in use in England.

BL Seeberg, Elizabeth S, *English–Norwegian – Norwegian–English dictionary of archaeology. The archaeological terminology of Great Britain and the North up to and including the Anglo-Saxon period and the Viking Age*. Oslo: Univ Oslo Dept of Archaeol, Numis and Hist of Art, 2 rev edn 1993, 268 p. 82 7181 097 9 pb.
Originally devised to help Norwegian archaeologists to use correct terms when writing in English. Includes stave-church terminology.

Simek, Rudolf (transl A Hall), *Dictionary of northern mythology*. Cambridge: Brewer, 1993, xiv, 424 p, bibl. 0 85991 369 4.
Includes entries for (eg) burial customs, place-names, ships; updated and enlarged as well as translated; substantial bibliography pp 381–424.

Social history and industrial classification (SHIC), see entry in Section 4.9 Museum catalogues.

Thesaurus of archaeological site types, see Royal Commission . . . above.

Thornton, J H, 'A glossary of shoe terms (including boots)', in *Costume*, 11, 1977, pp 28–33

Turner, Jane (ed), *Dictionary of art*. London: Macmillan, 1995, 34 vols, bibls, index. 1 884446 00 0.
Contains 41,000 articles, 15,000 images, and includes information on 1,500 archaeological sites, plus architecture and decorative arts. Aims to be non-Eurocentric. Substantial bibliographies and massive index.

Who was who. London: A and C Black, 8 vols 1897–1990.

Williams, A, biographical dictionary of Dark Age Britain, see Section 6.11.5 Migration and early medieval.

Zupko, Ronald E, *A dictionary of English weights and measures, from Anglo-Saxon times to the 19th century*. Madison WI: Univ Wisconsin Press, 1968, xvi, 224 p, bibl. No ISBN.

—, *A dictionary of weights and measures for the British Isles; the Middle Ages to the twentieth century*. Philadelphia: Amer Phil Soc (= *Memoirs*, 168), 1985, xxxviii, 520 p, refs. 0 87169 168 X.
Gives definitions and traces changing standards.

—, *British weights and measures: a history from antiquity to the 17th century*. Madison WI: Univ Wisconsin Press, 1977, xvi, 248 p, bibl, index. 0 299 07340 8.
Covers Roman Britain, AS Britain, Norman Britain, medieval, Tudor; contains useful list (pp 103–39) of all manner of 16th and 17th century commodities from acacia to zedoaria, together with how each was measured – singly, in pairs, by the dozen, gross, thousand, barrel etc.

WALES

Lewis, Samuel, *Topographical dictionary of Wales*. London: S Lewis, 3 edn 1845.
Similar to his topographical dictionary of England, giving bibliographical references to many places.

SCOTLAND

Donaldson, Gordon and Morpeth, Robert S, *A dictionary of Scottish history*. Edinburgh: John Donald, 1977, 234 p. 0 85976 018 9.
Mostly names of people, but also includes entries for (eg) Dumbarton Rock, Glasgow Archaeol Soc, Whithorn, etc. A handy volume.

— and —, *Who's who in Scottish history*. Oxford: Blackwell, 1973, xx, 254 p, bibl. 0 631 14700 4.

Graham, John J, *The Shetland dictionary*. Stornoway: Thule, 1979, xxvii, 124 p. 0 906191 33 5.

Lewis, Samuel, *Topographical dictionary of Scotland . . . with historical and statistical descriptions*. London: Samuel Lewis, 2 edn 1849, 2 vols plus atlas.
Results of typical 19th century enquiry among the educated people of the region, with descriptions of each place and endeavouring to correct extant printed materials.

Robinson, Mairi (ed-in-chief), *The concise Scots dictionary*. Aberdeen: Aberdeen Univ Press, 1987, xli, 819 p. 0 08028 491 4 hb, 0 08028 492 2 pb.
'An updated distillation of the Scottish National Dictionary and the Dictionary of the Older Scottish tongue', and much more accessible.

IRELAND

Flanagan, Laurence, *Dictionary of Irish archaeology*. Dublin: Gill and Macmillan, 1992, 222 p. 0 7171 1835 5 hb, 0 7171 1928 9 pb.
Less of a dictionary than a mini-encyclopaedia, containing summaries, some quite lengthy, of current knowledge on many archaeological sites, Mesolithic to late medieval. Many important artefact and site types are not listed, there is a strong Ulster bias, and the bibliography disappoints.

Lewis, Samuel, *A topographical dictionary of Ireland*. London: S Lewis, 2 edn 1849, 2 vols plus atlas. (Also a 1984 reprint by Genealogical Publishing Co, Baltimore, MD).
The accompanying atlas, with general map of Ireland and separate county maps, shows barony boundaries much as they were in medieval times.

Room, Adrian, *A dictionary of Irish place-names*. Belfast: Appletree Press, 1986, 136 p, bibl. 0 86281 132 5.
Convenient guide, not quite pocketable.

Encyclopaedias and Chronologies

It is the nature of encyclopaedias to go out of date quickly, but these may give suitable leads into the desired topic.

Blackburn, Graham, *The illustrated encyclopaedia of woodworking handtools, instruments and devices*. London: John Murray, 1974, 238 p. 0 7195 3283 3 pb.

The Cambridge encyclopedia of human evolution (eds Steve Jones et al). CUP, 1992, xiii, 506 p, bibl, index. 0 521 32370 3 hb, 0 521 46786 1 pb.
Part 9, 'Early human behaviour and ecology', could be useful.

Curl, J S, *Encyclopaedia of architectural terms*. Wimbledon: Donhead, 1993, 364 p. 1 87339 404 7.
Mostly 'polite' rather than vernacular architecture.

de Breffny, B, *Ireland: a cultural encyclopaedia*. London: Thames and Hudson, 1983, 256 p. 0 500 01304 7.
Contains 45 contributions on aesthetics, intellectual and artistic achievements etc; most entries have bibliographical references. For background more than for archaeology.

Ehrich, Robert W (ed), *Chronologies in Old World archaeology*. Chicago: Univ Chicago Press, 3 edn, 1990, 2 vols, bibl, index. o 226 19447 7.
Covers from first food-producing settlements through to relatively recent times. Contains tables of radiocarbon dates etc.

Gaucher, Jakez, *Histoire chronologique des pays celtiques* [Chronology of Celtic countries]. Guerande (Brittany): Ass Keltica International, 1990, 396 p, bibl, index. 2 9504767 o 8.
Covers, in six-column format, events in Isle of Man, Ireland, Scotland, Wales, Brittany and Cornwall; from the beginning of the Christian era to date. Maps and illustrations.

Loyn, H R (general ed), *The Middle Ages: a concise encyclopaedia*. London: Thames and Hudson, 1989, 352 p. o 500 25103 7 hb, o 500 27645 5 pb.
Contains over 30 contributions, many by first-rank historians.

McNeil, Ian (ed), *An encyclopaedia of the history of technology*. London: Routledge, 1990, xv, 1062 p, bibl, indexes. o 415 01306 2.
Edited by a former Secretary of the Newcomen Society: contributions on (eg) non-ferrous metals, ferrous metals, power sources, agriculture, textiles.

Meally, Victor (ed), *Encyclopaedia of Ireland*. Dublin: Allen Figgis, 1968, 463 p, bibls, index. Rather old now, but still useful for general (not archaeological) purposes.

Medieval Scandinavia: an encyclopedia (eds Phillip Pulsiano et al). New York/London: Garland, 1993, xix, 768 p, bibls, index. o 8240 4787 7.
Contains entries from numerous well-known authorities.

Paintin, Elaine (ed), Glyn Daniel (consultant ed), *Encyclopaedia of archaeology*. London: Macmillan 1978.
If found on library shelves, best not used now.

Pinto, Edward, *Treen and other wooden bygones: an encyclopaedia and social history*. London: Bell, 1969, x, 458 p; reprint Bell and Hyman 1979. o 7135 1533 3.
Important for understanding lathe-turned products such as bowls, as well as other wooden items.

Porteous, Andrew, *Dictionary of environmental science and technology*. Buckingham: Open

Univ Press, 1991, xii, 399 p, index. o 335 09231 4 hb, o 335 09230 6 pb.

Sherratt, A (ed), *The Cambridge encyclopaedia of archaeology*. Cambridge: CUP, 1980, 495 p, bibl, index. o 521 22989 8.
Not the usual type of encyclopaedia but a series of stimulating articles, averaging eight pages in length, on various aspects of archaeological theory or areas of prehistory. In view of its age should be used with some care now.

Steinberg, S H revised by John Paxton, *Historical tables 58 BC–AD 1985*. London: Macmillan, 11 edn 1986, 320 p, index. o 333 40903 5.
Basic chronological data given in columnar fashion, by culture.

*Stillwell, Richard (ed) et al, *The Princeton encyclopaedia of classical sites*. Princeton: Princeton Univ Press, 1976, xxii, 1019 p, index. o 691 03542 3.
Gives over 200 entries on the archaeology of Greek and Roman civilisation from 750 BC TO AD 565, contributed by excavators and other authorities. Some of it will have been overtaken by more recent research.

Storey, R L, *Chronology of the medieval world 800 to 1491*. London: Barrie and Jenkins 1973, xii, 705 p, index. o 214 66806 1.
Basic framework of dated historical events.

Tasker, Edward G (ed John Beaumont), *Encyclopedia of medieval church art*. London: Batsford, 1993, 320 p, bibl, index. o 7134 6821 1.
Attractive book arranged by main topics, eg creatures, everyday scenes, saints.

***Trinder, Barrie (ed), *The Blackwell enyclopedia of industrial archaeology*.
Oxford: Blackwell, 1992, xxii, 964 p, bibl (pp 873–930). index. o 631 14216 9.
Over 50 specialist contributors cover the developed world; indispensable, despite the bibliography's typographical errors.

Wood, E S, *Collins field guide to archaeology*. London: Collins, 5 edn, 1979, 383 p, bibl, index. o oo 219235 7.
Many people cut their archaeological teeth on this compendium of British archaeology, and it still has its uses, especially for some offbeat subjects like mazes; but see now the next item.

**—, *Historical Britain*. London: Harvill Press, 1995, xxii, 624 p, bibl, indexes. 1 86046 031 3.
Encyclopaedic compilation on all aspects of the

physical remains of our past, starting with the physical background and proceeding through all kinds of settlement to the present day. A mass of well-assimilated knowledge gracefully presented.

Atlases

'Atlas', as used these days, tends to be given various interpretations, ranging from nothing-but-maps to almost-no-maps-at-all. World/European atlases are listed first, then those devoted to England, Wales, Scotland or Ireland.

WORLD OR EUROPE-WIDE ATLASES

Barraclough, Geoffrey (ed, rev Norman Stone), *The Times atlas of world history*. London: Times Books, 3 edn 1989, 358 p, bibl, index. 0 7230 0304 1.
From human origins to the 1980s: series of regional and world maps with explanatory historical text.

Chadwick, Henry and Evans, G R (eds), *Atlas of the Christian church*. Oxford: Phaidon, 1990, 240 p. 0 7148 2657 X.
Not an atlas in the strict sense, but a profusely illustrated survey of all aspects of the Christian faith from the Early Church to the present.

Cornell and Matthews, Atlas of the Roman world, see Section 6.11.4 Romano-British.

European Ethnological Atlas, see Section 4.2 Organisations.

Graham-Campbell, Cultural atlas of the Viking world, see Section 6.11.5 Migration and early medieval (under Vikings).

Hawkes, J (ed), *Atlas of ancient archaeology*. London: Heinemann, 1974, 272 p. 0 434 31405 6. Reprinted 1994.
Not easy to use, rather incomplete, and by now superseded.

Haywood, Penguin historical atlas of the Vikings, see Section 6.11.5 Migration and early medieval (under Vikings).

McEvedy, Colin, *The new Penguin atlas of medieval history*. London: Penguin Books, revised and expanded edn 1992, 112 p, few refs, index. 0 14 051249 7.
Covers the period AD 362 to 1478, and the area from Britain to the River Oxus.

Manley, John, *Atlas of past worlds: a comparative*

chronology of human history 2000 BC–AD 1500. London: Cassell, 1994, 224 p, bibl, index. 0 304 34456 7 pb.
Mainly pictures and text with a few maps: useful articles on Flag Fen, Stonehenge, London at AD 1500, etc.

Matthew, Donald, *Atlas of medieval Europe*. New York: Facts on File, 1992, 240 p. 0 87196 133 4.
Text and colour pictures with a few maps.

***Scarre, Chris (ed), *Past worlds: the Times atlas of archaeology*. [London]: Times Books, rev edn 1995, 320 p, glossary, bibl, index. 0 7230 0810 8.
From human origins through to AD 1800; probably the best archaeological atlas currently available.

Whitehouse, David and Whitehouse, Ruth, *Archaeological atlas of the world*. London: Thames and Hudson, 1975, 272 p, bibls, index. 0 500 78005 6 hb, 0 500 79005 1 pb.
Still in print at 1993 and extremely useful for some areas of the world, though needs to be used in conjunction with more recent information.

ENGLAND (SOMETIMES INCLUDING WALES AND/OR SCOTLAND)

British atlas of historic towns, see under Lobel below.

*Butler, Jeremy, *Dartmoor atlas of antiquities* (4 vols: *East, North, Southwest, Southeast*). [Exeter]: Devon Books, 1991–3.
Contains an introductory text and a series of maps, colour photographs from the air and ground level, gazetteer of sites by category, from Neolithic to 19th century. Each map covers 4km square and there are plans of settlements, fields and so on.

Clout, Hugh (ed), *The Times London history atlas*. London: Times Books, 1991, 191 p, bibl, index. 0 7230 0342 4.
Introduces itself as 'a visual celebration of two thousand years of urban settlement.' Gives the geological and Thames background, followed by chapters on Roman through to Victorian and between-war London. Themes such as building fabric and bridges are also considered.

Coppock, Agricultural atlas of England and Wales, see Section 6.14 Landscape (under Vegetation).

Dymond, David and Martin, Edward (eds), *An historical atlas of Suffolk.* Ipswich: Suffolk County Council Planning Dept/ Suffolk Institute of Archaeology and History, 2 rev edn 1989. o 86055 124 5 hb, o 86055 129 6 pb. Archaeology, history and vernacular architecture, with maps and descriptive text.

Falkus, Malcolm and Gillingham, John, *Historical atlas of Britain.* London: Kingfisher Books 1987. 086272 295 o hb, o 86272 294 2 pb. Contributors include R J Bradley, Wendy Davies, F M L Thompson. Treatment is both chronological and thematic, from 4000 BC to modern. Again, is less of an atlas than an illustrated text with sections on such topics as Stonehenge and Avebury, metalwork, RB life, the coming of the English, etc.

**Goudie, Andrew and Brunsden, Denys, *The environment of the British Isles: an atlas.* Oxford: OUP, 1994, 144 p, 63 p maps, bibl. o 19 874172 3 hb, o 19 874173 1 pb. Gives a vivid picture of the physical nature of our islands: covers geology, geomorphology, hydrology, climatology, soils, biogeography, and human impact on each.

Hill, *Atlas of Anglo-Saxon England, see Section 6.11.5 Migration and early medieval (under Anglo-Saxon).*

Jones and Mattingly, *Atlas of Roman Britain, see Section 6.11.4 Romano-British.*

***Lobel, Mary D and Johns, W H (eds), *The British atlas of historic towns. Maps and plans of towns and cities in the British Isles, with historical commentaries, from earliest times to 1800.* Three volumes so far:
Vol. I: *Historic towns* [Banbury, Caernarvon, Glasgow, Gloucester, Hereford, Nottingham, Reading, Salisbury]. London/Oxford: Lovell Johns – Cook, Hammond and Kell Organization, 1969.
Vol.II: *The atlas of historic towns. Bristol, Cambridge, Coventry, Norwich.* London: Scolar Press/Historic Towns Trust, 1975. o 85967 185 2.
Vol.III: *British atlas of historic towns. The City of London from prehistoric times to c. 1520.* Oxford: OUP for Historic Towns Trust, 1989. o 19 822979 8.
Acclaimed for its high standards of research and cartography, this is an invaluable series for the urban researcher, whether archaeologist or

historian. Full-colour street maps, gazetteer, textual commentary for each town.

*Manley, John, *Atlas of prehistoric Britain.* Oxford: Phaidon, 1989, 160 p. o 7148 2569 7. Again, not an atlas in the normal sense; the maps contain a 'highly selective fraction' of the known sites and mainly illustrate concentrations of evidence. David Lyons' beautiful photographs accompany a text which is 'a very selective summary' of the period from c. 500,000 BC to AD 43. Suggests sites to visit and gives date charts and a very short bibliography.

Maxwell, I S (comp), *Historical atlas of West Penwith.* Sheffield: Univ Sheffield Dept Geography, 1976, vii, 20 p maps. No ISBN. Contains 20 map sheets showing historical and archaeological sites of a particularly interesting part of Cornwall.

Newman, *Atlas of the Civil War, see Section 6.11.7 Post-medieval.*

Ordnance Survey, *National atlas of Great Britain.* Southampton: Ordnance Survey, 1986, 256 p. o 600 33316 7.

Royal Commission on the Historical Monuments of England, *Northamptonshire: an archaeological atlas.* London: RCHME (= Suppl ser, 2, 1980, bibl. o 9507236 o 6. Scale 1:250,000. This one really is an atlas, with text and 18 transparent overlay maps to accompany the five volumes of the Northants Inventory; text by C C Taylor and P J Fowler.

Sylvester, D and Nulty, G (eds), *The historical atlas of Cheshire.* Chester: Cheshire Community Council, 1958, 64 p, bibl. Rather out of date in view of new discoveries, and the arrangement is not helpful (eg Roman and Medieval Chester maps follow industrial Cheshire map).

Wade-Martins, Peter (ed), *An historical atlas of Norfolk.* Norwich: Norfolk Mus Service, 2 edn 1994, 207 p, bibl, place-name index. o 903 1016 o 2 pb. Follows the Suffolk model (Dymond above), with 93 maps and explanatory texts on themes from Palaeolithic/Mesolithic to modern times, including listed buildings, scheduled ancient monuments and so on.

WALES

Carter, H (ed), *National atlas of Wales.* Cardiff:

Univ Wales Press for Board of Celtic Studies, 1989. 0 7083 0775 2.
Folded A2 sheets loose in portfolio, with explanatory text in Welsh and English. No historical element apart from a very little in the Settlement section; but shows physical environment (eg geology, climate, soils, vegetation), political development, culture (language and religion), economic history (eg mining, transport), land use and agriculture (crops, farming-type regions, livestock distributions). Uses are limited by the relatively small scale of the maps, 1:500 000 at best.

Coppock, Agricultural atlas of England and Wales, see Section 6.14 Landscape (under Vegetation).

Davies, Robert, Estate maps, see Section 2.2 Guides to . . . manuscripts . . .

Rees, William, *An historical atlas of Wales.* London: Faber and Faber, new edn 1972, vii, 71 p, 70 pls, undocumented. 0 571 08059 6 hb, 0 571 09976 9 pb.
Covers early dynasties, Celtic monasticism, Llewellyn the Great's Wales, and so on; but now out of date in its archaeology at least.

Richards, Melville (ed), *An atlas of Anglesey.* Anglesey Community Council 1972, 160 pp.
Contains distribution maps and descriptive texts by various hands. Attractive and scholarly, but would need supplementing by more up-to-date information (eg Lynch in Section 6.4 Regional surveys).

Robinson, David M and Thomas, Roger S, *Wales: castles and historic places.* Cardiff: Cadw/Wales Tourist Board, 1990, 136 p. 1 85013 030 2.
Includes a map of Welsh historic sites.

Williams, Atlas of Cistercian lands in Wales, see Section 6.11.7 Post-medieval.

SCOTLAND

McNeill, Peter and Nicholson, Ranald, *An historical atlas of Scotland c. 400 – c. 1600.* [St Andrews]: Atlas Committee of the Conference of Scottish Medievalists, 1975, x, 213 p, bibls, index. 0 9503904 0 2.
Maps, with descriptive text for each, on topics like place-name evidence, Pictish monuments and archaeological sites, Dalriadic Scots, Viking graves, etc.

IRELAND

Atlas of Ireland prepared under the direction of the Irish National Committee for Geography. Dublin: Roy Ir Acad, 1979, 104p. 0 901714 13 5.
Maps are provided of soils, flora and fauna, place-names (Irish and English), together with one for each of three topics: prehistory and early history, Early Christian and medieval, and historic buildings of 16th to 19th centuries. The maps include symbols for (eg) megalith, rock art, monastic house, Martello tower, etc. The main maps show latitude/longitude, but six pages at small scale show the National Grid.

*Duffy, Patrick J with Keenan, James (cartography), *Landscapes of South Ulster: a parish atlas of the Diocese of Clogher.* Belfast: Inst Ir Stud, 1993, viii, 131 p, bibl, index of parishes and townlands.
Remarkable book giving intensive details for each parish, showing them in the wider context.

Edwards, Ruth Dudley, *An atlas of Irish history.* London: Methuen, 2 edn 1981, 286 p, bibl, index. 0 416 74820 1 hb, 0 416 74050 2 pb.
Mainly historical, but sections on communications (early roads etc), medieval trade, Tudor plantations and so on could be useful.

***Irish Historic Towns Atlas* (various compilers; general editors J H Andrews, H B Clarke and A Simms). Dublin: Royal Irish Academy.
  Vol I: *Kildare* (comp J H Andrews), 1986. 0 901714 51 8
  Vol II: *Carrickfergus* (comp Philip Robinson), 1986. 0 901714 52 6
  Vol III: *Bandon* (comp Patrick O'Flanagan), 1988. 0 901714 74 7
  Vol IV: *Kells* (comp Anngret and Katharine Simms), 1990. 0 901714 84 4
  Vol V: *Mullingar* (comp J H Andrews and K M Davies), 1992, 0 901714 51 8
  Vol VI: *Athlone* (comp P H Murtagh), 1994. 1 874045 13 5
The series, which also has tabulated topographical information, has been hailed as a 'goldmine for the archaeologist, historical geographer and local historian' (J Bradley in *Archaeol Ir* 6.2). Later, these six fascicules were combined in a single volume (eds Anngret Simms et al), as *Irish historic towns atlas Vol 1*, 1995, 88 p + 52 p maps.

Maps and Gazetteers

Here are listed finding aids and directories for maps as well as some individual maps. Some notes on map scales are given below in the Ordnance Survey entry. Note that most or all County Record Offices will have catalogues or indexes of their map collections and should be the best place to start on a piece of local research. England, Wales, Scotland and Ireland are treated separately below. For atlases see the immediately preceding subsection.

ENGLAND

Abbott, Richard, 'Maps and plans', in Michael Dewe (ed), *Local studies collections: a manual*, vol 2, Gower Publishing, 1991, pp 265–301. Surveys types of maps and their uses.

AERIAL PANORAMIC MAPS, from Contour Designs, 88 Hucclecote Road, Upton St Leonards, Gloucester GL3 3RU, tel 01452 610549. Full colour representations of relief, size 600mm x 430, annotated with places of interest and providing excellent visual aids to topography of wide areas. Some 30 'maps' are available.

****The A-Z of London* series: large-format volumes showing London's streets at various periods, enabling one to picture the city at each stage and locate individual streets through time. The first three are all from Lympne Castle: Harry Margary/Guildhall Library.
> *The A-Z of Elizabethan London* (comp Adrian Prockter and Robert Taylor, 1979)
> *The A-Z of Georgian London* (introductory notes by Ralph Hyde, 1981)
> *The A-Z of Regency London* (introduction by Paul Laxton, 1985)
> *The A-Z of Victorian London* (introduction by Ralph Hyde). *London Topographical Society publications*, 136, 1987
> *The A-Z of Restoration London* (introduction by Ralph Hyde). *London Topographical Society publications*, 145, 1992. Shows the City newly rebuilt after the Great Fire.

****Bartholomew's gazetteer of places in Britain* (comp Oliver Mason). London: Bartholomew, revised reprint 1986, xl, 270 p + 120 p maps. o 7028 0731 1.
Extremely useful place-finder, with 4-figure National Grid References given in text. Unfortunately no National Grid overlay is provided on the maps themselves, but otherwise this gazetteer is much more informative than the official OS version.

British Library, *The map collections of the British Library*. London: British Library, 1994, 20 p, bibl. (Free leaflet.)
The Map Library of the BL is the national repository. There is a computer file of cartographic materials, available via BLAISE, as well as a list on microfiche. The leaflet gives a general description, indicates catalogues available, further reading, manuscript collections, topographical prints and drawings.

British Museum (now = British Library), *Catalogue of manuscript maps . . . in the British Museum*. 3 vols, 1844–61, reprinted 1962.
> *Catalogue of printed maps, charts and plans, complete to 1964*. London: Trustees of the British Museum, 1967
also *Ten-year supplement 1965–1974* (1978), followed by:
> British Library, *Catalogue of cartographic materials in the British Library 1975–1988*. London: Saur, 1989, 3 vols. o 86291 765 4 (set).

Canterbury Archaeological Trust see below under Tatton-Brown.

Eden, Peter (ed), *Dictionary of land surveyors and local cartographers of Great Britain and Ireland 1550–1850*. Folkestone: Dawson, 1979, 528 p, refs, indexes. o 7129 0900 1.
Includes Irish plantation surveyors. (Second edition said to be in preparation.)

**Goad, Charles E Ltd, *Goad fire insurance plans catalogue 1995*. (Updated from time to time: apply to Charles E Goad Ltd, 8–12 Salisbury Square, Hatfield, Herts AL9 5BJ).
These detailed town plans are invaluable for historical/archaeological work; they cover the period from 1878 and have been described by Gwyn Rowley, *British fire insurance plans* (1984, o 947547 00 2, with bibl) and also in *Archives*, 17, 1985, pp 67–78.

***Harley, J B, *Ordnance Survey maps: a descriptive manual*. Southampton: Ordnance Survey, 1975, xvi, 201 p, refs, index. No ISBN
Standard reference work giving comprehensive information on the National Grid, map content, and interrelationships between various map scales; also describes the surveying, cartographic and printing processes. Now see also Oliver (below).

Harvey, P D A, *Maps in Tudor England*. London: Public Rec Off and Brit Lib, 1993, 120 p, further reading, index. 0 7123 0311 1.

**Hindle, B P, *Maps for local history*. London: Batsford, 1988, 160 p, bibl. 0 7134 5584 5.
Illustrates a wide range of maps and shows their uses.

—, *Medieval town plans*. Shire Archaeol, 62, 1990, 64 p, bibl, index. 0 7478 0065 0 pb.
Good introduction to the subject.

*Hodson, Yolande, *Ordnance Surveyors' drawings, 1789–c. 1840: the original manuscript maps of the 1st Ordnance Survey of England and Wales from the British Library Map Library*. Reading: Research Publns, 1989, 154 p, indexes, folded map in pocket. 0 86257 101 4 spiral-bound.
Description and list.

*Hyde, Ralph, *Gilded scenes and shining prospects: panoramic views of British towns 1575–1900*. New Haven CT: Yale Center for British Art, 1985, 207 p, index of towns. 0 930606 49 3.
Catalogue of an exhibition; reproductions and extended captions.

Jolly, David C, *Maps in British periodicals: Part 1, Major monthlies before 1800; Part 2, Annuals, scientific periodicals and miscellaneous magazines mostly before 1800*. Brookline, MA: David C Jolly, 1990, 2 vols, indexes. 0 911775 51 X.
Indicates 'hidden' sources and may help to identify loose map sheets. Good details, references to other bibliographies, and much useful prefatory matter.

Lewis, Samuel, topographical dictionaries, see above in sub-section on dictionaries.

Lobel, M D (ed), British atlas of historic towns, see the immediately preceding sub-section.

Maltman, A, *Geological maps: an introduction*. Milton Keynes: Open University Press, 1990, viii, 184 pp, bibl, index. 0 335 15222 8.
How to read and use geological maps.

**Maps and plans in the Public Record Office, Vol 1, British Isles 1410–1860*.
London: PRO, 1967, xv, 648 p, index. 0 11 440170 5.
Includes Ireland, Scotland and Wales (pp 547–625): arranged by region and county; said

by Hoskins to be 'full of remarkable treasures – ignore at peril'.

*O'Donoghue, Yolande, *William Roy, 1726–1790: pioneer of the Ordnance Survey*. London: Brit Mus Publns for Brit Lib, 1977, 56 p. 0 7141 0387 x pb.
Catalogue of exhibition; essential for the history of map-making in Britain.

***Oliver, Richard, *Ordnance Survey maps: a concise guide for historians*. London: Charles Close Soc, 1993, 192 p, bibl, index. 0 870598 13 x pb.
Covers the development of the Ordnance Survey, the scales used and the map characteristics, OS mapping of towns (this section is over one-third of the book), county mapping at 1:10 560 and larger scales, and coverage of air photos and air photo mosaics. Invaluable.

ORDNANCE SURVEY

OS map scales, for practical purposes, are:
   1:625,000 (1 inch to 10 miles or 1 cm to 6.25 km) *Travelmaster* Sheet 1
   1:250,000 (1 inch to 4 miles or 1 cm to 2.5 km) *Travelmaster* Sheets 2–9
   1:50,000 (1¼ inch to 1 mile or 2 cm to 1 km) *Landranger*
   1:25,000 (2½ inch to 1 mile or 4 cm to 1 km) *Pathfinder*
(Note that Landranger and Pathfinder maps do not show parish boundaries.)
See OS catalogues for fuller details, including other types of map: for instance, OS can provide, to customer order, facsimile copies of early 19th century maps at the full range of scales from 1:500 to 1:625,000.

OS can also transform readings from field workers' GPS (Global Positioning System) satellite observations into National Grid coordinates: apply to OS Survey Contracts (01703 792285) for details.

The following are all from OS Southampton except where otherwise noted:

The Ordnance Survey Gazetteer of Britain: all names from the 1:50,000 Landranger Map Series. London: Macmillan, 3 edn 1992, 808 p. 0 319 00336 1.
Gives name, county, 4-figure NGR, lat/long, map number for over 250,000 place names. Also a feature code, eg A for non-Roman Antiquity, R for Roman antiquity, etc. For

some purposes Bartholomew's gazetteer may be preferred.

Ordnance Survey historical/archaeological maps:
(with RCHME/RCAMW/RCAHMS), *Ancient Britain.* 4 edn 1990. 0 319 29024 7. Scale 1:625,000, printed both sides, accompanying illustrated text.
  Map of southern Britain in the Iron Age. 1962.
Still in use for lack of an up-to-date replacement. Scale 1:625,000.
  Roman Britain. 4 rev edn, 1994. 0 319 29027 1. Scale 1:625,000, printed both sides, accompanying illustrated text.
  Hadrian's Wall. 1990. 0 319 29018 2.
Not recommended: prefer the small-scale (5mm to 1km or $^5/_{16}$ inch to 1 mile) sketch map with gazetteer of sites and excellent text by Brian Dobson (1990) available free (for sae) from The National Trust, Northumbria Regional Office, Scots' Gap, Morpeth, Northumberland NE61 4EG. The same leaflet also has other useful information, eg tourist information centres.
  Map of Britain in the Dark Ages, AD 410–870. 2 edn 1966 (OP).
  Map of monastic Britain. 2 edn 1954/5 (OP). Scale 1:625,000.

Other historical maps and guides, OS with other bodies:
Folded sheets with illustrations, overprinted on base map, scale 1:2,500 –
  (with RCHME/Bath Archaeological Trust), *Roman and medieval Bath.* 1989. 0 319 29022 0
  Georgian Bath. 1989. 0 319 29023 9
  (with RCHME/Canterbury Archaeological Trust), *Roman and medieval Canterbury.* 1990. 0 319 29026 3
  (with Mus of London), *Londinium: a descriptive map and guide to Roman London.* 2 edn 1983. 0 319 29015 8
  (with RCHME/York Archaeological Trust), *Roman and Anglian York.* 1988. 0 319 29017 4
  Viking and Medieval York. 1988. 0 319 29016 6

Phillips, C W, *Archaeology in the Ordnance Survey 1791–1965.* London: CBA, 1980, vii, 64 p, bibl. 0 900312 90 4 pb.
History and description.

Public Record Office list of maps and plans, see

Section 2.2 Guides to specific sources of manuscripts . . .

Smith, David, *Maps and plans for the local historian and collector: a guide to types of maps of the British Isles produced before 1914 valuable to local and other historians and mostly available to collectors.* London: Batsford, 1988, 240 p, bibl, index. 0 7134 5191 2.
Mainly about printed maps, with information on their likely sources.

TABULA IMPERII ROMANI Map of the Roman Empire: see Section 6.11.4 Romano- British.

Tatton-Brown, T (for Canterbury Archaeol Trust), *Topographical maps of Canterbury, AD 400, 1050, 1200, 1500 and 1700.* Canterbury: CAT, 2 rev edn 1982. 5 maps in portfolio, no ISBN.
Combining archaeological and historical evidence.

***Wallis, Helen (gen ed), *Historian's guide to early British maps: a guide to the location of pre-1900 maps of the British Isles preserved in the United Kingdom and Ireland.* London: Boydell for Roy Hist Soc (= *RHS guides and handbooks,* 18), 1994, ix, 465 p, location index. 0 86193 141 6.
Indispensable (although some editorial oversights have been noted): lists each repository with details of address, access, whether an index etc, types of maps held. Part I, on the history and purpose of maps, has short pieces by specialists on (eg) military surveys, town plans, estate maps, the history of special mapping of archaeological sites from late 16th century, etc. Notes the Goad fire insurance plans as 'the single most important cartographic source for . . . the development of the major British towns and cities . . . 1885–1970.'

WALES

The **National Library of Wales at Aberystwyth** is a rich source of map materials.

Davies, Robert, on estate maps of Wales 1600–1836, see Section 2.2 Guides to specific sources of manuscripts . . .

Map of Wales: a map and gazetteer to the ancient and historic sites in the care of Cadw: Welsh Historic Monuments. Cardiff: Cadw, rev edn 1993, folded A1 sheet. 0 948329 93 9.

Place-names, see Ordnance Survey under Scotland below.

SCOTLAND

The **National Monuments Record of Scotland** holds a complete microfilm set of First Edition 6-inch OS maps at 1:10,560, and microfilm copies of the OS Name Books relating to those maps. The National Library of Scotland Map Library collection is only to be used when local sources have been checked.

Index of Scottish Place-names from the 1981 Census with location and population. Edinburgh: HMSO, 1990, x, 161 p. 0 11 494106 8 pb.
Essentially a gazetteer of place-names, each with administrative category, old county, District, civil parish, population, NGR.

Lewis, Samuel, topographical dictionary, see above in sub-section on dictionaries.

Messenger, Guy, *Ordnance Survey one-inch map of Scotland: third edition in colour.* London: Charles Close Soc, 1991, 36 p. 1 870598 07 5 pb.

Moir, D G, *The early maps of Scotland to 1850.* Edinburgh: Roy Scott Geogr Soc, 2 vols, 1973, 1983.

Moore, John N, *The historical cartography of Scotland: a guide to the literature of Scottish maps and mapping prior to the Ordnance Survey.* Aberdeen: Dept Geography Univ Aberdeen (*O'Dell memorial monogr*, 24), 2 rev edn 1991, 95 p, indexes. ISSN 0141-1454.
Thematic arrangement. Suggests that the most comprehensive library listing is the British Museum's 'Scotland' in their *Catalogue of printed maps . . . to 1964*, (see above under British Museum), vol 13, pp 105–62.

Ordnance Survey, *Place-names on maps of Scotland and Wales.* Southampton: Ordnance Survey, corr repr 1981/1990, 23 p.

IRELAND

Note that some of the National Library's early maps have been inaccessible, partly for conservation reasons; this situation may now have improved.

Andrews, J H, *Ireland in maps: an introduction, with a catalogue of an exhibition . . . 1961.* Dublin: Dolmen Press, 1961, 36 p, refs.
See also this author's bibliographical postscript in *Ir geogr*, 4.4, 1962, pp 234–43.

—, *History in the Ordnance Map: an introduction*

for Irish readers. Newtown, Montgomery: David Archer, 2 edn 1993, 72p. 0 951757 92 X.
A thorough guide to maps 1824–1922, with extracts of 18 maps at original scale plus 7 national maps.

—, *A paper landscape: the Ordnance Survey in 19th century Ireland.* Oxford: Clarendon Press, 1975, xxiv, 350 p, index. 0 19 823209 8.
Detailed history of how the mapping was done.

Bartholomew's ¼-inch Travel Maps – not on National Grid. Five cover the whole island and megalithic tombs are marked.

British Museum catalogue of manuscript maps, see earlier in this sub-section under England.

Census of Ireland 1851. General alphabetical index to townlands and towns, parishes, and baronies of Ireland, showing the number of the sheet of the Ordnance Survey maps in which they appear. Dublin: Alex Thom for HMSO, 1861 [1862].
The 'Townland Index', mainly used for place-name studies but also sometimes for archaeological work. Further editions appeared after the 1871 Census (1877), 1901 Census ('General topographical index' 1904), with a supplement to the last appearing in 1913 from HMSO in London. *See also Ordnance Survey.*

Colby, Thomas, [sometimes catalogued under Larcom, T A], *Ordnance Survey of the County of Londonderry: memoir of the city and North-western Liberties of Londonderry, Parish of Templemore.* Dublin: Hodges and Smith, 1837, 364 p, index.
Only this one volume ever appeared (but see below under Ordnance Survey Memoirs for work going on to computerise the manuscript memoirs). Antiquities form one section among botany, economy, etc treated here.

Dublin c.840–c. 1540: the medieval town in the modern city. Map to 1:2,500 scale (comp H B Clarke for Friends of Medieval Dublin). Dublin: Ordnance Survey, 1978, 15 p of accompanying text.

Eden, Peter, dictionary of land surveyors including Irish, see under England earlier in this sub-section.

Edwards, R W Dudley and O'Dowd, Mary, chapter on 'Maps and drawings' in their *Sources for early modern Irish history, 1534–1641* (CUP, 1985).

Ferguson, Paul, *Irish map history: a select bibliography of secondary works, 1850–1983, on the history of cartography in Ireland.* Dublin: Univ Coll Dublin Dept Geogr (for Tenth Int Conference on the History of Cartography), 1983, vi, 26 p. 0 9509040 0 7 pb. (Second edn in preparation.)

Gazetteer of Ireland: names of centres of population and physical features. Dublin: Stationery Office for Place-Names branch of Ordnance Survey, 1989, xxxiv, 283 p. 0 7076 0076 6.
Gives 6-figure NGR, Irish spelling and English pronunciation, and English version, in both Irish and English alphabetical orders.

Godfrey reprint maps (Alan Godfrey, 12 The Off Quay Building, Foundry Lane, Newcastle on Tyne NE6 1LH. Tel 0191 276 1155, fax 0191 224 0080.)
Publishes large scale town and village reprints: 18 for N Ireland, one for the south. One side of the map has the complete one-inch map for the district, the other side a reduced-scale town plan.

Hadcock, R N, *Map of monastic Ireland.* Scale 1:625,000 or 1 inch to 9.86 miles. Dublin: Ordnance Survey Office, 2 edn 1965.
A distribution map of all known religious houses c AD 450–1600, overprinted with National Grid, main contours, modern roads and railways etc.

Hayes-McCoy, G A, *Ulster and other Irish maps c. 1600.* Dublin: Stationery Office for Irish Manuscripts Commission, 1964.
Facsimile of manuscript map showing houses, fortifications etc: 'may be used with caution for the later middle ages'.

'Index to townlands and towns', see above under Census.

Kissane, Noel (comp), *Historic Dublin maps.* Dublin: National Library, 1988, 13 maps in pocket and commentary. 0 907328 14 8 pb.
Includes nine historic maps from Speed to Rocque, and four maps showing the medieval development of Dublin.

Law, Andrew Bonar, *The printed maps of Ireland to 1612.* Morristown NJ: Eagle Press, 1983, 37 p.
Descriptive catalogue: forerunner of a much larger work in progress.

Lewis, Samuel, *topographical dictionary*, see above in sub-section on dictionaries.

Michelin Sheet 405, *Motoring map of Ireland.* Scale 1:400,000 or 1 inch to 6.3 miles; for general purposes is the best of the small-scale maps, very clear and with good index.

ORDNANCE SURVEY MEMOIRS OF IRELAND. The Memoirs of the N Ireland surveyors (compiled in 1830s and a rich source of parish information) have been published for the first time by the Institute of Irish Studies of The Queen's University of Belfast (in association with the Royal Irish Academy). The full series of 38 or 40 volumes (including four for the Republic) should be complete by now. (Contact Angelique Day at IIS for latest list.) The related computer databank, with every significant word indexed, will in due course become available to authorised users via Environment and Heritage Service: Historic Monuments and Buildings in Belfast. *(Note that virtually all the Memoirs for S Ireland, transferred long ago to Southampton OS, were destroyed in WW II bombing. However, some letters survive in the Royal Irish Academy: see OS Letters below.)*

Ordnance Survey of Ireland, *Townland survey.* Scale 1:10,560, or 6 inches to 1 mile. First edition shows barony and civil parishes approximately as in medieval times. Index at one-half or one-third mile scale also shows civil parish boundaries.

—, *Discovery series* maps at 1:50,000 (replacing old one-inch maps): 33 sheets for the Republic by the end of 1995, and continuing. These give the most up-to-date cover since the original 6-inch survey in the 19th century. (See also *Discoverer* series for N Ireland, noted below.)

Note that 25 half-inch maps covering the whole of Ireland are being superseded by the Discovery/ Discoverer series.

—, *Showing county boundaries [and] barony boundaries.* Scale 1:63,600 or 1 inch to 10 miles. Dublin: Ordnance Survey Office 1938. The 'barony map'. Use in conjunction with Lewis's atlas and the Townland Survey, because of late 19th century boundary changes.

—, *An illustrated record of the Ordnance Survey in Ireland, researched and compiled by the staff of both Ordnance Surveys in Ireland.* Dublin: OS of Ireland, 1991, 108 p. 0 904996 02 6.

—, 'Letters containing information relative to the antiquities of various counties collected during the progress of the OS in 1837–8' (typescript edition, Bray, 1927–8, held at Royal Irish Academy).

—, *Catalogue of the large-scale maps with dates of survey and latest revision shown on the indexes to each county.* Dublin: OS, 1964 [there appears to be no up-to-date catalogue]

—, *Urban maps at 1:1,000 scale*

—, *Rural maps at 1:2,500 scale*

(Note that Phoenix Maps – last known at 26 Ashington Avenue, Navan Road, Dublin 7, tel Dublin 838 3579 – reprinted all 205 sheets of the original one-inch OS map; six-inch cover for most parts of Dublin in c 1843 and c 1912; and reduced-scale 19th/20th century plans of 15 provincial towns.)

Ordnance Survey [of Northern Ireland], *Gazetteer of Northern Ireland: listing all the names that appear on the sheets of the one-inch map (3rd series) . . .* Belfast: HMSO, 1969.
Includes 4-figure National Grid References.
—, *Half-inch second series maps* (4 sheets: obsolete)
—, *One-inch third series maps* at 1:63,360 (9 sheets, going out of print)
—, *Discoverer series* (replaces old one-inch maps) at 1:50,000 (18 sheets for N Ireland: see also the *Discovery* series for the Republic, noted above.)
(Also various large-scale maps eg 1:10,000, 1:2,500, maps for administrative purposes, Areas of Natural Beauty, country parks etc.)
—, *OS road atlas of Ireland* (includes antiquities, museums, listed buildings etc).
See also current Map Catalogue produced by OS N Ireland.

'The Ordnance Survey and the local historian', as Vol 14.2 of *Ulster local studies*, 1992; contains various papers on the uses of maps.

For more information on the Ordnance Survey in both Republic and Northern Ireland, see Section 4.2 Organisations.

Robinson, Tim, *The Aran Islands: a map and guide.* Kilronan, Aran: author, 1980. o 9504002 2 X.
A short text on the history of the islands off Co Galway accompanies finely drawn, innovative maps at 2.2 inch to 1 mile of the archaeological and natural features.

—, *The Burren: a map of the uplands of County Clare, Eire.* [Kilronan, Aran]: author, 1977, folded map and accompanying text. o 9504002 1 1 pb.
Similarly innovative contribution to mapping.

Stout, Matthew, 'Plans from plans: an analysis of the 1:2,500 OS Series as a source for ringfort morphology', in *Proc Roy Ir Acad*, **92C**, 1992, pp 37–53 (on the usefulness of the turn-of-the-century large-scale maps for determining ringfort characteristics with a reasonable degree of accuracy).

_____

Addendum on 'Historic Landscapes' and similar maps
These maps, pioneered by the Cornwall Archaeological Unit, are increasingly being followed by other counties; they demonstrate the historic character of large tracts of landscape (as opposed to individual sites) and thus give planners more realistic advice on the historic landscape.
The Countryside Commission is publishing a special map in December 1996, entitled *The character of England: its landscape, wildlife and natural features.* It offers a generalised summary which will be followed during 1997 by more detailed landscape descriptions (including the historic environment).
Cadw for Wales uses the approach of 'listing' individual historic landscapes of special importance, but this process has only advisory force.

6.2
Introductory Texts

British

The fastest way to gain an introduction to British archaeology is through the short texts in the *Shire archaeology* series; slightly variable in quality, but most are very good, and all offer some titles for further reading.

*Bewley, Robert, *Prehistoric settlements*. London: Batsford/EH, 1994, 144 p, sites to visit, index. 0 7134 6857 2 hb, 0 7134 6853 x pb.
On the latest finds, many discovered from the air, and giving an introduction to archaeological techniques.

Champion, T C et al, *Prehistoric Europe*. London: Academic Press, 1984, vii, 359 p, bibl, index. 0 12 167550 5.
Student textbook.

*Cunliffe, Barry (ed), *The Oxford illustrated prehistory of Europe*. Oxford: OUP, 1994, 532 p, narrative bibls by chapter, index. 0 19 814395 0.
Various contributors provide 12 chapters, with the changing landscape and ecology as the recurrent theme. Covers up to AD 700 in fact.

Darvill, Timothy, *Prehistoric Britain*. London: Batsford, 1987, 223 p, bibl, glossary, index. 0 7134 5179 3 hb, 0 7134 5180 7 pb.
Traces six themes from the Ice Age to just before the Roman Conquest.

**Greene, Kevin, *Archaeology: an introduction: the history, principles and methods of modern archaeology*. London: Batsford, 3 edn fully revised 1995, 208 p, bibl, index. 0 7134 7636 2 limp.
Not a textbook, avowedly treats author's own interests, but a good introduction for students. The chapter on theoretical archaeology is mainly new.

***Longworth, I H and Cherry, John (eds), *Archaeology in Britain since 1945: new directions*. London: Brit Mus Publs, 1986, 248 p, bibl, glossary, index. 0 7141 2035 9 pb.
Attractive work designed to show the tremen-dous advances made since WWII in under-standing prehistoric to medieval archaeology.

*Megaw, J V S and Simpson, D D A (eds), *Introduction to British prehistory from the arrival of Homo sapiens to the Claudian invasion*. Leicester: Leics UP, 1979, xv, 560 p, bibl, index. 0 7185 1122 0 hb, 0 7185 1172 7 pb.
Basic textbook, kept in print though now partly out of date.

**Wass, Stephen, *Amateur archaeologist*. London: Batsford, 1992, 160 p, bibl, index. 0 7134 6896 3.
For the individual who wants to join in; gives simple explanations of fieldwalking, study of standing buildings, excavation techniques, survey, legislation, careers. Recommended.

***Wheeler, Mortimer, *Archaeology from the earth*. Oxford: Clarendon, 1954, xi, 221 p, index.
Still one of the best introductions to the discipline; the source of the famous dictum that we must search for the human dimension since 'dead archaeology is the driest dust that blows.'

Irish

A new series from Town House and Country House of Dublin offers short, authoritative texts on single topics, rather like the British series from *Shire archaeology*. The *Irish heritage* series from Eason (Dublin) is a popular and inexpensive collection of short introductions also covering single topics.

Bardon, Jonathan, *A history of Ulster*. Belfast: Blackstaff Press, 1992, 914 p, bibl, index. 0 85640 466 7 hb, 0 85640 476 4 pb.
Mainly for the later periods as is very light on prehistory and early history.

Bradley, R, Altering the earth, see Section 6.12 History and theory.

Cooney, Gabriel and Grogan, Eoin, *Irish prehistory: a social perspective*. Dublin: Wordwell, 1994, xiii, 251 p, bibl, index. 1 869857 11 9.
Not an easy book, but a good summary of present understanding, and refreshingly unobsessed with artefacts.

Harbison, Peter, *The archaeology of Ireland*. London: Bodley Head, 1976, 120 p, bibl, index. 0 370 01596 7.
Introduction for general reader; b/w and some

colour illustrations, line drawings and reconstruction drawings.

***—, *Pre-Christian Ireland: from the first settlers to the early Celts.* London: Thames and Hudson (= *Ancient peoples and places*, 104), 1988, 208 p, bibl, index. 0 500 02110 4 hb, 0 500 27809 1 pb.
Well-deserved winner of the British Archaeological Award for the best archaeological book of 1988; covers the period up to the Iron Age hillforts.

—, Potterton, H and Sheehy, J, *Irish art and architecture from prehistory to the present.* London: Thames and Hudson, pb edn 1993, 272 p, bibl, index. 0 500 27707 9. (Original edition was 1978.)
Another attractive introduction.

Herity, Michael and Eogan, George, *Ireland in prehistory.* London: Routledge and Kegan Paul, 1977, xvi, 302 p, bibl, index. 0 7100 8413 7.
Rather overtaken now by theoretical developments and new evidence, but with a very useful and extensive bibliography.

Moody, T W, Martin, F X and Byrne, F J (eds), *A new history of Ireland: VIII, a chronology of Irish history to 1976. A companion to Irish history, part I.* Oxford: Clarendon, 1982, xii, 591 p. 0 19 821744 2.
Dates and events from the earliest datable times. (Some of the other seven volumes are listed under their appropriate sections here, eg Cosgrove in Medieval.)

O'Kelly, Michael J, *Early Ireland: an introduction to Irish prehistory.* Cambridge: CUP, 1989, xiii, 375 p, bibl, index. 0 521 33489 6 hb, 0 521 33687 2 pb.
From the Ice Age to the Iron Age.

Ó Ríordáin, Sean P (revised by R de Valera), *Antiquities of the Irish countryside.* London: Methuen, 5 edn 1979, xvi, 182 p. 0 416 85630 6 hb, 0 416 85610 1 pb.
A classic companion, but should be read in conjunction with much more recent work.

***Ryan, Michael (ed), *Irish archaeology illustrated.* Dublin: Town House and Country House, rev edn 1994 (former title *Illustrated archaeology of Ireland*), 224 p, glossary, bibl, index. 0 946172 33 1 pb.
37 specialists write on their own subjects, aided by superb photographs.

**[— (ed)], *Treasures of Ireland: Irish art 3000 BC-1500 AD. Dublin: Royal Irish Academy,* 1983, 203 p, bibl. 0 901714 28 3.
Exhibition catalogue, originally prepared for Paris (*Trésors d'Irlande*, publ Assoc Française d'Action Artistique) and then Germany (*Irische Kunst aus drei Jahrtausenden*, Mainz 1983). The Irish edition is to be preferred and should not be confused with two similarly-titled but quite different works prepared for the New York Metropolitan Museum of Art's much earlier exhibition,, *Treasures of [early] Irish art 1500 BC-1500 AD* (1977).

6.3
Guides to Archaeological Sites

Listed here are guidebooks intended explicitly for archaeological tourists. (More explanatory, narrative texts will be found in the Regional Surveys section which follows.) Even if partly out of date, these guidebooks still offer the best chance of locating a site.

England, also more general guides covering Britain and Ireland together

Adkins, L and Adkins, R, *A field guide to Somerset archaeology*. Stanbridge: Dovecote Press, 1992, 138 p, bibl. 0 946159 94 7 pb.
Sites arranged by period.

Ashmore, O, on industrial sites in NW England, see Section 6.15 Archaeology of industrial processes.

Bailey, Brian, *The Ordnance Survey guide to great British ruins*. London: Cassell, 1991, 224 p, glossary, indexes to persons and places. 0 304 31855 8.
Well illustrated, with brief history of each ruin and access details together with portion of relevant OS map.

***Buildings of England series* (Harmondsworth: Penguin, ed N Pevsner followed by Bridget Cherry; 46 volumes under steady revision). The justly famed 'Pevsners' without which many people refuse to go on a journey: each county of England has a volume or more describing not only the buildings of note but also (in an introductory chapter) the principal prehistoric and Roman monuments of the county. (Parallel series for Wales, Scotland and Ireland appear under those countries below.) There is also a limited edition publication, from the Buildings of England office, which may be found in specialist libraries:
Blackshaw, T, Cherry, B and Williamson, E, *The Buildings of England further reading: a select bibliography* (London: Penguin, 1990). This is a list of non-local secondary sources mainly from 1945 onwards, including books and articles from major periodicals up to 1989–90 but excluding monographs on buildings or local studies.
A CD-ROM from OUP Electronic Publish-

ing, *A compendium of Pevsner's Buildings of England* (comp Michael Good, 0 19 268221 0) gives rapid computerised access to the 300,000 entries (buildings and artefacts) in the 46-volume series.

***Burl, Aubrey, *A guide to the stone circles of Britain, Ireland and Brittany*. London: Yale Univ Press, 1995, 276 p, bibl, index. 0 300 06331 8 semi-stiff cloth.
Nearly 400 sites listed by county.

Castleden, Rodney, *Neolithic Britain: New Stone Age sites of England, Scotland and Wales*. London: Routledge, 1992, xiv, 432 p, bibl, index. 0 415 05845 7.
Brief descriptions and map references.

Children, G and Nash, G, *Prehistoric sites of Herefordshire*. Almeley (Heref): Logaston Press (= *Monuments in the landscape*, 1), 1994, x, 133 p, bibl. 1 873827 09 1 pb.
Guide to the monuments, and general discussion of prehistoric British settlement.

CIVIL ENGINEERING HERITAGE see entries in Section 6.15 Archaeology of industrial processes.

Dyer, James, *The Penguin guide to prehistoric England and Wales*. London: Allen Lane 1981, 384 p, bibl, index. 0 7139 1164 6 (also Penguin: 0 14 046351 8 pb).

–, *Southern England: an archaeological guide. The prehistoric and Roman remains*. London: Faber and Faber, 1973, xlv, 380 p, index. 0 571 10317 0 hb, 0 571 10334 0 pb.
Visitable sites arranged by county, short reference list for each.

Ellis, P Berresford, *A guide to early Celtic remains in Britain*. London: Constable, 1991, 272 p, glossary, bibl, site index. 0 09 469200 9 hb, 0 09 471110 0 pvc covers.
Iron Age sites, in the usual Constable pocketable format.

English Heritage, *Guide to English Heritage properties*. London: English Heritage, issued annually to members.
Gives information (opening times, location etc) on over 350 properties in care. English Heritage also issues individual guide booklets to most of the sites in its care; list available from them. Their Battlefields Register is noted in Section 6.11.7 Post-medieval.

Exploring England's Heritage: regional series in

11 volumes. London: HMSO in association with English Heritage, 1991–.

These volumes aim to take visitors off the beaten track; they cover the best archaeological and architectural sites by region: eg Devon and Cornwall, London, Cumbria to Northumberland, Dorset to Gloucestershire, Yorkshire to Humberside, Oxfordshire to Buckinghamshire, Hertfordshire to Norfolk (etc).

Falconer, K, see 6.15 Archaeology of industrial processes.

Harbison, Robert, *Shell guide to English parish churches*. London: André Deutsch, 1994, 320 p. 0 233 98893 9 pb.

Hudson, Kenneth and Nicholls, Ann, *The Cambridge guide to the historic places of Britain and Ireland*. Cambridge: CUP, 1989, viii, 326 p, indexes. 0 521 36077 3.
Treats 1567 monuments and buildings, with colour illustrations and maps.

*Kerr, Nigel and Mary, *A guide to Anglo-Saxon sites*. London: Granada, 1982, 207 p, glossary, index. 0 246 11775 3.
This and the next two titles are very selective but extremely useful; it is a pity they contain no reading lists.

*– *A guide to Norman sites in Britain*. London: Granada, 1984, 192 p, glossary, index. 0 246 11976 4 hb, 0 586 08445 2 pb.

*–, *A guide to medieval sites in Britain*. London: Grafton Books, 1988, 270 p, glossary, index. 0 246 12470 9 hb, 0 586 08496 7 pb.

Lloyd, David W, *Historic towns of south-east England*. London: Gollancz, 1987, 160 p, bibl, index. 0 575 03689 3.
Gazetteer noting the significance of street plans and selected buildings in Kent, Surrey, Sussex and Hampshire.

Maxfield, V, Saxon Shore gazetteer, see Section 6.11.4 Romano-British.

Muir, Richard, *Shell guide to reading the Celtic landscapes*. London: Michael Joseph, 1985, 288 p. 0 7181 2533 9.
Covers Scotland, Ireland, Wales and Cornwall.

—, *National Trust guide to Dark Age and medieval Britain, 400–1350*. London: George Philip/Nat Trust, 1985, 256 p, bibl, index. 0 540 01090 1.

— and Welfare, Humphrey, *The National Trust guide to prehistoric and Roman Britain*. London: George Philip, 1983, 272 p, bibl, index. 0 540 01706 6.
Maps included.

New, Anthony, *A guide to the abbeys of England and Wales*. London: Constable, 1985, 465 p. 0 09 463520 X.
Pocketable book presenting 243 sites in alphabetical order with plans for most of them and an introduction.

Ottaway, Patrick and Cyprien, Michael (photographer), *A traveller's guide to Roman Britain*. London: Routledge and Kegan Paul, 1987, 0 7102 0943 6.
Fine black-and-white photographs accompany a rather dense but usefully fact-full text.

Pewsey, Stephen and Brooks, Andrew, *East Saxon heritage: an Essex gazetteer*. Stroud: Alan Sutton, 1993, xxi, 129 p, bibl. 0 7509 0290 6 pb.

The **Prehistoric Society** issues field guides to participants in its regular excursions, containing much useful information often not readily available elsewhere; most regions of Britain and Ireland have been covered and copies can sometimes be found in archaeology libraries.

Ratcliffe, Jeanette, *Scilly's archaeological heritage*. Truro: Twelveheads Press, 1992, 53 p. Authoritative guide.

Rowley, Trevor and Cyprien, M (photographer), *A traveller's guide to Norman Britain*. London: Routledge and Kegan Paul, 1986, 128 p. 0 7102 0687 9.
Covers 105 sites.

*The **Royal Archaeological Institute** holds summer conferences in a different region each year and produces a substantial handbook issued alongside (formerly bound with) *Archaeological journal*. Emphasis is on post-Roman.

Salter, Mick: has produced a large number of regional guide booklets to castles, too many to list here: Folly Publications, Malvern.

Smurthwaite, David, *Complete guide to the battlefields of Britain, with OS maps*. Camberley: Webb and Bower, 1984, 224 p, bibl, index. 0 86350 157 5 pb.
Describes and locates over 100 battlefields, from Roman [sic] to the Battle of Britain. (More accessible than the official English Heritage battlefields register.)

*Thomas, Nicholas, *A guide to prehistoric England*. London: Batsford, 2 edn 1976, 270 p, bibl, site index. 0 7134 3267 5.
Somewhat overtaken by archaeological events now, but remains useful for its site bibliographies. County arrangement.

Tomalin, David, *Roman Wight: a guide catalogue to 'The island of Vectis, very near to Britannia'*. Newport IoW: IoW County Council, 1987, 128 p, bibl, index. 0 906328 37 3 pb.
Survey of island sites and finds, with chapters on the Newport and Brading villas, and general discussion.

Wainwright, Richard, *A guide to the prehistoric remains in Britain (South and East)*. London: Constable, 1978, 325 p, bibl, index. 0 09 460320 0.

Wilson, Roger J A, *A guide to the Roman remains in Britain*. London: Constable, 3 edn 1988, xiii, 453 p, bibl, index. 0 09 468680 7.

Wales

Buildings of Wales series. The Welsh version of 'the Pevsners' (published from Harmondsworth by Penguin, and each with bibliography and index) includes so far:
Powys (Montgomeryshire, Radnorshire, Breconshire) (Richard Haslam, 1979, 436 p). 0 14 071051 5.
Clwyd (Denbighshire and Flintshire) (Edward Hubbard, 1986, 518 p). 0 14 071052 3. (Frances Lynch provided the prehistoric and Roman chapter in each.)
Glamorgan (John Newman, 1995, 717 p). 0 14 071056 6. (A Ward provided the prehistoric and Roman introduction and Stephen Hughes covered the industrial buildings.)

Burnham, Helen (ed Sian Rees), *A guide to ancient and historic Wales: Clwyd and Powys*. London: HMSO for Cadw, 1995, x, 220 p, bibl, glossary, index. 0 11 701575 X pb.
Describes 150 monuments to visit, from Palaeolithic onwards.

Cadw (Welsh Historic Monuments) issues individual guide booklets to many of its sites in care; list available from Cadw (address in Section 4.2 Organisations).

Dyer, James, *Penguin guide to prehistoric England and Wales*, see under England above.

Houlder, Christopher, *Wales – an archaeological guide: the prehistoric, Roman and early medieval field monuments*. London: Faber and Faber, 1974, 207 p, bibl, indexes. 0 571 08221 1.

Lynch, Frances, *A guide to ancient and historic Wales: Gwynedd*. London: HMSO/Cadw, 1995, x, 220 p, bibl, glossary, index. 0 11 701574 1 pb.
Gives 150 sites to visit from Mesolithic to medieval, with directions on reaching them.

Macinnes, Lesley, *Anglesey: a guide to ancient and historic sites on the Isle of Anglesey*. Cardiff: Cadw 1989, 44 p, refs. 0 948329 12 2 pb.
Covers 23 monuments and gives three suggested tours.

New, Anthony, *guide to abbeys*, see under England above.

Rees, Sian, *A guide to ancient and historic Wales: Dyfed*. London: HMSO/Cadw, 1992, x, 241 p, glossary, bibl, index. 0 11 701220 3 pb.
Period gazetteer and 'other' (ie remoter) sites, map; Palaeolithic onwards, though medieval sites occupy about half of the book.

Robinson, David, *Heritage in Wales: a guide to the ancient and historic sites in the care of Cadw: Welsh Historic Monuments*. London: Macdonald, Queen Anne Press, 1989, 208 p, glossary, bibl, index. 0 356 17278 3.
Describes the work of Cadw and gives an A–Z county descriptive gazetteer.

Whittle, Elizabeth, *A guide to ancient and historic Wales: Glamorgan and Gwent*. London: HMSO/Cadw, 1992, viii, 216 p, glossary, bibl, index. 0 11 701221 1 pb.
Period gazetteer and 'other' (ie remoter) sites, maps; Palaeolithic onwards, though medieval sites occupy about half the book.

Scotland

Breeze, D J, *guide to Roman remains*, see Section 6.11.4 Romano-British.

Buildings of Scotland series The 'McPevsners' nickname does not necessarily imply that these books have gained the respect given to the elder series. The five titles to date, general editor C McWilliam, all come from Penguin Books in London. They also contain a chapter on prehistoric and later monuments, a glossary and index. The later volumes are published in association with the Buildings of Scotland Trust. The five so far available are:

Edinburgh (John Gifford, 1984, 732 p). 0 14 071068 x

Fife (John Gifford, 1988, 468 p). 0 14 017077 9

Highland and Islands (Colin McWilliam, 1992, 683 p). 0 14 071071 x

Lothian (except Edinburgh) (Colin McWilliam, 1978, 523 p). 0 14 071066 3

Glasgow (Elizabeth Williamson et al, 1990, 701 p). 0 14 071069 8

Burl, A, on stone circles, see under England above.

Dunbar, John and Fisher, Ian, *Iona*. Edinburgh: HMSO for RCAHMS, 2 edn 1995, 32 p. 0 11 495269 8 pb.
Well illustrated guide to the island's history from St Columba (AD 563) to the present.

****Exploring Scotland's Heritage* (regional series in eight volumes), edited by Anna Ritchie. Edinburgh: HMSO for RCAHMS, new edition in progress 1995–. All are paperbacks at least 180 pages long, with an introductory survey followed by monument descriptions arranged in period groups, suggested excursion routes, bibliography and index. Expect to find new editions for the following areas:

Aberdeen and NE Scotland (Ian Shepherd, 1996). 0 11 495290 6 pb

Argyll and the Western Isles (Graham Ritchie and Mary Harman, 1996). 0 11 495287 6 pb

Dumfries and Galloway (Geoffrey Stell, 1996). 0 11 495294 9 pb

Edinburgh, Lothian and the Borders (John R Baldwin, 1996). 0 11 495292 2 pb

Fife, Perthshire and Angus (Bruce Walker and Graham Ritchie, 1996). 0 11 495286 8 pb.

Glasgow, Clydeside and Stirling (Jack Stevenson, 1995). 0 11 495291 4 pb

The Highlands (Joanna Close-Brooks, 1996). 0 11 495293 0 pb

Orkney (Anna Ritchie, 1996). 0 11 495288 4 pb.

Shetland (Anna Ritchie, 1996). 0 11 495289 2 pb

Feachem, Richard W, *A guide to prehistoric Scotland*. London: Batsford, 2 edn 1977, last reprinted 1992, 223 p, bibl, index. 0 7134 3264 0 pb.
Invaluable in its day; is kept in print but not up to date, so the *Exploring Scotland's Heritage* series should be used for preference.

*Fojut, Noel and Pringle, Denys, *The ancient monuments of Shetland*. Edinburgh: HMSO/ Historic Scotland, 1993, 64 p. 0 11 494200 5 pb.
Eight monuments selected to illustrate the span from Neolithic structure to 18th century fort; attractively illustrated.

*—, Pringle, Denys and Walker, Bruce, *The ancient monuments of the Western Isles: a visitors' guide to the principal historic sites and monuments*. Edinburgh: HMSO, 1994, 72 p. 0 11 495201 9 pb.

Historic Scotland issues individual guide booklets to many of the sites in its care; list available from Historic Scotland (address in Section 4.2 Organisations).

Horan, Martin, *Scottish castles*. Edinburgh: Chambers (Miniguides series), 1994, vi, 126 p. 0 550 20073 8 pb.

Jackson, Anthony, *The Pictish trail: a traveller's guide to the old Pictish kingdoms*. Kirkwall: Orkney Press, 1989, 64 p. 0 907618 18 9 pb.

Keppie, Lawrence, *Scotland's Roman remains: an introduction and handbook*. Edinburgh: John Donald, 1986, ix, 188 p, bibl, index. 0 85976 157 6.

MacKie, E W, *Scotland: an archaeological guide from earliest times to the 12th century AD*. London: Faber and Faber, 1975, 309 p, bibl, index. 0 571 09871 1 hb, 0 571 10735 4 pb.
Rather overtaken by events, so the *Exploring Scotland's Heritage* series is preferable.

Macnie, Donald L (ed), *New Shell guide to Scotland*. London: Ebury Press, 1977 edn, 479 p, bibl, index. [0] 7181 3036 7.

Muir, Richard, Shell guide to reading the Celtic landscapes, see under England above.

New, Anthony, *A guide to the abbeys of Scotland, with priories and collegiate churches*. London: Constable, 1988, 313 p. 0 09 467190 7.

Prentice, Robin (comp), *The National Trust for Scotland guide*. London: Cape, 1976, 316 p, index. 0 224 01239 8.

**Ritchie, Anna and Graham (ed P Ashmore), *The ancient monuments of Orkney*. Edinburgh: HMSO for Historic Scotland and Orkney Island Council, 1995, 76 p. 0 11 495734 7 pb.

The official guide to selected monuments, in colour throughout.

**Royal Incorporation of Architects in Scotland (address given in Section 4.2 Organisations) issues a series of very good repute, *Illustrated architectural guides to Scotland*. D Moody relishes the 'swashbuckling' tone of their descriptions.

Royal Society of Antiquaries of Ireland, Antiquarian Handbook series: IV, *Report of an excursion to the western islands of Scotland, Orkney and Caithness, 1900*.
Well illustrated, and even now not just a curiosity.

Whyte, Ian and Kathleen, *Exploring Scotland's historic landscapes*. Edinburgh: John Donald, 1987, 314 p, bibl, index. 0 85976 166 5 pb.
Not to be confused with the *Exploring Scotland's Heritage* series described above, this is a single work offering 18 trails over a range of Neolithic to modern landscape features to illuminate the way in which Scotland's landscape has developed.

Isle of Man

[Cubbon, A M], *The ancient and historic monuments of the Isle of Man: a general guide including a selected list with notes*. Douglas: Manx Museum and National Trust, 3 rev edn 1967, 20 p (regularly reprinted).
See also Cubbon on art of the Manx crosses in Section 6.11.5 Migration and early medieval.

Channel Islands

Hobbs, James and Kinnes, Ian, *The dolmens of Jersey: a guide*. Le Haule (Jersey): La Haule Books, 1988, ix, 89 p. 0 86120 021 7 pb.

Johnston, David E, *The Channel Islands: an archaeological guide*. Chichester: Phillimore, 1981, xiv, 144 p, bibl, index. 0 85033 395 4.

Ireland

AA Images of Ireland. Basingstoke: Automobile Ass, 1992, 191 p. 0 7495 0580 X.
Text by Peter Harbison accompanies large numbers of illustrations.

Bhreathnach, Edel and Newman, Conor, *Tara*

[guide to]. Dublin: Office of Public Works, 1995, 56 p. 0 7076 1695 6.

Buildings of Ireland series (Harmondsworth: Penguin, edited by Alistair Rowan, all with glossary and index but without the prehistoric chapters usual in the English and Scottish series. Nine volumes projected.)
North West Ulster: the counties of Londonderry, Donegal, Fermanagh and Tyrone (Alistair Rowan, 1979, 564 p). 0 14 071081 7.
North Leinster: the counties of Longford, Louth, Meath and Westmeath (Christine Casey and Alistair Rowan, 1993, 576 p). 0 14 071085 X.
(Antrim–Down–Belfast volume in preparation)

Burl, Aubrey, on stone circles, see under England above.

Connolly, Michael, *Kerry County Museum: a guide to the archaeology and history of County Kerry*. Tralee: Tralee UDC, 1992, 36 p.
Good guide with many illustrations.

Crowl, Philip, *The intelligent traveller's guide to Ireland*. Dublin: Gill and Macmillan, 1992, vii, 517 p. 0 8092 4062 9 hb, 0 7171 1974 2 pb.

*Environment Service (N Ireland) Historic Monuments and Buildings, *Historic monuments of Northern Ireland: an introduction and guide*. Belfast: HMSO, 1987, (2nd impression of 6 edn 1983), 170 p. 0 337 08180 8 pb.
General introduction and county-by-county guide to monuments in the Six Counties.

***Evans, E Estyn, *Prehistoric and early Christian Ireland: a guide*. London: Batsford, 1966, xiv, 241 p, glossary, bibl, index.
Out of date in some respects, but still a valuable guide to finding excavated and some other sites.

Gosling, Paul, *Carlingford town: an antiquarian's guide*. Carlingford Lough Heritage Trust, 1992, xii, 68 p. 0 952075 10 5.

—, *on Dundalk, see entry in Section 6.11.6 Medieval.*

Grogan, Eoin and Hillery, Tom, *A guide to the archaeology of County Wicklow*. Wicklow: Wicklow County Tourism, 1993, 56 p. 0 9519754 0 4 pb.
Covers 67 sites in seven trails, Neolithic to medieval.

***Harbison, Peter, *Guide to national and his-

toric monuments of Ireland, including a selection of other monuments not in State care. Dublin: Gill and Macmillan, 3 edn 1992, xiv, 377 p, bibl, index. 0 7171 1956 4 pb.
This edition includes the Six Counties of Northern Ireland for the first time; it is a very detailed guide with location maps, index, short bibliography. Illustrations are drawn from mainly 18th and 19th century sources.

Herity, Michael, *Rathcroghan and Carnfree: Celtic royal residence of Maeve and inauguration place of the O'Conors.* Dublin: Na Clocha Breaca, 1991, 40 p, bibl. No ISBN.

—, *Gleanncholmcille* [Donegal coast area]. Dublin: Na Clocha Breaca, 1995, 64 p, bibl. 1 873173 00 8 pb.

Hudson, Kenneth and Nicholls, Ann, see their *Cambridge guide to the historic places of Britain and Ireland, listed under England (etc) above.*

***Killanin, Lord and Duignan, Michael V, *Shell guide to Ireland.* London: Ebury Press, 2 edn 1967, 512 p, bibl.
Attractively illustrated with b/w and some colour photographs, and a very comprehensive guide (eg including the smaller sites which can be visited from main centres). This early edn is much fuller in details, and in side journeys, than the 3rd edn which followed it two decades later, revised by Peter Harbison with more colour illustrations (from Macmillan, and Gill and Macmillan, 1989, 0 333 46957 7).

**Mitchell, Frank, *Shell guide to reading the Irish landscape.* Dublin: Country House, 1990, xv, 228 p, bibl, index. 0 946172 06 4 hb, 0 946172 19 6 pb.
Revision of the 1976 classic work.

Muir, Richard, *Shell guide to the Celtic landscapes, see under England (etc) above.*

Northern Ireland Tourist Board, *Industrial heritage.* Belfast: Tourist Board, 1993. Wallchart (folded to A5) with map, descriptions and illustrations of the principal industrial heritage attractions, listed by county.

O'Kelly, M J and C, *Illustrated guide to Lough Gur, Co Limerick.* Blackrock (Co Cork): privately publ, 1978, 44 p. No ISBN.
On the prehistoric and Early Christian complex of monuments around the lake – which now also includes a visitor centre.

O'Kelly, Claire, *Illustrated guide to Newgrange and the other Boyne monuments.* Blackrock (Co Clare): privately publ, 3 edn rev and enlarged, 1978, 139 p, bibl, index. 0 9506267 0 8 pb.

Patton, Marcus, *Central Belfast: a historical gazetteer.* Belfast: Ulster Architectural Heritage Soc, 1993, xiv, 354 p. 0 900457 45 7 pb.
Street by street survey.

Royal Society of Antiquaries of Ireland, *Antiquarian handbook series* (Dublin: Hodges, Figgis, 1895–1916).
These were produced for the extensive summer tours of RSAI, were well illustrated and are still found useful: the six titles (under various editors) are –
I *Dunsany, Tara and Glendalough,* 1895
II *The Western Islands and Galway, Athenry, Roscommon, etc,* 1897
III *The Western Islands (continued),* 1898
[IV *Report of an excursion to the western islands of Scotland, Orkney and Caithness,* 1900, also listed under Scotland above]
V *The antiquities of the northern portion of the County Clare . . . ,* 1900
VI *Illustrated guide to the northern, western and southern islands,* 1905
VII *The antiquities of Limerick and its neighbourhood . . . ,* 1916

Salter, Mike, *Castles and stronghouses of Ireland.* Malvern: Folly Publs, 1993, 160 p, bibl. 1 871731 15 1 pb.
A volume in a very long series of castle guides by this author.

Tarrant, Bernadette and O'Connell, Grainne, *Exploring the rich heritage of the North Kerry landscape.* Listowel: Fóras Aiseanna Saothar, 1990, xiv, 209 p. 0 9516103 0 9 hb, 0 9516103 1 7 pb.
Archaeology, history and folklore set out by the N Kerry Archaeology Survey team.

Wakeman, W F, *A survey of the antiquarian remains on the island of Inismurray (Inis Muireadhaigh).* London/Edinburgh: Williams and Norgate/RSAI, 1893.
Useful drawings, some photographs.

—, *A handbook of Irish antiquities, pagan and Christian, especially of such as are easy of access from the Irish metropolis.* Dublin: Hodges, Figgis, 1848, 2 edn 1891. Also 3 edn by John Cooke published as *Wakeman's handbook of*

Irish antiquities – Dublin/London: Hodges, Figgis/John Murray, 1903; and further reprinted by Bracken (London), 1995, 1 85891 256 3
Inextinguishable classic.

Weir, Anthony, *Early Ireland: a field guide*. Dundonald, Belfast: Blackstaff Press, 1980, vii, 245 p, bibl, index. 0 85640 212 5.
A personal selection of monuments, intended (as the author says) to fill the gap left when E E Evans' classic work (above) went out of print. Glossary, short bibliography, index to places.

Williams, Jeremy, *A companion guide to architecture in Ireland, 1837–1921*. Dublin: Ir Acad Press, 1994, 424 p, indexes. 0 7165 2513 5.
Describes the Victorian and later buildings in county order.

6.4
Regional Surveys

In contrast to the guidebooks listed in the previous section, the books listed here offer deeper and wider archaeological studies, whether of counties or larger regions. They are best read before visiting the region concerned. The arrangement below gives Scotland first, then CBA regions (roughly north to south), with the Isle of Man and Ireland at the end. Note that most CBA Regions have newsletters or bulletins to keep their members up to date with new developments.

For England, a justly famed series called 'The making of the English landscape' flourished mainly in the 1970s; several of the volumes opened up surprising new vistas at the time, but such has been the subsequent progress in landscape history that only a few of the 'MEL' series have seemed worth listing here. Omitted for similar reasons are the annual volumes of the British Association for the Advancement of Science, which provided from 1949 to 1972 multidisciplinary essays as background to the area in which that year's 'British Ass' conference was held; one or more archaeological contributions were always included. (The volumes are listed in W G V Balchin's 'Regional surveys of the British Association for the Advancement of Science', *Geography*, 58, 1973, 237–41.) Some volumes listed below appeared in an incomplete series from Longman called 'Regional history of England'. A new series 'Origins of the Shire' (Manchester University Press) began with volumes for Cheshire, Lancashire, Norfolk and Somerset; it is worth watching for more. See also Section 6.14 Landscape, and also the books listed in Section 5.2 Air photographs.

Scotland

See also the RCAHMS county inventories noted in Section 6.5 Lists of monuments; and the Scottish Burgh Surveys noted in Section 6.11.6 Medieval.

Armit, Ian, *The archaeology of Skye and the Western Isles*. Edinburgh: EUP, 1996, viii, 264 p, bibl, index. 0 7486 0640 8 pb.
Describes the environmental setting and the archaeological periods from Neolithic to the Lords of the Isles; a list of radiocarbon dates is included.

Baldwin, John R (ed), *Caithness: a cultural cross-roads*. Edinburgh: Scot Soc for Northern Studies and Edina Press, 1982, 214 p. o 9505994 1 7 and o 905695 26 7.
Includes papers on the making of the landscape, Freswick Late Norse site, Scots and Scandinavians 1266–1375, Scandinavian and Celtic place-names, etc.

—, (ed), *Firthlands of Ross and Sutherland*. Edinburgh: Scott Soc Northern Studies, 1986, ix, 220 p, bibl. o 9505994 4 1.
Short papers with bibls.

Breeze, D J (ed), *Studies in Scottish antiquity presented to Stewart Cruden*. Edinburgh: John Donald, 1984, xiii, 488 p, bibls. o 85976 075 8.
Essays in tribute to a leading scholar range from Callanish Neolithic site through to the wartime defences of the Firth of Forth, concluding with a survey of popular archaeology 1945–75.

Calder, Jenni (ed), *The wealth of a nation in the National Museums of Scotland*. Edinburgh: National Museums of Scotland, 1989, 208 p. o 86267 267 8 hb, o 86267 265 1 pb.
Encyclopaedic arrangement of information on Scotland's geology, archaeology, industry, agriculture, social history, arts, science and technology.

Chapman, J C and Mytum, H (eds), *Settlement in North Britain 1000 BC – AD 1000. Papers presented to George Jobey . . . BARBS*, 118, 1983, xii, 356 p, bibls. o 86054 224 6 pb.
Papers range from the physical environment through to Pictish Scotland.

Coutts, Herbert, *Ancient monuments of Tayside*. Dundee: Dundee Museum and Art Gallery, 1970, 83 p.

Hanson, W S and Slater, E A (eds), *Scottish archaeology: new perceptions*.
Aberdeen: Aberdeen Univ Press, 1991, xi, 228 p, bibls. o 08 041212 2 pb.
A fresh look at some problems.

MacSween, Ann with Mick Sharp photos, *Prehistoric Scotland*. London: Batsford, 1989, 192 p, bibl. o 7134 6173 X.
Perceptive descriptions and superb photographs, but the organisation and index could have been better.

Magnusson, Magnus and White, Graham (eds), *The nature of Scotland: landscape, wild life and people*. Edinburgh: Canongate Press, 1991, 250 p. o 862413 33 8.
For a rare treat archaeology is treated on a par with the natural world!

Miket, R and Burgess, C (eds), *Between and beyond the Walls: essays on the prehistory and history of North Britain in honour of George Jobey*. Edinburgh: John Donald, 1984, xii, 424 p, bibl, index. o 85975 087 1.
Over 20 papers contributed by friends of an esteemed northern archaeologist.

O'Connor, Anne and Clarke, D V (eds), *From the Stone Age to the 'Forty-five: studies presented to R B K Stevenson . . .* Edinburgh: John Donald, 1983, xiii, 621 p, bibl. o 85976 046 4.
Contains 38 papers on Mesolithic to 18th century subjects and some general topics.

Oram, Richard and Stell, Geoffrey (eds), *Galloway: land and lordship*. Edinburgh: *Scot Soc for Northern Studies publs*, 5, 1991, x, 172 p, bibls. o 9505994 6 8.
Includes essays on Whithorn's Hiberno-Norse settlement and early medieval period; pre-Norman sculpture; Viking evidence; Scandinavian evidence; medieval buildings and secular lordship, etc.

**Piggott, Stuart, with J N G Ritchie, *Scotland before history*. Edinburgh: EUP, rev edn 1982, Polygon repr 1992, vii, 195 p. o 85224 348 0.
Introduction to Scotland's prehistory in Piggott's masterly style, with appended brief guide to sites.

**Renfrew, A Colin (ed), *The prehistory of Orkney*. Edinburgh: EUP, rev edn 1994, 320 p, bibl, index. o 7486 0238 0 pb.
The principal source for the new surge of work on Orkney that began in the 1970s.

*Ritchie, Anna, *Scotland BC*. Edinburgh: HMSO, 1988, 80 p, bibl, index. o 11 493427 4 pb.
Excellent introduction.

—, *Prehistoric Orkney*. London: Historic Scotland/Batsford, 1995, 128 p, bibl, index. o 7134 7593 5 pb.
Covers the period 4000 BC to AD 800.

***Ritchie, Graham and Ritchie, Anna, *Scotland: archaeology and early history*. Edinburgh: EUP, rev edn 1991, 206 p, bibl, index. o 7486 0291 7 pb.
Still the nearest thing to a textbook for Scotland's archaeology; and this new edition adds

fresh material in notes and extra (excellent) bibliography. The essential starting point.

Sellar, W D H (ed), *Moray: province and people*. Edinburgh: Scot Soc for Northern Studies, 1993, vi, 264 p. 0 9505994 6 8 hb, 0 9505994 7 6 pb.
From the geological background through human settlement to vernacular architecture.

Smith, Brian (ed), *Shetland archaeology: new work in Shetland in the 1970s*. Lerwick: Shetland Times, 1985, 220 p. 0 900662 47 6.
Eight contributions cover all periods of the islands' archaeology; but there has been much new work since the 1970s.

Wales (CBA Wales)

Davies, J L and Kirby, D P (eds), *Cardiganshire county history: Volume 1, from the earliest times to the coming of the Normans*. Cardiff: Univ Wales Press for Cardigans Antiq Soc/ RCAHMW, 1994, xx, 441 p, footnotes, index. 0 7083 1170 9.
The first of three projected volumes offers 15 contributions ranging from the physical background, vegetation history and fauna through the Stone Age to the Norman Conquest. A catalogue of Early Christian monuments is included.

Huw Owen, D (ed), *Settlement and society in Wales*. Cardiff: Univ Wales Press, 1989, xii, 315 p, bibl, index of places and names. 0 7083 0985 2.
Includes sections by H N Savory (archaeology), G R J Jones (Dark Ages), Peter Smith (houses), W Linnard (vegetation), D Q Bowen (landforms) and G Pierce (place-names).

Lynch, Frances, *Prehistoric Anglesey: the archaeology of the island to the Roman Conquest*. Anglesey Antiquarian Society and Field Club, 1991, 411 p, footnotes, index. 0 95001997 6 pb.
Reprint of 1970 edition with six new chapters reviewing 20 years' work plus new introduction.

Manley, John et al (eds), *The archaeology of Clwyd*. Mold: Clwyd Co Co Archaeology Service, 1991, 252 p, bibl, index. 0 904449 42 4 pb.

Moore, Donald and Austin, David (eds), *Welsh archaeological heritage: the proceedings of a*

conference . . . 1985. Lampeter: Cambrian Archaeol Ass/St David's Univ College, 1986, 171 p. 0 905285 08 5 pb.
Archaeological sites and their preservation.

RCAHMW Inventories see Section 6.5 Lists of monuments.

Robinson, David M, *South Glamorgan's heritage: the archaeology of a county*. [s l]: Glamorgan-Gwent Archaeol Trust, 1985, 144 p, short bibl, index. 0 9506950 8 4.
Profusely illustrated introduction to the county with list of sites to visit.

Savory, H N (ed), *Glamorgan county history Vol II: Early Glamorgan, pre-history and early history*. Cardiff: Glam Co Hist Trust, 1984, xx, 506 p, notes index.
Sets the environmental background before treating the periods from Palaeolithic to AD 1100, with an appendix on place-names.

Stanford, S C on Welsh Marches, see Section 6.14 Landscape.

CBA North (Cleveland, Cumbria, Durham, Northumberland, Tyne and Wear)

Bewley, Robert H, *Prehistoric and Romano-British settlement in the Solway plain, Cumbria*. Oxbow monogr, 36, 1994, 100 p, bibl, air-photo list. 0 946897 66 2 pb.
An examination of air photographic and field-walking evidence aims to correct the previous heavy bias towards Roman occupation in this area.

Higham, N, *The northern counties to AD 1000*. London: Longman, 1986, xv, 392 p, bibl, index. 0 582 49275 0 hb; 0 582 49276 9 pb.

CBA Yorkshire and Humberside

*Ellis, S and Crowther, D R (eds), *Humber perspectives: a region through the ages*. Hull: Hull Univ Press, 1990, xvi, 444 p, bibl, index. 0 85058 484 4 pb.
Wide-ranging interdisciplinary perspectives, from wetlands to modern urban settlement.

Faull, M L and Moorhouse, S (eds), *West Yorkshire: an archaeological survey to AD 1500*. Wakefield: W Yorks Metropol Co Co, 4 vols, 1981. 0 86181 001 5.
Comprehensive (and weighty) history of the

county using documentary, excavated, survey and aerial photographic evidence.

Higham, N see under CBA North above.

Hodges, R see under CBA East Midlands below.

Manby, T G (ed), *Archaeology in eastern Yorkshire: essays in honour of T C M Brewster.* Sheffield: Univ Sheffield Dept Archaeol Prehist, 1988, vi, 202 p, bibl. 0 906090 30 x pb.
14 papers on various aspects, from Star Carr through Heslerton to medieval settlement.

*Spratt, Donald, *Prehistoric and Roman archaeology of North-East Yorkshire.* Revised edn as CBA res rep, 87, 1993, ix, 188 p, bibl, index. 0 872414 28 1 pb.
This award-winning book provides data and offers explanations.

CBA North West (Cheshire, Greater Manchester, Lancashire, Merseyside)

Higham, N, *The origins of Cheshire.* Manchester: Manchester UP, 1993, xvi, 241 p, bibl, index. 0 7190 3159 1 hb, 0 7190 3160 5 pb. (Origins of the shire series.)

—, *see also under CBA North above.*

Kenyon, Denise, *The origins of Lancashire.* Manchester: Manchester UP, 1991, xi, 202 p, bibl, index. 0 7190 3546 5 pb. (Origins of the shire series.)

Nevell, Michael, *Tameside before 1066: a history and archaeology of Tameside.* Tameside Metropolitan Borough Council, 1992, xi, 129 p, bibl, index. 1 87132 407 6 pb.

—, *Tameside 1066–1700*. . . 1991, ix, 155 p, bibl, index. 1 87132 406 8 pb.

—, *Tameside 1700–1930*. . . 1993. 1 87132 408 4 pb.

Tomlinson, Philippa and Warhurst, Margaret (eds), *The archaeology of Merseyside: papers from the seminar held to celebrate ten years of archaeology in Merseyside, 15 March 1986.* Printed as *J Merseyside Archaeol Soc*, 7, 1986–7.

CBA East Anglia (Norfolk and Suffolk)

Darby, H C, *The changing Fenland.* Cambridge: CUP, 1983, xv, 267 p, bibl, index. 0 521 24606 7.
Traces the progressive draining of a landscape

from Roman times to the 20th century. [Archaeological knowledge has greatly increased since this book appeared.]

Dymond, David, *The Norfolk landscape.* London: Hodder and Stoughton (The making of the English landscape), 1985, 279 p, bibl, index. 0 340 04332 6 pb.

Williamson, Tom, *The origins of Norfolk.* Manchester: Manchester UP, 1993, x, 208 p, bibl, index. 0 7190 3401 9 (Origins of the shire series.)

CBA Mid-Anglia (Cambridgeshire, Essex, Hertfordshire, London north of the Thames)

Biddle, M, Hudson, D and Heighway, C M, *The future of London's past: a survey of the archaeological implications of planning and development in the nation's capital.* Worcester: RESCUE Publ, 4, 1973, 83 p, bibl, loose overlay maps, all in portfolio. 0 903789 01 9 pb.
Archaeological knowledge has increased enormously since this work appeared, but it was a landmark volume in how to perform an urban archaeological study, and also had developers, as well archaeologists, entranced with the various combinations of data revealed by shuffling the overlay maps.

Buckley, D G (ed), *Archaeology in Essex to AD 1500. CBA res rep*, 34, 1980, 130 p, bibl. 0 900312 83 1 pb.
Papers from a conference; again, subsequent research has changed the picture.

Fox, Cyril, *The archaeology of the Cambridge region: a topographical study of the Bronze, early Iron, Roman and Anglo-Saxon ages, with an introductory note on the Neolithic.* Cambridge: CUP, 1923, xxv, 360 p, bibl, index.
Included here sheerly for its classic status as a pioneering study of the 'total archaeology' of a region.

Munby, Lionel, *The Hertfordshire landscape.* London: Hodder and Stoughton (The making of the English landscape), 1977, 267 p, bibl, index. 0 340 04459 4.

Taylor, Christopher, *The Cambridgeshire landscape: Cambridgeshire and the southern fens.* London: Hodder and Stoughton (The making of the English landscape), 1973, 286 p, bibl, index. 0 340 15460 8.

An early volume in this series, but a seminal study by a leading landscape archaeologist-historian.

CBA West Midlands (Hereford and Worcester, Shropshire, Staffordshire, Warwickshire, West Midlands)

Gibson A *see under CBA East Midlands below.*

Rowlands, Marie B, *The West Midlands from AD 1000.* London: Longman (Regional history of England series), 1987, xxii, 436 p, bibl, index. o 582 49215 7 hb, o 582 49216 5 pb.
Largely historical evidence for Staffordshire and Warwickshire.

Stanford S C on Welsh Marches, see in Section 6.14 Landscape.

CBA South Midlands (Bedfordshire, Buckinghamshire, Northamptonshire, Oxfordshire)

Bigmore, P, *The Bedfordshire and Huntingdonshire landscape.* London: Hodder and Stoughton (The making of the English landscape), 1979, 240 p, bibl, index. o 340 24149 7.

Emery, F, *The Oxfordshire landscape.* London: Hodder and Stoughton (The making of the English landscape), 1974, 240 p, footnotes, index. o 340 04301 6.

Reed, Michael, *The Buckinghamshire landscape.* London: Hodder and Stoughton (The making of the English landscape), 1979, 288 p, bibl, index. o 340 19044 2.

Steane, J, *The Northamptonshire landscape: Northamptonshire and the Soke of Peterborough.* London: Hodder and Stoughton (The making of the English landscape), 1974, 320 p, footnotes, index. o 340 15867 o.
The best of this region's bunch!

CBA South-East (Kent, Surrey, Sussex, London south of the Thames)

Bird, J and D G (eds), *The archaeology of Surrey to 1540.* Guildford: Surrey Archaeol Soc, 1987, 289 p, bibl, index. o 9501345 6 2 pb.
From the Palaeolithic to AD 1540.

Drewett, Peter, Rudling, D and Gardiner, M, *The south-east to AD 1000.* London: Longman,

1988, xvi, 384 p, bibl, index. o 582 49271 8 hb, o 582 49272 6 pb.
A volume in the Regional history of England series.

CBA Wessex (Berkshire, Dorset, Hampshire, Wiltshire, Isle of Wight, Channel Islands)

Coles, B J (ed) see under CBA South-West below.

Cunliffe, B W, *Wessex to AD 1000.* Harlow: Longman, 1993, xvii, 388 p, bibl, index. o 582 49279 3 hb, o 582 49280 7 pb.
A volume in the Regional history of England series.

Johnston, Peter (ed), *The archaeology of the Channel Islands.* Chichester: Phillimore, 1986, xix, 232 p, bibls, index. o 85033 498 5.
Fifteen papers, from Palaeolithic to medieval.

Patton, Mark, *Jersey in prehistory.* La Haule (Jersey, CI): La Haule Books, 1987, x, 153 p, short bibl. o 86120 017 9.

Taylor, Christopher, *Dorset.* London: Hodder and Stoughton (The making of the English landscape), 1970, 215 p, bibl, index. o 340 10962 9.
Well worth study for the methodology even though there have been great increases in archaeological knowledge since this book appeared.

CBA South-West (Avon, Cornwall, Devon, Gloucestershire, Somerset)

Allden, Alison et al, *Handbook of Gloucestershire archaeology.* Gloucester: Comm for Archaeol in Gloucestershire (BGAS), 1985, 48 p, bibl. o 900197 21 8 pb.
Treats selected monuments; sources and resources for study in the county; societies etc; field survey techniques.

Ashbee, Paul, *Ancient Scilly from the first farmers to the Early Christians: an introduction and survey.* Newton Abbot: David and Charles, 1974, 352 p, bibl, indexes. o 7153 6568 1.

Aston, Mick, *The archaeology of Avon: a review from the Neolithic to the Middle Ages.* Bristol: Avon Co Co, [1987], xi, 191 p, bibl, index. o 86063 282 2 pb.

–, and Burrow I (eds), *The archaeology of*

Somerset. Bridgwater: Somerset Co Co, 1991, 146 p. 0 86183 028 8 pb.

Coles, B J (ed), *Organic archaeological remains in southwest Britain: a survey of the available evidence*. Exeter: *WARP occas pap*, 4, 1990, 92 p, bibl. ISSN 0950-8244 pb.
(Includes Wiltshire.)

— and Coles, John, *Sweet Track to Glastonbury: the Somerset Levels in prehistory*. London: Thames and Hudson, 1986, 200 p, bibl, index. 0 500 39022 3.

Coles, J M (ed), *Somerset Levels Papers*, 15, 1989. Final report of the Somerset Levels Project for archaeology.

Costen, Michael, *The origins of Somerset*. Manchester: Manchester UP, 1992, xvi, 202 p, bibl, index. 0 7190 3399 3. (Origins of the shire series.)

Darvill, Timothy, *Prehistoric Gloucestershire*. Gloucester: Alan Sutton, 1987, viii, 216 p, bibl, index. 0 86299 460 8 pb.

Heighway, Carolyn, *Anglo-Saxon Gloucestershire*. Gloucester: Alan Sutton/Glos Co Lib, 1987, xii, 180 p, bibl, index. 0 86299 364 4 pb.

Johnson, Nicholas and Rose, Peter (ed D Bonney), *Bodmin Moor: an archaeological survey. Vol. 1: the human landscape to c. 1800*. Engl Heritage archaeol rep, [old ser] 24, 1994, xv, 131 p, bibl, index. 1 85074 381 9 pb.

Saville, Alan (ed), *Archaeology in Gloucestershire from the earliest hunters to the Industrial Age*. Cheltenham: Cheltenham Art Gallery and Museums/BGAS, 1984, 352 p, bibl, index. 0 905157 09 5 pb.
Essays dedicated to two pioneers of the county's archaeology, Helen O'Neil and Elsie Clifford.

Thomas, Charles, *Exploration of a drowned landscape: archaeology and history of the Isles of Scilly*. London: Batsford, 1985, 320 p, bibl, index. 0 7134 4852 0.
Detailed survey of all archaeological features plus a proffered date (post-Roman, mainly Tudor) for the drowning of the islands.

Todd, Malcolm, *The south-west to AD 1000*. London: Longman, 1987, xv, 338 p, bibl, index. 0 582 49273 4 hb; 0 582 49274 2 pb.
Covers Devon, Cornwall and the Isles of Scilly.

CBA East Midlands (Derbyshire, Leicestershire, Lincolnshire, Nottinghamshire)

Gibson, Alex (ed), *Midlands prehistory: some recent and current researches into the prehistory of central England. BARBS*, 204, 1989, x, 226 p, bibl. 0 86054 611 x pb.
Illustrates that the area is not, as once thought, a prehistoric blank.

Hodges, Richard and Smith, Ken (eds) *Recent developments in the archaeology of the Peak District*. Sheffield: J R Collis Publs, 1991, viii, 134 p. 0 906090 38 5.

Vince, Alan (ed), *Pre-Viking Lindsey. Lincoln archaeol stud*, 1, 1993, 156 p, bibl, index. 0 9514987 7 0 pb.
Papers from a 1990 conference on part of Lincs.

Isle of Man

Davey, P J (ed), *Man and environment in the Isle of Man. BARBS*, 54, 1978, 2 vols, 428 p, chapter bibls. 0 86054 034 0 pb.
Papers from a conference intended to link archaeological and environmental studies.

Ireland

See also county surveys and bibliographies for the Republic listed in Section 1.2 County bibliographies.

Evans, E Estyn, *The personality of Ireland: habitat, heritage and history*. Dublin: Lilliput Press, revised reprint 1992, xiv, 130 p. 0 946640 81 5.
New foreword (Paul Durcan) and updated bibliography for a classic work.

Hickey, Helen, *Images of stone: figure sculpture of the Lough Erne Basin*. Fermanagh: Fermanagh District Council/Arts Council Northern Ireland, 2 edn, 1985, 119 p. 0 85640 110 2 pb.

McDonald, Theresa, *Achill: 5000 BC to 1900 AD. Archaeology, history, folklore*. [s l]: IAS Publns, n d [1992], 223 p, bibl, folding map, index. 0 9519974 0 8 pb.
Results of ten years' fieldwork and research.

McDonogh, Steve, *The Dingle Peninsula: history, folklore, archaeology*. Dingle: Brandon, 1993, 256 p. 0 863221 59 9 pb.

Mallory, J P and McNeill, T E, *The archaeology of Ulster from colonization to plantation.* Belfast: Institute of Irish Studies, 1991, x, 367 p, bibl, index. o 85389 352 7 hb; o 85389 353 5 pb.
For the general reader, 'especially the beleaguered teacher suddenly thrust into teaching "cultural heritage"' (from preface).

Mould, Daphne D C Pochin, *The Aran Islands.* Newton Abbot: David and Charles, 1972, 171 p, bibl, index. o 7153 5782 4.
Environmental background, the great stone forts, Aran of the Saints, etc to 19th and 20th centuries.

—, *Discovering Cork.* Dingle: Brandon, 1991, 307 p, endpaper maps. o 863221 29 7 pb.
Chronological list and description of monuments together with thematic chapters such as industry, ships.

Norman, E R and St Joseph, J K S, *The early development of Irish society: the evidence of aerial photography.* Cambridge: CUP, 1969, xi, 126 p, bibl, index.
A pioneering survey.

Rynne, Colin, *The archaeology of Cork city and harbour from the earliest times to industrialisation.* Cork: The Collins Press, 1993, viii, 110 p, bibl, index. o 9513036 8 x pb.
The first general study of the area, starting in 5000 BC.

Shee Twohig, Elizabeth and Ronayne, Margaret, *Past perceptions: the prehistoric archaeology of south west Ireland.* Cork: Cork Univ Press, 1993, 183 p, bibl, index. 1 902561 89 8 pb.
An important contribution to understanding this area.

Swinfen, Averil, *Forgotten stones: ancient church sites of the Burren.* Dublin: Lilliput Press, 1992, viii, 151 p. 1 874675 01 5 pb. Foreword by Peter Harbison.

6.5
Lists of Monuments

This section notes the more or less formal lists of ancient monuments produced, in varying forms, by the Royal Commissions on Ancient/Historical Monuments, English Heritage, Historic Scotland, Cadw Welsh Historic Monuments, DoENI, and the Republic's Office of Public Works, plus a few other inventory-style publications.

World Heritage sites within these islands are:
UK – City of Bath; Blenheim Palace; Canterbury Cathedral, St Augustine's Abbey and St Martin's Church; Durham Cathedral and Castle; Fountains Abbey and Studley Royal Park; Giants' Causeway and Causeway Coast, Northern Ireland (a natural site); Castles and town walls of Edward I in Gwynedd; Hadrian's Wall military zone; Ironbridge Gorge; Overton Down, Wiltshire; St Kilda; Stonehenge, Avebury and associated megalithic sites; Tower of London; Westminster Palace, Westminster Abbey and St Margaret's Church.
Irish Republic – Boyne Valley; Skellig Michael.

England

Guardianship sites are listed in English Heritage's annual directory for members. County lists of scheduled sites in England are issued regularly by English Heritage.

Royal Commission on the Historical Monuments of England: The *Inventory* series ran from 1910, each volume providing an introduction, a list of buildings recommended for preservation, and an illustrated inventory of the buildings and monuments inspected. The counties treated were: *Buckinghamshire* (2 vols, 1912–13); *Cambridgeshire* (2 vols, 1968, 1972); *City of Cambridge* (1959); *Dorset* (5 vols 1952–75); *Essex* (4 vols, 1916–23); *Gloucestershire* (1 vol completed, 1977); *Herefordshire* (3 vols, 1931–34); *Hertfordshire* (1910); *Huntingdonshire* (1926); *Lincolnshire: Town of Stamford* (1977); *London* (5 vols 1924–30); *Middlesex* (1937); *Northamptonshire* (6 vols 1975–84); *City of Oxford* (1939); *Westmorland* (1936); *Wiltshire: City of Salisbury* (1980–); *Yorkshire* (5 vols 1962–81).
The older volumes, ie those appearing before about 1960, should be seen in the light of much more modern and more complete information available today.

During the 1980s the Commission moved away from the slow-moving production of county inventories and began to produce thematic volumes on such topics as non-conformist chapels and meeting houses; textile factories; industrial housing; rural houses, and so on. Some of these thematic volumes have been entered at the appropriate points elsewhere in this bibliography. A list of all RCHME publications in print is available from the National Monuments Record Centre, Swindon.

Thacker, Christopher (comp), *Register of parks and gardens of special historic interest in England*. London: English Heritage, 46 parts by county, 1984–8, informally bound.
Under continuous revision, and now held on computer; the data have also been absorbed into county SMRs.

Wales

Cadw, *Schedule of ancient monuments of national importance in Wales*. Cardiff: Cadw, 1993, 8 parts (by county).

Royal Commission on the Ancient and Historical Monuments in Wales, *Inventories*. These took the same form as those for England (see above) and began in 1911. The counties treated were: *Anglesey* (1937); *Brecknock Vol 1ii* (1986); *Caernarvonshire* (3 vols 1956–64); *Carmarthen* (1917); *Denbigh* (1914); *Flint* (1912); *Glamorgan* (1976–); *Merioneth* (1921); *Montgomery* (1911); *Pembroke* (1925); *Radnor* (1913).
The older volumes, ie those appearing before about 1960, should be used in the light of much more modern and more complete information available today.

Scotland

Cross, Morag, *Bibliography of monuments in the care of the Secretary of State for Scotland. Dept Archaeol Univ Glasgow occas pap ser*, 2, 1994, xxiv, 602 p.
Essentially a management tool, not produced in market quantity; constrained by its tight focus and the listed items are not evaluated.

Historic Scotland, *List of ancient monuments in Scotland*. Edinburgh: Hist Scotland, 1995, 60 p. 1 900168 14 6 (or any later issue).
Basic list in order of regional, Island and District Council areas, and then by monument category with 6-figure map references.

Land Use Consultants, inventory of Scottish

gardens and designed landscapes, see Section 6.16 Garden archaeology and history.

Royal Commission on the Ancient and Historical Monuments of Scotland: RCAHMS *Inventories* exist for the following 'old' (ie pre-1973) counties. Volumes published before about 1960 should be used in the light of much more modern and more complete information available today.

Argyll (7 vols 1971–90); *County of Berwick* (1909, 1915); *Caithness* (1911); *County of Dumfries* (1920); *East Lothian* (1924); *City of Edinburgh* (1951); *Counties of Fife, Kinross and Clackmannan* (1933); *Galloway* (= *Kirkcudbright and Wigtownshire*, 2 vols, 1912–14); *Lanarkshire* (Prehistoric and Roman, 1978); *Midlothian and West Lothian* (1929); *Orkney and Shetland* (1946); *Outer Hebrides, Skye and the small isles* (1928); *Peeblesshire* (1967); *Roxburghshire* (2 vols, 1956); *Selkirkshire* (1957); *Stirlingshire* (1963); *Sutherland* (1911). A new style of presentation began in 1990 with *North-East Perth: an archaeological landscape* (1990); *South-East Perth* (1994).

RCAHMS, *The archaeological sites and monuments of Scotland* (series).
These are lists, compiled by administrative district, from the Sites and Monuments Record, from 1970 onward; contact RCAHMS for complete list of those available.

Scottish Burgh Surveys, see Section 6.11.6 Medieval for those volumes issued so far.

Ireland

Here are Surveys and Inventories: note carefully the distinction. For the Republic, the *Surveys* are detailed whereas the *Inventories* are briefer lists intended for quick dissemination for planning authority purposes. Both types are prepared by the Office of Public Works (OPW). There are also some local surveys (Dingle, Donegal, Ikerrin, Iveragh) done to similar standards. The only N Irish volume is that for Co Down, although the surveys for Counties Armagh and Fermanagh are in an advanced state of preparation at the time of writing.

For quick reference:
Office of Public Works, *Heritage sites*. Dublin: Stationery Office, 1990, informally produced (plastic spiral-bound).

Basic list for the Republic of guardianship sites, preservation orders and the like. Gives 'easy reference to heritage sites owned, controlled or protected by OPW', including Parks, National Monuments, wildlife, waterways, and architecturally significant buildings.

The following Survey and Inventory volumes (N Ireland and Republic) are arranged in county order:

County Carlow
Brindley, Anna L and Kilfeather, A, *Archaeological inventory of County Carlow*. Dublin: Stationery Office, 1993, x, 128 p, bibl, index. o 7076 0324 2.

County Cavan
O'Donovan, Patrick, *The archaeological inventory of County Cavan*. Dublin: Stationery Office, 1995, x, 296 p, bibl, index. o 7076 1694 8.
Lists over 1,900 sites, Neolithic to post-medieval.

County Cork
Power, Denis et al, *Archaeological inventory of County Cork, Vol I - West Cork*. Dublin: Stationery Office, 1992, 478 pp, refs, indexes. o 7076 0175 4 and *Vol II, East and South Cork*, 1995, xii, 432 p, bibl, indexes. o 7076 0323 4. The first two volumes of four planned for the county log large numbers of sites, including those later than AD 1700.

County Donegal
Lacy, Brian et al, *Archaeological survey of County Donegal: a description of the field antiquities of the County from the Mesolithic period to the 17th century AD*. Lifford: Donegal Co Co, 1983, xvii, 401 p, bibl, index. o 9508407 0 X.

County Down
Archaeological Survey of Northern Ireland, *An archaeological survey of County Down*. Belfast: HMSO, 1966, xxiv, 478 p, glossary, short bibl, index.
Definitive (at its time) record, Meso to 19th century; resurvey of the county is in progress. *For industrial archaeology of Co Down see under Green in Section 6.15 Archaeology of industrial processes.*

County Galway
Gosling, Paul, *Archaeological inventory of County Galway, vol. 1: West Galway*. Dublin:

Stationery Office, 1993, xii, 242 p, bibl, indexes. o 7076 0322 6.

County Kerry: Dingle
Cuppage, Judith et al, *Archaeological survey of the Dingle Peninsula. A description of the field antiquities of the Barony of Corca Dhuibhne from the Mesolithic period to the 17th century AD*. Ballyferriter: Oidhreacht Chorca Dhuibhne, 1986, xxi, 462 p, bibl, index. o 906096 06 5.
  North Kerry
Toal, Caroline, *The North Kerry archaeological survey*. Dingle: Brandon Book Publrs, 1995, 335 p, bibl, place-name index. o 86322 186 6.
  South Kerry
O'Sullivan, Ann and Sheehan, John, *The Iveragh Peninsula: an archaeological survey of South Kerry*. Cork: Cork Univ Press, 1996, xxi, 461 p, bibl, glossary, indexes. o 902561 84 7.
Covers over 1500 sites.

County Laois
Sweetman, P David, Alcock O and Moran, B, *Archaeological inventory of County Laois*. Dublin: Stationery Office, 1995, x, 171 p, bibl, index. o 7076 1631 X.

County Louth
Buckley, Victor M, *Archaeological inventory of County Louth*. Dublin: Stationery Office, 1986, x, 135 p, bibl, index. o 7076 0028 6.

— and Sweetman, P David, *Archaeological survey of County Louth*. Dublin: Stationery Office, 1991, 407 p, bibl, index. o 7076 0168 1.
The fuller version of the preceding title.

County Mayo
Lavelle, Diarmuid et al, *An archeological survey of Ballinrobe [S Mayo] and district including Lough Mask and Lough Carra*. Ballinrobe: Lough Mask and Lough Cara Tourism Devel Ass, 1994, 124 p, bibl, glossary, index. o 9517091 3 5 hb, o 9517091 2 7 pb.

O'Hara, Bernard, *The archaeological heritage of Killasser, Co Mayo*. Galway: Research and Devel Unit, Galway Regional Tech Coll, 1991, 227 p, bibl, index. o 9517270 0 1 hb, o 9517270 0 X pb.
Systematic account by monument type.

County Meath
Moore, Michael J (comp), *Archaeological inventory of County Meath*. Dublin: Stationery Office, 1987, 230 p, index. o 7076 0031 6.

County Monaghan

Brindley, Anna L (comp), *Archaeological inventory of County Monaghan*. Dublin: Stationery Office, 1986, x, 131 p, bibl, index. 0 7076 0029 4.
Monuments inventoried in classified order.

County Tipperary

Stout, Geraldine T in assoc with the Roscrea Heritage Society, *Archaeological survey of the Barony of Ikerrin* [= NE Tipperary]. Roscrea: Roscrea Heritage Soc/AnCO – the Industrial Training Authority, 1984 (1985), xii, 146 p, bibl, index. no ISBN.

Inventories still to come for the Republic are: in near future, counties Offaly, Wexford, Wicklow; then Mid-Cork, Waterford, Kildare, Longford, Leitrim, Sligo, South and North Galway; followed by Kilkenny and East Galway (from information available at early 1996).

Isle of Man

Kermode, P M C, *List of Manx antiquities*. Douglas: Meyer, 1930, 87 p, refs.
Classified within parishes.

—, *The Manx Archaeological Survey*. A reissue of the first five reports (1909–18):
Keeils and burial grounds in the sheadings of Glenfaba, Michael, Ayre, Garff and Middle, drawn up by P M C Kermode (et al) for Isle of Man Natural History and Antiquarian Society, and published by The Manx Museum and National Trust, 1968.

Bruce, J R, *Sixth report 1966. Keeils and burial grounds in the Sheading of Rushen*. The Manx Museum and National Trust, 1968.

6.6
Legislation and Planning

Sections 6.7 on Archaeological Heritage Management and 6.8 on Conservation of Buildings should also be consulted, as should Section 6.9, subsection on Excavation preliminaries and conduct. Paul Spoerry kindly read the UK part of this section for me, but is not responsible for any remaining errors or misinterpretations.

The following sub-sections will be found:
Periodicals
General remarks on legislation (ancient monuments, listed buildings, scheduled monuments, archaeology in Parliament, European law on cultural heritage, World Heritage Sites, Treasure Trove)
Below-ground archaeology
Standing buildings
Treasure Trove, portable antiquities and metal detecting
Scotland
Ireland

Periodicals

The best periodical sources to use for keeping generally in touch with legislative developments affecting archaeology in the UK are the CBA's *British archaeology* (1357-4442, 10/yr), English Heritage's *Conservation bulletin* (0953-8674, 3/yr), and the monthly journal *Planning and environment law* (0307-4870). For Scotland there is a news sheet, *Scottish planning and environmental law* (0144-8196). For Ireland, see *Irish planning and environmental law journal* (Brehon Publishing, 1994-).

General remarks on legislation

As the legislative situation in Scotland, N. Ireland and the Irish Republic differs from that in England and Wales, their references are entered separately at the end of this section. A very brief sketch of the British situation follows. The exhaustive reference book on legislation world-wide is O'Keefe and Prott, listed below.

The essential reading for **ancient monuments** in the UK is David Breeze's 'Ancient monuments legislation' in J Hunter and I Ralston (ed),

Archaeological resource management in the United Kingdom: an introduction (1993, pp 44–55): in particular he clarifies legislative differences between the separate nations of the United Kingdom. Another very useful work is Paul Spoerry's *Archaeology and legislation in Britain* (entered below) which includes a clear description of the means whereby archaeology can be properly represented within the development plan for each area.

Listed buildings – those registered as of special architectural or historic interest – are a central government responsibility borne by the Secretary of State for the Department of National Heritage. The lists, produced area by area, are readily available in planning authorities, sites and monuments records, the National Monuments Record, and main public libraries; each property is briefly described with its location and most important features. A good text here is R W Suddards' 'Listed buildings', pp 77–88 in Hunter and Ralston (above), but his 1988 book is fuller (see below).

The records of '**Scheduled monuments**' (UK only) are in the charge of English Heritage, Historic Scotland and Cadw respectively. Such monuments are judged to be of national importance and therefore subject to protective measures. In N Ireland the authority is Environment and Heritage Service (see Hamlin under Ireland below). For the Republic see Ryan under Irish Republic below.

For **objects**, the Hunter and Ralston volume (above) has Ian Longworth's 'Portable antiquities', pp 56–64, dealing with the separate situations in England/Wales, Scotland, Isle of Man and Northern Ireland.

The Government circular which currently has most effect on archaeological evaluation and excavation is *Planning policy guidance note 16* (1990; see below), while another circular, *PPG 15* (1994), sets out the conditions affecting standing buildings. Both of these have equivalents for Scotland, but the Welsh situation is unclear at the time of writing. See also the papers by Carrington and by O'Sullivan (below).

Archaeology in Parliament: Parliamentary debates and questions relevant to archaeology were listed for several years in *British archaeological abstracts*, 6.1, 1973 – 14.1, 1981; the service then lapsed for lack of resources, but began again in the successor abstracting service *British archaeological bibliography* which has, from volume 1.2

(1992) onwards, presented relevant extracts from the Parliamentary computer database POLIS.

European law on cultural heritage: Three organisations, the Council of Europe, the European Commission, and the European Parliament all have a role in conservation, explained by Duncan Simpson in *[English Heritage] Conservation bulletin*, 22, 1994, pp 6–7. Note that EC Directive on Environmental Protection 90/313/EC (23 June 1990) requires member states to provide freedom of access to information on the environment, which includes information from sites and monuments records (SMRs).

For fuller details of European legislation, the best starting point is the special section in *Antiquity*, 67, 1993, pp 400–45 (ed Henry Cleere). Briefly indicated here are the main European documents:

1. *Charter for the Protection and Management of the Archaeological Heritage* (Lausanne 1990). It covers planning, legislation and economy, sites and monuments records, research, presentation and the like. It was devised by ICAHM, a division of ICOMOS, and its text is given in *Antiquity*, 67, 1993, pp 402–5.

2. *European Convention on the Protection of the Archaeological Heritage* (Valetta 1992: European Treaty Series 143). See H F Cleere's commentary in *Antiquity*, 66, 1992, pp 287–8, and P J O'Keefe's in *Antiquity*, 67, 1993, pp 401–13. The Convention came into force on 25 May 1995 but the UK and some other European states have not yet (at the time of writing) ratified it.

3. *Convention for the Protection of the Architectural Heritage of Europe* (1985: European Treaty Series 121).

Two further conventions which have not yet been proceeded with deal with (a) offences related to cultural property, and (b) the underwater cultural heritage.

World Heritage Sites: The 1972 UNESCO Convention for the Protection of the World Cultural and Natural Heritage came into force in 1975 and was ratified by the UK in 1984. (There are a dozen or so World Heritage Sites in the UK so far, and two in the Republic of Ireland: see list at the start of Section 6.5 Lists of monuments.)

For **Treasure Trove law, portable antiquities and metal detectors** see separate sub-section below. Legislation for **maritime sites** is given in Section

6.19 Maritime, nautical and underwater archaeology.

Below-ground archaeology

****Archaeological code of practice* is published by the British Archaeologists' and Developers' Liaison Group (revised 1991, obtainable for £1 post-free from British Property Federation, 35 Catherine Place, London SW1E 6DY or from SCAUM (for which see Section 4.2 Organisations).

****Archaeological investigations code of practice for mineral operators* (revised 1991) obtainable from Confederation of British Industry, Centre Point, 103 New Oxford Street, London WC1A 1DU (price £4 for CBI members, £8 for non-members, postage extra).

Association of County Archaeological Officers, *The future of county archaeological services in England* (1993: obtain from current ACAO Secretary – see Section 4.2 Organisations).

— (comp David Baker et al), *Model briefs and specifications for archaeological assessments and field evaluations.* [s l]: ACAO, 1993, 24 p. 0 9510695 19. (Obtain from Bedford County Planning Office, County Hall, Bedford MK42 9AP.)

**Association of County Councils, *Archaeological heritage. The ancient monuments legislation: a review by the Association of County Archaeological Officers.* London: Ass County Councils Publications, 1993, 18 p. 1 85862 002 3.
Outlines present deficiencies and suggests the need for a new legislative code.

Association of District Councils, *Towards unitary authorities: Vol. 2, Archaeology.* London: ADC, 1993. (Not seen by compiler.)

Carman, J, *Valuing ancient things: archaeology and law.* London: Leicester Univ Press, 1996, x, 246 p, bibl, index. 0 7185 0012 1.
The first full-length study to investigate English heritage laws during and since the 19th century, tracing their effect on the development of archaeology and on archaeologists' thinking about their subject.

Carrington, Peter (ed), *Evaluations in rescue archaeology: PPG16 three years on.* Chester Archaeol Service occas pap, 1, 1993, iv, 21 p. 1 872587 02 X pb.

Cleere, H F (ed), 'Heritage and the ICAHM Charter', in *Antiquity*, 67, 1993, pp 400–26.
Includes discussion of the European Convention on the Protection of the Archaeological Heritage.

****Competitive tendering in archaeology.* Hertford: RESCUE and SCAUM, 1991.
Papers from the 1990 conference with a statement by English Heritage and a copy of IFA's *Code of approved practice for the regulation of contractual arrangements in field archaeology.*

Conservation issues in strategic plans (Countryside Commission/English Heritage/English Nature, CCP 420, 1993). Available from Countryside Commission Postal Sales, PO Box 124, Walgrave, Northampton NN6 9TL. 0 86170 383 9.
Aims to assist local authorities with the preparation of development plans at strategic level, with the theme 'conservation is sustainable'.
An equivalent document for conservation issues in local plans is due in 1996.

Corporation of London, *Archaeology and planning in the City of London.* London: The Corporation, 1993, 28 p, maps. 0 85203 037 1.
Aims at preventing the destruction of potentially valuable archaeological remains when sites are developed, and at supporting every opportunity for the investigation and recording of such sites.

Disused Burial Grounds Acts, 1884, 1981 are described by Spoerry (below). See also the work by Garratt-Frost in Section 6.9, sub-section on excavation preliminaries and conduct.

***DoE and Welsh Office, *Environmental assessment,* DoE Circular 15/88, Welsh Office Circular 23/88, Joint Circular July 1988.

Dromgoole, S on underwater cultural property, see Section 6.19 Maritime, nautical and underwater archaeology.

***Hunter, J and Ralston, I (eds), *Archaeological resource management in the United Kingdom: an introduction.* Stroud: Alan Sutton for IFA, 1993, x, 277 p, bibl, index. 0 7509 0275 2.
Essential reading: papers from 22 contributors on all aspects of the subject.

***McGill, Greg, *Building on the past: a guide to the archaeology and development process.* London: Spon, 1995, xx, 371 p, chapter refs and further reading, index. 0 419 17690 X.

(*Note: there are two other books with the same main title as this one: one, by Hyde, is listed under Ireland below.*)
Essential guide for planners, developers, architects and archaeologists, showing both sides of the development process: analyses the conflicts, defines how legislation works to protect remains, explains risks and duties, cost implications and contracts.

**O'Keefe, P J and Prott, L V, *Law and the cultural heritage*. 3 vols: I, *Discovery and excavation* (Abingdon: Professional Books, 1984, xxviii, 434 p. 0 86205 060 X. II *(to come)*. III, *Movement* (London: Butterworths, 1989, xliv, 1049 p. 0 406 12071 4.
Massive world-wide survey of current legislation. See also Prott below.

O'Sullivan, Helen, '82–90 Park Lane, Croydon: a planning case-study', *London archaeol*, 7.16, 1996, pp 424–31.
The public inquiry about the Anglo-Saxon cemetery site here raised several very important policy issues (excavate or try to preserve?) and revealed severe deficiencies in the operation of *PPG 16*.

Peacock, Sir Alan, *The political economy of heritage*. Keynes Lecture (British Academy) for 1994, reported briefly in *Conservation bulletin*, 25, 1995.
Attacks the notion put forward by archaeologists and others that the heritage is beyond price; whereas consumer preference ought to rule, at present the key decisions are taken by experts and consumers have no choice. Moreover, all museums and galleries should charge entrance fees.

***Planning policy guidance note 16: Archaeology and planning* (PPG 16). HMSO, 1990. 0 11 752353 4 pb.
Draws together the existing relevant advice to planning authorities in England, property owners, developers, archaeologists, amenity societies and the general public. There is a useful explanation by G J Wainwright in *Conservation bull*, 17, 1992, pp 23–5, and an 8-page commentary by P V Addyman in *Yorkshire Philosophical Society annual report* for 1992, as well as in Spoerry's book and in Pugh-Smith and Samuels (below). Two reports were commissioned from Pagoda Projects (1992, 1995) by English Heritage to examine the workings of

PPG 16, while SCOLA reported in 1995 on its workings within the Greater London area.

Pugh-Smith, John and Samuels, John, '*PPG 16* two years on', *J plann envir law*, Mar 1993, pp 203–10.

Simpson, Duncan, 'Council of Europe, European Parliament, and European Commission', *[English Heritage] Conservation bulletin*, 22, 1994, pp 6–7.
Explains who does what, and how, in the field of conservation in Europe. Mentions Article 128 of the Maastricht Treaty which gives the European Union a specific remit for cultural affairs including the historic environment.

***Spoerry, Paul, *Archaeology and legislation in Britain*. Hertford: RESCUE, 1993, 43 p. [o] 903789 16 7 pb.
Brief but very valuable account of the various pieces of legislation that affect UK archaeology, indicating where to find fuller details, with a bibliography of all source documents.

WALES
Welsh Affairs Committee of the House of Commons. *The preservation of historic buildings and ancient monuments*. 9 June 1993. 2 vols: I, *Report and proceedings*; II, *Minutes of evidence and appendices*. 0 10 020693 X pb.
Offers 39 recommendations relating to listed buildings, provision of conservation expertise, archaeology of churches and chapels, and archaeological landscapes.
Also (same title), the Government's response to this report (Cm 2416, November 1993, 15 p, 0 10 124162 3 pb).

Standing buildings

'LISTED BUILDINGS'
The regulations are highly complex and the reader should consult the references below under, respectively, Cambridgeshire; Cooling et al; Jackson-Stops; Suddards; *PPG 15*. Spoerry (in subsection above) also deals with listed building legislation. In the section below dealing with Ireland, the two main references are Hamlin (for NI) and Ryan (for the Republic).

For **Church of England buildings**, Ecclesiastical Exemption and the Faculty Jurisdiction are explained by Halsey and Carter (see below).

Refer also to Section 6.8 Conservation of buildings.

BOOKS AND REFERENCE WORKS

Bourn, John, *Protecting and managing England's heritage property; report by the Comptroller and Auditor-General, National Audit Office.* London: HMSO, 1992. 0 10 213293 3 pb.
Official examination of the work of English Heritage, the National Heritage Memorial Fund, the Historic Royal Palaces Agency, Royal Armouries, and RCHME; with recommendations for action.

The Cambridgeshire guide to historic buildings law. Cambridge: Cambs Co Co, rev edn 1995, 231 + separate updating page. 1 870724 19 4 pb.
The new edition (by R Walker) takes *PPG 15* into account.

Care of Churches and Ecclesiastical Jurisdiction Measure: code of practice. London: Church House Publishing, 1993, 133 p. 0 7151 3753 0 pb.
On the proper protection of churches which are listed buildings.

Cooling, Penelope, Shacklock, V and Scarrett, D, *Legislation for the built environment: a concise guide.* London: Donhead, 1993, x, 308 p, index. 1 873394 03 9.
Collects together many dispersed provisions on planning, conservation, the building control system, statutory responsibilities of builder, financial aid and the like.

Council for the Protection of Rural England, *The campaigners' guide to local plans.* London: CPRE, 1992.
On the importance of local plans, their likely contents and legal requirements, how to press for environmental (including archaeological) improvements. See also *Responding to planning applications* (1993) and *Index of national planning policies* from CPRE and CPRW, 'the most detailed index of planning policies ever published', including all PPGs, MPGs etc: over 400 entries under subject headings. *Understanding planning applications* is a free leaflet, 1993.

***Dept of National Heritage, *The Ecclesiastical Exemption: what it is and how it works.* London: DNH, 1994, c 40 p, bibl.
Sets out which faiths can now determine their own applications for alterations, additions or demolitions, as against those faiths which are subject to normal planning controls.

Faculty Jurisdiction Commission, *The continuing care of churches and cathedrals.* London: CIO Publishing, 1984, viii, 226 p. 0 7151 3696 8 pb.
Examined the secular planning legislation in so far as it affected the Church of England at that date.

Gowers, Sir Ernest (Chairman), *Houses of outstanding historic or architectural interest: report of the Committee.* London: HMSO, 1950, iv, 80 p.
Historic document, the original spur to the listing process.

Halsey, Richard and Carter, Howard, 'Ecclesiastical Exemption and Faculty Jurisdiction', *[English Heritage] Conservation bulletin*, 22, 1994, pp 10–11.
Article explaining the operation of these two procedures.

Hyde, D, Building on the past, see Irish section below.

Jackson-Stops and Staff, *A guide to the legislation relating to listed buildings.* London: Simmons and Simmons, 1992, 28 p.
Although not, apparently, accurate in every detail, this small guide is much more approachable than the Cambridge and Suddards guides.

Le-Las, Wendy, *Playing the public inquiry game: an objector's guide.* Mirfield (W Yorks): Osmosis Publishing, 1987, vii, 98 p. 1 870459 00 8 pb.
How to appeal against (eg) Listed Building Consent and the like.

McGill, G, Building on the past, see in Below-ground sub-section above.

Parnell, A C, *Building legislation and historic buildings: a guide to the application of the Building Regulations, the Public Health Acts, the Fire Precautions Act, the Housing Act and other legislation relevant to historic buildings.* London: Architectural Press, 1987, 149 p. 0 85139 790 5.
Includes case studies.

****Planning Policy Guidance note 15: Planning and the historic environment* (PPG 15), DoE/DNH, 1994, ii, 64 p, bibl, index. 0 11 752944 3 pb.
The Government document which explains, inter alia, the 'presumption in favour of pre-

servation' of (a) listed buildings and (b) unlisted buildings that contribute to the character of a conservation area. It marks an important change in the climate for historic buildings. Note however that the version for Wales (1996) is being seen as a backward step.

Richards, Ruth, *Conservation planning: a guide to planning legislation concerning our architectural heritage*. London: Planning Aid for London, 1990, vi, 44 p. 1 872063 40 3 pb.

Ross, Michael, *Planning and the heritage: policy and procedures*. London: Spon, 1991, ix, 188 p, short bibl, index. 0 419 15100 1 pb.
Discusses the development of UK heritage legislation and current implications for architects, developers, planners and conservationists; now somewhat overtaken by *PPGs* 15 and 16.

Simpson D on European matters, see in Below-ground sub-section above.

Speer, Roy and Dade, Michael, *How to stop and influence planning permission*. London: Dent, 1994, 160 p. 0 460 86194 8 pb.
Practical advice and list of useful addresses.

***Suddards, Roger W (et al), *Listed buildings: the law and practice of historic buildings, ancient monuments, and conservation areas*. London: Sweet and Maxwell, 3 rev edn 1995, 502 p, index. 0 421 43260 8.

Wales: *see entry at end of Below-ground sub-section above.*

Treasure Trove, portable antiquities and metal detecting

Responsibility for Treasure Trove in **England and Wales** was transferred from the Treasury to the Dept of National Heritage on 1 April 1993. Lord Perth's 'Treasure Bill', which aims to bring the medieval law of Treasure Trove (for England and Wales) into a state more suitable for the 21st century, failed in Parliament in 1995. A separate, private member's bill produced by Sir Anthony Grant won an unopposed second reading in March 1996 and may proceed further. (Note the discussion document listed under Dept of National Heritage below.) The situation in **Scotland** remains unchanged (a leaflet describing it is available from the National Museums of Scotland, Queen St, Edinburgh EH2 1JD). **Northern Ireland, the Republic of Ireland and the Isle of Man** all have their own legislation. The whole situation is

very complex and readers should initially consult Longworth (below).

The CBA provides the secretariat for the **Standing Conference on Portable Antiquities**, representing nearly 30 organisations from ACAO to Ulster Museum.

Export of Works of Art. Annual reports of the Reviewing Committee appointed by the Chancellor of the Exchequer are published by HMSO; while mostly concerned with objects of art-historical interest, they also give aggregate figures for archaeological materials.

The Thesaurus Group Ltd archives have over 15 million auction lots on record, and all items listed as missing in the 73 issues of *Trace*. Address: 76 Gloucester Place, London W1H 3HN, tel 0171 487 3401.

UNIDROIT's draft convention on stolen or illegally exported cultural objects has not so far been approved by the European Union.

JOURNALS
To keep in touch, consult (as well as the CBA newsletter and *Antiquity*) the *International journal of cultural property* (0940-7391, 1992-, 2 issues/yr, de Gruyter in Berlin): it covers policy, ethics, economics and law of cultural property, and gives news of documents, judicial decisions, bibliography and events. There is also a series of articles dealing with European Union law on the free movement of cultural goods. The periodical *Trace* (0969-1388, The Thesaurus Group) gives monthly lists of stolen cultural property.

BOOKS AND OTHER REFERENCES
CBA, Mus Ass, Soc Antiq London, 'Portable antiquities: a statement of principles', *International journal of cultural property*, 3, 1994, pp 187-9.
Set out four tenets for bringing portable antiquities within the law in England and Wales.

Convention on the means of prohibiting and preventing the illicit import, export and transfer of ownership of cultural property. Paris: UNESCO, 14 Nov 1970.
Not yet ratified by Britain, and a further draft convention is still under consideration by the European Union (see UNIDROIT above).

Country Landowners' Association: guidance note

on metal detectors, in *International journal of cultural property*, 4.1, 1995, pp 157–64.

Department of National Heritage, *Portable antiquities: a discussion document*. London: DNH, 1996, 8 p (= DNH J0154 RP).
Sought (by mid-1996) views of interested parties on possible measures to improve the recording of all archaeological objects (not just those covered by the law of Treasure Trove or its proposed replacement).

Dobinson, Colin and Denison, Simon (et 2 al), *Metal detecting and archaeology in England*. London/York: English Heritage/CBA, 1995, xi, 102 p, bibl, index. 1 872414 54 0 pb ringbound.
A survey of museums, units, metal detector clubs and detectorists revealed much information about the scale and effects of metal-detector looting of sites; data are given in many tables and appendices. It is argued that in the right hands metal detectors can reveal immensely valuable information, hence archaeologists should overcome their distaste and make much more use of them.

Greenfield, Jeanette, *The return of cultural treasures*. Cambridge: CUP, 2 edn 1996, xxi, 351 p, bibl, index. 0 521 47746 8 pb.
Discusses a vexed issue with reference to the practice in various countries.

Hanworth, Rosamond, 'New approaches to legislation on Treasure Trove', *Museum archaeologist*, 18, 1993, pp 22–4.

Institute of Field Archaeologists, 'Portable antiquities: the Institute's response to the DoE/Welsh Office consultative paper on portable antiquities', *Field archaeologist*, 9, 1988, pp 139–42.
Includes the text of the DoE/WO paper.

Longworth, I H, 'Portable antiquities', in J Hunter and I Ralston (eds), *Archaeological resource management in the United Kingdom* (1993), pp 56–64.
Convenient summary of situation in England/Wales, Scotland, Isle of Man and Northern Ireland.

Palmer, Andrew, *The metal detector book*. London: Seaby (Batsford), 1995, c. 180 p. 0 7134 7810 1 pb.
Bound to upset some archaeologists, though author lays stress on the importance of good relations with museums, accurate recording,

safe cleaning and preservation of finds, and explains the laws of Treasure Trove in England and Scotland.

Palmer, Norman E, 'Treasure Trove and title to discovered antiquities', *International journal of cultural property*, 2, 1993, pp 275–318.
Useful article amounting to a bibliography of cases, in addition to explaining the law and its potential for injustice. Appendices give back-up data.

Prott, L V and O'Keefe, P J, *Handbook of national regulations concerning the export of cultural property*. [Paris]: UNESCO, 1988, 239 p, bibl. No ISBN.
See also under O'Keefe in sub-section Belowground above.

Schadla-Hall, Tim, 'Antiquities legislation: a proper basis?', in G T Denford (ed), *Museum archaeology: what's new?* (= *Mus archaeol*, 21, for 1994), pp 12–16.
Critique of the 'Treasure Bill 1994'.

Tubb, K W (ed), *Antiquities: trade or betrayed. Legal, ethical and conservation issues*. London: Archetype Books/UKIC Archaeol Section, 1996, xxi, 263 p. 1 873132 70 0.
Contains 26 papers from an international seminar held in London at the end of 1993: contributions come from archaeologists, conservators, the police, lawyers, dealers, government officials and private individuals.

Scotland

Below-ground archaeology, listed buildings and Treasure Trove are merged in a single sequence here.

Ancient Monuments Board, 'The preservation of monuments in State care', as Appendix 3, pp 23–34, in [Scottish] *Ancient Monuments Board annual report*, 44, 1994.
Discusses general principles governing the preservation of monuments; specific principles for stone, mortar, harling, timberwork, historic decoration, earthworks etc.

*** *Archaeology and planning. National planning policy guideline (NPPG)* 5 (Scotland). Edinburgh: Scottish Office Envir Dept, Jan. 1994, 12 p. 0 7480 0829 2.
This and the next are the two official notices.

*** *Archaeology: the planning process and scheduled monument procedures. Planning advice* *note (PAN)* 42 (Scotland). Edinburgh: Scottish Office Envir Dept, Jan 1994, 24 p. 0 7480 0833 0.

Brand, C M and Cant, R G, *Modern legislation for the protection of history: the Ancient Monuments and Archaeological Areas Act 1979.* Glasgow: The Planning Exchange (*Scottish planning law and practice occas pap*, 2), 1980.

Garratt-Frost, on regulations relating to Scottish burial finds, see Section 6.9 on excavation preliminaries and conduct.

Historic Scotland, *Scotland's listed buildings: a guide to their protection.* Edinburgh: Hist Scotl, 1993, 3 rev edn, 15 p.
Informal guide to legislation and how Historic Scotland and the planning authorities administer it.

—, *Memorandum of guidance on listed buildings and conservation areas.* Edinburgh, 1995, 134 p. 0 7480 4972 X.

Macinnes, Lesley, 'Ancient monuments in the Scottish countryside: their protection and management', *Scottish archaeological review*, 7, 1990, pp 131–8.

—, 'Preserving the past for the future' in W S Hanson and E A Slater (eds), *Scottish archaeology: new perceptions* (Aberdeen Univ Press, 1991), pp 196–217.

Scottish planning and environmental law (0144-8196) (news sheet). The Planning Exchange, 186 Bath St, Glasgow G2 4HG. (Mostly cases, but also news items relevant to rural archaeology.)

Sheridan, Alison, 'Portable antiquities legislation in Scotland', in K W Tubb (ed), *Antiquities: trade or betrayed* (1996, pp 193–204; see full reference under Tubb in Treasure Trove subsection above.)

—, 'The Scottish "Treasure Trove" system: a suitable case for emulation?', in G T Denford (ed), *Museum archaeology: what's new?* (= *Mus archaeol*, 21 for 1994), pp 4–11.

Ireland

Below-ground archaeology and standing buildings are not separated out here, but N Ireland and the Republic are because of their different legislative arrangements.

NORTHERN IRELAND

The following three papers describe the situation in the Six Counties. More recently the Historic Monuments and Archaeological Objects (NI) Order 1995 has come into force: this order requires landowners to make advance application for written permission to carry out any works affecting the condition of a scheduled historic monument. The order also allows, in certain circumstances, management agreements and grant-aid for increasing the protection of a monument. See the Environment and Heritage Service's free leaflet, *Scheduled historic monuments in Northern Ireland: advice to landowners on new legal measures.*

***Hamlin, Ann, 'Legislation in Northern Ireland', in J Hunter and I Ralston (eds), *Archaeological resource management in the UK* (1993), pp 134–5.

—, 'Government archaeology in Northern Ireland', in H Cleere (ed), *Heritage management in the modern world* (1989), pp 171–81.

Lynn, Chris, 'Archaeology in Northern Ireland', *Rescue news*, 57, 1992, pp 4–5

REPUBLIC OF IRELAND

(Thanks are due to Dr Ann Lynch for advice on this sub-section, though any remaining errors are the compiler's own.)

Important here is the National Monuments (Amendment) Act 1994 which includes several new provisions relating to the protection of portable antiquities: see advertisements in *Archaeology Ireland* during 1994. The National Monuments Advisory Council was not reconstituted after 1990, but the *Heritage Act 1995* established a Heritage Council on a statutory basis, with its own staffing and finance; this came into being in November 1995. The same Act also transferred the heritage functions of the Office of Public Works to the Ministry of Arts, Culture and the Gaeltacht (being implemented at the time of writing). The 1994 Act also requires the Commissioners of Public Works to establish and maintain a record of monuments which in effect gives blanket legal protection to all SMR sites.

To keep up with legislative developments, see *Irish planning and environmental law journal* (Brehon Publishing, 1994–).

The National Museum of Ireland has a leaflet *Protecting our past: a short guide to the National*

Monuments (Amendment) Act 1994; this explains what to do if archaeological objects are found.

Books for the Republic

***Hyde, Douglas, *Building on the past: urban change and archaeology*. Dublin: Environmental Inst, Univ College Dublin, 1993, xvii, 125 p. bibl, index. 1 898473 02 1 pb *NB: do not confuse with two other books having same main title.*

Examines the present planning system (policy and practice) in the Republic, indicating the complexities of Irish law in this context, and comparing policy in England-Wales and Scotland. Discusses current problems of managing the urban archaeological resource during urban renewal, and offers suggestions for improvement under the heads of planning regulations, policies, case studies, codes of practice.

Kelly, E P, 'Treasure hunting in Ireland: its rise and fall', in *Antiquity*, **67**, 1993, pp 378–81.

Cheerful piece indicating several improvements in public attitudes to the buried (and drowned) heritage in the Republic; notes that the Republic has signed the European Convention on the Protection of the Archaeological Heritage (Valletta 1992: details earlier in this section).

—, 'Protecting Ireland's archaeological heritage', in K W Tubb (ed), *Antiquities: trade or betrayed* (1996, pp 235–43: see full reference under Tubb in Treasure Trove above.)

Ryan, Michael, 'Irish archaeological legislation', in *Antiquity*, **62**, 1988, pp 284–5.

Describes the National Monuments (Amendments) Act 1987 making provision for historic wrecks, inland waterways, metal detecting, and the concept of the archaeological area.

6.7
Archaeological Heritage Management

See also Section 6.6 Legislation and planning, and Section 6.8 Conservation of Buildings.

This section incorporates some suggestions made by Dr Henry Cleere, who should be absolved from any remaining errors. Titles on standing buildings are included as well as below-ground archaeology.

Organisations

(UK countries and Ireland in single sequence)
Where no address is given below, look in Section 4.2 Organisations for the full entry.

CONSERVARE nv The European Heritage Forum (Troonstaat 66, B-8400 Oostende, Belgium, tel +(32) 59 556611). Organised the event Conservare '93 at Ostend as 'the first European forum to consider the preservation, protection, restoration and presentation of our heritage'.

European Forum for Arts and Heritage (EFAH), 1 rue Defacqz, 1050 Brussels, Belgium (tel +(32) 2 534 4300, fax +(32) 2 534 5275). This is a representative forum for arts and heritage organisations, associations and cultural networks across Europe. It is in liaison with the European Commission, the European Parliament, other European organisations including the Council of Europe, and with UNESCO.

European Heritage Group, c/o Europa Nostra, Lange Voorhout 35, 2414 EC, The Hague, The Netherlands (tel +(31) 70 356 0333, fax +(31) 70 361 7865). This group was created in 1995 to ensure the representation of heritage organisation interests at European level.

ICAHM (International Committee on Archaeological Heritage Management) maintains an international *Directory of archaeological heritage management organizations* (new edn 1996 published by ICOMOS Canada, PO Box 737, Station B, Ottawa, Ontario, Canada KIP 5R4; ISBN 0 969897 10 3, 223 p). Further information on ICAHM is in Section 4.2 Organisations.

Institute of Advanced Architectural Studies: Landscapes and Gardens

Institute of Environmental Assessment, Gregorycroft House, Fen Road, East Kirkby, Lincs

PE23 4DB (tel 01790 763613) is compiling a nationwide database of completed environmental statements.

Joint Centre for Heritage Conservation and Management

Periodicals

Conservation Bulletin (0953–8674). 1987–. English Heritage Conservation Group. (Mostly concerned with listed buildings but covers some archaeological matters, together with historic parks and gardens and the like.) Cumulative index to first 20 issues appeared in 1993.

Conservation and management of archaeological sites (1350–5033). 1995–. James and James Science Publishers. International in scope.

International journal of heritage studies (1352–7258). 1994–. 4/yr. Intellect, Exeter. Academic level; includes natural as well as archaeological heritage.

Journal of planning and environment law (0307–4870). Monthly with cumulating index. Sweet and Maxwell.

Sanctuary, the Ministry of Defence conservation magazine. Regular contributions on archaeological sites within defence training areas. Tel 0181 391 3028/9.

Books

The main reference here is Hunter and Ralston (below). For management of the industrial heritage, see Alfrey and Putnam in Section 6.15 Archaeology of industrial processes. The lecture by Biddle (below) is important.

Archaeology and society. Large scale rescue operations – their possibilities and problems. Stockholm: ICAHM, 1989, 338 p. 91 7192 786 7.
Papers from the first world conference on archaeological heritage management (Stockholm, September 1988).

Baker, David, *Living with the past: the historic environment.* Bedford: the author, 1983, 174 p, bibl, index. 0 9508681 0 8 hb, 0 9508681 1 6 pb.
Perhaps now showing its age, but was the first complete and rounded explanation of the below- and above-ground historic environment.

Berry, André and Brown, Ian W (eds), *Managing ancient monuments: an integrated approach.* Mold: Clwyd Archaeol Service/ACAO, 1995, xiv, 238 p. 0 900121 99 8 pb.
Principles and practice discussed by archaeologists for National Parks, local authorities, heritage/conservation bodies; includes consideration of underwater and wetland as well as normal terrestrial sites. Directory of c. 200 environmental organisations in the UK.

**— and — (eds), *Erosion on archaeological earthworks: its prevention, control and repair.* Mold: Clwyd Archaeol Service/ACAO/IFA, 1994, xiii, 159 p. 0 900121 57 2 pb.
Papers from a 1992 conference which recorded failures and successes; a product list guides selection of the best stabilisation method.

**Biddle, Martin, *What future for British archaeology?* Oxford: *Oxbow lecture, 1,* 1994, 20 p, refs.
Sets out the problems arising from *PPG16* and suggests a method for its reform. Particular attention is drawn to the impact of piled structures on archaeological deposits.

Bourke, Edward et al, *The care and conservation of graveyards.* Dublin: Office of Public Works, 1995, 23 p, bibl. 0 7076 1614 X pb.

Bourn, J, *Protecting and managing England's heritage property: report by the Comptroller and Auditor-General, National Audit Office.* London: HMSO, 1992. 0 10 213293 3 pb.
Official examination of the work of English Heritage, the National Heritage Memorial Fund, the Historic Royal Palaces Agency, Royal Armouries, and RCHME, with recommendations for action.

Boyle, Anne et al, *Ruins and remains: Edinburgh's neglected heritage. A commentary on Edinburgh's graveyards and cemeteries.* Edinburgh: Scotland's Cultural Heritage (History of Medicine and Science Unit), 1985, 143 p, bibls. 0 907692 81 8 pb.
Nine papers, mostly on 17th century onwards.

Brisbane, Mark and Wood, John, *A future for the past? An introduction to heritage studies.* London: English Heritage, 1995, 96 p. 1 85074 491 2.
Examines the conflicting issues of safeguarding versus making accessible: for sixth forms and upwards.

Burman, P, Feilden, B and Kennet, Lord (eds),

Managing World Heritage sites in Britain: proceedings of a seminar held in York in November 1991. London: ICOMOS UK, 1993, c. 150 p. 0 9517677 3 9 pb (not seen).

— and Stapleton, Henry, *The churchyards handbook: advice on the history and significance of churchyards, their care, improvement and maintenance.* London: Church House Publishing, 3 rev edn 1988, 200 p. 0 7151 7554 8 limp.
Includes a chapter on the archaeological value of churchyards, lichens as dating evidence and so on.

Carver, M O H (ed), Arguments in stone, see Section 6.12 History and theory of archaeology.

CBA Countryside Committee, *The past in tomorrow's landscape.* York: CBA, 1993, 16 p. 1 872414 48 6 pb.
A revision of the 1988 'Policy for the countryside', arguing forcefully for the formation of a strategy for the protection, management and interpretation of the landscape as a whole.

CBA Historic Buildings Committee, 'Historic farm buildings', *Brit archaeol news*, 3, 1988, p 23.
Approaches to their definition and preservation.

—, 'The ancillary structures of great houses', *Brit archaeol news*, 3, 1988, p 71.
Conservation guidelines.

Champion, T, see under English Heritage below.

**Cleere, Henry (ed), *Approaches to the archaeological heritage: a comparative study of world cultural resource management systems.* Cambridge: CUP, 1984, x, 138 p, bibl, index. 0 521 24305 X.
The editor treats Britain, and W D Lipe's excellent paper on value and meaning in cultural resources should also be read; the other dozen contributors take one country each.

***— (ed), *Archaeological heritage management in the modern world.* London: Unwin Hyman (= One World Archaeology, 9), 1989, xxiv, 318 p, bibl, index. 0 04 445028 1 hb, 0 04 445914 9 pb.
Contributions from 18 different countries discuss the rationale and practice of protecting the archaeological heritage, including case studies and training in management. Several papers deal with the UK situation including two on

Stonehenge and one on the role of the professional institution.

**— (ed), 'Managing the archaeological heritage', in *Antiquity*, 67, 1993, pp 400–45. Includes 1. the text of the Charter for the Protection and Management of the Archaeological Heritage (ICOMOS); 2. commentaries on the Revised Convention on the Protection of the Archaeological Heritage (Council of Europe, Valletta 1992); 3. papers by G Wainwright, W Startin.

Clubb, Nigel, 'Computerising the list of historic buildings in England: a historical case study on initiating a national project', in J Huggett and N Ryan (eds), *Computer applications and quantitative methods in archaeology 1994.* BAR Int Ser, 600, 1995, pp 193–202.
Notes the numerous successive feasibility studies which were necessary before this very large scheme could begin to be realised.

Cooper, Malcolm et al (eds), *Managing archaeology.* London: Routledge, 1995, xviii, 259 p, bibl, glossary, index. 0 415 10674 5.
The character of the archaeological heritage, how concepts of 'value' arise, how useful are general management approaches for the archaeological case? Sixteen papers plus conclusion.

Cullen, Ian and Hunter, Paul, *The investment performance of listed buildings.* London: English Heritage/RICS and Investment Property Databank, 1995 edn, 15 p. 0 85406 730 2 pb.
Demonstrates that listed buildings can be attractive investments.

Dartington Amenity Research Trust for Countryside Commission, *Hadrian's Wall: a strategy for conservation and visitor services.* DART Publ 25/CCP 98, 1976, 151 p. 0 902590 38 3 pb.
Discusses the setting, the Wall and related features, visitors, strategic considerations, detailed proposals etc. [The Hadrian's Wall Walk was approved in 1994, in the face of much opposition from archaeologists and others.]

*Darvill, Timothy, *The archaeology of the uplands: a rapid assessment of archaeological knowledge and practice.* London: RCHME/CBA, 1986, x, 101 p, bibl, glossary. 0 906780 63 2 pb.
On the nature and extent of upland archaeology, threats to it, its value as resource and for recreation and tourism, etc.

*—, (for Ancient Monuments Division, English Heritage), *Ancient monuments in the country-*

side: *an archaeological management review*. London: *English Heritage archaeol rep*, (old series) 5, 1987, viii, 188 p. 1 85074 167 0 pb. Gives the background to the recognition, investigation and management of the rural archaeological resource; assesses current knowledge and threats, and discusses ways of exploiting and conserving the resource. A shorter illustrated guide (same author and main title) was also produced.

—, *Valuing Britain's archaeological resource*. Bournemouth: Bournemouth Univ, 1993, 30 p, refs. 1 858990 01 7 pb.
Inaugural lecture on changing perceptions of 'value' of ancient monuments over the years.

—, Gerrard, C and Startin, Bill, 'Identifying and protecting historic landscapes', in *Antiquity*, 67, 1993, pp 563–74.
Arises from the MPP (Monuments Protection Programme) need to define 'relict cultural landscapes' and judge their relative values.

— and Wainwright, G J, 'The Monuments at Risk Survey: an introduction', in *Antiquity*, 68, 1994, pp 820–4.

*—, Burrow, S and Wildgust, D-A, *The assessment gazetteer 1981–1991: resumés and bibliographic details for completed archaeological assessments, field evaluation reports, and environmental statements. Suppl 1 to Brit archaeol bibl*, Oct 1994, vi, 287 p, indexes. No ISBN.
Guide to reports otherwise very hard to locate. *See also under English Heritage below.*

Dunk, Julie and Rugg, Julie, *The management of old cemetery land: now and the future. A report of the University of York Cemetery Research Group*. Crayford: Shaw and Sons, 1994, 105 p, bibl. 0 7219 1370 9 pb.

English Heritage, *Planning for the past*. Three volumes under this main title, all 1995:
Vol. 1, Trow, Stephen, *A review of archaeological assessment procedures in England 1982–91*. London: EH, 17 p. 1 85074 526 9 (Covers the period leading up to and immediately following *PPG 16*.)
Vol. 2, Darvill, T, Burrow, Stephen and Wildgust, D-A, *An assessment of archaeological assessments, 1982–91*. Bournemouth: the University/EH, 52 p, bibl. 1 85899 003 3 (Covers desk-based and field evaluations, environmental assessments etc.)
Vol. 3, Champion, T, Shennan, S and

Cuming, P, *Decision-making and field methods in archaeological evaluation*. Southampton: the University/EH, 64 p, bibl. 1 85432 531 X pb (Covers the development and current state of the process and methodology of evaluation, etc.)

English Heritage/ADAS, *Farming historic landscapes and people*. London: English Heritage/ADAS, 1991?, available free from English Heritage or from local ADAS offices.
Gives advice to farmers on caring for our 6000-year-old countryside; how to identify and conserve sites as part of good agricultural practice.

English Heritage/London Planning Advisory Committee, *Conservation in London: a study of strategic planning policy in London*. London: EH, 1995, 83 p, bibl. 1 85074 522 6 pb.
Indicates that London's historic environment contributes significantly to its economic success and to the quality of London life. Recommends six key policy initiatives for central government and boroughs.

English Historic Towns Forum, *Townscape in trouble: conservation areas – the case for change*. Bath: EHTF, 1992, 24 p. No ISBN.
Calls for a more holistic approach and stronger controls if urban character is to be maintained.

Evans, Dai Morgan, *Survey grants for presentation purposes: a guide for applicants*. London: English Heritage, [1988], 12 p.
Free advice for farmers who wish to identify monuments on their land for possible presentation to the public.

—, Salway, Peter and Thackray, David (eds), 'The remains of distant times': archaeology and the National Trust*. Woodbridge: Boydell Press for Soc Antiq London and Nat Trust, 1996, ix, 235 p, bibls, index. 0 85115 671 1.
Numerous papers illustrate how the Trust has become aware, over the last couple of decades in particular, of its responsibilities to its very considerable holdings of ancient monuments.

**Feilden, B M and Jokilehto, J, *Management guidelines for World Cultural Heritage sites*. Rome: ICCROM, 1993, xi, 122 p, bibl. 92 9077 110 X.
Offers guiding principles, general policy of the Convention, evaluation for conservation, and so on. Gives a list of World Heritage sites.

Feist, Andrew and Hutchinson, Robert, *Cultural trends in the eighties*. London: Policy Studies

Inst, 1990 (= *PSI spec rep*, 4), 69 p. 0 85374 455 6 pb.
Includes analysis of figures for attendance at historic properties etc. (Twice as many people visit the UK largely to see monuments as come for the theatre etc.) See also Jeremy Eckstein (ed), 'The built heritage', in *Cultural trends*, 4.3, 1992, pp 21–57.

Fladmark, J M (ed), *Heritage: conservation, interpretation and enterprise; papers presented at the Robert Gordon University Heritage Convention, 1993*. London: Donhead, 1993, xvi, 355 p, bibls. 1 873394 13 6.
Papers consider (mainly with Scottish focus) the built and natural environment, the future of green tourism, museums, arts and crafts, etc.

Foley, Claire, *Understanding historic monuments on the farm*. Belfast: DOENI/Dept Agriculture N Ireland, [1988], 20 p. No ISBN.
Booklet of advice for farmers, available free from Environment Service Historic Monuments and Buildings (DOENI).

Forest Service [Ireland], *Forestry and archaeology guidelines*. Dublin: Forest Service, 1992.

Fowler P J, *The past in contemporary society: then, now*. London: Routledge (Heritage: Care–Preservation–Management), 1992, xvii, 192 p, bibl, index. 0 415 06726 X hb, 0 415 07130 5 pb.
Making extensive use of media coverage, examines the treatment of the past in contemporary society.

—, 'Archaeology in Trust', in Howard Newby (ed), *The National Trust: the next hundred years*. London: National Trust, 1995, pp 104–16.
Documents the 'long way' that the Trust has come over the last half-century in understanding its archaeological holdings.

Gilg, A W, *Countryside planning policies for the 1990s*. Wallingford: CAB International, 1991, x, 290 p. 0 85198 744 3.
A reference work for professionals involved in rural planning, for organisations concerned with environmental issues, and for students in associated disciplines.

Goulty, S, on heritage garden management, see Section 6.16 Garden archaeology and history.

Hamlin, A, *The care of graveyards*. Belfast: DOENI, 1993.

Harrison, R, *Manual of heritage management*. Oxford: Butterworth/Heinemann, 1994, xiv, 425 p, bibl, index. 0 7506 0822 6.
Fully detailed reference work with over 60 papers, covering the natural and human-made heritage. Discusses general strategies and principles, with the addition of many short case-studies. One section deals with financial and operational management and others with interpretation and presentation of sites, and recording and conservation.

**Heighway, C M (ed), *The erosion of history: archaeology and planning in towns. A study of historic towns affected by modern development in England, Wales and Scotland*. London: CBA, 1972, vii, 126 p. 0 900312 15 7 pb.
A landmark volume which, although now out of date in many respects, is still highly influential for its classification of towns by relative importance in archaeological and historical terms.

Hingley, Richard (ed), *Medieval or later rural settlement in Scotland: management and preservation . . . a seminar organised by Historic Scotland. HS Anc Monuments Div occas pap*, 1, 1993, 70 p, bibl. 0 7480 0672 9 pb.
Discussions on how to choose the most suitable settlements to preserve, from the myriad numbers across Scotland. HS subsequently set up an advisory group for the protection and management of such sites.

House of Commons Environment Committee, *Historic buildings and ancient monuments*. (First report, Session 1986–87.) 3 vols, 1987.
Comprises the Report, Evidence and Minutes, Appendices. (See also Government responses as *First, second and third special reports on historic buildings and ancient monuments*, printed as House of Commons Papers in 1988 and 1989.)

House of Commons Welsh Affairs Committee, *Second report: the preservation of historic buildings and ancient monuments*. House of Commons, 1993, 2 vols. 0 10 020693 X pb and 0 10 020973 4 pb.
and the Government's response, Nov 1993, Cm 2416. 0 10 124162 3 pb.

***Hunter, John and Ralston, Ian (eds), *Archaeological resource management in the UK: an introduction*. Stroud: Alan Sutton/IFA, 1993, x, 277 p, bibl, index. 0 7509 0275 2.
Indispensable handbook which takes stock of

current archaeological practice in Britain. It aims to assist professionals in neighbouring subjects, and the 22 contributors discuss heritage management, legislation (including Scotland and N Ireland), planning controls, changing land use, pressures of public interest, etc. Extensive bibliography.

Jackson, Angela M, *Forestry and archaeology: a study in survival of field monuments in southwest Scotland*. Hertford: Rescue, 1978, 52 p, bibl. 0 903789 06 x pb.
Brought to attention the effects of deep ploughing for afforestation on archaeological sites. (*See also Proudfoot below.*)

Kennet, Wayland, *Preservation*. London: Temple Smith, 1972, 224 p, bibl, index. 0 85117 022 6.
A pioneering work in this field.

*Lambrick, George (ed), *Archaeology and nature conservation*. Oxford: Oxford Univ Dept External Stud, 1985, 121 p, bibls. 0 903736 19 5 pb.
16 papers from a 1984 conference on aspects of the relationship between archaeology and ecology: the first of the 'green' statements for archaeology.

Lowenthal, David, *The past is a foreign country*. Cambridge: CUP, 1985, xxvii, 489 p, bibl, index. 0 521 22415 2 hb, 0 521 29480 0 pb.
How do we recognise and cope with the weighty heritage of the past – what does it cost, what are the benefits; and how do we reshape it for modern needs. Remains useful.

Macinnes, Lesley, 'Preserving the past for the future', in W S Hanson and E S Slater (eds), *Scottish archaeology: new perceptions* (1991), pp 196–217.
Comments of an Ancient Monuments Inspector in Scotland.

**— and Wickham-Jones, C, *All natural things: archaeology and the green debate*. Oxford: Oxbow monogr, 21, 1992, viii, 213 p, bibls. 0 946897 45 x pb.
The human side and the time depth of the environmental argument.

Methodist Church Property Division, *A charge to keep? a Methodist response to listed buildings and conservation*. Manchester: Methodist Church Property Div, 1990. No ISBN.
Booklet showing how it is possible to achieve solutions for listed buildings which meet the needs of the Church and of conservationists

through co-operation with planning bodies and amenity societies.

Murray, David, *An archaeological survey of the United Kingdom: the preservation and protection of our ancient monuments*. Glasgow: MacLehose, 1896.
Of historic interest as an early plea for conservation.

Mynors, Charles, *Listed buildings and conservation areas*. London: Longman, 2 rev edn 1994, xxx, 351 p, bibl. 0 85121 902 0.
Guide to a very complex area of law.

National Audit Office see under Bourn above.

Palmer and Neaverson on managing the industrial heritage, see Section 6.15 Archaeology of industrial processes.

Pearce, Graham, Hems, L and Hennessy, B, *The conservation areas of England*. London: English Heritage, 1990.
5-volume set covering respectively London and the southeast, the West Midlands and southwest, the east of England, the north of England, plus a summary volume. Covers 6,300 conservation areas in all.

Planning Policy Guidance Notes 15 and 16 see Section 6.6 Legislation and planning.

Prehistoric Society, *Saving our prehistoric heritage* [policy statement]. London: Prehistoric Society, 1988.

Pressouyre, Léon, *La convention du patrimoine mondial, vingt ans après*. Paris: Éditions UNESCO, 1993, 63 p. 92 3 202893 x (English version forthcoming).
A perceptive analysis of the strengths and weaknesses of the 1972 UNESCO Convention.

*Proudfoot, E V W (ed), *Our vanishing heritage: forestry and archaeology. Proceedings of a conference, Inverness, April 1987*. Edinburgh: CSA occas pap, 2, 1989, 36 p, bibl. 0 901352 10 1 pb.
Papers from a conference which at last led to improved treatment of archaeological remains by Scottish and other forestry authorities. (*See also Jackson above.*)

RCAHMS, *Afforestable land surveys*. [Short booklets in same format as regional SMR lists, 1994-]
Detailed fieldwork over land due for planting.

Startin, Bill, 'The Monuments Protection Programme: archaeological records', in U Larsen (ed), *Sites and monuments; national archaeological records* (Copenhagen, 1992), pp 201–6.

*Swain, Hedley (ed), *Rescuing the historic environment: proceedings of a conference held at Leicester. . . 1993*. Hertford: Rescue, 1993, 99 p, bibls. 0 903789 17 5 pb.
The 20 papers discussed the natural and historic environments, the role of the various conservation bodies, management case studies, the campaign for change.

Thompson, M W, *Ruins: their preservation and display*. London: Brit Mus Publs (Colonnade), 1981, 104 p, bibl, index. 0 7141 8034 3.

Trow, S see under English Heritage above.

***UNESCO, *Conventions and recommendations of UNESCO concerning the protection of the cultural heritage*. Paris: UNESCO, 1985, 239 p. 92 3 102101 X.
Contains texts of Conventions on the protection of cultural property in the event of armed conflict (1954), illicit trade in cultural property (1970), and the protection of the world cultural and natural heritage (1972).

Ward, Pamela (ed), *Conservation and development in historic towns and cities*. Newcastle: Oriel Press, 1968, 275 p, index. 0 85362 046 6.
A seminal volume from nearly 30 years ago expressing concern about the scale of destruction of historic urban sites.

See also list of UK World Heritage Sites in Section 6.5 Lists of monuments.

6.8
Conservation of Buildings

This section deals with physical conservation rather than legal provisions (which are treated in Sections 6.6 Legislation and planning, and 6.7 Archaeological heritage management). See also Section 6.18 Vernacular architecture.

Organisations with interests in building conservation

Addresses and other details will be found in Section 4.2 Organisations if not given below.

Ancient Monuments Society
Association for Studies in the Conservation of Historic Buildings
Brooking Collection (of architectural details). Univ of Greenwich at Dartford, Kent DA1 2SZ, tel 0181 316 9896
Building Conservation Trust see now UPKEEP
Building Research Establishment Heritage Support Service
Cathedrals Fabric Commission for England
Churches Conservation Trust (formerly Redundant Churches Fund)
Civic Trust
Council for British Archaeology
English Heritage (including Architectural Study Collection)
Farmsteads Survey (RCHME)
Friends of Friendless Churches
Georgian Group
Guild of Master Craftsmen, 166 High Street, Lewes, E Sussex BN7 1XU, tel 01273 478449, fax 01273 478606. Produces an annual *Directory of Members* listing over 27,000 members in nearly 400 trades: building and allied, other crafts, artist-craftsmen. Also publishes *Care and Repair* (1989).
Historic Chapels Trust
Historic Farm Buildings Group
Institute of Advanced Architectural Studies: Landscapes and Gardens (formerly Centre for the Conservation of Historic Parks and Gardens)
ICOMOS UK
ICOMOS (International Council on Monuments and Sites)
Joint Centre for Heritage Conservation and Management (Bournemouth)

Landmark Trust
National Trust
Redundant Churches Fund *see* Churches Conservation Trust
Royal Commission on the Historical Monuments of England
Royal Institute of British Architects
Royal Institution of Chartered Surveyors
SAVE Britain's Heritage
Society of Antiquaries of London
Society for the Protection of Ancient Buildings
UPKEEP (formerly Building Conservation Trust)
Vernacular Architecture Group

Periodicals

Association for Studies in the Conservation of Historic Buldings/Transactions (0142–5803). 1973–. Annual.
Churchscape (0262–4966). 1982–. Annual. Council for the Care of Churches.
Conservation bulletin (0953–8674). 1987–. 3/yr. English Heritage.
Context, Journal of the Association of Conservation Officers.
English heritage monitor 19..: a yearly analysis of trends affecting England's architectural heritage. Annual. English Tourist Board.
Journal of architectural conservation (1355–207). 1995–. 3/yr. London: Donhead
Journal of the Historic Farm Buildings Group (0952–5513). 1987–. Annual.

Directories and bibliographies

The building conservation directory: a guide to specialist suppliers, consultants and craftsmen . . . . Annual. London/Tisbury: Cathedral Communications Ltd.
Includes a few archaeological consultants, c. 600 suppliers, 150 amenity societies and groups, glossary, etc.

Conservation Unit MGC, *The conservation sourcebook.* London: Museums and Galleries Commission, 1991, 122 p, index. 0 11 290493 9 pb.
Alphabetical directory of organisations concerned with conserving buildings and objects in the UK.

English Heritage, *Directory of public sources of grants for the repair and conversion of historic buildings.* London: English Heritage, rev edn 1990, looseleaf sheets. 0 85074 180 8 (Revision under consideration at time of writing.)
Eligibility, location, size of grant, where to apply.

Smith, John F (comp), *A critical bibliography of building conservation: historic towns, buildings, their furnishings and fittings.* London: Mansell, 1978, 207 p, indexes. 0 7201 0707 5.
Classified arrangement covering numerous topics including other bibliographies and directories.

Books

(Of the technical manuals, only the principal ones are included; and in a rapidly developing field only the most recent titles are mentioned.)

Ashurst, John and Nicola, *Practical building conservation.* Aldershot: English Heritage/ Gower Technical Press, 1988, 5 vols on different materials.

Bailey, *Sir Alan, see under Fire Protection Association below.*

Binney, Marcus and Watson-Smyth, M, *The SAVE Britain's Heritage action guide.* London: Collins and Brown, 1991, 160 p, index. 1 85585 056 7.
The story of SAVE plus many case histories illustrating the use of publicity to stir up effective public reaction.

Brand, Vanessa (ed), *Buildings at risk: a sample survey.* London: English Heritage, 1992, 24 p. 1 85074 364 9 pb.
Condition survey of over 40, 000 listed buildings in England.

Brereton, Christopher, *The repair of historic buildings: advice on principles and methods.* London: English Heritage (*Aspects of conservation,* 4), rev edn 1995, 67 p. 1 85074 527 7 pb.
Comprehensive advice on how to avoid damage by inadequate or misguided maintenance and repair.

Brooke, C J, 'Ground-based remote sensing for archaeological information recovery in historic buildings', *Int j remote sensing,* 8, 1987, pp 1039–48.
For recovering invisible features on excavations as well as sub-plaster anomalies in buildings, gravestone inscriptions etc.

Buchanan, Terry, *Photographing historic buildings for the record.* London: HMSO for

RCHME, 1983, 108 p, index. 0 11 701123 1 pb.
Guide from an experienced RCHME photographer.

Burman, Peter (ed), *Treasures on earth: a good housekeeping guide to churches and their contents*. London: Donhead, 1994, x, 304 p. 1 873394 10 1.
Problems of cleaning and repair, hazards of non-specialist treatment, etc; 16 papers, mostly on contents rather than church fabric, but adds a discussion on floors.

Cathedral Communications Ltd (ed J Taylor), *The conservation and repair of ecclesiastical buildings*. London: Cathedral Comms (= *Building Conserv Dir spec rep*, 1) 1994, 44 p. 0 9520080 3 3 pb.
Contains articles by Thomas Cocke, Matthew Saunders, Carol Pyrah, Pamela Ward and others, as well as advertisements for suppliers etc.

Charles, F W B and M, *Conservation of timber buildings*. London: Hutchinson, 1984, 256 p, bibl, index. 0 09 145090 X (Repr Donhead 1995 as 1 873394 17 9).
Background, office practice, case studies.

Church security: this useful document by Staffordshire Police is obtainable from English Heritage (London Division).

Civic Trust, *Traffic measures in historic towns*. London: Civic Trust, 1993, 24 p. 1 870257 70 7 pb.

Cocke, R et al on recording a church, see Section 6.9 Excavation preliminaries and conduct, subsection Drawing (etc).

Code of practice for dealers in architectural salvage. Obtain from SALVO, Ford Woodhouse, Berwick-upon-Tweed TD15 2QF, tel 01668 216494.

Council for the Care of Churches, *How to look after your church*. London: CCC, 3 rev edn, 1991, 36 p. 0 7151 7561 0 pb.

Cunnington, Pamela, *Change of use: conversion of old buildings*. London: A and C Black, 1988, 256 p, bibl, index. 0 7136 3020 5.

—, *Care for old houses*. London: A and C Black, 2 edn 1991, 256 p, bibl, index. 0 7136 3318 2.
Gives the historical background to conservation, current legal position, financial aid, principles of repair and alteration, etc.

Darley, Gillian, *A future for farm buildings*. London: SAVE, 1988, 84 p, bibl. 0 905978 26 9.
Legislation and grants, planning policies, conversions, recommendations for action by relevant agencies including government.

Davey, Ken, *Building conservation contracts and grant aid: a practical guide*. London: Spon, 1992, vii, 231 p, index. 0 419 17140 1.

Davey, N, *Building stones of England and Wales*. London: Bedford Square Press for SCLH, 1976, 47 p. 0 7199 0912 0 pb.
Covers rock types, quarry types, erratics used for building, etc.

Davies, Philip and Keate, Delcia, *In the public interest: London's civic architecture at risk*. London: EH, 1995, 82 p, bibl, index. 1 85074 516 1 pb.
Illustrated gazetteer of a wide range of publicly owned London buildings suffering neglect and mismanagement.

Eckstein, Jeremy, 'The built heritage', *Cultural trends 1992*, 15, pp 21–57.
Independent review for Policy Studies Institute examined statistics relating to historic properties (eg trading statistics) and to the various bodies concerned with historic buildings and/or ancient monuments (English Heritage, Historic Scotland, Cadw, the Royal Commissions), the grants available, etc.

English Heritage publishes a very wide range of advisory books and leaflets on topics ranging from churches to farm buildings, and from appropriate window types to insurance matters and the effects of listing on economic value.

Feilden, Bernard M, *Conservation of historic buildings*. London: Butterworth Sci, 1982, x, 472 p, bibl, glossary, indexes. 0 408 10782 0 hb. (Paperback edn 1994 from Butterworth Heinemann, 0 7506 1739 X pb.)
Conveys the fruits of a lifetime's experience.

Fire Protection Association, *Heritage under fire: a guide to the protection of historic buildings*. London: FPA, 2 edn 1995, 76 p. 0 902167 90 1 pb.
Advice on reducing the possibility of fire breaking out, and on reducing the impact if it does; action plan, safety checklist. Includes full text of

the 'Bailey Report' on fire safety in royal palaces.

Fowler, Daryl, *Church floors and floor coverings*. London: Church House Publishing for Council for the Care of Churches, 1992, 31 p. 0 7151 7563 7 pb.
Draws attention to the archaeological and art-historical aspects of many floors, and describes maintenance methods.

Harvey, Nigel, *Redundant farm buildings – present liabilities, future assets: problems, possibilities and procedures*. London: privately by author, 1993, no ISBN. £4.50 pb from N Harvey, 41 Coningham Road, London NW11 7BS.

Heyman, Jacques, *The stone skeleton: structural engineering of masonry architecture*. Cambridge: CUP, 1995, x, 160 p, bibl, index. 0 521 47270 9.
Examines matters relevant to the upkeep of old stone buildings.

International index on training in conservation of cultural property (comp Cynthia Rockwell). Marina del Rey: Getty Conservation Institute, 1987, 96 p. 0 89236 127 1 pb.

Kennet, Wayland on preservation, see Section 6.7 Archaeological heritage management.

Kindred, Bob, *Listed building repairs notices: a study . . . 1984–90 . . . .* Ipswich: Assoc of Conservation Officers, 1992, 64 p. 0 9519300 1 pb.
A survey of the use of repairs notices found them to be a severely under-used option. Guidance is given on repair schedules, with suggestions for improving the process.

Michell, Eleanor, *Emergency repairs for historic buildings*. London: English Heritage, 1989, 128 p. 1 85074 227 8.

Newsom, G H and Newsom, G L, *Faculty jurisdiction of the Church of England: [the care of churches and churchyards]*. London: Sweet and Maxwell, 2 edn 1993, xxxiv, 334 p. 0 421 43960 2.

Parnell, on building legislation, see Section 6.6 Legislation and planning.

Parsons, D, on investigating churches and chapels, see Section 6.9 The excavator's task, under Drawing . . .

Pearson, Gordon T, *Conservation of clay and chalk buildings*. London: Donhead, 1992, 224 p. 1 873394 00 4.

RCHME (ed John Bold), *Recording historic buildings: a symposium, London, May 1991*. London: RCHME, 1991, 75p. 1 87359 203 5 pb.

— and RIBA, *Architectural records in national and local collections – guidance notes for archivists and record offices*. London: RCHME, 1987.
Informal publication on how to collect drawings etc from local architects for archiving.

Redundant Churches Fund, *Churches in retirement: a gazetteer*. London: HMSO, 1990, xi, 162 p. 0 11 701452 4. (The RCF is now the Churches Conservation Trust.)

SAVE Britain's Heritage publishes a wide range of books on buildings at risk, for example historic naval and military architecture; not individually listed here.

Suddards, on listed buildings law, see Section 6.6 Legislation and planning.

Swallow, P, Watt, D and Ashton, R, *Measurement and recording of historic buildings*. London: Donhead, 1993, 176 p. 1 873394 08 X.

Swindells, D J and Hutchings, M, *A checklist for the structural survey of period timber-framed buildings*. London: RICS, 1993, 40 p. 0 85406 543 1 spiral-bound.
Essential basic help for chartered surveyors.

URBED (Urban and Economic Development) Ltd, *Re-using redundant buildings: case studies of good practice in urban regeneration*. London: HMSO for DoE Inner Cities Directorate, 1987, 15 p. 0 11 752011 X.
Gives 14 case studies from public, private and voluntary sectors.

Wade Martins, Susanna (ed), *Old farm buildings in a new countryside: redundancy, conversion and conservation in the 1990s*. Reading: Historic Farm Buildings Group, 1991, 48 p. 0 9517503 0 5 pb.
A 1990 conference drew attention to the historic value of farm buildings and suggested improved strategies for protecting them.

Watt, D, *Surveying historic buildings*. London: Donhead, due 1995/6, c 300 p. 1 87339 416 0.

Weir, Hilary, *How to rescue a ruin by setting up a local Buildings Preservation Trust*. London:

Archit Heritage Fund, 1989, 72 p, bibl. o 9515468 0 5.

Wood, Jason (ed), *Buildings archaeology: applications in practice. Oxbow monogr*, **43**, 1994, vii, 263 p, bibls. o 946897 75 1.
Contains papers from the IFA Buildings Group (1993) designed to underpin conservation and management policies. Sections are: academic and legislative frameworks; extensive survey; intensive survey (selective and comprehensive).

Wright, Adela, *Craft techniques for traditional buildings*. London: Batsford, 1991, 176 p. o 7134 6419 4.
Guide to the repair and conservation of walling and roofing.

___

Wales

Organisations concerned with historic buildings conservation include:
Cadw, Capel, Civic Trust for Wales, RCAHMW, Welsh Mills Society, whose addresses are in Section 4.2 Organisations.

___

Scotland

Organisations concerned with historic buildings conservation include:

Architectural Heritage Society of Scotland
Cairdean nan Taighean Tugha (Friends of Thatched Houses)
Church of Scotland Advisory Committee on Artistic Matters
Cockburn Association
Council for Scottish Archaeology
Glasgow West Conservation Trust
Historic Scotland
National Trust for Scotland
Royal Commission on the Ancient and Historical Monuments of Scotland
Royal Incorporation of Architects in Scotland
Royal Institution of Chartered Surveyors in Scotland
Royal Town Planning Institute Scotland
Saltire Society
Scottish Burgh Survey
Scottish Civic Trust
Scottish Historic Buildings Trust
Scottish Industrial Heritage Society
Scottish Vernacular Buildings Working Group
Society of Antiquaries of Scotland

Addresses are in Section 4.2 Organisations.

BOOKS

Historic Scotland, *Memorandum of guidance on listed buildings and conservation areas*. Edinburgh, 1995, 134 p. o 7480 4972 X.
(Historic Scotland issues a number of works, some substantial, some pamphlets, on technical aspects of building conservation.)

Scottish Civic Trust for SDD, *New uses for older buildings in Scotland: a manual of practical encouragement*. Edinburgh: HMSO, 1981, 164 p, bibl, index. o 11 491691694 2.

___

Ireland

Organisations concerned with historic buildings conservation include:

(for Northern Ireland)
Belfast Civic Trust
Environment and Heritage Service: Historic Monuments and Buildings
HEARTH
Historic Buildings Council
Historic Monuments Council
National Trust (NI)
Ulster Architectural Heritage Society (UAHS)

(for Republic of Ireland)
Heritage Council
Irish Georgian Society
Office of Public Works
Royal Society of Antiquaries of Ireland
An Taisce

Addresses are in Section 4.2 Organisations.

BOOKS

Bourke, Edward et al, *The care and conservation of graveyards*. Dublin: Office of Public Works, 1995, 23 p, bibl. o 7076 1614 X pb.

Hamlin, Ann, *The care of graveyards*. Belfast: Dept of Environment NI, 1993.

Ulster Architectural Heritage Society, *Buildings at risk: a catalogue of buildings at risk in Northern Ireland*. Belfast: UAHS, 1993, 119 p. No ISBN, pb.

6.9
The Excavator's Training, Career and Tasks

This section contains principal sub-sections as follows:

Training (Britain), including summer schools and information for school teachers; Irish Republic information

Excavation preliminaries and conduct

Reporting, publishing, interpreting.

Training

Britain and abroad

A very full list of **UK universities** and the archaeology courses they offer (for first and postgraduate degrees, and for formal adult qualifications) is provided in the CBA's *British archaeological yearbook*; very brief indications of both UK and Irish universities will be found above in Section 4.7 Universities.

For those who wish to work abroad, or to gain additional experience, the **Archaeology Abroad Service**, 31–34 Gordon Square, London WC1H OPY issues regular bulletins of information. The American bimonthly journal *Archaeology* (0003–8113, published by the Archaeological Institute of America, 15 Park Row, New York, NY 10038, USA) contains regular advertisements of excavations requiring volunteers.

Cathedral Camps, 16 Glebe Avenue, Flitwick, Beds MK45 1HS (tel 01525 716237). For working holidays doing minor maintenance work in cathedrals, similar to the National Trust's Acorn Camps: not primarily for training, although volunteers (aged 16–30) can progress on the job.

Centre for Environmental Interpretation (address in Section 4.2 Organisations) offers a regular *Directory of training opportunities in the UK*.

COSQUEC, Council for Occupational Standards and Qualifications in Environmental Conservation: see Section 4.2 Organisations.

European Heritage School, Universidad Autonoma, Barcelona, offers short training and professional courses; has links with PACT (see Section 4.2 Organisations).

International Academic Projects Summer Schools offer numerous short intensive courses, at various centres in the UK, Continental Europe and the USA, designed mostly for conservators but with some courses on archaeological survey, drawing, faunal bone identification and so on. For details of the current year's programme apply to International Academic Projects, c/o James Black, UCL Institute of Archaeology, 31–34 Gordon Square, London WC1H OPY, 0171 387 9651, fax 0171 388 0283, Internet home page http://www.ucl.ac.uk/~tcfa313/

For archaeological summer schools consult *Briefing* (bimonthly supplement to the CBA's *British archaeology*). Considerable variety is likely to be on offer: just a few of those currently available are –

Castell Henllys training excavation, Dyfed – apply to H C Mytum, Univ York Dept Archaeology

Compton Bassett Area Research Project (field course) – Institute of Archaeology, London (address as in previous paragraph)

Essex – Cressing Temple, Witham Road, Braintree, Essex CM7 8PD (site archaeologist 01376 583220)

Sussex – Bignor Roman Villa (field courses) – apply to Mrs Sheila Maltby, Archaeology South-East, 1 West Street, Ditchling, Hassocks, W Sussex BN6 8TS (tel 01273 845497)

Scotland – apply to either the Centre for Continuing Education (tel 0131 650 1000) or the Centre for Field Archaeology (tel 0131 650 8197) at the University of Edinburgh.

For Irish universities, summer schools and teaching materials see below under Irish Republic.

BOOKS

Apelt, Mary L and Apelt, H-P, *Reading knowledge in German: a course for art historians and archaeologists*. Berlin: Erich Schmidt, 2 rev edn, 1984, 152 p. 3 503 02228 7.
Not enough British archaeologists read German and this course gives them less excuse!

Bahn, Paul, *Bluff your way in archaeology*. Horsham: Ravette Books, 1989, 62 p. 1 85304 102 5.
Well worth acquiring for its clear-eyed advice as well as numerous good jokes.

Greene, Kevin, *Archaeology: an introduction. The history, principles and methods of modern*

archaeology. London: Batsford, 3 edn fully revised 1995, 208 p, bibl, index. 0 7134 7636 2 limp.
Excellent introduction for students.

Morris, Elaine, *Women in British archaeology*. *IFA occas pap*, 4, 1992. 0 948393 86 6 pb.
A report from the working party on equal opportunities in archaeology.

Steane, John and Dix, B F, *Peopling past landscapes: a handbook introducing archaeological fieldwork techniques in rural areas*. London: CBA, 1978, 94 p. 0 900312 81 5 pb.
Still a useful initial training guide.

***Wass, Stephen, *The amateur archaeologist*. London: Batsford, 1992, 160 p, bibl, index. 0 7134 6896 3.
Very useful information for the beginner: treats surveying, legislation, careers etc.

INFORMATION FOR SCHOOL TEACHERS
Organisations
The **CBA,** with its Education Officer supported by regional education liaison officers, is the best general source of current information: see *Brit archaeol yearbook* for a basic list of schools and colleges offering archaeological courses. The CBA has also produced a 64-page booklet listing educational software for archaeology and history.

Educational information (much of it closely geared to the National Curriculum) is also supplied by:

English Heritage Education Service, 429 Oxford Street, London W1R 2HD (tel 0171 973 3442/3, fax 0171 973 3430) under Mike Corbishley: also has regional education officers and supplies a very wide variety of course materials (including booklets on using historic buildings for National Curriculum work in – eg – English, science, maths; also GCSE materials, advice on free site visits etc.) There are also EH videos, Family Discovery Packs and a magazine, *Heritage learning* (1355–7572, 3/yr). Catalogue available.

Council for Scottish Archaeology, c/o National Museum of Scotland, Queen Street, Edinburgh EH2 1JD (tel 0131 225 7534 ext 311): developing its own educational programme in close liaison with the CBA.

The National Trust's education service is steadily increasing its output of school materials as part of its MINERVA programme (life-long learning through the resources of its properties). Teachers' pack, Education Supplement, and lists of publications and events from Education Dept, The National Trust, 36 Queen Anne's Gate, London SW1H 9AS (tel 0171 222 9251).

The National Trust for Scotland's Education Department (5 Charlotte Square, Edinburgh EH2 4DU, tel 0131 226 5922) has leaflets and special teachers' guidebooks for individual properties of the NTS.

The **Royal Anthropological Institute** issues a teachers' resource guide (4 edn 1990, new edition due 1996), naturally dealing mainly with anthropology but containing some material related to archaeological work.

Books for teachers
Corbishley, Mike (ed), *Archaeology in the National Curriculum*. London: CBA/EH, 1992, 17 p. 0 85074 385 1 pb. (Also a version in Welsh published by CBA Wales.)
Papers on Key Stages 1, 2, 3/4, plus three other useful contributions; case studies and ideas.

Cracknell, Stephen and Corbishley, M (eds), *Presenting archaeology to young people*. CBA *res rep*, 64, 1986, vi, 50p, bibl. 0 906780 61 6 pb.
Several papers offer practical ideas for, and a rationale for, teaching archaeology in schools. Includes making videos, pottery firing, computer modelling etc.

Gallagher, Carmel et al, *Making sense of history: evidence in Ireland for the young historian*. Belfast: Ulster Historical Foundation, 1990, 63 p. 0 901905 43 7.

Keith, Crispin, *A teacher's guide to using listed buildings*. London: English Heritage, 1991, 36 p. 1 85074 297 9 pb.
Explains what listing means, and looks at the issues raised by conservation and the conflicts of interest which can arise.

Moloney, Norah (ed), *The Young Oxford book of archaeology*. Oxford: OUP, 1995, 160 p. 0 19 910067 5.
Plenty here for adults too!

Stone, Peter and MacKenzie, Robert (eds), *The excluded past: archaeology in education*. London: Routledge (= *One world archaeology*, 17), 1994, xxxiii, 316 p, bibl. 0 415 10545 5.
Papers from a conference.

Willetts, Susan J (comp), *Resources guide to*

audiovisual material for the classics. London: Inst Classical Stud, 1995, 72 p. 0 9527347 0 2 pb.
Lists the material with sources and suppliers.

IRISH REPUBLIC

Universities: see list in Section 4.7 Universities.

Summer schools:

Bord Fáilte (Baggot St Bridge, Dublin 2) can provide a leaflet on cultural courses (including archaeology). There are, however, summer schools available at:

Burren Field School, details from Roscrea Heritage Centre, Co Tipperary

UC Cork, details from Seamus O'Tuama, Summer Campus Coordinator, Dept of Adult and Continuing Education, UCC: tel (Cork) +(21) 276871 ext 2631/2302

Glencolmcille, Co Donegal (contact Oideas Gael, Gleann Cholm Cille, Co Dhún na nGall for brochure; tel (Donegal) +(73) 30248, e-mail oidsgael@iol.ia

Rathmichael Historical Society: contact Rosemary Beckett, 25 Flower Grove, Glenageary, Co Dublin, tel Dublin 285 7625

Achill, Co Mayo: contact Theresa McDonald, St O'Hara's Hill, Tullamore, Co Offaly, tel (Tullamore) +(506) 21627

Dúchas Inis Óirr, Arainn, Co Galway, tel +(99) 75008.

For regular information on training opportunities in Ireland see the quarterly magazine *Archaeology Ireland* (0790–982x), which also contains regular information of interest to **teachers**, including lists of events. See for example the 16-page Education Supplement included in its autumn 1993 issue (vol. 7.3).

The **Discovery Programme Ltd** (13–15 Hatch Street, Dublin 2, tel Dublin 661 3111 ext 3144) is developing a range of teaching materials related to the sites it is exploring.

Excavation preliminaries and conduct

This sub-section contains:
Evaluations and safety requirements
Survey and reconnaissance (with journals, bibliographies and books)
Excavation techniques
Drawing, recording and photography

Colour charts and other aids for soil and pottery examination
Post-excavation processes (including on-site conservation and archive preparation)

EVALUATIONS AND SAFETY REQUIREMENTS

This part includes procedures for formal evaluations (environmental impact assessment and the like) and requirements for safe field archaeology. For technical details of survey operations see under Survey/ Reconnaissance below.

For **Ireland**, it is important to realise that no excavation may be carried out there, whether north or south of the border, without a licence obtained from the relevant authority/ies (which will require firm evidence of competence in the field). In **Northern Ireland** this authority is the Environment and Heritage Service: Historic Monuments and Buildings (5–33 Hill Street, Belfast BT1 2LA, tel Belfast 235000). In the **Republic**, following the National Monuments Amendment Act 1994, two authorities must now be approached: the National Monuments Service, Office of Public Works (51 St Stephen's Green, Dublin 2, tel Dublin 661 3111), and also the Irish Antiquities Division of the National Museum of Ireland, Kildare Street, Dublin 2 (tel Dublin 661 8811).

See also Section 6.6 Legislation and planning.

Books and other references

***ACAO (comp David Baker et al), *Model briefs and specifications for archaeological assessments and field evaluations*. [s l]: ACAO, 1993, 24 p. 0 9510695 1 9. (Obtain from Bedford County Planning Office, County Hall, Bedford MK42 9AP.)

***Allen, J L, Andrews, W H and Holt, A St John, *Health and safety in field archaeology*. [s l]: SCAUM, 2 edn 1992, viii, 55 p. 0 9511407 0 1 pb.
Essential guide which covers: a roundup of health and safety law; excavations; plant, equipment and tools; welfare facilities; health hazards; offices; reporting of injuries, diseases and dangerous occurrences; substances hazardous to health; asbestos; noise.

Archaeological investigations; code of practice for mineral operators. New edn 1991. (Obtain from CBI, Centre Point, 103 New Oxford Street, London WC1A 1DU, tel 0171 379 7400)

***BADLG, *Code of practice of the British*

Archaeologists' and Developers' Liaison Group. 1991 or later edn: obtain from British Property Federation, 35 Catherine Place, London SW1E 6DY. (Model agreements also obtainable.)

Biddle, M, on practical problems of PPG 16, see Section 6.7 Archaeological heritage management.

Carrington, P (ed), *Evaluations in rescue archaeology: PPG16 three years on.* Chester Archaeol Service occas pap, 1, 1993, iv, 21 p. 1 872587 02 x pb.

*Carver, Martin and Sheldon, David, 'The innocent archaeologist in court, or A bad year at Earl Bottom', in *Field archaeologist*, 17, 1992, pp 329–32.
A witty, dreadful warning of the legal disasters that could befall the unwary archaeologist.

Darvill, T, on valuing Britain's archaeological resource, see Section 6.7 Archaeological heritage management; where also is Darvill et al, gazetteer of assessments 1982–91.

— and Atkins, Meryl, *Regulating archaeological work by contract.* Inst Fld Archaeol techn pap, 8, 1991, 16 p. 0 948393 08 4 pb.
Offers guidance on drawing up contracts, whether for comprehensive development agreement or for particular archaeological operations. Includes a model contract.

— and Gerrard, C, *Evaluating archaeological sites: the Cotswold Trust approach.* Cotswold Archaeol Trust annu rev, 2, 1990. (Not available to compiler.)

Garratt-Frost, Stephen, *The law and burial archaeology.* IFA techn pap, 11, 1992, 16 p, bibl. 0 948393 11 4 pb.
Appraises the current situation, with appendices on applying for licences, procedures relating to ecclesiastical jurisdiction, and Scottish differences.

Institute of Field Archaeologists, *Code of approved practice for the regulation of contractual arrangements in field archaeology.* Birmingham: IFA, By-law 1991, 6 p.
Offers guidance on professional conduct, with particular reference to work carried out as part of development controlled by the planning process. (This and the next item are both set out within the current IFA Directory of Members.)

—, *The IFA Code of conduct.* Birmingham: Inst Fld Archaeol, By-Law 1993.

IFA also publishes the following (all 1994):
Standard and guidance for archaeological desk-based assessments
Standard and guidance for archaeological watching briefs
Standard and guidance for archaeological field evaluations
Draft standard and guidance for archaeological excavations.

[Keene, D J and others], 'The use of documentary sources by the archaeologist', British Records Ass symposium published in *Archives*, 13, 1978, pp 196–215.
Includes papers by (as well as Keene), B J N Edwards, Brian S Smith, G G Simpson, and a record of a discussion on 'The preservation and use of archaeological excavation reports and records'.

McGill, G, Building on the past, see Section 6.6 Legislation and planning.

National Monuments Advisory Council [of Irish Republic], *Guidelines for planning authorities, developers and archaeologists: urban archaeology guidelines.* Dublin: NMAC, 1989, 12 p.

Olivier, Adrian, *Safety in archaeological fieldwork.* CBA prac handb archaeol, 6, 1989, 36 p. 0 906780 80 2 pb.
General principles, fieldwork in various environments, buildings, working abroad.

Ralston, Ian and Thomas, Roger (eds), *Environmental assessment and archaeology: papers presented to the 6th Annual Conference of IFA, April 1992.* IFA occas pap, 5, 1993, viii, 36 p. 0 048393 87 4 pb.

Swain, Hedley (ed), *Competitive tendering in archaeology: papers presented at a one-day conference in June 1990.* Hertford: Rescue and SCAUM, 1991, 56 p. 0 903789 14 0 pb.
Includes IFA guidelines, a model specification, and an English Heritage statement.

SURVEY AND RECONAISSANCE
Journals
Archaeological prospection (1075–2196). 1994–. 2/yr. Chichester: Wiley
Geoarchaeology (0883–6353). 1986–. 6/yr. New York: Wiley

BIBLIOGRAPHY

Petrie, Lyn et al (eds), *GIS in archaeology: an annotated bibliography. Sydney Univ Archaeol Methods Ser*, 1, 1994?/5, ?p, index. 0 86758 965 5.

Not available to compiler: said to contain c 350 references on Geographical Information Systems, mostly from archaeological literature and dealing with applications; theory; overview.

BOOKS

This can only be a small selection from a wealth of material on the preliminary work for and conduct of an excavation.

Aston, M and Rowley, T, *Landscape archaeology: an introduction to fieldwork techniques on post-Roman landscapes.* Newton Abbot: David and Charles, 1974, 217 p, bibl, index. 0 7153 6670 X.

Bailey, R N, Cambridge, E and Briggs, H D, *Dowsing and church archaeology.* Wimborne: Intercept, 1988, xv, 192 p, bibl, index. 0 946707 13 8.
Cites numerous instances in the north of England where features suggested by the unconventional technique of dowsing were confirmed by excavation, although some results were negative. Ten-page bibliography.

Bettess, Fred, *Surveying for archaeologists.* Durham: Univ Durham, 2 rev edn 1992, x, 136 p, short bibl, index. 0 905096 09 6 pb.
The new edn includes a chapter on EDM (electronic distance measurement).

Brooke, C J, *Ground-based remote sensing. IFA techn pap*, 7, 1989, 8 p, bibl. 0 948393 07 6 pb.
On photographic survey techniques for recovering non-visible information from buildings and archaeological sites.

Brown, A E, *Fieldwork for archaeologists and local historians.* London: Batsford, 1987, 159 p, bibl, index. 0 7134 4841 5 hb, 0 7134 4842 3 pb.

Clark, Anthony, *Seeing beneath the soil: prospecting methods in archaeology.* London: Batsford, 1990, 176 p, bibl, glossary, index. 0 7134 5858 5. (Also a 1996 revision.)

Cocke, T et al on recording a church, see subsection below on Drawing (etc).

Crawford, O G S, *Archaeology in the field.* London: Phoenix, 4 rev impression, 1960, 280 p, bibl, index.

Classic work by one of the fathers of archaeological fieldwork.

David, Andrew (comp), *Geophysical survey in archaeological field evaluation.* Free from EH Ancient Monuments Lab.
Guidelines for developers, planners and archaeological geophysicists on: standards for conduct and reporting; choice of survey type; good practice.

English Heritage Geophysical Survey Database: see *Archaeol prospection*, 1.1, 1994, pp 71–2.
Experimental project to put the last 25 years of AML survey data on ORACLE, so as to facilitate desktop evaluations and allow the monitoring of country-wide survey.

Farrar, Raymond, *Survey by prismatic compass, with an appendix on earthwork profiles by clinometer. CBA prac handb archaeol*, 2, rev edn 1987, 24 p. 0 906780 72 1 pb.
On one of the simplest surveying techniques.

Gaffney, Chris et al, *The use of geophysical techniques in archaeological evaluations. IFA techn pap*, 9, 1991, 12 p. 0 948393 09 2 pb.
Introductory paper indicating limitations and suitability for specific situations; also brief discussion of sampling, data display and legal points.

Gaffney, V and Tingle, M, *The Maddle Farm Project: an integrated survey of prehistoric and Roman landscapes on the Berkshire Downs. BARBS*, 200, 1989, ix, 262 p. 0 86054 604 7 pb.
Thorough landscape survey of changing settlement patterns.

Gurney, D A, *Phosphate analysis of soils: a guide for the field archaeologist. IFA techn pap*, 3, 1985, 8 p. 0 948393 02 6 pb.

Haselgrove, Colin et al (eds), *Archaeology from the ploughsoil: studies in the collection and interpretation of field survey data.* Sheffield: Dept Archaeol Hist Univ Sheffield, 1985, v, 119 p, bibl, index. 0 906090 24 5 pb.
Symposium papers on how to make the best use of the valuable archaeological resource that is the topsoil.

Hogg, A H A, *Surveying for archaeologists and other fieldworkers.* London: Croom Helm, 1980, 315 p, index. 0 85664 767 5 hb, 0 7099 0185 2 pb.
Much fuller than Bettess (above), but the chain

methods advocated are now only used by those with no access to electronic survey equipment. Also includes methods for 'rough surveys'.

Joukowsky, Martha, *A complete manual of field archaeology: tools and techniques of field work for archaeologists*. Englewood Cliffs, NJ: Prentice Hall, 1980, x, 630 p, bibl, index. 0 13 162164 5 hb, 0 13 162156 4 pb.
Entered here for completeness, although opinions differ on its usefulness in the British/Irish situation, despite the presence of some examples from Old World archaeology.

Leach, Peter, *The surveying of archaeological sites*. London: Institute of Archaeology Publns, 1988 (repr 1994 with improved illustrations), 46 p. 1 873132 35 2 pb.
Includes buildings.

Ordnance Survey, *Field archaeology in Great Britain*. Southampton: OS, 5 edn 1973, 184 p, bibl, index. 0 319 00022 2 pb.
Highly influential in its time, and still a useful primer, even though out of date in many respects. An earlier edn (1963) may also be found: it gave grid references for a large number of sites.

Palmer, Rog and Cox, Chris, *Uses of aerial photography in archaeological evaluations*. IFA techn pap, 12, 1993, 12 p. 0 948393 12 2 pb.

Schofield, A J (ed), *Interpreting artefact scatters: contributions to ploughzone archaeology*. Oxbow monogr, 4, 1991, v, 151 p, bibl, index. 0 946897 25 5 pb.
Contains 12 papers in four sections, from research design through landscape processes to presentation of results.

Scollar, I et al, *Archaeological prospecting and remote sensing*. Cambridge: CUP (= *Topics in remote sensing*, 2), 1990, 674 p, bibl, index. 0 521 32050 X.
Technical details for those trained in physical sciences; first chapter useful to all archaeologists.

Spoerry, Paul (ed), *Geoprospection in the archaeological landscape [papers from a 1989 conference in Bournemouth]*. Oxbow monogr, 18, 1992, 154 p, bibl. 0 946897 42 5 pb.
Ten papers on new techniques and on whole-landscape study.

Welfare, Humphrey and Mercer, Roger (eds),

'Archaeological field survey in the 1990s', in *Field archaeologist*, 12, 1990, pp 202–10
Brief statements from all the principal bodies concerned in Britain and N Ireland: the Royal Commissions, National Trust, Forestry Commission, English Heritage, Cadw, and Historic Scotland.

See also references to soils in Section 6.14 Landscape.

EXCAVATION TECHNIQUES

Barber, J (ed), *Interpreting stratigraphy*. Edinburgh: AOC (Scotl), 1993, 75 p. 0 9519344 2 2 pb.

Barker, Philip A, *Techniques of archaeological excavation*. London: Batsford, rev edn 1993, 285 p, bibl, index. 0 7134 7169 7.
The 'bible' for many, by one of our very finest excavators.

—, *Understanding archaeological excavation*. London: Batsford, 1986, 190 p, bibl, glossary, index. 0 7134 3631 X hb, 0 7134 3632 8 pb.
On the formation of sites, development of techniques for recovery, pre-excavation research etc.

Bell, M, Fowler, P J and Hillson, S W (eds), *The experimental earthwork project 1960–1992. CBA res rep*, 100, forthcoming 1996.
This will be the first report for nearly 30 years on this pioneering experiment to investigate the way in which the archaeological record is formed and how buried materials change and decay. Two earthworks were built, at Overton Down, Wilts (on chalk) and Wareham Heath, Dorset (on acidic sandy soil) and sampled at intervals thereafter, providing valuable information to assist interpretation on archaeological sites. (The first report on the Overton Down earthwork was edited by P A Jewell in 1963.)

Biddle, Martin, 'Site recording, phasing, and processing the finds', in M Biddle (ed), *Object and economy in medieval Winchester* (Clarendon Press, 1990), pp 9–23.
A classic site where recording was based on Wheelerian principles, adapted for urban Winchester and adding a regular 'viewing' of all the finds trays to provide a strong measure of quality control.

Canti, Matthew, *Particle size analysis: a revised interpretation guide for excavators*. Anc Mon Lab rep, 1/91.

Central Archaeology Service (English Heritage, Fort Cumberland): new field manual reportedly in preparation.

Courty, M, Goldberg, P and Macphail, R, *Soils and micromorphology in archaeology*. Cambridge: CUP, 1990, xx, 344 p, bibl, index. 0 521 32419 X.
Reference handbook for archaeologists and environmentalists; includes case study on 'dark earth'. *See also more about soils on p.231–2 below and also in Section 6.14 Landscape.*

Coy, Jennie, *First aid for animal bones*. Hertford: Rescue, 1978, 40 p, bibl. 0 903789 07 8 pb (OP).
How to collect bones during excavation and prepare them for specialist examination.

Fasham, P J, *Groundwater pumping techniques for excavation. IFA techn pap*, 1, 1984, 4 p. 0 948393 00 9 pb.

Hunter, John, Roberts, Charlotte and Martin, Anthony (eds), *Studies in crime: an introduction to forensic archaeology*. London: Batsford, 1996, 174 p, bibl, index. 0 7134 7901 9.
How to locate buried (human) remains and achieve the maximum recovery of evidence, with particular reference to police investigations. Includes use of DNA and other techniques for obtaining additional evidence.

Levitan, B, *Excavations at West Hill Uley, 1979: the sieving and sampling programme*. Bristol: *Western Archaeol Trust occas pap*, 10, 1982, 32 p. 0 904918 12 2 pb.
Results of a designed comparison between sieving and manual recovery.

Payton, Robert (ed), *Retrieval of objects from archaeological sites*. Denbigh: Archetype, 1992, vii, 166 p, bibl. 1 873132 30 1.
Some dozen contributions to a seminar covering situations in which conservators are involved, eg lifting of grave goods, Roman floor and wall structures, kilns, timber structures and boats, etc.

Pryor, Francis, *Earthmoving on open archaeological sites. IFA techn pap*, 4, 1986, 11 p. 0 948393 03 3 pb.
On the use of mechanical excavators.

Webster, Graham, *Practical archaeology: an introduction to archaeological fieldwork and excavation*. London: A and C Black, 2 edn 1974, xii, 164 p. 0 7136 1179 0.

Influential in its day but now over twenty years old.

DRAWING, RECORDING AND PHOTOGRAPHY

This section lists books about drawing and photographing excavation plans and sections, and finds; some cartographic materials are also included. The relevant journal is *Graphic archaeology*, the journal of the Association of Archaeological Illustrators and Surveyors (1351–9175, 1988–); published by AAI&S, c/o University of Exeter, Dept of History and Archaeology, Queen's Building, The Queen's Drive, Exeter EX4 4QH. AAI&S can also supply a list of courses in archaeological illustration currently available at various institutions. Manuals on the recording of historic buildings are entered in Section 6.18 Vernacular and general architecture, where that seems more appropriate.

Addington, Lucile R, *Lithic illustration: drawing flaked stone artifacts for publication*. Chicago/London: Univ Chicago Press, 1986, xviii, 139 p, bibl, glossary, index. 0 226 00634 4 hb, 0 226 00635 2 pb.
Gives conventions, symbols and so on, with examples (USA-based).

Adkins, L and R A, *Archaeological illustration*. Cambridge: CUP (Cambridge Manuals in Archaeology), 1989, xv, 259 p, bibl, index. 0 521 35478 1.
All aspects of how to illustrate, with both good and bad practice shown.

Allen, Steven J, *The illustration of wooden artefacts: an introduction and guide to the depiction of wooden objects. AAI&S techn pap*, 11, 1994, 24 p, bibl, glossary. 0 9516721 3 4 pb.

Cocke, Thomas et al, *Recording a church: an illustrated glossary. CBA prac handb archaeol*, 7, 3 edn 1996, 51 p. 1 872414 56 7 pb.

Dallas, R A, *Photogrammetry and rectified photography. AAI&S techn pap*, 6, 1981, (reprinted articles with various paginations).

Dorrell, Peter G, *Photography in archaeology and conservation*. Cambridge: CUP, 2 edn 1994, xvi, 266 p, bibl, index. 0 521 45534 0 hb, 0 521 45554 5 pb.
Comprehensive guide to work in the field and indoors.

Friendship-Taylor, D E et al, *Recent research in*

archaeological footwear. AAI&S techn pap, 8, 1987, 49 p.
Mainly on how to draw shoe-parts.

Griffiths, Nick et al, *Drawing archaeological finds: a handbook*. London: *Inst Archaeol UCL occas pap*, 13, 1990, 120 p, bibl. 1 873132 00 X pb.
From equipment and materials to the finished artwork; suggests various techniques for translating 3-dimensional objects to two dimensions.

Harris, Edward C, *Principles of archaeological stratigraphy*. London: Academic Press, 2 edn 1989, xiv, 170 p, bibl, glossary, index. 0 12 326651 3.
Concepts, techniques, laws of archaeological stratigraphy, plans and sections, phasing, post-excavation analysis etc.

—, Brown, M R (III) and Brown, G J (eds), *Practices of archaeological stratigraphy*. London: Academic Press, 1993, viii, 296 p, bibl, index. 0 12 326445 6.
Contains 17 essays on the development and use of the Harris matrix, using data originating in sites from medieval Europe to Colonial Williamsburg.

Hope-Taylor, B, 'Archaeological draughtsmanship: principles and practice', *Antiquity*, 41, 1967, pp 181–9.
Valuable advice from an eminent illustrator.

Jones, Jeremy, *How to record graveyards*. London: CBA/RESCUE, 3 edn 1984, 39 p, bibl. 0 906780 43 8 pb.

Kenworthy, Mary Anne et al, *Preserving field records: archival techniques for archaeologists and anthropologists*. Philadelphia: Univ Pennsylvania Museum, Univ, 1985, x, 102 p, bibl. 0 934718 72 5.

Lapidary Working Party, *Recording worked stones. CBA prac handb archaeol*, 1, 1987, 47 p, bibl. 0 906780 71 3 pb.
On the handling, cleaning and marking of architectural materials, including guidance on personal safety, record cards, publication, computer records.

Martingell, Hazel and Saville, Alan, *The illustration of lithic artefacts: a guide to drawing stone tools for specialist reports. Lithic Stud Soc occas pap*, 3/*AAI&S techn pap*, 9, 1988, 30 p, bibl. pb.

Practical advice and examples, equipment, materials, etc.

Parsons, David, *Churches and chapels: investigating places of worship. CBA prac handb archaeol*, 8, 1989, 78 p, bibl. 0 906780 86 1 pb.
A study aid on fabric, fixtures and fittings, documentary evidence, and recording.

Philo, C and Swann, A, *Preparation of art work for publication. IFA techn pap*, 10/*AAI&S techn pap*, 4, 1992, 12 p.

Renow, Sidney, *Vertical archaeological photography. IFA techn pap*, 2, 1985, 4 p. 0 948393 01 7 pb.

Stopford, Jenny, *Recording medieval floor tiles. CBA prac handb archaeol*, 10, 1990, iv, 46 p, 1 872414 03 6 pb.

Tufte, Edward R, *The visual display of quantitative information*. Cheshire (Conn): Graphics Press, 1983, 197 p, footnotes, index. No ISBN.
How to make the most effective presentation of numerical data; a most attractive book in its own right.

Vitoria, Mary, *The archaeological illustrator and the law of copyright. AAI&S techn pap*, 5, [1984], 4 p.

Westman, Andrew (ed), *Archaeological site manual*. London: Mus of London Dept of Urban Archaeol, 3 edn 1994, unnumbered pages in looseleaf binder. 0 904818 40 3.
Guide to compilation of the drawn and written record, based on the single-context recording system. Includes environmental sampling, masonry, timber, skeletons, coffins etc; also photographs and archives.

White, Susan and King, David, *The illustration of excavated window glass: suggestions for methods and materials. AAI&S techn pap*, 10, 1990, 4 pp.

SOIL REFERENCE HANDBOOKS AND COLOUR CHARTS

See also Section 6.14 Landscape, for works on soils by: Bell and Boardman 1992; Courty 1990; Fitzpatrick 1986 and 1993; and Limbrey 1975.

Barham, A F and Macphail, R I (eds), *Archaeological sediments and soils: analysis and interpretation*. London: Inst Archaeol UCL, 1995, 240 p. 0 905853 31 8 pb.
Ten papers from the 1989 AEA conference deal with the analysis, interpretation and manage-

ment of soils, with particular reference to care in their excavation.

Keeley, H M and Macphail, R, *A soil handbook for archaeologists.* Offprinted from *Bull Inst Archaeol Univ London,* 18, 1981, pp 225–44. Includes colour illustrations.

Munsell Soil Color Charts, rev edn 1994. As well as soils, allows user to judge colour of rocks, archaeological specimens, animal skins, and other natural products in this colour range. Looseleaf binder with set of nine charts containing permanently mounted matte colour chips (hues 10R – 5Y plus Gley), colour-name diagrams, instructions, masks. Obtainable from D G Colour Ltd, 121 Bouverie Avenue South, Salisbury, Wilts SP2 8EA (tel 01722 323840, fax 01722 414341).

CBA/RESCUE Pottery colour chart, obtainable from RESCUE, 15A Bull Plain, Hertford, Herts SG14 1DX (tel 01992 553377).

There are also German and French versions of colour charts: details given in C R Orton et al, Pottery in archaeology (1993) – listed below.

POST-EXCAVATION PROCESSES (INCLUDING ON-SITE CONSERVATION AND ARCHIVE PREPARATIONS)

*Blake, H and Davey, P (eds), *Guidelines for the processing and publication of medieval pottery from excavations. Report by a working party of the Medieval Pottery Research Group and the Dept of the Environment.* London: DoE (= *DAMHB occas pap,* 5), 1983, 70 p, bibl.

Brinch-Madsen, Helga, *Handbook of field conservation.* [s l]: Roy Danish Acad Fine Arts School of Conservation, 1994, 124 p, bibl. 87 89730 10 0.
Discusses soil as preserver/destroyer; recovery techniques; pottery, glass and stone; metals; organic materials.

**Carver, M O H, *Underneath English towns: interpreting urban archaeology.* London: Batsford, 1987, 160 p, bibl, index. 0 7134 3637 9 hb, 0 7134 3638 7 pb.
Covers the achievements and potential of urban archaeology for the period AD 40–1540, offering many new concepts, new means of graphical representation, and the like.

***Davies, B J, Richardson, B and Tomber, R S, *A dated corpus of early Roman pottery from the City of London (The archaeology of Roman*

London, 5). CBA res rep, 98, 1995, xviii, 283 p, bibl, index. 1 872414 00 1 pb.
Should form the model for Roman pottery reporting: combines former DUA fabric/quantification with the DGLA formalised typology in fabric groups.

Dowman, Elizabeth, *Conservation in field archaeology.* London: Methuen, 1970, ix, 170 p, bibl. 0 416 16330 0.
On-site techniques for non-specialists.

Ferguson, L and Murray, D, *The preparation, curation and storage of archaeological documentary archives. IFA techn pap* (forthcoming).

Fulford, M G and Huddleston, K, *The current state of Romano-British pottery studies: a review for English Heritage.* London: English Heritage, 1991, 59 p, bibl. 1 85074 340 1 pb.

Historic Scotland, *A policy statement for the allocation and disposal of artefacts.* Edinburgh: HS, 1994.

Hodges, H M W (ed), *In-situ archaeological conservation.* Los Angeles: Getty Conservation Inst, 1993, viii, 205 p, bibls. 0 941103 03 X.

Hunter, Kate, *Excavated artefacts and conservation: UK sites. UKIC conserv guidelines,* 1, rev edn 1988, 8 p. No ISBN.
Brief manual of procedures for ensuring the preservation and recovery of information potentially available in archaeological objects.

Institute of Field Archaeologists, Finds Special Interest Group:
    Guidelines for finds work (ed V Buteux)
    Directory of finds study and special interest groups (ed V Buteux)
Offer standards for good practice in the administration and implementation of finds work.

**McKinley, J I and Roberts, C, *Excavation and post-excavation treatment of cremated and inhumed human remains. IFA techn pap,* 13, 1993, 12 p, bibl. 0 948393 13 0 pb.

***Orton, Clive, Tyers, Paul, and Vince, Alan, *Pottery in archaeology.* Cambridge: CUP (Cambridge Manuals in Archaeology), 1993, xvii, 269 p, bibl, index. 0 521 25715 8 hb, 0 521 44597 3 pb.
Well-received and indispensable technical manual covering the history and potential of pottery studies, a guide to processing and recording, and themes in ceramic studies.

**Owen, Janet (ed) for Soc Mus Archaeol, *Towards an accessible archaeological archive: the transfer of archaeological archives to museums: guidelines for use in England, Northern Ireland, Scotland and Wales*. Winchester: Soc Mus Archaeol, 1995, ii, 78 p, bibl. 1 871855 09 8 pb.
Papers argue the need to incorporate long-term archive needs into the archive creation process, and to ensure more efficient use of resources. Also deals with copyright, ownership rights, gifts of title, role of the museum archaeologist in society, etc, explaining the inter-county differences as well as enunciating legal, ethical and procedural principles.

Prehistoric Ceramics Research Group (double volume):
The study of later prehistoric pottery: general policies and guidelines for analysis and publication. PCRG occas pap, 1 and 2, 1995, 61 p. 0 9518489 2 5 pb (reissue of previously separate parts from 1991 and 1992).

***Rice, Prudence M, *Pottery analysis: a sourcebook*. Chicago: Univ Chicago Press, 1987, xxiv, 559 p, bibl, glossary, index. 0 226 71118 8.
Another essential work on the properties of raw materials, history of potting, characterisation, definitions, etc.

Roman Finds Group and Finds Research Group AD 700–1700, *Guidelines for the preparation of site archives and assessment for all finds other than clay vessels – a survival guide to MAP 2*. RFG/FRG, 1992 (not seen).

Sease, Catherine, *A conservation manual for the field archaeologist*. Los Angeles: UCLA monogr archaeol, 3 edn 1994, v, 114 p, bibl, index. 0 917956 82 6.
New edn of a well-established work.

Study Group for Roman Pottery, *Draft guidelines for the archiving of Roman pottery*. SGRP, 1994 (not seen).

***Walker, Kirsten, *Guidelines for the preparation of excavation archives for long-term storage*. London: UKIC Archaeol Section, 1990, 29 p. 1 871656 06 0 pb.

Watkinson, David (ed), *First aid for finds*. [Hertford]: Rescue/UKIC, 2 edn 1987, 114 p, index. 0 903789 13 2 (new edn in preparation).
Looseleaf binder with polyart paper: how to cope with objects of various materials, lifting of fragile objects, list of suppliers.

Young, C J (ed), *Guidelines for the processing and publication of Roman pottery from excavations*. London: DoE (= DAMHB occas pap, 4), 1980, 40 p, bibl.
Now superseded by practices demonstrated in (eg) Davies above.

(The CBA Handbook of scientific aids and evidence for archaeologists (1970) has been totally superseded by other works now.)

Reporting, publishing, interpreting

The excavator has not completed work until a full archive has been prepared and a publishable report completed; often an interpretation for the general public is also required. This sub-section offers some pointers to help with those tasks under the following heads:
Preparation of archaeological reports for publication
Publishing methods (including desktop publication, indexing and copyright)
Site interpretation and presentation.

It is noticeable that microfiche, once thought to be the saviour of archaeological budgets, is much less used now and greater reliance is placed on the site archive (which may or may not be readily accessible). See Owen on archives in the previous sub-section, and also the thoughtful piece by Hills below.

For monograph authors or publishers requiring an index, bear in mind that computers can only 'index' at a very crude and unsatisfactory level, usually producing a concordance of words rather than a true retrieval aid. Far better to engage an experienced archaeological indexer using computer-assisted human intelligence, for which the **Archaeological Indexers' Panel** may be consulted: L and R Adkins, Longstone Lodge, Aller, Langport, Somerset TA10 0QT (tel 01458 250075). They may also be able to find archaeologically experienced copy-editors or proofreaders; otherwise apply to **Society of Freelance Editors and Proofreaders** (SFEP, founded 1988), Mermaid House, 1 Mermaid Court, London SE1 1HR (tel 0171 403 5141).

Anyone publishing a work should 1. obtain from Whitakers (12 Dyott Street, London WC1A 1DF) an ISBN (International Standard Book Number) which ensures entry in the lists and catalogues which many librarians use for deciding on purchases, 2. comply with the Legal Deposit Requirements (see note at end of this section). If starting a new journal, apply to British Library Document Supply Centre for an ISSN (International Standard Serial Number): address BLDSS, Boston Spa, Wetherby, W Yorks LS23 7BQ. These numbers are not a bureaucratic ploy: they ensure that your publication is readily locatable all over the world.

PREPARATION OF ARCHAEOLOGICAL REPORTS FOR PUBLICATION

Adkins, L and R A, Talking archaeology, see under Interpretation below.

**Alcock, L, 'Excavation and publication: some comments', Proc Soc Antiq Scotl, 109, 1977–8 (1980), pp 1–6.
An early attempt to grapple with the increasing costs and complexity of publishing excavation reports.

**Ashmore, Patrick, 'Historic Scotland's requirements of the (Data) Structure Report', in J W Barber (ed), Interpreting stratigraphy (AOC Scotland, 1993, pp 69–71).
The Structure Report is the contractually required immediate product of a Historic Scotland-funded excavation, providing a narrative and lists of contexts etc which will guide the planning of post-excavation work, including archiving and finds dispersal.

Carver, Martin et al, 'Archaeological publication, archives and collections: towards a national policy', published as insert in Brit archaeol news, 7.2, March 1992.
Attempts to set out problems needing solutions, arising from the increased pressure of excavation, publication and finds storage.

***CBA Publications Committee, Signposts for archaeological publication: a guide to good practice in the presentation and printing of archaeological periodicals and monographs. London: CBA, 3 edn 1991, 90 p, bibl. 1 872414 04 4 pb.
Third edition of the standard work, covering every stage of the process from presentation and estimates through production to deposit copies and sales. Includes the CBA's notes for authors; notes on preparation of microfiche; standard list of abbreviations for titles of current periodicals and series; and guidelines for publishing scientific contributions to archaeological reports.

*Cunliffe, B (chmn), The publication of archaeological excavations: the report of a joint working party of the Council for British Archaeology and the Department of the Environment. London: Dept of Environment, 1983, ii, 11 p.
The 'Cunliffe Report', second attempt (see under Frere below) to introduce a rationale into the publication process.

English Heritage, Academic and specialist publications: preparing your illustrations for publication. nd, available free from English Heritage.
Intended primarily for English Heritage's own Archaeological report series, but applicable to others; gives guidance on page size, foldouts, captions, maps/plans/sections, maximising use of space for artwork, use of second colour, photographs (including colour), artefact drawings.

Frere, S S (chmn), Principles of publication in rescue archaeology. Report by a working party of the Ancient Monuments Board for England, Committee for Rescue Archaeology. London: Dept of Environment, 1975.
The 'Frere Report', first attempt to rationalise the publication process (see also Cunliffe above).

Grinsell, L V, Rahtz, P and Williams, D P, The preparation of archaeological reports. London: Baker, 2 edn 1974, 105 p, bibl, index.
A valuable manual in its day, covering all stages in the preparation of a report, this book has been largely overtaken by the complexities of modern excavations. If used, it should be read in conjunction with the Frere and Cunliffe reports (see above) and Hills (next item below).

Hills, Catherine, 'The dissemination of information', in J Hunter and I Ralston (eds), Archaeological resource management in the UK (1993), pp 215–24.
A wide-ranging and thoughtful piece which analyses the difficulties experienced nowadays in publishing archaeological reports: 'somehow, somewhere an awful lot of basic, boring information has to be both on record and properly digested to produce a clearly argued and fully supported story.'

Owen, J, on accessible archives, see entry in subsection on post-excavation processes (above).

Philo, Chris and Swann, Andy (for AAIS), Preparation of artwork for publication. IFA techn pap, 10, 1992, 12 p. 0 948393 10 0 pb.

General guidance, description of printing process and printers' requirements.

***Shepherd, I A G, 'Editorial: The Society of Antiquaries of Scotland: a policy for publication', *Proc Soc Antiq Scotl*, 113, 1983, pp vii-xi
Explains the Society's policy for two-level simultaneous publication of excavation reports, with microfiche supplementing print.

PUBLISHING METHODS (INCLUDING DESKTOP PUBLISHING, INDEXING AND COPYRGHT)

All editors should consult the guidelines on serial (journal) publications listed under UK Serials Group below. A journal useful for the general background of publishing, and which occasionally has articles applicable to the archaeological situation, is *Learned publishing*, Journal of the Association of Learned and Professional Society Publishers (0953-1513, 1988-; former title *Bulletin of ALPSP*, 0260-9428). There is also *Scholarly publishing* (0036-634x) from Univ Toronto Press (name changed in 1994 to *Journal of scholarly publishing*).

Adkins, Lesley and Roy, 'First catch your indexer', *Learned publishing*, 6.3, July 1993, pp 30-1.
How to find, and treat, indexers!

Aslib guide to copyright (eds R A Wall and C Oppenheim). London: Aslib, the Association for Information Management, 1994 and 1995. Looseleaf binder in three releases and 15 sections. 0 85142 311 6.
Includes a good bibliography.

Baron, D N (ed), *Units, symbols and abbreviations: a guide for biological and medical editors and authors*. London: Roy Soc Medicine Press, 5 edn 1994, 64 p, bibl. 1 85315 217 X pb.
Useful for any work involving scientific symbols, eg weights and measures; also gives basic proof correction marks.

Clark, Charles, *Photocopying from books and journals: a guide for all users of copyright literary works*. London: British Copyright Council, 1990, 12 p. 0 901737 06 2 pb.
This is just one of several works on what may and may not be done at the photocopier.

Dorner, Jane, *Writing on disk: an A-Z handbook of terms, tips and techniques for authors and publishers*. Hatfield: John Taylor Book Ventures, 1992, 240 p, software list, index. 1 87224 11 X hb, 1 87224 12 8 pb spiral-bound.

Hart's Rules for compositors and readers at the

University Press, Oxford (last edn was 39th, reprinted 1995). 0 19 212983 X.

Lavell, C, 'Problems of archaeological indexing', *The Indexer*, 12, 1981, pp 175-84.
Indexing of publications is too often neglected, or at best left to the last minute, whereas responsibility for publishing should also include providing the means for easy retrieval of all that costly information. This paper should help those who consult indexes as well as those who construct them. *See also* Trial trench *below*.

McAllister, S, [review of available DTP software], *Learned publishing*, 6.3, July 1993, pp 63-71.
Reviews three popular programs: Aldus Pagemaker, Timeworks Publisher 2, and QuarkXpress.

St Aubyn, John, 'Questions of photocopying and the CLA', *Learned publishing*, 6.3, 1993, pp 3-7.
Explains how publishers can mandate the PLS (Publishers' Licensing Society) to allow the Copyright Licensing Agency to collect copying fees on their behalf.

Society of Authors: Quick Guide series, for example:
   1. *Copyright and moral rights* (1996)
   8. *Publishing contracts* (1995)
(84 Drayton Gardens, London SW10 9SB)

Taylor, John and Heale, Shirley, *Editing for desktop publishing: a guide to writing and editing on the personal computer*. Hatfield: John Taylor Book Ventures, 1992, 205 p, bibl, glossary, index. 1 871224 04 7 spiral bound.
Describes what editing is, house style, preparing text and illustrations for printing, makeup, budget, etc.

Trial trench: a newsletter for archaeological indexers (0969-1502). 1992-. Published approximately yearly under the auspices of the Society of Indexers and edited by Cherry Lavell.
Offers views, advice, problems, reviews and useful references, as much for editors who commission indexes as for the indexers themselves; includes a copy-editor's corner.

***UK Serials Group, *Serial publications: guidelines for good practice in publishing printed journals and other serial publications*. Witney: UKSG, 1994, 48 p, refs, index. 0 906148 10 3 pb.
Essential for editors of county and other jour-

nals: covers all aspects of the information that should be presented to readers – changes of title, numbering and dating of publications, bibliographies, spine information, index cumulation and a host of other matters.

Wall, Raymond A, *Copyright made easier*. London: Aslib, 1993, 393 p, bibl, index. 0 85142 310 8 pb.

SITE INTERPRETATION AND PRESENTATION
Journals
Environmental interpretation: the bulletin of the Centre for Environmental Interpretation (0950–0995). 1980–. 3/yr.

Interpretation (0265–3664 OR 0964–6337, title varies: eg *Heritage interpretation; Interpretation journal*). 1975–. 3/yr. Society for the Interpretation of Britain's Heritage

Books
Adkins, L and R, *Talking archaeology: a handbook for lecturers and organisers. CBA prac handb archaeol*, 9, 1990, vi, 42 p. 0 906780 87 x pb.
How to communicate and handle projection equipment (etc) effectively.

[Aldridge, Don], *Site interpretation: a practical guide*. Edinburgh: Scot Tourist Board, 1993, no ISBN.

Ambrose, Timothy (ed), *on presenting Scotland's story*, see entry in Section 4.8 Museum directories.

Binks, Gillian, Dyke, J and Dagnall, P, *Visitors welcome: a manual on the presentation and interpretation of archaeological excavations*. London: HMSO, 1988, 162 p, bibl, index. 0 11 701210 6 pb.
Covers all aspects, from costs of a visitor centre to video productions, with emphasis on effective presentation at low cost.

De Cicco, Gabriel, 'A public relations primer', in *American antiquity*, 53, 1988, pp 840–56.
How to handle press and public; written for the USA but much of it universally applicable.

Fowler, Peter, *The past in contemporary society: then, now*. London: Routledge, 1993, xvii, 192 p, bibl, index. 0 415 06726 x hb, 0 415 07130 5 pb.
Discusses the British cult of nostalgia and the concomitant rise of the heritage industry.

Hodder, Ian et al (eds), *Interpreting archaeology:*

finding meaning in the past. London: Routledge, 1995, ix, 275 p, bibl, index. 0 415 07330 8.
Papers discuss philosophical issues; origins of meaning; interpreting, writing and presenting the past; archaeology and history; material culture, etc.

Hughes, Mike and Rowley, Linda (eds), *The management and presentation of field monuments*. Oxford: Oxford Univ Dept External Stud, 1986, 133 p, bibl. 0 903736 21 7 pb.
Papers from a conference: some general considerations (such as legal aspects) and some regional or case studies.

Parker Pearson, Mike, 'Visitors welcome', in J Hunter and I Ralston (eds), *Archaeological resource management in the UK* (1993), pp 225–31.
Offers 14 discussion points on how we should be presenting archaeology to the public.

Southworth, Edmund (ed), *The interpretation of archaeological sites and monuments: Society of Museum Archaeologists . . . annual conference, Salisbury 1985. Museum archaeologist*, 12, 1988, iv, 33 p. 1 871855 00 4 pb.

—, *Ready for the new millennium? Futures for museum archaeology. Museum archaeologist*, 17, 73 p, bibls. 1 871855 04 7 pb.

Uzzell, David (ed), *Heritage interpretation*. London: Belhaven Press (Pinter) 1989, 2 vols.
1. *Natural and built environment*, xv, 237 p, bibl, index. 1 85293 077 2.
Contains 27 papers from around the world: includes visible monuments, ruins, and historic buildings still in use.
2. *The visitor experience*, xi, 220 p, bibl, index. 1 85293 078 0.
On the organisation of heritage sites, marketing, funding, education and publication; 24 papers from around the world.

FINALLY: All publishers, no matter how homegrown, have a legal obligation to send one copy of their publications (including one copy of *each* issue of a serial publication) to the Legal Deposit Office, The British Library, Boston Spa, Wetherby, W Yorks LS23 7BY. This must be done within one month of publication. The Agent for the other five copyright libraries (Bodleian, Cambridge University Library, National Libraries of Scotland and of Wales, Trinity College Dublin) may request a further five copies from the publisher, who must comply if so asked.

6.10
Science-based Archaeology

Over the last few decades science-based archaeology has become of fundamental importance to the conduct of most archaeological work; accordingly this section tries to identify the main sources of assistance in fields which may be unfamiliar to many archaeologists. It covers:

Multi-topic treatments of science-based archaeology, and relevant organisations

Physical and chemical examination including dating methods, and radiocarbon, thermoluminescence and archaeomagnetic dating laboratories active in UK

Laboratory conservation

Biological and environmental examination

Computing and statistics.

Within each of those sub-sections, relevant organisations, bibliographies and journals are listed first.

Archaeometry is defined by C W Beck as the application of science and engineering to interpret material retrieved through active archaeological investigation.

For geological and pedological matters see Section 6.14 Landscape; some Quaternary materials will also be found in Section 6.11.1 Quaternary/ Palaeolithic.

Thanks are due to Sebastian Payne for considerable help with this section, but final responsibility is the compiler's alone.

Multi-topic treatments of science-based archaeology, and relevant organisations

Serial bibliography

Art and archaeology technical abstracts (0004-2994). 1955–. Mainly for conservators, but also includes abstracts on dating methods, data and record handling, analysis, archaeometry, site location, site preservation and management, geoarchaeology, environment and archaeozoology. Available online through the bibliographic database BCIN of Conservation Information Network, a joint project of the Getty Conservation Institute and the Department of Canadian Heritage.

Organisations
Ancient Monuments Laboratory, English Heritage, 23 Savile Row, London W1X 1AB, tel 0171 973 3000, fax 0171 973 3330. Provides archaeological science services and advice, and undertakes scientific research (mainly for EH-funded projects). It has branches for Environmental Studies, Conservation and Technology, and Archaeometry, and issues regular abstracts of research projects: *see AML entry below under Books.*

British Museum Department of Scientific Research, London WC1B 3DG, tel (main BM switchboard) 0171 636 1555, fax 0171 323 8276. Head: Dr Sheridan Bowman. Undertakes scientific and computing research, including radiocarbon dating, applicable to understanding the Museum's collections; external work is only undertaken if relevant to current research aims.

COPUS, Committee on the Public Understanding of Science of the Royal Society, Royal Institution, and British Association for the Advancement of Science. This committee was formed to encourage better dissemination of scientific work to the general public; it can sometimes offer small grants to assist projects in the public understanding of science – enquiries to COPUS at the Royal Society, 6 Carlton House Terrace, London SW1Y 5AG.

European Science Foundation: aims to strengthen science through the increased mobility of scientists within Europe. 'ESF Networks' include one on the Palaeolithic Occupation of Europe (set up 1993 to fund three workshops and some discussion meetings aimed at identifying reasons for the human colonisation of Europe). ESF issued in the 1980s four handbooks for archaeologists, treating different aspects of archaeological science: *see entry for ESF under Books below.*

Fund for Applied Science in Archaeology *see Section 4.6 Grants and Awards under British Academy.*

GMPCA, Groupement des Méthodes Pluridisciplinaires Contribuant à l'Archéologie, Université de Rennes 1, Ille-et-Vilaine, France.

PACT (= European Study Group on Physical, Chemical and Mathematical Techniques applied to Archaeology). Founded in 1975 to improve communication between involved scientists. Enquiries to Tony Hackens, 28a ave Léopold, B-1330 Rixensart, Belgium. (1993 info.) *See also Soustelle under Books below.*

Research Laboratory for Archaeology and the History of Art, 6 Keble Road, Oxford OX1 3QJ (tel. 01865 515211, fax 01865 273932). Director: Professor Michael Tite. Founded 1955 to develop scientific techniques for these subjects. Publishes the journal *Archaeometry* (see below). Research topics include chemical analysis, radiocarbon dating, DNA detection in bone, etc.

Science-Based Archaeology Committee (discontinued: see now entry for NERC, Natural Environment Research Council, in Section 4.2 Organisations.)

Society for Archaeological Sciences, c/o R E Taylor (General Secretary), Radiocarbon Laboratory, Dept of Anthropology, Univ California at Riverside, Riverside, CA 92521, USA, tel +(1) 909 787 5521.

JOURNALS

Journal of archaeological science (0305-4403). 1974–. 6/yr. Academic Press. International coverage of the whole range of science-based archaeology.

PACT (0257-8727). 1977–. Irreg. Strasbourg/Rixensart. Publishes conferences and some major monographs, various aspects of science-based archaeology.

Science and archaeology (0586-9668). 1970-91. Ceased.

Science-based archaeology newsletter (available from David Gale at NERC: address given in Section 4.2 Organisations). Indispensable news service for all aspects of the discipline.

BOOKS COVERING MORE THAN ONE ASPECT OF SCIENCE-BASED ARCHAEOLOGY

Allibone, T E (org), *The impact of the natural sciences on archaeology: a joint symposium of the Royal Society and the British Academy*. London: OUP for Brit Acad, 1970, vii, 185 p, bibls. (Also issued as *Phil trans Roy Soc London (B)*, B269, 1970.)
A landmark review of the ways in which scientific studies have altered archaeological perceptions. *For the follow-up conference see Pollard below.*

*Ancient Monuments Laboratory Reports (from 1986) are 6-monthly summaries of recent work done in the English Heritage Laboratory's various sections. The abstracts can be used to request photocopies of the full reports.

Archaeol rev Cambridge, 10.1, Spring 1991 took 'Interpreting archaeological science' as its spe-

cial theme, with eight papers on various aspects. (ISSN 0261-4332.)

'Archaeological Science Review' is a regular feature from 1993 in the *Journal of field archaeology* (US 0093-4690). Edited by Julian Henderson of Sheffield University it replaces the 'Archaeometric Clearing House' (compiled by C W Beck) which ran for 26 issues, between 1975 and 1993, in the same journal.

Brothwell, D R and Higgs, E S (eds), *Science in archaeology: a survey of progress and research*. London: Thames and Hudson, 2 edn 1969, 720 p, bibl, index. 0 500 05011 2 pb.
Classic work, though overtaken in many sections by now.

Budd, P et al (eds), *Archaeological sciences 1989: proceedings of a conference on the application of scientific techniques to archaeology, Bradford, September 1989*. Oxbow monogr, 9, 1991, xviii, 390 p, bibls. 0 946897 29 8 pb.
Entered here as just one example of this regular conference.

CBA Archaeological Science Committee, 'Excavators and archaeological scientists', *Brit archaeol news*, 5, 1990, pp 51-2 and 54.
Guidelines on the relationship between excavators and specialists working on scientific aspects of excavations.

Centre de Recherches Archéologiques, *Notes et monographies techniques*, occasional publications on archaeometry and the like; has contained material on organic and inorganic materials, artefact studies, etc.

European Science Foundation Handbooks for Archaeologists (Strasbourg: ESF)
   1. *Thermoluminescence dating* (G A Wagner et al, 1983)
   2. *Dendrochronological dating* (D Eckstein, 1984)
   3. *Radiocarbon dating* (W G Mook and H T Waterbolk, 1985)
   4. *Archaeobotany* (J Greig et al, 1989)
All these handy introductions are still available (Archetype Books, 31-34 Gordon Square, London WC1H 0PY) but should now be used with care in view of their age. *See also under Verhaeghe below.*

Fletcher, Mike and Lock, Gary, Digging numbers, see entry under Computing and statistics (towards the end of this section).

Hodges, H M W on artefacts, see Section 6.15 Archaeology of industrial processes.

Mellars, Paul (ed for CBA Archaeol Sci Committee), *Research priorities for archaeological science*. London: CBA, 1987, 51 p. o 906780 67 5 pb.
Contributions dealt with 16 main divisions of archaeological science, setting out needs and priorities for the following 5–10 years.

Musty, John, 'Science Diary' regularly in *Current archaeology*, notes selected items of interest.

Phillips, Pat (ed), *The archaeologist and the laboratory*. CBA res rep, 58, 1985, vii, 70 p, bibls, index, microfiche. o 906780 45 4 pb.
Fifteen papers from an Oxford conference in 1983.

Pollard, A M (ed), *New developments in archaeological science: a joint symposium of the Royal Society and the British Academy, February 1991*. Proc Brit Acad, 77, 1992.
Review containing sections on past human environments, artefact studies, food evidence, site survey techniques, human remains. A C Renfrew's summarising remarks (pp 285–93), 'The identity and future of archaeological science', include a 13-point sketch programme for future investigations.

*Soustelle, Jacques and Hackens, Tony, *PACT: European networks of scientific co-operation in the field of physical, chemical, mathematical, and biological techniques applied to archaeology*. [Strasbourg]: PACT, [1988], 16 p.
Describes 17 networks set up to foster cooperation and communication in numerous topics from archaeological wood through building and statuary stone to osteology and underwater archaeology.

Tite, M S, 'Archaeological science – past achievements and future prospects', *Archaeometry*, 33, 1991, pp 139–51.
The professor's inaugural lecture, Oxford 1990, concentrates on dating methods, artefact studies, humans and environment.

Verhaeghe, F (comp), *Archaeology, natural science and technology: the European situation*. Strasbourg: European Science Foundation, 1979, 3 vols.
This early attempt to co-ordinate and focus European efforts in archaeological science listed the relevant institutions by country (111 given

for Britain, including subjects like geology and photogrammetry).

Physical and chemical examination including dating methods

JOURNALS ON SCIENTIFIC DATING, MATERIALS EXAMINATION AND GEOPHYSICAL PROSPECTION

Ancient TL (0735–1348). 1979–. Various publishers: from 1996 is at Laboratoire de Physique Corpusculaire, IN2P3-CNRS, Univ Blaise-Pascal, 63177 Aubière Cedex, France. Technical papers with occasional bibliographies and results of luminescence and electron spin resonance dating.

Archaeological prospection (1075–2196). 1994–. 2/yr. Chichester: Wiley.

Archaeometry (0003–813X). 1958–. 2/yr. Research Laboratory for Archaeology and History of Art, Univ Oxford. Technical papers, mostly on physical and chemical analysis with occasional dendrochronological analysis and tephra.

Archeomaterials (0891–2920). 1986–. 2/yr. Rockville, MD, USA. Mostly physics, with occasional dendrochronological papers.

Berliner Beiträge zur Archäometrie (0344–5081). 1976–. Berlin: Staatliche Museen, Preussischer Kulturbesitz. Physics, chemistry, conservation.

Corpus vitrearum newsletter (0308–2237). Centre Suisse de Recherche et d'Information sur le Vitrail, Romont, Switzerland. Technical information on window glass.

Radiocarbon (0033–8222). 1959–. (Currently) Univ Arizona Dept of Geosciences, Tucson, Arizona, USA. Technical papers and (until vol 36, 1994) date-lists from certain participating laboratories. Now offers only technical articles on radiocarbon.

Revue d'archéometrie (0399–1237). 1977–. Rennes: GMPCA (Groupement des Méthodes Pluridisciplinaires Contribuant à l'Archéologie, Univ de Rennes I).

BIBLIOGRAPHIES

Anon, 'Bibliographie der Deutschsprachigen Literatur zur Archäometrie (1985–9)', in *Berliner Beitr z Archäometrie*, 11, 1992, pp 275–315.
A five-year listing of German-language literature.

Bleck, R-D, *Bibliographie der archäologisch-chemischen Literatur, Beiheft zu Alt-Thüringen*, (Weimar) 1966; also 1971, 269 p.

Brandt, A-C and Riederer, J, 'Die Anfänge der Archäometrie-Literatur im 18. und 19. Jahrhundert', in *Berliner Beitr z Archäometrie*, 3, 1978, pp 162–73.
Valuable retrospective list of about 200 references from 1779 to 1899 on science-based archaeology; mostly German language but with a sprinkling of British and Irish references.

Lewin, S Z and Alexander, S M, 'The composition and structure of natural patinas: I, copper and copper alloys', in *Art archaeol techn abstr*, 6.4, 1967 suppl pp 201–83; 7.1, 1968 suppl pp 279–370.

— and —, 'II, zinc and zinc alloys', and 'III, tin, lead and their alloys', both in *Art archaeol techn abstr*, 7.2, 1968 suppl pp 149–92.

Polach, Dilette, *Radiocarbon dating literature: the first 21 years, 1947–1968. Annotated bibliography*. London: Academic Press, 1988, x, 370 p, bibl, indexes. 0 12 559290 6.
Theory, techniques and applications of radiocarbon dating (English-language materials only); is not a finding aid to sites dated.

Riedel, E, 'Bibliographie zu Material, Technologie und Restaurierung kulturgeschichtlicher Glasobjekte', in *Berliner Beitr z Archäometrie*, 11, 1992, pp 237–74
Mostly covers publications from 1950s with a few earlier items: glass from earliest examples through Mediterranean cultures to recent times.

Riederer, J, 'Bibliographie zur Material und Technologie kulturgeschichtlicher Goldobjekte', in *Berliner Beitr z Archäometrie*, 3, 1978, pp 175–90.
This series also went on to treat silver, copper, iron, glass etc in subsequent years, various compilers.

BOOKS ON SCIENCE-BASED DATING AND MATERIALS EXAMINATION

Aitken, M J, *Science-based dating in archaeology*. London: Longman, 1990, xix, 274 p, bibl, index. 0 582 05498 2 hb, 0 582 49309 9 pb.
Written mainly for the non-specialist, but with technical appendices. Deals with methods which depend on climate records, radiocarbon, potassium-argon, U-series, fission track, thermoluminescence, electron spin resonance, amino-acid, chemical analysis, and magnetism.

Baillie, M G L, *A slice through time: dendrochronology and precision dating*. London: Batsford, 1995, 176 p, bibl, index. 0 7134 7654 0 pb.
Advocates tree rings as the essential starting point for studying the detail of the past: 'the trees don't lie – and they were there,' whereas radiocarbon dating cannot provide precision to any degree.

Bayley, Justine, *Archaeometallurgical guidelines* (= [English Heritage] *Research and professional services guidelines*, 2, 1995, 3 p.
Where to find specialist advice.

Beck, Curt and Shennan, Stephen, *Amber in prehistoric Britain. Oxbow monogr*, 8, 1991, 232 p, bibl. 0 946897 30 1 pb.
Discusses analyses and provenances, with special reference to the European amber trade, and gives a corpus of examples.

Bowman, Sheridan, *Radiocarbon dating*. London: Brit Mus Publns (Interpreting the Past), 1990, 64 p, bibl, index. 0 7141 2047 2.
Introductory text: see also her 'Using radiocarbon: an update' in *Antiquity*, 68, 1994, pp 838–43.

***— (ed), *Science and the past*. London: Brit Mus, 1991, 192 p, bibl, index. 0 7141 2071 5.
Chapters give the most comprehensive summary of current techniques in the various branches of science-based archaeology.

Brooke, C J, *Ground-based remote sensing, see Section 6.9 The excavator's training (under survey and reconnaissance).*

Clark, Tony, *Seeing beneath the soil: prospecting methods in archaeology*. London: Batsford, rev. edn 1996, 192 p, bibl, index. 0 7134 7994 9.
Notes the historical development of the subject and discusses resistivity, magnetometry, magnetic susceptibility, ground-penetrating radar, phosphate detection, metal detection, dowsing, etc. Possibly somewhat over-simplified.

David, Andrew (comp), *Geophysical survey in archaeological field evaluation. Research and professional services guidelines*, 1, 1995, 39 p, bibl.

Eighmy, J L and Steinberg, R S, *Archaeomagnetic dating*. Tucson: Univ Arizona Press, 1990, xvi, 446 p, bibl, index. 0 8165 1132 2.
American focus but useful bibliography.

Frank, Susan, *Glass and archaeology*. London: Academic Press (Studies in Archaeological

Science), 1982, xii, 155 p, bibls, index. o 12 265620 2.
Technical approach to manufacture, composition, archaeological glass finds.

Gillespie, Richard, *Radiocarbon user's handbook*. Oxford: OUCA monogr, 3, corr reprint 1986, 36 p, bibl. o 947816 03 8 pb.
Includes AMS dating; use now in conjunction with newer information.

Gowlett, J A J and Hedges, R E M, *Archaeological results from accelerator dating*. Oxford: OUCA monogr, 11, 1986, 170 p, bibls. o 947816 11 9.
AMS or accelerator mass spectrometry dating has been almost routine since 1983 and this volume gave some case studies for assessment in their archaeological context. From early domestication to Bronze Age materials.

Historical Metallurgy Society, *Archaeological data sheets* (available for £1 from D Starley at the Ancient Monuments Laboratory (address at head of this section). This series of about a dozen numbers covers ironworking processes, crucibles and moulds, precious metal refining, etc.

Mook, W G and Waterbolk, H T (eds), *Proceedings of the 2nd International Symposium on Archaeology and C14, Groningen 1987*. PACT, 29, 1990, 459 p, bibls.

Scollar, I et al (eds), *Archaeological prospecting and remote sensing*. Cambridge: CUP, 1990, xv, 674 p, bibl, index. o 521 32050 x.
Technical information on low-level air photography and prospection by magnetic, thermal, electric and electromagnetic means.

Vernacular architecture has published dendrochronological results for timber-framed buildings in UK since volume 11 (1980), becoming regular at volume 15. Volume 18 (1987) has a cumulative index to the dates published 1976–87; vol 24 (1993) one for 1988–92. *See also Baillie above; also Section 6.18 Vernacular architecture (especially Laxton and Litton on the East Midlands master tree-ring chronology). See Section 2.3 Databases for an entry on tree-ring databases. Laboratories working currently on dendrochronology include Nottingham University Tree Ring Dating Laboratory; Sheffield University Dept of Archaeology and Prehistory; Godwin Laboratory Cambridge; MOLAS (Museum of London).*

DATING LABORATORIES: RADIOCARBON, THERMOLUMINESCENCE, ARCHAEOMAGNETISM

The official organ for the publication of **radiocarbon** dates was, until 1994, the journal *Radiocarbon* (details given above under Journals). However, many laboratories never submitted their date lists for publication, so it was always a very imperfect means for discovering which sites have been dated. Over the years many different radiocarbon laboratories have dated British and Irish materials, but those currently active in Britain and Ireland are (with their lab codes) Belfast (UB), British Museum (BM), Cambridge (Q), Cardiff (CAR), Glasgow (SRR), Oxford Accelerator (OxA), and RCD Radiocarbon Dating (RCD). (Harwell – HAR – is no longer active.) Outside these islands Groningen (Gro, then GrN) does considerable work on Irish sites, and American laboratories (eg BETA) are called upon from time to time. For accelerator dates, lists from the Oxford AMS laboratory appear fairly regularly in *Archaeometry* (starting in 1984; and see also the entry under Gowlett above).

The first attempt to bring British and Irish radiocarbon dates under bibliographic control was the CBA's *Archaeological site index to radiocarbon dates for Great Britain and Ireland*, 1971 with four sets of addenda (1972, 1974, 1977, 1982). This looseleaf compilation was discontinued for lack of resources to continue updating it, but all of it, together with many post-1982 determinations, has been transferred to a computer database using Harwell Computer Power's STATUS program. At the time of writing the work is in abeyance, but a means of continuing it and making it available is being sought.

Recently English Heritage issued a list of dates it had funded:
Jordan, D, Haddon-Reece, D and Bayliss, A (comp), *Radiocarbon dates from samples funded by English Heritage and dated before 1981*. London: English Heritage, 1994, 283 p, bibl, indexes. 1 85074 471 8 pb.
This consists of dates prepared at Harwell only, and the restriction to EH-funded dates considerably mars its usefulness as a guide to which English (let alone Welsh, Scottish and Irish) sites have been dated.

Occasional lists of French, Dutch (etc) dates appear in Continental journals but it has not been possible to collect them here.

Thermoluminescence dating
Two laboratories are currently active: at University of **Durham** and the **Oxford** Research Laboratory for Archaeology and the History of Art. A third is being planned at the Centre for Environmental Change and Quaternary Research, Cheltenham.

Archaeomagnetic dating
Besides the **Oxford** Research Laboratory and the **University of Bradford**'s Dept of Archaeological Sciences, a new laboratory has opened at the **Museum of London** Archaeological Service (Dr Bill McCann, MOLAS, Walker House, 87 Queen Victoria Street,London EC4V 4AB, tel 0171 410 2200, fax 0171 410 2201, e-mail ajclark@molas.demon.co.uk).

Laboratory conservation

This sub-section contains names of some useful organisations, some bibliographies, and some basic texts for the fieldworker. It does not pretend to be a guide for the laboratory conservator, merely an indication to the practising archaeologist of some likely sources of advice.

ORGANISATIONS
(Where no address is given below, see Section 4.2 Organisations)

UK
Heritage Biocare: consultancy in biodeterioration (basically fungal and insect attack). Apply to Dr Joan Kelley, International Mycological Institute, Bakeham Lane, Egham, Surrey TW20 9TY, tel 01784 470111.
Historic Scotland Conservation Centre Stenhouse (Edinburgh)
ICOM International Council on Museums (London: for conservation advice)
Museums and Galleries Commission: Conservation Unit (London)
Scottish Society for Conservation and Restoration
Textile Conservation Centre, Apt 22, Hampton Court Palace, East Molesey, Surrey KT8 9AU, tel 0181 977 4943. (Founded 1975)
UK Institute for the Conservation of Historic and Artistic Works ('UKIC') (London)
York Archaeological Wood Centre, c/o York Archaeological Trust, Cromwell House, 11–13 Ogleforth, York YO1 2JG, tel 01904 612529 (conserves large timbers from excavations.)

Ireland
Institute for the Conservation of Historic and Artistic Works in Ireland (ICHAWI)
Irish Professional Conservators and Restorers' Association (IPCRA)

BIBLIOGRAPHIES
Art and archaeology technical abstracts (0004–2994). 1955–. With its earlier versions, is the main bibliographic source for conservation; as well as the six-monthly issues, occasional specialist supplements are produced on such topics as patinas or the preservation of natural stone.

CHIN, Canadian Heritage Information Network. Homepage www.chin.doc.ca for pilot version of databases on conservation. Full version planned to be available by early summer 1996.

Druzik, James R (comp), *Research abstracts of the scientific program*. Marina del Rey: Getty Conservation Inst, 1989 and subsequent issues. Technical summaries of all aspects of GCI work: conservation of objects, of archaeological sites, museum environments, and new technologies.

BOOKS
Some books which describe first aid for excavation finds – eg those by E Dowman, Kate Hunter, Catherine Sease, David Watkinson (respectively) – are listed in Section 6.9 The excavator's training, career and tasks.

Conservation sourcebook. London: Museums and Galleries Commission, rev ed 1991, 122 p, subject index. 0 11 290493 9 pb.
Authoritative directory of information on organisations concerned with conservation, whether of buildings or objects. For each organisation is listed its address, publications, information services, technical advice, any grants offered.

Cronyn, Janey, *The elements of archaeological conservation*. London: Routledge, 1990, xx, 326 p, bibl, index. 0 415 01206 6 hb, 0 415 01207 4 pb.

English Heritage Ancient Monuments Laboratory, *Guidelines for the care of waterlogged archaeological leather. Scientific and technical guidelines*, 4, (available on English Heritage Archaeological Division's Web Home Page).

Irish Professional Conservators' and Restorers'

Association, *Irish conservation directory* (2 edn due c. 1996).

O'Connor, S A and Brooks, M M (ed), *Archaeological textiles. UKIC Occas Pap*, 10, 1990, 62 p. 1 871656 07 9.
Papers from a conference on textiles for the archaeological conservator.

Plenderleith, H J and Werner, A E A, *The conservation of antiquities and works of art: treatment, repair and restoration*. Oxford: OUP, 2 edn 1971, xix, 394 p, refs, index. 0 19 212960 0.
The principal authority, to be used in conjunction with more recent specialist texts in a rapidly developing subject.

Robinson, Wendy, *First aid for marine finds, see Section 6.19 Maritime, nautical and underwater archaeology.*

Tait, Gillian (ed), *Scottish conservation directory: a guide to businesses in Scotland working in the conservation and restoration of historic artefacts and cultural property*. Edinburgh: Hist Scotl SCB, 1991. 0 9517989 0 1 pb.
Lists relevant firms with short descriptions of their work.

White, R and Todd, V (eds), *Archaeological conservation: training and employment. UKIC occas pap*, 12, 1992, 28 p.
Particulars of some individual courses in conservation (eg London Institute, Durham etc) and some more general papers.

Biological and environmental examination

(*For geology and soils, see Section 6.14 Landscape*)

ORGANISATIONS
(Where no address is given below see Section 4.2 Organisations)
Ancient Monuments Laboratory (Environmental Studies), English Heritage
Association of Environmental Archaeologists
Centre for Environmental Change and Quaternary Research, Cheltenham
International Council for Archaeozoology
Stirling University, Dept of Environmental Sciences, Stirling FK9 4LA, tel 01786 467840, fax 01786 467843: specialises in soil thin sections from archaeological sites

University of Wales Lampeter, Dept of Archaeology, St David's University College, Lampeter, Dyfed SA48 7ED, tel 01570 424732: performs analyses in environmental archaeology

PERIODICALS
Archaeofauna. 1994–. Madrid: International Council for Archaeozoology
ArchaeoZoologia (0299–3600). 1987–. Grenoble: Pensée Sauvage. Contains running bibliography by H. Müller.
Circaea, bulletin of the Association for Environmental Archaeology (0268-425X). 1982–. Frequency varies, 1 or 2/yr
The Holocene (0959–6836). 1991–. 3/yr. London: Edward Arnold
International journal of osteoarchaeology (1047–482X). 1991–. 4/yr. Chichester: Wiley
Ossa, international journal of skeletal research (0345–8865). 1974–. Solna (Sweden): Univ Stockholm Osteological Research Lab
Paleopathology newsletter (0148–4737). 1973–. 4/yr. Detroit: Paleopathology Association. (Includes abstracts of recent articles)
Vegetatio, the international journal of plant ecology (0042–3106). 1948–. Dordrecht: Kluwer
Vegetation history and archaeobotany (0939–6314). 1992–. 4/yr. Wilhelmshaven: Springer International

BIBLIOGRAPHIES AND REFERENCE WORKS
Archaeobotanical computer database at York, see Section 2.3 Databases.

Association for Environmental Archaeology newsletter has substantial lists of published references.

Bibliography of European palaeobotany and palynology. Cardiff: Nat Mus Wales Dept Botany. Started 1990–91, with a 1988/9 report treating British publications only. Annotated bibliography.

Buckland, P C and Coope, G R, *A bibliography and literature review of Quaternary entomology.* Sheffield: J R Collis Publs, 1991, 85 p. 0 906090 35 0 pb.
A 24-page review plus bibliography of over a thousand items.

Desse-Berset, Nathalie (comp), *Répertoire International de l'Archéozoologie / International archaeozoological directory.* Paris: CNRS (=

Dossier de documentation archéologique, 11), 1986, 2 vols. 2 222 03862 6.
Lists researchers and their specialisms on five continents, with indexes by specialism, orientation, sites worked, etc. (contact Jean Desse at Centre Recherche Archéologique, CNRS, Sophia Antipolis, 06560 Valbonne Cedex, France).

Lange, Martina et al (comp), 'A bibliography of cremation / Leichenbrand-Bibliographie'. Strasbourg: *PACT*, 19, 1987, 168 p, bibl, indexes.

Müller, H-H, *Bibliographie zur Archäologie und Geschichte der Haustiere* [Bibliography on the archaeology and history of domestic animals]. Berlin: Akad Wiss DDR Zentralinst Alte Geschichte Archäologie. Ceased: appeared 1971–91 but covered material from 1955. The references are still collected, but now for the periodical *ArchaeoZoologia*.

Schultze-Motel, J, 'Literature on archaeological remains of cultivated plants (1991/2)', in *Vegetation history and archaeobotany*, 3.1, 1994, pp 33–61. (Two more lists in 1992 and 1993 issues of that journal; before that, lists were in *Kulturpflanze* annually up to 1990.)
References are listed by species as the main breakdown, and by country and age within that.

Schwidetzky, I, 'Bibliographien zur prähistorischen Anthropologie' [Bibliographies on prehistoric physical anthropology], in *Archäologische Naturwissenschaften* for 1977, pp 49–52.
Annotated references classified by material, period and country.

Stampfli, H R and Schibler, J, *Bibliography of archaeozoology*. Bellach and Basel: [privately], 1991, 39 p + 6 microfiches.
Covers pre-1989 material, internationally, with author and subject indexes. Also available on two discs; updates planned. Apply to PD Dr J Schibler, Seminar f. Ur und Frühgeschichte, Petersgraben 9–11, CH-4051 Basel, Switzerland.

Tomlinson, Philippa (comp), bibliography of environmental archaeology reports; available as AML Report with three disks, also available on Internet at http://www.eng-h.gov.uk/
This covers all substantial environmental reports for sites in England published after 1950 in county journals; period archaeological journals; and major excavation monograph series.

Unpublished reports, other than AML, are not included. Topics covered include biological work on excavated materials, non-human invertebrate remains, plant remains, insects, mollusca, soils.

see also Caseldine and Keeley (respectively) below.

BOOKS
(*The Association of Environmental Archaeologists annual conferences are published under various editorships, usually in the* BAR *or* OUCA *monograph series.*)

Baker, John R and Brothwell, D, *Animal diseases in archaeology.* London: Academic Press, 1980, ix, 235 p. 0 12 074150 4.

Bass, W H, *Human osteology: a laboratory and field manual.* Columbia, Mo: Missouri Archaeol Soc, 3 edn 1987, 327 p. 0 943414 68 7 spiral bound, 0 943414 67 9 pb (reprinted 1992).

Berglund, Holocene handbook, see Section 6.14 Landscape.

Bintliff, John, Davidson, D A and Grant, E G (eds), *Conceptual issues in environmental archaeology.* Edinburgh: EUP, 1988, 320 p, bibls, index. 0 85224 545 9.
Papers from the 1985 symposium in Oxford.

Birks, H J and Birks, H, *Quaternary palaeoecology.* London: Edward Arnold, 1980, viii, 289 p, bibl, index. 0 7131 2781 3.

Boddington, A, Garland, A N and Janaway, R C, *Death, decay and reconstruction: approaches to archaeological and forensic science.* Manchester: Manchester Univ Press, 1987, viii, 249 p, bibl, index. 0 7190 2303 3.
Contains 17 papers in four sections: survival and decay; analytical approaches to decay; approaches to reconstruction; archaeology and forensic science.

Brothwell, D R, *Digging up bones: the excavation, treatment, and study of human skeletal remains.* Oxford: OUP, 3 edn 1981 (reprinted 1993), 208 p, bibl, index. 0 19 858504 7 hb, 0 19 858510 1 pb.
The burial-excavator's bible.

Buikstra, J E and Ubelaker, D H, *Standards for data collection from human skeletal remains: proceedings of a seminar at the Field Museum of Natural History.* Arkansas Archeol Survey res ser, **44**, 1994, 202 p + unpag appendices, bibl, index. 1 56349 075 7 spiral-bound.

Caseldine, A, *Environmental archaeology in Wales*. Lampeter: St David's University College, 1990, iv, 197 p, bibl. 0 905285 26 3 pb.
Includes 56-page bibliography.

Chamberlain, Andrew, *Human remains*. London: Brit Mus Press, 1994 (Interpreting the past), 64 p, bibl, index. 0 7141 2092 8 pb.
Introduction to the identification and analysis of bones. *See also Waldron (below)*

Chaplin, R E, *The study of animal bones from archaeological sites*. London/New York: Seminar Press, 1971, ix, 170 p, bibl, index. 0 12 816050 0.
Standard work.

Clutton-Brock, Juliet, *A natural history of domesticated animals*. Cambridge: CUP, 1987, 208 p, bibl, index. 0 521 34697 5.

Cohen, Alan and Serjeantson, Dale, *A manual for the identification of bird bones from archaeological sites*. London: Archetype, rev edn 1996, 116 p, bibl, European glossary. 1 873132 90 5 spiral-bound card.
Illustrates separate bones from numerous species of post-glacial birds in the British Isles.

Corke, E, Davis, S and Payne, S, *A list of vertebrate skeletons in the comparative collection of the Ancient Monuments Laboratory, London*. AML Rep, **6/94**, 1994, 24 p, refs. (no ISBN).
Lists a total of 1,546 specimens (over 1,200 complete skeletons) including 68 species of mammal, 149 of bird, 48 of fish, etc.

Courty, Marie-Agnes et al on soils and micromorphology, see under Soils in Section 6.14 Landscape.

Davis, Simon J M, *The archaeology of animals*. London: Batsford, 1987, 224 p, bibl, index. 0 7134 4571 8 hb, 0 7134 4572 6 pb.
Methods and problems in zooarchaeology, from Palaeolithic to postmedieval material.

Desse, Jean and Desse-Berset, Nathalie, *Fiches d'ostéologie animal pour l'archéologie*. Sophia Antipolis: in progress.
Three series: A, *Fish* (8 numbers issued, 4 in preparation); B, *Mammals* (5 numbers issued, 3 in preparation); C, *Birds* (in preparation).
From the Laboratoire d'Archéozoologie, Centre Rech Archéol, CNRS, Sophia Antipolis, 06560 Valbonne Cedex, France.

Dickson, J H and Mill, R R (eds), *Plants and people: economic botany in Northern Europe AD 800–1800*. Botanical j Scotl, **46**.4, 1994, pp 519–706. 0 7486 0526 6 pb.
Papers on archaeobotany, early gardens and herbaria, medieval plants and herbals, woodmanship and wood use, etc.

Dimbleby, G W, *The palynology of archaeological sites*. London: Academic Press, 1985, xiii, 176 p, bibl, index. 0 12 216480 6.
Principles and techniques for the study of soil pollen; waterlogged sites; old ground surfaces; interpretation of structures; open sites; caves and rock shelters etc.

Dobney, K M, Jaques, S D and Irving, B G, *Of butchers and breeds: report on vertebrate remains from . . . Lincoln. Lincoln archaeol stud*, **5**, 1996, c 150 p. 1 899641 00 9 pb.
Combining evidence from numerous sites, this work erects a city-wide framework of economic-industrial-social organisation, Roman to post-medieval, wild and domestic species and including fish.

Driesch, A von den, *A guide to the measurement of animal bones from archaeological sites*. Cambridge, Mass: Peabody Mus Bull, **1**, Harvard Univ, 1976, 136 p, bibl. 0 87365 950 3.

Godwin, H, *The history of the British flora: a factual basis for phytogeography*. Cambridge: CUP, 2 edn 1975, x, 541 p, bibl, index. 0 521 20254 X.
Classic reference work.

Goudie, Andrew, *Environmental change*. Oxford: OUP, 3 edn 1992, xx, 329 p, bibl, index. 0 19 874166 9 hb, 0 19 874167 7 pb.

Greig, J et al, *Archaeobotany*. Strasbourg: European Science Foundation (= *Handbooks for Archaeol*, **4**), 1989, iv, 93 p. 2 903148 56 2 pb.
One of the ESF basic guides.

Hillson, Simon, *Mammal bones and teeth: an introductory guide to methods of identification*. London: UCL Inst Archaeol, 1992, c 150 p. 0 905853 30 X spiral-bound.
Avowedly a basic guide only: should be used alongside a reference collection and with zooarchaeological tuition.

—, *Teeth*. Cambridge: CUP, 1986, xix, 379 p. 0 521 30405 9.

Treats 150 genera.

Hunter, John, Roberts, Charlotte and Martin, Anthony, *Studies in crime: an introduction to forensic archaeology*. London: Batsford, 1996, 174 p, bibl, index. 0 7134 7901 9.
How to locate buried human remains and achieve maximum recovery of evidence, including DNA: particular reference to police work.

Huntley, B J and Birks, H J B, *An atlas of past and present pollen maps for Europe 0–13,000 years ago*. Cambridge: CUP, 1983.

Jones, Martin (ed), *Archaeology and the flora of the British Isles: human influence on the evolution of plant communities*. Oxford: OUCA monogr, 14, 1988, 122 p, bibls. 0 94716 14 3 pb.
Papers from a joint conference in 1984 of the Botanical Society of the British Isles and the AEA.
See also Jones M, England before Domesday in Section 6.14 Landscape.

Keeley, H C M (ed), *Environmental archaeology: a regional review*. (2 vols.) London: *DAMHB occas pap*, 6, 1984, 181 p, bibls; *HBMCE occas pap*, 1, 1987, 379 p, bibl. 1 85074 040 2 pb.
Authoritative surveys, by region, of available data.

Kenward, H K et al, 'A tested set of techniques for the extraction of plant and animal macrofossils from waterlogged archaeological deposits', *Science and archaeology*, 22, 1980, pp 3–15.
The nearest thing to a 'sieving bible' that we have?

Kiple, K F (ed), *The Cambridge world history of human disease*. Cambridge: CUP, 1993, xxiv, 1176 p, bibls, index. 0 521 33286 9.
Mainly historical evidence but archaeology also figures.

Lyman, R Lee, *Vertebrate taphonomy*. Cambridge: CUP (Cambridge Manuals in Archaeology), 1994, 524 p, bibls, index. 0 521 45215 5 hb, 0 521 45540 4 pb.
Referred to as an 'encyclopaedic reference volume' this treats topics from the structure of skeletons, through butchering, to burial as a taphonomic process and diagenesis.

Moore, P D, Webb, J A and Collinson, M E, *Pollen analysis*. Oxford: Blackwell, 2 edn 1991, viii, 216 p, bibl, index. 0 632 02176 4.
The principal text, with very good bibliography.

Pennington, W on British vegetation, see Section 6.14 Landscape.

Polunin, O and Walker, M on vegetation of Britain and Europe, see Section 6.14 Landscape.

Prummel, Wietske, *Atlas for the identification of foetal skeletal elements of cattle, horse, sheep and pig*. Two parts, in *ArchaeoZoologia*, 1.1, 1987, pp 23–30 and 1.2, 1987, pp 11–41 (respectively).

Rackham, James, *Animal bones*. London: Brit Mus Press (Interpreting the Past), 1994, 64 p, bibl, index. 0 7141 2057 X pb.
Introduction to what bones can reveal.

Roberts, Charlotte, Lee, F and Bintliff, J (eds), *Burial archaeology: current research, methods and developments*. BARBS, 211, 1989, x, 293 p, bibls. 0 86054 671 3 pb.
About 20 papers from a 1988 conference at Bradford on topics from the philosophy of skeletal study through to case studies.

— and Manchester, Keith, *The archaeology of disease*. Stroud: A Sutton, 2 rev edn 1995, x, 243 p, bibl, index. 0 7509 0595 6.

Rogers, Juliet and Waldron, Tony, *A field guide to joint disease in archaeology*. Chichester: Wiley, 1995, viii, 119 p, bibl, index. 0 471 95506 X pb.

Schmid, Elisabeth, *Atlas of animal bones for prehistorians, archaeologists and Quaternary geologists*. Amsterdam: Elsevier, 1972, vii, 159 p, bibl, index. 0 444 40831 2.
Parallel English/German text.

Serjeantson, D and Waldron, T (eds), *Diet and crafts in towns: the evidence of animal remains from the Roman to the post-medieval period*. BARBS, 199, 1989, 223 p, bibls. 0 86054 598 9 pb.
Twelve papers from a conference.

Shackley, Myra, *Using environmental archaeology*. London: Batsford, 1985, 162 p, bibl, index. 0 7134 4346 4.
Introductory text.

Stuart, A J, *Pleistocene vertebrates in the British Isles*. London/New York: Longman, 1982, ix, 212 p, bibl, index. 0 582 30069 X.

Tansley, A G, *The British Islands and their vegetation*. Cambridge: CUP, 1939, xxxviii, 930 p, chapter bibls, index.

Classic work, to be used now in conjunction with newer studies.

Turner, R C and Scaife, R G, *Bog bodies: new discoveries and new perspectives*. London: Brit Mus Press, 1995, 256 p, bibl, indexes. 0 7141 2305 6.

A wide range of scientific and historic expertise is applied by 27 contributors to bodies from Lindow Moss and many other sites. Provides valuable 'life style' data and includes gazetteer of British Isles bog bodies; 18-page bibliography.

Ubelaker, D H, *Human skeletal remains: excavation, analysis, interpretation*. Washington DC: Taraxacum Press, (= *Manuals in archaeology* 2), 2 edn 1989, x, 172 p, bibl, index. 0 9602822 6 2.

Veen, M Van der, on crop husbandry regimes, see in Section 6.14 *Landscape*.

Waldron, Tony, *Counting the dead: the epidemiology of skeletal populations*. Chichester: Wiley, 1994, xiv, 109 p, bibl, index. 0 471 95138 2.

On the nature of palaeopathology, diagnosis, analytical epidemiology, and a guide to best practice.

Wheeler, Alwyne and Jones, A K G, *Fishes*. Cambridge: CUP (Cambridge Manuals in Archaeology), 1989, xiv, 210 p, bibl, index. 0 521 30407 5.

Practical introduction to the recovery, identification and interpretation of fish bones from archaeological sites.

White, T D and Folkens, P A, *Human osteology*. San Diego: Academic Press, 1990, xix, 455 p, bibl, index. 0 12 746610 X.

For archaeologists and forensic scientists, etc; designed to assist identification of fragmentary remains and to use these to learn something about the individuals so represented.

Wilson, B, Grigson, C and Payne, S (eds), *Ageing and sexing animal bones from archaeological sites. BARBS*, 109, 1982, 268 p, bibl. 0 86054 192 4 pb.

Contains 17 papers on various aspects of methodology and results.

Computing and statistics

See the introduction to this volume for some **Internet** addresses and information.

ORGANISATION

CTICH, Computers in Teaching Initiative Centre for History with Archaeology and Art History. 1 University Gardens, Glasgow G12 8QQ, tel 0141 339 8855 ext 6336/6446/4942; e-mail ctich@uk.ac.glasgow

Established to promote computer use in history and (since 1990) in archaeology, ancient history, church history, etc. Handles software exchange, teaching materials etc, and publishes *Craft* (see below).

PERIODICALS

Archaeological computing newsletter (0952–3332). Dec 1984–. 4/yr then 2/yr. C/o Institute of Archaeology, 36 Beaumont Street, Oxford OX1 2PG

Archeologia e calcolatori, c/o Istituto per l'Archeologia Etrusco-Italica del CNR, Viale di Villa Massimo 29, 00161 Roma, Italy

Computers and texts: newsletter (0963–1763). 1991–. (Previously *Computers and literature*.) Published by the Computers in Teaching Initiative (and others), c/o Oxford University Computer Service, 13 Banbury Road, Oxford OX2 6NN. Deals mainly with manipulation of literary texts, and replaced *Humanities communication newsletter* in 1991.

Craft, the newsletter of the CTI Centre for History with Archaeology and Art History (0958–8183). 3/yr. Address as for CTICH (above under Organisation). Contains numerous items of archaeological interest

History and computing (0957–0144). 1989–. Edinburgh Univ Press (formerly from OUP)

Humanities communication newsletter, replaced by *Computers and texts* (above)

CONFERENCES

Computer applications in archaeology (title varies, also **Computers and quantitative methods in archaeology**); an annual conference on all aspects of computer and statistical archaeology, held and published in various locations (originally Birmingham University) and latterly published in *BAR international series*.

BOOKS

Baxter, Mike, *Exploratory multivariate analysis in archaeology*. Edinburgh: EUP, 1994, xiii, 307 p, bibl, index. 0 7486 0423 5.

Booth, B K W, Grant, S A V and Richards, J D (eds), *Computer usage in British archaeology.*

IFA occas pap, 3, 2 edn 1989, various pagings. o 948393 82 6 pb.

Tabulated responses to a questionnaire on hardware and software in use in archaeological organisations of all kinds. Mainly of historic interest now.

Djindjian, F and Ducasse, H (eds), *Data processing and mathematics applied to archaeology (= PACT, 16, 1987; ISSN 0257-8727)*. Ravello: Council of Europe.

Fletcher, Mike and Lock, Gary, *Digging numbers: elementary statistics for archaeologists. OUCA monogr*, 33, 2 corr impression 1994, ix, 187 p, bibl, index. o 947816 33 X.

Aims to induce readers to try statistics for themselves, illustrating the most popular techniques with reference to a data set of 40 bronze spearheads, manipulable on computer. Includes annotated catalogue of statistical software.

Floud, R, *An introduction to quantitative methods for historians*. London: Methuen, 2 edn 1979, xii, 237 p, bibl, index. o 416 71670 9 pb.

Lock, Gary and Wilcock, John, *Computer archaeology. Shire archaeol*, 51, 1987, 64 p, bibl, glossary, index. o 85263 877 9 pb..

A concise introduction to hardware, software, data, archaeological uses.

Mawdsley, E and Munck, T, *Computing for historians: an introductory guide*. Manchester: Manchester UP, 1993, xvi, 231 p. o 7190 3547 3 hb, o 7190 3548 1 pb.

Museum Documentation Association, on computers in museums, see Section 4.9 Museum catalogues.

Orton, C R, *Mathematics in archaeology*. London: Collins, 1980, 248 p, bibl, index. o oo 216226 1. (Reprinted by CUP, 1982, o 521 28922 X.)

Essential reading, whether or not you think you are doing mathematical archaeology!

Rahtz, Sebastian, 'Ten commandments for archaeological computing', in *Archaeol comput newslett*, 36, 1993, pp 1–2

Reilly, Paul and Rahtz, S (eds), *Archaeology and the information age: a global perspective*. London/ New York: Routledge, 1992 (= *One world archaeology*, 21), xxiv, 395 p, bibl, index. o 415 07858 X.

Contains papers on various aspects, including GIS, three-dimensional modelling, an expert system, and 'dynamic archaeological publications'.

Richards, J S and Ryan, N S, *Data processing in archaeology*. Cambridge: CUP (Cambridge manuals in archaeology), 1985, vii, 232 p, bibl, index. o 521 25769 7.

Still a useful introduction to basic principles.

Ross, Seamus, et al (eds), *Computing for archaeologists. OUCA monogr*, 18, 1991, xiii, 207 p, bibl. o 947816 18 6 pb.

Contains 11 papers on computer applications: site-based, database fundamentals, graphics, introductory statistics, etc.

Shennan, Stephen, *Quantifying archaeology: an introductory text*. Edinburgh: EUP, 1988, x, 364 p, bibl, index. o 85224 460 6.

For first-year undergraduates.

Spaeth, Donald A, *A guide to software for historians*. Glasgow: CTICH, 1991, v, 98 p, bibl, index. o 9517514 0 9 pb.

For teachers and researchers; includes some archaeological programs among the 300 or so listed.

6.11
Period Treatments

This section is subdivided on fairly conventional lines:

6.11.1 Quaternary, Palaeolithic and Mesolithic
6.11.2 Neolithic and Bronze Age
6.11.3 Iron Age
6.11.4 Romano-British
6.11.5 Migration and early medieval:
  Anglo-Saxon to Late Saxon England
  'Sub-Roman', Late Celtic and Early Christian Britain
  Viking Age/Norse/Scandinavian Britain
  Isle of Man
  Wales: Celtic; Viking and Late Saxon
  Scotland: Late Celtic, Early Christian, Pictish, Viking/Norse
  Ireland: Late Celtic, Early Christian, Viking
6.11.6 Medieval
6.11.7 Post-Medieval

Items in this 'period' section are generally presented in the order – societies, periodicals, bibliographies and reference works, books. Where necessary, material relating to Wales, Scotland, Channel Islands and Ireland is set out separately. The recurrent abbreviation 'BARBS' stands for 'British Archaeological Reports, British Series' – the ubiquitous A4 series with blue paper covers in which so many archaeologists publish their work. Another series now appearing in increasing numbers is published by Batsford for English Heritage; an equivalent series for Scotland arises from Batsford's collaboration with Historic Scotland. Not all of their titles could be listed here, but most are of high quality and the series is worth looking out for.

6.11.1
Quaternary, Palaeolithic and Mesolithic

This section owes much to improvements made by John Wymer, though any faults remain those of the compiler.
Britain (including the Channel Islands) is treated first, then Ireland. See also relevant material in Section 6.14 Landscape.

Societies

(details in Section 4.2 Organisations)

Irish Association for Quaternary Studies
Lithic Studies Society
Prehistoric Society
Quaternary Research Association

Periodicals

Bulletin of primitive technology (1078-4845). 1991-. 2/yr. Rexburg, Idaho.
Lithics (0262-7817). 1980-. Annual
Proceedings of the Prehistoric Society (0079-497X). 1935-. Annual
Quaternary newsletter (0143-2826). 1970-. Exeter: Quaternary Research Association
Quaternary perspectives (0965-1357). Newsletter of the International Union for Quaternary Research, INQUA. Elsevier Scientific (from 1996)
Quaternary research (0038-5894). 1970-. 6/yr. Seattle: Quaternary Research Center
Quaternary science reviews (0277-3791). 1982-. 10/yr. Oxford: Pergamon/Elsevier

Bibliographies

The journal *Lithics* sometimes lists recently published works.

A useful survey of current knowledge on the Palaeolithic will be found (though it is not easy to get hold of) in Derek Roe's 'portmanteau' review of excavation reports on Hoxne, High Lodge and Hengistbury in the American periodical *Quarterly review of archaeology* (Salem, Mass), 14.2, Fall 1993, pp 1–9; the same periodical's issue 16.1 for Spring 1995 contains his review of the two books by Bridgland and Gibbard respectively (see below).

There is also P Rowley-Conwy's useful general survey in 'Palaeolithic and Mesolithic: from culture to behaviour' in B Vyner (ed), *Building on the past: papers celebrating 150 years of the Royal Archaeological Institute* (RAI, 1994), pp 75–89; strongest on Mesolithic.

Kidson, C (ed), *Bibliography of the Quaternary history of the Irish Sea coasts*. Aberystwyth: Dept Geogr Univ Coll Aberystwyth, 1977, 81 p, pb.

Mansfield, R W and Donovan, D T, 'Palaeolithic and Pleistocene sites of the Mendip, Bath and Bristol areas: recent bibliography', in *Proc Univ Bristol Spelaeol Soc*, 18.3, 1989, pp 367–89.
Update of earlier lists (eg that by Hawkins and Tratman covering 1964–77, in vol 14.3, 1977, pp 197–232 of same periodical).

Books

QUATERNARY
(*See also Geology within Section 6.14 Landscape*).

Note the extremely useful series of Field Guides (to Britain) published by the Quaternary Research Association. To date there have appeared guides to: E Yorks; Pliocene-Mid Pleistocene E Anglia; West Midlands; Glen Roy; Beauly to Nairn; Central E Anglia; Isle of Skye; Western Pennines; SW Scottish Highlands; Isle of Man; Jersey; Shetland. A full list is obtainable from QRA's Assistant Secretary (Publications), Dr W A Mitchell, School of Geological and Environmental Sciences, University of Luton, Park Square, Luton LU1 3JU. There is a similar series listed below under Ireland.

Andrews, Peter, *Owls, caves and fossils: predation, preservation and accumulation of small mammal bones in caves, with an analysis of the Pleistocene cave fauna from Westbury-sub-Mendip, Somerset, UK*. Chicago: Univ Chicago Press, 1990, viii, 231 p, bibl, index. 0 226 02037 1.
Useful contribution to cave studies relating to 350,000 years ago.

Bell, Martin and Walker, M J C, *Late Quaternary environmental change: physical and human perspectives*. Harlow: Longman Sci Techn, 1992, xiv, 273 p, bibl, index. 0 582 04514 2 pb.
Discusses interactions, on both spatial and temporal scales, of people, environment and climate in the northern temperate zone.

Berglund, Holocene handbook, see Section 6.14 Landscape.

Birks, H J B and Birks, H H, *Quaternary palaeoecology*. London: Edward Arnold, 1980, viii, 289 p, bibl, index. 0 7131 2781 3.
The standard work on Quaternary vegetation.

Bowen, D Q, *Quaternary geology: a stratigraphic framework for multidisciplinary work*. Oxford: Pergamon Press, 1978, xi, 221 p, bibl, index. 0 08 020409 0 pb.

Bridgland, D R, *Quaternary of the Thames*. London: Chapman and Hall (= *Geol conservation review ser*, 7), 1994, xiv, 441 p, bibl. 0 412 48830 2.
Roe (see introduction above) found this both forward-looking and useful.

Gibbard, P L, *The Pleistocene history of the Middle Thames Valley*. Cambridge: CUP, 1985, vii, 155 p, bibl, index. 0 521 26578 9.

—, *Pleistocene history of the Lower Thames Valley*. Cambridge: CUP, 1994, 200 p. 0 521 40209 3.

Kidson, C and Tooley, M J (eds), *The Quaternary history of the Irish Sea*. Liverpool: Seel House Press (= *Geol j special issue*, 7), 1977, 345 p, bibl, index. 0 902354 07 8.

Preece, R C (ed), *Island Britain: a Quaternary perspective*. London: Geol Soc (= *Geol Soc special publ*, 96), 1995, 274 p, bibl, index. 1 897799 40 3.
Contains 16 conference papers on geology, flora and fauna; sealevels; insularity. Includes Ireland.

PALAEOLITHIC BRITAIN
**Ashton, N M, Cook, J, Lewis, S G and Rose, J, *High Lodge: excavations by G de G Sieveking, 1962–8 and J Cook, 1988*. London: British Museum Publs, 1992, 192 p. 0 7141 1369 7.
The long-awaited report on a very early (Lower Palaeolithic) occupation site.

— and David, A (eds), *Stories in stone: proceedings of anniversary conference . . . Oxford 1993. Lithic Studies occas pap*, 4, 1994, 218 p, bibls. 0 9513246 1 6 pb.
The sections of this work cover dating and scientific techniques; raw materials and petrology; resource management; technology and use-wear analysis; typology.

Barton, N, *Hengistbury Head, Dorset, vol 2: the*

Late Upper Palaeolithic and Early Mesolithic sites. OUCA monogr, **34**, 1992, xii, 299 p, bibl, index. 0 947816 34 8.
Excavations on an important site in S England; good illustrated glossary of stone tools etc.

—, Roberts, A J and Roe, D A (eds), *The Late Glacial in north-west Europe: human adaptation and environmental change at the end of the Pleistocene. CBA res rep*, **77**, 1991, xii, 279 p, bibl, index. 1 872414 15 X.
Conference papers.

Berglund, Holocene handbook, see Section 6.14 Landscape.

Bonsall, C J, Upper Palaeolithic gazetteer, see under Wymer in the Mesolithic section below.

Callow, P and Cornford, J M, *La Cotte de St Brelade 1961–1978: excavations by C B M McBurney*. Norwich: Geo Books, 1986, xix, 433 p, bibl, index. 0 86094 207 4.
Important excavations of Palaeolithic kill-site in a Jersey cave whose deposits cover a quarter of a million years.

**Campbell, J B, *The Upper Palaeolithic of Britain: a study of man and nature in the late Ice Age*. Oxford: Clarendon Press, 1977, 2 vols, bibl, index. 0 19 813188 7.
Contains the fullest (so far) bibliography for this period, and a gazetteer of sites.

Collcutt, S N (ed), *The Palaeolithic of Britain and its nearest neighbours: recent trends*. Sheffield: Univ Sheffield Dept Archaeol Prehist, 1986, iv, 109 p, bibl, place-name index. 0 906090 27 X pb.
Contains 25 short papers on knowledge up to 1986.

*Conway, Bernard, McNabb, John and Ashton, Nick, *Excavations at Barnfield Pit, Swanscombe 1968–72. Brit Mus occas pap*, **94**, 1996, vii, 266 p, bibl. 0 861590 94 5 pb.
First publication of this classic Lower Palaeolithic site; with environmental and archaeological studies.

Coulson, Sheila D, *Middle Palaeolithic industries of Great Britain*. Bonn: Holos (= *Studies in modern archaeol*, **4**), 1990, 415 p, bibl. 3 926216 97 2.

*Debénath, A and Dibble, Harold L, *Handbook of Paleolithic typology. Vol 1: Lower and Middle Paleolithic of Europe*. Philadelphia: Univ Museum, Univ Philadelphia, 1994, ix,

202 p, bibl, index of tool types. 0 924171 23 5 limp.

Evans, John, *The ancient stone implements, weapons and ornaments of Great Britain*. London: Longmans Green, 2 edn 1897, xviii, 747 p, refs, indexes.
Classic volume which still contains much useful information.

Gamble, Clive, *The Palaeolithic settlement of Europe*. Cambridge: CUP, 1986, xix, 471 p, bibl, index. 0 521 24514 1 hb, 0 521 28764 2 pb.
Takes a behavioural approach and a worldwide frame; considers energy needs, resource strategies etc.

— and Lawson, Andrew J (eds), *The English Palaeolithic reviewed. Papers from a one-day conference held . . . 1994*. [Salisbury]: Trust for Wessex Archaeology Ltd, 1996, vi, 76 p, bibls, index. 1 974350 17 5 pb.
The papers arise from the English Rivers Palaeolithic Survey (*see under Wymer below*); and include one on the Boxgrove hominid.

Garrod, D A E, *The Upper Palaeolithic age in Britain*. Oxford: Clarendon, 1926, 211 p, bibl, index.
Important pioneer work which inter alia coined the term 'Creswellian'.

Green, H Stephen [H S Aldhouse-Green], *Pontnewydd Cave, a Lower Palaeolithic hominid site in Wales: the first report*. Cardiff: Nat Mus Wales, 1984, xvii, 227 p, bibl, index. 0 7200 0282 6.
On a brief seasonal occupation by hominids of the period approximately 250,000 to 225,000 years ago: handaxe, Levallois and scraper industry of NW European importance.

— and Walker, Elizabeth, *Ice Age hunters: Neanderthals and early modern hunters in Wales*. Cardiff: Nat Mus Wales, 1991, 72 p, illus incl. colour. 0 7200 0358 X pb.
Introduction to evidence for Neanderthal and early modern humans in Welsh caves, from Paviland in the south to Pontnewydd in the north.

Jones, R L and Keen, D H, *Pleistocene environments in the British Isles*. London: Chapman and Hall, 1993, 346 p, bibl, index. 0 41244 190 X pb.
Includes a long chapter on the Flandrian, with a

short section taking the archaeological stages into medieval times.

Lord, John, *The nature and subsequent uses of flint. Vol 1: the basics of lithic technology.* Brandon: the author, 1993, 60 p. 0 9521356 0 4 pb.
Posits that the best way to learn about flint is to knap it; discusses geology, terminology, tool selection, etc.

McComb, Patricia, *Upper Palaeolithic osseous artifacts from Britain and Belgium: an inventory and technological description. BAR int ser,* S481, 1989, 361 p, bibl. 0 86054 618 7 pb.
Boneworking shown as a central element in the toolkit.

Roberts, Mark, 'Excavation of the Lower Palaeolithic site in Amey's Eartham Pit, Boxgrove, West Sussex: a preliminary report', *Proc Prehist Soc,* 52, 1986, pp 215–45.
On a long-running excavation of a highly important in-situ working floor from 500,000 years ago. Further reports are eagerly awaited from this site which later yielded remains of 'Boxgrove Man', the earliest hominid in Europe.

—, 'A hominid tibia from the Middle Pleistocene sediments of Boxgrove, UK', *Nature,* 369, 1994, pp 311–12.
First inkling of the size and type of the individuals using this site.

Roe, D A (comp), *A gazetteer of British Lower and Middle Palaeolithic sites. CBA res rep,* 8, 1968, xviii, 355 p. Pb.
Brief details of over 3000 sites. The original card index for this compilation was lodged at RCHME Swindon and the data incorporated into sites and monuments records (which will themselves now contain additional sites).

—, *The Lower and Middle Palaeolithic periods in Britain.* London: Routledge and Kegan Paul, 1981, (= *Archaeology of Britain,* 3), xvi, 324 p, bibl, index. 0 7100 0600 4.

— (ed), *Studies in the Upper Palaeolithic of Britain and Northwest Europe. BAR int ser,* S296, 1986, x, 249 p, bibl, index. 0 86054 380 3 pb.
Contains 14 papers on various aspects.

Sampson, C G (ed), *Paleoecology and archeology of an Acheulian site at Caddington, England.* Dallas: Southern Methodist Univ Dept Anthropol, 1978, 158 p, bibl. 0 89643 000 7.

Sieveking, Ann, *A catalogue of Palaeolithic art in the British Museum.* London: Brit Mus Publ, 1987, xvii, 115p + 131 pls, bibl, index. 0 7141 1376 X.
Includes a handful of pieces from Creswell Crags.

Sieveking, G de G and Newcomer, M H (eds), *The human uses of flint and chert: proceedings of the 4th International Flint Symposium . . . Brighton, 1983.* Cambridge: CUP, 1987, xiii, 263 p, bibls. 0 521 26253 4 pb.

*Singer, Ronald, Gladfelter, B G and Wymer, J J, *The Lower Paleolithic site at Hoxne, England.* Chicago/London: Chicago Univ Press, 1993, 236 p, bibl, ind, 0 226 76111 8.
Important excavation report on one of the few sites with early hominid artefacts and other types of data in primary context.

Smith, Christopher, *Late Stone Age hunters of the British Isles.* London: Routledge, 1992, x, 206 p, bibl, index. 0 415 03161 3 hb, 0 415 03202 6 pb.
Not universally well received, but offers a welcome concentration on ways of life rather than stone tool studies; covers Late Upper Palaeo to Mesolithic.

Stringer, C, 'The British Isles', in R Orban (ed), *Hominid remains: an up-date. British Isles and Eastern Germany.* (Brussels: suppl to *Bull Soc Royale d'anthropologie et préhistoire,* 3), 1990, pp 1–40.
Adds new cave finds to the earlier *Catalogue of fossil hominids* – Gough's Cave, Pontnewydd, Tornewton – and adds fresh data for 18 previously listed sites.

Tixier, Jacques et al, *Préhistoire de la pierre taillée: 2, terminologie et technologie.* Antibes: Cercle de Recherches et d'Etudes Préhistoriques, 1980, 120 p, bibl. 2 903516 01 4 pb.
The nature of raw materials, how to make observations, the processes of flaking and retouching stone; plus illustrated lexicon with French/English and English/French technological terms. (A second volume with same main title, published 1984, contains papers from a conference on technology and lithic flaking experiments.)

**Wymer, J J, *Lower Palaeolithic archaeology in*

Britain as represented by the Thames Valley.
London: John Baker, 1968, 429 p, bibl, indexes.
Classic gazetteer and discussion which is a
pleasure to handle, read and use.

—, *The Palaeolithic age.* London: Croom Helm,
1982, 310 p, bibl, index. 0 7099 2710 X.
Textbook, worldwide treatment.

—, *The Palaeolithic sites of East Anglia.* Norwich:
Geo Books, 1985, x, 440 p, bibl, indexes. 0
86094 147 7 hb, 0 86094 178 7 pb.
Describes an area important in this period.

—, for Wessex Archaeology, *The Southern Rivers
Palaeolithic Project. Report No. 1, 1991–1992,
The Upper Thames Valley, the Kennet Valley
and the Solent drainage system.*
*Report No. 2, 1992–1993, The southwest and
south of the Thames.*
*Report No. 3, 1993–1994, The Sussex raised
beaches and the Bristol Avon.*
Salisbury: Trust for Wessex Archaeology,
1993–4, 222 + 234 + 141 p. (Copies held in
the relevant SMRs.)
This is a massive study of all recorded Lower
and Middle Palaeolithic discoveries in the area
south of Severn and Thames; discoveries are
related to their geological contexts and made
available for academic and management purposes.

MESOLITHIC BRITAIN

*Bonsall, Clive, *The Mesolithic in Europe: papers
presented at the Third International Symposium, Edinburgh 1985 (UISPP Mesolithic Commission).* Edinburgh: John Donald, [1989], xii,
645 p, bibl, site index. 0 85976 205 X.
Nearly half of the 62 papers relate to British and
Irish material.

*Clark, J G D, *Excavations at Star Carr.* Cambridge: CUP, 1954, xxiii, 200 p, refs, index.
The classic British Mesolithic site, on the
interpretation of which debate still continues.

—, *Star Carr: a case study in bioarchaeology.*
Reading (Mass): *Addison Wesley modules in
anthropology,* 10, 1972, 42 p, bibl.
The excavator was the first to reinterpret his
own site.

Lacaille, A D, *The Stone Age in Scotland.* London:
OUP for Wellcome Hist Medicine Mus (= *Publ,*
5), 1954, xxii, 345 p, bibl, index.
Seminal work, with good illustrations; now
overtaken by more recent studies.

Legge, A J and Rowley-Conwy, P A, *Star Carr
revisited: a re-analysis of the larger mammals.*
London: Birkbeck Coll Centre for Extra-Mural
Stud, 1988, vii, 145 p, bibl. 0 7187 0876 8 pb.
Offers some different conclusions from those of
the original excavator.

Lynch, Frances, *Excavations in the Brenig Valley:
a Mesolithic and Bronze Age landscape in
North Wales.* [Bangor]: Cambrian Archaeol
Ass (= *Cambrian archaeol monogr,* 5), 1993,
234 p, bibl, fiche. 0 947846 04 2 pb.
From 6th millennium BC through to a medieval
shieling.

Mellars, P A (ed), *The early post-glacial settlement
of northern Europe: an ecological perspective.*
London: Duckworth, 1978, ix, 411 p, bibl,
index. 0 7156 1297 2.
Symposium on Mesolithic studies, still useful
despite its age.

*—, *Excavations on Oronsay: prehistoric human
ecology on a small island.* Edinburgh: EUP,
1987, viii, 306 p, bibl, index. 0 85224 544 0.
An important series of excavation seasons here
threw much light on the earliest of Scotland's
inhabitants.

Morrison, Alex, *Early man in Britain and Ireland:
an introduction to Palaeolithic and Mesolithic
cultures.* London: Croom Helm, 1980, 209 p,
bibl, index. 0 85664 084 0 hb, 0 85664 089 1.
Textbook emphasising the multidisciplinary
approach needed to understand these periods.

Palmer, Susann, *Mesolithic cultures of Britain.*
Poole: Dolphin Press, 1977, 230 p, bibl, index.
Not universally applauded but has some useful
information, concentrating on coastal sites in S
England.

Pollard, Tony and Morrison, Alex (eds), *The early
prehistory of Scotland.* Edinburgh: EUP for
Univ Glasgow (= *Dalrymple monogr,* 3),
1996, vii, 300 p, bibls. 0 7486 0677 7.
Scottish (and N English) studies offer a reassessment of the Mesolithic in the light of freshly
excavated evidence and environmental studies.

Rowley-Conwy, P, Zvelebil, M and Blankholm,
H-P (eds), *Mesolithic northwest Europe – recent
trends.* Sheffield: Dept Archaeol Prehist Univ
Sheffield, 1987, v, 170 p, bibl, index. 0 906090
28 8.
Contains 15 papers on various aspects, from
data recovery to regional syntheses, especially
Vale of Pickering, Gwithian, and Ireland.

*Wickham-Jones, Caroline, *Rhum: Mesolithic and later sites at Kinloch: excavations 1984–86*. Edinburgh: *Soc Antiq Scotl monogr*, 7, 1990, 183 p, bibl, index, 3 fiches. 0 903903 07 5 pb.
Another important site with repercussions for the whole Scottish Mesolithic.

—, *Scotland's first settlers*. London: Batsford/Hist Scotl, 1994, 128 p, bibl, glossary, index. 0 7134 7371 1 pb.
A more accessible account of the Mesolithic in Scotland.

Woodman, P C, 'A review of the Scottish Mesolithic: a plea for normality', in *Proc Soc Antiq Scotl*, 119, 1989, pp 1–32.

Wymer, J, *Mesolithic Britain*. Princes Risborough: *Shire archaeol*, 65, 1991, 64 p, bibl, index, o 7478 0121 5 pb.
Introduction to the topic.

— (ed) with Bonsall, C J, *Gazetteer of Mesolithic sites in England and Wales, with a gazetteer of Upper Palaeolithic sites in England and Wales*. Geo Abstracts/CBA res rep, 20, 1977, xxvi, 511 p, bibl, index.
County by county tabulation of sites: a landmark in its time, the first revelation of the number and density of Mesolithic traces in Britain. The original card index is held at RCHME Swindon, the data incorporated in the sites and monuments record.

Ireland

BIBLIOGRAPHY
Lithics, 13, 1992, pp 69–75 has recent bibliography of Irish lithics.

QUATERNARY OF IRELAND
Edwards, Kevin J and Warren, W P (eds), *The Quaternary history of Ireland*. London: Academic Press, 1985, xxii, 382 p, bibl. 0 12 232730 6.
Discusses human effects on vegetation; vertebrates; prehistoric settlement and environment; chronology; economy.
See also Preece (ed), under main Quaternary sub-section above.

Just as for Britain (above), Ireland has a very useful series of Field Guides produced annually since 1978 by the Irish Association for Quaternary Studies, covering the areas (respec-

tively): South County Down, Galtees, Co Tyrone, Co Wexford (S and E coasts), SW Iveragh, NE Co Donegal and NW Co Londonderry, Sligo and W Leitrim, Corca Dhuibhne, Offaly and W Kildare, Connemara, Waterford and E Cork, N Antrim and Londonderry, N Mayo, The Burren, S Fermanagh, Clare Island, Inishbofin, NW Donegal, etc. (Those still in print are obtainable from IQUA, c/o Catherine Delaney, Coastal Resources Centre, Dept of Geography, Univ College Cork.)

MESOLITHIC IRELAND
Bonsall, C J (ed), see entry under Mesolithic Britain above.

Green, S W and Zvelebil, M, 'Interpreting Ireland's prehistoric landscape: the Bally Lough archaeological project', in P Bogucki (ed), *Case studies in European prehistory* (Boca Raton: CRC Press, 1994), pp 1–29.
On the Meso-BA sites discovered in the SE Ireland survey.

Movius, Hallam, *The Irish Stone Age: its chronology, development and relationships*. Cambridge: CUP, 1942, 339 p, bibl, index.
Much overtaken by recent research, but a classic work.

Woodman, Peter C, *The Mesolithic in Ireland: hunter-gatherers in an insular environment*. *BARBS*, 58, 1978, 360 p, bibl. 0 86054 042 1 pb.
A pioneer work which put the Irish Mesolithic on a secure footing.

—, *Excavations at Mount Sandel 1973–77, County Londonderry*. Belfast: HMSO (= N Ireland archaeol monogr, 2), 1985, xvi, 204 p, bibl. 0 337 08194 8.
Ireland's principal excavated Mesolithic site.

6.11.2
Neolithic and Bronze Age

Because the dividing line between Neolithic and Bronze Age is somewhat arbitrary, they are treated together here. In fact authors increasingly prefer the terms 'fourth millennium BC', 'second millennium BC' etc when writing of this era. The dividing line at the end of the Bronze Age is also blurred; some books listed here run into the Iron Age (EIA) or later.

The most recent summaries of the state of research come from the Royal Archaeological Institute's volume *Building on the past*, edited by Blaise Vyner (1994). In this volume, Ian Kinnes treats 'The Neolithic in Britain' (pp 90–102), covering developments since Piggott's landmark 1954 volume; and John Barrett surveys 'The Bronze Age' (pp 103–22), discussing the history of the concept of a Bronze Age and offering a possible way ahead. All the other works cited in this section should be considered in the light of these two important papers. The year 1995 was **European Year of the Bronze Age**, of which one tangible result is the published conference *Ireland in the Bronze Age*, listed under Waddell at the end of Ireland (below).

Societies and journals

The main national societies dealing with this period are:

The Cambrian Archaeological Association (Wales: publishes *Archaeologia Cambrensis*)

The Prehistoric Society (publishes *Proceedings . . .*)

Royal Archaeological Institute (publishes *Archaeological journal*)

Royal Irish Academy (publishes *Proceedings . . .*)

Royal Society of Antiquaries of Ireland (publishes *Journal . . .*)

Society of Antiquaries of London (publishes *Antiquaries journal*)

Society of Antiquaries of Scotland (publishes *Proceedings . . .*)

Lithic Studies Society, a small specialist group, publishes *Lithics* annually.

Bibliography and reference

Ars Praehistorica: Anuario internacional de arte prehistorico (0212–7288). Sabadell (Barcelona): Editorial AUSA. 1980–.
Includes an annual bibliography, with abstracts, of (mainly rock) art, world-wide scope.

Who's who in rock art. Directory of specialists, scholars and technicians (ed A Fradkin Anati). ICOMOS-CAR and CCSP. Capo di Ponte: Edizioni del Centro Camuno di Studi Preistorici, 1985, 161 pp.

The periodical *Lithics* sometimes lists recent publications on stone tools.

Books

First are listed books which cover both Britain and Ireland; then come works specific to Wales, Scotland, the Channel Islands and Ireland respectively.

BRITAIN AND IRELAND, GENERAL WORKS

Abercromby, John, *A study of the Bronze Age pottery of Great Britain and Ireland and its associated grave goods.* Oxford: Clarendon, 1912, 2 vols, refs, index.
Classic pioneering work, still consulted for its illustrations and basic data.

Annable, F K and Simpson, D D A, *Guide catalogue of the Neolithic and Bronze Age collections in Devizes Museum.* Devizes: Wilts Archaeol Natur Hist Soc, 1964, vii, 133 p.
Details of these important items.

Ashbee, Paul, *The earthen long barrow in Britain: an introduction to the study of the funerary practice and culture of the Neolithic people of the third millennium BC.* Norwich: Geo Books, 2 rev edn, 1984, xlv, 208 p, bibl, index. 0 86094 170 1.
This and the next item remain classics.

—, *The Bronze Age round barrow in Britain: an introduction to the study of the funerary practice and culture of the British and Irish single-grave people of the second millennium BC.* London: Phoenix House, 1960, 222 p, bibl, index.

Ashton and David (eds), Studies in stone, see Section 6.11.1 Quaternary . . . Mesolithic.

Atkinson, R J C, *Stonehenge.* Harmondsworth: Penguin, rev edn 1979, 224 p, bibl, index. 0 14 020450 4 pb.
Still worth reading for the quality of the writing alone, although now somewhat eclipsed by the full publication by Cleal et al (see below) of 20th century studies of this most celebrated monument. In particular Atkinson's phasing has been considerably revised.

Barnatt, J, *Stone circles of Britain: taxonomic and distributional analyses and a catalogue of sites in England, Scotland and Wales. BARBS,* 215(i–ii), 2 vols, 1989, 555 p, bibl, site index. 0 86054 701 9 pb.

Barrett, J C, *Fragments from antiquity: an archaeology of social life in Britain, 2900–1200 BC.*

Oxford: Blackwell, 1993, x, 190 p, bibl, index. 0 631 18953 x hb, 0 631 18954 8 pb.
A fresh approach to a formative period.

— and Bradley, Richard (eds), *Settlement and society in the British Later Bronze Age. BARBS*, 83(i-ii), 1980, 500 p, bibl. 0 86054 108 8 pb.
Papers aiming to discover the relationship between the settlements and the artefacts; post-Wessex Culture changes in subsistence and society.

— and Kinnes, I A (eds), *The archaeology of context in the Neolithic and Bronze Age: recent trends.* Sheffield: Univ Sheffield Dept Archaeol Prehist (*Recent trends*, 3), 1988, iii, 143 p, bibl, index. 0 906090 31 8 pb.
Twelve papers on English and Scottish material.

**—, Bradley, R and Green, Martin, *Landscape, monuments and society: the prehistory of Cranborne Chase* ... Cambridge: CUP, 1991, x, 255 p, bibl. 0 521 32128 x.

**— , Bradley, R and Hall, Melanie (eds), *Papers on the prehistoric archaeology of Cranborne Chase. Oxbow monogr*, 11, 1991, iv, 251 p, bibl. 0 946897 31 x.
This and the previous volume have been welcomed as essential reading for all serious students of later prehistory.

Beckensall, S, *Rock carvings of northern Britain.* Princes Risborough: *Shire archaeol*, 47, 1986, 64 p, index. 0 85263 760 8 pb.
Introduction to a subject which is gaining increased attention as attempts are made to read its symbolism.

Blick, on early metal working, see Section 6.15 Archaeology of industrial processes.

Blore, Frances, Hitchen, Miles and Vallender, John, *Archaeological assessment of the Stonehenge World Heritage site and its surviving landscape.* London: Engl Heritage, 1995, 28 p + 500 p + 20 p, bibl. 5 ring binders + spiral-bound adjuncts. No ISBN.
Comprises gazetteers of the recorded archaeology within the site and its surrounding landscape, and of the survey and evaluation work undertaken in the same area. Sets out constraints and policy frameworks.

Bradley, Richard and Edmonds, Mark, *Interpreting the axe trade: production and exchange in Neolithic Britain.* Cambridge: CUP, 1993, xiv,
236 p, bibl, index. 0 521 43446 7 (New studies in archaeology).
Studies changes in the character of Lake District axe production and examines changing patterns in trade elsewhere in the country.

— et al (eds), *Prehistoric land divisions on Salisbury Plain: the work of the Wessex Linear Ditches Project.* London: English Heritage (= *Archaeol rep*, 2), 1994, [viii], 181 p, bibl, index. 1 87504 477 4 pb.
Traces a long development of these divisions.

BRITISH BRONZE AGE METALWORK ASSOCIATED FINDS SERIES (British Museum Publications):
A1–A6, Needham, S P et al, *Early Bronze Age hoards.* 1985, six cards. 0 7141 1380 8
A7–A16, Kinnes, I A, *Beaker and Early Bronze Age grave groups.* 1985, ten cards. 0 7141 1381 6
A17–A30, Kinnnes, I A, *Beaker and Early Bronze Age grave groups (continued).* 1995, 14 cards. 0 7141 2302 1
These three sets provide drawings and basic data for some important hoards in each category.

Buckley, Victor (comp), *Burnt offerings: international contributions to burnt mound archaeology.* Dublin: Wordwell, 1990, 195 p, bibl. 1 869857 07 0 pb.
Numerous papers on the distribution, function, dating and nature of these still-enigmatic monuments. See also Hodder below.

Burgess, Colin et al, *Enclosures and defences in the Neolithic of western Europe. BAR int ser*, S403(i–ii), 1988, x, 445 p, bibl. 0 86054 518 0 pb.
Includes both general and site-specific papers (eg Crickley Hill, Hambledon Hill, Etton, Haddenham).

—, *Bronze Age metalwork in Northern England, c. 1000 to 700 BC.* Newcastle upon Tyne: Oriel Press, 1968, 74 p, bibl, index. Pb.
Discussion of archaeological and metallurgical information, and definition of Wallington and Wilburton complexes of bronze implements.

***—, *The age of Stonehenge.* London: Dent, 1980, 402 p, bibl, index. 0 460 04254 8.
University level text covering the period c. 3200 – c. 1200 BC, with emphasis on continuity through the five phases defined, and with particular attention to changes in burial, ritual

and society over the period. Still indispensable though later work now needs to be taken into account.

— and Gerloff, S, *The dirks and rapiers of Great Britain and Ireland*. München: C H Beck, (= *Prähistorische Bronzefunde*, **IV**.7), 1981, 141 p, bibl, index. 3 406 07083 3.
Corpus of known items; a volume in the German series which aims to cover all European bronze finds.

— and Miket, R (eds), *Settlement and economy in the third and second millennia BC: papers delivered ... January 1976*. BARBS, 33, 1976, bibls. 0 904531 52 X.
Showing its age now but a seminal work.

**Burl, H A W (Aubrey), *The stone circles of the British Isles*. New Haven/London: Yale Univ Press, 1976, xxii, 410 p, bibl, index. 0 300 01972 6.
Synthesis discussing origins, social implications, possible astronomical significance etc, and providing regional surveys, concordance and gazetteer.

*—, *Prehistoric Avebury*. New York/London: Yale Univ Press, 1979, x, 275 p, bibl, index. 0 300 02368 5.
Presents the known facts and sets the great monument into its local and wider context, with special attention to daily life of its people.

*—, *From Carnac to Callanish: the prehistoric stone rows of Britain, Ireland and Brittany*. New Haven: Yale Univ Press, 1993, 296 p, bibl, index. 0 300 05575 7.
History of research, distribution, circles, avenues; gazetteers by class of monument.
And see Burl in Section 6.3 Guides.

Castleden, R, see Section 6.3 Guides.

Champion, T C and Megaw, J V S (eds), *Settlement and society: aspects of West European prehistory in the first millennium BC*. Leicester: Leicester Univ Press, 1985, viii, 243 p, bibl, index. 0 7185 1232 4 hb, 0 7185 1256 1 pb.
Late Bronze Age and Iron Age papers.

***Chippindale, Christopher, *Stonehenge complete*. London: Thames and Hudson, rev edn 1994, 296 pp, bibl, index. 0 500 27750 8 pb.
Invaluable, profusely illustrated conspectus of antiquarian to modern records; but now to be read in the light of Cleal et al (below).

Clarke, David L, *Beaker pottery of Great Britain*

and Ireland. Cambridge; CUP, 1970, 2 vols, xix, 575 p, bibl. 0 521 07249 2.
In its time a pioneering corpus of the material; very difficult to use because of the cataloguing system, and the conclusions have been regularly reassessed (see, eg, Lanting and van der Waals below).

Clarke, David V, Cowie, T G and Foxon, A, *Symbols of power at the time of Stonehenge*. Edinburgh: Nat Mus Antiquities Scotland/ HMSO, 1985, xvi, 334 p, bibl, index. 0 11 492455 4 pb.
Superbly illustrated catalogue of an exhibition which presented artefacts and monuments as symbols of the ideology of domination; also useful discussion of the craft skills of third and second millennia BC.

Cleal, R M J, Montague, R and Walker, K E, *Stonehenge in its landscape: twentieth century excavations*. English Heritage archaeol rep, [new ser] 10, 1995, [xxii], 618 p, bibl, index. 1 85074 605 2.
The definitive recension of this century's investigations of the monument. (*See also Blore et al above.*)

Clough, T H McK and Cummins, W A (eds), *Stone axe studies: archaeological, petrological, experimental, and ethnographic* [Vol.1]. CBA res rep, 23, 1979, 137 p, bibl, index. 0 900312 63 7 pb.
This and the next work are volumes of specialist papers in the continuing process of examining the source rocks for Neo/BA implements.

— and —, *Stone axe studies, vol 2: The petrology of prehistoric stone implements from the British isles*. CBA res rep, 67, 1988, ix, 297 p, bibl, index. 0 906780 52 7 pb.

Coles, J M and Coles, B J, *Sweet Track to Glastonbury: the Somerset levels in prehistory*. London: Thames and Hudson, 1986, 200 p, bibl, index. 0 500 39022 3.
Displays the richness of the wetlands for providing information on housebuilding, crafts, industries, daily life, woodland management; also treats experimental archaeology.

— and Harding, A F, *The Bronze Age in Europe: an introduction to the prehistory of Europe, c 2000–700 BC*. London: Methuen, 1979, xviii, 581 p, bibl, index.

Colquohoun, Ian and Burgess, Colin, *The swords of Britain*. München: C H Beck, (= *Prähistor-*

ische Bronzefunde, **IV**.5), 1988, x, 163 p, bibl, indexes. 3 406 30500 8.
Another in the German-origin series which aims to catalogue all the bronzes of Europe.

Craddock, Paul T, *Early metal mining and production*. Edinburgh: Edin UP, 1995, xix, 363 p, bibl, index. 0 7486 0498 7.
Highly technical work which treats native metals, inception and development of metal smelting processes, lead and silver, iron and steel, volatile metals and other alloys. Its emphasis lies outside Britain.

Crew, Peter and Susan (eds), *Early mining in the British Isles: proceedings of the Early Mining workshop at Plas Tan y Bwlch . . . November 1989. Plas Tan y Bwlch occas pap*, 1, 1990, iv, 80 p, bibl. 0 9512373 7 3 pb.
Mainly Welsh sites, offering evidence that mining began in the Bronze Age.

Edmonds, Mark, *Stone tools and society: working stone in Neolithic and Bronze Age Britain*. London: Batsford, 1995, 208 p, bibl, glossary, index. 0 7134 7140 9 hb, 0 7134 7141 7 pb.
Treats theoretical considerations, reassesses some principal horizons of change, and examines production/exchange contexts and competition with metal.

Eogan, George, *The accomplished art: gold and gold-working in Britain and Ireland during the Bronze Age c. 2300 – 650 BC. Oxbow monogr*, 42, 1994, x, 199 p. 0 946897 72 7.
Evaluation and interpretation of the four main Bronze Age phases from Beaker to Final Bronze Age, based on about 1,600 objects.

Evans, John, *The ancient stone implements, weapons and ornaments of Great Britain*. London: Longmans Green, 2 rev edn 1897, xviii, 747 p, refs, indexes. Classic, pioneering work treating essentially Palaeolithic to Beaker evidence.

—, *The ancient bronze implements, weapons, and ornaments of Great Britain and Ireland*. London: Longmans Green, 1881, xix, 509 p, refs, indexes.
Another classic and pioneering study.

*Fleming, Andrew, *The Dartmoor reaves: investigating prehistoric land divisions*. London: Batsford, 1988, 135 p, bibl, index. 0 7134 5665 5.
Rediscovery by painstaking fieldwork of the ancient stone boundary walls which parcelled Dartmoor up in the Bronze Age.

Gallay, Gretel, *Die mittel- und spätbronze – sowie ältereisenzeitlichen Bronzedolche in Frankreich und auf den Britischen Kanalinseln* [The MBA, LBA and EIA bronze daggers in France and the Channel Islands]. München: C H Beck, (= *Prähistorische Bronzefunde*, **VI**.7), 1988, ix, 202 p, bibl, indexes. 3 406 31774 X.
This and the next volume are two more in the important 'PBF' series of full drawings and descriptions.

Gerloff, S, *The Early Bronze Age daggers in Great Britain and a reconsideration of the Wessex Culture*. München: C H Beck (= *Prähistorische Bronzefunde*, **VI**.2), 1975, viii, 298 p, bibl, indexes. 3 406 00756 2.

Gibson, Alex M, *Beaker domestic sites: a study of the domestic pottery of the late 3rd and early 2nd millennia BC in the British Isles. BARBS*, 107(i-ii), 1982, 553 p, bibl. 0 86054 189 4 pb.

Greenwell, W and Rolleston, G, *British barrows . . .* Oxford: Clarendon Press, 1877, xiii, 763 p.
Classic early excavation work from which researchers still try to wring essential data.

Grimes, W F, *Excavations on defence sites, 1939–45: I, mainly Neolithic–Bronze Age*. London: HMSO, (= *Min Works archaeol rep*, 3, 1960, 259 p, refs, index.
The principal publication left to us by one of our finest excavators (and illustrators) records his wartime excavations; included here largely for the model illustrations.

Grinsell, L V, *The ancient burial mounds of England*. London: Methuen, 2 edn 1953, xviii, 278 p, refs, index. (Reprinted Westport, Conn: Greenwood Press, 1975, xxiv, 281 p.)
Pioneering classic whose value possibly even gains as more and more barrows disappear from the countryside; covers Roman and Saxon as well as prehistoric barrows. See relevant county journals for author's detailed and updated lists; and see also author's attractive introduction in the *Shire archaeol* series (3 edn 1990).

Harding, A F with Lee, G E, *Henge monuments and related sites of Great Britain: air photographic evidence and catalogue. BARBS*, 175, 1987, ii, 443 p, bibl. 0 86054 470 2 pb.

Hayes, John W, *Ancient metal axes and other tools in the Royal Ontario Museum: European*

and *Mediterranean types*. Toronto: Roy Ont Mus, 1991, xiii, 105 p, bibl. 0 88854 393 x.
Catalogue including a few British examples, together with amendments to the Pryor 1980 work (below).

Heggie, Douglas, *Megalithic science: ancient mathematics and astronomy in north-west Europe*. London: Thames and Hudson, 1981, 256 p, bibl, index. 0 500 05036 8.
Searching analysis, by an astronomer, of claims (from Lockyer to Thom and MacKie) for the astronomical uses of megalithic settings.

Hodder, M and Barfield, L, *Burnt mounds and hot stone technology. Papers from the Second International Burnt Mounds conference, Sandwell 12–14 October 1990*. Sandwell: Sandwell Metrop Borough Council, 1991, ii, 111 p, bibl. 0 9517419 0 x pb.
A follow-up volume to Buckley 1990 (above).

Kinnes, Ian, *Non-megalithic long barrows and allied structures in the British Neolithic. Brit Mus occas pap*, 52, 1992, 250 p, bibl. 0 86159 052 x pb.
Gazetteer and discussion.

—, *Round barrows and ring ditches in the British Neolithic. Brit Mus occas pap*, 7, 1979, 140 p, bibl. 0 86159 006 6 pb.
Register of sites, and synthesis.

— and Varndell, G (eds), '*Unbaked urns of rudely shape': essays on British and Irish pottery for Ian Longworth*. Oxbow monogr, 55, 1995, 218 p, bibls. 0 946897 94 8.
Neolithic and Bronze Age pottery treated by 19 contributors.

Lanting, J N and van der Waals, J D, 'British beakers as seen from the Continent: a review article', *Helinium* (Wetteren), 12, 1972, pp 20–46.
A response to D L Clarke's Corpus (above), offering a revised scheme.

Longworth, I H, *Collared urns of the Bronze Age in Great Britain and Ireland*. Cambridge: CUP, 1984, xiv, 338 p. (Gulbenkian archaeol series). 0 521 08596 9.
Corpus of a common pottery form.

Lynch, Frances and Burgess, Colin (eds), *Prehistoric man in Wales and the West: essays in honour of Lily F Chitty*. Bath: Adams and Dart, 1972, viii, 368 p, bibls, index. 0 239 00071 4.

Collection in honour of a noted Bronze Age scholar.

MacKie, E W, *Science and society in prehistoric Britain*. London: Elek, 1977, xii, 252 p, bibl, index. 0 236 40041 x.
Sets out a controversial theory that the great ritual monuments like Silbury Hill, Stonehenge, Brodgar, were devised and built by a priestly elite.

**Mercer, R J, *Hambledon Hill: a Neolithic landscape*. Edinburgh: Edin UP, 1980, 71 pp, refs. 0 85224 406 1 pb.
While the excavation report is still awaited, this booklet gives a summary view of the causewayed camp and surrounding features.

Milles, Annie et al, The beginnings of agriculture, see Section 6.14 Landscape . . . agriculture.

Moore, C N and Rowlands, M J, *Bronze Age metalwork in Salisbury Museum*. Salisbury: Salisbury and S Wilts Museum, 1972, 72 + 16 p, bibl. 0 9502338 0 3.

Mortimer, J R, *Forty years' researches in British and Saxon burial mounds of Yorkshire*. London: Brown, 1905, lxxxvi, 452 p, index.
Classic volume from which researchers are still trying to extract vital details.

*Needham, Stuart, *Excavation and salvage at Runnymede Bridge, 1978: the Late Bronze Age waterfront site*. London: Brit Mus Publ/ English Heritage, 1991, 388 p, bibl. 0 7141 1397 2 pb.
Report on an important site, notable chiefly for the preservation of waterlogged organic and environmental materials.

Nicholson, S M, *Catalogue of the prehistoric metalwork in Merseyside County Museums*. Liverpool: Merseyside County Museums/Univ Liverpool *Work Notes*, 2, 1980, 148 p.
Mainly Bronze Age objects from the British Isles (and Central Europe).

Norwich Castle Museum, *Bronze Age metalwork in Norwich Castle Museum*. [Norwich]: Norfolk Museums Service, 2 rev edn 1977, 64 p, bibl, index. Pb.

Oddy, W A (ed), on early metallurgy, see Section 6.15 Archaeology of industrial processes.

Parker Pearson, Michael, *English Heritage book of Bronze Age Britain*. Batsford/English Heri-

tage, 1992, 152 p, bibl, index. 0 7134 6801 7 hb, 0 7134 6856 4 pb.
Survey covering the period from 4000 to 900 BC; lists sites to visit.

Pearce, Susan, *The Bronze Age metalwork of south-western Britain. BARBS, 120*, 1983, 2 vols. 0 86054 242 4 pb.
Corpus of the material.

*Piggott, Stuart, *Neolithic cultures of the British Isles*. Cambridge: CUP, 1954, xix, 420 p, bibl, index. (Reprint edn 0 521 07781 8.)
Classic work which, although now outdated in much of its theory, remains an indispensable – and beautifully written – source of basic data on Neolithic sites and artefacts.

*—, *The West Kennet long barrow: excavations 1955-6*. London: HMSO, 1962 (= *Min Publ Bldg Works archaeol rep*, **4**), xii, 103 p, refs, index. 0 11 670558 2.
Another classic work on an important monument in the Avebury area.

Powell, T G E et al (eds), *Megalithic enquiries in the West of Britain: a Liverpool symposium*. Liverpool Univ Press, 1969, 357 p, bibl, index.
Important papers on monuments in N Wales, the Clyde cairns of Scotland, and Cotswold-Severn tombs.

PRÄHISTORISCHE BRONZEFUNDE SERIES see entries under (respectively) Burgess and Gerloff, Colquohoun and Burgess, Gerloff, Harbison (in Irish section), and Schmidt and Burgess.

**Pryor, Francis, *Flag Fen: prehistoric Fenland centre*. London: Batsford/English Heritage, 1991, 143 p, bibl, glossary, index. 0 7134 6752 5 hb, 0 7134 6753 3 pb.
Important wetland site near Peterborough with BA structures and ritual depositions. Novel excavation techniques, study of landscape development, etc.

—, *A catalogue of British and Irish prehistoric bronzes in the Royal Ontario Museum*. Toronto: Roy Ont Mus, 1980, 80p, bibl, index. 0 88854 240 2.
Material which found its way across the Atlantic includes all types of axe, weaponry, ornaments, LBA shield etc. Some corrections noted in Hayes (above).

Richards, Julian, *English Heritage book of Stone-*

henge. London: Batsford/English Heritage, 1991, 141 p, bibl, index. 0 7134 6142 X.
Summarises current knowledge of the World Heritage monument in its landscape.

Royal Commission on the Historical Monuments of England, *Long barrows in Hampshire and the Isle of Wight*. London: HMSO, 1979, xxxvi, 77 pp, bibl, index. 0 11 700837 0 pb.
Inventory to familiar RCHME standards, with discussion.

Ruggles, C L N (ed), *Records in stone: papers in memory of Alexander Thom*. Cambridge: CUP, 1988, xvii, 519 p, bibl. 0 521 33381 4.
Contains 21 papers on megalithic circles and their implications for Neo/BA metrology, geometry and astronomy.

— and Whittle, A W R (eds), *Astronomy and society in Britain during the period 4000–1500 BC. BARBS, 88*, 1981, 342 p, bibl. 0 86054 130 4 pb.
Sober examination of the evidence, in ten papers.

Schmidt, P K and Burgess, C B, *The axes of Scotland and northern England*. München: C H Beck (= *Prähistorische Bronzefunde*, **IX**.7), 1981, xi, 297 p, bibl, index. 3 406 04001 2.
Another in the German-origin series of catalogues of bronzes.

Sharples, Niall on Maiden Castle Neolithic, see entry in Section 6.11.3 Iron Age.

— and Sheridan, Alison (eds), *Vessels for the ancestors: essays on the Neolithic of Britain and Ireland in honour of Audrey Henshall*. Edinburgh: EUP, 1992, vi, 366 p, bibl, index. 0 7486 0341 7.
A good introductory summary of current Neolithic studies in these islands is followed by sections on funerary studies, decorated stones, and artefact studies.

Shee-Twohig, Elizabeth, *The megalithic art of western Europe*. Oxford: Clarendon Press, 1981, 259 p, bibl, index. 0 19 813193 3.
Catalogue and full discussion of the geometric and other art associated with megalithic tombs from Iberia to Ireland and Orkney.

Simpson, D D A (ed), *Economy and settlement in Neolithic and Early Bronze Age Britain and Europe: papers delivered at a conference . . . 1969*. Leicester: Leicester Univ Press, 1971, 186 p, bibl, site index. 0 7185 1094 1.

Smith, I F, *Windmill Hill and Avebury: excavations by Alexander Keiller 1925–1939.* Oxford: Clarendon Press, 1965, xxx, 265 p, bibl, index. Exemplary recension of the prewar excavations on what is now a World Heritage Site. To be read now in the light of Ucko et al below. *NB: this book sometimes found catalogued under Keiller.*

Stig Sørenson, M L and Thomas, Roger (eds), *The Bronze Age-Iron Age transition in Europe: aspects of continuity and change in European societies c. 1200 to 500 BC. BAR int ser,* S483(i-ii), 1989, x, 492 p, bibl. 0 86054 620 9 pb. Includes several papers with British reference.

Taylor, Joan J, *Bronze Age goldwork of the British Isles.* Cambridge: CUP, 1980, xiv, 199 p, bibl, index. 0 521 20802 5. Corpus (with fine photographs of detail) and discussion of the workmanship of lunulae, other gold sheetwork, massive ornaments of LBA.

Taylor, Robin J, *Hoards of the Bronze Age in southern Britain: analysis and interpretation. BARBS,* 228, 1993, x, 116 p, bibl, 5 fiches. 0 86054 748 5 pb.

Thom, Alexander, *Megalithic sites in Britain.* Oxford: Clarendon Press, 1967, 174 p. No ISBN.

—, *Megalithic lunar observatories.* Oxford: Clarendon Press, 1971, 127 p. 0 19 858132 7. Both these works demand a great deal from the reader in terms of mathematical and astronomical ability, but were fundamental in forcing a total reassessment of the intellectual capabilities of Neolithic people. Thom was also the first person to make detailed theodolite surveys of a large number of megalithic circles and other settings; his plans are preserved in the next item. The work was mostly concerned with Scotland but was later extended to some English sites.

—, and Thom, A S (ed A Burl), *Megalithic rings: plans and data from 229 monuments in Britain. BARBS,* 81, 1980, 405 p, refs, site index. 0 86054 094 4 pb. The Thoms' high-quality surveys, presented with archaeological notes by Burl.

Thomas, Julian, *Rethinking the Neolithic.* Cambridge: CUP, 1991, xv, 211 p, bibl, index. 0 521 40377 4. (New studies in archaeology.) Controversial post-processual interpretation of the S English Neolithic.

Tylecote, R F, *The prehistory of metallurgy in the British Isles.* London: Institute of Metals, 1986, xiv, 257 p, refs, glossary, indexes. 0 904357 72 4. Covers the development of metallurgical skills from the beginnings into the medieval period.

*Ucko, P, Hunter, M, Clark, A J and David, A, *Avebury reconsidered: from the 1660s to the 1990s.* London: Unwin Hyman, 1991, xiv, 293 p, bibl, index. 0 04 445919 X. Rediscovery of forgotten 17th-century plans provoked this re-examination of evidence for various features at Avebury, and a revaluation of Stukeley's work.

*Wainwright, G J, with I H Longworth, *Durrington Walls excavations, 1966–1968. Rep Res Comm Soc Antiq London,* 29, 1971, xiv, 421 p, bibl, index. 0 85431 218 8. Very large-scale excavation which began a new era in the understanding of henge monuments.

—, *Mount Pleasant, Dorset: excavations 1970–71. Rep Res Comm Soc Antiq London,* 37, 1979, xiv, 265 p, bibl, index. 0 500 99029 8. The second large-scale henge excavation.

**—, *The henge monuments: ceremony and society in prehistoric Britain.* London: Thames and Hudson, 1989, 176 p, bibl, index. (New aspects of antiquity series). 0 500 39025 8. Synthesis of knowledge derived from exploration of a number of chalk downland sites.

Warne, Charles, *The Celtic tumuli of Dorset. . . .* London: J R Smith, 1866, c. 180 p. Early, classic, survey of the burial mounds predating the Roman Conquest.

Whittle, Alasdair, *Europe in the Neolithic: the creation of new worlds.* Cambridge: CUP, 1996, 443 p, bibl, index. 0 521 44476 4 hb, 0 521 44920 0 pb. Revision of author's 1985 work: challenges conventional views and argues that the Neolithic phenomenon had strong roots in foraging peoples, with gradual adoption of new ideas on sacred sites and the like. Covers the period 7000–2500 BC.

—, *Problems in Neolithic archaeology.* Cambridge: CUP, 1988, xiii, 232 p, bibl, index. 0 521 35121 9. Covers NW Europe from mid-6th to mid-3rd millennium.

WALES: ie BOOKS SPECIFIC TO WALES ALONE

Barker, C T, *The chambered tombs of southwest Wales: a reassessment of the Neolithic burial monuments of Carmarthenshire and Pembrokeshire*. Oxbow monogr, 14, 1992, viii, 88 p, bibl. o 946897 33 6 pb.
Survey, gazetteer and discussion.

Britnell, W J and Savory, H N, *Gwernvale and Penywyrlod: two Neolithic long cairns in the Black Mountains of Brecknock*. Cambrian archaeol monogr, 2, 1984, viii, 163 p, refs, index. o 947846 o o pb.
Two modern excavations.

Fox, (Sir) Cyril, *Life and death in the Bronze Age: an archaeologist's field work*. London: Routledge and Kegan Paul, 1959, xxvii, 193 p, bibl, indexes.
Classic work on the excavation of several Welsh barrows, remarkable for its exercise of creative imagination about prehistoric ritual practices.

Griffith, John E, *Portfolio of photographs of the cromlechs of Anglesey and Carnarvonshire [sic] reproduced in collotype*. Bangor: privately, 1900, c. 45 photographs in landscape format.
These megalithic tombs were foresightedly photographed as a record for posterity.

Lynch, Frances, see Brenig Valley volume (including Bronze Age barrows) in Section 6.11.1 Quaternary . . . Mesolithic.

— and Burgess, C (eds), on prehistoric man in Wales and the West, see above in Britain and Ireland general.

Powell, T G E and Daniel, G, *Barclodiad y Gawres: the excavation of a megalithic chamber tomb in Anglesey 1952–1953*. Liverpool: Liverpool Univ Press, 1956, 80 p, refs, index.
The tomb contained mural art of great interest. Includes a short note by J L Forde-Johnston on the Calderstones, Liverpool.

**Royal Commission on the Ancient and Historical Monuments of Wales, *An inventory of the ancient monuments in Glamorgan: vol I(i), The Stone and Bronze Ages*. London: HMSO, 1976, xxx, 144 p, notes, index. o 11 700588 6.
The official record.

Savory, H N, *Guide catalogue of the Bronze Age collections*. Cardiff: Nat Mus Wales, 1980, 258 p, bibl, index. o 7200 0219 2.
Includes a summary of archaeometallurgical studies.

Smith, C A and Lynch, F, *Trefignath and Din Dryfol: the excavation of two megalithic tombs on Anglesey*. Cambrian archaeol monogr, 3, 1987, xvi, 135 p, bibl. o 947846 01 8 pb.

SCOTLAND: ie BOOKS SPECIFIC TO SCOTLAND AND THE BORDERS

Anderson, Joseph, *Scotland in pagan times: the Bronze and Stone Ages. The Rhind Lectures in Archaeology for 1882*. Edinburgh: David Douglas, 1886, xii, 397 p.
An early classic.

Ashmore, Patrick, *Calanais [Callanish]: the standing stones*. [n p]: Urras nan Tursachan, 1995, 52 p, bibl. o 86152 161 7 pb.
Fine booklet on the well-known ceremonial site on the Isle of Lewis.

Barclay, Gordon, *Balfarg: the prehistoric ceremonial complex*. Edinburgh: Hist Scot, 1993, 35 p. 1 872162 01 0 pb.
Souvenir booklet, brief account of this extremely important set of monuments, now fully reported in *Proc Soc Antiq Scot*, 123, 1993, pp 43–210.

Burgess and Gerloff corpus of dirks and rapiers, see above under Britain and Ireland general.

Clarke, D V and Maguire, P, *Skara Brae: northern Europe's best preserved prehistoric village*. [Edinburgh: HBMS], 1989, 28 p. o 7480 0190 5 pb.
Booklet in advance of the definitive report.

Cowie, T G, *Bronze Age food vessel urns in northern Britain*. BARBS, 55, 1978, 173 p, bibl. o 86054 031 6 pb.
Corpus of known examples.

Cowie, Trevor, *Magic metal: early metalworkers in the north-east*. Aberdeen: Anthropol Mus, Univ Aberdeen, 1988, 56 p, refs. ISBN missing.
Written to accompany an important exhibition: a useful conspectus of available information on the earliest Bronze Age in the Grampian area.

*Davidson, J L and Henshall, A S, *The chambered cairns of Orkney: an inventory of the structures and their contents*. Edinburgh: EUP, 1989, 198 p, bibl, index. o 85224 547 5.
This and the next entry, plus Henshall and Ritchie (below) are the definitive inventories.

*— and —, *The chambered cairns of Caithness: an inventory of the structures and their contents*.

Edinburgh: EUP, 1991, 177 p, bibl, index. o 7486 0256 9.

Hedges, J W, *Isbister: a chambered tomb in Orkney*. BARBS, 115, 1983, xx, 313 p, bibl. o 86054 213 o pb.

—, *Tomb of the eagles: a window on Stone Age tribal Britain*. London: Murray, 1984, xii, 244 p, bibl, index. o 7195 4119 o.
A more approachable (and more speculative) version of the Isbister work.

*Henshall, A S, *The chambered tombs of Scotland*. Edinburgh: EUP, 2 vols, 1963 and 1972, xv, 456 + 656 p, refs, index. o 85224 190 9.
To use in conjunction with the two more up-to-date volumes above (under Davidson and Henshall) and with the next entry.

— and Ritchie, J N G, *The chambered cairns of Sutherland: an inventory of the structures and their contents*. Edinburgh: EUP, 1995, vi, 168 p, bibl, index. o 7486 0609 2.

Morris, R W B, *Prehistoric rock art of Galloway and the Isle of Man*. Poole: Blandford Press, 1979, 192 p, bibl, site index. o 7137 0974 x hb, o 7137 0975 8 pb.
This work and the next are factual, illustrated records of extended field surveys.

—, *The prehistoric rock art of Argyll*. Poole: Dolphin, 1977, 128 p, bibl. o 85642 043 3 hb, o 85642 059 x pb.

*Renfrew, A C, *Investigations in Orkney. Rep Res Comm Soc Antiq London*, 38, 1979, xvi, 234 p, bibl, index. o 500 99028 x.
Important excavations on megalithic tombs etc.

Schmidt P, on bronze axes, see above under Britain and Ireland general.

Sharples, Niall and Sheridan, Alison (eds), Vessels for the ancestors, see above under Britain and Ireland general.

Shepherd, I A G, *Powerful pots: Beakers in northeast prehistory*. Aberdeen: Anthropol Mus, Univ of Aberdeen, 1986, 42 p, bibl. o 951141 10 4 pb.
Uniform with the Cowie booklet above; record of another important exhibition.

Smith, Beverley Ballin (ed), *Howe: four millennia of Orkney prehistory: excavations 1978–1982*. *Soc Antiq Scotl monogr*, 9, 1994, xx, 305 p, bibl, index, 3 microfiche. o 903903 09 1 pb.
The site was occupied from 4th millennium to

late Iron Age by, successively, Neolithic tombs (including Maes Howe type), Neo house (Knap of Howar type), and an Iron Age sequence.

Thom, Alexander, on stone circles, see above under Britain and Ireland general.

Yates, M J, *Bronze Age round cairns in Dumfriesshire and Galloway: an inventory and discussion*. BARBS, 132, 1984, x, 258 p, bibl. o 86054 286 6 pb.

CHANNEL ISLANDS

Patton, Mark, *Neolithic communities of the Channel Islands*. BARBS, 240, 1995, 194 p, bibl. o 86054 776 o pb.
Pays particular attention to the effects of insularity on historical and cultural development.

IRELAND

For recent bibliography of Irish lithics, see *Lithics*, 13, 1992, pp 69–75.

See also the following authors listed above under Britain and Ireland general: Buckley, Burgess and Gerloff, Burl, Clarke D L, Eogan, Longworth, Kinnes and Varndell, Sharples and Sheridan, Shee Twohig, Taylor J J.

Bergh, Stefan, *Landscape of the monuments: a study of the passage tombs in the Cúil Irra region, Co Sligo, Ireland*. Stockholm: Riksantikvarieämbetet, Archeologiska undersokningar, Skrifter 6, 1995, 256 p, bibl. 91 7192 945 2 pb.
Regional and spatial analysis of the tombs of this area: one of the products of Scandinavian interest here.

Borlase, W C, *The dolmens of Ireland*. 3 vols. London: Chapman and Hall, 1897.
Classic early study.

Brennan, Martin, *The stars and the stones: ancient art and astronomy in Ireland*. London: Thames and Hudson, 1983, 208 p. o 500 27283 2.
Attractively illustrated with photographs and drawings of stone circles and tombs and their art; was well received.

Caulfield, Seamas, *Céide Fields, Ballycastle, Co Mayo*. [s l]: [Céide Fields Visitor Centre, 1992], 15 pp. No ISBN, pb.
Guide to the Neolithic/Bronze Age field system which lies below the bog here.

Coffey, George, *The Bronze Age in Ireland*.

Dublin/London: Hodges, Figgis/ Simpkin, Marshall, 1913, 107 p, footnotes, index.
Classic early work.

***De Valera, R and Ó Nualláin, S (eds), *Survey of the megalithic tombs of Ireland* (5 volumes to date). Dublin: Stationery Office, 1961– (last volume so far 1989).
These are the definitive accounts of megalithic tombs, with full descriptions and illustrations, discussion and bibliography. Counties covered so far are (vol 1) Clare; (vol 2) Mayo; (vol 3) Galway, Roscommon, Leitrim, Longford, Westmeath, Laoighis, Offaly, Kildare, Cavan; (vol 4) Cork, Kerry, Limerick, Tipperary; (vol 5 – by second author alone) Sligo.

Eogan, George, *Catalogue of Irish bronze swords*. Dublin: Stationery Office, 1965, xxxix, 190 p, bibl.

*—, *The hoards of the Irish Later Bronze Age*. Dublin: UCD, 1983, xxv, 331 p, bibl, index. o 901120 77 4.
Important catalogue of the finds.

**—, *Knowth and the passage tombs of Ireland*. London: Thames and Hudson, 1986, 247 p, bibl, index. o 500 39023 1 (New aspects of antiquity series).
Attractive account of 25 years' excavation at a classic Irish site.

Evans, Emyr Estyn, *Lyles Hill, a late Neolithic site in County Antrim*. Belfast: HMSO (*Archaeol res publ N Ireland*, 2), 1953, 71 pp, refs.
Classic Neolithic site on which investigations have recently been renewed.

Harbison, Peter, *Bracers and V-perforated buttons in the Beaker and Food Vessel cultures of Ireland*. Bad Bramstedt (West Germany): Moreland Editions (= *Archaeologica Atlantica res rep*, 1), 1976, 95 p, refs. No ISBN.
Catalogue of these attractive personal pieces.

—, *The axes of the Early Bronze Age in Ireland*. München: C H Beck (= *Prähistorische Bronzefunde*, 9.1), 1969, viii, 108 p, bibl, indexes.

—, *The daggers and the halberds of the Early Bronze Age in Ireland*. München: C H Beck, (= *Prähistorische Bronzefunde*, 6.1), 1969, x, 76 p, bibl, indexes.

Herity, Michael, *Irish passage graves: Neolithic tomb builders in Ireland and Britain 2500 BC*. Dublin: Irish Univ Press, 1974, xi, 308 p, bibl, index. o 7165 2167 9.

*Lynch, Ann, *Man and environment in southwest Ireland, 4000 BC–AD 800: a study of man's impact on the development of soil and vegetation*. BARBS, 85, 1981, vi, 175 p, bibl. o 86054 112 6 pb.
Important environmental study.

Moloney, Aonghus and Jennings, D, *Excavations at Clonfinlough, Co Offaly*. Dublin: Crannog Publication (*Ir Archaeol Wetland Unit/Trans*, 2), 1993, x, 131 p, refs.
An LBA palisaded settlement.

— et 5 al, *Blackwater survey and excavations: artefact deterioration in peatlands; Lough More, Co Mayo*. Dublin: *Ir Archaeol Wetland Unit/Trans*, 4, 1995, vi, 205 p, bibl. Pb.
Treats 252 newly discovered sites, a study of physical and chemical deterioration of metal and bone in raised bogs, and excavation of a metal-working crannog.

O'Brien, William, *Mount Gabriel: Bronze Age mining in Ireland*. Galway: Galway Univ Press (= *Bronze Age studies*, 3), 1994, xiv, 371 p, bibl. o 907775 51 9 hb, o 907775 56 x pb.
Investigation of a copper mining area in West County Cork.

Ó Drisceoil, Diarmuid, 'Fulachta fiadh: a general statement', in *N Munster antiq j*, 33, 1991, pp 3–6.
Radiocarbon dating suggests an EBA/MBA date for these 'cooking pits' of an impoverished 2nd millennium economy.

**O'Kelly, M J, *Newgrange: archaeology, art and legend*. London: Thames and Hudson, 1982, 240 p, bibl, index. o 500 39015 0 (New aspects of antiquity series).
Attractive account of a classic site.

— (per Claire O'Kelly), *Early Ireland: an introduction to Irish prehistory*. Cambridge: CUP, 1989, xiii, 375 p, bibl, index. o 521 33489 6 hb, o 521 33687 2 pb.
By the then doyen of Irish prehistory.

Ó Nualláin, Seán, *Stone circles*. Dublin: Town House and Country House, 1995, 48 p, glossary, refs, index. o 946172 45 5 pb.
Introductory booklet.

Ó Ríordáin, Breandán and Waddell, John, *The funerary bowls and vases of the Irish Bronze Age*. Galway: Galway Univ Press for NMI (= *Bronze Age studies*), 1993, xxv, 289 p, bibl. o 907715 46 2.

Corpus of examples.

O'Sullivan, Muiris (photos by John Scarry), *Megalithic art in Ireland*. Dublin: Town House and Country House, 1993, 46 p. 0 946172 36 6 pb.
General survey of this art, placing it in context and discussing current views of its symbolism.

*Raftery, Barry, *Trackways through time: archaeological investigations on Irish bog roads, 1985–1989*. Rush, Co Dublin: Headline, 1990, ii, 75 p, bibl. 0 9515761 0 0 pb.
Introductory text with colour and b/w photographs, dendrochronological dates.

—, *Mountdillon excavations 1985–91*. Ir Archaeol Wetland Unit/Trans, 3), due 1996.
Neo to Early Christian period trackway; woodworking, palynology and palaeobotany.

Shee Twohig, E, *Irish megalithic tombs*. Princes Risborough: *Shire archaeology*, 63, 1990, 72 p, bibl, index. 0 7478 0094 4 pb.
Good introduction.

Waddell, John, *The Bronze Age burials of Ireland*. Galway: Galway Univ Press, 1990, 166 p, bibl. 0 907775 36 5.
Corpus and gazetteer of discoveries to 1980.

— and Shee Twohig, Elizabeth (eds), *Ireland in the Bronze Age: proceedings of the Dublin conference, April 1995*. Dublin: Stationery Office, 1995, xii, 169 p, bibls. 0 7076 2311 1 pb.
For the European Year of the Bronze Age: papers on the radiocarbon chronology, dendrochronology, copper mining, bronze- and goldwork, the Navan complex, timber circles, cemeteries, rock art, wedge tombs, and cross-sea relations.

6.11.3
Iron Age

This period is taken to run from about the seventh century BC to the Roman Conquest in AD 43. The most recent summary of research over the last five decades is in John Collis's chapter 'The Iron Age' in B Vyner (ed), *Building on the past* (Roy Archaeol Inst, 1994), pp 123–48, with good bibliography. This section has been much improved by Dr A P Fitzpatrick, though any remaining faults are the compiler's own.

Societies and journals

The main national societies dealing with this period are those listed in the previous section on Neolithic and Bronze Age.

Bibliographies

[Feugère, M (ed)], *Bibliographies sur l'Age du Fer (BTA 1–8)*. Montagnan: Edns Monique Mergoil (*Bibliographies thématiques en archéologie*), 1988, unnumbered pages. 2 907303 00 7 pb.
European scope, with geographical and thematic indexes, but by no means comprehensive.

***Hogg, A H A, *British hillforts: an index*. BARBS, 62, 1979, 237 p, bibl, index. 0 86054 046 4 pb.
List of the sites and their main references, with introductory discussion.

— et al, 'Hillfort abstracts for Welsh archaeological periodicals', *Bull Board Celtic Stud*, 33, 1986, pp 291–386.
Very detailed, coded analyses of a large number of sites, with abstracts of some.

Lorenz, H and Frey, O-H (subsequently U Müller), *Kommentierte Bibliographie zur Archäologie der Kelten*. Marburg: Vorgeschichtliches Seminar der Philipps-Univ Marburg. 1976/7–.
At least five numbers were issued. (Note that occasional bibliographic round-ups are given in the rather inaccessible *Études celtiques*.)

Books
ENGLAND, AND FOUR-NATION WORKS GENERALLY

**Alcock, Leslie, *By South Cadbury is that Camelot . . . The excavation of Cadbury Castle 1966–1970*. London: Thames and Hudson, 1972, 224 p, notes, index. 0 500 39011 8 hb, 0 500 27029 5 pb.
Highly readable account of how an excavation unfolds from season to season; treats Neolithic and post-Roman evidence as well as the Iron Age hillfort. The conclusions have been revised in the forthcoming report.

Allen, D F, 'The origins of coinage in Britain: a reappraisal', in Frere (1961, below), pp 97–308.
A classic work on Iron Age coinage, still regularly used by specialists though it placed more emphasis on invasions than is accepted now. See also Haselgrove (below).

Arnold, Bettina and Gibson, D Blair (eds), *Celtic chiefdom, Celtic state: the evolution of complex social systems in prehistoric Europe.* Cambridge: CUP, 1995, xii, 159 p, bibl, index. o 521 44469 2.

Audouze, F and Büchsenschütz, O (transl H Cleere), *Towns, villages and countryside of Celtic Europe: from the beginning of the second millennium to the end of the first century* BC. London: Batsford, 1991, 256 p, bibl, index. o 7134 6523 9.
A clear and useful synthesis, marred by an inadequately checked bibliography.

Barrett, J C et al on Cranborne Chase, see Section 6.11.2 Neolithic–Bronze Age.

Blick, on early metallurgy, see Section 6.15 Archaeology of industrial processes.

Bradley, Richard, see relevant chapters in two of his works: *The social foundations of prehistoric Europe* (Longman, 1984); *Passage of arms* (CUP, 1990).

*Brailsford, J W, *Early Celtic masterpieces from Britain in the British Museum.* London: Brit Mus Publs, 1975, 103 p, refs, glossary, index. o 7141 1362 X hb, o 7141 1363 8 pb.
Fine illustrations of selected pieces, with commentary.

*Brothwell, Don, *The Bog Man and the archaeology of people.* London: Brit Mus Publs, 1986, 128 p, bibl, index. o 7141 1384 o pb.
On the peat-preserved corpse of 'Lindow Man' and comparable bodies: see also under Stead et al and Turner (respectively) below.

[Champion, T C], 'The Iron Age: A, Southern Britain and Ireland', in J V S Megaw and D D A Simpson (eds), *Introduction to British prehistory . . .*, 1979, pp 344–421.
Introduction for students; should now be taken along with newer works.

— and Megaw, J V S (eds), *Settlement and society: aspects of West European prehistory in the first millennium* BC. Leicester: Leicester Univ Press, 1985, viii, 243 p, bibl, index. o 7185 1232 4 hb, o 7185 1256 1 pb.

Cleere and Crossley on Wealden iron, see Section 6.15 Archaeology of industrial processes.

Coles, J M (ed), *Meare Village East: the excavations of A Bulleid and H St George Gray 1932–1956.* Exeter: Somerset Levels Project (= *Som Levels pap*, 13), 1987, 260 p, bibl. (landscape format).
Retrieves previously unpublished work on an important wetland settlement.

*— and Minnitt, Stephen, *'Industrious and fairly civilized': the Glastonbury lake village.* Taunton: Somerset Levels Papers/Somerset County Council Museums Service, 1995, 213 p, bibl. o 9507122 2 1 pb.
The long-awaited synthesis of old and recent excavations of a famous settlement in the Somerset wetlands.

Collis, John, *The European Iron Age.* London: Batsford, 1984, 192 p, bibl, index. o 7134 3451 1 hb, o 7134 3452 X pb.
Focuses on the socio-economics of production and exchange.

***Cunliffe, B W, *Iron age communities in Britain: an account of England, Scotland and Wales from the 7th century* BC *until the Roman Conquest.* London: Routledge, 3 edn 1991, xii, 685 p, bibl, index. o 415 05416 8.
Third in the series Archaeology of Britain: indispensable text book. For an easier introduction the same author's *Iron Age Britain* in the Batsford/EH series, 1995, is recommended.

***—, *Danebury: anatomy of an Iron Age hillfort.* London: English Heritage/Batsford, 2 edn 1993, 136 p, bibl, index. o 7134 6885 8 hb, o 7134 6886 6 pb.
Extensively revised edition of this accessible introduction to a famous hillfort, more fully described in the volumes below. Danebury must surely be reckoned the principal Iron Age project of the late twentieth century, notable inter alia for its extensive application of archaeological science in almost every aspect.

**—, *Danebury: an Iron Age hillfort in Hampshire.* Vol 1, *The excavations, 1969–78: the site; vol 2, . . . the finds* (both published as *CBA res rep*, 52, 1984, viii, ix, 568 p, bibl, index, 17 fiches. o 906780 27 6 pb (the set). (First series excavations.)
Vol 3, see below under Palmer.
Vols 4 and 5 (with Cynthia Poole), *The excavations 1979–88: the site / the finds* (both published as *CBA res rep*, 73, 1991, ix, v, 493 p, bibl, index, fiches.) 1 872414 21 4 pb (the set.). (Second series excavations.)
Vol 6, *A hillfort community perspective. CBA*

res rep, 102, 1995, xi, 296 p, bibls, index, fiche. 1 872414 58 3.

—, 'Danebury: the anatomy of a hillfort re-exposed', in P Bogucki (ed), *Case studies in European prehistory* (Boca Raton: CRC Press, 1994), pp 259–86 (0 8493 8882 1).

—, *The Celtic world*. London: Constable, 1992, 224 p, bibl, index. 0 09 47164 0.
General European survey in large format.

— and Miles D (eds), *Aspects of the Iron Age in central southern Britain*. OUCA monogr, 2, 1984, vi, 209 p, bibl, indexes. 0 947816 02 X.
Collected papers from an Oxford conference on settlement, farming, metallurgy, pottery and coins.

Cunnington, M E, *The Early Iron Age inhabited site at All Cannings Cross Farm, Wiltshire*. Devizes: Simpson and Co, 1923, 204 p, refs, index.
Classic site.

Elsdon, Sheila, *Later prehistoric pottery in England and Wales*. Princes Risborough: *Shire archaeol*, 58, 1989, 68 p, refs, index. 0 7478 0004 9 pb.
Attractive primer and introduction.

Eluère, Christiane, *The Celts: first masters of Europe*. London: Thames and Hudson (New horizons series), 1993, 175 p. 0 500 30034 8 pb.

Fitzpatrick, A P and Morris, Elaine L (eds), *The Iron Age in Wessex: recent work*. Salisbury: Assoc Française d'Étude de l'Age du Fer/Trust for Wessex Archaeol, 1994, xii, 124 p, bibl. 1 874350 11 6 pb.
Pre-conference publication for an Anglo-French conference.

Fox, Cyril, *Pattern and purpose: a survey of Early Celtic art in Britain*. Cardiff: Nat Mus Wales, 1958, xxix, 160 p, refs, index.
Art-historical approach analysing individual elements on metalwork and other fine pieces; rather dated now, but still the best all-round survey.

Frere, S S (ed), *Problems of the Iron Age in southern Britain: papers given at a CBA conference held at the Institute of Archaeology Dec 12–14 1958*. London: *Univ London Inst Archaeol occas pap*, 11, [1961], xii, 308 p, refs.
A landmark conference: contains the only record so far in print for some sites even now, and still regularly cited.

Green, Miranda, *The gods of the Celts*. Gloucester: Alan Sutton, 1986, x, 257 p, bibl. 0 86299 292 3.
One of several books on Celtic religion by this author; bibliography not easy to use.

— (ed), *The Celtic world*. London: Routledge, 1995, xxiv, 839 p, bibl, index. 0 415 05764 7 hb, 0 415 14627 5 pb.
Massive survey with 41 papers of variable quality under the headings: Celtic origins; warriors and warfare; society and social life; settlement and environment; economy; technology and craftsmanship; art; pagan Celtic religion; Celts in Europe, and on the edge of the Western world; Celtic survival. Britain is well represented. Can be regarded as a counterpart of Wacher's *The Roman world* (see next section, Roman Britain). Some scholars have preferred the Moscati (ed) volume noted below.

Guido, Margaret, *The glass beads of the prehistoric and Roman periods in Britain and Ireland*. *Rep Res Comm Soc Antiq London*, 35, 1978, xxxi, 250 p, bibl, index. 0 500 99026 3.
Complex typology and gazetteer of a ubiquitous and often attractive ornament.

Gwilt, Adam and Haselgrove, Colin (eds), *Reconstructing Iron Age societies: new approaches to the British Iron Age*. Oxford: *Oxbow monogr* forthcoming (1996).
Important collection of 30 papers from a Durham meeting in 1994, debating and synthesising various aspects of the period.

**Harding, D W (ed), *Hillforts: later prehistoric earthworks in Britain and Ireland*. London: Academic Press, 1976, xiv, 579 p, bibl, indexes. 0 12 324750 0.
Symposium volume containing the only reports, in some cases, for excavations on hillforts (eg Salmonsbury, Blewburton, Scottish vitrified forts, etc).

*—, Blake, I M and Reynolds, P J, *An Iron Age settlement in Dorset: excavation and reconstruction*. Univ Edinburgh Dept Archaeol monogr, 1, 1993, 113 p, bibl. ISSN (only) 0968-0500.
Pimperne is the site name, unaccountably omitted from the title: previous to this long-delayed publication the site had been better known for houses experimentally built to its excavation plan, and for other experimental

work described here (including the dismantling of the original Butser Ancient Farm 'replica').

Haselgrove, C, *Iron Age coinage in south-east England: the archaeological context. BARBS*, **174**, 1987, 2 vols, ix, 524 p, bibl. o 86054 461 3 pb.
Gazetteer of recorded finds together with models of coin use and trade. (See also Allen 1961 above, and Haselgrove's 'The development of British Iron-Age coinage' in *Numismatic chronicle*, 153, pp 31–64.)

Hattatt, Richard, *Ancient and Romano-British brooches*. Sherborne: Dorset Publ Co, 1982, 221 p, index. o 902129 39 2.
The first of the author's four guides to brooches in his extensive collection, all unfortunately from non-archaeologically controlled sources. They are additional to the Hull corpus (see below), and are well drawn, with some discussion of development/typology. The other three titles are:
> *Iron Age and Roman brooches: a second selection of brooches from the author's collection*. Oxford: Oxbow Books, 1985 (repr 1993), 242 p, bibl, index. o 946897 07 7
> *Brooches of antiquity: a third selection . . .* Oxford: Oxbow Books, 1987 (repr 1994), 406 p, index. o 946897 11 5
> *Ancient brooches and other artefacts: a fourth selection . . .* Oxford: Oxbow Books 1989, 520 p. o 946897 17 4 (Includes a 'visual catalogue' – ie representative drawings of the various types.)

*Hawkes, C F C and Hull, M R, *Camulodunum. Rep Res Comm Soc Antiq London*, **14**, 1947, xix, 362 p, bibl, index.
Classic report on the Late Iron Age 'oppidum' next to what became the Roman fortress and colony of Colchester. Reassessed in C F C Hawkes and Philip Crummy, *Camulodunum 2. Colchester Archaeol Rep*, **11**, 1995, xiv, 186 p, bibl, index. o 897719 03 5.

Hill, David and Jesson, M (eds), *The Iron Age and its hillforts: papers presented to Sir Mortimer Wheeler . . .* Southampton: Southampton Univ Archaeol Soc, 1971, xii, 220 p, bibl, index.
Papers by eminent scholars (and those who later became so) in honour of modern archaeology's founding father.

Hogg, A H A, *A guide to the hillforts of Britain*. London: Paladin, 2 edn 1984, xv, 304 p, bibl, index. o 586 08460 6 pb.
Updated preface and bibliography.

Hull, M R and Hawkes, C F C, *Corpus of ancient brooches in Britain: pre-Roman bow brooches (PBB). BARBS*, **168**, 1987, 236 p, bibl, site index. o 86054 450 8 pb.
Terminology, introductory material on Bronze Age and Iron Age, then brooches up to La Tène III. (A further volume, on the later types, is forthcoming.)

James, Simon, *Exploring the world of the Celts*. London: Thames and Hudson, 1993, 192 p, bibl, glossary, indexes. o 500 05067 8.
Accessible introduction which includes a gazetteer of sites and museums.

**Jones, Martin, *England before Domesday*. London: Batsford, 1986, 174 p, bibl, index. o 7134 2555 5 hb, o 7134 2556 3 pb.
Numerous Iron Age examples are given in this general introduction to landscape and environmental archaeology.

*Macready, S and Thompson, F H (eds), *Cross-Channel trade between Gaul and Britain in the pre-Roman Iron Age. Soc Antiq London occas pap*, **4**, 1984, vii, 114 p, bibl, index. o 500 99036 0 pb.
Conference papers setting out the extent of the busy Channel traffic at this time.

Mays, Melinda (ed), *Celtic coinage: Britain and beyond. The eleventh Oxford Symposium on Coinage and Monetary History. BARBS*, **222**, 1992, xvi, 302 p, bibls. o 86054 732 9.
Contains 17 papers reporting the latest research on various aspects of the coinage.

*Megaw, J V S, *Art of the Iron Age: a study of the elusive image*. Bath: Adams and Dart, 1970, 195 p, bibl, index. o 239 00019 6.
Europe-wide survey and analysis of this ambiguous art, profusely illustrated.

**Megaw, R and V, *Celtic art: from its beginning to the Book of Kells*. London: Thames and Hudson, 1989, 288 p, bibl, index. o 500 05050 3.
Reviews previous studies and surveys the whole period, with an epilogue on the Early Christian period.

*Moscati, S (coordinator), Frey, O H, Kruta, V, Raftery, B and Szabo, M (eds), *The Celts*.

London: Thames and Hudson, 1993 reprint, 711 p. 0 500 01524 4 (Also New York: Rizzoli, 1991.)
Over 1,100 illustrations, many in colour, accompany contributions from over 100 scholars from all around Europe. The book is based on a large exhibition mounted in Venice in 1991, whose aim was to present a 'definitive record of a people who, in great part, *are* Europe'. (More than one version has been published, carefully distinguished in J V S Megaw's review in *Antiquity*, 66, 1992, pp 254–60.)

*Nash, Daphne, *Coinage in the Celtic world*. London: Seaby, 1987, 153 p, bibl, index. 0 900652 85 3.
Accessible introduction, from 4th century BC Mediterranean background to mid-1st century AD Britain, in the historical context.

*Palmer, Rog, *Danebury: an Iron Age hillfort in Hampshire. Vol 3, An aerial photographic interpretation of its environs. RCHME suppl ser*, 6, 1984, 133 p, bibl. 0 9507236 1 4 pb.
A graphic, and seminal, presentation of the startling increase in archaeological knowledge obtainable from air photographs, as applied to central Wessex.

Parfitt, Keith (et al), *Iron Age burials from Mill Hill, Deal*. London: Brit Mus Press, 1995, 215 p, bibl. 0 7141 2304 8.
Iron Age cemetery with one of the most important single inhumations in Britain, an individual buried with his regalia.

*Piggott, Stuart, *The Druids*. London: Thames and Hudson (= *Ancient peoples and places*, 63), 1985 (pb edn), 214 p, bibl, index. 0 500 27363 4 pb.
The *real* Druids, as discoverable from Iron Age and Roman sources, with a historiography of their study, written in this author's elegant style.

— and Allen, Derek, *Early Celtic art*. Edinburgh: Edin UP for Arts Council Great Britain, 1970, 42 p. 0 85224 198 4 pb.
Well illustrated exhibition catalogue of British and other European pieces.

Powell, T G E, *The Celts*. London: Thames and Hudson, new edn 1980, 232 p, bibl, index. 0 500 02094 9 hb, 0 500 27275 1 pb (Ancient peoples and places, 6).
This book, first published in 1968 and dated in some aspects, remains a concise and lucid introduction.

Raftery, Barry et al (ed), *Celtic art*. [Paris]: Unesco/Flammarion (distrib Thames and Hudson), 1990, 171 p, bibl, glossary, index. 2 08 013509 0.
Survey (in the UNESCO Art Album series) by an international team of specialists, with many colour illustrations; Britain and Ireland are treated by A Sherratt and B Raftery, and Celtic Christian art by M Ryan.

— (ed, with Vincent Megaw and Val Rigby), *Sites and sights of the Iron Age. Essays on fieldwork and museum research presented to Ian Mathieson Stead. Oxbow monogr*, 56, 179 p, bibls, index. 0 900188 00 7 pb.
Contributions on coins, metalwork, chariots, ornaments, weaponry, pits, Irish pottery and some Roman material.

Reid, M on prehistoric houses, see Section 6.13 Topic surveys.

Reynolds, Peter, see Butser Ancient Farm items in Section 6.14 Landscape . . . agriculture.

Ritchie, W F and Ritchie, J N G, *Celtic warriors*. Princes Risborough: *Shire archaeol*, 41, 1985, 56 p, bibl, index. 0 85263 714 4 pb.
Authoritative and accessible introduction.

Scott, B G, on early Irish ironworking, see under Ireland at end of this section; and on blacksmithing, see Section 6.15 Archaeology of industrial processes.

Sharples, Niall, *Maiden Castle*. London: Batsford/English Heritage, 1991, 143 p, bibl, index. 0 7134 6079 2.
Introduction to the site, more general than same author's excavation report for English Heritage (1991).

**Stead, I M, *Celtic art in Britain before the Roman conquest*. London: Brit Mus Publs, 1985, 72 p, bibl, index. 0 7141 2031 6 pb.
Sets out a clear framework and considers the material thematically, drawing many examples from the British Museum's fine collections.

*—, *Iron Age cemeteries in East Yorkshire: excavations at Burton Fleming, Rudston, Garton-on-the-Wold, and Kirkburn. HBMCE archaeol rep*, old series 22, 1991, ix, 237 p, bibl, index. 1 85074 351 7 pb.
Important excavations of 267 burials of 'La Tène Arras Culture', including two cart-burials, with reassessment of cart construction and description of a mail tunic.

—, Bourke, J C and Brothwell, D, *Lindow man: the body in the bog*. London: Brit Mus Publs, 1986, 208 p, bibl, index. 0 7141 1386 7.
Exhaustive examination of a human body of Iron Age or early Roman date. (*See also under Brothwell above and Turner below*.)

Turner, R C and Scaife, R G (eds), *Bog bodies: new discoveries and new perspectives*. London: Brit Mus Press, 1995, 256 p, bibl, index. 0 7141 2305 6.
Numerous papers present the results of a decade of research since 'Lindow Man' was discovered. Bog bodies from Ireland and the Netherlands have been systematically studied for the information they can convey on past life-styles.

Van Arsdell, R D, *Celtic coinage of Britain*. London: Spink, 1989, xvi, 584 p, bibl, index. 0 907605 24 9.
Catalogue of 800 coin types, well illustrated and intended to replace Mack's 1975 list, though the groupings and chronology have not found general acceptance. Glossary, concordance, maps, metrological and metallurgical information, modern forgeries.

Veen, Marijke van der, *Crop husbandry regimes: an archaeobotanical study of farming in northern England 1000 BC – AD 500*. Sheffield archaeol monogr, 3, 1992, xvii, 227 p, bibl. 0 906090 41 5.
Important ecological and statistical approach.

Wainwright, G J et al, *Gussage All Saints: an Iron Age settlement in Dorset*. London: HMSO (= Dept Environment archaeol rep, old series 10), 1979, xi, 202 p, bibl, index. 0 11 670831 X.
Full excavation of a 'classic Little Woodbury' type of farmstead, covering 3 acres and including an important bronze-founder's deposit.

Wheeler, R E M, *Maiden Castle, Dorset. Rep Res Comm Soc Antiq London*, 12, 1943, xx, 399 p, refs, index.
The classic 1930s excavation, reassessed today (eg Sharples above), but highly influential for at least a generation, and still entertaining. Neolithic and Iron Age.

Woodward, A on Uley temples, see Section 6.11.4 Romano-British.

WALES

(*See also more general books under England above*).

Alcock, Leslie, *Dinas Powys: an Iron Age, Dark Age and medieval settlement in Glamorgan*. Cardiff: Univ Wales Press, 1963, xxviii, 230 p, refs, index.
Excavation report on a key site in S Wales.
See also his book on economy, society and warfare in Section 6.11.5 Migration and early medieval.

Davies, J L, 'The early Celts in Wales', in Miranda Green (ed), *The Celtic world* (referenced above), pp 671–700.
Up-to-date survey.

Fox, Cyril, *A find of the Early Iron Age from Llyn Cerrig Bach, Anglesey*. Cardiff: Nat Mus Wales, 1946, viii, 98 p, refs.
Rich 'hoard' of metalwork from a lake or bog, found during preparations for a wartime airfield.

Jarrett, M G and Wrathmell, S, *Whitton: an Iron Age and Roman farmstead in South Glamorgan*. Cardiff: Univ Wales Press, 1981, xv, 262 p, bibl. 0 7083 0765 5.
First total excavation by modern methods of a Romanised farm in S Wales.

Lloyd-Jones, M, *Society and settlement in Wales and the Marches, 500 BC to AD 1100. BARBS*, 121, 1984, 2 vols, 247 p, 52-page bibl. 0 86054 248 3.

Musson, C R et al, *The Breiddin hillfort: a later prehistoric settlement in the Welsh Marches. CBA res rep*, 76, 1991, x, 223 p, bibl, index, fiches. 1 872414 12 5 pb.
Includes some Meso, Neo, substantial LBA, Iron Age and RB occupation. Also a wet deposit covering Late Glacial to beginning EIA and containing wooden artefacts.

Royal Commission on the Ancient and Historical Monuments of Wales, *An inventory of the ancient monuments in Brecknock (Brycheiniog). The prehistoric and Roman monuments: part ii, Hillforts and Roman remains*. London: HMSO, 1986, xxxii, 196 p, refs, glossary, index. 0 11 300003 0.
Inventory of 77 sites (hillforts, Roman military and civilian sites, roads).
And see Glamorgan Iron Age and Roman volume in Section 6.4 Regional surveys.

Savory, H N, *Excavations at Dinorben 1965–9*. Cardiff: Nat Mus Wales, 1971, x, 85 p, refs, index.
Important hillfort in N Wales, still subject to debate.

—, *Guide catalogue of the Iron Age collections* [of the Nat Mus of Wales]. Cardiff: Nat Mus Wales, 1976, 119 p, footnotes, indexes. o 7200 0089 0.
Many illustrations, subject and topographical index by old counties.

SCOTLAND
(See also more general books under England above).

Allen, J Romilly. *Celtic art in pagan and Christian times.* London: Bracken Books reprint 1993 of 1912 edition, xviii, 315 p (with additional bibliography). 1 85892 075 7.
Classic early study; much of the earlier material receives more modern treatment from MacGregor (below).

Anderson, Joseph, *Scotland in pagan times: the Iron Age. The Rhind lectures in archaeology for 1881.* Edinburgh: David Douglas, 1883, xx, 314 p, index.
A further classic from this pioneering author.

Armit, Ian (ed), *Beyond the brochs: changing perspectives on the Atlantic Scottish Iron Age.* Edinburgh: EUP, 1991, 228 p, bibl, index. o 7486 0197 X.
Papers from a Scottish Archaeological Forum conference, providing the most up-to-date survey of recent work.

—, *The later prehistory of the Western Isles of Scotland. BARBS,* 221, 1992, vi, 185 p, bibl. o 86054 731 0 pb
Covers the first millennium BC to AD 800 and offers a synthesis with a catalogue of sites.

Fairhurst, Horace et al, *Excavations at Crosskirk Broch, Caithness. Soc Antiq Scotl monogr ser,* 3, 1984, 187 p, bibl. o 903903 03 2.
Describes the complex sequence of pre-broch fort, external settlement, environment, some artefacts, economic evidence, radiocarbon dates.

Hamilton, J R C, *Excavations at Jarlshof, Shetland. Min Works archaeol rep,* 1, 1956, xiii, 228 p, bibl, index.
Complex sequence with Neo, LBA evidence, round houses and souterrains, Iron Age, Viking and later Norse occupation, medieval farm, the Old House (late med) of Jarlshof.

—, *Excavations at Clickhimin, Shetland. MPBW archaeol rep,* 6, 1968, xv, 193 p, bibl, index.
LBA farmstead, Iron Age farmstead and fort, broch, wheelhouse, late wheelhouse occupation.

Harding, D W (ed), *Later prehistoric settlement in south-east Scotland. Univ Edinburgh Dept Archaeol occas pap,* 8, 1982, vii, 210 p, bibl. [ISSN only] pb.
Contains 13 papers on settlement patterns, hillforts, artefacts and animal husbandry.

Lamb, R G, *Iron Age promontory forts in the Northern Isles. BARBS,* 79, 1980, 102 p, bibl, index. o 86054 087 1 pb.

MacGregor, Morna, *Early Celtic art in North Britain: a study of decorative metalwork from the third century BC to the third century AD.* Leicester: the Univ Press, 1976, 2 vols, c.450 p, bibl, index. o 7185 1135 2 the set.
Detailed catalogue and discussion, developed from author's thesis.

Morrison, Ian, *Landscape with lake dwellings: the crannogs of Scotland.* Edinburgh: EUP, 1985, o 85224 472 X hb, o 85224 522 X pb.
(These settlements cover a two-and-a-half millennium span in fact.)

Munro, R, *Ancient Scottish lake dwellings or crannogs: with a supplementary chapter on remains of lake dwellings in England.* Edinburgh: David Douglas, 1882, xx, 326 p, refs, index.
To be read in conjunction with the Morrison work above.

Piggott and Allen on early Celtic art, see above under England.

Ralston, I B M, 'The Iron Age. B: Northern Britain', in J V S Megaw and D D A Simpson (eds), *Introduction to British prehistory . . . ,* 1979, pp 446–96.
Clear introduction for students.

Rideout, J S et al (eds), *Hillforts of southern Scotland.* Edinburgh: AOC monogr, 1, 1992, vi, 175 p, bibl, index. o 9519344 1 4 pb.
Important excavation reports on this area.

Ritchie, J N G, *Brochs of Scotland.* Princes Risborough: *Shire archaeology,* 53, 1988, 56 p, bibl, index. o 85263 928 7 pb.

Rivet, A L F (ed), *The Iron Age in northern Britain.* Edinburgh: EUP, 1966, viii, 155 p, bibl.
May be found on library shelves but has largely been overtaken by events.

Smith, Beverley Ballin (ed), *Howe: four millennia*

of Orkney prehistory. Edinburgh (= *Soc Antiq Scotl monogr*, 9), 1994, xxii, 305 p, bibl, index, 3 fiche. 0 903903 09 1 pb.

Full report of the first total excavation of a series of Iron Age settlements in the Northern Isles. (Also Neo-BA occupation levels here.)

ISLE OF MAN

(See also more general works above under England.)

Bersu, Gerhard (ed C A R Radford), *Three Iron Age round houses in the Isle of Man.* Douglas: Manx Mus and National Trust, 1977, xii, 96 p, bibl.

Sites dug by the excavator who taught us to recognise posthole structures; the editor supplies a revision of Bersu's dating.

IRELAND

(See also the more general books above under England. The journal Emania *carries a number of articles on the Irish Iron Age.)*

Byrne, F J, *Irish kings and high-kings.* London: Batsford, rev edn 1987, 342 p, bibl, index. 0 7134 5813 5.

The main, definitive source for the background to monuments like Tara.

Dumville, D N et al, see in Section 6.11.5 Migration and early medieval, for material on the Iron Age sites of Emain Macha and Ard Macha.

Guido, M, corpus of glass beads, see above under England.

Harding, D W, Hillforts of the British Isles, see above under England.

Jackson, K H, *The oldest Irish tradition: a window on the Iron Age (Rede lecture 1964).* Cambridge: CUP, 1964, vi, 56 p.

Suggested how the Irish epics allow us to visualise life in the Celtic Iron Age; but the theory has since been extensively questioned.

Macalister, R A S, *Tara: a pagan sanctuary of ancient Ireland.* London: Scribner, 1931, 208 p, notes, index.

This and the next entry are currently being overtaken by more detailed recent work.

Ó Ríordáin, S P, *Tara: the monuments on the hill.* Dundalk: Dundalgan Press, 1971, 23 p. *See also Bhreathnach's Tara bibliography in Section 6.11.5 Migration and early medieval.*

Raftery, Barry, *A catalogue of Irish Iron Age antiquities.* Marburg: *Veröffentlichung der Vorgeschichtlichen Seminar Marburg, Sonderband* 1, 2 vols, 1983, bibl, place-name indexes. 3 924222 00 2 pb.

Catalogue raisonné.

—, *La Tène in Ireland: problems of origin and chronology.* Marburg: *Veröffentlichung der Vorgeschichtlichen Seminar Marburg, Sonderband* 2, 1984, xxiv, 396 p, bibl, indexes. 3 924222 01 0.

Discusses, as a companion volume to the entry above, how and when the distinctive Iron Age style arrived in Ireland.

**—, *Pagan Celtic Ireland: the enigma of the Irish Iron Age.* London: Thames and Hudson, 1994, 240 p, annot bibl, index. 0 500 05072 4.

Important new statement with fresh information on sites like Navan and Tara.

Scott, B G, *Early Irish iron working.* Belfast: *Ulster Museum publ*, 266, [1990], xi, 238 p, bibl. 0 900761 25 3.

How iron working came to Ireland and how it developed; ores, mining, slags, furnace structures; evidence of language and literature.

Warner, R B et al, 'Irish Early Iron Age sites: a provisional map of absolute dated sites', *Emania*, 7, 1990, pp 46–50.

Wood-Martin, W G, *Pagan Ireland, an archaeological sketch: a handbook of Irish pre-Christian antiquities.* London: Longmans Green, 1895, 689 p, bibl, index.

Classic source book with good bibliography (pp 595–655).

Also relevant

Brunaux, Jean-Louis (transl D Nash), *The Celtic Gauls: gods, rites and sanctuaries.* London: Seaby, 1988, vi, 154 p, bibl, index. 1 85264 009 X.

Translation of *Les Gaulois*; includes Britain.

6.11.4
Romano-British

This period is taken as starting in AD 43 with the Roman Conquest and continuing until about AD 410 with Rome's formal abdication from control over Britain's defence. In fact the preceding and following periods are of great interest. In the period before the Roman conquest increasing Romanisation is seen in SE Britain; and the period which followed the withdrawal of the last remnants of the Roman legions, with the Anglo-Saxon incursions (whether in great or small numbers) is one of the most tantalisingly obscure phases in Britain's history. It should also be remembered that Britain was but a small part of the Roman Empire, so that developments far from these islands had their repercussions here too; Wacher (ed) *The Roman world* is probably best for showing the wider context. An important continuing German series, *Aufstieg und Niedergang der römischen Welt*, often contains state-of-the-art papers (usually in English when dealing with British material) on various aspects of the rise and decline of the Roman world.

The most recent summary of the last ninety years or so of research on Roman Britain is by W S Hanson, 'Dealing with barbarians: the Romanization of Britain' in B Vyner (ed), *Building on the past* (Roy Archaeol Inst, 1994), pp 149–63. Apart from that, a recent comment by W S Hanson indicated a general scarcity of useful general works on Roman Britain.

Societies, journals and bibliographies are listed first, followed by works on Britain and the Roman Empire generally; then come works specific to Wales, Scotland and Ireland respectively.

This section has been much improved by Dr Joan P Alcock, but any remaining faults are those of the compiler.

Societies

Numerous societies deal with Roman studies in Britain: the main ones are listed below (addresses will be found in Section 4.2 Organisations).

Association for Roman Archaeology
Association for the Study and Preservation of Roman Mosaics
Roman Military Equipment Conference
Society for the Promotion of Roman Studies
Study Group for Roman Pottery

Journals

Britannia (0068–113X) 1970–. Society for the Promotion of Roman Studies (Contains the extremely valuable annual roundup 'Roman Britain in 19XX'.)
Coin hoards from Roman Britain (0140–1149).

1975–. Royal Numismatic Society for Internat Numis Commission
Journal of Roman archaeology (1047–7594). 1988–. Ann Arbor
Journal of Roman military equipment studies (0961–3684). 1990–. Roman Military Equipment Conference
Journal of Roman pottery studies (0958–3491). 1988–. Oxbow Books
Journal of Roman studies (0075–4358). 1911–. Society for the Promotion of Roman Studies. (Up to 1969 contained the annual roundup that was then transferred to *Britannia*.)
Journal of theoretical Roman archaeology (0965–1861). 1993–. Oxbow Books

Bibliographies and sourcebooks

Three works may be singled out as containing particularly useful bibliographies of this period: Jones and Mattingley (1990); Salway (1993); and Potter and Johns (1992). Bonser's bibliography can be useful within its time-frame. The principal source for **inscriptions** is 'RIB', listed as *ROMAN INSCRIPTIONS OF BRITAIN* below. For **texts** refer to Moore or Ireland, and for **sculptures** see *CORPUS SIGNORUM IMPERII ROMANI* below.

Adkins, L and Adkins, R, *Handbook to life in Ancient Rome*. New York: Facts on File, 1994, xi, 404 p, bibl, index. 0 816027 55 2.
Includes the Roman Empire generally, so references to Roman Britain are necessarily scattered.

— and —, *Dictionary of Roman religion*. New York: Facts on File, 1996, xvi, 288 p, glossary, bibl, index. 0 8160 3005 7.

Bonser, Wilfrid, A Romano-British bibliography (55 BC–AD 449). Oxford: Blackwell, 1964, 2 vols, xliii, 442 p + 95 p indexes.
Contains over 9,000 entries, classified and indexed by subjects and authors; unselective and occasionally odd, but can be useful for finding and checking references up to about 1960.

*Cameron, F, 'Dictionary of Roman pottery terms', in *J Roman pottery studies*, 1, 1986, pp 58–79.
Gives the commoner current terms in English with French, Italian, Spanish, German and Dutch equivalents.

*Campbell, Brian, *The Roman army, 31 BC–AD 337: a sourcebook*. London: Routledge, 1994, 288 p, bibl, index. 0 415 07172 0 hb, 0 415 07173 9 pb.
On military organisation and practice, and the role of soldiers in social, political and economic life, drawn from literary, epigraphic, coin and artefactual evidence.

*Cornell, Tim and Matthews, John, *Atlas of the Roman world*. Oxford: Phaidon, 1982, 240 p, bibl, gazetteer, index. 0 7148 2152 7 (repr Facts on File, 1992, 0 87196 652 2).

***CORPUS SIGNORUM IMPERII ROMANI* (Corpus of sculpture of the Roman world). Oxford: OUP/Brit Academy. Volume 1 covers Great Britain, of which eight fascicules have appeared, by various authors:
Fascicule 1, *Corbridge, Hadrian's Wall east of the North Tyne* (E J Phillips, 1977)
Fasc. 2, *Bath and the rest of Wessex* (B W Cunliffe and M Fulford, 1982)
Fasc. 3, *Yorkshire* (S R Tufi, 1983)
Fasc. 4, *Scotland* (L J F Keppie and B J Arnold, 1984)
Fasc. 5, *Wales* (R J Brewer, 1986)
Fasc. 6, *Hadrian's Wall west of the N Tyne* (J C Coulston and E J Phillips, 1988)
Fasc. 7, *Roman sculpture from the Cotswold region with Devon and Cornwall* (M Henig, 1993)
Fasc. 8, *Roman sculpture from eastern England* (J Huskinson, 1994)

Fletcher, Richard, *Who's who in Roman Britain and Anglo-Saxon England*. London: Shepheard-Walwyn, 1989, xxv, 245 p, glossary, index. 0 85683 089 5 hb, 0 85683 114 X pb.
Short biographies of individuals, up to Harold II.

*Hammond, N G L and Scullard, H H (eds), *Oxford classical dictionary*. Oxford: Clarendon, 2 edn 1970, xxii, 1176 p. 0 19 869117 3.

**Ireland, S, *Roman Britain: a sourcebook*. London: Routledge, 2 edn 1996, 280p, bibl indexes. 0 415 13134 0 pb.
A collection of literary, numismatic, epigraphic and similar evidence in English translation, spanning the period from Caesar to Gildas.

***Jones, Barri and Mattingly, David, *An atlas of Roman Britain*. Oxford: Blackwell, 1990, x, 341 p, bibl, index. 0 631 13791 2; also 1993, 0 631 18786 3 pb.
Narrative text on the progress and nature of Roman settlement with many maps, plans, photographs and data tables, and excellent bibliography.

Jones, John Melville, *A dictionary of ancient Roman coins*. London: Seaby, 1990, 329 p. 1 85264 026 X.
A supplement to S W Stevenson's 19th century work; defines coin-related words such as 'aes', 'follis', 'debasement'; covers to end of reign of Anastasius I.

Lyell, Arthur, *A bibliographical list descriptive of Romano-British architectural remains in Great Britain*. Cambridge: CUP, 1912, xii, 156 p, place-name index.
An early attempt, with compact, sensible layout by county, unfortunately no subject index; includes a list of works consulted. It excludes sites where (eg) roof tiles but no foundations were discovered.

*Maxfield, Valerie A and Dobson, Brian, *Inscriptions of Roman Britain*. LACTOR 4, 3 edn 1995, 160 p, glossary, bibl, indexes. 0 903625 23 7 pb.
Includes short explanatory papers on religion and on the source-value of coinage. A small selection of the wooden and curse tablets is included.

Moore, R W (ed), *The Romans in Britain: a selection of Latin texts with commentary*. London: Methuen, 3 edn 1954 (revised W V Wade), 214 p.
Basic material for understanding the Roman occupation; the only sourcebook to give the Latin texts.

Potter and Johns see in main sequence below.

***Rivet, A L F and Smith, C, *The place names of Roman Britain*. London: Batsford, 1979, xviii, 526 p, refs, glossary, index. 0 7134 2077 4.
Definitive account and discussion of names as recorded in classical sources.

***THE ROMAN INSCRIPTIONS OF BRITAIN*: series edited by R G Collingwood and R P Wright (Oxford: OUP), followed by S S Frere and R S O Tomlin (Stroud: Alan Sutton). Volumes available so far are:
1. *Inscriptions on stone* (Collingwood and Wright, 1965; reprinted with additional material, Alan Sutton, 1995)
plus *Epigraphic Indexes* (comp Roger Goodburn and Helen Waugh, 1983; reprinted 1990)

II. *Instrumentum domesticum: fascicule I, The military diplomata, metal ingots, tesserae, dress labels and lead sealings, RIB 2401–2411* (ed Frere et al, 1990)

fasc. II *Weights, gold, silver, bronze, lead, pewter, shale, glass vessels, spoons, RIB 2412–2420* (ed Frere et al, 1991)

fasc. III, *Brooches, rings, gems, bracelets, helmets, shields, weapons, iron tools, baldric fittings, votives in gold, silver and bronze, lead pipes, roundels, sheets and other lead objects, stone roundels, pottery and bone roundels, other objects of bone, RIB 2421–2441* (Frere and Tomlin, 1991)

fasc. IV, *Wooden barrels, stilus-tablets, misc. objects of wood, leather objects, oculists' stamps, wall plaster, mosaics, handmills, stone tablets, stone balls, stone pebbles, small stone votives, misc. objects of stone, jet figurines, clay figurines, misc. clay objects, antefixes, tile stamps . . . , RIB 2442–2480* (Frere and Tomlin, 1992)

fasc. V, *Tile-stamps . . . , RIB 2481–2491* (Frere and Tomlin, 1993)

fasc. VI, *Dipinti and graffiti on amphorae . . . on mortaria . . . in barbotine . . . , RIB 2492–2500* (Frere, Tomlin and Hassall, 1994)

fasc. VII, *Graffiti on samian ware (RIB 2501)* (Frere, Tomlin and Hassall, 1995)

fasc. VIII, *Graffiti on coarse pottery: addenda and corrigenda* (ed Frere and Tomlin, 1995)

Indexes and concordances to RIB II (fascicules I–VII), 1995, 93 p (comp S S Frere: contains 16 separate indexes)

Salway see in main sequence below.

Symonds, R (comp), 'Roman pottery bibliography' (annually in *J Roman pottery studies* from 1986 onwards).

Books

BRITAIN AND ROMAN EMPIRE GENERALLY

Works with a strong military emphasis are signalled by (M) before the author's name.

*Adam, Jean-Pierre, *Roman building: materials and techniques* (transl Anthony Mathews). London: Batsford, 1993, 360 p, bibl, index. 0 7134 7167 0.

Alcock, J P, *Life in Roman Britain*. London: Batsford, due late 1996.

*Allason-Jones, Lindsay, *Women in Roman Britain*. London: Brit Mus Publs, 1989, 208 p, bibl, index. 0 7141 1392 1 pb.
Well-received, balanced account.

(M) —, *A guide to the inscriptions and sculptured stones in the Museum of Antiquities of the University and Society of Antiquaries of Newcastle upon Tyne*. Newcastle upon Tyne: Dept of Archaeol Univ Newcastle, 1989, 48 p, bibl, glossary. 1 872447 01 5 pb.
Description of 89 items.

THE ARCHAEOLOGY OF CANTERBURY: monograph series in progress from Canterbury Archaeological Trust; covers from Belgic period onwards.

THE ARCHAEOLOGY OF ROMAN LONDON: in *CBA res rep* series, vols **69–70**, **88**, **98** etc.
Treated in thematic or topographical divisions.

THE ARCHAEOLOGY OF YORK (general editor P V Addyman, published by CBA and York Archaeol Trust): 19 volumes in preparation of which vols 1 and 3–6, together with some fascicules of later volumes, deal with Roman York.

Bailey, Donald M, *A catalogue of the lamps in the British Museum: III, Roman provincial lamps*. London: Brit Mus Publs, 1988, xv, 560 p, bibl, index. 0 7141 1278 X.

Barley, M W and Hanson, R P C (eds), *Christianity in Britain, 300–700: papers presented to the conference on Christianity in Roman and sub-Roman Britain . . .* Leicester: Leicester Univ Press, 1968, 221 p, bibls, index. 0 7185 1077 1.
A ground-breaking conference at the time, and its papers still of use, though Thomas (below) would be preferred for most purposes now.

Bassett, S (ed), on death in towns, see Section 6.13 *Topic surveys (under Society).*

(M) *Birley, Anthony R, *The fasti of Roman Britain*. Oxford: Clarendon Press, 1981, xii, 476 p, bibl, index. 0 19 814821 6.
Gives the careers of known officials of the province.

*—, *The people of Roman Britain*. London: Batsford, 1979, 224 p, bibl, indexes. 0 7134 0580 5.
Information from inscriptions and references of all kinds brings to life the people who lived here.

(M) *Birley, Eric, *Roman Britain and the Roman army: collected papers*. Kendal: Titus Wilson, 1953, xi, 196 p, refs, indexes.
Classic collection from the late doyen of RB military studies.

(M) Birley, Robin (and others), *Vindolanda research reports, new series*. Hexham: Roman Army Museum Publications for Vindolanda Trust.
Seven volumes are planned to report on the excavations of this frontier fort; several have been published so far.

(M) *—, *Vindolanda: a Roman frontier post on Hadrian's Wall*. London: Thames and Hudson, 1977, 184 p, bibl, index. 0 500 39014 2.
Attractive account for a wider audience than the previous title.

(M) **Bishop, M and Coulston, J C N, *Roman military equipment from the Punic wars to the fall of Rome*. London: Batsford, 1993, 256 p, bibl, index. 0 7134 6637 5 (also a pb version 1994).
Indispensable for military studies; treats the appearance of the equipment, how it was used, the place of the army in society and so on; some colour pictures and good drawings.

Blagg, T F C and Millett, Martin (eds), *The early Roman Empire in the West*. Oxford: Oxbow, 1990, 241 p, bibl, index. 0 946897 22 0 pb.
Contains about 15 papers on conquest, integration, urban development, trade development, agriculture, and the like.

*Bland, Roger and Johns, Catherine, *The Hoxne Treasure: an illustrated introduction*. London: Brit Mus Press, 1993, 32 pp. 0 7141 2301 3 pb.
Brief description of the early 5th century treasure found, and properly excavated, in 1992; nearly 15,000 coins and 200 gold and silver objects were retrieved and studied.

Blick, on early metallurgy, see Section 6.15 Archaeology of industrial processes.

*Boon, G C, *Silchester: the Roman town of Calleva*. London: David and Charles, rev edn 1974, 379 p, bibl, index. 0 7153 6339 5.
The most complete account so far of any RB town; dug in early 20th century 'like potatoes' in Wheeler's phrase, but still capable of yielding valuable information. New excavations by M Fulford are improving the contextual framework for the town.

(M) **Bowman, A K, *Life and letters on the Roman frontier: Vindolanda and its people*. London: Brit Mus Press, 1994, 159 p, bibl, index. 0 7141 1389 1.
An important book showing the wide range of information, both military and domestic, that has been extracted from the Chesterholm writing tablets. Includes texts of 34 key tablets. *See also R Birley above.*

(M) — and Thomas, J D, *The Vindolanda writing tablets: Tabulae Vindulandenses* II. London: Brit Mus Press, 1994, 440 p, bibl, index. 0 7141 2300 5.
Fuller details of this important find.

Branigan, K and Dearne, M J (eds), *Romano-British cavemen: cave use in Roman Britain*. Oxbow monogr, 19, 1992, 118 p, bibl. 0 946897 43 3 pb.
Opens up a long-neglected subject with a summary gazetteer of caves with RB material in England and Wales and discussion of cave environments, usage, etc.

(M) ***Breeze, D J, *The northern frontiers of Roman Britain*. London: Batsford, 1982 (repr 1993), 188 p, bibl, index. 0 7134 7256 1 pb.
Indispensable for understanding the Roman North.

(M) ***— and Dobson, B, *Hadrian's Wall*. Harmondsworth: Penguin, 3 edn 1987, viii, 325 p, bibl, index. 0 14 022672 9 pb.
The standard work: dissolves many cherished beliefs about the Wall's purpose and history.

(M) — *Roman officers and frontiers*. Stuttgart: Franz Steiner (= *Mavors Roman Army Researches*, 10), 1993, 631 p, bibls, index. 3 315 06181 9.
Useful reprint collection of papers written 1966–91.

Brodribb, Gerald, *Roman brick and tile*. Gloucester: Alan Sutton, 1987, ix, 164 p, bibl, glossary. 0 86299 363 6.
Illustrates and discusses many different forms.

Brown, A E (ed), *Roman small towns in eastern England and beyond*. Oxbow monogr, 52, 1995, 208 p, bibls. 0 946897 90 5 pb.
Contains 19 papers from a 1992 conference at Leicester, offering theoretical and practical approaches plus contextual studies.

(M) Bruce, J Collingwood (ed Charles Daniels), *Handbook to the Roman Wall with the Cum-*

brian coast and outpost forts. Newcastle upon Tyne: Harold Hill and Son, 13 rev and enlarged edn, 1978, x, 355 p, bibl, index. o 900463 32 5. Classic pocket guide, partly overtaken by later research (see, eg, the shorter guide listed below under Daniels).

Carson, R A G, *Coins of the Roman Empire.* London: Routledge, 1990, xiv, 367 p, bibl, index. o 415 01591 x in slip case.
From 31 BC to AD 498: monetary systems, mint histories, techniques, sources of metal etc.

Chevallier, R, *Roman roads [Les voies romaines],* transl N H Field. London: Batsford, 1976, 272 p, bibl, index. o 7134 3039 7.
Classic work on Roman Empire communications.

Cleere and Crossley on Wealden iron, see Section 6.15 Archaeology of industrial processes.

Collingwood, R G and Myres, J N L, *Roman Britain and the English settlements.* Oxford: OUP, 2 edn 1937, xxv, 515 p, refs, index. o 19 821703 x.
Classic work, very much out of date in approach and details, but still unsurpassed in many ways and greatly admired for the quality of its writing.

— and Richmond, I A, *The archaeology of Roman Britain.* London: Methuen, rev edn 1969, xxv, 350 p, bibl, index. o 416 27580 x.
Another classic, also partly out of date, but often found in libraries and can be used in conjunction with more recent works.

(M) — *and Wright, R P, on Roman inscriptions in Britain ('RIB') see under ROMAN in bibliographic sub-section above.*

(M) Cool, H E M, Lloyd-Morgan, G and Hooley, A D, *Finds from the fortress.* York: CBA (= *Archaeol of York,* 17.10), 1995, pp 1513–1686, bibl. 1 872414 53 2 pb.
Reports the largest collection of non-pottery artefacts from Roman York: both military and civilian. Uses correspondence analysis to compare the assemblage with that from Caerleon.

— and Price, Jennifer, *Roman vessel glass from excavations in Colchester, 1971–85. Colchester archaeol rep,* 8, 1995, xii, 256 p, bibl, indexes, 1 m'fiche. 1 897719 02 7.
Covers the whole RB period in the Colchester area, with a particularly strong mid-1st century collection.

**Cunliffe, B W (ed), *The temple of Sulis Minerva at Bath. Vol. 1 – The site.* Oxford: OUCA monogr, 7, 1985, xv, 194 p, bibl, index. o 947816 07 0.
Vol. 11 – The finds from the sacred spring. OUCA monogr, 16, 1988, vii, 362 p, bibl, index of tablets. o 947816 16 x.
Many important findings of votive objects here, for instance leaden curse-tablets which throw much light on religious and social attitudes of the time.

(M) Daniels, Charles (comp), *The eleventh pilgrimage of Hadrian's Wall . . . 1989.* [s l]: Soc Antiquaries Newcastle upon Tyne etc, 1989, 95 p, refs.
Review of work up to that date and guide to sites.

Davey, N and Ling, R, *Wall painting in Roman Britain. Britannia monogr,* 3, 1982, 231 p, bibl, index, colour m'fiche. o 904387 96 8 pb.
On experiences in restoring the paintings, with art-historical comment, including social implications and organisation of the works.

***Davies, Barbara, Richardson, Beth and Tomber, Roberta, *The archaeology of London vol. 5: A dated corpus of early Roman pottery from the City of London. CBA res rep,* 98, 1994, xviii, 283 p, bibl, index. 1 872414 00 1 pb.
Both the methodology and the content of this report render it of the first importance; date, fabric, forms and (where possible) source are given for each potting industry or fabric. Covers London's most important period, AD 50–160.

(M) *Davies, Roy (ed D Breeze and V Maxfield), *Service in the Roman army.* Edinburgh: EUP, 1989, xii, 336 p, bibl, glossary, index. o 85224 495 9.
Reprint of ten important papers on Roman military administration and military routines.

de la Bédoyère, Guy, *The finds of Roman Britain.* London: Batsford, 1989, 242 p, bibl, index. o 7134 6082 2.
Not universally liked, but provides illustrations of the various types of object.

—, *English Heritage book of Roman towns in Britain.* London: Batsford, 1992, 143 p, bibl, glossary, index. o 7134 6894 7 pb.
From early developments through to the final demise of RB towns; includes list of towns to visit.

(M) Dixon, Karen P and Southern, P, *The Roman*

cavalry from the 1st to the 3rd century AD London: Batsford, 1992, 256 p, bibl, glossary, index. 0 7134 6396 1.
Treats the units in peace and war, the supply of horses, stables and grooming, water and food supply, welfare, baggage animals.

**Esmonde Cleary, A S, *The ending of Roman Britain*. London: Batsford, 1989, xi, 242 p, bibl, index. 0 7134 5275 7.
Good account of a difficult period.

*Farwell, D E and Molleson, T, *Excavations at Poundbury 1966–80, vol 2: the cemeteries*. *Dorset Natur Hist Archaeol Soc monogr*, 11, 1993, xii, 303 p, bibl. 0 900341 35 1 pb.
Important anthropological study of a large RB population.

***Frere, Sheppard, *Britannia: a history of Roman Britain*. London: Routledge, 3 edn 1987, xvi, 423 p, chapter notes, index. 0 7102 1215 1 (also Pimlico, 0 7126 5027 X pb).
The standard textbook, indispensable.

**— and St Joseph, J K S, *Roman Britain from the air*. Cambridge: CUP, 1983, xvii, 232 p, refs, index. 0 521 25088 9.
The bird's eye view of many important sites.

— et al, *Verulamium excavations*. 3 vols:
    1. *Rep Res Soc Antiq London*, 28, 1972, xiv, 384 p, bibl, index. no ISBN
    2. *Rep Res Soc Antiq London*, 41, 1983, xv, 346 p, bibl, index. 0 500 99034 4
    3. *OUCA monogr*, 1, 1984, viii, 299 p, bibl, mini-index. 0 947816 01 1
Long excavation campaign on an important Roman town.

Fulford, M G, 'The landscape of Roman Britain: a review', in *Landscape history*, 12, 1990, pp 25–31.
Article drawing together the evidence and discussing the problems of distinguishing a 400-year dynamic landscape from its prehistoric predecessors and Anglo-Saxon successors.

— and Huddleston, K, *The current state of Romano-British pottery studies: a review for English Heritage*. *Engl Heritage occas pap*, 1, 1991. 1 85074 340 1 pb.
Rapid survey of 20 years' study and recommendations for future policy.

Gaffney and Tingle on Maddle Farm project see Section 6.9 The excavator's training . . . under Survey and reconnaissance.

**Greene, Kevin, *The archaeology of the Roman economy*. London: Batsford, 1986, 192 p, bibl, index. 0 7134 4593 9 hb, 0 7134 4594 7 pb.
Empire-wide survey of trade, agriculture and production.

Greenwell Collection, see under Kinnes in Section 4.9 Museum catalogues.

Grimes, W F, *The excavation of Roman and medieval London*. London: Routledge and Kegan Paul, 1968, xxi, 261 p, index.
Summary reports on bomb-site excavations: includes the Mithras Temple, the Cripplegate fort, and other important discoveries. Grimes's London excavations are currently being prepared as a fully-archived report by the Museum of London.

Hanson, W S and Maxwell, G, on Antonine Wall, see Scottish sub-section below.

Hattatt on brooches, see Section 6.11.3 Iron Age.

*Haverfield, F (revised George Macdonald), *The Romanization of Roman Britain*. Oxford: Clarendon, rev edn 1923, 91 p, footnotes, index.
Classic work, which has been the starting point for many studies. This edition includes a 20-page bibliography of Haverfield's writings.

Hayfield, C, *An archaeological survey of the parish of Wharram Percy, East Yorkshire: 1, the evolution of the Roman landscape*. BARBS, 172, 1987, xiv, 206 p, bibl. 0 86054 463 X pb.
Shows that Wharram was settled long before the famous deserted medieval village appeared.

***Henig, Martin, *Art of Roman Britain*. London: Batsford, 1995, 224 p, bibl, glossary, index. 0 7134 5430 X.
This and the next are masterly discussions of two prominent aspects of the Romans in Britain.

***—, *Religion in Roman Britain*. London: Batsford, 1984, 263 p, bibl, index. 0 7134 1220 8.

*Hingley, Richard, *Rural settlement in Roman Britain*. London: Seaby, 1989, 192 p, bibl, index. 1 85264 017 0.
Takes a fresh look, especially at non-villa settlement.

*Horsley, J, *Britannia Roma or the Roman antiquities of Britain*. Newcastle upon Tyne: Frank Graham reprint, 1974, vi, xxii, 520 p, indexes.

Classic 18th century work reprinted with an introduction by Eric Birley; well illustrated, especially for the Hadrian's Wall area.

Jackson, Ralph, *Camerton: late Iron Age and early Roman metalwork*. London: Brit Mus Publs, 1990, 96 p, bibl. 0 7141 1395 6.
Catalogue of important pre-Flavian hoard (probably from a Roman fort) with some Bronze Age and medieval pieces also found.

*Johns, Catherine, *The jewellery of Roman Britain*. London: UCL Press, due 1996. 1 85728 566 2.
The pieces demonstrate vividly the interaction of Roman and Celtic traditions, and also prompt a discussion of the significance of personal ornament in various cultures.

*— and Potter, Timothy, *The Thetford treasure: Roman jewellery and silver*. London: Brit Mus Publs, 1983, 136 p, bibl, index. 0 7141 1372 7.
Full catalogue and discussion of late 4th century hoard of gold, silver and other items; debates the ambiguous symbolism of the pieces.

(M) Johnson, Stephen, *English Heritage book of Hadrian's Wall*. London: Batsford/English Heritage, 1989, 143 p, bibl, index. 0 7134 5957 3 hb, 0 7134 5958 1 pb.
Accessible introduction.

Johnson, Peter (ed, with Ian Haynes), *Architecture in Roman Britain*. CBA res rep, **94**, 1996, xii, 173 p, bibl, index. 1 872414 39 7 pb.
Notable among the papers from this 1991 conference is new evidence for two-storey buildings.

(M) Jones, Michael J, *Roman fort defences to AD 117, with special reference to Britain*. BARBS, 21, 1975, 192 p, bibl. 0 904531 24 4 pb.
The bibliography was particularly noted at the time as having future uses.

Jones and Dimbleby on environment, Iron Age to Saxon, see Section 6.14 Landscape.

Jones, R F J (ed), *Britain in the Roman period: recent trends*. Sheffield: J R Collis Publs (= *Recent trends*, 5), 1991, vii, 120 pp, bibls. 0 906090 39 3 pb.
Sixteen papers on various aspects: buildings, money, urbanism, soldiers and settlement in Wales and Scotland, the Hayling Island temple.

**Kennedy, D (ed), *Into the sun: essays in air photography in archaeology in honour of*

Derrick Riley. Sheffield: Dept of Archaeol, 1989, x, 211 p, bibls, index. 0 906090 36 9 pb.
Includes papers regarded as essential reading for Roman Britain in particular.

Kent, J P C and Painter, K S (eds), *Wealth of the Roman world AD 300–700*. London: Brit Mus Publs, 1977, 192 p, bibl. 0 7141 0062 5 hb, 0 7141 0061 7 pb.
Exhibition catalogue, with several British sites represented (Traprain Law, Coleraine, New Grange, Sutton Hoo, Anglo-Saxon and Germanic jewellery).

(M) ***Keppie, Lawrence, *Understanding Roman inscriptions*. Batsford, 1991, 158 p, bibl, index. 0 7134 5692 2 hb, 0 7134 5693 0 pb.
Vital guide to a crucial but often perplexing source of evidence.

*King, Anthony, *Roman Gaul and Germany*. London: Brit Mus Publs (Exploring the Roman World series), 1990, 240 p, bibl, index. 0 7141 2044 8.
Useful for setting Roman Britain into context.

Ling, Roger, *Romano-British wall painting*. Princes Risborough: *Shire archaeol*, 42, 1985, 64 p, bibl, index. 0 856263 715 2 pb.
Accessible introduction.

Lysons, Samuel, *An account of Roman antiquities discovered at Woodchester in the county of Gloucester*. London, 1797, 21 pp, 40 pls (some coloured).
Classic drawings and antiquarian report on a Gloucestershire villa with an exceptional Orpheus pavement: only in specialist libraries but well worth looking at.

*Maloney, John and Hobley, Brian (eds), *Roman urban defences in the west: a review of current research on urban defences in the Roman Empire with special reference to the western provinces . . . CBA res rep*, 51, 1983, 147 p, bibls, index. 0 906780 23 3 pb.
Papers from a 1980 conference.

*Manning, W H, *Catalogue of the Romano-British iron tools, fittings and weapons in the British Museum*. London: Brit Mus Publs, 1985, xvii, 197 p, bibl. 0 7141 1370 0.
Seminal work whose centrepiece is the Hod Hill collection, with the Waltham Abbey hoard also included. Appended is a list of major collections and sites.

—, *Catalogue of Romano-British ironwork in the*

Museum of Antiquities, Newcastle upon Tyne. Newcastle upon Tyne: Dept of Archaeol Newcastle Univ, 1976, iv, 61 p, bibl, index.
Another important work from an artefact-rich area of Roman Britain.

**Margary, Ivan D, *Roman roads in Britain.* London: John Baker, 3 edn 1973, 550 p, bibl, index. 0 212 97001 1.
Magisterial survey which, though amplified in detail by others, has not yet been superseded.

*Marsden, P R V, *Ships of the Port of London, first to eleventh centuries AD. Engl Herit archaeol rep,* 3, 1994, 237 p, bibl, glossary, index. 1 85074 470 x pb.
The first survey of ships to take such a long and detailed sweep of historical and archaeological evidence.

(M) **Maxfield, Valerie (ed), *The Saxon Shore: a handbook produced on the occasion of the 15th International Congress of Roman Frontier Studies ... 1989. Exeter studies in history,* 25, 1989, vi, 178 p, bibl. 0 85989 330 8 pb.
Essays and a gazetteer of sites. *See also Roman Frontier Studies entry below.*

***Merrifield, Ralph, *London: city of the Romans.* London: Batsford, 1983, xi, 288 p, bibl, index. 0 7134 2745 0.
Classic by the late doyen of Roman London studies.

***—, *The Roman city of London.* London: Benn, 1965, xvii, 344 p, refs, gazetteer, index.
Still a basic reference work for the City.

*Millett, Martin, *The Romanization of Roman Britain: an essay in archaeological interpretation.* Cambridge: CUP, 1990, xvi, 255 p, bibl, index. 0 521 36084 6 hb, 0 521 42864 5 pb.
Textbook presenting quantities of data and offering explanations.

—, *English Heritage book of Roman Britain.* London: Batsford, 1995, 144 p, narrative bibl, index. 0 7134 7792 x hb, 0 7134 7793 8 pb.
Provides a useful survey of the political and economic history of Roman Britain, setting it in context of the Roman world.

***Milne, Gustav, *The port of Roman London.* London: Batsford, 1985 (repr 1993), 160 p, bibl, index, 0 7134 4364 2 hb, 0 7134 4365 0 pb.
Attractive description of the Roman harbour, first London bridge, quays, warehouses, fishing industry and shipping, all from excavations 1979–82 in the Billingsgate area.

— (ed), *From Roman basilica to medieval market: archaeology in action in the City of London.* London: HMSO for Mus of London, 1992, xiv, 143 p, bibl. 0 11 290446 7.
Essays on different aspects and periods of the Leadenhall Court excavation.

—, *English Heritage book of Roman London: urban archaeology in the nation's capital.* London: Batsford, 1995, 128 p, short bibl, glossary, index. 0 7134 6851 3 hb, 0 7134 6852 1 pb.
Includes the radical reinterpretation of the Governor's Palace induced by recent excavations, and considers social and cultural aspects.

Neal, D S, *Roman mosaics in Britain: an introduction to their schemes and a catalogue of paintings. Britannia monogr,* 1, 1981, 127, 88 p, 2 fiches. 0 904387 64 x pb.
Author's superb reproduction paintings and analytical text.

(M) Ogilvie, R M and Richmond, I A (eds), *Cornelii Taciti De Vita Agricolae* [Tacitus's Life of Agricola]. Oxford: Clarendon Press, 1967, xii, 344 p.
Basic source for the Conquest, with authoritative commentary. Note that Agricola has been the subject of considerable reassessment in recent years: eg W S Hanson in the Scottish section below.

Ordnance Survey, *Roman Britain: historical map and guide at 1:625,000.* Southampton: OS, 4 rev edn 1991. Printed both sides and folded. 0 319 29027 1.
Accompanied by short text and illustrations. Some authorities still prefer the 1978 edition! And note that, by common consent, the 1990 OS map of *Hadrian's Wall* is no substitute for the much older edition (1972).

Oswald, Felix, *Index of the potters' stamps on terra sigillata 'samian ware'* ... East Bridgford: author, 1931, xxiii, 428 p. Limited edn of 275 copies.
Classic work, still regularly consulted.

— and Pryce, T D, *An introduction to the study of terra sigillata treated from a chronological standpoint.* London: Longmans Green, 1920, xii, 286 p, 85 pls, bibl, index.
Classic work which demonstrated the potential

of 'samian' ware for dating purposes; but hard to obtain.

Painter, K, *The Water Newton Early Christian silver*. London: Brit Mus Publs, 1977, 48 p. 0 7141 1364 6 pb.

—, *The Mildenhall Treasure: Roman silver from East Anglia*. London: Brit Mus Publs, 1977, 79 p, bibl. 0 7141 1365 4 pb.
These two booklets describe important hoards of fine silverwork.

Peacock, D P S and Williams, D F, *Amphorae and the Roman economy; an introductory guide*. London: Longman, 1986, xix, 239 p, bibl, index. 0 582 49304 8.
Traces one of the main indicators of trade contacts.

PEOPLES OF ROMAN BRITAIN SERIES. (1) London: Duckworth; (2) Stroud: Alan Sutton. These books, though variable in quality and some now showing their age, treat individual tribes and tribal areas, in a standardised format and all about 150–220 pages long with bibliographies and indexes. The individual tribes are: *Brigantes* (B R Hartley and L Fitts, 1988); *Cantiaci* (A P Detsicas, 1984); *Carvetii* (N Higham and G D B Jones, 1984); *Catuvellauni* (K Branigan, 1985); *Coritani* (M Todd, 1991); *Cornovii* (G Webster, rev edn 1991); *Parisi* (H Ramm, 1978); *Regni* (B W Cunliffe, 1973); *Trinovantes* (B R K Dunnett, 1975)

(M) Peterson, Daniel, *The Roman legions recreated in colour photographs*. London: Windrow and Greene (= Europa Militaria special, 2), 1992, 96 p. 1 872004 06 7 pb.
Five of the research groups (British and Continental) which specialise in studying, reproducing and wearing Roman armour provide a vivid picture of how the military units may have looked.

Phillips, C W et al (ed), *The Fenland in Roman times: studies of a major area of peasant colonization with a gazetteer . . .* London: *Royal Geogr Soc res ser*, 5, 1970, xii, 360 p, bibl, indexes.
Classic and pioneering study, using aerial reconnaissance, of sites which were still well preserved at that time, so only partly overtaken by more recent Fenland research; hard to obtain.

Phillips and Heywood on York fortress, see Section 6.11.5 Migration and early medieval.

**Philpott, Robert, *Burial practices in Roman Britain: a survey of grave treatment and furnishing AD 43–410*. BARBS, 219, 1991, viii, 472 p, bibl. 0 86054 725 6 pb.
Invaluable for reference purposes, though reticent on mortuary behaviour.

**Potter, T W and Johns, Catherine. *Roman Britain*. London: Brit Mus Press (Exploring the Roman World series), 1992, 239 p, bibl, index. 0 7141 2045 6.
Dense text, with emphasis on material culture and not much on economy or society.

*Price, Jennifer and Wilson, P R, with others (eds), *Recent research in Roman Yorkshire. Studies in honour of Mary Kitson Clark (Mrs Derwas Chitty)*. BARBS, 193, 1988, xi, 406 p, bibls. 0 86054 555 5 pb.
Valuable study of the Roman North, with good bibliographies

Rainey, Anne, *Mosaics in Roman Britain: a gazetteer*. Newton Abbot: David and Charles, 1973, 205 p, refs. 0 7153 5791 3.
Gives basic information on each, including those lost and those in museums.

**Reece, R M, *My Roman Britain*. Cirencester: Cotswold Studies, 1988, iv, 148 p. 0 905853 21 0 pb.
Idiosyncratic but invigorating!

— (ed), *Burial in the Roman world*. CBA res rep, 22, 1977, vi, 66 p, bibl, index. 0 900312 47 5 pb.
Contains nine papers from a 1974 seminar.

—, *Coinage in Roman Britain*. London: Seaby, 1987, 144 p, bibl, indexes. 0 900652 86 1.

—, *Roman coins from 140 sites in Britain*. Cirencester: *Cotswold studies*, 4, 1991, 107 p.
Reference work giving coin tables, with explanation and commentary, arranged to allow 'an interpretation of coins from a site which is totally consistent with the evidence available . . .'

*Rees, Sian, *Agricultural implements in prehistoric and Roman Britain*. BARBS, 69, 1979, 772 p, bibl. 0 86054 064 2 pb.
Catalogue of the equipment available for breaking and tilling the soil.

*Rich, John (ed), *The city in late antiquity*. London: Routledge, 1992, x, 204 p, bibl, index. 0 415 06855 X.

Includes two papers on the end of RB cities, by R Reece and by P W Dixon.

Rivet, A L F (ed), *The Roman villa in Britain*. London: Routledge and Kegan Paul, 1969, 299 p, bibl, indexes.
A number of studies which still retain their importance.

(M) *Robinson, H Russell, *What the soldiers wore on Hadrian's Wall*. Newcastle upon Tyne: Graham, 3 edn 1985, 40 p.
Presents and discusses well-researched colour reconstruction paintings by Ronald Embleton.

Rodwell, W (ed), *Temples, churches and religion: recent research in Roman Britain, with a gazetteer of Romano-Celtic temples in Continental Europe*. BARBS, 77, 1980, 2 vols, 585 p, bibls. 0 86054 085 5 pb.
Papers on various aspects providing a fundamental reference work, but now getting somewhat out of date.

— and Rodwell, Kirsty, *Rivenhall: Vol. I, Investigation of a villa, church and village 1950–77*. CBA res rep, 55, 1985, 150 p, bibl. 0 906780 48 9 pb. *Vol. II, Specialist studies and index to both vols*. CBA res rep, 80, 1993, x, 261 p, bibl, index, fiche. 1 872414 10 9 pb.
Important reports showing development of an area from Roman Britain through the Anglo-Saxon period.

(M) ROMAN FRONTIER STUDIES CONGRESS (LIMESKONGRESS), held every 2 or 4 years, once a decade coming to Britain: published as follows (year of publication in brackets, various publishers):
1949, Newcastle-upon Tyne (1952); 1959, Durham (not published); 1969, Cardiff (1974); 1979, Stirling (1980); 1989, Canterbury (published 1991)

ROMAN IMPERIAL COINAGE (instituted by Mattingley and Sydenham); 10 volumes published (Spink) 1923–94, Augustus to fall of the Western Empire.

Rook, Tony, *Roman baths in Britain*. Princes Risborough: *Shire archaeol*, 69, 1992, 64 p, bibl, index. 0 7478 0157 6 pb.
Introduction.

Rule, Margaret and Monaghan, Jason, *A Gallo-Roman trading vessel from Guernsey: the excavation and recovery of a third-century shipwreck*. *Guernsey Mus monogr*, 5, 1993, xv, 157 p, bibl, glossary. 1 871560 03 9 pb.
The vessel recovered from the harbour mouth at St Peter Port provides important evidence for cross-Channel trade.

***Salway, Peter, *The Oxford illustrated history of Roman Britain*. Oxford: OUP, 1993, xiii, 563 p, bibl, index. 0 19 822984 4.
Thoroughly recast from the unillustrated 1981 edition, incorporating a wealth of fresh evidence and stressing the two-way influence between Britain and Rome. Good bibliography, but textual statements not always well referenced.

—, *The frontier people of Roman Britain*. Cambridge: CUP, 2 edn 1967, xviii, 286 p, bibl, index.
On civilian settlements: broke new ground in its day, but needs to be read in the light of newer work.

Scott, Eleanor, (ed), *Theoretical Roman archaeology: first conference proceedings*. Aldershot: Avebury, 1993, 186 p, bibls. 1 85628 703 3.
Contains 14 papers, mostly on Roman Britain, illustrating a movement to provide a theorizing basis for the subject. The second conference proceedings were edited by Peter Rush (Avebury Publ, 1995, 1 85628 713 0), and the fourth by Sally Cottam (Oxbow, 1995). (Third conference proceedings in preparation.)

(M) Shotton, David, *Romans and Britons in north-west England*. Lancaster: Centre for NW Regional Studies (Univ Lancaster), 1993, xi, 115 p. 0 901800 19 8 pb.
Useful introduction to the area, with appendices giving data on troop dispositions, dated building inscriptions, documentary sources.

Snape, M E, *Roman brooches from North Britain: a classification and catalogue of brooches from sites on the Stanegate*. BARBS, 235, 1993, v, 123 p, bibl. 0 86054 762 0 pb.

(M) Southern, Pat and Dixon, Karen Ramsey, *The Late Roman army*. London: Batsford, 1996, xvii, 206 p, glossary, bibl, index. 0 7134 7047 X.
Well-illustrated reference work giving chronological tables, emperor lists, discussion of sources, followed by an account of developments from late second century, conditions of service, etc.

Stanfield, J A and Simpson, G, *Central Gaulish*

potters. London: OUP, 1958, liii, 300 p, bibl, index.
This classic work is now available in a completely revised edition (in French as *Les potiers de la Gaule centrale*) with extra illustrations and bibliography covering 1959–89: published at Gonfaron by Revue Archéol Sites (= *Hors-série*, 37), 1990, 450 p.

Strong, Donald and Brown, David (eds), *Roman crafts*. London: Duckworth, 1976, 256 p, bibl, index. 0 7156 0781 2.
Studies of how things were made in all kinds of materials from precious metals to textiles and mosaics.

—, *Roman art*. Prepared for press by J M C Toynbee, 2 edn revised and annotated under editorship of Roger Ling. New Haven: Yale UP, 1995, 406 p, bibl, index. 0 300 05293 6 pb (Pelican history of art).

Swan, Vivien G, *The pottery kilns of Roman Britain*. London: HMSO (= *RCHME suppl ser*, 5), 1984, 179 p, bibl, fiches. 0 11 701203 3 pb.
Inventory and discussion of all known sites.

—, *Pottery in Roman Britain*. Princes Risborough: *Shire archaeol*, 3, 4 rev edn, 1988, 72 p, bibl, index. 0 85263 912 0 pb.
Popular work kept under continuous revision.

Symonds, R, *Rhenish wares: fine dark-coloured pottery from Gaul and Germany*. Oxford: *OUCA monogr*, 23, 1992, [vi], 121 p, bibl. 0 947816 23 2 pb.
Catalogue, typology and dating of these regularly-encountered imports.

***TABULA IMPERII ROMANI*, Map of the Roman Empire, published by OUP for British Academy/Union Académique Internationale:
Condate–Glevum–Londinium–Lutetia.
Sheets M.30/part of M.31, 1983, xvi, 109 p. 0 19 726020 9
Britannia Septentrionalis [ie from Kenchester/Cambridge north to Orkney]. Sheets N.30 and O.30/parts of N.29, N.31, O.29. 1987, xvi, 94 p. 0 19 726059 4
The sheets are based on the 1:1,000,000 international map of the world; loose maps folded inside soft cover gazetteer giving brief descriptions and bibliographical references. Layouts of the most important towns and forts are illustrated.

Taylor, Joan du Plat and Cleere, H F (eds), *Roman shipping and trade: Britain and the Rhine*

provinces. CBA res rep, 24, 1978, viii, 86 p, bibls, index. 0 906780 62 9 pb.
Papers from a seminal symposium in 1977, but now rather overtaken.

THEORETICAL ROMAN ARCHAEOLOGY CONFERENCE see above under Scott.

***Thomas, Charles, *Christianity in Roman Britain to AD 500*. London: Batsford, 1993, 416 p, bibl, index. 0 7134 1443 X (pb edn of 1981 work).

***Todd, Malcolm (ed), *Studies in the Romano-British villa*. Leicester: Leicester Univ Press, 1978, 244 p, bibl, indexes. 0 7185 1149 2.
Papers from a Nottingham conference in 1976; includes index of villas and good bibliography for its time.

— (ed), *Research on Roman Britain 1960–89*. *Britannia monogr*, 11, 1989, xi, 271 p, bibl, indexes. 0 907764 13 4 pb.
Important conspectus in which sixteen contributors illustrate the changing patterns of research objectives over the three decades.

Toynbee, Jocelyn, *Art in Britain under the Romans*. Oxford: Clarendon, 1964, xxiv, 473 p, bibl, index.
Classic work listing nearly everything known at that time, with 94 pp of monochrome plates.

***Tyers, Paul, *Roman pottery in Britain*. London: Batsford, due mid-1996.
Reference work with maps of nearly 100 different classes of pottery, British and Continental, and studies of fabric, form, stamps, etc.

VINDOLANDA RESEARCH SERIES see above under Birley, R.

**Wacher, John, *The towns of Roman Britain*. London: Batsford, 2 edn 1995, 480 p, bibl, index. 0 7134 7319 3.
Town-by-town factual survey, with discussion of general issues: completely rewritten and re-illustrated to incorporate two decades of new evidence.

**— (ed), *The Roman world*. London: Routledge, 1990, 2 vols, l, 872 p, bibls, glossary, index. 0 415 05231 8 the set (pb).
Encyclopaedic work in 11 sections, treating every aspect of Rome over the period 8th century BC to the collapse of the Western Empire in AD 476.

*Watts, Dorothy, *Christians and pagans in Ro-

man Britain. London: Routledge, 1991, xii, 302
p, bibl, (index). 0 415 05071 5.
Centres on identifying Christian sites and
related evidence, and examines links with pagan
religions and practices.

(M) Webster, Graham, *The conquest of Britain*
(trilogy, new pb editions from Batsford in
1993):
  The Roman invasion of Britain. 224 p, refs,
  glossary, index. 0 7134 7253 7 pb
  *Rome against Caratacus: the Roman cam-
  paigns in Britain AD 48–58.* 181 p, refs,
  glossary, index. 0 7134 7254 5 pb
  Boudica: the British revolt against Rome, AD
  60. 152 p, refs, index. 0 7134 7255 3 pb.

(M) —, *The Roman imperial army of the 1st and
2nd centuries AD.* London: A and C Black, 3 edn
1985, xv, 343 p, bibl, index. 0 7136 2697 6.

Webster, Peter, with contributions by G B Dan-
nell, *Roman samian pottery in Britain. CBA
prac handb archaeol,* 13, 1996, vi, 138 p, bibl,
glossary, index.
Practical introduction to allow estimation of
pottery date range and assessment of the quality
of potential information, with a key to published works.

(M) Welfare, Humphrey and Swan, Vivien, *Roman camps in England: the field archaeology.*
London: HMSO, 1995, xii, 196 p, bibl, index. 0
11 300039 1 pb.
Descriptions and detailed ground surveys or air
photograph transcriptions of over 130 temporary camps.

*White, K D, *Agricultural implements of the
Roman world.* Cambridge: CUP, 1967, 232
p, bibl, index.
Survey of the known material, with rather small
marginal illustrations and some photographs.
Covers equipment up to the point of removal of
crops for storing/processing. Use in the light of
Rees (above).

*—, *Farm equipment of the Roman world.* Cambridge: CUP, 1975, xvii, 258 p, bibl, glossary,
index. 0 521 20333 3.
Complements the previous volume, covering
(eg) fencing, cordage, basketry and other uten-
sils. Again, small drawings in margins and some
plates. Combines classical evidence with archaeological material where available.

Wild, J P, *Textile manufacture in the northern

Roman provinces. Cambridge: CUP, 1970, xxii,
190 p, bibl, indexes. 0 521 07491 6.
Deals with fibres, their preparation, weaving
and finishing.

Wilson, Roger J A, *A guide to the Roman remains
in Britain.* London: Constable, 3 edn 1988, xiii,
453 p, bibl, indexes. 0 09 468680 7.
Standard pocket guide.

Woodward, Ann, *English Heritage book of
shrines and sacrifice.* London: Batsford, 1992,
143 p, bibl, index. 0 7134 6080 6 hb, 0 7134
6084 9 pb.
Examines the continuity, or otherwise, of ritual
sites, cult, symbolism etc, with particular reference to the Uley shrines.

**—, and Leach, Peter, *The Uley shrines: excava-
tion of a ritual complex on West Hill, Uley,
Gloucestershire 1977-79. Engl Heritage archaeol rep,* 17, (in assoc with Brit Mus Press),
1993, bibl, index, fiche. 1 85074 303 7 pb.
Academic report on the site, a focus of ritual
activity from the Neolithic period through Iron
Age and Roman times to the 7th or 8th century
AD.

Yegül, Fikret, *Baths and bathing in classical
antiquity.* New York/Cambridge MA: Architectural History Foundation/MIT Press, 1992,
ix, 501 p, bibl, glossary, index. 0 262 24035 1
hb.
Although concentrating on the Mediterranean
world and Asia Minor, has useful technological
appendices on heating and water supply, architectural elements and the like.

Young, C (ed), *Guidelines for the processing and
publication of Roman pottery from excavations. Dir Anc Monum Hist Build occas pap,* 4,
1980, 40 p, bibl. No ISBN.
Research has moved on since this research aid
appeared; Davies (above) may be found helpful
in addition.

WALES
(M) *Annual Caerleon Lectures* (Nat Mus Wales):
  1. W H Manning, *Early Roman campaigns
  in the southwest of Britain* (1988)
  2. D J Breeze, *The Second Augustan Legion
  in North Britain* (1989)
  3. A Birley, *Officers of the Second Augustan
  Legion in Britain* (1990)
  4. P J Casey, *The legions in the later Roman
  Empire* (1991)

5. M Speidel, *The framework of an Imperial legion* (1992)
6. L Keppie, *The origins and early history of the Second Augustan Legion* (1993)
7. M G Jarrett, *Early Roman campaigns in Wales* (1994)
(and continuing)

(M) *Boon, G C, *Isca: the Roman legionary fortress at Caerleon, Monmouthshire*. Cardiff: Nat Mus Wales, 3 rev edn, 1972, 142 p, refs, index. 0 7200 0049 1.
The official account.

Brewer, R J, see entry under CORPUS SIGNORUM IMPERII ROMANI in Bibliographies above.

Browne, David M, *An index of illustrations of Roman objects from Welsh journals*. Suppl to *Archaeol in Wales*, 27, 1987, 7 p.
Material is extracted from over 30 journals (1,155 volumes in all) and sorted by function within material.

(M) *Burnham, Barry C and Davies, J L (eds), *Conquest, co-existence and change: recent work in Roman Wales*. Trivium, 25, 1990, 202 p, bibls. 0 905285 27 1.
22 mainly short papers.

Greene, Kevin, see under Manning below.

Jarrett and Wrathmell on Whitton, see Section 6.11.3 Iron Age (under Wales).

Lloyd-Jones, M on Marches, see Section 6.11.3 Iron Age (under Wales).

(M) ***Manning, W H (ed), *Report on the excavations at Usk 1965–1976*. Cardiff: Univ Wales Press for Board of Celtic Studies, eight volumes:
   The pre-Flavian fine wares (Kevin Greene, 1979, 0 7083 0733 7)
   The fortress excavations 1968–1971 (W H Manning, 1981, 0 7083 0774 4)
   The coins, inscriptions and graffiti (G C Boon and M Hassall, 1982, 0 7083 0789 2)
   The fortress excavations 1972–1974 . . . (W H Manning and I R Scott, 1989)
   The Roman pottery (W H Manning, 1993, 0 7083 1173 3)
   The Roman small finds (W H Manning, J Price and J Webster, 1995, 0 7083 1302 7)
   The later Roman occupation (W H Manning, forthcoming)

(and see Courtney in Section 6.11.6 Medieval under Wales.)
Detailed excavation reports on an important site for Roman Wales.

Musson et al on Breiddin, see Section 6.11.3 Iron Age (under Wales).

(M) ***Nash-Williams, V E, revised by M G Jarrett (ed), *The Roman frontier in Wales*. Cardiff: Univ Wales Press, 2 rev edn 1969, xv, 206 p, bibl, index.
The basic reference work for the Roman military in Wales: descriptive gazetteer and supporting discussions.

RCAHMW, see Brecon and Glamorgan entries in Section 6.11.3 Iron Age (under Wales).

Wainwright, G J, *Coygan Camp: a prehistoric, Romano-British and Dark Age settlement in Carmarthenshire*. [Cardiff]: Cambrian Archaeol Ass, 1967, xii, 213 p, refs, index.
Extensively explored settlement site.

SCOTLAND

As most of this material has a strong military emphasis it has not been specially annotated. Further material on Hadrian's Wall material is in the main UK sequence above, notably under Breeze, and is not repeated below.

*Breeze, D J, *Roman Scotland: a guide to the visible remains*. Newcastle upon Tyne: Frank Graham, 1979, 62 p, bibl. 0 85983 150 7 pb.

*Clarke, D V, Breeze, D J and Mackay, G, *The Romans in Scotland: an introduction to the collections of the National Museum of Antiquities of Scotland*. Edinburgh: Nat Mus Antiq Scotl, 1980, 79 p, bibl. 0 11 491637 3 pb.

Curle, A O, *The treasure of Traprain: a Scottish hoard of Roman silver plate*. Glasgow: MacLehose, 1923, xv, 131 p, bibl.

Curle, James, *A Roman frontier post and its people: the fort of Newstead in the parish of Melrose*. Glasgow: MacLehose, 1911, xix, 431 p.
A pioneering excavation which produced much of interest. (Note that RCAHMS has bound photocopies of Curle's excavation notebooks.)

**Hanson, W S, *Agricola and the conquest of the North*. London: Batsford, 1987, 210 p, bibl, index. 0 7134 0607 0.
A rather dismissive reassessment of the famous commander.

**— and Maxwell, G S, *Rome's northwest frontier: the Antonine Wall*. Edinburgh: EUP, 1986, xiv, 250 p, bibl, index. 0 85224 525 4 pb (has short addenda to 1983 hardback).

Keppie and Arnold, see under CORPUS SIGNORUM IMPERII ROMANI under Bibliographies above.

MacDonald, G, *The Roman wall in Scotland*. Oxford: Clarendon, rev edn 1934, xvi, 492 p. Classic, but hard to find.

**Maxwell, Gordon, *The Romans in Scotland*. Edinburgh: James Thin The Mercat Press, 1989, 200 p, bibl, index. 0 901824 76 3.

Miller, S N (ed), *The Roman occupation of SW Scotland*. Glasgow: MacLehose/University Press, 1952, xix, 246 p, bibl, index. Discusses roads, forts etc.

**Ordnance Survey, *The Antonine Wall* (folded map at 1:25,000 scale). Southampton: Ordnance Survey, 1969.

**—, *Hadrian's Wall* (folded map slightly reduced from 1:25,000 scale base). Southampton: Ordnance Survey, 2 edn 1972.
(This edition, if it can be found now, is preferable to the 1989 one, which many people have found unsatisfactory.)

Richmond, I A (ed), *Roman and native in north Britain*. Edinburgh/London: Nelson, 1958, 174 p, bibl, index.
An old classic which must be read in conjunction with modern ideas, especially as regards pastoralism in the north.

Ritchie, Anna and Breeze, David J, *Invaders of Scotland: an introduction to the archaeology of the Romans, Scots, Angles and Vikings . . . .* Edinburgh: HMSO, 1991, 58 p, bibl, index. 0 11 494136 x pb.

**Robertson, Anne S (rev and ed L Keppie), *The Antonine Wall: a handbook to the surviving remains*. Glasgow: Glasgow Archaeol Soc, 4 rev edn 1990, v, 113 p. 0 904254 12 7 pb.
The essential guide for exploring this northern frontier of Rome.

Roy, William, *The military antiquities of the Romans in North Britain and particularly their ancient system of castrametation . . .* London: Society of Antiquaries, 1793, 2 vols, xvi, 206 p. (Reprinted Gregg, 1969, 2 vols.)
In this classic, monumental work the 'father' of

the Ordnance Survey plotted Roman forts and endeavoured to trace Agricola's conquering progress.

Salway, on frontier people, see entry in main UK section above.

Skinner, D N, *The countryside of the Antonine Wall: a survey and recommended policy statement*. Perth: Countryside Commission for Scotland, 1973, iv, 71 p, maps. 0 902226 20 7.
Includes the OS 2½ inch map of the Wall in rear pocket. Gives background, appearance today, charts of relevant data, proposals affecting future, etc.

IRELAND

There is still debate about the extent of Roman influence in Ireland; in any event the Irish Iron Age continued well into the 1st millennium AD.

Bateson, J, 'Roman material in Ireland: a reconsideration', *Proc Roy Ir Acad*, 73C, 1973, pp 21–97; also 'Further Roman material from Ireland', *Proc Roy Ir Acad*, 76C, 1976, pp 171–80.
Catalogue and discussion of the real significance of Roman finds in Ireland.

Several works listed in Section 6.11.5 Migration and Early Medieval discuss the extent of Roman contacts in Ireland: B Raftery's *Pagan Celtic Ireland*, Mytum's *Origins of Early Christian Ireland*, and N Edwards's *Archaeology of early medieval Ireland*; see also a continuing debate about the significance of Drumanagh in the pages of (eg) *Archaeology Ireland*, 10.1–2, 1996 (article and subsequent letters column); and *British archaeology*, 14, May 1996, p 6.

6.11.5
Migration and Early Medieval

This is conventionally the period between the withdrawal of Roman control and the Norman Conquest at AD 1066. Inevitably it is a complex period, with a ferment of Europe-wide change; and it attracts a very large share of scholarly effort. In England the period is mainly associated with Anglo-Saxon and Viking incomers; the Celtic West (Wales, Scotland and Ireland) sees little or nothing of the Anglo-Saxons but undergoes considerable Viking/Norse/Scandinavian influence.

Accordingly (apart from the societies and periodicals) the entries in this section are split under the headings:

General British
Anglo-Saxon to Late Saxon England
'Sub-Roman', Late Celtic and early Christian Britain
Viking Age and Norse/Scandinavian Britain plus Isle of Man
Wales (Late Celtic, Early Christian, Viking)
Scotland (Late Celtic, Early Christian, Pictish, Viking/Norse)
Ireland (Late Celtic, Early Christian, Viking/Norse)

However, such divisions are largely artificial and oversimplified, especially as many books span two or more of them. 'Saxo-Norman' matters will be found in Section 6.11.6 Medieval.

The most recent summary of the last three decades of research is by Helena Hamerow, 'Migration theory and the migration period' in B Vyner (ed), *Building on the past* (Roy Archaeol Inst, 1994), pp 164–77.

As this period essentially began with the withdrawal of Roman power, consult the works in the previous section which deal with that phase, especially Esmonde-Cleary 1989 and Maxfield 1989.

A European Science Foundation Project '"The Transformation of the Roman World": new approaches to the emergence of early medieval Europe' is to run for five years from January 1993 and cover the 4th to 9th centuries.

Professors Richard Bailey and Charles Thomas, and Dr David Hill all gave valuable help with this section, but should not be held responsible for its final form or faults.

Societies

(details given in Section 4.2 Organisations)

Dark Ages Society
Pictish Arts Society
Society for Medieval Archaeology
Viking Society for Northern Research

Periodicals

The principal periodicals and series devoted to this period are:

Anglo-Saxon England (0263–6751). 1972–. Contains valuable annual bibliographies, helpfully classified.

Anglo-Saxon studies in archaeology and history (0264–5254). 1979–, irregular.
Cambrian (formerly *Cambridge*) *medieval Celtic studies* (0260–5600). 1981–93, then title changed, 1993–.
Early medieval Europe (0963–9462). 1992–. (Mostly historical but some other source materials in addition.)
Medieval archaeology (0076–6097). 1957–. (The 5-year cumulative indexes are particularly valuable).
Medieval Scandinavia. 1968–88. Odense.
Peritia, journal of the Medieval Academy of Ireland. (0332–1592). 1982–.
Pictish Arts Society journal (0966–1115). 1992–.
Studia Celtica (0081–6353). 1966–. (Absorbed *Bulletin of the Board of Celtic Studies* at 1994.)

Bibliography and reference works (for all the 'cultural' divisions above)

'Anglo-Saxon bibliography' annually in the hardback journal *Anglo-Saxon England*, from 1972 onwards.

***ARTHURIAN PERIOD SOURCES* (ed John Morris). Chichester: Phillimore, various dates.
1. *Introduction, notes and index*; 2. *Annals and charters*; 3. *Persons*; 4. *Places and Saxon archaeology*; 5. *Genealogies and texts*; 6. *Studies in Dark Age history* (all six were 1995 issues); 7. *Gildas* (ed M Winterbottom, 1978); 8. *Nennius* (ed J Morris, 1978); 9. *St Patrick* (ed A B E Hood, 1978).

**Bonser, Wilfrid, *An Anglo-Saxon and Celtic bibliography (AD 450–1087)*. Oxford: Blackwell, 1957, 2 vols, xxxvii, 574 p; indexes 123 p. Has its oddities but is very full up to 1953, and a good starting point.

Deshman, Robert, *Anglo-Saxon art and Anglo-Scandinavian art: an annotated bibliography*. Boston (Mass): G K Hall, 1984, 125 p. 0 8161 8344 9.
Covers the 9th to 12th centuries.

Gaucher, J, chronology of Celtic lands, see Section 6.1 General reference works, under Encyclopaedias and chronologies.

*Haywood, John, *The Penguin historical atlas of the Vikings*. London: Penguin, 1995, 144 p, bibl, index. 0 14 051328 0 pb.
Produced in the modern style with 'boxes' detailing particular topics.

***Hill, David, *An atlas of Anglo-Saxon England.* Oxford: Blackwell, 1981, 180 p, bibl, place-name index. 0 631 11181 6 (regularly reprinted).
A genuine 'atlas' with maps aplenty, but really an invaluable collection of data of all kinds, brilliantly expressed in maps and graphs with supporting text; covers everything from climate to bishops, in sections treating background, events, administration, economy and Church.

Meaney, A S, *Gazetteer of early Anglo-Saxon burial sites.* London: Allen and Unwin, 1964, 304 p, bibl.
Still a good source of basic information about the cemeteries known at that date.

Rosenthal, J T, *Anglo-Saxon history: an annotated bibliography 450–1066.* New York: Amer Medieval Soc Press, 1985, 177 p, author index. 0 404 61437 X.
Classified selective bibliography, not much liked by reviewers.

Werner, Martin, *Insular art: an annotated bibliography.* Boston, Mass: G K Hall (Reference publications in art history), 1984, xxxiv, 395 p. 0 8161 8327 9.
Deals with 7th to 10th century Hiberno-Saxon works.

'The year's work in Old English studies', annual bibliography in *Old English newsletter* (Binghamton, NY).

Books

GENERAL BRITISH

**Alcock, Leslie, *Arthur's Britain: history and archaeology AD 367–634.* London: Penguin, revised reprint 1989, xvii, 437 p, narrative bibl, index. 0 14 013605 3 pb.
Wide-ranging survey of the conditions in Britain at this time: texts, historical data, material culture of Roman Britain, Picts, Scots and ancestral English. Includes a valuable survey of the nature of archaeological evidence. The reprint edition admits that the case for a historical Arthur has been 'largely undermined' if not destroyed in recent years. See also next item.

— (in collaboration with S J Stevens and C R Musson), *Cadbury Castle, Somerset: the early medieval archaeology.* Cardiff: Univ Wales Press, 1995, x, 188 p, bibl, index. 0 7083 1275 6.
Supersedes previous accounts: treats two distinct periods, the 'Arthurian' phase and the Ethelredan occupation.

Allen, J Romilly, *Early Christian symbolism in Britain and Ireland. The Rhind Lectures for 1885.* Modern reprint of classic, Lampeter: Llanerch Publishers, 1994, 3 vols:
   1. *The Romano-British period and Celtic monuments* (0 947992 95 2)
   2. *The high crosses of Ireland* (0 947992 90 1)
   3. *Norman sculpture and the medieval bestiaries* (0 947992 96 0)

Barley, M W (ed), *European towns: their archaeology and early history.* London: Academic Press for CBA, 1977, xxvii, 523 p, bibl, index. 0 12 078850 0.
Papers from an important conference which considered the topic of urban formation from RB times onward; papers on English, Scotland, Wales and Ireland.

Brenan, Jane, *Hanging bowls and their contexts: an archaeological survey of their socio-economic significance from the fifth to seventh centuries AD. BARBS,* 220, 1991, ix, 305 p, bibl. 0 86054 724 8 pb.
Catalogue and discussion of fine vessels from 78 sites covering a wide range of function.

Chadwick, Nora K (ed), *Celt and Saxon: studies in the early British border.* Cambridge: CUP, 1963, viii, 367 p, footnotes, index.
Contains papers by K Jackson, the Taylors, etc, on topics such as Nennius, pre-Norman churches of the Border, Celtic background of early Anglo-Saxon England, etc.

*Deanesley, Margaret, *The pre-Conquest church in England.* London: A and C Black, 1961, vii, 374 p, bibl, index.
Classic work on the historical background to both Anglo-Saxon and Celtic Christianity.

*Dixon, P W, *Barbarian Europe.* Oxford: Elsevier-Phaidon, 1976, 151 p, glossary, index. 0 7290 0011 7 (The Making of the Past series).
Excellent text and beautiful book-production, lavishly illustrated, treating the dislocation of the Roman world by the movements of the Goths, Franks and Saxons; then the Charlemagne era; and finally the Viking disruptions.

*Driscoll, S T and Nieke, M R (eds), *Power and*

politics in early medieval Britain and Ireland. Edinburgh: EUP, 1988, 218 p, bibls, index. o 85224 520 3.

Important work with papers on Dalriada, Celtic British potentates, early Irish kingship, Northumbria, mid-Saxon power and exchange, early Scottish towns, Anglo-Saxon polities in S England, Anglo-Saxon cremation burial variability, style and sociopolitics, and artefacts/documents/power.

Dumville, David N, *Histories and pseudo-histories of the Insular Middle Ages.* Aldershot: Variorum (Gower Publ), 1990, various pagings, bibls, indexes. o 86078 264 6.

Reprints of papers on sub-Roman Britain, the Historia Brittonum, Welsh Latin annals, Picts in Orkney, kingship and genealogies, etc.

FINDS RESEARCH GROUP 700–1700: publishes Data Sheets on various types of find.

Gelling, Margaret, *The West Midlands in the early Middle Ages.* London: Leicester Univ Press, 1992, ix, 221 p, bibl, index. o 7185 1170 0 hb, o 7185 1395 9 pb.

Treats the natural background, end of RB, the British people of the area, Church and state, town and country, and the evolution of settlement and landscape over the period AD 400–1066, for Cheshire, Shrops, Staffs, Herefs and Warks.

Henderson, George, *From Durrow to Kells: the Insular gospel-books 650–800.* London: Thames and Hudson, 1987, 224 p. o 500 23474 4.

Introduction to these great art-works of Britain and Ireland.

*Hodges, Richard, *Dark Age economics.* London: Duckworth, 2 edn 1989, 230 p, bibl, index. o 7156 1666 8 pb.

Important discussion of Western European towns and trade, AD 600–1000.

—, and Hobley, Brian (eds), *The rebirth of towns in the west, AD 700–1050: a review of current research . . . CBA res rep,* 68, 1988, ix, 135 p, bibl, index. o 906780 74 8 pb.

Papers from a joint CBA/DUA international conference in 1986.

Hope-Taylor, Brian, *Yeavering: an Anglo-British centre of early Northumbria. Dept of Environment archaeol rep,* 7, 1977, xix, 392 p, bibl, index. o 11 670552 3.

The principal structures belonged to a post-Roman township with remarkable halls, temple and arena; there was also Bronze Age and Roman Iron Age occupation evidence.

*Jackson, K H, *Language and history in early Britain: a chronological survey of the Brittonic languages 1st century to 12th century AD.* Dublin: Four Courts Press, 1994, xxvi, 752 p, bibl, indexes. 1 85182 140 6.

Reissue of the 1953 classic philological work on the British language, Early Christian inscriptions, and the incoming Saxons. William Gillies's new introduction explains that, despite much intervening work, it was Jackson who 'set up the ground rules and remains the starting point for discussion'.

Morris, R K, *The church in British archaeology. CBA res rep,* 47, 1983, viii, 124 p, bibl, index. o 906780 17 9 pb.

Seminal volume on the nature of the evidence and what can be gained from it.

Ottaway, P, on archaeology in British towns, see Section 6.13 Topic surveys.

ANGLO-SAXON TO LATE SAXON ENGLAND

With such a profusion of books and excavation reports, this can only be a sample to start off one's search; and note the bibliographies at the head of this section.

Akerman, J Y, *Remains of pagan Saxondom.* 1855.

Classic early collection of information.

***THE ARCHAEOLOGY OF YORK (general ed P V Addyman). Published by CBA for York Archaeological Trust, 1976–. 19 volumes in progress, each with a number of separate fascicules; vols 7–8 deal with this period

***Backhouse, Janet et al (eds), *The golden age of Anglo-Saxon art 966–1066.* London: Brit Mus Publs, 1984, 216 p, bibl. o 7141 0532 5.

Catalogue of an important exhibition.

*Baldwin Brown, G, *The arts in early England.* Six volumes. London: Murray, 2 1915–37.

Massive, classic source still in regular use; the six volumes are:

1. *The life of Saxon England in its relation to the arts* (2 edn 1926)
2. *Anglo-Saxon architecture* (2 edn 1925)
3. and 4. *Saxon art and industry in the pagan period* (1915)
5. *The Ruthwell and Bewcastle crosses . . .* (1921)

6(1) *Completion of the study of [Northumbrian monuments]* (1930)

6(2) *Anglo-Saxon sculpture* (1937)

Barley and Hanson (eds) on early Christianity in Britain, see Section 6.11.4 Romano-British.

Bassett, S (ed), *The origins of Anglo-Saxon kingdoms*. London: Leicester Univ Press (Pinter), 1989, xii, 300 p, bibl, index. 0 7158 1317 7.
Contains 14 papers on how and why kingship developed, with some general explanations of processes of state formation in the 5th to 7th centuries.

Blair, John, *Anglo-Saxon Oxfordshire*. Stroud: A Sutton, 1994, xxv, 230 p, bibl, index. 0 7509 0147 0.
Treats the development of landscape and society in a border county (Wessex/Mercia) with the important town of Oxford at its political and economic heart.

British Museum (comp R A Smith), *A guide to Anglo-Saxon and foreign Teutonic antiquities in the ... British Museum*. London: Brit Mus, 1923, xi, 179 p, index. (Reprinted Anglia Publishing 1993.)
The first formal identification guide for this period, and still useful.

Brown, Michelle, *Anglo-Saxon manuscripts*. London: Brit Lib, 1991, 80 p, bibl. 0 7123 0266 2 pb.
Introductory text.

***Bruce-Mitford, R L S, *The Sutton Hoo ship burial* (3 vols). London: Brit Mus Press. 0 7141 1331 X the set.
1. *Excavations, background, the ship, dating and inventory* (1975)
2. *Arms, armour and regalia* (1978)
3. (ed A Care Evans), *Late Roman and Byzantine silver, hanging bowls [etc]* (1983)
The full, and long-awaited, publication of perhaps the most important (and most debated?) single find in the history of these islands.

***Butler, L A S and Morris, R K (eds), *The Anglo-Saxon church: papers on history, architecture and archaeology in honour of Dr H M Taylor*. CBA res rep, 60, 1986, xi, 226 p, bibls, index. 0 906780 54 3 pb.
Papers from a conference which built on Dr Taylor's seminal studies in this field.

***Campbell, James (ed), *The Anglo-Saxons*. Harmondsworth: Penguin, 1991 reprint of 1982 (Phaidon) edn, 272 p, bibl, index. 0 14 014395 5.
Large format chronological survey by historians together with 'picture essays' on the archaeological evidence.

Carver, Martin (ed), *The age of Sutton Hoo*. Woodbridge: Boydell Press, 1992, 432 p, bibls, index. 0 85115 330 5 (also pb edn 1994).
Contains 24 essays on material culture and society in NW Europe, 5th to 8th centuries, including Snape, Sutton Hoo, kingship, burial practices etc.

*Clapham, Sir A W, *English Romanesque architecture: before the Conquest*. Oxford: Clarendon, 1930, xx, 168 p, refs, index.
Classic study.

Clark, Ann, *Excavations at Mucking. Vol. 1: the site atlas*. English Heritage archaeol rep, 20, 1993, 42 p + plans, boxed, index. 1 85074 276 6.
Set of 25 unbound plans with explanatory text setting the scene for the full report on this important early AS settlement. (*See Hamerow below*.)

Colgrave, B and Mynors, R A B (eds), *Bede's Ecclesiastical history of the English people*. Oxford: Clarendon, corrected reprint 1991, lxxvi, 618 p, bibl, indexes. 0 19 822202 5.
Classic edition of our first historian, best used now in conjunction with Wallace-Hadrill 1993 (*see below*).

Collingwood, W G on Northumbrian crosses, see below in Viking Age sub-section.

****CORPUS OF ANGLO-SAXON STONE SCULPTURE*. General editor R Cramp. OUP for Brit Academy:
Grammar of Anglo-Saxon ornament (R Cramp, 1991; previously as *General Introduction to the Corpus* ... , 1984)
Vol 1. *Counties Durham and Northumberland* (R Cramp, 1984)
Vol 2. *Cumberland, Westmorland, Lancashire-North-of-Sands* (R N Bailey, R Cramp et al, 1988)
Vol 3 *York and eastern Yorkshire* (J Lang et al, 1991)

Crabtree, Pam J, 'The economy of an early Anglo-Saxon village: zooarchaeological research at West Stow', in P Bogucki (ed), *Case studies in European prehistory* (Boca Raton: CRC Press, 1994, pp 287–307).

Cramp, Rosemary, *Studies in Anglo-Saxon sculpture*. London: Pindar, 1993, 386 p + 262 illus, bibls, index. 0 907132 61 8.
Collected essays from thirty years' work by this scholar, concentrating on the Northumbrian region and making full use of the archaeological evidence. *See also CORPUS above.*

*Davidson, H R Ellis, *The sword in Anglo-Saxon England: its archaeology and literature.* Woodbridge: Boydell, corr reprint 1994, xxvii, 239 p, footnotes, index. 0 85115 355 0.
Classic work on how swords were made and used.

DEERHURST LECTURES. Series about the important Saxon church in Gloucestershire: those published so far are by P Wormald, D Parsons, M Berry, M Hare, D Hooke. Obtainable from Oxbow Books, Oxford.

Dickinson, Tania and Härke, H, *Early Anglo-Saxon shields. Archaeologia,* 110, 1992, ix, 94 p, bibl, index. 0 85431 260 9.
Catalogue and discussion.

**EARLY CHARTERS SERIES.* All from Leicester Univ Press:
by H P R Finberg: *Devon and Cornwall* (1953); *West Midlands* (1961); *Wessex* (1964)
by Cyril Hart: *Essex* (1957); *Eastern England* (1966); *Northern England and North Midlands* (1975)
by M Gelling: *Thames Valley* (1979)
These are all clear, easy to use, and a good starting point for topographical and area studies; thought preferable to either the Sawyer set or the British Academy series.

Elliott, R W V, *Runes: an introduction.* Manchester/New York: Manchester Univ Press/St Martin's Press, 2 edn 1989, xiv, 151 p, bibl, index. 0 7190 3008 0.

*Evans, Angela Care, *The Sutton Hoo ship burial.* London: Brit Mus Publs, new edn 1994, 128 p, bibl, index. 0 7141 0575 9 pb.
Summary handbook, including evidence from the most recent excavations, on a classic site (*see also definitive publication under Bruce-Mitford above*).

Farrell, Robert and Neuman de Vegvar, Carol, *Sutton Hoo: fifty years after.* Oxford (Ohio): Miami Univ (= *American early medieval studies,* 2), 1992, 198 p, bibl. 1 879836 02 7 pb.
Contains 13 conference papers on various aspects of the site.

**Fenwick, Valerie (ed), *The Graveney boat: a tenth-century find from Kent. BARBS,* 53, 1978, xx, 348 p, bibl, glossary, index. 0 86054 030 8 pb.
Thorough excavation and reporting made this an exemplar for boat and ship archaeological research, putting it on a truly professional footing.

Fletcher, Richard, see Section 6.11.4 Romano-British for his 'Who's who' guide to Roman Britain and Anglo-Saxon England.

Garmonsway, G N (transl and ed), *The Anglo-Saxon Chronicle.* London: Dent, 1992 reprint of 1972 edn, xlix, 295 p, bibl, index.
The principal historical source for the period.

*Hamerow, Helena, *Excavations at Mucking, 2: The Anglo-Saxon settlement: excavations by M U Jones and W T Jones. Engl Heritage archaeol rep,* old ser 21, 1993, xii, 329 p, bibl, index. 1 85074 274 X pb.
Important early settlement on the Thames estuary: large numbers of buildings and two cemeteries were extensively excavated 1965–78.

Harden, D B (ed), *Dark Age Britain: studies presented to E T Leeds.* London: Methuen, 1956, xxii, 270 p, refs, index.
The Festschrift for the then doyen of Anglo-Saxon studies contains numerous landmark papers.

Härke, Heinrich, *Angelsächsische Waffengräber des 5. bis 7. Jahrhunderts* [Anglo-Saxon weapon graves from the 5th to the 7th century]. Cologne: Rheinland Verlag + Habelt, 1992 (= *Beih der Zeitschrift für Archäologie des Mittelalters,* 6), 290 p, refs, index. 3 7927 1217 2.
Deals with 1,600 inhumations from 47 cemeteries spanning Kent to Yorkshire, in relation to the ritual and social background of the weapon-burying rite. Establishes that not all those so buried were actual soldiers.

Haslam, Jeremy (ed), *Anglo-Saxon towns in southern England.* Chichester: Phillimore, 1984, xviii, 429 p, bibls, index. 0 85033 438 1.
Collection of the evidence available at that time.

—, *Early medieval towns in Britain c. 700–1140.* Princes Risborough: *Shire archaeol,* 45, 1985, 64 p, bibl, index. 0 85263 758 6 pb.
Introduction to the subject.

Hawkes, S C (ed), *Weapons and warfare in Anglo-*

Saxon England. OUCA monogr, 21, 1989, 213 p, bibl. o 947816 21 6 pb.
Thirteen papers from a conference.

Higham, N J, *The kingdom of Northumbria AD 350–1100*. Stroud: A Sutton, 1993, ix, 296 p, bibl, index. o 86299 730 5.
A rather heavy text, using more historical than archaeological evidence, some problems skated over, and references not easy to follow up, but lusciously illustrated.

Hill, D and Metcalf, D (eds), *Sceattas in England and on the Continent: the 7th Oxford symposium on coinage and monetary history*. BARBS, 128, 1984, 209 p, bibl. o 86054 266 1 pb.
Contains 20 papers on a crucial period.

Hills, Catherine (ed), *Spong Hill excavations* (all published in the *East Anglian Archaeology* [EAA] series):
    1. (Anglo-Saxon cremations), as EAA 6, C Hills, 1977; 2, (more cremations), as EAA 11, C Hills and K Penn, 1981; 3, (Inhumations), as EAA 21, C Hills et al, 1984; 4, (The cremations 1), as EAA 34, C Hills et al, 1987; 5, (The cremations 2), as EAA 67, C Hills et al, 1993; 6, (Occupation from 7th to 2nd millennium), as EAA 39, F Healy, 1988; 7, (Iron Age, Roman, early Saxon settlement), as EAA 73, R Rickett, 1995; 8, (The cremations), as EAA 69, J I McKinley, 1994.

Hinton, D A, *Archaeology, economy and society: England from the 5th to the 15th century*. London: Seaby, 1990, viii, 245 p, bibl, index. 1 85264 049 9.
General introduction to the period, well received.

—, *A catalogue of the Anglo-Saxon ornamental metalwork 700–1100 in the Department of Antiquities, Ashmolean Museum*. Oxford: Clarendon Press, 1974, 81 p, bibl, index. o 19 813187 9.

Hodges, Richard, *The Anglo-Saxon achievement: archaeology and the beginnings of English society*. London: Duckworth, 1989, xii, 212 p, bibl, index. o 7156 2130 0.
Stimulating and controversial treatment of early trading 'emporia', and the beginnings of capitalism and 'commoditisation'.

Hooke, Della (ed), *Anglo-Saxon settlements*. Oxford: Blackwell, 1988, 320 p, bibl, index. o 631 15454 X.
Papers from a Birmingham seminar in 1986.

— and Burnell, Simon (eds), *Landscape and settlement in Britain AD 400–1066*. Exeter: Univ Exeter Press, 1995, xi, 156 p, bibls, index. o 85989 386 3 pb.
Papers from a conference which included consideration of monastic effects on the landscape among other topics.

JARROW LECTURES. Annual series celebrating the life and work of the Venerable Bede, available as separates or (now) as a collected double volume *Bede and his world: the collected Jarrow Lectures 1958–1993* with a preface by Michael Lapidge. Variorum, 1994, 1,000 p, index. o 86078 449 5 (£135).

Jessup, Ronald, *Anglo-Saxon jewellery*. London: Faber, 1950, 148 p, refs, index.

—, *Anglo-Saxon jewellery*. Princes Risborough: *Shire archaeol*, 1, 1974, 96 p, index. o 85263 261 4 hb, o 85263 262 2 pb.

Kendall, C B and Wells, P S (eds), *Voyage to the other world: the legacy of Sutton Hoo*. Minneapolis: Univ Minnesota Press (= *Medieval studies at Minnesota*, 5), 1992, xix, 222 p, bibls, index. o 8166 2023 7 pb.
Several important papers in this volume, eg one arguing that the coins in the Sutton Hoo purse are not a 'special collection' at all; while others argue for a severance of the long-supposed links between Sutton Hoo and *Beowulf*.

Kendrick, Thomas, *Late Saxon and Viking art*. London: Methuen, 1949, xv, 152 p, refs, index.
Classic study still in use.

Kerr, Mary and Nigel, *Anglo-Saxon architecture*. Princes Risborough: *Shire Archaeol*, 18, 1983, 72 p, bibl, index. o 85263 570 2 pb.
Best seen as an introduction to the 3-volume work by the Taylors (below).

Kirby, D P, *Bede's Historia ecclesiastica gentis anglorum: its contemporary setting*. Jarrow Lecture for 1992, 22 p.
Background for Bede's History of the English Church and People (see also Wallace-Hadrill below).

*Lang, James T (ed), *Anglo-Saxon and Viking-age sculpture and its context: papers from the Collingwood symposium on insular sculpture from 800 to 1066*. BARBS, 49, 1978, 216 p, bibls. o 86054 017 0 pb.
Important colloquium examining recent progress in this topic.

—, *Anglo-Saxon sculpture.* Princes Risborough: *Shire archaeol*, 52, 1988, 60 p, bibl, index. o 85263 927 9 pb.
Brief introduction.

Leeds, E T, *The archaeology of the Anglo-Saxon settlements.* Oxford: Clarendon, 1913 (repr 1970), 144 p, refs, index. o 19 813161 5.
Remains a classic despite much work since the war.

—, *Early Anglo-Saxon art and archaeology (Rhind Lectures, Edinburgh 1935).* Oxford: Clarendon, 1936, xii, 130 p, refs, index.
Classic and highly influential work.

—, *A corpus of Early Anglo-Saxon great square-headed brooches.* Oxford: Clarendon, 1949, xv, 138 p, bibl, indexes.

Loyn, H R, *Anglo-Saxon England and the Norman conquest.* Harlow: Longman, 2 edn 1991, xvii, 433 p, bibl, index. o 582 07297 2 hb, o 582 07296 4 pb.
Simplified from the first edition.

MacGregor, Arthur and Bolick, Ellen, *A summary catalogue of the Anglo-Saxon collections [of the Ashmolean Museum].* Oxford: BARBS, 230, 1993, 277 p, bibl. o 86054 751 5 pb.
Complete inventory of some 1,200 items, with chemical analyses for many, but not shown in grave-groups, and photographs rather than drawings.

Matthew, Donald et al (eds), *Stenton's 'Anglo-Saxon England' fifty years on. Papers given . . . 1993.* Reading: Univ Reading Dept History (= *Reading hist studies*, 1), 1994, viii, 134 p, notes. o 7049 0448 9 pb.
Includes numerous papers reassessing Stenton's contribution in the light of fresh information; topics include place-names, numismatics as well as more general reviews.

Mellor, M, on MEM and medieval pottery, see Section 6.11.6 Medieval.

Milne, Gustav and Richards, Julian D, *Two Anglo-Saxon buildings and associated finds. (= Wharram: a study of settlement on the Yorkshire Wolds, 7/York Univ archaeol publ, 9),* 1992, iv, 114 p. o 946722 09 9 pb.
Also contains the indexes for Wharram volumes II, IV, VI and VII.

Morris, R, on cathedrals and abbeys, see Section 6.11.6 Medieval.

Mortimer, J R, on Saxon burial mounds of Yorkshire, see Section 6.11.2 Neolithic-Bronze Age.

Morton, A D (ed), *Excavations at Hamwic, vol 1: excavations 1946–83, excluding Six Dials and Melbourne Street.* CBA res rep, 84, 1992, xiii, 237 p. 1 872414 32 X pb.
Gives a broad synthesis of evidence for the Saxon town gleaned over 37 years' work.

Myres, J N L, *A corpus of Anglo-Saxon pottery: pagan period.* Cambridge: CUP, 1977, 2 vols, xxxvi, 358 + 376 p, bibl, index. o 521 21285 5.
Fruit of a lifetime's study; mostly cemetery pottery.

Noble, F, on Offa's Dyke, see under Wales below.

North, J J, *English hammered coinage: Vol 1, Early Anglo-Saxon to Henry III, c 650–1272.* London: Spink, 3 rev edn, 1994, 218 p + pls, bibl, index.

Ohlgren, Thomas H, *Insular and Anglo-Saxon illuminated manuscripts: an iconographic catalogue c. AD 625 to 1100.* New York/London: Garland, 1986, xxvii, 400 p, bibl, indexes. o 8240 8651 1.
An aid to locating particular scenes, eg Evangelical symbols, agricultural tools, animal depictions, household objects and the like.

—, *Anglo-Saxon textual illustration. Photographs of 16 manuscripts with descriptions and index.* Kalamazoo: Western Michigan Univ/ Medieval Inst Publs, 1992, xiv, 576 p, index. 1 879288 10 9.
Builds on his previous work, with 454 photographs of MSS such as the Bury, Athelstan and Harley Psalters; again a finding aid for depictions of agricultural activities, church furnishings, buildings etc.

Okasha, Elizabeth, *Handlist of Anglo-Saxon non-runic inscriptions.* Cambridge: CUP, 1971, xiii, 159 p, bibl, indexes. o 521 07904 7.
See also decennial supplements to this list in the periodical *Anglo-Saxon England*, vol 11, 1983, pp 83–118; and vol. 21, 1992, pp 37–85.

Page, R I, *Runes.* London: Brit Mus Publ, 1987, 64 p, bibl, index. o 7141 8065 3 pb (Reading the Past series).
Introductory text.

Painter, Kenneth (ed), *'Churches built in ancient times': recent studies in Early Christian archae-*

ology. *Soc Antiq London occas pap*, **16**, 1994, xxvii, 362 p, bibls, index. 1 873415 10 9 pb.
Includes papers on Anglo-Saxon topics by R Cramp, W Rodwell, M J Jones; together with A C Thomas on the western provinces and M Ryan on Irish metalwork of the time.

*Rackham, James (ed), *Environment and economy in Anglo-Saxon England: a review of recent work* . . . . *CBA res rep*, **89**, 1994, vi, 151 p, bibls, index. 1 872414 33 8 pb.
Rural and urban topics are covered in these papers.

*Rahtz, Philip et al, *The Saxon and medieval palaces at Cheddar: excavations 1960–62.* *BARBS*, **65**, 1979, x, 411 p, bibl. 0 86054 055 3 pb.
Mainly 9th to 14th century: from hall complex to the documented royal palace of the 10th century charters; later alterations up to 17th century, surviving ruin.

*— and Meeson, Robert, *An Anglo-Saxon water mill at Tamworth: excavations . . . 1971 and 1978.* *CBA res rep*, **83**, 1992, xiii, 167 p, 5 fiches, bibl, index. 0 906780 94 2 pb.
The first excavation to recover timberwork of this period in situ, and a prime contribution to mill studies.

Sawyer, P H, *Anglo-Saxon charters: an annotated list and bibliography.* London: *Roy Hist Soc guides and handbooks*, 8, 1968, xiii, 538 p, bibl, index.
Important, but less easy to use than the 'Early Charters' listed above.

Smith, R A, see under British Museum above.

Southworth, Edmund (ed), *Anglo-Saxon cemeteries: a reappraisal. Proceedings of a conference held at Liverpool Museum 1986.* Stroud: Alan Sutton, 1990, vii, 199 p, bibls. 0 86299 818 2 pb.
The Joseph Mayer centenary conference: papers on various aspects.

Speake, G, *Anglo-Saxon animal art and its Germanic background.* Oxford: Clarendon, 1980, xi, 116 p, bibl, index. 0 19 813194 1.
From author's thesis on the development and significance of 6th–7th century Salin's Style II art; includes its appearance in the Sutton Hoo and Taplow burials.

SPONG HILL CEMETERY see above under Hills.

SUTTON HOO PROJECT (1983–93). To be published in three ways: Research Reports forthcoming in the Soc Antiq London series; Field Reports (Level III) in binders, to be deposited in various institutions in 1997; Field Records (Level II) and finds to go to British Museum in about 1997. Enquire of M O H Carver at York University about the finds index in dBase III and on disk.

Sutton Hoo Research Committee (ed M O H Carver): *Bulletins 1983–1993* (0953–6191). Woodbridge: Boydell Press, 1993, various pagings. 0 85115 341 0.
A bound set of the 11 years' issues covering the recent excavation campaigns.

Swanton, M J, *The spearheads of the Anglo-Saxon settlements.* *RAI monogr*, 1973, xi, 215 p, bibl. 0 903986 01 9 pb.
Catalogue and discussion of a large number of examples.

Szarmach, P E (ed), *Sources of Anglo-Saxon culture.* Kalamazoo: *Studies in Medieval Culture*, 20, 1986, 457 p, bibls. 0 918720 67 2 hb, 0 918720 68 0 pb.
Some seminal papers on art and craft topics.

***Taylor, Joan and Harold M, *Anglo-Saxon architecture.* 3 volumes. Cambridge: CUP, (vols 1–2), 1965 (pb edn 1980); (vol 3), 1978, xxxvi + xx, 1118 p, bibl, index.
These three volumes make up one of the few works that justify the term 'monumental'; they provide detailed descriptions of all the churches in which AS fabric can be found, together with full discussion and synthesis.

Temple, Elzbieta, *Anglo-Saxon manuscripts 900–1066.* London: Harvey Miller (= *Survey of manuscripts illuminated in the British Isles*, 2), 1976, 243 p, bibl, glossary, index. 0 85602 016 8.
Relevant to ornamental metalwork of this period.

*Tweddle, Dominic, *The Anglian helmet from 16–22 Coppergate.* York: CBA/YAT (= *Archaeol of York*, 17.8), 1992, pp 851–1200, bibl, index, wallet of unbound illustrations. 1 872414 19 2 pb.
Complete description and analysis of this important find.

Vince, Alan, *Saxon London: an archaeological investigation.* London: Seaby, 1990, xii, 160 p, bibl, index. 1 85264 019 7.

Location and economy of the newly located Saxon settlement.

Wallace-Hadrill, J M, *Bede's Ecclesiastical history of the English people: a historical commentary*. Oxford: Clarendon, (Oxford medieval texts), 1988, xxxv, 299 p, bibl. 0 19 82222 69 6 (Pb edn 1993, 0 19 822174 6).
Complements and adds to the standard Colgrave and Mynors edition of 1969 (see above).

Webster, Leslie, 'Stylistic aspects of the Franks Casket', in R T Farrell (ed), *The Vikings*, (1982), pp 20–32.
The best treatment of this important carved whalebone piece.

***— and Backhouse, Janet, *The making of England: Anglo-Saxon art and culture AD 600–900*. London: Brit Mus Press, 1991, 312 p, refs, glossary. 0 7141 0555 4 pb.
Catalogue of an important exhibition: excellent bibliography.

Welch, Martin, *English Heritage book of Anglo-Saxon England*. London: Batsford/EH, 1992, 144 p, bibl, index. 0 7134 6566 2 pb.
General introduction.

*Whitelock, Dorothy (ed), *English historical documents: 1, c. 500–1042*. London: Eyre Methuen, 2 rev edn 1979, xxxi, 952 p, index. 0 413 32490 7.
Texts of and commentaries on the crucial early documents.

Williams, Ann, Smyth, Alfred P and Kirby, D P, *A biographical dictionary of Dark Age Britain: England, Scotland and Wales c. 500–c. 1050*. London: Seaby, 1991, xlii, 253 p, bibl, glossary. 1 85264 04 7.

Wilson, David, *Anglo-Saxon paganism*. London/New York: Routledge, 1992, xiii, 197 p, bibl, index. 0 415 01897 8.
Considers place-names, temples and shrines, burial rites, Sutton Hoo.

Wilson, David M (ed), *The archaeology of Anglo-Saxon England*. London: Methuen, 1976, xvi, 532 p, bibl, index. Reprint by CUP, 1981, 0 521 28390 6 pb.
Indispensable volume on all aspects of Anglo-Saxon life: should now be read in the light of newer research.

—, *Anglo-Saxon art from the 7th century to the Norman Conquest*. London: Thames and Hudson, 1984, 224 p, bibl, index. 0 500 23392 6.

The first general survey since Kendrick (1938) of England's 'Golden Age'.

'SUB-ROMAN', LATE CELTIC AND EARLY CHRISTIAN BRITAIN

see also separate sections below for Wales, Scotland, Ireland.

Alcock, see above under General British.

Alexander, J J G, *Insular manuscripts 6th to the 9th century*. London: Harvey Miller (= *Survey of manuscripts illuminated in the British Isles*, 1), 1978, 219 p, bibl, index. 0 905203 01 1.
Lavishly illustrated work of relevance to ornamental metalwork.

Bourke, Cormac (ed), *From the isles of the north: early medieval art in Ireland and Britain*. Belfast: HMSO for Ulster Museum, 1996, xi, 280 p, bibls. 0 337 11207 X hb, 0 337 11201 0 pb.
Thirty essays from the Belfast conference held in April 1994.

Collingwood, W G, on Northumbrian crosses, see in Viking Age sub-section below.

Dillon, Myles and Chadwick, N K, *The Celtic realms*. London: Cardinal, reprint 1973, xii, 355 p, refs, index.
From Early Iron Age through Roman Britain to the Celtic revival; mainly historical.

Dodwell, C R, *The pictorial arts of the West 800–1200*. New Haven/London: Yale Univ Press (Pelican History of Art), 1993, xii, 461 p, bibl, indexes.
Profusely illustrated survey of all kinds of art, from embroidery to stained glass: includes Kells, Anglo-Saxon manuscript art, etc.

Dumville, D on Saint Patrick, see under Ireland below.

*Hughes, Kathleen (ed David Dumville), *Celtic Britain in the early middle Ages: studies in Scottish and Welsh sources*. Woodbridge: Boydell, 1980, ix, 123 p, bibl, index. 0 85115 127 2.
Discusses fundamental questions of the principal source materials, source criticism and historical analysis.

Karkov, Catherine and Farrell, Robert (eds), *Studies in Insular art and archaeology*. Oxford (Ohio): (= *American early medieval stud*, 1), 1991, i, 161 p, bibl. 1 879836 00 9 pb.
Contains papers by R Bailey, C Batey, C D Morris, E P Kelly, M Kenny, M Ryan, C Farr,

and the editors; subjects range from St Wilfrid to Picts, Vikings and Norse in the North, plus crannogs and lake dwellings.

Laing, Lloyd, *A catalogue of Celtic ornamental metalwork in the British Isles c. AD 400–1200.* BARBS, 229, 1993, 120 pp, refs. 0 86054 750 7 pb (Also as *Nottingham monogr archaeol, 5*). Indifferent illustrations mar this work.

Leeds, E T, *Celtic ornament in the British Isles down to AD 700.* Oxford: Clarendon, 1933, xix, 170 p, refs, index.
Classic volume still consulted.

Macalister, R A S, see under Ireland below.

Okasha, Elizabeth, *Corpus of Early Christian inscribed stones of southwest Britain.* London: Leicester Univ Press, 1993, vi, 374 p, bibl. 0 7185 1475 0.
Descriptions and discussion of the stones; not well received.

Painter, Kenneth (ed), see entry on churches in Anglo-Saxon sub-section above.

Pearce, Susan (ed), The early church in western Britain and Ireland, see under Ireland below.

Rahtz, P A et al, *Cadbury-Congresbury 1968–73: a late and post-Roman hilltop settlement in Somerset.* BARBS, 223, 1992, xi, 262 p. 0 86054735 3 pb.
Important West Country site.

Thomas, Charles, *Celtic Britain.* London: Thames and Hudson, (= *Ancient peoples and places*, 103), 1986, 200 p, bibl, index. 0 500 02107 4.
To the end of 7th century.

**—, *English Heritage book of Tintagel: Arthur and archaeology.* London: Batsford, 1993, 144 p, bibl, glossary, index. 0 7134 6689 8 hb, 0 7134 6690 1 pb.
Offers a visitor's guide and attempts to separate fact and myth with the help of recent excavations.

—, *And shall these mute stones speak? Post-Roman inscriptions in western Britain.* Cardiff: Univ Wales Press, (= *Dalrymple archaeol monogr, 2*), 1994, xxiv, 353 p, bibl, indexes. 0 7083 1160 1.
Not a catalogue, but an enquiry in depth.

Williams, Ann et al, see biographical dictionary near end of Anglo-Saxon section above.

***Youngs, Susan (ed), *The work of angels: masterpieces of Celtic metalwork, 6th–9th centuries AD.* London: Brit Mus Publs, 1989, 223 p, bibl. 0 7141 0554 6 pb.
Catalogue of an important exhibition.

Further relevant material will be found under Wales, Scotland and Ireland below.

VIKING AGE, NORSE/SCANDINAVIAN BRITAIN
An enormous number of books treat this period: below is a selection only, but further references are listed under Wales, Scotland and Ireland below. An interactive laserdisc, *The world of the Vikings*, with 2,500 colour pictures and 20 minutes of video and sound in ten themes, and two interactive CD-ROMS, come from Past Forward Ltd, Merchant Chambers, 44-46 Fossgate, York YO1 2TF (tel 01904 670707 fax 01904 670825).

**Bailey, Richard N, *Viking Age sculpture in northern England.* London: Collins, 1980, 288 p, bibl, index. 0 00 216228 8.
These important pieces show the interaction between pagan and Christian belief in the late 9th and 10th centuries.

*Baldwin, J R and Whyte, I D (eds), *The Scandinavians in Cumbria.* Edinburgh: Scot Soc. for Northern Studies, 1985, vi, 167 p, bibls. 0 9505994 2 5.
Effects of the Scandinavian settlement on the previous landscape.

Blunt, C E et al, *Coinage in tenth-century England from Edward the Elder to Edgar's reform.* Oxford: OUP for Brit Acad, 1989, xxxiii, 372 p, bibl, index.

**Clarke, Helen and Ambrosiani, Björn, *Towns in the Viking Age.* Leicester: Leicester Univ Press, 1991, xii, 207 p, bibl, index. 0 7185 1307 X (also 0 7185 1792 2 pb, 1995 corrected reprint).
Discusses the process of urbanisation in the three centuries from AD 700, from Dublin to Kiev but with North Sea and Baltic emphases. Good bibliography; the 1995 paperback has a revised bibliography and postscript update.

Collingwood, W G, *Northumbrian crosses of the pre-Norman age.* London: 1927, (reprinted 1989), 196 p, index.
Classic volume still valued for its drawings: shows an 'artist's instinctive understanding of the mind of the medieval sculptor' (R N Bailey).

*Cramp, R and Miket, R, *Catalogue of the Anglo-Saxon and Viking antiquities in the Museum of Antiquities, Newcastle on Tyne.* Newcastle on

Tyne: Museum of Antiquities, 1982, viii, 25, [xxxv] p, bibl, index.

Crawford, Barbara E (ed) on Scandinavian settlement in northern Britain, see Section 6.17 Place-names and local history (sub-section on Scotland).

*Farrell, R T (ed), The Vikings. London: Phillimore, 1982, xiv, 306 p, bibl, index. 0 85033 436 5.
A dozen papers on various aspects; from an important conference.

**Graham-Campbell, James (ed), Cultural atlas of the Viking world. New York: Facts on File, 1994, 240 p, gazetteer, glossary, bibl, index. 0 8160 3004 9.
Large format with many photographs and other illustrations, information 'boxes' on many pages; covers all aspects of Viking culture.

**—, Viking artefacts: a select catalogue. London: Brit Mus Publs, 1980, 312 p, bibl. 0 7141 1354 9.
From a major exhibition.

*— (ed), Viking treasure from the northwest: the Cuerdale hoard in its context. Selected papers from the Vikings of the Irish Sea conference, Liverpool, 18–20 May 1990. Liverpool: Nat Museums and Galleries on Merseyside occas pap, 5, viii, 115 p, bibls. 0 906367 50 6.
Nine wide-ranging essays treating place-names, trading, metallurgy, and the important Cuerdale hoard (c. AD 905) itself. (See also Philpott below.)

*—, The Viking world. Leicester: Windward, 1989, 220 p, bibl. (Revised reprint of 1980 edn.) 0 7112 0571 X.

*Hall, R, English Heritage book of Viking Age York. London: Batsford, 1994, 128 p, bibl, index. 0 7134 7013 5 hb, 0 7134 7014 3 pb.

*Haywood, John, The Penguin historical atlas of the Vikings. London: Penguin Books, 1995, 144 p, short bibl, index. 0 14 051328 0 pb.
Lively presentation in diagrams and boxes.

Jones, Gwyn, A history of the Vikings. Oxford: OUP, 2 edn 1984, xviii, 504 p, bibl, index. 0 19 285139 X pb.
Massive and authoritative work, now somewhat dated.

Lang, J T (ed), on Viking sculpture, see under Anglo-Saxon above.

Loyn, H R, The Vikings in Britain. London: Batsford, 1977, 176 p, bibl, index. 0 7134 0293 8 hb, 0 7134 0294 6 pb.
Compact, handy and easily approachable work, though now in need of revision.

—, The Vikings of Britain. Oxford: Blackwell, (Historical Ass studies), 1995, 128 p. 0 6311 8712 X pb.
Lays emphasis on the complexity of the raiding and settlement movements in England, Scotland, Wales and Ireland, up to AD 1100.

Phillips, Derek and Heywood, Brenda (ed M O H Carver), Excavations at York Minster Vol 1: From Roman fortress to Norman cathedral. Pt 1: the site. Pt 2: the finds. London: HMSO, 1995, 2 parts in slipcase, xxiii, 658 p, chapter bibls, index. 0 11 300001 4.
A salvage excavation (carried out in extremely difficult circumstances during engineering works on the tower) recovered an enormous amount of vital data on the Roman fortress, the Anglian, Viking and Norman occupation, and the social, economic and ideological changes which took place over the period. (But the immediate post-Roman period, before the Anglian revival, remains enigmatic apart from the sculpture finds.)

Philpott, Fiona A (ed James Graham-Campbell), A silver saga: Viking treasure from the northwest. Liverpool: Nat Galleries and Museums on Merseyside, 1990, 87 p. 0 906367 41 7 pb.
Fully illustrated exhibition catalogue; relates to the J Graham-Campbell work on the Cuerdale hoard listed above.

Richards, Julian D, English Heritage book of Viking Age England. London: Batsford, 1991, 144 p, bibl, index. 0 7134 6520 4.

Roesdahl, Else et al, The Vikings in England and in their Danish homeland. London: Anglo-Danish Viking Project, 1981, 192 p, bibl, index. 0 9507432 0 8 pb.
Illustrated catalogue of exhibition held at York and elsewhere.

— and Wilson, D M (gen eds), From Viking to Crusader: the Scandinavians and Europe 800–1200. New York: Rizzoli, 1992, 428 p, bibl, indexes. 0 8478 1625 7 (also Nordic Council of Ministers, 87 7303 558 0).
Heavily illustrated catalogue of 22nd Council of Europe Exhibition (Paris, Berlin, Copenhagen).

*Shetelig, Haakon (ed), Viking antiquities in

Great Britain and Ireland. Oslo: Aschehoug (Nygaard). Five volumes issued in 1940 and a final one in 1954:
I. *An introduction to the Viking history of Western Europe* (Shetelig); II. *Viking antiquities in Scotland* (Sigurd Greig); III. *Norse antiquities in Ireland* (Johs Bøe); IV. *Viking antiquities in England* (A Bjørn and Shetelig); V. *British antiquities of the Viking period found in Norway* (J Petersen); VI. *Civilization of the Viking settlers in relation to their old and new countries* (A O Curle et al).
Classic source, each volume having references and site index.

Smyth, Alfred P, *Scandinavian York and Dublin: the history and archaeology of two related Viking kingdoms*. 2 vols. 1, Dublin: Templekieran Press, 1975, 116 p, refs. 2, New Jersey/Dublin: Humanities Press/Templekieran Press, 1979, 361 p, bibls, index. 0 391 01049 2 pb.
Many of his conclusions are thought contentious.

VIKING CONGRESS, held every few years, various editors and venues.

Wilson, D (ed), *The northern world: the history and heritage of northern Europe AD 400–1100*. London: Thames and Hudson, 1980, 248 p, refs, index. 0 500 25070 7.
Large-format survey with many colour photographs conveying the vitality of this period.

— and Klindt-Jensen, O, *Viking art*. London: Allen and Unwin, 2 edn 1980, 173 p, bibl, index. 0 04 709018 9.
Still unsurpassed as a general survey.

Isle of Man

Bersu, Gerhard and Wilson, D M, *Three Viking graves in the Isle of Man. Soc Medieval archaeol monogr*, 1, 1966, xiv, 100 p, bibl, index.

Cubbon, A M, *The art of the Manx crosses: a selection of photographs with notes*. Douglas: Manx Mus and Nat Trust, 1971, 41 p, parish index, pb.
Booklet with excellent photographs and short text.

Fell, Christine et al (eds), *The Viking age in the Isle of Man: select papers from the 9th Viking Congress . . . 1981*. London: Vik Soc Northern Res, 1983, 187 p, bibls. 0 903521 16 4.

Kermode, P C M, *Manx crosses . . . from the end*

of the 5th to the beginning of the 13th century. London, 1907, xxii, 221 p, refs, index. Reprinted, with introd by D M Wilson, by Pinkfoot Press (Balgavies, Forfar), 1994, XX, xx, 222 + 42 p apps, bibls, indexes. 1 874012 07 5 hb, 1 874012 08 3 pb.
This reprint is a reduced facsimile of the original classic, which remains the basic corpus.

Wilson, D M, *The Viking Age in the Isle of Man: the archaeological evidence*. Odense: Odense Univ Press, 1974, 48 p. 87 7492 096 0.

Wales – Late Celtic, Early Christian and Viking

Alcock, Leslie, *Economy, society and warfare among the Britons and Saxons*. Cardiff: Univ Wales Press, 1987, 352 p, bibl, index. 0 7083 0963 1.
Concentrates on Wales and Dumnonia, with the addition of material on S Cadbury and reprints of earlier works on economy, society and warfare.

Davies, Wendy, *Wales in the early Middle Ages*. [Leicester]: Leicester UP, 1982, xii, 263 p, bibl, index. (Studies in the early history of Britain). 0 7185 1163 8.
This and the next item are important, mainly historical, syntheses.

—, *Patterns of power in early Wales*. Oxford: Clarendon Press, 1990, viii, 103 p, bibl, index. 0 19 820153 2.

Edwards, Nancy and Lane, Alan (eds), *Early medieval settlements in Wales AD 400–1100: a critical reassessment and gazetteer of the archaeological evidence for secular settlements in Wales*. Bangor: Res Centre Wales of Univ Coll N Wales, 1988, 157 p, bibl. 0 9511834 1 9.
Introduction and gazetteer compiled by the Early Medieval Wales Archaeological Research Group.

— and —, (eds), *The early church in Wales and the West: recent work in Early Christian archaeology, history and place-names*. Oxbow monogr, 16, 1992, viii, 168 p, bibl, index. 0 946897 37 9 pb.
Contains 15 contributions from a 1989 Cardiff conference: area covered is Wales, Scotland, the SW peninsula of England.

Fox, Cyril, *Offa's Dyke: a field survey of the western frontier-works of Mercia in the 7th and*

8th centuries AD. London: OUP *for Brit Acad*, 1955, xxvii, 317 p, refs, index.
Pioneering work now at least partly superseded by later work, especially that of F Noble (see below) and David Hill (eg 'The inter-relation of Offa's and Wat's Dykes', *Antiquity*, **48**, 1974, pp 309–17).

Jarman, A O H (transl and ed), *Aneirin-y Gododdin: Britain's oldest heroic poem*. Llandysul: Gomer Press, 1988, ciii, 205 p. 0 86383 354 3. Parallel Welsh/English texts of this important source for the Battle of Catraeth and other events of British history.

Loyn, Henry, *The Vikings in Wales*. London: Viking Soc for Northern Res/UCL, 1976, 22 p. No ISBN. The Dorothea Coke Memorial Lecture.
Mostly historical and place-name evidence, some from coins and sculpture.

Nash-Williams, V E, *The Early Christian monuments of Wales*. Cardiff: Univ Wales Press, 1950, xxiii, 258 p, refs, indexes.
Corpus of the monuments with Christian inscriptions.

Noble, F (ed M Gelling), *Offa's Dyke reviewed: a detailed consideration of the course of the Dyke through the Diocese of Hereford, with a critical reassessment . . . BARBS*, **114**, 1983, 109 p, bibl. 0 86054 210 6 pb.

Redknap, Mark, *The Christian Celts: treasures of Late Celtic Wales*. Cardiff: Nat Mus Wales, 1991, 88 p, some refs, glossary. 0 7200 0354 7 pb.
Accessible introduction, dealing mainly with the crosses, but including crafts and settlements: gives locations of collections and a list of casts in Nat Mus Wales.

Rees, Alwyn and Rees, Brinley, *Celtic heritage: ancient tradition in Ireland and Wales*. London: Thames and Hudson, 1961 (repr 1989), 428 p, bibl, index. 0 500 27039 2.
Classic work.

Royal Commission on the Ancient and Historical Monuments of Wales, *An inventory of the ancient monuments in Glamorgan. Vol 1: Pre-Norman. Pt 3: the Early Christian period*. Cardiff: HMSO, 1976, xxx, 80 p, footnotes, index. 0 11 700590 8.

Victory, Siân, *The Celtic church in Wales*. London: SPCK, 1977, xii, 146 p, bibl, index. 0 281 02945 8.
A useful if somewhat slight work.

Wainwright, G J, on Coygan Camp, see Section 6.11.4 Romano-British under Wales.

Williams, Ann et al, see biographical dictionary entry near end of Anglo-Saxon section above.

Scotland – Late Celtic, Early Christian, Pictish and Viking/Norse

Note that several publishers are producing reprints of 'classic' 19th-century works about this period in Scotland; these are mostly not listed here, partly for reasons of space, but also because their use requires a good knowledge of modern research, and the originals may be traced through modern studies if need be. The few 'classic reprints' listed below either have modern introductions or other good reasons for inclusion.
There is a particularly good bibliography on Pictish materials in Nicoll (ed) listed below.

Alcock, L, *The neighbours of the Picts: Angles, Britons and Scots at war and at home*. [Rosemarkie]: Groam House Mus Trust, 1993, 48 p, refs. 0 9515778 2 4 pb.
A Groam House Lecture.

—, *Bede, Eddius and the forts of the North Britons*. Jarrow Lecture 1988.

(*See also his Economy, society and warfare under Wales earlier in this section.*)

— and Alcock, E A, 'Reconnaissance excavations on Early Historic fortifications and other royal sites in Scotland . . .', *Proc Soc Antiq Scot*, **120**, 1990, pp 95–149 (contains gazetteer of coastal and inland sites, AD 450–850, as pp 130–8).

Allen, J Romilly and Anderson, J, *The Early Christian monuments of Scotland*. 2 vols. Reprinted, with introduction by Isabel Henderson, by The Pinkfoot Press (Balgavies, Forfar), 1993, 48 + 418 + 522 p. 1 874012 05 9.
This reprint of the 1903 classic is a photo-reduction and scales are now incorrect.

Anderson, A O, *Early sources of Scottish history AD 500–1286* (2 vols). Edinburgh: EUP, 1922, clviii, 604 + 805 p, refs, index.
An important sourcebook.

— and Anderson, M O (eds), *Adomnan's Life of Columba, edited with translation and notes by Alan Orr Anderson and Marjorie Ogilvie*

Anderson. Oxford: Clarendon, rev edn 1991, lxxxiv, 263 p, refs. (Oxford Medieval Texts). On the saint who settled in Iona AD 563 and founded an important religious settlement with a profound effect on British Early Christianity. Now, prefer the newer translation and notes by Sharpe (below).

Anderson, M O, *Kings and kingship in early Scotland*. Edinburgh/London: Scot Acad Press, 1973, xviii, 310 p, footnotes, index. Historical evidence.

Armit, I, on later prehistory of the Western Isles to AD 800, see entry in Section 6.11.3 Iron Age.

Bannerman, J, *Studies in the history of Dalriada*. Edinburgh/London: Scott Acad Press, 1974, ix, 178 p, refs, index. 0 7011 2040 1. The arrival of the Scotti from N Ireland and their later history.

**Batey, C E, Jesch, J and Morris, C D (eds), *The Viking Age in Caithness, Orkney and the North Atlantic*. Edinburgh: EUP, 1993, xvi, 554 p, bibls. 0 7486 0430 8. Contains 35 papers from the Eleventh Viking Congress (1989), treating topics from place-names to insects via hoards, settlements and sagas.

Brooke, Daphne, *Wild men and holy places: St Ninian, Whithorn and the medieval realm of Galloway*. Edinburgh: Canongate Press, 1996, viii, 216 p, bibl, index. 0 86241 479 2.

Close-Brooks, J, *Pictish stones in Dunrobin Castle Museum*. Sutherland: Sutherland Trust/Pilgrim Press, 1989, 16 p, bibl. 0 900594 90 X (A Groam House lecture.)

— and Stevenson, R B K, *Dark Age sculpture: a selection from the collections of the National Museum of Antiquities of Scotland*. Edinburgh: HMSO, 1982, 48 p, short bibl. 0 11 492015 X pb.

Crawford, Barbara E, *Scandinavian Scotland*. Leicester: Leics Univ Press, 1987, xii, 274 p, bibl. index. 0 7185 1282 0 pb (recently reprinted). (Studies in the Early History of Britain/Scotland in the Early Middle Ages, 2.)

—, *Earl and Mormaer: Norse–Pictish relationships in northern Scotland*. Rosemarkie: Groam House Museum, 1994. A Groam House Lecture.

—, *Scotland in Dark Age Europe: the proceedings of a day conference held 20 February 1993*. St Andrews: Committee for Dark Age Studies (= *St John's House Papers*, 5), 1994, 115 p, bibls. 0 9512573 2 3 pb. Six contributions on different aspects, starting with the Roman legacy.

— (ed), *Northern Isles connections: essays from Orkney and Shetland presented to Per Sveaas Andersen*. Kirkwall: Orkney Press, 1995. 0 907618 35 9. (Not available to compiler.)

— (ed), *Scotland in Dark Age Britain*. Aberdeen: Scot Cultural Press (= *St John's House Papers*, 6), 1996, xii, 160 p, bibl. 1 898218 61 7 pb. Essays on place-name studies and other aspects, up to AD 1057; includes Wales and SW Britain.

See also her edited volume on Scandinavian settlement in Northern Britain in Section 6.17 Placenames and local history.

Cruden, Stewart, *The Early Christian and Pictish monuments of Scotland*. Edinburgh: HMSO, 2 edn, 1964, 28 p + 51 pls. [o] 11 490858 3. An illustrated introduction with illustrated and descriptive catalogues of the Meigle and St Vigeans collections; photos are good but small.

Curle, C L, *Pictish and Norse finds from the Brough of Birsay 1934–74*. Soc Antiq Scotl Monogr, 1, 1982, 141 p, bibl. 0 903903 01 6 pb.

Driscoll and Nieke (ed) on power and politics, see entry in General British section above.

**Fenton, Alexander and Pálsson, Hermann (eds), *The Northern and Western Isles in the Viking world: survival, continuity and change*. Edinburgh: John Donald, 1984, x, 347 p, bibl. 0 85976 101 0. Papers from an Edinburgh conference (1981) on material culture (archaeology and ethnology); place-names and history; language, literature and oral traditions; interpretation.

Foster, Sally M, *Picts, Gaels and Scots*. Edinburgh: Batsford/Historic Scotland, 1996, 128 p, bibl, index. 0 7134 7485 8 hb, 0 7134 7486 6 pb. Discusses the origins of the Picts and Dal Riata (Gaels), how they became Scots, the significance of the Pictish symbols, and various aspects of politics, religion and daily life.

Friell, J G P and Watson, W G (eds), *Pictish studies: settlement, burial and art in Dark Age Northern Britain*. BARBS, 125, 1984, x, 216 p, bibl. 0 86054 262 9 pb.

Graham-Campbell, J, *The Viking Age gold and silver of Scotland (AD 850–1100)*. Edinburgh: Royal Museum Scotland, 1995, viii, 260 p, bibl, index. 0 948636 62 9.
Fully illustrated catalogue of the remains of 14 gold and silver hoards plus single finds; specialist contributions, new analysis. Not coins.

GROAM HOUSE LECTURE SERIES: these are annual lectures delivered at, and published by, Groam House Museum, the award-winning Pictish centre in Rosemarkie (Highland). See (eg) Henderson below.

Hamilton, J R C, *Jarlshof, see Section 6.11.3 Iron Age under Scotland.*

Harbison's volumes on Irish high crosses also have relevance to this area: see under Ireland below.

***Henderson, Isabel, *The Picts*. London: Thames and Hudson, 1967, 228 p, bibl, index. (Ancient Peoples and Places). No ISBN.
Has attained classic status.

—, *The art and function of Rosemarkie's Pictish monuments*. Rosemarkie: *Groam House Museum Lecture*, 1, 1990, 29 p. 0 9515778 0 8 pb.

Hill, Peter, *Whithorn and St Ninian: the excavations of a monastic town 1984–91*. Stroud: Alan Sutton, due 1996. 0 7509 0912 9.
The excavated sequence spanned the period AD 500 to the present day.

Hughes, Kathleen, *Early Christianity in Pictland*. Jarrow Lecture 1970.

[Inverness Field Club, ed E Meldrum], *The Dark Ages in the Highlands: ancient peoples, local history, archaeology*. Inverness: Inverness Field Club, 1971, 90 p, bibl. No ISBN, pb.
Essays cover the Late Iron Age to Pictish and Viking period (brochs, Celtic church, N Pictland, symbol stones, Vikings).

Jackson, Anthony, *The symbol stones of Scotland: a social anthropological resolution of the problem of the Picts*. Kirkwall: Orkney Press, 1984 (2 impr 1990), 254 p, bibl. 0 907618 10 3 hb, 0 907618 16 2 pb.
The new interpretations offered here are rejected by some archaeologists.

Jackson, K H, *Language and history . . . , see entry in General British section above. Also note that his version (1969) of The Gododdin has now been supplanted by Jarman, A O H, Aneirin-y Gododdin, in Welsh section above.*

Karkov C and Farrell R (eds) see in 'Sub-Roman', Late Celtic and Early Christian Britain subsection above.

MacDonald, Aidan, *Curadán, Boniface and the early church of Rosemarkie*. Rosemarkie: Groam House Museum Trust (= Third Groam House Lecture), 1992, 48 p. 0 9515778 1 6 pb.

MacQueen, John, *St Nynia, with a translation of the Miracula Nynie Episcopi and the Vita Niniani by Winifred MacQueen*. Edinburgh: Polygon, 1990, vii, 141 p. 07486 6048 8.
A study of Scotland's earliest named saint (Ninian): for the site associated with him at Whithorn see P Hill (above).

**Morris, C D, *Viking and Late Norse Orkney: an update and bibliography*. Acta Archaeologica, (Copenhagen) 62, 1991 (1992), pp 123–50.
Survey and classified bibliography covering years 1982–9; follows on from similar survey in Renfrew (ed) 1985, below.

—, 'Viking Orkney', in A C Renfrew (ed), *The prehistory of Orkney* (Edinburgh UP, 1985), pp 210–42.

**— (ed), *Norse and later settlement and subsistence in the North Atlantic*. Glasgow: Univ Glasgow Dept Archaeol, 1992, x, 230 p, bibls. 1 873132 40 9.

—, Batey, C E and Rackham, D J, *Freswick Links, Caithness: excavations and survey of a Norse settlement*. Edinburgh: Historic Scotland, 1995, xxix, 295 p, bibl, index, fiche. 0 874253 01 3 (= N Atlantic Biocultural Organisation monogr, 1, and Highland archaeology monogr, 1).
Includes detailed study of the environmental evidence derived from middens.

Nicoll, E H (ed), *A Pictish panorama: the story of the Picts and a Pictish bibliography*. Forfar: Pinkfoot Press/Pictish Arts Soc, 1995, xii, 188 p, bibl, indexes. 1 874012 10 5.
Contains six brief but authoritative essays on various aspects: documentary history, language, place-names, art, archaeological evidence for daily life, and early Christianity. The main part of the book is a notable and substantial indexed bibliography by J R F Burt.

Ralston, I and Inglis, J, *Foul hordes: the Picts in the North East and their background*. Aberdeen: Anthropol Mus Univ Aberdeen, 1984, 64 p, bibl. no ISBN, pb.
Record of important exhibition.

***Ritchie, Anna, *Picts: an introduction to the life of the Picts and the carved stones in the care of the Secretary of State for Scotland*. Edinburgh: HMSO, 1989, 64 p, bibl, site index. o 11 493491 6 pb.
This and the next volume are both finely written and well-illustrated introductions.

***—, *Viking Scotland*. London: Batsford/Historic Scotland, 1993, 143 p, glossary, bibl, index. o 7134 7225 1 hb, o 7134 7316 9 pb.

—, *Perceptions of the Picts: from Eumenius to John Buchan*. Rosemarkie: Groam House Mus Trust, 1994, 30 p, refs. o 9515778 4 0 pb.

**—, (ed), *Govan and its early medieval sculpture*. Stroud: Alan Sutton, 1994, xiv, 168 p, bibl, index. o 7509 0717 7.
Contains 15 papers on a key collection of Early Christian sculpture: from a 1992 conference.

— *and Breeze, on invaders of Scotland see Section 6.11.4 under Scotland.*

Royal Commission on the Ancient and Historical Monuments of Scotland (comp G Ritchie and I Fraser), *Pictish symbol stones: a handlist 1994*. Edinburgh: RCAHMS, 1994, 32 p, bibl, index of places.
List by region, with some illustrations, forming a working catalogue and bibliography.

Ryan, M (ed), Cork conference on Insular art, see under Ireland below.

Sharpe, Richard (transl and ed), *Adomnán of Iona: Life of St Columba*. London: Penguin Classics, 1995, xx, 406 p, bibl, index. o 14 044462 9 pb.
This new translation with extended notes has largely supplanted the Andersons' one (above).

Small, Alan, Thomas, C and Wilson, D M, *St Ninian's Isle and its treasure*. Oxford: OUP for Univ Aberdeen, 1973, 2 vols, x, 193 p + pls, bibl, index. o 19 714101 3.

— (ed), *The Picts: a new look at old problems*. Dundee: [G Hunter Foundation], 1987, 92 p. o 903674 09 2 pb.

Smyth, A P, *Warlords and holy men: Scotland AD 80–1000*. Edinburgh: EUP, repr 1989 of 1984 edn, viii, 279 p, bibl, index, chronol. o 7131 6305 4.

Spearman, R Michael and Higgitt, John (eds), *The age of migrating ideas: early medieval art in Northern Britain and Ireland. Proceedings of the 2nd International Conference on Insular Art held in the National Museums of Scotland in Edinburgh, 3–6 January 1991*. Edinburgh/ Stroud: Nat Mus of Scotland/Alan Sutton, 1993, x, 267 p, bibl. o 7509 0357 0.
Contains 32 papers on the migration of ideas, centres of patronage and production, and Insular manuscripts, metalwork and sculpture.

Stevenson, R B K, 'Sculpture in Scotland in the 6th–9th centuries AD', in V Elbern and V Milojcic (eds), *Kolloq über spätantike und frühmittelalterliche Skulptur II, Heidelberg, 1970*, (Mainz: von Zabern, 1971), pp 65–74.
An important paper available as an offprint in some archaeological libraries.

Stuart, John, *The sculptured stones of Scotland*. 2 vols. Aberdeen: Spalding Club, 1856, xxx, 44 p + 138 pls, index; and Edinburgh: Spalding Club, 1867, 52 p + cii + 131 pls, index.
Classic volume containing very fine drawn plates, and also dealing with metalwork, shrines, ornaments, Early Christian plaques, etc.

**Sutherland, Elizabeth, *In search of the Picts: a Celtic Dark Age nation*. London: Constable, 1994, 263 p, bibl, index. o 09 473650 2.
Survey of the Pictish kingdom, its symbol stones, Christian evidence, Pictish language and arts, daily life, the end of Pictland.

***Thomas, A C, *The early Christian archaeology of North Britain: University of Glasgow Hunter Marshall Lectures 1968*. Oxford: OUP, 1971, xvi, 253 p, bibl, index. o 19 214102 3.

Wainwright, F T, *The problem of the Picts*. Edinburgh: Nelson, repr 1955, xi, 187 p, bibl, index.
Classic attempt to understand an enigmatic people; much progress has since been made on understanding them. (*See for example Ritchie or Sutherland above.*)

—, *The souterrains of southern Pictland*. London: Routledge and Kegan Paul, 1963 (repr 1983), viii, 234 p, bibl, index.

See also Young (ed), Work of angels, in 'Sub-Roman', Late Celtic and Early Christian section above, and Williams, A et al, biographical dictionary, in Anglo-Saxon section above.

Ireland – Late Celtic, Early Christian and Viking

Barrow, G L, *The round towers of Ireland: a study and gazetteer.* Dublin: Academy Press, 1979, 232 p, bibl. 0 906187 04 4.

Bhreathnach, Edel, *Tara: a select bibliography.* Dublin: Roy Ir Acad (= *Discovery Programme report*, 3), 1995, ix, 173 p, indexes. 1 874045 35 6.
Annotated references. *See also Section 6.11.3 Iron Age for some works on Tara.*

**Bieler, Ludwig, *Ireland: harbinger of the Middle Ages.* London: OUP, 1966 (corrected reprint), 148 p, bibl.
A lovely book, with good colour and b/w illustrations of Late Celtic art, with very pleasantly written scholarly text on Irish monasticism. Well worth seeking out.

Bitel, Lisa M, *Isle of the Saints: monastic settlement and Christian community in early Ireland.* Cornell Univ, 1990. (Paperback version from Cork Univ, 1993, xiv, 268 p, bibl, indexes. 0 8014 2371 2.)
Combines historical, archaeological and anthropological evidence for the period 800–1200 to see why monks and saints so dominated the social and spiritual life of the population. Warmly recommended by A C Thomas (*Antiquity* Dec 94).

Bøe, Johs, see below under Shetelig.

*Bourke, Cormac, *Patrick: the archaeology of a saint.* Belfast: HMSO/Ulster Mus, 1993, x, 62 p. 0 337 08311 8 pb.
Derived from an exhibition at the Ulster Museum; more important than its modest size suggests, eg describes Shanmullagh hoard and is well illustrated in colour.

— (ed), *'From the isles of the north, see under 'Sub-Roman', Late Celtic and Early Christian Britain (above).*

Bradley, John (ed), *Viking Dublin exposed: the Wood Quay saga.* Dublin: O'Brien Press, 1984, 184 p. 0 86278 066 7.
Record of a three-year saga when the people of Dublin rose up in protest at the redevelopment of this waterlogged site, excavation of which brought about a complete rewriting of Dublin's history.

—, *Walled towns in Ireland.* Dublin: Town House and Country House, 1995, 48 p, glossary, bibl, index. 0 946172 46 3 pb.
From the monastic period to the Plantation.

—, *Urbanization in early medieval Ireland* (forthcoming).

Champneys, A C, *Irish ecclesiastical architecture, with some notice of similar or related work in England, Scotland and elsewhere.* London/Dublin: G Bell and Sons/Hodges, Figgis, 1910, reprinted Shannon: Irish University Press, 1970, 258 p, bibl, indexes; with introduction by Liam de Paor. [0] 7165 0016 7.
Classic work on 'primitive' to 16th century buildings.

*Clarke, H B and Simms, A (eds), *The comparative history of urban origins in non-Roman Europe: Ireland, Wales, Denmark, Germany, Poland and Russia from the 9th to the 13th century.* Oxford: *BAR Int Ser*, S255(i-ii), 1985, xxxi, 748 p, bibl. 0 86054 326 9 pb.
Includes seven papers on Irish towns.

—, Ni Mhaonaigh, Máire, and Ó Floinn, Raghnall (eds), *Ireland and Scandinavia in the early Viking Age.* Blackrock, Co Dublin: Four Courts Press, due autumn 1996, c 400 p. 1 85182 235 6.
Proceedings of an important international conference in 1995 which examined current research on the history, literary and material culture.

Clarke, Helen and Ambrosiani, B on towns of the Viking Age, see entry above under Viking Age Britain.

de Paor, Liam, *Saint Patrick's world: the Christian culture of Ireland's apostolic age* (translation and commentaries by author). Blackrock, Co Dublin: Four Courts Press, 1993, x, 335 p, bibl, index. 1 85182 118 X hb, 1 85182 144 9 pb.
Mostly literary evidence: ancient and medieval writings selected 'to offer a picture of the conversion of Ireland to Christianity as it was seen through the eyes of contemporaries' and those of later writers.

de Paor, Maire and Liam, *Early Christian Ireland.* London: Thames and Hudson, rev edn 1978, 264 p, bibl, index.
One of the classic introductions to the period.

**Dublin 1000: Discovery and excavation in Dublin, 1842–1981*, by P F Wallace and R Ó

Floinn. Dublin: Nat Mus Ireland, 1988, 30 p. No ISBN.
Exhibition catalogue of nearly 700 items, including the Thomas Ray collection (1900–81).

Dumville, David N *et al*, *Saint Patrick, AD 493–1993*. Woodbridge: Boydell Press, 1993, ix, 334 p, bibl, indexes. 0 85115 332 1 (= *Studies in Celtic history*, 13).
These 34 essays received mixed reviews.

Dunraven, (Edwin), Third Earl of (ed Margaret Stokes), *Notes on Irish architecture*. London, 1875–7, 2 vols (127 p + c.245 p, index).
Classic early work with good photographs and drawings. Vol. 1 treats pagan forts and early Christian monasteries plus churches; vol. 2 covers round towers and the Irish Romanesque.

*Edwards, Nancy, *The archaeology of early medieval Ireland*. London: Batsford, 1990, xiii, 226 p, bibl, index. 0 7134 5367 2 hb, 0 7134 7995 7 pb.
Synthetic work assessing much new information.

Fanning, Thomas, *Viking Age ringed pins from Dublin*. Dublin: Roy Ir Acad (*Medieval Dublin excavations 1962–81, Series B vol* 4), 1994, xi, 140 p, bibl. 1 874045 27 5 hb, 1 874045 28 3 pb.
A collection which forms about one-third of all known ringed pins of this period.

Hamlin, A, 'The early Irish church: problems of identification' in N Edwards and A Lane (eds), *The early church in Wales and the West* (*Oxbow monogr*, 16), 1992, pp 138–44.

— and Hughes, K, *The modern traveller to the early Irish church*. Blackrock, Co Dublin: Four Courts Press, new edn due 1996, c. 144 p. 1 85182 194 5 pb.
Explains the function, sites, economy, buildings, stone-carvings of the early church sites and discusses monks and laymen from 5th to 12th century. Lists recommended sites to visit, by county.

***Harbison, Peter, *Irish high crosses*. Mainz: RGZM/Roy Ir Academy, 1992, 3 vols, bibl, index. 3 7749 2536 4. (Distributed in Ireland by Roy Ir Acad.)
Long-awaited photographic catalogue and analysis of these magnificent pieces, and of the comparative material. A more popular version on selected monuments, with the same title,

comes from Boyne Valley Honey Co, 1994, 111 p, 0 9517823 7 1 pb.

—, *Pilgrimage in Ireland: the monuments and the people*. London: Barrie and Jenkins, 1991, 256 p, bibl, index. 0 7126 4732 5.
Discusses who the pilgrims were and where they went on the Continent; the pilgrimage places in Ireland; and the associated monuments and artefacts (round towers, reliquaries and the like). Excellent bibliography.

Henry, Françoise, *Early Christian Irish art*. Cork: Mercier Press, 3 edn 1979, 66 p, bibl. 0 85342 462 4.

(next three all London: Methuen)
***—, *Irish art in the Early Christian period (to 800 AD)*. 2 edn 1965, xvi, 256 p, bibl.
***—, *Irish art during the Viking invasions (800–1020 AD)*. 1967, xvi, 236 p, bibls.
***—, *Irish art in the Romanesque period (1020–1170 AD)*. 1970, xvi, 240 p, bibl.
Indispensable works, all well illustrated, for the study of this period. This scholar's papers were also collected together and republished in three volumes by Pindar Press (London) as follows: *Studies in Early Christian and medieval Irish art*:

1. *Enamels and metalwork*. 1983, 0 907132 12 X
2. (with G Marsh-Micheli) *Manuscript illumination*. 1984, 0 907132 22 7
3. *Sculpture and architecture*. 1985, 0 907132 23 5

*—, *The Book of Kells: reproductions from the manuscript in Trinity College, Dublin with a study of the manuscript by Françoise Henry*. London: Thames and Hudson, 1974, 230 p, 126 colour pls etc. 0 500 23213 X.
Extensive selection of pages reproduced in colour with enlargements of details.

Higgins, J G, *The Early Christian cross slabs, pillar stones and related monuments of Co Galway, Ireland*. BAR Int Ser S375, 2 vols, 1987, xxv, 422 p, bibl. 0 86054 483 4 pb.
Catalogue and discussion.

Higgitt, J see Spearman and Higgitt under Scotland above.

Hughes, Kathleen, *The Church in early Irish society*. London: Methuen, 1966, xii, 303 p, bibl, index. 0 416 74390 0.

*—, *Early Christian Ireland: introduction to the*

sources. Cambridge: CUP, 1977, 320 p, bibl, index. 0 521 21451 3.

Historical, numismatic and aerial photography sources.

And see Hamlin and Hughes above.

Karkov and Farrell (eds), on Insular art, see under 'Sub-Roman' (etc) above.

Kelly, E P, *Early Celtic art in Ireland*. Dublin: Town House and Country House, 1993, 47 p. 0 946172 34 X pb.

Short handbook with colour and b/w photos and glossary.

Kenney, J F, on sources for the early history of Ireland, see Section 1.1 Guides to literature.

Lang, James T and Caulfield, D, *Viking-Age decorated wood: a study of its ornament and style*. Dublin: Roy Ir Acad for Nat Mus Ireland (*Medieval Dublin excavations 1962–81*, Series B, 1), 1988, ix, 102 p, bibl. 0 901714 68 2 hb, 0 901714 69 0 pb.

Study of the carved wood from the waterlogged levels in Dublin allows a refined dating for the art styles of the period.

Lucas, A T, *Cattle in ancient Ireland*. (Based on his Rhind Lectures). Kilkenny: Boethius, 1989, 290 p. 0 86314 146 3 hb, 0 86314 145 5 pb.

Explores the basic form of wealth in the early economy.

Lynn, Chris, 'A bibliography of northern linear earthworks', *Emania*, 6, 1989, pp 18–21.

Macalister, R A S, *Corpus inscriptionum insularum celticarum*. Dublin: Irish Manuscripts Commission, 2 vols 1945, 1949. (Vol 1 to be reprinted 1997: 1 85182 242 9.)

Catalogue of the inscriptions on stone in Ireland, Great Britain and surrounding islands. Volume 1 deals with oghams, 11 with half-uncial inscriptions.

—, *The memorial slabs of Clonmacnois, King's County* [Offaly]. Dublin: Univ Press, 1909, 158 pp, refs.

McManus, Damian, *A guide to ogam*. Maynooth: An Sagart (St Patrick's College), (= *Maynooth monogr*, 4), 1991, 223 p, bibl, indexes. 1 870684 17 6 pb.

Much liked in A C Thomas's review: scholarly work but usable by anyone.

Mahr, Adolf, *Christian art in ancient Ireland: selected objects illustrated and described*. Vol 1.

Dublin: Stationery Office, 1932, xxvii + 80 pls. (See Raftery below for vol 2.)

Has 'classic' status although most items in it are now more fully published elsewhere.

Mallory, J P (ed), *Aspects of the Táin*. Belfast: the Universities Press, 1992, 159 p, bibl. 0 9517068 2 9 pb.

Alas for hopes: analysis of the material culture depicted in the folk tale fails to support an Iron Age date for the story.

— and Stockman, Gerard (eds), *ULIDIA* (Proc 1st Internat Conference on the Ulster Cycle of Tales (Belfast 1994). Belfast: December Publrs, 1994, 321 p, bibl. 0 9517068 6 1 pb.

Contains 35 papers, including several on archaeological aspects.

Manning, Conleth, *Early Irish monasteries*. Dublin: Town House and Country House, 1995, 48 p, glossary, select bibl, index. 0 946172 48 X pb.

Basic introduction.

Meehan, Bernard, *The book of Kells*. London: Thames and Hudson, 1994, 96 p. 0 500 27790 7 pb.

The Keeper of Manuscripts at Trinity College Dublin reproduces the most important of the fully decorated pages together with enlargements of detail; the text analyses the work and its milieu.

Mitchell, G Frank and others, *Archaeology and environment in early Dublin*. Dublin: Roy Ir Acad (*Medieval Dublin excavations, 1962–81*, Ser C, 1), 1987, 40 p, bibl. 0 901714 65 8 hb, 0 901714 61 5 pb.

Analyses of quantities of organic refuse, shedding light on the earliest levels of the city.

Mytum, Harold, *The origins of early Christian Ireland*. London: Routledge, 1992, xiii, 301 p, bibl, index. 0 415 03258 X.

Ní Chatháin, P and Richter, M (eds), *Irland und Europa. Die Kirche im Frühmittelalter* [Ireland and Europe: the church in the early middle ages]. Stuttgart: Klett-Cotta, 1984, xvii, 458 p, bibl, index. 3 608 91549 4.

Includes papers (in English) on aspects of Early Christian Ireland by Deirdre Flanagan, Charles Doherty, Michael Herity, Ann Hamlin, Hilary Richardson and Michael Ryan.

Ó Corráin, Donncha, *Ireland before the Normans*. Dublin: Gill and Macmillan (Gill History

of Ireland, 2), 1972, [14], 210 p, bibl, index. o 7171 0559 8.
Largely historical work on political divisions of 9th century, structure of society and economy, Viking and Irish wars, etc. Good narrative-type bibliography. Now 20 years old but was seminal for offering a new view of the Vikings in Ireland.

Ó Cróinín, D, *Early medieval Ireland 400–1200*. London: Longman, 1995, xvi, 379 p, bibl, glossary, index. o 582 01566 9 hb, o 582 01565 0 pb.
Well-regarded first volume in the new Longman History of Ireland series: intended to give the student and general reader a picture of all aspects of Irish society. Incorporates archaeological evidence in a mainly historical text; substantial bibliography.

Okasha, Elizabeth, on Early Christian inscribed stones, see under Sub-Roman (etc) section above.

O'Mahony, Felicity (ed), *The Book of Kells: proceedings of a conference at Trinity College Dublin, 6–9 September 1992*. Aldershot: Scolar Press for Trinity Coll Library, 1994, xiv, 603 p, bibl, some colour pls. o 85967 967 5.
Papers discuss the background, technical examination (pigments, skins etc), palaeography, and art (eg in relation to stone crosses and metalwork).

O'Meadhra, Uaininn, *Early Christian, Viking and Romanesque art motif-pieces from Ireland.*
1: *An illustrated and descriptive catalogue of the so-called artists' 'trial-pieces' from c. 5th to 12th centuries AD found in Ireland c. 1830–1973.* Stockholm/Atlantic Highlands NJ: Almqvist and Wiksell Internat/Humanities Press, (*Theses and papers in North European archaeology*, 7), 1979, 202 p, bibl. 91 22 00270 7 pb.
Beautiful photographs and drawings illustrate this catalogue of practice pieces made by fine craftsmen in Dublin and elsewhere in Ireland.
2: *A discussion on aspects of find-context and function.* Stockholm: Almqvist and Wiksell (*Theses and Papers in North European Archaeology*, 17), 1987, 200 p, bibl. 91 22 00892 6 pb.

*Pearce, Susan (ed), *The early church in western Britain and Ireland. BARBS, 102, 1982, 388 p, bibl, index. o 86054 182 7 pb.

Conference papers include five relevant to Ireland.

Petrie, G, *The ecclesiastical architecture of Ireland, anterior to the Anglo-Norman invasion, comprising an essay on the origin and uses of the round towers of Ireland*. Dublin: Hodges and Smith, 2 edn 1845, 520 p, index.
Classic early work. There is also a 1970 Irish Univ Press edition with introduction by L de Paor (xxvi, 525 p).

— (ed M Stokes), *Christian inscriptions in the Irish language*. 2 vols. Dublin: Roy Hist and Archaeol Ass Ireland, 1872 and 1878.

Porter, Arthur K, *The crosses and culture of Ireland*. New Haven: Yale UP, 1931, xxiii, 143 pp, refs. (subsequently reprinted by Arno Press).
Treats St Patrick; Columcille; the great missionaries; fall of the Celtic church; Vikings in Ireland.

Raftery, Barry, on Mountdillon see Section 6.11.2 Neolithic–Bronze Age.

Raftery, Joseph, *Christian art in ancient Ireland: selected objects illustrated and described*. Vol 2. Dublin: Stationery Office, 1941, 184 p.
Many photographs. See Mahr above for vol 1.

Rees, Alwyn and Rees, Brinley, *Celtic heritage: ancient tradition in Ireland and Wales*. London: Thames and Hudson, 1961 (repr 1989), 428 p, bibl, index. o 500 27039 2.
Classic work.

Richardson, Hilary and Scarry, John, *An introduction to Irish high crosses*. Dublin: Mercier Press, 1990, 152 p, bibl. o 85342 941 3 hb, o 85342 954 5 pb.
This may serve if one cannot lay hands on the 3-volume Harbison work or his shorter work (above), but it fails to take into account a great deal of recent research and its illustrations are said not to do justice to the monuments.

***Ryan, Michael, *The Derrynaflan Hoard I: a preliminary account*. Dublin: Nat Mus Ireland, 1983, iv, 65 p + colour pls, bibl. o 901777 07 2 pb.
The provisional publication of this astonishing hoard of 8th and 9th century church plate from the monastic site in Tipperary.

*— (ed), *Ireland and insular art AD 500–1200: ·proceedings of a conference at University Col-

lege Cork . . . 1985. Dublin: Roy Ir Acad, 1987, viii, 187 p. 0 901714 54 2 pb.
Twenty-six papers treating the period from La Tène to 12th century.

—, *Metal craftsmanship in early Ireland*. Dublin: Town House and Country House, 1993, 47 p, glossary. 0 946172 37 4 pb.
Short survey, c. AD 450–1200, with colour and b/w illustrations.

Rynne, E (ed), *Figures from the past: studies on figurative art in Christian Ireland*. Dublin: Glendale Press for RSAI, 1987, 328 p, bibls. 0 907606 44 X.
Papers in honour of Helen M Roe, doyenne of the study of this topic.

Shetelig, Haakon (gen ed): Bøe, Johs, *Norse antiquities in Ireland*. Oslo: Aschehoug (Ny-gaard), 1940 (= *Viking antiquities in Great Britain and Ireland*, III), 137 p, index of places. Text with photographs (no drawings of objects).

Smyth, A P, *Celtic Leinster: towards an historical geography of early Irish civilisation*. Blackrock, Co Dublin: Ir Acad Press, 1982, xvi, 197 p. 0 7165 0097 3.

—, *on Scandinavian York and Dublin see under Viking Age Britain above.*

Spearman and Higgitt, on Age of migrating ideas see under Scotland above.

Stokes, Margaret, *Early Christian architecture in Ireland*. London: Bell, 1878, 160 p, refs, index. This and the next come from a generally underrated author; fine woodcut illustrations.

—, *Early Christian art in Ireland*. London: Chapman and Hall, 1887, 210 p, index.

Wallace, P F, *Dublin 840–1300: an archaeological bibliography*. Dublin: Roy Ir Acad (*Medieval Dublin excavations 1962–81*, Series B, 2/Miscellanea 1), 1988, pp 1–6.

—, *The Viking Age buildings of Dublin*. Dublin: Roy Ir Acad (*Medieval Dublin excavations 1962–81*, Series A, vol 1(1–2), 1992, 2 vols (text + illus). 1 874045 00 3 hb, 1 874045 01 1 pb.
Description and discussion of the well-preserved wooden buildings from waterlogged sites in the city. Includes 12-page glossary.

Warner, R B, 'The archaeology of Early Historic Irish kingship', in S T Driscoll and M R Nieke (eds), *Power and politics in early medieval Britain and Ireland* (1988), pp 47–68.

Whitelock, Dorothy, McKitterick, Rosamond and Dumville, David (eds), *Ireland in early mediaeval Europe: studies in memory of Kathleen Hughes*. Cambridge: CUP, 1982, x, 406 p, bibl, index. 0 521 23547 2.
Includes pieces on Pictish art and Kells, Dalriada and the kingdom of the Scots, the Vikings in Ireland, etc.

Wood-Martin, W G, *The lake dwellings of Ireland . . . crannogs*. Reprint of 1886 edn, Dublin: Crannog Edns, 1983, xxiii, 318 p, errata list.
This and the next two are early classics.

—, *Traces of the elder faiths of Ireland: a folklore sketch*. Reprint of 1902 edn, London: Kenniket Press, 2 vols.
Contains 908 bibliographic items on subjects from amber to wooden objects via bronze, caves, fictilia, glass, gold, jade, jet, raths/souterrains, etc.

Youngs, S (ed), Work of angels, see under 'Sub-Roman' (etc) Britain above.

6.11.6
Medieval

This period conventionally starts with the Norman Conquest at 1066 (including Late Saxon material) and ends with the accession of the Tudors in 1485, but the boundaries at both ends are of course indistinct and debatable. Three useful summaries cover this period in B Vyner (ed), *Building on the past* (Roy Archaeol Inst 1994):

Coad, Jonathan, 'Medieval fortifications and post-medieval artillery defences: developments in post-war research and future trends' (pp 215–27)

Schofield, John, 'Medieval and later towns' (pp 195–214)

Wrathmell, Stuart, 'Rural settlements in medieval England: perspectives and perceptions' (pp 178–94).

The full surveys by Clarke and by Steane (under General works below) form good introductions to the period.

The principal relevant society is the **Society for Medieval Archaeology**; also important is the **Medieval Settlement Research Group**. In addition the **British Archaeological Association, Cambrian Archaeological Association, Royal Archaeological Institute, Royal Irish Academy, Royal Society of Antiquaries of Ireland, Society of Antiquaries of London,** and **Society of Antiquaries of Scotland** embrace the medieval period within their wider interests. Addresses for all are in Section 4.2 Organisations.

The contents of this section are:

Principal periodicals and series
Bibliography and reference
General works on Britain and Ireland, and
  those on England alone
Wales
Scotland
Isle of Man
Ireland

Principal periodicals and series

Château Gaillard annual conference volumes
Medieval archaeology (0076–6097). 1957–. Annual. Society for Medieval Archaeology. Contains annual roundup of excavations and discoveries.
Medieval ceramics (ISBNs only). 1977–. Medieval Ceramics Research Group
Medieval history (0960–0752). 1991–. Bangor, Headstart History
Medieval and later pottery in Wales (0142–7555). 1978–. Annual.
Medieval life (1357–6291). 1995– [replaced the short-lived *Medieval world*]
Medieval Settlement Research Group annual report (0959–2474)
Source: the holy wells journal. (T G Hulse, Pen-y-Bont, Bont Newydd, Cefn, St Asaph, LL17 0HH)
Urban history (0963–9268). 1992–. CUP (Previously *Urban history yearbook* (0306–0845), 1974–91)

Bibliography and reference works

***Barclay, K and Davey, P: annual ceramic bibliographies starting in Vol 8, 1984 of *Medieval ceramics* (see above), with an initial list in vol 1, 1977.

Bates, David, *A bibliography of Domesday Book* [materials published 1886–1984]. Woodbridge: Boydell Press, 1986, xi, 166 p, index. 0 85115 433 6.

Brown, Shirley Ann, *The Bayeux Tapestry: history and bibliography*. Woodbridge: Boydell and

Brewer, 1988, xi, 186 p, refs, index. 0 85115 509 X.

***Colvin, H M (gen ed), *The history of the King's Works*. 6 vols. London: HMSO, 1963–82:
Vols 1 and 2. *The Middle Ages* (R A Brown, H M Colvin and A J Taylor, 1963)
Vols 3 and 4. *1485–1660* (H M Colvin et al, 1975 and 1982)
Vol 5. *1660–1782* (H M Colvin et al, 1976)
Vol 6. *1782–1851* (J M Crook et al, 1973)
The architectural historian's basic reference work.

CORPUS OF ROMANESQUE SCULPTURE IN BRITAIN AND IRELAND: British Academy project for a database (for publication on CD-ROM) of all examples.

CORPUS VITREARUM MEDII AEVI: corpus of medieval stained glass under auspices of Comité International d'Histoire de l'Art, Union Académique International, British Academy, and RCHME. Its aim is the systematic recording and publication of all surviving European medieval stained glass (including that now surviving in N America). Catalogues are produced to a common format and there is a CVMA newsletter produced at Romont, Switzerland (ISSN 0308–2237). The British national archive is maintained by RCHME at Swindon.

European Castles Bibliography, 1950–. Based at Verona (Castell Vecchio Museum) using the castellology collection of the late Prof Piero Gazzola; computer printout and disc access planned. (No recent information available to compiler.)

Evans, Davis, *A bibliography of stained glass*. Cambridge: D S Brewer, 1982, 201 p, index. 085991 087 3.

Fernie, E C, 'Contrasts in methodology and interpretation of medieval ecclesiastical architecture', in *Archaeol j*, 145, 1988, pp 344–64 (includes 7-page bibliography).

Harvey, John, *English medieval architects: a biographical dictionary down to 1550*. Gloucester: A Sutton, rev edn 1984, xxxviii, 479 p, indexes. 0 86299 034 3; plus *Supplement to revised edn* (Pinhorn, 1987, 16 pp pamphlet, 0 901262 24 2).

***Kenyon, J R, *Castles, town defences, and artillery fortifications in Britain: a bibliography* (3 vols in *CBA res rep series*: vol 1 covering

1945–77 as *CBA res rep*, **25**, 1978; vol 2 covering 1977–82, plus new section on Ireland, as *CBA res rep*, **53**, 1983; and vol 3 covering 1983–9 as *CBA res rep*, **72**, 1990. Continuing.

***King, D J Cathcart, *Castellarium Anglicanum: an index and bibliography of the castles in England, Wales and the Islands*. New York: Kraus Internat, 1983, 2 vols, lxviii, 676 p, bibl, index. 0 527 50110 7.
Important reference work; and see under King in next sub-section.

*Knowles, David and Hadcock, R Neville, *Medieval religious houses*. London: Longman, 1994, 584 p. 0 582 11230 3.
A reissue of the expanded 1971 edn 'in response to insistent scholarly demand' for this exhaustive catalogue of monastic houses.

Loyn, Henry (gen ed), *The Middle Ages: a concise encyclopaedia*. London: Thames and Hudson, 1989, 352 p, refs. 0 500 25103 7 hb, 0 500 27645 5 pb.
Covers AD 400 to 1500, Scandinavia to Middle East, with nearly 1,000 entries by a team of scholars. Includes discussion of themes like science and war, biographies of important figures, artistic achievements, etc.

Medieval Settlement Research Group annual report (see above under Journals); from 1987 contains annual bibliography.

Nicolle, David, *Medieval warfare sourcebook: 1, Warfare in western Christendom*. London: Arms and Armour Press, 1995, 320 p, bibl, glossary, index. 1 85409 196 4 (NB: ISBN on dustwrapper differs).
Semi-encyclopaedic treatment of fortifications, weaponry, strategy and warfare types. Good classified bibliography. Volume 2, forthcoming, will cover Christian Europe and its neighbours.

Platt, C P S, *Medieval archaeology in England: a guide to the historical sources*. Shalfleet, IoW: Pinhorns, 1969, 32 p.
Descriptive bibliography giving classes of document available in PRO and Brit Mus, printed sources, manuscript material, etc.

Tyson, Rachel and Clark, John (comp), *Bibliography of medieval glass vessels for British sites AD 1200–1500*. [s l]: Assoc for the Hist of Glass Ltd, 1994, 24 p. (No ISBN).
Covers general and regional surveys and reports, other countries, other sources of evidence.

Williams, Harry F, *An index of mediaeval studies published in Festschriften 1865–1946, with special reference to Romanic material*. Berkeley (Calif): UCAL Press, 1951, x, 165 p.
Covers art, customs, history, language, literature and science of Western Europe. Celtic material is on pp 22–4, English on 25–34, and Scandinavian on 108–14; mostly marginal to archaeology.

General works on Britain and Ireland and those on England alone

Aberg, F A (ed), *Medieval moated sites. CBA res rep*, **17**, 1978, iv, 93 p, bibl. 0 900312 58 0 pb.
This collective volume opened up the subject and its bibliography did not claim exhaustivity even at that time.

Andrews, D D and Milne, G, *Wharram: a study of settlement in the Yorkshire Wolds. Vol 1: domestic settlement; part 1, areas 10 and 6. Soc Medieval Archaeol monogr ser*, **8, 1979, x, 157 p, bibl, index.
First report from this pioneering decades-long excavation of a deserted village (DMV). *See also Beresford and Hurst below.*

THE ARCHAEOLOGY OF YORK (general ed P V Addyman). In progress. Published by CBA for York Archaeological Trust; vols **9–12** deal with medieval York.

Armitage, Ella, *Early Norman castles of the British Isles*. London: Murray, 1912, xvi, 408 p.
Classic volume still regularly resorted to.

*ASPECTS OF SAXO-NORMAN LONDON. *London and Middlesex Archaeol Soc spec pap* **11**, **12** and **14** respectively.
1. *Building and street development* (V Horsman, G and C Milne, 1988, 123 p). 0 903290 36 7 pb.
2. *Finds and environmental evidence* (ed A Vince, 1991, 451 p). 0 903290 37 5 pb.
3. *The bridgehead and Billingsgate to 1200* (K Steedman, T Dyson and J Schofield, 1992, 216 p; plus consolidated index to all three volumes). 0 903290 40 5 pb.

Astill, G G, *A medieval industrial complex and its landscape: the metalworking watermills and workshops of Bordesley Abbey. CBA res rep*, **92**, 1993, 316 p, bibl, index, fiche. 1 872414 43 5 pb.

Important 12th–14th century site illuminating early medieval waterpowered iron-smithing.

*— and Grant, Annie (eds), *The countryside of medieval England.* Oxford: Blackwell, 1988, xi, 282 p, bibl, index. 0 631 15091 9 hb, 0 631 18442 2 pb.
Multidisciplinary contributions to a fuller understanding of landscape and agriculture.

Aston, Mick, *Monasteries.* London: Batsford (Know the Landscape series), 1993, 176 p, bibl, index. 0 7134 6709 6 pb.
Discusses the influence on the landscape of these important early medieval and later buildings. Good bibliography.

— (ed), *Medieval fish, fisheries and fishponds in England.* BARBS, 182, 1988, 2 vols, ix, 484 p, bibls. 0 86054 509 1 pb.
Case studies and discussions which opened up a new subject.

— and Bond, James, *The landscape of towns.* London: Dent (Archaeology in the Field series), 1976, 255 p, bibl, index. 0 460 04194 0.
Why towns are sited where they are, their later development, and why they look as they do.

*—, Austin, David and Dyer, C (eds), *The rural settlements of medieval England: studies dedicated to Maurice Beresford and John Hurst.* Oxford: Blackwell, 1989, xi, 318 p, refs, index. 0 631 15903 7.
Essays noting advances since the seminal volume of 1971 (see under Beresford and Hurst below).

*— and Lewis, Carenza (eds), *The medieval landscape of Wessex. Oxbow monogr,* 46, viii, 280 p, bibl, index. 0 946897 78 6 pb.
Contains 13 papers on 5th to 11th century settlement, agriculture, wetland reclamation, and protection of sites.

Ayton, E, *Knights and warhorses: military service and the English aristocracy under Edward III.* Woodbridge: Boydell, 1994, ix, 304 p, bibl, index. 0 85115 568 5.
Largely historical data but throws much light on the material evidence of horsegear and the like (*for which see Clark below*).

*Barley, M W (ed), *The plans and topography of medieval towns in England and Wales. CBA res rep,* 14, 1976, vi, 92 p, bibl, index. 0 900312 33 5 pb.
Seminal collection of papers on town evolution, sources for town topography, defences, and so on.

Bassett, Steven (ed), *on death in towns AD 100–1600,* see Section 6.13 Topic surveys (under Society).

Beresford, M, *New towns of the Middle Ages: town plantation in England, Wales and Gascony.* Gloucester: Alan Sutton, 2 edn 1988, xxi, 670 p, bibl, index. 0 86299 430 6.
Reprint with new preface of the 1967 classic.

***— and Hurst, J G (eds), *Deserted medieval villages: studies.* Gloucester: Alan Sutton, 1989, xx, 340 p, refs, index. 0 86299 655 4.
Facsimile reprint, with new preface, of the 1971 classic which opened up this whole subject. *See also Aston, Austin and Dyer (eds) above.*

—, *English Heritage book of Wharram Percy deserted medieval village.* London: Batsford/ Engl Heritage, 1990, 144 p, refs, glossary, index. 0 7134 6133 6 hb; 0 7134 6114 4 pb.
Records the highly influential 40-year programme of research excavation: includes prehistoric and RB material through medieval to post-desertion landscape. *See also Andrews (above) and Wrathmell (below).*

— and St Joseph, J K S, *Medieval England: an aerial survey.* Cambridge: CUP, 2 rev edn 1979, 286 p.
The new edn contains some revised commentaries and several new photographs.

***Biddle, Martin et al, *Object and economy in medieval Winchester.* Oxford: Clarendon (= *Winchester studies,* 7), 1990, 2 vols, cxii, 1271 p, bibl, concordances, indexes. 0 19 813175 5.
Valuable for the number (6,600) and range of objects catalogued by function, with discussion of their implications for industrial development.

**Blair, John and Ramsay, Nigel (eds), *English medieval industries: craftsmen, techniques, products.* London: Hambledon Press, 1991, xxxiv, 446 p, bibl, index. 0 907628 87 7.
Chapters on the various materials.

Brown, R Allen, *Castles from the air, with photographs from the University of Cambridge collection.* Cambridge: CUP, 1989, 246 p, index. 0 521 32932 9.
Commentaries on photographs of over 100 English and Welsh castles.

—, *Architecture of castles: a visual guide*. London: Batsford, 1984, 120 p, index. 0 7134 4089 9. Includes many plans plus some details (eg turrets, gateways, cutaways).

Campbell, Bruce et al, *A medieval capital and its grain supply: agrarian production and distribution in the London region c. 1300*. London: Inst Brit Geogr (= *Hist geogr res ser*, 30, 1993, x, 233 p, bibl, index. 1 870074 12 2. Useful data on the relationship between a city and its hinterland.

Cantor, L M, *The medieval parks of England: a gazetteer*. Loughborough: Loughborough Univ Dept Educ, 1983, 95 p, bibl. 0 946348 00 6 pb.

Cherry, John, 'The National Reference Collection of medieval pottery', in *Medieval ceramics*, 10, 1986, pp 125–30 and 13, 1989, pp 9–11.

*Clapham, Sir A W, *English romanesque architecture*. Oxford: Clarendon Press, 1930–4, 2 vols, footnotes, indexes. Classic volumes, the first treating pre-conquest and the second post-conquest to 12th century.

Clark, John, *Saxon and Norman London*. London: HMSO, 1989, 48 p. 0 11 290458 0 pb. Introduction incorporating new data.

—, *The medieval horse and its equipment c. 1150–c. 1450*. London: HMSO (= *Medieval finds from excavations in London*, 5), 1995, xii, 185 p, bibl. 0 11 290485 8 pb. Catalogue of horsegear of all kinds.

Clarke, Helen, *The archaeology of medieval England*. London: Brit Mus Publs (Colonnade), 1984, 224 p, bibl, index. 0 631 15293 8. Wide-ranging text.

Cocke, T et al on recording a church, see Section 6.8 Conservation of buildings.

Coleman-Smith, Richard and Pearson, Terry, *Excavations in the Donyatt potteries*. Chichester: Phillimore, 1988, 428 p, bibl, indexes, 2 fiches. 0 85033 502 7. Despite its SW Somerset locale, this book was welcomed as the most comprehensive and useful catalogue of pottery forms then available. Covers 13th to 20th centuries.

Coppack, Glyn, *English Heritage book of abbeys and priories*. London: Batsford/Engl Heritage, 1990, 159 p, gazetteer, index. 0 7134 6308 2 hb, 0 7134 6309 0 pb.

To the Suppression and beyond; includes a whole chapter on sanitation.

Cowgill, J, de Neergaard, M and Griffiths, N, *Knives and scabbards*. London: HMSO (= *Medieval finds from excavations in London*, 1), 1987, x, 169 p, refs. 0 11 290440 8 pb. Illustrated catalogue showing over 300 knives, 100 leather scabbards, 50 pairs of shears and scissors dating 12th to mid-15th century.

Crewe, Sarah, *Stained glass in England 1180–1540*. HMSO for RCHME, 1987, 104 p, glossary, bibl, index. 0 11 300015 4 pb. Covers techniques and subjects.

Crossley, D W, *The Bewl Valley ironworks, Kent c. 1300–1730. Roy Archaeol Inst monogr*, 1975, 98 p, bibl. no ISBN, pb. Excavation report and discussion on the water-powered Chingley forge and furnace.

— (ed), *Medieval industry. CBA res rep*, 40, 1981, vii, 156 p, bibls, index. 0 906780 07 1 pb. Papers from a seminal conference which discussed various industries. *See also now Blair and Ramsay (above).*

Crowfoot, E, Pritchard, F and Staniland, K, *Textiles and clothing c. 1150–c. 1450*. London: HMSO (= *Medieval finds from excavations in London*, 4), 1992, x, 223 p, refs, glossary, concordance. 0 11 290445 9 pb. The first synthesis of medieval materials previously known only from paintings, sculpture etc. Discusses techniques of manufacture etc.

Davey, P J and Hodges, R (eds), *Ceramics and trade: the production and distribution of later medieval pottery in northwest Europe*. Sheffield: Dept Prehist and Archaeol, 1983, x, 305 p, bibl, index. 0 906090 10 5 pb. Fourteen papers from the Hull conference, 1980.

DOMESDAY BOOK (gen ed John Morris). Edition of 35 county-by-county volumes, with the original Latin paralleled by English translations; each volume complete with introduction and notes etc. Also 3-volume index to places, persons, and subjects respectively (J McN Dodgson and others). Chichester: Phillimore, 1975–92.

Dyer, C C (chmn), *Medieval archaeology in the 1990s. Proposals . . . towards the HBMCE five-year plan, 1991–6*. Society for Medieval Archaeol, 1989.

Informally-produced document offering general themes as prime candidates for rescue archaeology funding.

Eames, E S, *Catalogue of medieval lead-glazed earthenware tiles*. London: Brit Mus, 1980, 2 vols, 793 p + plates vol. o 7141 1338 7 (set.) Magisterial survey, with bibliographic updates provided in *Bulletin of the Census of Medieval Tiles*.

Egan, Geoff and Pritchard, Frances, *Dress accessories c. 1150–c. 1450*. London: HMSO (= *Medieval finds from excavations in London*, 3), 1991, xi, 410 p, bibl. o 11 290444 o pb.
Over 2000 items are catalogued, with special aspects like conservation and metallographic analysis considered.

Ellis, Mary, *Using manorial records*. London: PRO Publns/Roy Comm Hist MSS (= *PRO readers' guides*, 6), 1994, viii, 110 p. 1 873162 12 x pb.
Explains the records held by the Public Record Office and the Manorial Documents Register held by Roy Comm Hist MSS.

Evans, D H and Tomlinson, D G, *Excavations at 33–35 Eastgate, Beverley, 1983–6*. Sheffield excavation rep, 3, 1992, xix, 299 p, bibl, 2 fiche with abbrev. index. o 906090 44 x pb.
This is the most detailed excavation of a medieval dyeworks in Britain, with eight phases of activity.

Evison V I, Hodges, H and Hurst, J G (eds), *Medieval pottery from excavations: studies presented to Gerald Clough Dunning . . .* London: John Baker, 1974, 262 p, refs, index. o 212 97009 7
Includes papers on Anglo-Saxon as well as medieval and post-medieval pottery.

Fehring, G P (transl Ross Samson), *The archaeology of medieval Germany: an introduction*. London: Routledge, 1991, 266 p, bibl. o 415 04062 o.
Considered a valuable source book by reviewers, with some patterns paralleling English evidence.

FINDS RESEARCH GROUP AD 700–1700. Issues occasional *Data sheets* on specific topics.

Ford, Boris (ed), *Cambridge cultural history of Britain: 2, The Middle Ages*. Cambridge: CUP, pb edn 1992, bibl, index. o 521 42882 3 pb.
Essays covering the arts from AD 1100–1500;

note that the bibliography in the earlier hardback edn (1988) is much larger.

Gaimster, David and Redknap, Mark (eds), *Everyday and exotic pottery from Europe c. 650–1900: studies in honour of John G Hurst*. Oxford: Oxbow, 1992, 382 p, bibls. o 946897 47 6.
Collection of 33 papers from the Medieval Pottery Research Group.

Gilchrist, Roberta and Mytum, Harold (eds), *The archaeology of rural monasteries*. BARBS, 203, 1989, vi, 361 p, bibl. o 86054 610 1 pb.
Sixteen papers from a 1988 conference in York.

— (eds), *Advances in monastic archaeology*. BARBS, 227, 1993, ii, 148 p, bibls. o 86054 746 9 pb.
The more general papers from this 1989 conference cover recording worked stone, urban monasteries, water management in urban monasteries, the potential of tiles, and pottery and glass.

*Greene, J Patrick, *Medieval monasteries*. Leicester: Leicester Univ Press, 1992, xi, 255 p, bibl, glossary, index. o 7185 1296 o hb, o 7185 2229 x pb.
Received slightly mixed reviews but contains much information for the visitor, archaeologist and buildings conserver.

*—, *Norton Priory: the archaeology of a medieval religious house*. Cambridge: CUP, 1989, xii, 167 p, bibl, index. o 521 33054 8.
Archaeological, architectural and documentary evidence derived from a 12-year campaign, the first thorough investigation of a monastic house (Augustinian in this case).

Grew, F and de Neergaard, M, *Shoes and pattens*. London: HMSO (= *Medieval finds from excavations in London*, 2), 1988, vi, 145 p, bibl. o 11 290443 2 pb.
Treats nearly 2,000 shoes from AD 1100–1450.

Grierson, Philip, *The coins of medieval Europe*. London: Seaby, 1991, ix, 248 p, bibl, glossary, index. 1 85264 058 8.

Grimes, W F, *The excavation of Roman and medieval London*. London: Routledge and Kegan Paul, 1968, xxi, 261 p, refs, index.
So far the only account from the extensive postwar excavations, although the Museum of London has a full report in preparation.

Hall, David, *Medieval fields. Shire archaeol*, 28, 1982, 56 p, refs, index. 0 85263 599 0 pb.
How to identify them on the ground.

Hallam, H E (ed), *The agrarian history of England and Wales* II: *1042–1350*. Cambridge: CUP, 1988, xxxix. 1086 p, bibls, indexes. 0 521 20073 3.
Includes chapters on rural building in England by J G Hurst (pp 854–930) and in Wales by L A S Butler (pp 931–65).

Hammond, P W, *Food and feast in medieval England*. Stroud: Alan Sutton, 1993, 176 p, bibl, index. 0 86299 794 1.
Where food came from, town and country foods, the gentry, adulteration and nutrition, etc.

Harvey, John H, *Medieval craftsmen*. London: Batsford, 1975, vii, 231 p, bibl, index. 0 7134 2934 8.
Mainly documents, with some material evidence.

—, *Cathedrals of England and Wales*. London: Batsford, rev edn 1974, 272 p, bibl. 0 7134 0616 X.

Harvey, P D A, *Manorial records*. London: Brit Records Ass (= *Archives and the user*, 5), 1984, viii, 81 p, notes, index. 0 900222 06 9 pb.

Haslam, Jeremy, *Medieval pottery. Shire archaeol*, 6, 2 edn 1984, 64 p, bibl, index. 0 85263 670 9 pb.
Introduces a highly complex subject.

*Higham, Robert and Barker, Philip, *Timber castles*. London: Batsford, 1992, 390 p, bibl, site index. 0 7134 2189 4.
Discussion includes gazetteer of excavated sites in Britain and Ireland and some notes on vocabulary of medieval sources on castles. The last chapter treats Hen Domen, the most extensively excavated timber castle. A reference work 'written with verve and skill' (M W Thompson).

Hindle, B P, *Medieval town plans. Shire archaeol*, 62, 1990, 64 p, bibl, index. 0 7478 0065 0 pb.

Hinton, D A (ed), *Twenty-five years of medieval archaeology*. Sheffield: Dept of Prehistory and Archaeol/Soc Medieval Archaeol, 1983, 135 p, chapter bibls. No ISBN.
Fourteen papers celebrated the silver jubilee of the Society for Medieval Archaeology; Celtic West and Anglo-Saxon materials are included.

Dismissed by one critic as 'scholars talking to one another'.

See also Hinton's entries in Section 6.11.5 Migration and early medieval (under Anglo-Saxon).

Holt, Richard, *The mills of medieval England*. Oxford: Blackwell, 1988, x, 202 p, bibl, index. 0 631 15692 5.
Covers both wind- and watermills, AD 600–1550.

Hooke, Della (ed), *Medieval villages: a review of current work. OUCA monogr*, 5, 1985, 223 p, bibls. 0 947816 05 4 pb.
Papers on archaeological, geographical and historical aspects, England–Wales–Scotland.

Hurst, J G, see Hallam above.

Hutchinson, Gillian, *Medieval ships and shipping*. London: Leicester Univ Press (series The archaeology of medieval Britain), 1994, xi, 219 p, bibl, glossary, index. 0 7185 1413 0.
Three chapters on the ships themselves, and seven on their context (trade, ports, inland water transport, fishing, warfare, pilotage/navigation, etc).

Hyland, Ann, *The medieval warhorse from Byzantium to the Crusades*. Stroud: A Sutton, 1995, xii, 204 p, bibl, index. 0 86299 983 9.
Historical and material evidence.

Jennings, Sara, *Medieval pottery in the Yorkshire Museum*. York: Yorkshire Mus, 1992, 56 p, glossary, bibl. 0 905807 04 9 pb.
Some 200 pots are illustrated in colour photos and marginal drawings; both informative and attractive for a lay audience, but not well arranged for the serious pottery worker.

*Kenyon, John R, *Medieval fortifications*. Leicester/London: Leicester Univ Press (Pinter), 1990, xvi, 233 p, bibl, index. 0 7185 1289 8 hb; 1991 pb 0 7185 1392 4 (with bibliographic update in preface).
Concentrates on the large volume of archaeological research since 1945; covers all aspects of castles, town defences, and the decline of the castle.

*King, D J Cathcart, *The castle in England and Wales: an interpretative history*. London: Croom Helm (Routledge), 1988, 210 p, bibl, index. 0 7099 4829 8.
On the character, origins, development and influence of castles; a companion to his refer-

ence work (listed under Bibliographies earlier in this section).

Knowles, D and St Joseph, J K S, *Monastic sites from the air*. Cambridge: CUP, 1952, xxviii, 281 p, footnotes, site index.
Selected sites are shown with short commentaries.

Lightbown, R W, *Medieval jewellery in western Europe*. London: Gollancz, 1991, 589 p, bibl, index. 0 948107 87 1.
Massive, wide ranging and important study; includes catalogue of the Victoria and Albert Museum collection c. 800–c. 1500.

London Museum medieval catalogue 1940 (comp J B Ward-Perkins; modern reprint introduced by John Clark). Ipswich: Anglia Publishing, 1993 reprint, xii, 324 p. 1 897874 01 4.
Unrevised reprint.

*McCarthy, Michael and Brooks, Catherine M, *Medieval pottery in Britain*, AD 900–1600. Leicester: Leicester Univ Press, 1988, xx, 521 p, refs, index. 0 7185 1254 5 hb, 0 7185 1271 5 pb.
Fundamental work which includes a select gazetteer; emphasis is on social and industrialisation aspects more than dating. One reviewer criticised it for lack of cross-referencing and poor indexing, but there is an immense amount of information in it.

McNeill, Tom, *English Heritage book of castles*. London: Batsford/EH, 1992, 142 p, bibl, index. 0 7134 7025 9 pb.

Man, Elizabeth, 'The Medieval Village Research Group Archive: an introduction', in *Medieval Sett Res Grp annu rep*, 5, 1990, pp 5–6.
Outlines the material accumulated from 1952 to 1987 which is deposited at NMR (Swindon).

Margeson, Sue, *Norwich households: the medieval and post-medieval finds from Norwich Survey excavations 1971–8. E Anglian archaeol rep*, 58, 1993, xii, 266 p, bibl, index. 0 9520695 0 4 pb.
A rich mine of finds of all kinds except pottery, grouped by function or trade, from dress accessories to building fittings.

Mayes, Philip and Scott, Keith (ed Shirley Johnson), *Pottery kilns at Chilvers Coton, Nuneaton. Soc Medieval Archaeol monogr*, 10, 1984, xi, 197 p, bibl. (No ISBN.)

Excavation of complex of 42 kilns, in production from 13th to 17th century.

MEDIEVAL ART AND ARCHITECTURE SERIES: annual reports from Brit Archaeol Ass meetings in cathedral cities. Mostly architectural with some archaeological information.

Medieval Settlement Research Group archive, see Elizabeth Man above.

*Mellor, Maureen (ed) for MPRG, *Medieval ceramic studies in England: a review for English Heritage*. London: Engl Heritage, 1994, vii, 76 p, refs. 1 85074 483 1 pb.
Review of progress in the discipline and identification of areas where resources need to be applied. Covers the period from end of Roman Britain to 17th century, excluding post-medieval fine ware industries. Highly selective bibliography of key reports for each region up to 1992; recommendations for action.

Milne, Gustav and Milne, Chrissie, *Medieval waterfront development at Trig Lane, London. London and Middx Archaeol Soc spec pap*, 5, 1982, v, 114 p, bibl, glossary, index. 0 903290 24 3 pb.
Record of the first large waterfront excavation in Britain, showing how the Thames foreshore was steadily reclaimed for the development of docks, warehouses and the like.

*—, with Trevor Brigham et al, *Timber building techniques in London c. 900–1400: an archaeological study of waterfront installations and related material. London and Middx Archaeol Soc spec pap*, 15, 1992, 152 p, bibl, index. 0 903290 41 3 pb.
Important study advancing knowledge of carpentry techniques, particularly on the transition from earthfast timbers to framing techniques.

see also Milne on Leadenhall Court excavations in Section 6.11.4 Romano-British.

Morris, Richard, *Cathedrals and abbeys of England and Wales: the building church, 600–1540*. London: Dent, 1979, 294 p, bibl, glossary, index. 0 460 04334 X.
On the origins of 33 cathedrals and 42 great churches, their architecture, how they were used, and so on.

— (ed), *The church in British archaeology. CBA res rep*, 47, 1983, 124 p, bibl, index. 0 906780 17 9 pb.
Covers Roman Britain to post-Reformation at a

time when the discipline of church study was being transformed by the introduction of archaeological methods. Includes a list of church excavations 1955–80.

**—, *Churches in the landscape*. London: Dent, 1989, 508 p, bibl, index. 0 460 04509 1.
A wide and deep survey using all sources of evidence, from St Augustine at Canterbury to the social upheavals of 18th/19th centuries; the best book to read on the influence of churches on the surrounding landscapes and parishes.

Ordnance Survey maps for monastic Britain, see Section 6.1 General reference works (under Maps).

Parnell, Geoffrey, *The Tower of London*. London: Batsford/Engl Heritage, 1993, 128 p, bibl, index. 0 7134 6863 7 hb, 0 7134 6864 5 pb.
History of the Tower including results of recent research and throwing light on military architecture and the purposes of castle buildings.

Pearce, Jacqueline and Vince, Alan (and others), *A dated type series of London medieval pottery: part 4, Surrey whitewares*. London and Middx Archaeol Soc spec pap, [10], 1988, 192 p, bibl. 0 903290 34 0 pb.
Some earlier parts in this series were originally published in the Society's *Transactions*, also available as offprints: part 1 (1982) dealt with Mill Green Ware; part 2 (*spec pap* 6, 1985) with London-type ware; part 3 (1983) with a late medieval Hertfordshire glazed ware.

Pearson, S et al, on medieval Kentish houses, see Section 6.18 Vernacular architecture.

Pevsner, N and Metcalf, Priscilla, *The cathedrals of England*. Harmondsworth: Viking, 2 vols, 1985, 399 + 381 p, bibl, glossary, index to each. 0 670 80125 9 hb, 0 670 80124 0 pb.
One volume treats Midland, Eastern and Northern England; the other, Southern England. Information was collected and brought up to date from the Buildings of England series.

Platt, Colin, *Medieval England: a social history and archaeology from the Conquest to AD 1600*. London: Routledge, 1995, xvii, 292 p, bibl, index. 0 415 11915 4 hb, 0 415 12913 3 pb.
Revision of 1978 original.

—, *Medieval Britain from the air*. London: George Philip, 1984, 239 p, bibl, index. 0 540 01077 4.
Social and historical comment on a series of aerial photographs.

*Renn, D F, *Norman castles in Britain*. London: John Baker, 2 edn 1973, xii, 369 p, bibl, index. 0 212 97002 X.
Classic survey.

*Roberts, B K, *The making of the English village: a study in historical geography*. Harlow: Longman, 1987, 288 p, bibl, index. 0 582 30143 2.
Pioneer work on the use of village plans to construct geographical models.

Rodwell, Warwick, *English Heritage book of church archaeology*. London: Batsford/Engl Heritage, 1989, 208 p, bibl, index. 0 7134 2590 3.
New edn of book formerly published as *The archaeology of the English church* (1981).

Rouse, E Clive, *Medieval wall paintings*. Princes Risborough: Shire, 4 edn 1991, 80 p, bibl, index. 0 7478 0144 9 pb.
By the doyen of wall painting studies.

Rowley, T, *The Norman heritage 1066–1200*. London: Routledge and Kegan Paul, 1983, xiv, 210 p, bibl, index. 0 7100 9413 2.
Cultural survey.

— and Wood, John, *Deserted villages*. Shire archaeol, 23, rev edn 1995, 72 p, bibl, index. 0 7478 0283 1 pb.
Good introduction, but omits Welsh examples.

Royal Commission on the Ancient and Historical Monuments of England (per H G Ramm, R W McDowall and E Mercer), *Shielings and bastles*. London: HMSO, 1970, xv, 104 p, footnote refs, index. 0 11 700468 5.
These defensive Border structures date from 14th to 17th centuries. Note also P W Dixon's review-article reconsidering some of the problems in *Archaeologia Aeliana* (4th series), 50, 1972, pp 249–58.

Salzman, L F, *English industries of the middle ages: being an introduction to the industrial history of medieval England*. Oxford: OUP, 2 edn 1923, xx, 360 p, footnotes, index.
Classic and pioneering volume based largely on documentary evidence which should now be read in the light of much newer, more archaeological evidence (eg Blair and Ramsay or Crossley, above).

Saunders, Andrew, on fortresses, see Section 6.11.7 Post-medieval.

Saunders, Peter and Saunders, Eleanor, *Salisbury Museum medieval catalogue: part 1*. Salisbury:

Salisbury and S Wilts Museum, 1991, 191 p, refs, index. 0 947535 13 6 pb.
Harness pendants, seals, rings, etc. (*See under Spencer for Part 2.*)

Scarisbrick, Diana, *Jewellery in Britain 1066–1837: a documentary, social, literary and artistic survey*. Wilby (Norwich): Michael Russell, 1994, xxiii, 431 p, bibl, index. 0 85955 190 3.

*Schofield, John, *The building of London from the Conquest to the Great Fire*. London: Brit Mus Publs/Mus of London, rev edn 1993, 190 p. 0 7141 1733 1 pb.
Important study of the development of the city; includes gazetteer and map of surviving fragments of Roman and medieval London.

–, *Medieval London houses*. London: Yale Univ Press for Paul Mellor Centre for Studies in British Art, 1995, 272 p, bibl, index. 0 300 05578 1.
Discusses, for the period c. 1200 to 1666, the houses, shops, almshouses, inns, livery halls; topography, selective gazetteer, townscape formation processes, constructional details.

— and Vince, Alan, *Medieval towns*. London: Leicester Univ Press, 1994, xii, 243 p, bibl, index. 0 7185 1294 4 hb, 0 7185 1971 X pb.
From Saxon times to 16th century, offers a synthesis from three decades of research covering topography, houses and streets, crafts and industries, trade and commerce, churches and religious houses, cemeteries, the environment.

Simpson, W D, *Castles from the air*. London: Country Life, 1949, 128 p.
Over a hundred half-page photographs with long captions; the first book to take advantage of the new technique of air photography for better understanding of buildings in their landscape. (Not to be confused with R Allen Brown's similarly-titled 1989 book.)

Slater, T R (ed), *The built form of western cities: essays for M R G Conzen on the occasion of his eightieth birthday*. London: Leicester Univ Press, 1990, xviii, 445 p, bibls, index. 0 7185 1295 2.
Includes papers by C J Bond (on Thame), Harold Carter (Welsh towns), George Gordon (Scottish cities from Georgian times), the editor (medieval Midlands towns), and J Bradley (town plan analysis for medieval Irish towns); also four papers on townscape conservation.

Spencer, Brian, *Pilgrim souvenirs and secular badges. Salisbury Mus medieval catalogue part 2*. Salisbury: Salisbury and S Wilts Museum, 1990, 144 p, bibl, name index. 0 947535 12 8 pb.

***Steane, J M, *The archaeology of medieval England and Wales*. London: Croom Helm, 1985, xvi, 302 p, bibl, index. 0 7099 2385 6.
Essential thematic guide.

—, *The archaeology of the English monarchy*. London: Batsford, 1993, 226 p, bibl, index. 0 7134 7246 4.
Deals with symbols of power, burials of the medieval royal family, royal accommodation, palaces and castle gardens, hunting etc.

Stopford, J on recording medieval tiles, see Section 6.9 The excavator's training (etc) under Drawing.

Stuart, Dennis on manorial records transcription, see Section 6.17 Place-names and local history.

**Taylor, Chris, *Fieldwork in medieval archaeology*. London: Batsford, 1974, 176 p, bibl, index. 0 7134 2850 3 hb, 0 7134 2872 4 limp. Classic 'how to do it' guide.

Thompson, A H, *Military architecture in England during the middle ages*. Oxford: OUP, 1912, xxi, 384 p, bibl, indexes.
Classic framework for castle studies.

Thompson, M W, *The rise of the castle*. Cambridge: CUP, 1991, ix, 205 p, bibl, index. 0 521 37544 4.
On the domestic and the fortified functions, sometimes combined, sometimes separated.

—, *The decline of the castle*. Cambridge: CUP, 1987, viii, 211 p, bibl, index. 0 521 32194 8.

Vyner, B E (ed), *Medieval rural settlement in north-east England. Architect Archaeol Soc Durham and Northumberland res pap, 2*, 1990, vii, 150 p, bibl. 0 9510388 1 8 pb. (Not available to compiler.)
Nine papers from a 1989 day school, some on individual sites and some more general.

Wrathmell, Stuart et al, *Wharram: a study of settlement on the Yorkshire Wolds. Vol 6, Domestic settlement; part 2, medieval peasant farmsteads. York Univ archaeol publs, 8*, 1989, viii, 59 p, bibl, one fiche.
Excavation report from this classic site. (*See*

also Andrews, and Beresford and Hurst, respectively, above).

Wales

BIBLIOGRAPHY

*SURVEY OF MEDIEVAL POTTERY IN WALES (Board of Celtic Studies major project): Papazian, C and Campbell, E, *Medieval pottery and roof tile in Wales AD 1100–1600*, published as special issue of *Medieval and later pottery in Wales*, 13, 1992, pp 1–107. Includes list of sites with medieval pottery, location of collections, archive and site records in Nat Mus Wales, ten-page bibliography.

In addition *Medieval and later pottery in Wales* has provided regular bibliographies of Welsh medieval and post-medieval ceramics, from its inception in 1978.

BOOKS

Avent, Richard, *Castles of the princes of Gwynedd/Cestyll Tywysogion Gwynedd*. Cardiff: Cadw, 1983, vi, 41 p. 0 11 671134 5 pb. Introductory booklet.

***Barker, Philip and Higham, Robert, *Hen Domen, Montgomery: a timber castle on the English-Welsh border*. London: Roy Archaeol Inst, 1982, 98 p, bibl. 0 903986 10 8. First of two planned volumes on a motte-and-bailey castle of AD 1071/86 to 1300, excavated to exemplary standards over many seasons: massively timber-framed with subsequent rebuilds, five motte bridges, etc.

Brown, R Allen, on castles from the air, see entry under General works (above).

Butler, L A S, see Hallam under General works (above).

Courtney, Paul, *Medieval and later Usk* (vol 5 of *Report on the fortress excavations at Usk 1965–76*, ed W H Manning). Cardiff: Univ Wales Press, 1994, xx, 165 p, bibl, index. 0 7083 1245 4.

Davis, Paul R and Lloyd-Fern, Susan, *Lost churches of Wales and the Marches*. Stroud: Sutton, 1991, xix, 168 p, index. 0 86299 564 7 pb.

Gresham, Colin A, *Medieval stone carving in North Wales: sepulchral slabs and effigies of the 13th and 14th centuries*. Cardiff: Univ Wales Press, 1968, xxiv, 264 p, refs, glossary, index.

Harvey, John, on cathedrals of England and Wales, see entry under General works (above).

Humphries, P H, *Castles of Edward the First in Wales*. Cardiff: Cadw, 1983, 48 p. 0 11 790262 4 pb. Souvenir booklet.

Jack, R Ian, *Medieval Wales*. London: The Sources of History Ltd/Hodder and Stoughton, 1972, 255 p, refs, index. 0 340 12693 0. Description of the sources for Welsh medieval history.

*Kenyon, J R and Avent, R (eds), *Castles in Wales and the Marches: essays in honour of D J Cathcart King*. Cardiff; Univ Wales Press, 1987, x, 248 p, bibls. 0 7083 0948 8. Festschrift containing 15 papers.

King, D J Cathcart-, on the castle in England and Wales, see entry under General works (above).

Lewis, J M, *Welsh medieval paving tiles*. Cardiff: Nat Mus Wales, 1976, 36 p. 0 7200 0057 2 pb. Introductory booklet.

—, *Welsh monumental brasses*. Cardiff: Nat Mus Wales, 1974, 112 p. 0 7200 0054 8 pb. Illustrates all the Welsh figure brasses up to mid-19th century.

—, *Medieval pottery and metalware in Wales*. Cardiff, Nat Mus Wales, 1978, 36 p. 0 7200 0209 5. Illustrates a wide range.

Royal Commission on the Ancient and Historical Monuments of Wales, *An inventory of the ancient monuments of Glamorgan, III. Medieval secular monuments: part IA, The early castles (to 1217)*. London: HMSO, 1991, xv, 391 p, footnotes, glossary, site index. 0 11 300035 9.
Part II, Non-defensive. Cardiff: HMSO, 1982, xxxviii, 398 p, footnotes, glossary, index. 0 11 701141 X. Definitive records in 'Inventory' style.

Robinson, David M, *Cowbridge: the archaeology and topography of a small market town in the Vale of Glamorgan*. Swansea: GGAT, 1980 (= Town survey 1), 85 p, bibl, index. 0 9506950 1 7 pb. Full analysis of topographical development, prehistoric to modern.

Soulsby, Ian, *The towns of medieval Wales: a study of their history, archaeology and early topography*. Chichester; Phillimore, 1983, xiii, 276 p, index. 0 85033 437 3.

Steane, J M, on archaeology of medieval England and Wales, see under General works (above).

Taylor, A J, *The Welsh castles of Edward I.* London: Hambledon Press, 1986, vi, 129 p, refs. 0 907628 71 0.
Revised and re-edited version of material originally published in the *History of the king's works* (1963), and secondly in *The king's works in Wales 1277–1330*, HMSO 1974. Mainly historical but includes castle plans.

Vyner, B and Wrathmell, S (eds), *Studies in medieval and later pottery in Wales presented to J M Lewis.* Cardiff: Univ Coll Cardiff Dept Extra-Mural Stud, 1987, viii, 252 p, bibl. 0 946045 32 1 pb.
Contains 16 papers on typology, production and trade.

Williams, David H, *Atlas of Cistercian lands in Wales.* Cardiff: Univ Wales Press, 1990, xv, 153 p, bibl, index. 0 7083 1007 9.
Introductory chapters, inventory, maps, plans and plates.

Scotland

Caldwell, D H, on weapons and fortifications, see Section 6.11.7 Post-Medieval.

Cant, R G, *The medieval churches and chapels of Shetland.* Lerwick: Shetland Archaeol Hist Soc, 1975, 50 p. 0 9504744 0 1 pb.

Cowan, Ian B and Easson, David E, *Medieval religious houses in Scotland with an appendix on the houses in the Isle of Man.* London/New York: Longman, 2 edn 1976, xxviii, 252 p, maps, refs, index. 0 582 12069 1.
Gives basic historical data on monasteries.

*Cruden, Stewart, *The Scottish castle.* Edinburgh: Spurbooks, 3 edn 1981, 272 p, index. 0 7157 2088 0.

Ewan, Elizabeth, *Town life in 14th century Scotland.* Edinburgh: EUP, 1990, ix, 201 p, bibl, index. 0 7486 0128 7 pb.
Documentary and archaeological evidence used to offer a rounded picture of the urban economy.

Fawcett, Richard, *Scottish medieval churches: an introduction to the ecclesiastical architecture of the twelfth to sixteenth centuries.* Edinburgh:

Historic Scotland, 1985, 64 p, short bibl, index. 0 11 492385 X pb.
Attractive and accessible work, almost a 'souvenir guide'.

—, *Scottish abbeys and priories.* London: Batsford/Hist Scotl, 1994, 144 p, short bibl, gazetteer, index. 0 7134 7440 8 hb, 0 7134 7372 X pb.

—, *Scottish architecture from the accession of the Stuarts to the Reformation, 1371–1560.* Edinburgh: EUP / Hist Scotl, 1994, xxi, 386 p, bibl, index. 0 7486 0465 0.
Ecclesiastical and royal buildings, castles, domestic, artillery fortifications.

Hingley, R on Scottish medieval and later rural settlement, see Section 6.7 Archaeological heritage management.

Holdsworth, P (ed), *Excavations in the medieval burgh of Perth, 1979–1981.* Soc Antiq Scotl monogr, 5, 1987, 219 p, bibl, 3 microfiches. 0 903903 05 9 pb.
Three principal areas of the town, mainly 14th and 15th century, were examined, making this the most extensively explored Scottish burgh.

Inverness Field Club [ed L MacLean], *The Middle Ages in the Highlands.* Inverness: Inverness Field Club, 1981, 179 p. 0 9502612 1 1 pb.
Symposium volume.

Lewis, John and Ewart, Gordon, *Jedburgh Abbey.* Soc Antiq Scot monogr, 10, 1995, 182 p, bibl, index. 0 903903 10 5 pb.
Report on the 1984 excavation which revealed much about the history, society and topographical context as well as the daily life of the Beauvais-founded abbey.

Lynch, Michael, Spearman, Michael and Stell, Geoffrey (eds), *The Scottish medieval town.* Edinburgh: John Donald, 1988, ix, 344 p, bibl, index. 0 85976 170 3.
Three papers have archaeological content.

MacGibbon, D and Ross, T, *The castellated and domestic architecture of Scotland from the twelfth to the eighteenth century.* Edinburgh: David Douglas, 5 vols 1887–92.
This and the next are classic early works, profusely illustrated in line.

—, *The ecclesiastical architecture of Scotland.* Edinburgh: David Douglas, 3 vols 1896–7.

MacIvor, Iain, *Edinburgh Castle.* London: Bats-

ford/Historic Scotland, 1993, 143 p, glossary, short bibl, index. 0 7134 7295 2 pb.
Includes mention of the earliest (Bronze Age occupation) of the castle and takes the story through the royal fortress and palace, military garrison, and tourist attraction.

National Museum of Antiquities of Scotland, *Angels, nobles and unicorns: art and patronage in medieval Scotland*. Edinburgh: Nat Mus Antiq Scotl, 1982, 120 p, bibl. 0 9503117 1 5 pb.
Exhibition catalogue.

RCAHMS, on late medieval sculpture, see Steer and Bannerman below.

RCHME, on shielings and bastles, see under General works (above).

Salter, Mike, *Discovering Scottish castles*. Princes Risborough: Shire *Discovering* 279, 1985, 160 p, index. 0 85263 749 7 pb.
Gazetteer of over 1,000 castles.

Simpson, A T T and Stevenson, S, *Town houses and structures in medieval Scotland: a seminar*. [Glasgow]: Univ Glasgow Dept Archaeol, 1980, 52 p, bibls. (No ISBN).
Treats both upstanding and excavated buildings.

Smith, J S (ed), *New light on medieval Aberdeen*. Aberdeen: Aberdeen Univ Press, 1985, xi, 66 p, bibl. 0 08 032449 5 pb.
Six papers on documentary and archaeological aspects.

— (ed), *North east castles: castles in the landscape of north east Scotland*. Aberdeen: Aberdeen Univ Press, 1990, ix, 126 p, bibl. 0 08 040931 8.
Contributions on castle landscapes, tower houses (especially restorations), castle restoration, the shift from castle to defensible residence.

Steer, K A and Bannerman, J W M, *Late medieval monumental sculpture in the Western Highlands*. Edinburgh: HMSO for RCAHMS, 1977, xxvi, 230 p, bibl, index. 0 11 491383 8.
Describes over 600 crosses, grave slabs and effigies, 14th to 16th centuries.

*Stones, J A (ed), *Three Scottish Carmelite friaries: excavations at Aberdeen, Linlithgow and Perth, 1980–86*. Soc Antiq Scotl monogr, 6, 1989, 175 p, bibl, 13 fiches. 0 903903 06 7 pb.
This volume helps rectify a lack of extensive excavation in Scottish friaries.

SURVEY OF SCOTTISH BURGHS, by E P Dennison Torrie and Russel Coleman. 1995–.
Geographical and topographical background to the settlement of each burgh, with archaeological and historical evidence for its layout and development. Already published: *Historic Stranraer; Historic Kirkcaldy; Historic Cumnock*. Published by Historic Scotland/Scottish Cultural Press.

Tabraham, Christopher, *Scottish castles and fortifications*. Edinburgh: Historic Scotland, 1986, 80 p, index. 0 11 492475 9 pb.
Well-illustrated official guide.

Taylor, Michael, *The Lewis chessmen*. London: British Museum, 1978, 16 p. 0 7141 1347 6 pb.
Introduction to these popular and much-reproduced ivory pieces.

Torrie, E P Dennison and Coleman, Russel, see SURVEY OF SCOTTISH BURGHS above.

*Yeoman, Peter, *Medieval Scotland: an archaeological perspective*. London: Batsford/Hist Scotland, 1995, 128 p, bibl, glossary, index. 0 7134 7464 5 hb, 0 7134 7465 3 pb.
Reviews the results of two decades of excavations in burghs, the countryside and ecclesiastical foundations; considers social roles and offers many new illustrations.

Isle of Man

see Cowan and Easson under Scotland above.

Ireland: from Anglo-Norman period onwards

BIBLIOGRAPHY

**Asplin, P W A, *Medieval Ireland c.1170–1495: a bibliography of secondary works*. Dublin: Roy Ir Acad, 1971, 154 p, index. 0 901714 01 1 pb.
Very useful for sources up to the 1960s, including details of serials, essays and Festschriften; see also under Cosgrove below.

BOOKS

Barry, T B, *The medieval moated sites of southeastern Ireland: Counties Carlow, Kilkenny, Tipperary and Wexford. BARBS*, 35, 1977, 247 p, bibl. 0 904531 69 4 pb.

—, 'Medieval moated sites in Ireland: some new conclusions on their chronology and function', in G MacNiocaill and P Wallace (eds), *Keimelia* (see entry below), pp 525–35; updates previous item.

*—, *The archaeology of medieval Ireland*. London: Methuen, 1987, xvii, 234 p, bibl, indexes. 0 416 30360 9; then Routledge 1988, 0 415 01104 3.
First treatment of this period from pre-Norman settlement to the later middle ages.

Bradley, John (ed), *Settlement and society in medieval Ireland: studies presented to F X Martin, osa*. Kilkenny: Boethius Press, 1988, xviii, 524 p, bibls. 0 86314 143 9.
Papers on early historic and Viking Ireland, Anglo-Norman Ireland, late medieval.

—, *see also under Slater in General British works (above).*

Butlin, R (ed), *The development of the Irish town*. London: Croom Helm, 1977, 144 p, bibl, index. 0 87471 979 8.

Cairns, C T, *Irish tower houses: a County Tipperary case study*. [s l]: Group for the Study of Ir Hist Sett (= *Ir sett stud*, 2), 1987, 35 p. No ISBN, pb.

*Clarke, Howard (ed), *Medieval Dublin: the making of a metropolis*. Blackrock, Co Dublin: Ir Acad Press, 1990, 313 p, bibl, index. 0 7165 2459 7.
Reprinted essays by various authors, with emphasis on Dublin as a European city.

— (ed), *Medieval Dublin: the living city*. Blackrock, Co Dublin: Ir Acad Press, 1990, 241 p, bibl, index. 0 7165 2460 0.
Mainly historical sources; includes several monastic topics.

— and Simms, A (eds), *see entry for Irish urban origins in Section 6.11.5 Migration and early medieval (under Ireland).*

Coffey, G, *Catalogue of Irish coins in the collection of the Royal Irish Academy . . . Dublin. Pt 2, Anglo-Irish*. Dublin: Dept of Sci and Art of the Committee of Council on Education, 1895, 123 p.

Cosgrove, Art (ed), *A new history of Ireland: II, Medieval Ireland 1169–1534*. Oxford: Clarendon, 2 edn 1993, lxii, 1002 p, bibl, index. 0 19 821755 2.
Includes several articles relevant to archaeologists, as well as a substantial bibliography.

Cunningham, George, *The Anglo-Norman advance into the south-west midlands of Ireland 1185–1221*. Roscrea: Parkmore Press, 1987, xxviii, 195 p, bibl, index. 0 9505368 4 9.
Illustrated with many photographs, aerial views, maps and plans of monuments.

de Breffny, Brian, *Castles of Ireland*. London: Thames and Hudson, 1977, 208 p, unreferenced, castle-name index. 0 500 24100 7; (1986 pb) 0 500 27398 7.

— and Mott, George, *The churches and abbeys of Ireland*. London: Thames and Hudson, 1976, 208 p, bibl, index. 0 500 24096 5.
Chronological survey of about 300 sites from Celtic times to the present, with some useful data in appendices.

Dolley, R H M and Seaby, W A, *Anglo-Irish coins: John–Edward III, Ulster Museum, Belfast*. London: OUP for Brit Acad/Ulster Mus (= *Sylloge of coins of the British Isles*, 10), 1968, lvii, 33 p + 16 pls.

Eames, Elizabeth and Fanning, Thomas, *Irish medieval tiles: decorated medieval paving tiles in Ireland with an inventory of sites and designs and a visual index*. Roy Ir Acad monogr archaeol, 2, 1988, vii, 144 p, bibl, site index. 0 911714 62 3.
Covers 88 sites with 505 individual designs from about 1250 to 1550.

Feehan, J (ed), *Environment and development in Ireland*. Dublin: Environmental Inst Univ Coll Dublin, 1992, xii, 620 p, bibls. 1 870089 76 6.
Includes G Cooney, 'The archaeological endowment' (pp 70–80) and J Bradley, 'Archaeology and development in Ireland's medieval cities and towns' (pp 81–6).

Galloway, Peter, *The cathedrals of Ireland*. Belfast: Inst Ir Stud, 1992, xxiv, 231 p. 0 85389 422 3.
The first guide to the history and architecture of all cathedral churches of Ireland.

Glasscock, R, 'The study of deserted medieval settlements in Ireland (to 1968)', in M W Beresford and J G Hurst (eds), *Deserted medieval villages* (Alan Sutton 1989 reprint), pp 279–301 including gazetteer.

Gosling, Paul, *From Dún Delca to Dundalk: the topography and archaeology of a medieval frontier town c. 1187–1700*. Co Louth Archaeol Hist Soc, 1993, 132 p. 0 9521456 0 X pb.

Reviews archaeological, documentary and cartographic sources for the early development of the town. (Reprinted from *Co Louth archaeol hist j*, 22.3, 1991.)

Graham, B J, *Anglo-Norman settlement in Ireland*. [s l]: Group for the Study of Ir Hist Sett (*Ir sett stud*, 1), 1985, 40 p, refs. No ISBN, pb.

Gwynn, Aubrey and Hadcock, R Neville, *Medieval religious houses: Ireland, with an appendix to early sites*. London: Longman, 1970, xii, 479 p. [o] 582 11229 X (Repr Ir Academic Press, 1988, 0 7165 2416 3).
Basic research tool listing the historical evidence arranged by religious order – Benedictine, Cluniac, Cistercian etc.

Hadcock, R N, *map of monastic Ireland, see Section 6.1 General reference (under Maps)*.

Healy, J N, *The castles of County Cork*. Cork: Mercier Press, 1988, 450 p, bibl, index. 0 85342 876 8.

Hunt, John (with contributions from Peter Harbison), *Irish medieval figure sculpture 1200–1600: a study of Irish tombs with notes on costume and armour*. Dublin/London: Irish Univ Press/Sotheby Parke Bernet, 1974, 2 vols, bibl, index. 0 85667 012 X.
Major corpus of medieval funerary monuments.

IRISH MEDIEVAL ART CONFERENCE BELFAST 1994 see under Bourke (ed) in Section 6.11.5 Migration and early medieval (under 'Sub-Roman' etc).

*Leask, H G, *Irish castles and castellated houses*. Dundalk: Dundealgan Press, rev edn 1951, 170 p, glossary, index.
This and the next entry are classic studies.

*—, *Irish churches and monastic buildings*. 3 vols: I, *The first phases and the Romanesque* (1955); II, *Gothic architecture to AD 1400* (1958); III, *Medieval Gothic: the last phase* (1960) (all Dundalk: Dundealgan Press).

McGrail, Sean, *Medieval boat and ship timbers from Dublin, see Section 6.19 Maritime, nautical and underwater archaeology*.

McNeill, T E, *Anglo-Norman Ulster: the history and archaeology of an Irish barony, 1177–1400*. Edinburgh: John Donald for Inst Ir Stud, 1980, ix, 157 p, bibl, index. 0 85976 057 X.

Mostly historical work, with some castle archaeology; a thesis-based text.

—, *Carrickfergus Castle, County Antrim*. Belfast: HMSO (= N Ireland archaeol monogr, 1), 1981, xiii, 88 p. 0 337 08164 6.
Excavation report on this castle whose history spans 12th to 20th century.

*MacNiocaill, Gearóid and Wallace, Patrick F (eds), *Keimelia: studies in medieval archaeology and history in memory of Tom Delaney*. Galway: Galway Univ Press, 1988, xvi, 622 p, bibl. 0 907775 33 0.
34 papers in tribute to a highly accomplished archaeologist who died tragically young.

Ó Floinn, Raghnall, *Irish shrines and reliquaries of the Middle Ages*. Dublin: Town House and Country House, 1994, 46 p, bibl. 0 946172 40 4 pb.
Short introduction.

O'Neill, Timothy, *Merchants and mariners in medieval Ireland*. Dublin: Ir Acad Press, 1987, 164 p, bibl, index. 0 7165 2398 1 hb, 0 7165 2399 X pb.
Mainly historical, with 10-page bibliography.

Richter, Michael, *Medieval Ireland: the enduring tradition*. Dublin: Gill and Macmillan (= New Gill history of Ireland, 1), 1988, 214 p, bibl, glossary, index. 0 7171 1606 9 hb, 0 7171 1616 6 pb.
English translation of his *Irland im Mittelalter*; shows the continuity from prehistory and through the first millennium to AD 1500.

Saunders, A on fortresses, see General British works (above).

Simms, K, *From kings to warlords: the changing political structure of Gaelic Ireland in the later Middle Ages*. Woodbridge: Boydell Press, 1987, 191 p, glossary, bibl, indexes. 0 85115 420 4.
Historical background.

Stalley, Roger, *Architecture and sculpture in Ireland 1150–1350*. Dublin: Gill and Macmillan, 1971, vi, 149 p, bibl. [o] 7171 0554 7.

—, *The Cistercian monasteries of Ireland: an account of the history, art and architecture of the White Monks in Ireland from 1142 to 1540*. London/New Haven: Yale Univ Press, 1987, vi, 295p, bibl, glossary, index. 0 300 03737 6.

Sweetman, David, *Irish castles and fortified houses*. Dublin: Town House and Country

House, 1995, 47 p, glossary, index. 0 946172 49 8 pb.
Illustrated introduction.

Thomas, Avril, *The walled towns of Ireland*. Blackrock, Co Dublin: Ir Acad Press, 1992, 2 vols, bibl, index. 0 7165 2481 3 (set).
Mostly documentary evidence, plus reference to surviving structures. Good bibliography.

6.11.7
Post-Medieval

Conventionally the post-medieval period begins with the accession of Henry VII in 1485, though some authorities prefer 1450. Industrial archaeology is given its own section (6.15) rather than being included here. For books on houses of this period, the section on Vernacular Architecture (6.18) should be consulted. Material on ships and maritime sites will be found in Section 6.19 Maritime, nautical and underwater archaeology; and that on early gardens in Section 6.16 Garden archaeology and history.

A good introduction to the post-medieval period is in David Gaimster's paper 'The archaeology of post-medieval society, c 1450–1750: material culture studies in Britain since the war', in B Vyner (ed), *Building on the past* (Roy Archaeol Inst 1994), pp 283–312 (with over six pages of bibliography).

The section is divided thus:
Journals
Bibliographies
General British
Wales
Scotland
Ireland

Journals

Medieval and later pottery in Wales (0142–7555). 1978–.
Post-medieval archaeology (0079–4236). 1967–
Transactions of the English Ceramic Circle (0071–0547). 1933–

Bibliographies

Atkin, Susanne (ed), *Bibliography of clay pipe studies. Topographical: British Isles*. [s l]: Soc

for Clay Pipe Research, 1989, 63 p, refs. No ISBN.
List of publications by county and selected other publications (eg on Dutch and French pipes etc).

Bell, Edward L, *Vestiges of mortality and remembrance: a bibliography of the historical archaeology of cemeteries*. Metuchen, NJ: Scarecrow Press, 1994, xix, 419 p, bibl, indexes. 0 8108 2893 6.
Treats cemeteries of 15th to 20th century, including some British.

Britton on delftware see Section 4.9 Museum catalogues (under Bristol).

Charleston, R J and Griffiths, D M, 'The literature of English post-medieval pottery', in *Post-medieval archaeol*, 3, 1969, pp 219–26.
Useful critical review of the literature from 1850 onwards; and in fact *Post-medieval archaeology* has regular bibliographies for all post-medieval topics.

General British

*Beamon, Sylvia and Roaf, Susan, *The ice houses of Britain*. London: Routledge, 1990, xvii, 553 p, bibl, index. 0 415 03301 2.
County gazetteer introduced by a history of ice houses from Mesopotamia and the classical world through to the 20th century.

Brooks, Chris et al, *Mortal remains: the history and present state of the Victorian and Edwardian cemetery*. Exeter: Wheaton for Vic Soc, 1989, vi, 186 p, bibl, index. 0 08 037098 5 hb.
Includes gazetteer of historic cemeteries and strategies for their management and conservation.

*Burgess, Frederick K, *English churchyard memorials*. London: Lutterworth, 1963, 362 p, glossary, indexes. (Repr SPCK 1979, 0 281 03662 4.)
Classic work on the history, design and techniques of manufacture.

Buxbaum, Tim, *Icehouses. Shire albums*, 278, 1992, 32 p. 0 7478 0150 9 pb.
An introduction, more accessible than the Beamon/Roaf volume.

Chandler, John, *John Leland's itinerary: travels in Tudor England*. Stroud: Sutton, 1993, xxxvi, 601 p, bibl, indexes of names and places. 0 86299 957 X.
Records made by the first and only King's

Antiquary, here put into modern English, sorted into county order and illustrated. Much less full, but much easier to use, than the Lucy Toulmin Smith version (*noted in Section 6.12 History and theory of archaeology*).

Chatwin, Amina, *Cheltenham's ornamental ironwork: a guide and history*. Cheltenham: author, 2 edn 1984, 94 p, bibl, index. 0 9503820 0 0 pb. Well-illustrated booklet concentrating on Regency buildings, with uses well outside its own area.

Coleman-Smith and Pearson on Donyatt potteries, see Section 6.11.6 Medieval.

Colvin, H M, *Biographical dictionary of British architects 1600–1840*. London: Yale Univ Press for Paul Mellon Centre for British Art, 3 edn 1995, 1264 p, bibl, indexes. 0 300 06091 2.

Crellin, J K on the Wellcome Collection of medical glass and ceramics, see Section 4.9 Museum catalogues (under 'specific catalogues').

***Crossley, David, *Post-medieval archaeology in Britain*. London: Leicester Univ Press/Pinter, 1990, ix, 328 p, bibl, index. 0 7185 1285 5 hb, 0 7185 1433 5 pb (1994).
Gives the current state of knowledge and a guide to the literature on salient points. Treats the rural and urban situations, churches, fortifications, shipwrecks, power sources, metals, mining and quarrying, glass, ceramics, etc.

Davey, P J, *The archaeology of the clay tobacco pipe: Britain*. Various *BARBS* issues (63, 78, 97, 100, 146, 178, 192, 239) from 1979 onwards, covering the different regions of Britain to provide catalogues of known pieces.

Draper, Jo, *Post-medieval pottery 1650–1800*. *Shire archaeol*, 40, 1984, 64 p, bibl, index. 0 85263 681 4 pb.
Introduction to a complex subject.

Eden, Peter, dictionary of surveyors 1550–1850, see Section 6.1 Reference works (under Maps).

Egan, Geoffrey, *Lead cloth seals and related items in the British Museum. Brit Mus occas pap*, 93, 1994, 199 p. 0 86159 093 7.
Introduces and catalogues the Museum's collection of over 350 cloth seals (quality control marks) and matrices from England and the Continent.

English Heritage, *Register of historic battlefields.*

London: EH, [1995], unnumbered pp in ring binder.
Sites are listed in alphabetical order, with a list in date order in addition.

Evison, V et al (eds), Gerald Dunning Festschrift, see Section 6.11.6 Medieval.

Harrington, Peter, *Archaeology of the English Civil War. Shire archaeol*, 68, 1992, 64 p, bibl, index. 0 7478 0156 8 pb.
Artefacts, structures, battlefields.

Hobhouse, Hermione and Saunders, Anne, *Good and proper materials: the fabric of London since the Great Fire*. London: RCHME/ *London Topogr Soc*, 140, 1989, viii, 70 p, refs. 0 902087 27 4 pb.
Papers on building materials from a conference organised by the Survey of London office, 1988.

Hornsby, P R G et al, *Pewter: a celebration of the craft 1200–1700*. London: Mus London, 1989, 112 p, bibl. 0 904818 36 5 pb.
Catalogue of 150 exhibition items, with introduction to the craft.

Keene, Derek and Harding, Vanessa, *A survey of documentary sources for property holding in London before the Great Fire. London Rec Soc publs*, 22, 1985, xix, 248 p. 0 900952 22 9.

Lemmen, Hans van, *Delftware tiles. Shire albums*, 179, 1986, 32 p. 0 85263 834 5 pb.
Introduction to these ubiquitous blue-and-white decorative tiles.

Lowry, Bernard (ed), *Twentieth century defences in Britain: an introductory guide. Handbook of the Defence of Britain project. CBA prac handb archaeol*, 12, 1995, xii, 144 p, short bibl, addresses. 1 872414 57 5 pb.
Offers advice in recording pill-boxes and other defensive installations.

Molleson, Theya and Cox, Margaret, *The Spitalfields Project, vol 2: the middling sort. CBA res rep*, 86, 1993, 223 p, refs, index. 1 872414 08 7 pb.
A well-documented burial vault group dating 1646–1852 allowed an exceptional opportunity for anthropological and historical analyses of an urban population, of mainly Huguenot descent. Of the 1,000 skeletons, nearly 400 were identifiable via coffin plates. *See also Reeve below.*

Moorhouse, Stephen and Roberts, Ian, *Wrenthorpe potteries. Excavations of six-*

teenth- and seventeenth-century potting tenements near Wakefield, 1983–86. Yorkshire Archaeol, 2, 1992, x, 189 p, bibl, index. 1 870453 03 4 pb.
Reports the 'Potovens' site excavated by W Yorks Archaeol Service, a significant and detailed contribution to post-med pottery studies.

Mullett, Michael, Sources for the history of English non-conformity 1660–1830. London: Brit Rec Ass (= Archives and the user, 8), 1991, 116 p. 0 900222 09 3 pb.
An aid to chapels research.

Newman, Peter, Atlas of the English Civil War. London: Croom Helm, 1985, 126 p, bibl, index. 0 7099 1811 9 pb.
Contains 56 maps tracing the course of the war, its strongholds, battles, etc.

Non-Conformist Working Party (ed C Stell), Hallelujah: recording chapels and meeting houses. London: CBA, 1985, 61 p, bibl. 0 906780 49 7 pb.
Practical handbook on the history and architectural background, relevant legislation, researching, recording, etc.

Parsons, David, 'The church and its architecture before and after the Reformation', in B Vyner (ed), Building on the past (RAI, 1994), pp 264–82.
Historiography from 1845 onwards.

Pearce, Jacqueline. Border wares. London: HMSO for Mus of London (= Post-medieval pottery in London 1500–1700, 1), 1992, xii, 137 p, bibl, index. 0 11 290494 7 pb.
The title is unhelpful: it has nothing to do with the Scottish or Welsh borders, but deals with the Surrey-Hampshire wares supplying London in 16th–17th centuries.

Platt, Colin, The Great Rebuildings of Tudor and Stuart England: revolutions in architectural taste. London: UCL Press, 1994, viii, 230 p, notes, index. 1 85728 315 5 hb, 1 85728 316 3 pb.
Argues (from literary and architectural evidence) that the period after the Civil War was even more important for rebuilding than that identified by Hoskins, and that the effects of Tudor–Jacobean courtiers travelling abroad and developing a need for privacy began the trend towards modern houses.

RCHME on shielings and bastles, see Section 6.11.6 Medieval.

Reeve, Jez and Adams, Max, The Spitalfields Project, Vol 1: Across the Styx. CBA res rep, 85, 1993, 167 p, bibliog, index. 1 872414 07 8 pb.
(See also Molleson above.) Report on the excavation process for the vaults of Christchurch, Spitalfields which recovered the 1,000 burials made between 1729 and 1852. Important for the pioneering methodology which had to deal with dangers like lead poisoning and smallpox as well as retrieving the sequence of the crammed-together coffins.

Saunders, Andrew, Fortress Britain: artillery fortification in the British Isles and Ireland. Liphook: Beaufort Publ, 1989, 256 p, bibl, glossary, index. Reissued Oxbow 1995, 0 94689 779 4.
Comprehensive and very readable survey from 14th century to WWII, with gazetteer of visitable sites.

Smith, Lucy Toulmin, edition of Leland, see Section 6.12 History and theory of archaeology.

Society for Post-Medieval Archaeology, Research priorities for post-medieval archaeology. [s l]: SPMA, 1988, 9 pp.
Policy document to aid future research directions.

Stell, Christopher, Non-conformist chapels and meeting houses in Central England. London: RCHME, 1986, xviii, 276 p, bibl, index. 0 11 701181 9.
This Commission-style Inventory of a previously-neglected important type of building, from Quaker meeting houses to Salvation Army citadels (up to 1914) was followed by others for different parts of the country: South-West England in 1991; North of England in 1994; and Eastern England due 1996.
See also under Non-Conformist Working Party (above).

Weinstein, Rosemary, Tudor London. London: HMSO for Mus of London, 1994, 56 p. 0 11 290495 5 pb.
Draws on recent archaeological evidence and the oldest maps of, and guides to, London.

Wales

Davies, Robert, on estate maps 1600–1836, see Section 2.2 Guides to specific sources (under Wales).

Numerous titles relevant to Wales are in Section 6.15 Archaeology of industrial processes, and 6.18 Vernacular architecture.

Scotland

Adams, Ian H, *The making of urban Scotland.* London: Croom Helm, 1978, 303 p, refs, glossary, index. 0 85664 518 4.

Boyle et al, on graveyards, see Section 6.7 Archaeological heritage management.

Breeze, David, *A queen's progress.* Edinburgh: Historic Scotland, 1987, 80 p, bibl, index. 0 11 493343 x pb.
Buildings associated with Mary Stuart; many colour illustrations.

Burnett, C J and Tabraham, C J, *The honours of Scotland: the story of the Scottish crown jewels.* Edinburgh: Historic Scotland, 1993, 57 p, bibl. 0 7480 0626 5.
Popular presentation.

Caldwell, D H (ed), *Scottish weapons and fortifications 1100–1800.* Edinburgh: John Donald, 1981, xviii, 452 p, bibls, index. 0 85976 047 2.
Papers from two conferences, 1976 and 1978.

Douglas, G J et al, *A survey of Scottish brickmarks.* Glasgow: Scot Industr Archaeol Survey, 1985, 60 p. No ISBN.

Haldane, A R B, *The drove roads of Scotland.* Newton Abbot: David and Charles, new edn 1973, xiii, 266 p, bibl, index. 0 7153 6107 4.

Howard, Deborah, *Scottish architecture: Reformation to Restoration 1560–1660.* Edinburgh: EUP (The Architectural History of Scotland), 1995, xvi, 270 p, bibl, index. 0 7486 0530 4.
Describes how the Scottish style evolved from the integration of continental classicism with the native traditions; a very innovative period.

Knox, Susan A, *The making of the Shetland landscape.* Edinburgh: John Donald, 1985, x, 255 p, bibl, index. 085976 108 8.
Essentially treats the late 18th century onwards.

Stell, Geoffrey and Harman, Mary, *Buildings of St Kilda.* Edinburgh: HMSO for RCAHM, 1988, x, 58 p, map in pocket. 0 11 493391 x pb.
Survey of the settlement that was finally evacuated (because of destitution) in 1930. A poignant story, finely recorded. A World Heritage Site.

Tabraham, Chris and Grove, Doreen, *Fortress Scotland and the Jacobites.* London: Batsford/ Historic Scotland, 1995, 128 p, glossary, bibl, index. 0 7134 7483 1 hb, 0 7134 7484 x pb.
The historical events 1650–1750 (ie Cromwell to Culloden), the buildings and the fighting men. List of places to visit.

Taylor, W, *The military roads in Scotland.* Newton Abbot: David and Charles, 1976, 197 p, bibl, index. 0 7153 7067 7.

Whyte, Ian and Kathleen, *The changing Scottish landscape 1500-1800.* London: Routledge, 1991, x, 251 p, bibl, index. 0 415 02992 9.

Willsher, Betty, 'Scottish churchyard memorials in the eighteenth century', *Local historian,* 23.2, May 1993, pp 66–84, bibl.
Well illustrated and attractive article on a still-neglected subject.

—, (ed E Proudfoot), *How to record Scottish graveyards: a companion to 'Understanding Scottish graveyards'.* Edinburgh: CBA Scotland, 1985, 46 p, refs. 0 901352 09 8 pb.

—, *Understanding Scottish graveyards: an interpretative approach.* Edinburgh: reprinted Canongate Books, 1995, viii, 72 p, bibl, glossary, index. 0 86241 560 8 pb (Originally published 1985.)

Ireland

Bell and Watson on Irish farming tools, see Section 6.14 Landscape . . . agriculture.

Beranger's views of Ireland: a collection of drawings of the principal antique buildings of Ireland designed on the spot and collected by Gabriel Beranger. Dublin: Roy Ir Acad, 1991, 111 p. 0 901714 93 3 hb, 0 901714 94 1 pb.
Peter Harbison's text accompanying the 47 watercolour sketches reproduced here explains that Beranger gives 'a good cross-section of our monumental heritage as it was in the 18th century, often preserving for posterity illustrations of certain buildings which have entirely disappeared and of which no other record exists'; this is a 'treasury for architects, art historians and archaeologists'. (Another volume in preparation.)

Bradley, J on walled towns, see Section 6.11.5 Migration and early medieval, under Ireland.-

Curl, James Stevens, *The Londonderry Plantation 1609–1914. The history, architecture and
planning of the estates of the City of London
and its livery companies in Ulster*. Chichester:
Phillimore, 1986, 503 p, bibl, index. 0 85033
577 9.

Enoch, V J, *The Martello towers of Ireland*.
Dublin: the author, 1975, 33 p. 0 9504382 0
0 pb.

*Flanagan, L, on Armada wrecks, see Section 6.19
Maritime, nautical and underwater archaeology.*

Foster, R F, *Modern Ireland 1600–1972*. London:
Allen Lane, 1988 and Penguin, 1989, 688 p,
bibliographic essay, indexes. 0 14 013250 3 pb.
Mainly useful to archaeologists for the Plantation period.

Grose, Daniel, *The antiquities of Ireland, a
supplement to Francis Grose* (ed Roger Stalley).
Dublin: Irish Architectural Archive, 1991, xxiv,
214 p. 0 9515536 4 x.
This contains watercolours and other depictions by Francis Grose's nephew, now published
for the first time. Stalley's commentary indicates that the pictures are not always accurate,
but they do show many monuments now
altered, ruined or vanished (see also Beranger
above).

Grose, Francis (ed by Edward Ledwich), *The
antiquities of Ireland*. 2 vols. London, 1791,
1795 (also a 1982 reprint from Wellbrook Press
(Kilkenny) with introduction by Liam de Paor)
Engravings are plentiful and good.

*Howley, James, on follies etc, see Section 6.16
Garden archaeology and history.*

Kerrigan, Paul, *Castles and fortifications in Ireland 1485–1945*. Cork: Collins Press, 1995, ix,
302 p, bibl, index. 1 898256 12 8.
This will be the standard work now.

McCracken, Eileen, *The Irish woods since Tudor
times: distribution and exploitation*. Newton
Abbot: David and Charles (for IIS Belfast),
1971, 184 p, refs, index. 0 7153 5008 0.

*Malins, Edward and The Knight of Glin on
landscape gardening, see Section 6.16 Garden
archaeology and history.*

*Mallory and McNeill on Plantation Ulster, see
Section 6.4 Regional surveys (under Ireland).*

Reynolds, Mairead, 'Irish fine-ceramic potteries,
1769–96', in *Post-medieval archaeol*, 18, 1984,
pp 251–61.

Robinson, Philip S, *The plantation of Ulster:
British settlement in an Irish landscape
1600–1670*. Belfast: Ulster Historical Foundation, 1994, xxx, 254 p, notes, glossary, index. 0
901905 62 3 (a reprint, with introduction by
Nicholas Canny, of the 1984 edn by Gill and
Macmillan.)
Mostly history, but some physical evidence (eg
houses, settlement patterns).

*Saunders, A on fortresses, see under England
above.*

6.12
History and Theory of Archaeology

History of archaeology

The principal relevant journal is *Antiquity*, containing not only occasional articles on the history of archaeology but also editorials providing a lively and sometimes provocative running commentary on contemporary movements in archaeology. For museology the *Journal of the history of collections* will be found useful. The books listed here include some biographies and autobiographies of noted archaeologists as well as more general histories of the discipline.

Bell, A S (ed), *The Scottish antiquarian tradition: essays to mark the bicentenary of the Society of Antiquaries of Scotland, 1780–1980*. Edinburgh: John Donald, 1981, 286 p, bibl, index. 0 85976 080 4.
Includes eight papers treating the ideas, organisation and principal personalities of SAS.

*Bowden, Mark, *Pitt Rivers: the life and archaeological work of Lt-General Augustus Henry Lane Fox Pitt Rivers, DCL, FRS, FSA*. Cambridge: CUP, 1991, xv, 182 p, bibl, index. 0 521 40077 5.
Biography of a much quoted but often misrepresented archaeologist, first Inspector of Ancient Monuments, commonly seen as the father of our modern discipline. (*See also M W Thompson below.*)

Carman, John, *Valuing ancient things: archaeology and law*. London: Leicester Univ Press, 1996, x, 246 p, bibl, index. 0 7185 0012 1.
Traces the effects of English heritage laws on the development of archaeology.

Champion, T, see under Díaz-Andrew below.

Chandler, John, *John Leland's Itinerary: travels in Tudor England*. Stroud: Alan Sutton, 1993, xxxvi, 601 p, indexes. 0 86299 957 X.
New one-volume version of the travels of the first (and only) King's Antiquary. *See also fuller version under Smith below.*

Cooney, G, see under Díaz-Andrew below.

Crawford, O G S, *Said and done: the autobio-graphy of an archaeologist*. London: Weidenfeld and Nicolson, 1955, ix, 316 pp.
Life and philosophy of the founder of *Antiquity* and head of the former Ordnance Survey Archaeological Division.

Cunnington, R H (ed James Dyer), *From antiquary to archaeologist: a biography of William Cunnington, 1754–1810*. Princes Risborough: Shire, 1975, xviii, 178 p, refs. 0 85263 265 7.
Cunnington was employed by Sir Richard Colt Hoare to excavate barrows on his Wiltshire estates. This book traces the development of Cunnington's increasingly scientific approach over the period 1800–10, and shows how the germ of many modern ideas can be traced to him.

Daniel, Glyn, *A hundred and fifty years of archaeology*. London: Duckworth, 2 edn 1975, 410 p, refs, index. (No ISBN.)
Worldwide view, dense factual text.

*— and Renfrew, C, *The idea of prehistory*. Edinburgh: Edin UP, 2 edn 1988, 221 p, bibl, index. 0 85224 532 7.
On the history of archaeological theory from the early antiquarians to the present day.

**— and Chippindale, Christopher (eds), *The pastmasters: eleven modern pioneers of archaeology*. London: Thames and Hudson, 1989, 176 p, bibl. 0 500 05051 1.
Short pieces on Gordon Childe, Stuart Piggott, Charles Phillips, Christopher Hawkes, plus seven others whose work was outside Britain.

Díaz-Andrew, Margarita and Champion, Timothy, *Nationalism and archaeology in Europe*. London: UCL Press, 1996, vi, 314 p, bibls, index. 1 85728 289 2.
Two of the contributions consider the interactions of national identity and archaeology in, respectively, Britain (Tim Champion, pp 119–45) and Ireland (G Cooney, pp 146–63).

Evans, Joan, *A history of the Society of Antiquaries*. Oxford: OUP for Soc Antiq London, 1956, xv, 487 p, bibl, index.
The standard history of our premier society.

Evans, J D et al (eds), *Antiquity of man: essays in honour of Glyn Daniel*. London: Thames and Hudson, 1981, 256 p, bibls, index. 0 500 05040 6.
Papers are gathered into separate sections: History of archaeology; Rude stone monuments

in Europe; Archaeology and the public; the Editor of *Antiquity*.

'Gildas' (pseud.), 'De excidio', in *Brit archaeol news*, 4.1, Jan 1989, pp 2–3.
The best analysis of the effect on archaeological work of cuts in Government funding at the time. Reprinted from a pseudonymously-written piece in a French bulletin.

Green, Sally, *Prehistorian: a biography of V Gordon Childe*. Bradford-on-Avon: Moonraker, 1981, xxii, 200 p, bibl, index. 0 239 00206 7.
One of several books to celebrate one of the most influential thinkers of 20th century archaeology.

Hawkes, Jacquetta, *Mortimer Wheeler: adventurer in archaeology*. London: Weidenfeld and Nicolson, 1982, xii, 387 p, index. 0 297 78056 5.
A racy account of a colourful personality, but it fails to convey why he was so important in 20th century archaeology.

Hoare, Richard Colt, *The ancient history of North Wiltshire*. London, 1819, 128 p; and *The ancient history of South Wiltshire*. London, 1812, 259 p.
Classic early works by a pioneering field archaeologist. (*See also Cunnington above*.)

Hudson, Kenneth, *A social history of archaeology: the British experience*. London: Macmillan, 1981, viii, 197 p, bibl, index. 0 333 25679 4.
Discusses public perceptions of archaeology from Victorian times onwards; a partly polemical attempt to relate archaeological practice to social conditions of the time.

*Levine, Philippa, *The amateur and the professional: antiquarians, historians and archaeologists in Victorian England 1838–1886*. Cambridge: CUP, 1986, x, 210 p, bibl, index. 0 521 30635 3.
Analyses the social milieux of the early practitioners, tracing the rise of the professional and the sidelining of the gentleman amateur, examining also the theological and technical barriers to the development of archaeology.

Marsden, Barry, *The early barrow diggers*. Aylesbury: Shire, 1974, ix, 126 p, bibl, index. 0 85263 242 8.
On the 18th- and 19th- century barrow-openers.

**Piggott, Stuart, *William Stukeley: an eighteenth-century antiquary*. London: Thames and Hudson, 2 edn 1985, 191 p, refs, index. 0 500 01360 8.
Study of one of the (colourful) founding fathers of archaeology.

—, *Antiquity depicted: aspects of archaeological illustration (Walter Neurath memorial lecture 10)*. London: Thames and Hudson, 1978, 64 p, bibl.
A remarkable short history of archaeological draughtsmanship, treating developments from late medieval times.

—, 'The origins of the English county archaeological societies', in *Trans Birmingham Warwickshire Archaeol Soc*, 86, 1974, pp 1–15.
Explores the social and cultural conditions that led to the surge in the establishment of the county societies in the middle third of the nineteenth century.

—, *Ruins in a landscape: essays in antiquarianism*. Edinburgh: EUP, 1976, viii, 212 p, bibl, index. 0 85224 303 0 hb, 0 85224 311 1 pb.
Nine essays on the history of antiquarian thought, 16th to 19th centuries; includes the ancestry of Sir Walter Scott's romantic antiquarianism, and a study of antiquarian thought about Celts and Saxons.

—, *Ancient Britons and the antiquarian imagination: ideas from the Renaissance to the Regency*. London: Thames and Hudson, 1989, 175 p, bibl, index. 0 500 01470 1.
How British scholars of that period sought to visualise their pre-Roman ancestors.

— and Robertson, Marjorie, *Three centuries of Scottish archaeology: George Buchanan to Lord Abercromby*. Edinburgh: EUP, 1977, 68 p, bibl. 0 85224 327 8.
Catalogue of books and manuscripts exhibited to celebrate 50 years of the Abercromby Chair of Archaeology in Edinburgh, 1927–77.

Royal Commission on the Historical Monuments of England, *50 years of the National Buildings Record 1941–1991*. Beckenham: Trigon Press/RCHME, 1991, 68 p, index. 0 904929 27 2 hb, 0 904929 28 0 pb.
Sir John Summerson introduces this celebratory volume.

Smith, Lucy Toulmin, *The itinerary of John Leland in or about the years 1535–1543*. London: Bell, 1907–10, 11 parts in 5 vols, indexes.

The first edition of Leland to have maps indicating the course of his journeys; but the use of Latin and Tudor English render it difficult for modern readers, and Chandler's edition (above) may be preferred, initially at least.

Thompson, M W, *General Pitt-Rivers: evolution and archaeology in the nineteenth century.* Bradford-on-Avon: Moonraker, 1977, 164 p, refs, index. [o] 239 00162 1.
Presents the facts of his life and attempts to understand why he did what he did. (*See also Bowden above.*)

**Trigger, Bruce, *A history of archaeological thought.* Cambridge: CUP, 1990, xv, 500 p, bibl, index. o 521 32878 o hb, o 521 33818 2 pb.
Worldwide perspective, from medieval antiquarians to modern archaeologists.

**—, *Gordon Childe: revolutions in archaeology.* London: Thames and Hudson, 1980, 207 p, bibl, index. o 500 05034 1.
Extended study of Childe's developing thought.

***Vyner, Blaise (ed), *Building on the past: papers celebrating 150 years of the Royal Archaeological Institute.* London: RAI, 1994, 319 p, bibls, index.
Important series of papers on the RAI's own history and on the progress of studies in each main archaeological period from Palaeolithic to the early industrial age. (Individual papers have been noted at the head of each relevant section of this book.)

Wheeler, Mortimer, *Still digging: interleaves from an antiquary's notebook.* London: Michael Joseph, 1955, 236 p, index.
Memoirs of this century's most charismatic archaeologist.

*—, *Alms for oblivion: an antiquary's scrapbook.* London: Weidenfeld and Nicolson, 1966, 175 p.
Avowedly contains 'sundry scraps' of reminiscence, but also useful chapters on what matters in archaeology and on the transmission of ideas in the past. *See also his Archaeology from the earth in Section 6.2.*

Archaeological theory

This section lists some of the more approachable works on archaeological theory, from which

readers may explore further. Particularly recommended are the titles by (respectively) Bradley, Champion, and Renfrew & Bahn. Note that interesting ideas are often to be found in the inaugural lectures given by professors of archaeology on taking up their chairs (a list was prepared for this volume but discarded for lack of space).

A new periodical on this theme, *Journal of theoretical archaeology* (0965–1861), began publication in 1991 (Cruithne Press, Skelmorlie, Strathclyde), and another, *Journal of archaeological research* (1059–0161), began in 1993 (Plenum Press). In 1996 another new periodical was promised: *Journal of material culture* (edited by Dr Christopher Tilley of Univ College London).

Allen, Kathleen M S et al (eds), *Interpreting space: GIS and archaeology.* London: Taylor and Francis, 1990, xiv, 398 p, bibls, index. o 85066 824 7.
Papers examining the use of Geographical Information Systems in archaeology.

Anon (aka Donn Bayard), *New light on biodegradable byways to the day before yesterday: invitations to the study of sociocultural exoskeletons (with a preface by L D L Binclarke).* Phu Wiang/Dunedin/Honolulu: Pooh Wiang Univ Press Publs in Scientific Prehistory, 2, 1974.
Spoof on The New Archaeology; very rare faded copies may sometimes be found in the remoter corners of university lecturers' studies.

Barber, J W (ed), *Interpreting stratigraphy: conference proceedings 25 November 1992, Edinburgh.* Leith: AOCC (Scotland), 1993, iv, 75 p. o 9519344 2 2 pb.
On the evolution of procedures for post-excavation processing on very large sites; evaluation on deep stratified sites; micromorphology; attribute analysis; land use diagrams, etc. Includes guidance on Historic Scotland's requirements for immediate post-excavation structure (*on which see also Ashmore in Section 6.9 The excavator's training . . . under Preparation of archaeological reports*).

***Bradley, Richard, *Altering the earth: the origins of monuments in Britain and Continental Europe. The Rhind lectures 1991–2.* Scot Antiq Scotl monogr, 8, 1993, xv, 150 p, bibl, index. o 903903 08 3 pb.
Important study of the origins and workings of monuments; and of their post-construction history.

**Carver, Martin, *Arguments in stone: archaeological research and the European town in the first millennium* (Dalrymple lectures for 1990, Glasgow Archaeol Soc and Univ Glasgow). *Oxbow monogr*, 29, 1993, ix, 123 p. 0 946897 57 3.
On the philosophy and practice of archaeology: what is it, are we doing it for good reasons and in the right way? How to dig up and document our past. Argues for research rather than rescue archaeology to be the driving force.

**Champion, Tim, 'Theoretical archaeology in Britain', in I Hodder (ed), *Archaeological theory in Europe*, p 129–60 with 6-page bibl (see below under Hodder).

**Clark, Grahame, *Economic prehistory: papers on archaeology*. Cambridge: CUP, 1989, xviii, 638 p, bibl, index. 0 521 34481 6.
Collected papers from a highly influential economic prehistorian, on topics as varied as bees, whaling, Star Carr, and the 'invasion hypothesis'.

Clarke, David L (revised B Chapman), *Analytical archaeology*. London: Routledge, rev edn 1978, xxi, 526 p, bibl, index. 0 416 85460 5.
Though highly influential for about a decade, has rather passed from favour.

— (ed), *Models in archaeology*. London: Methuen, 1972, xxiv, 1055 p, bibl, index. 0 416 16540 0.
Another influential volume, still a useful aid to the construction of theory.

*Collingwood, R G (with introduction by Jan van der Dussen), *The idea of history*. Oxford: OUP, rev edn 1994, liii, 510 p, bibl, index. 0 19 285306 6 pb.
Collingwood was notable for his insistence on asking specific questions in archaeological research; this edition of his important work includes lectures given in 1926–8. Collingwood's *Autobiography* is also well worth reading.

Cooney, Gabriel, 'Theory and practice in Irish archaeology', in P Ucko (ed), *Theory in archaeology: a world perspective* (1994), pp 263–77.

Cooper, Malcolm, see under Gamble below.

Dark, K R, *Theoretical archaeology*. London: Duckworth, 1995, x, 246 p, glossary, bibl, index. 0 7156 2634 5 hb, 0 7156 2670 1 pb.

An introduction to some main themes for undergraduates and non-specialists.

Gamble, Clive (general ed), *Theoretical Archaeology Group series*. London: Routledge, 1995–.
The first titles in the series are: *Managing archaeology* (eds Malcolm Cooper et al); *Cultural identity and archaeology* (eds P Graves-Brown et al: see next entry); *Theory in archaeology: a world perspective* (ed P J Ucko: see full entry below).

Graves-Brown, Paul, Jones, Sian and Gamble, Clive (eds), *Cultural identity and archaeology: the construction of European communities*. London: Routledge, 1996, xx, 284 p, bibls, index. 0 415 10676 1.
A volume in the Theoretical Archaeology Group series contains papers by A P Fitzpatrick on 'Celtic' Iron Age Europe; John Hines on Britain after Rome; and John Collis on Celts and politics.

Hodder, Ian (ed), *Archaeological theory in Europe: the last three decades*. London: Routledge, 1991, xi, 318 p, bibl, index. 0 415 06521 6.
Includes a chapter on Britain (see Champion above).

—, *Theory and practice in archaeology*. London: Routledge, 1992, xii, 285 p, bibl, index. 0 415 06520 8 hb, 0 415 12777 7 pb.
A collection of previously published papers to demonstrate the consistency and developmental coherence of author's work.

— and Orton, Clive, *Spatial analysis in archaeology*. Cambridge: CUP, 1979, ix, 270 p, bibl, index. 0 521 29738 9 pb.
Mathematical treatment of archaeological settlement data.

*Orme, Bryony, *Anthropology for archaeologists: an introduction*. London: Duckworth, 1981, x, 300 p, bibl, index. 0 7156 1442 7 hb, 0 7156 1481 9 pb.
How to use anthropological material to illuminate archaeological evidence for food and raw materials, settlement, social organisation, and so on.

***Renfrew, Colin and Bahn, Paul, *Archaeology: theories, methods, and practice*. London: Thames and Hudson, 2 edn 1996, 608 p, bibl, index. 0 500 05079 1 hb, 0 500 27867 9 pb.
This much-acclaimed work aims to provide a complete introduction to the history of archaeology, the nature of evidence, social archaeol-

ogy, techniques, publication, notable excavations; world-wide treatment and includes 30-page bibliography.

Thomas, Charles (ed), *Research objectives in British archaeology*. London: CBA, 1983, xiv, 56 p. 0 906780 32 2 pb.
Booklet compiled by the CBA specialist research committees on, respectively, aerial archaeology, churches, countryside, historic buildings, industrial archaeology, urban archaeology, and archaeological science.

Ucko, P J (ed),*Theory in archaeology: a world perspective*. London: Routledge, 1994, xx, 393 p, bibl, index. 0 415 10677 X.
Papers from the European Theoretical Archaeology Group, Southampton 1992. (*See Cooney, above, and Woodman, below for two relevant papers.*)

Woodman, Peter C, 'Irish archaeology today: a poverty amongst riches', in *The Irish review*, 12, spring-summer 1992, pp 34–9 (Belfast: Inst Ir Stud).
Review-article prompted by several popular works; there has been an extraordinary explosion of development (digging of gas pipelines etc) and consequent additions to archaeological data, but publication of the results lags a very long way behind and the significance of this new material is rarely discussed. Hence the government-funded Discovery Programme offers a welcome opportunity to look at key problems.

—, 'Filling in the spaces in Irish prehistory', in *Antiquity*, 66, 1992, pp 295–314; offers a 'radical re-evaluation of the traditional [1940s] paradigms of Irish prehistory'. (See also G Cooney's response in *Antiquity*, 67, 1993, pp 632–41, with a rejoinder by P Woodman.)

—, 'Who possesses Tara?', in P Ucko (ed), *Theory in archaeology* (1994), pp 278–97.

6.13
Topic Surveys: Multi-period or General

This section is for books which treat general topics or cover several archaeological periods. It is subdivided into:
Settlements
Society
Artefacts

Settlements

See Section 6.11.4 Romano-British for the following three town series:
THE ARCHAEOLOGY OF CANTERBURY
THE ARCHAEOLOGY OF ROMAN LONDON
THE ARCHAEOLOGY OF YORK

**Aston, Michael and Bond, James, *The landscape of towns*. London: Dent, 1976, 255 p, bibl, index. 0 460 04194 0. (Archaeology in the field series.)
Principles of archaeological fieldwork applied to towns.

[Cave archaeology]: nine papers in *Cave Science*, 16.3, 1989, pp 79–111, some on specific sites like Creswell, Thorpe Common, Ulva (Mull).

Crawford, Harriet, *Subterranean Britain: aspects of underground archaeology*. London: John Baker, 1980, 201 p. 0 212 97024 0.
Includes papers on Grimes Graves, Roman structures, Irish souterrains, early industrial structures, and medieval and later 'curiosities'.

Fenton, A and Stell, G (eds), *Loads and roads in Scotland and beyond: land transport over 6000 years*. Edinburgh: John Donald, 1984, vii, 144 p. 0 85976 107 X pb.
Contributions treat trackways and roads, bridges, wheelless transport, carts and wagons.

Hindle, Brian P, *Roads, tracks and their interpretation*. London: Batsford, 1993, 157 p, bibl, index. 0 7134 6598 0 pb.
A volume in the 'Know the Landscape' series; strong northern emphasis.

*Ottaway, Patrick, *Archaeology in British towns: from the Emperor Claudius to the Black Death*. London: Routledge, 1992, xvi, 249 p, bibl, index. 0 415 00068 8.
Covers the last 25 years of archaeology in

towns; urban archaeologists at work; then by period (Roman, Anglo-Saxon, medieval); and presenting the past to the public.

Reid, M L, *Prehistoric houses in Britain. Shire Archaeol*, 70, 1993, 72 p, bibl, index. 0 7478 0218 1 pb.

*Roberts, B K, *Landscapes of settlement: prehistory to the present*. London: Routledge, 1996, x, 181 p, bibl, index. 0 415 11967 7 hb, 0 415 11968 5 pb.
Settlements offer clues by which the history of a country may be read; many examples, worldwide as well as British.

Rodwell, Warwick and Rodwell, Kirsty A, *Rivenhall: investigations of a Roman villa, church and village, 1950–77. CBA res rep*, 55, 1985 and *CBA res rep*, 80, 1993.
An example of 'total archaeology', ie examination of all periods, from Mesolithic to medieval, represented in a single parish.

**Taylor, Christopher, *Roads and tracks of Britain*. London: Dent, 1979, xiv, 210 p, index. 0 460 04329 3.
Pitfalls of the evidence are explained and routeways of all periods are examined for their effect on settlement.

*—, *Village and farmstead: a history of rural settlement in England*. London: George Philip, 1983, 254 p, bibl, index. 0 540 01071 5.
Important study for every local worker.

Society

Bassett, Stephen (ed), *Death in towns: urban responses to the dying and the dead, 100–1600*. Leicester: Leics Univ Press, 1992, vi, 258 p, bibl, index. 0 7185 1418 1 hb, 0 7185 1280 x pb.
Contains 14 papers from a 1991 conference on various aspects of disposal and commemoration of the dead, from the Roman Empire to the Renaissance.

**Bradley, Richard, *The social foundations of prehistoric Britain: themes and variations in the archaeology of power*. London: Longman, 1984, x, 195 pp, bibl, index. 0 582 49164 9 pb.
Important synthetic and philosophical work covering broadly the Neolithic to the Roman conquest.

Brenneman, Walter L (Jr) and Brenneman, Mary G, *Crossing the circle at the holy wells of Ireland*. Charlottesville: Univ Press of Virginia, 1995, xii, 141 p, bibl, index. 0 8139 1548 1.
Studies 500 well sites in the context of religious practices, wells as sacred springs, merging of pagan and Christian belief, local and wider significance.

Chapman, Robert et al (eds), *The archaeology of death*. Cambridge: CUP, 1981, vii, 159 p, bibl, index. 0 521 23775 0 (New directions in archaeology series).
Papers relating to Britain treat megalithic tombs, Wessex Culture and Deverel-Rimbury burials. (Remaining papers are on USA and Denmark.)

Ehrenberg, Margaret, *Women in prehistory*. London: Brit Mus Publ, 1989, 208 p, bibl, index. 0 7141 1388 3 pb.
Examines the relationship between the economic role and social status of women, as gleaned from mainly archaeological and ethnographic evidence.

Garwood, Paul et al (eds), *Sacred and profane: proceedings of a conference on archaeology, ritual and religion, Oxford 1989. OUCA monogr*, 32, 1991, xvii, 171 p, bibl. 0 947816 32 1 pb.
Attempts to fill a gap in theoretical archaeology – the social significance of ritual and the criteria adopted for its material identification.

Hutton, Ronald, *The pagan religions of the ancient British Isles: their nature and legacy*. Oxford: Blackwell, 1991, 397 p, bibl, index. 0 631 17288 2.
Rather poorly illustrated, and one reviewer disagreed with 'every page', but it is included here for its stimulating quality.

Merrifield, Ralph, *The archaeology of ritual and magic*. London: Batsford, 1987, xiv, 224 p, bibl, index. 0 7134 4870 9.
A systematic examination of a topic some archaeologists prefer to dodge, with a plea for closer recording of observed phenomena to assist interpretation. From prehistory to modern survivals.

*Piggott, Stuart, *Ancient Europe from the beginnings of agriculture to classical antiquity: a survey*. Edinburgh: EUP, 1965, xxiii, 343 p, bibl, index.
Based on the Rhind Lectures for 1962, this beautifully written classic is a 'personal.estimate of certain factors which . . . contributed to the

eventual character of the ancient world which lay behind early historical Europe'. It conveys a wonderful sense of steadily unrolling history and every archaeologist should read it.

Renfrew, Colin, *Archaeology and language: the puzzle of Indo-European origins*. London: Cape, 1987, xiv, 346 p, bibl, index. 0 224 02495 7.
Argues that the first Indo-European speakers came to Europe from Anatolia c. 6000 BC, along with domesticated plants and animals, resulting in parallel development of Celtic-speaking peoples in the areas where they are found today.

— and Zubrow, Ezra B W (eds), *The ancient mind: elements of cognitive archaeology*. Cambridge: CUP, 1994, xiv, 195 p, bibls, index. 0 521 43488 2 hb, 0 521 45620 7 pb.
Contributions explore the possibility of developing a science of cognitive archaeology, looking at religion, funerary beliefs, petroglyphs and the like.

Rodwell, Warwick, *English Heritage book of church archaeology*. London: Batsford/English Heritage, 2 edn 1989, 208 p, bibl, index. 0 7134 6294 9 pb.

Scarre, Chris and Healy, Frances (eds), *Trade and exchange in prehistoric Europe*. Oxbow monogr, 33, 1993, 255 p, bibls. 0 946899 62 x pb.
Twenty-four papers from a Bristol conference (1992) on topics ranging from hunter-gatherer foraging through Bronze Age cross-Channel trade to the late pre-Roman Iron Age.

Sharp, Mick, *A land of gods and giants*. Gloucester: Alan Sutton, 1989, 191 p. 0 86299 664 3.
A beautiful book of colour photographs reminding us that archaeological sites can be 'dramatic and magical' places as well as sources of academic information.

Artefacts

(by material or type)

Section 4.9 Museum catalogues should also be consulted. See also Hodges on artefacts generally, in Section 6.15 Archaeology of industrial processes.

Amber

Beck, Curt and Shennan, Stephen, *Amber in prehistoric Britain*. Oxbow monogr, 8, 1991, 232 p, bibl. 0 946897 31 1 pb.
Corpus of drawings and catalogue which showed that amber was used locally to begin with, only later acquiring status value and becoming a long-distance trade item.

Clothing see *Footwear and Textiles respectively below*.

Coins see *Numismatics below*.

Culture general

Ford, Boris (ed), *Cambridge cultural history of Britain, vol. 1: Early Britain*. Cambridge: CUP, 1992, xi, 289 p, bibl, index. 0 521 300971 9 hb, 0 521 42881 5 pb.
Specialist essays on topics such as architecture, visual arts and crafts, literature. (A much fuller bibliography was supplied in the original 1988 edition entitled *Cambridge guide to the arts in Britain, vol. 1: Prehistoric, Roman and early medieval*.)

Food

Brears, P D C et al, *A taste of history*. London: English Heritage/Brit Mus Press, 1993, 352 p. 0 7141 1732 3.
A gastronomic history from prehistory through to 20th century. Recipes adapted for modern use are included. All but the last section are reprints of an earlier English Heritage series.

Footwear and leather

Friendship-Taylor, D E et al (eds), *Recent research in archaeological footwear*. AAIS techn pap, 8, 1987, 49 p.

Waterer, J W, *Leather and the warrior: an account of the importance of leather to the fighting man*. Northampton: Museum of Leathercraft, 1981, xx, 180 p.
From the ancient Greeks to WWII.

Glass

Harden, D B, *Ancient glass*. (Bound offprints of three seminal articles on pre-Roman, Roman, and post-Roman glass respectively, from *Archaeol j*, 125, 126 and 128; available from RAI.)

Hoards

*Bradley, Richard, *The passage of arms: an archaeological analysis of prehistoric hoards and votive deposits*. Cambridge: CUP, 1990, xvi, 234 pp, bibl, index. 0 521 38446 x.
A fresh examination of a recurrent phenomenon traces changing patterns of deposition.

Numismatics

(*general works only; books relating to a specific period, eg medieval, will be found under that period.*)

Numismatic Literature (0029–6031). 1947–.
World-wide abstracting service with author and brief subject indexes.

Price, Martin et al (eds), *A survey of numismatic research 1978–1984*. London: Internat Ass Professional Numismatists special publ, 9, 1986, 2 vols, no ISBN.
Various specialists provide bibliographic surveys.

Sylloge of Coins of the British Isles (general editor M A S Blackburn). 1, 1958–, irregular. London: (variously) British Academy or British Museum Press or OUP. 40+ volumes issued so far, with cumulative indexes to vols 1–20 (1981) and 21–40 (1992).
An important series which concentrates (though not exclusively) on the Anglo-Saxon period, listing British and overseas collections: a fundamental basic source for the study of coin issues and moneyers, hoards, personal and place-name forms.

Pottery

Gibson, Alex M and Woods, Ann, *Prehistoric pottery for the archaeologist, 4000 BC–AD 400*. London: Leicester Univ Press (Pinter), 1990, xxi, 293 p, bibl, glossary, index. 0 7185 1274 X hb, 0 7185 1304 5 'student edn', 0 7185 1954 X pb. (New edn due late 1996/7.)
Text for undergraduates.

Rice, Prudence M, *Pottery analysis: a sourcebook*. Chicago: Univ Chicago Press, 1987, xxiv, 559 p, bibl, glossary, index. 0 226 71118 8.
Considers the nature and properties of raw materials of potting, history of potting through to modern times, its use, trade and discard, characterisation studies.

Textiles and clothing

Bender Jørgensen, Lise, *North European textiles until AD1000*. Aarhus: Aarhus Univ Press, 1992, 285 p, bibl. 87 7288 416 9.
Large catalogue representing 2,500 years of textile history, with important bibliography. Britain and Ireland represented on pp 18–40.

Tarrant, Naomi, *The development of costume*. London/New York: Routledge/Nat Mus Scotland, 1994, xv, 176 p, bibl, index. 0 415 08018 5.

Covers a wide variety of aspects: development of costume, technical aspects of production (eg invention of needles, fastenings etc), how costume is to be understood, its display in museums, etc.

Walton, Penelope and Wild, J P (eds), *Textiles in northern archaeology*. London: IAP/Archetype, 1990, 231 p, bibl. 1 873132 05 0.
Several UK-origin papers appear in this volume from NESAT, the North European Symposium for Archaeological Textiles.

Wild, J P, *Textiles in archaeology. Shire archaeol*, 56, 1988, 68 p, bibl, index. 0 85263 931 7 pb.
Short introduction.

Wheeled transport

Piggott, Stuart, *Wagon, chariot and carriage: symbol and status in the history of transport*. London: Thames and Hudson, 1992, 184 p, bibl, index. 0 500 25114 2.
Focuses on wheeled vehicles as prestige items suitable for presentation to potentates or for them to be buried in.

Wooden artefacts

Earwood, Caroline, *Domestic wooden artefacts in Britain and Ireland from Neolithic to Viking times*. Exeter: Univ Exeter Press, 1993, 320 p, bibl, index. 0 85989 389 8.
Developments in manufacture, changing styles and decoration; includes many previously neglected objects and draws comparisons from across Europe as well as comparing wooden vessels with those made of other materials.

6.14
Landscape: Geology and Soils; Vegetation, Agriculture and Landscape Change

This section deals with landscape and the effects on it of human occupation through the millennia. The first part sets the scene with references on geology and soils; the second part deals with agricultural and other land use changes. The materials are presented in the following order:

Geology and soils:
Organisations
Periodicals
Bibliography and reference
Books: Britain generally; Wales; Scotland; Ireland
Vegetation, agriculture and landscape change:
Organisations
Periodicals
Bibliographies
Books: Britain generally; Wales; Scotland; Ireland

Some Quaternary references are listed here; others will be found in Section 6.11.1 Quaternary . . . where that seemed more appropriate. See also Section 6.16 Garden archaeology and history.

Geology and soils

ORGANISATIONS
(where no details are given below, see the appropriate entry in 4.2 Organisations)

British Geological Survey
Geologists' Association (noted under Geological Society in 4.2 Organisations)
INQUA, the International Quaternary Association
Irish Association for Quaternary Studies (IQUA)
Macaulay Land Use Research Institute
Quaternary Research Association (QRA)
Soil Survey and Land Research Centre

PERIODICALS
(a selection of the principal titles)

Geoarchaeology (0883–6353). 1986–. 6/yr. New York: Wiley
Geographical journal (0016–7398). 1898–. London: Royal Geogr Soc

The Holocene (0959–6836). 1991–. 3/yr. London: Edward Arnold
Institute of British Geographers/transactions (0020–2754). 1976– (n ser). London: Inst Brit Geogr
Proceedings of the Geologists' Association (0016–7878). 1859–. London: Geol Ass
Quaternary newsletter (0143–2826). 1970–. Exeter: Quat Res Ass
Quaternary research (0038–5894). 1970–. 6/yr. Seattle: Quat Res Center
Quaternary science reviews (0277–3791). 1982–. 10/yr. Pergamon (Elsevier)
Scottish geographical magazine (0036–9225). 1885–. 2/yr. Edinburgh: Scot Geogr Soc

BIBLIOGRAPHY AND REFERENCE WORKS
Abstracting services: see Section 1.5 Indexing and abstracting services.

Bibliography:
Miedema, Rienk and Mermut, Ahmet R (eds), *Soil micromorphology: an annotated bibliography 1968–1986*. Wallingford: CAB Internat/Internat Soc Soil Sci, 1990, 250 p, index. 0 85198 681 1 pb. Full abstracts for each reference, but very little specific to Britain or Ireland.

Directories:
The geologist's directory: a guide to the earth sciences in Britain. Annual. London/Bath: Geological Society. Comprehensive guide with sections on the Geological Society, government, education, consultants, specialist services such as borehole CCTV, map and air photograph suppliers, information services, etc.

Register of workers in soil micromorphology: being collected by Dr Anne Gebhardt, Laboratoire d'Anthropologie, Univ de Rennes, Beaulieu, 35042 Rennes, France.

BOOKS – BRITAIN GENERALLY
Bell, Martin and Boardman, John (eds), *Past and present soil erosion: archaeological and geographical perspectives*. Oxbow monogr, 22, 1992, v, 250 p, bibls, index. 0 946897 46 8. Papers from a 1991 conference; first eight chapters cover field studies in lowland Britain.

Berglund, B E (ed), *Handbook of Holocene palaeoecology and palaeohydrology*. Chichester: Wiley, 1986, xxiv, 869 p, bibls, index. 0 471 90691 3. (International Geological Correlation Programme.) Contains 41 papers ranging from research strategy, sampling and mapping through methodologies to numerical treatments of biostratigraphic data.

Bowen, D G et al, 'Correlation of Quaternary glaciations in England–Ireland–Scotland–Wales', in *Quat sci rev*, 5, 1986, pp 299–340.

BRITISH ASSOCIATION FOR THE ADVANCEMENT OF SCIENCE used to publish a volume of descriptive essays for each region in which it held its annual conferences: eg Leeds 1967. A list of the volumes published is in *Geography*, 58.3, 1973, pp 237–41.

British Geological Survey, *Geology of the country around . . .* These are Memoirs of the Survey, one for each geological sheet in England and Wales issued.

British regional geology. London: HMSO. 18 volumes were published covering different regions of Britain.

Brown, Eric H and Clayton, K (gen eds), *Geomorphology of the British Isles* (series). London: Methuen. Several volumes were issued, covering (eg) Eastern and Central England (Straw and Clayton, 1979); Ireland (Davies and Stephens, 1978); Scotland (Sissons, 1976); Northern England (King, 1976).

Courty, M, Goldberg, P and Macphail, R, *Soils and micromorphology in archaeology.* Cambridge: CUP, 1990, xx, 344 p, bibl, index. 0 521 32419 X.
Reference handbook for archaeologists and environmentalists; includes case study on 'dark earth' etc.

Devoy, J F N, 'Post-glacial environmental change and man in the Thames Estuary: a synopsis', in F H Thompson (ed), *Archaeology and coastal change. Soc Antiq London occas pap*, n ser 1, 1980, pp 134–48.

Ehlers, J, Gibbard, P L and Rose, J (eds), *Glacial deposits in Great Britain and Ireland.* Rotterdam/Brookfield VT: Balkema, 1991, 580 p, bibl (pp 503–44), index. 90 6191 875 8.
Contains 44 papers on the various regions including the Isle of Man and the Isles of Scilly.

Fitzpatrick, E A, *An introduction to soil science.* London: Longman, 2 edn 1986, x, 255 p, bibl, index. 0 582 30128 9 pb.
For first-year students.

—, *Soil microscopy and micromorphology.*

Chichester: Wiley, 1993, x, 304 p, bibl, index. 0 471 93859 9.

Geological Association (per Eric Robinson), *Geology in the churchyard.* London: Geol Ass, 1992, 4 p leaflet.
Describes gravestones with some notes on their geology, lichens, weathering etc.

Goudie, Andrew, *The landforms of England and Wales.* Oxford: Blackwell, 1990, xi, 394 p, bibl, index. 0 631 17306 4.
Includes, as last chapter, consideration of human impact on Pleistocene formations.

Goulty, George A, *A dictionary of landscape: a dictionary of terms used in the description of the world's land surface.* Aldershot: Avebury Technical, 1991, vi, 309 p. 1 85628 214 7.

Jones, D K C (ed), *The shaping of southern England.* London: Academic Press, (= *Inst Brit Geogr spec pap*, 11), 1980, xi, 274 p, bibls, index. 0 12 388950 2.

Limbrey, Susan, *Soil science and archaeology.* London: Academic Press (Studies in Archaeological Science), 1975, 384 p, bibl, index. 0 12 785477 0.
Textbook.

Maltman on geological maps see Section 6.1 General reference works (under Maps).

Mitchell, G F et al, *A correlation of Quaternary deposits in the British Isles. Geol Soc spec rep*, 4, 1973, 99 p, bibl. 0 7073 0052 5 pb.
Good bibliography for the time.

Roberts, Neil, *The Holocene: an environmental history.* Oxford: Blackwell, 1989, x, 227 p, bibl, index/glossary. 0 631 14575 3 hb, 0 631 16178 3 pb.
Covers the period from 10,000 BP to present.

Whittow, John, *Geology and scenery in Britain.* London: Chapman and Hall, 1992, xii, 478 p, bibl, index. 0 412 44380 5 pb.

WALES

Bowen, D Q, 'Studies in the Welsh Quaternary: a retrospect and prospect', in *Cambria*, 4, 1977, pp 2–9.

Campbell, S and Bowen, D Q, *Geological conservation review: Quaternary of Wales.* Peterborough: Nature Conservancy Council, 1989, 237 p, bibl, index. 0 86139 570 0.
Describes (by region) Quaternary rocks and landforms, including Pleistocene glaciations,

fluctuating sealevels, presence of ancient flora, fauna and humans. Full bibliography.

Lewis, Colin A (ed), *The glaciations of Wales and adjoining regions*. London: Longman, 1970, xv, 378 p, bibls, index. [o] 582 48154 6.
Twelve contributions; rather out of date by now but not yet replaced. Also includes Cheshire-Shropshire lowlands, Hereford Basin, Lower Severn Valley, the West country and (pp 267–314) southern Ireland.

Millward, Roy and Robinson, Adrian, *Landscapes of North Wales*. Newton Abbot: David and Charles, 1978, 207 p, bibl, index. 0 7153 7713 2

SCOTLAND

British Geological Survey (published by HMSO Scotland) volumes on:
The northern Highlands of Scotland (G S Johnstone and W Mykura, 4 edn 1990)
The Midland valley of Scotland (I B Cameron and D Stephenson, 3 edn 1985)
The Tertiary volcanic districts of Scotland (J E Richey rev by A G MacGregor and F W Anderson, 3 edn 1987)
Also *BGS memoirs*, 9 volumes by region.

Baird, W J, *The scenery of Scotland: the structure beneath*. Edinburgh: Nat Mus Scotl, 3 edn 1993, 36 p. 0 948636 24 6 pb.
Pamphlet with aerial photographic illustration.

Craig, G Y (ed), *Geology of Scotland*. London: Geol Soc, 1991, xii, 612 p, bibls, index. 0 903317 63 X hb, 0 903317 64 8 pb.
The Quaternary is covered on pp 503–43.

Gordon, J E and Sutherland, D G (eds), *Quaternary of Scotland*. London: Chapman and Hall, 1993, 695 p, bibl. 0 412 48840 X.
Introductory chapters and regional treatments.

Gray, J M and Lowe, J J (eds), *Studies in the Scottish Late Glacial environment*. Oxford: Pergamon, 1977, xiii, 197 p, bibl, index. 0 08 020498 8.

Sissons, J B, *Scotland*. London: Methuen, (Geomorphology of the British Isles series), 1976, [9], 150 p. 0 416 83990 8 hb, 0 416 84000 0 pb.

Whittow, J B, *Geology and scenery in Scotland*. Harmondsworth: Penguin, 1977, 362 p, bibl, index. 0 14 021867 X pb.

IRELAND

Information on soils can be obtained from Teagasc, part of the Irish Agricultural Institute (19 Sandymount Avenue, Dublin 4). A useful bibliography including soils is in Ann Lynch's *BARBS 85* (see Section 6.11.2 Neolithic–Bronze Age).

Periodicals

Biology and environment (0791–7945). 1993–. 3/yr. Royal Irish Academy's retitling of its former 'B' series of its Proceedings. Includes palaeoenvironmental articles and other matters of interest to archaeologists.
Irish geography (0075–0778). 1944–. Dublin: Geogr Soc Ireland.

Books

Gardiner, M J and Radford, T, *Soil associations of Ireland and their land use potential. Explanatory bulletin to Soil Map of Ireland 1980*. Dublin: Nat Soil Survey of Ireland, 1980, iv, 143 p, bibl.
Includes list of the 9 county soil surveys that had been done at that point.

— and Ryan, P, 'A new generalised soil map of Ireland and its land use interpretation', in *Ir j agric res*, **8**, 1969, 95–109 (not seen).

Herries Davies, G L and Stephens, Nicholas, *Ireland*. London: Methuen, 1978, xii, 250 p, bibl, index. 0 416 84640 8 hb; 0 416 84650 5 pb (Geomorphology of the British Isles series).

Holland, C H (ed), *A geology of Ireland*. Scot Acad Pr, 1981, x, 335 p, bibl, index. 0 7073 0269 2.

IRISH QUATERNARY ASSOCIATION FIELD GUIDES. Nearly twenty have been published to date: see brief list reproduced in Section 6.11.1 Quaternary .. Mesolithic, with address.

Jessen, Knud, *Studies in late Quaternary deposits and flora-history of Ireland*. Dublin: Proc Roy Ir Acad, ser B, **52.6**, 1949, pp 85-290.
Retains its classic status.

McCabe, A M and Hirons, K R, *Field guide to the Quaternary deposits of SE Ulster . . .* Cambridge: Quat Res Ass/Ir Ass for Quat Stud, 1986, 185 p.

Naylor, D, *Ireland* (Introduction to General Geology). Dublin: Roy Ir Acad, 1980. (Not available to compiler.)

Stephens, N, on Irish glaciations, see under Lewis in Wales above.

Whittow, J B, *Geology and scenery in Ireland*. Harmondsworth: Penguin, 1974, 301 p, glossary, index. o 14 021791 6 pb.

Wilson, H E, *Regional geology of Northern Ireland*. Belfast: HMSO, 1972, x, 105 p, bibl, index. [o] 337 06012 6.
Official publication.

———

Vegetation, agriculture and landscape change
ORGANISATIONS

(where no address is given see Section 4.2 Organisations)

Bede's World 'Anglo-Saxon' farm (The Museum, Church Bank, Jarrow, Tyne and Wear NE32 3DY)
British Agricultural History Society
Butser Ancient Farm Project
Society for Landscape Studies

PERIODICALS: BRITAIN AND IRELAND

Agricultural history review (0002–1490). 1953–. 2/yr. Reading: British Agricultural History Society. Contains annual bibliography (comp Raine Morgan) of published items on agricultural history
Biology and environment (0791–7945). 1993–. 3/yr. (Formerly *Proc Royal Irish Academy B*)
Geographical abstracts: human geography (0953–9611)
Journal of biogeography (0305–0270). 1974–. 6/yr. Oxford: Blackwell Science
Journal of historical geography (0305–7488). 1975–. 4/yr. London: Academic Press
Landscape history (0143–3768). 1979–. Annual. Society for Landscape Studies
Progress in human geography: international reviews of current research (0309–1325). 1977–. 4/yr. Edward Arnold
Rural history: economy, society, culture (0956–7933). 1990–. 2/yr. CUP
Scottish geographical magazine (0036–9225). 1885–. 2/yr. Edinburgh: Scottish Geographical Society
Tools and tillage: a journal of the history of the implements of cultivation and other agricultural processes (0563–8887). 1968–. Annual. Copenhagen: Nat Museum Denmark
Vegetatio, the international journal of plant ecology (0042–3106). 1948–. Dordrecht: Kluwer
See also Section 6.10 *Science-based archaeology (under Biological and environmental examination)*.

BIBLIOGRAPHIES

Brewer, J G, *Enclosures and the open fields: a bibliography*. Reading: Brit Agric Hist Soc, 1972, 32 p, author index. [o] 903269 00 7 pb.
Lists 355 items on general, regional and special topics.

Morgan, Raine (ed), *Farm tools, implements and machines in Britain, prehistory to 1945: a bibliography*. Reading: Univ Reading and Brit Agric Hist Soc, 1984, xxii, 275 p, index. o 7049 0707 0 pb.

White, K D, *A bibliography of Roman agriculture*. Reading: Univ Reading Inst of Agric Hist, 1970, xxviii, 63 p. o 900724 03 X.
Mostly Mediterranean, little Roman Britain.

Whitworth, Alan, *A comprehensive bibliography of dovecotes*. Whitby: author, 1995 (at 10 The Carrs, Sleights, Whitby, YO21 1RR)

BOOKS – BRITAIN GENERALLY

Allen, Tim et al, *Excavations at Roughground Farm, Lechlade: a prehistoric and Roman landscape*. Oxford: OUCA (= *Thames Valley Landscapes: the Cotswold Water Park*, 1), 1993, xxiii, 208 p, bibl, 4 fiche. o 947816 83 6.
Examination of 8 hectares, Late Neo to end of Roman period; at the time (1957–65) was one of the first landscape studies in this country.

Aston, Michael, *Interpreting the landscape: landscape archaeology in local studies*. London: Batsford, 1985, 168 p, bibl, index. o 7134 3649 2 hb, o 7134 3650 6 pb.
Fundamental textbook for England and Wales.

Baker, A R H and Butlin, R A (eds), *Studies of field systems in the British Isles*. Cambridge: CUP, 1973, xxvi, 702 p, bibl, index. o 521 20121 7.
Papers treat sources, methods, and area studies.

— and Harley, J B (eds), *Man made the land: essays in English historical geography*. Newton Abbot: David and Charles, 1973, 208 p, bibls, index. o 7153 5756 5 pb.
In view of its age, perhaps now best used for its excellent illustrations.

Barker, Graeme, *Prehistoric farming in Europe*.

Cambridge: CUP, 1985, 327 p, bibl, index. o 521 22810 7 hb, o 521 26969 5 pb.
Regional treatment.

Beswick, Pauline and Rotherham, I D (eds), *Ancient woodlands: their archaeology and ecology – a coincidence of interest.* Sheffield: Landscape Conservation Forum, 1993, vi, 113 p, bibls. (No ISBN: ISSN 1354-0262.)
Papers from a 1992 conference.

Birks, Hilary et al (eds), *The cultural landscape: past, present and future.* Cambridge: CUP, 1988, xviii, 521 p, bibl, index. o 521 34435 2.
Vegetational and landscape history. *See also Birks and Birks in Section 6.11.1 Quaternary . . . Mesolithic.*

Bowen, H C for Research Committee on Ancient Fields (BAAS), *Ancient fields: a tentative analysis of vanishing earthworks and landscapes.* Originally published 1961, reprinted Wakefield: SR Publishers, 1970, xii, 80 p, bibl, index.
Classic early description of 'Celtic' fields, strip lynchets, ridge-and-furrow.

— and Fowler, P J (eds), *Early land allotment in the British Isles: a survey of recent work.* BARBS, 48, 1978, v, 199 p, bibls. o 86054 015 4 pb.
Contributors treat Neolithic to medieval fields.

Bradley, R J, on altering the earth, see Section 6.12 History and theory (under Theory).

Chambers, F M (ed), *Climate change and human impact on the landscape.* London: Chapman and Hall, 1993, xxi, 303 p, bibl, index. o 412 46200 1.
Includes Wales and Ireland; excellent bibliography.

Coppock, J T, *An agricultural atlas of England and Wales.* London: Faber, rev edn 1976, 267 p, bibl, index. o 571 04829 3.
Offers a 'snapshot of agriculture . . . in 1970'; shows land-use and gives a general indication of productive land.

Council for the Protection of Rural England (per G Sinclair), *The lost land – land use change in England 1945–1990. A report to the CPRE.* London: CPRE, 1993, 80 p. o 946044 08 2 pb.
Shows rural land disappearing at over twice the rate given in government statistics.

Crawford, O G S, on ancient field systems, see Archaeology in the field in Section 6.9 The

excavator's training . . . *(under Survey and reconnaissance).*

Dodgshon, R A and Butlin, R A (eds), *An historical geography of England and Wales.* London: Academic Press, 2 edn 1990, xxiii, 589 p, bibl, index. o 12 219253 2 hb, o 12 219254 0 pb.
Important basic text, substantially enlarged and revised since the 1978 version; contains 19 sections on various aspects, including prehistoric.

Edwards, Peter, *Farming sources for local historians.* London: Batsford, 1991, 226 p, bibl, index. o 7134 5116 5.
Mainly documentary, some physical evidence.

Evans, George Ewart, *Ask the fellows who cut the hay.* London: Faber, 2 edn 1965, 262 p, bibl, index. o 571 08648 9 hb, o 571 06353 5 pb.
Suffolk emphasis, but full of illuminating details of hand-tool farming.

Evans, J G, *Environment of early man in the British Isles.* London: Elek, 1975, xvi, 216 p, bibl, index. o 236 30902 1 hb, o 236 40047 9 pb.
Pioneering work covering glaciation effects to modern times.

—, Limbrey, S and Cleere, H F (eds), *The effect of man on the landscape: the Highland Zone.* CBA res rep, 11, 1975, viii, 129 p, bibls. No ISBN, pb.
Twenty papers from a seminal conference at Lancaster. (For Lowland Zone see under Limbrey below.)

Everett, Alan, *Continuity and colonization: the evolution of Kentish settlement.* Leicester: Leicester Univ Press, 1986, xxi, 426 p, notes, index. o 7185 1255 3.
From end of Roman Britain to 13th/14th century: indicates places where continuity from RB occupation seems likely, using all available forms of evidence.

Finberg, H P R (ed), *The agrarian history of England and Wales: vol I(ii),* AD 43–1047. Cambridge: CUP, 1972, xviii, 566 p, bibl, index. o 521 08423 7.
Needs revision now, eg using Foster and Smout, Fowler or Mercer below.

Fisher, John L, *A medieval farming glossary of Latin and English words taken mainly from Essex records.* London: NCSS for SCLH, 1968, 41 p. [o] 7199 0752 7 pb.

Particularly useful for manorial records.

Foster, S and Smout, T C, *The history of soils and field systems*. Aberdeen: Scott Cultural Press, 1994, ix, 165 p, bibl, index. 1 898218 13 7 pb.
Offers 12 papers on various aspects from the Northern Isles to the English Midlands and from prehistory to modern (Rothamsted) soil experiments.

Fowler, P J, *The farming of prehistoric Britain*. Cambridge: CUP, 1983, x, 246 p, bibl, index. 0 521 27369 2.
Revision of 1981 paper in Piggott (ed) (*below*).

Fox, Cyril, *The personality of Britain: its influence on inhabitant and invader in prehistoric and early historic times*. Cardiff: Nat Mus Wales, 4 rev edn 1959, 99 p, refs, index.
Pioneering work, still regarded with some awe and affection even though many of its ideas have been displaced in the last 50 years.

Fulford, Michael and Nichols, E (eds), *Developing landscapes of lowland Britain: the archaeology of the British gravels, a review*. Soc Antiq occas pap, 14, 1992, xiii, 145 p, bibls. 0 85431 259 5 pb.

Hall, David, *The open fields of Northamptonshire*. Northampton: Northants Rec Soc, 1995, xi, 378 p, bibl, glossary, index. 0 901275 59 X.
Documentary and fieldwork evidence brought together in a survey with far more than local interest, eg the change from two- to three-field system.

Hallam, H E (ed), *The agrarian history of England and Wales, vol II: 1042–1350*. Cambridge: CUP, 1988, xxxix, 1086 p, bibls, indexes. 0 521 20073 3.
Standard work for the period.

Harvey, Nigel, *A history of farm buildings in England and Wales*. Newton Abbot: David and Charles, 2 edn 1984, 279 p, bibl, index. 0 7153 8383 3.
Narrative history and 'running sourcebook' for other relevant materials (hence for general reader and specialist alike).

—, *Historic farm buildings study: sources of information*. London: MAFF/CBA, 1985, 76 p. No ISBN.
Describes the historical importance of such buildings and summarises evidence on their number, type, age and rate of loss; published

and unpublished sources; recording; dating; buildings accessible to public.

Hayfield, C, on landscape of Wharram Percy, see Section 6.11.4 Romano-British.

Hodges, Richard, *Wall-to-wall history: the story of Royston Grange*. London: Duckworth, 1991, viii, 166 p. 1 7156 2342 7 pb.
Of much wider importance than its title would suggest: this was a crucial work demonstrating evidence of field layouts from Neolithic to modern times.

*Hoskins, W G, *Leicestershire: an illustrated essay on the history of the landscape*. London: Hodder and Stoughton, 1957, xvi, 138 p, bibl, index.
Classic, beautifully written work showing a whole new way of looking at the landscape: it inspired a whole series of volumes on The Making of the English Landscape (several of which are listed here in Section 6.4 Regional surveys).

***— (commentary by Chris Taylor), *The making of the English landscape*. London: Hodder and Stoughton, 3 edn 1988, 256 p, bib, index. 0 340 39971 6.
Seminal work updated by Hoskins's natural successor, who provides an introduction and new information as marginalia, with extra illustrations.

***Ingrouille, M, *Historical ecology of the British flora*. London: Chapman and Hall, 1995, xii, 347 p, bibl, index. 0 412 56150 6.
Includes main sections on the natural vegetation of the British Isles and the managed landscape.

Jewell, C Andrew (ed), *Victorian farming: a sourcebook*. Winchester: Shurlock, 1975, xx, 138 p, bibl, index. 0 903330 12 1.
Extracts from the 1870 Book of the Farm (Henry Stephens) with introduction explaining the anatomy of Victorian farming.

***Jones, Martin, *England before Domesday*. London: Batsford, 1986, 174 p, bibl, index. 0 7134 2555 5 hb, 0 7134 2556 3 pb.
Describes the development of the landscape from the last glaciation to AD 1086, using the methods of landscape and environmental archaeology.

— and Dimbleby, G (eds), *The environment of man: the Iron Age to the Anglo-Saxon period*.

BARBS, 87, 1981, 336 p, bibls. o 86054 128 2 pb.

Kain, R J P, *An atlas and index of the tithe files of mid-19th century England and Wales.* Cambridge: CUP, 1986, xxviii, 651 p, bibl, index. o 521 25716 6.
Analysis of nearly 15,000 tithe files in the PRO, with computer-generated maps and statistical tables.

— and Prince, H C, *The tithe surveys of England and Wales.* Cambridge: CUP (= *Cambridge studies in historical geography*, 6), 1985, xvi, 327 p, bibl, indexes. o 521 24681 4.
Describes the most comprehensive record of the agrarian landscape ever made, and explains its value for tracing land use, farming practices, field systems and so on.

Lamb, H H, *Climate: present, past and future.* London: Methuen, 1972, 1977, 2 vols, bibls, indexes. o 416 11530 6.

Langdon, John, *Horses, oxen and technological innovation: the use of draught animals in English farming from 1066 to 1500.* Cambridge: CUP, 1986, xvi, 331 p, bibl, index. o 521 26772 2.
Documentary evidence.

Limbrey, Susan and Evans, J G (eds), *The effect of man on the landscape: the Lowland Zone. CBA res rep*, 21, 1978, v, 153 p, bibl, index. o 900312 60 2 pb.
Papers from an important conference at Reading, 1975.

Mercer, Roger (ed), *Farming practice in British prehistory.* Edinburgh: EUP, 1981, xxvi, 245 p, bibls, index. o 85224 414 2 pb.
Papers from a 1980 conference.

Milles, Annie et al (eds), *The beginnings of agriculture. BAR int ser*, S496 */Symposia Ass Envir Archaeol*, 8, 1989, xii, 267 p, bibls. o 86054 636 5 pb
Papers in four sections, one treating the adoption of agriculture in the British Isles.

Partridge, Michael, *Farm tools through the ages.* Reading: Osprey, 1973, 240 p, bibl, index. [o] 85045 081 0.
Based on the collections of the Museum of English Rural Life and Rutland County Museum. Drawings and contemporary prints.

Pennington, Winifred (Mrs T G Tutin), *The history of British vegetation.* London: English Univs Press, 2 edn 1974, viii, 152 p, bibl, index. o 340 18667 4 hb, o 340 18666 6 pb.
Classic work.

Piggott, Stuart (ed), *The agrarian history of England and Wales, Vol 1(i), Prehistory.* Cambridge: CUP, 1981, xxi, 451 p, bibl, index. o 521 08741 4.
Three sections: early prehistory (S Piggott), later prehistory (P J Fowler), livestock (M J Ryder). Should now be read in the light of later works, eg Foster and Smout, Fowler, Mercer, all listed in this section.

Polunin, O and Walters, M, *A guide to the vegetation of Britain and Europe.* Oxford: OUP, 1985, ix, 238 p, bibl, glossary, indexes. o 19 217713 3.
Describes vegetation types, soils and climates; lists national parks and nature reserves.

Rackham, O, *Ancient woodland: its history, vegetation and uses in England.* London: Edward Arnold, 1980, 402 p, refs, index. o 7131 2723 6.
A seminal work covering prehistoric times to the present day: methodology, former and present biology, humans as agents of change.

—, *The history of the countryside.* London: Dent, 1986, xvi, 445 p, refs, index/glossary. o 460 04449 4.
Combines the evidence of climate, soils and landforms with those of plants and animals, archaeology, and documents. (New edition announced as: *Illustrated history of the countryside*, May 1996, o 297 83392 8.)

—, *Trees and woodland in the British landscape: the complete history of Britain's trees, woods and hedgerows.* London: Dent, rev edn 1993; also pb edn, Weidenfeld and Nicolson, 1995, xix, 234 p, bibl, index. o 297 81623 3 pb.
The new edn incorporates 13 years' recent work.

Renfrew, Jane (ed), *New light on early farming: recent developments in palaeoethnobotany.* Edinburgh: EUP, 1991, xii, 395 p, bibl, index. o 7486 0131 7.
Includes a study of archaeobotanical evidence from early historic Ireland plus three relating to coastal Essex, the Cambridgeshire Fens, and Saxon Hampshire.

Reynolds, Peter, *Ancient farming. Shire archaeol*, 50, 1987, 64 p, bibl, index. o 85263 876 0 pb.

—, *Iron Age farm: the Butser experiment*. London: Brit Mus (Colonnade), 1979, 112 p, index. 0 7141 8014 9 hb, 0 7141 8015 7 pb.
An early report on this important experimental work, still continuing, though now on a different site.

*Rodwell, J S (ed), *British plant communities*. Cambridge: CUP, 1990–, 5 vols planned. 0 521 23558 8.
Four volumes have appeared: 1. Woodland and scrub; 2. Mires and heaths; 3. Grasslands and montane; 4. Aquatic communities.

Rowley, Trevor, *Villages in the landscape*. London: Dent, 1978, 211 p, bibl, index. 0 460 04166 5. (Reprinted Orion Books, 1994, 1 85797 341 0 pb.)
Sets human settlements in their countryside, from prehistoric roots to 20th century village decline. (*See also Rowley under Wales below*.)

— (ed), *The evolution of marshland landscapes*. Oxford: Oxford Univ Dept External Stud, 1981, 177 p, bibls. 0 903736 12 8 pb.
Papers on prehistoric to 19th century evidence.

Simmons, I G and Tooley, M (eds), *The environment in British prehistory*. London: Duckworth, 1981, x, 334 p, bibl, index. 0 7156 1362 6 hb, 0 7156 1441 X pb.
Discusses the impact of the environment on successive peoples, from palaeolithic to Iron Age.

Stanford, S C, see under Wales below.

***Taylor, Chris, *Fields in the English landscape*. London: Dent (Archaeology in the Field series), 1975, 174 p, bibl, index. 0 460 02232 6.
Classic work tracing the evolution from prehistory to modern times, using physical evidence plus documents for later periods. Notes temporal and regional differences.

***—, *Village and farmstead: a history of rural settlement in England*. London: George Philip, 1983, 254 p, bibl, index. 0 540 01071 5.
Very useful bibliography accompanies this illuminating work.

Thirsk, Joan (gen ed), *The agrarian history of England and Wales*. Cambridge: CUP, 8 vols 1972–91.
For prehistory see under Piggott above; for AD 43–1047 see under Finberg above; for 1042–1350 see under Hallam above; other volumes treat the periods 1348–1500 (1991); 1500–1640 (1967); 1640–1750 (1984/5); 1750–1850 (1989); and 1914–39 (1978). (vol 7, 1850–1914 due 1997.)

Thompson, F H (ed), *Archaeology and coastal change: being the papers presented at meetings in London and Manchester. . . 1977*. Soc Antiq London occas pap, n ser 1, 1980, 154 p, bibl. 0 500 99031 X pb.
Traces sealevel alterations in Britain and the Netherlands, and their effects on settlement.

*Veen, Marijke van der, *Crop husbandry regimes: an archaeobotanical study of farming in northern England 1000 BC – AD 500*. Sheffield archaeol monogr, 3, 1992, xvii, 227 p, bibl. 0 906090 41 5.
Thesis-based synthesis of data on ancient agriculture, using an ecological and statistical approach.

Vincent, Peter, *The biogeography of the British Isles: an introduction*. London: Routledge, 1990, xv, 315 p, bibl, glossary, index. 0 415 03470 1 hb, 0 415 03471 X pb.
On the interpretation of plant and animal distributions in geographical space, and how we measure the impact of humans on the environment.

WALES

Caseldine, Astrid, *Environmental archaeology in Wales*. Lampeter: St David's Univ Coll, 1990, iv, 197 p, bibl. 0 905285 26 3 pb.
Important work with 56-page bibliography; sets context for Welsh archaeology.

Huw Owen, D (ed), on Welsh settlement (includes vegetation and landforms) see Section 6.4 Regional surveys (under Wales).

Jenkins, Geraint (ed), *Studies in folk life: essays in honour of Iorwerth C Peate*. London: Routledge and Kegan Paul, 1969, 361 p. 0 7100 6055 6.

Linnard, W, *Welsh woods and forests: history and utilisation*. Cardiff: Nat Mus Wales, 1982, xxi, 203 p. 0 7200 0245 1.

*Rowley, Trevor, *The landscape of the Welsh Marches*. London: Michael Joseph, 1986, xi, 257 p, index. 0 7181 2347 6.
Traces the evolution of the landscape from Stone Age to modern times.

Stanford, S C, *The archaeology of the Welsh

Marches. Ludlow: privately published, 2 rev edn 1991, 190 p, bibl, index. 0 9503271 5 8. Views the development of the Marches landscape from half a dozen key points. (Available from author at The Old Farm House, Leinthall Starkes, Shropshire SY8 2HP.)

Williams, Moelwyn, *The making of the South Wales landscape*. London: Hodder and Stoughton, 1975, 271 p, bibl, index. 0 340 15994 4.

SCOTLAND

Beck, Robert, *Scotland's native horse: its history, breeding and survival*. Wigtown: GC Book Publishers, 1992, 203 p, bibl, index. 1 872350 25 9.
Includes many illustrations of horses on Pictish monuments.

*Coppock, J T, *An agricultural atlas of Scotland*. Edinburgh: John Donald, 1976, xv, 242 p, bibl. 0 85976 016 2.

Fenton, Alex and Gillmor, Desmond (eds), *Rural land use on the Atlantic periphery of Europe: Scotland and Ireland*. Dublin: Roy Ir Acad, 1994, 219 p, bibl. 1 87404 509 7 pb.
Conference papers examine the factors that have historically influenced land use in both countries, with a look at emergent patterns within EU policies.

Millman, R N, *The making of the Scottish landscape*. London: Batsford, 1975, 264 p, bibl, index. 0 7134 2838 4.
Better on the post-AD 1100 period than the earlier; useful illustrations.

Parry, M L and Slater, T R (eds), *The making of the Scottish countryside*. London: Croom Helm, 1980, 327p, bibl, index. 0 85664 646 6.
Thirteen essays stressing agriculture as the main agent of change.

**Smout, T C (ed), *Scotland since prehistory: natural change and human impact*. Aberdeen: Scot Cultural Press, 1994, xx, 140 p, bibl, index. 1 89821 803 x pb.
Important new studies, eleven chapters covering the scene from climatic change and human impact on the prehistoric environment through pollen studies and woodland history to salmon catch data.

Spence, David, *Shetland's living landscape: a study in island plant ecology*. Sandwick: Thule Press, 1979, 152 p, bibl, index. 0 906191 14 9 hb, 0 906191 10 6 pb.

Walker, G J and Kirby, K J, *Inventories of ancient, long-established and semi-natural woodland for Scotland*. Peterborough: Nature Conservancy Council [English Nature], 1989, 63 p. 0 86139 564 6.
Information derived from early OS maps etc.

Whittington, G and Whyte, I D (eds), *An historical geography of Scotland*. London: Acad Press, 1983, viii, 282 p. 0 12 747360 2 hb, 0 12 747362 9 pb.

IRELAND

Aalen, F H A, *Man and the landscape in Ireland*. London/NY: Academic Press, 1978, xii, 343 p, bibl, index. 0 12 041350 7.
The natural habitat and its modification from Mesolithic through to modern times; in need of fresh edn to cover later research.

Andrews, J H, *Interpreting the Irish landscape: explorations in settlement history*. Blackrock, Co Dublin: Four Courts Press, forthcoming (1996), 96 pp. 1 85182 256 9.
Six papers, only one published previously: some new evidence and a new approach to settlement and agricultural history in Ireland.

*Bell, Jonathan and Watson, M, *Irish farming: implements and techniques 1750–1900*. Edinburgh: John Donald, 1986, viii, 256 p, bibl, index. 0 85976 164 9.
Extremely useful survey of traditional methods and tools, and the effects of recent changes.

British Association for the Advancement of Science (ed James Meenan and David A Webb), *A view of Ireland: twelve essays on different aspects of Irish life and the Irish countryside*. Dublin: the Association, 1957, xvi, 254 p.
Papers on physiography and climate, geology, botany, zoology, peat, archaeology, folklore, language, and the city of Dublin; now to be seen in the light of newer work.

Chambers, F M (ed), *Climate change and human impact on the landscape*. London: Chapman and Hall, 1993, xxi, 303 p, bibl, index. 0 412 46200 1.
Includes work on Irish palaeoenvironment.

Collins T (ed), *Decoding the landscape*. Galway: UCG Centre for Landscape Studies, 1994, x, 170 p, refs. 0 907775 7 0.
Papers from a 1990 inaugural conference: Irish Sea shores, the West of Ireland, and European Celtic identity among other studies.

Doyle, Gerry (ed), *Ecology and conservation of Irish peatlands*. Dublin: Roy Ir Acad, 1990, [8], ix, 221 p, bibl. 0 901714 87 9.
From a 1988 seminar: includes M O'Connell on origins of Irish lowland blanket bog.

Du Noyer, George Victor (ed F Croke), *Hidden landscapes: an exhibition to celebrate the sesquicentennial of the Geological Survey of Ireland*. Dublin: Nat Gallery Ireland, 1995, 88 p. 0 9031627 1 7 pb.
Selected illustrations by the 19th-century antiquary (1817–69) of ancient monuments as well as geological, botanical and palaeontological features.

Edwards, Kevin J and Warren, W P (eds), *The Quaternary history of Ireland*. London: Academic Press, 1985, xxii, 382 p, bibl. 0 12 232730 6.
Discusses human effects on vegetation; vertebrates; prehistoric settlement and environment; chronology; economy.

Evans, Emyr Estyn, *Irish folk ways*. London: Routledge and Kegan Paul, 1957, xvi, 324 p. (3 impr 1966, 0 7100 1344 2.)
An eminent ethnographer deals with all manner of rural life in Ireland.

Feehan, John (ed), *Climate variation and climate change in Ireland*. Dublin: Envir Inst Univ Coll Dublin, 1994, 151 p, bibls. 1 89847 310 2 pb.
Papers from a Dublin conference 1994.

Fenton and Gillmor (eds), on rural land use, see under Scotland above.

Gailey, Alan and Ó hÓgáin, Dáithi (eds), *Gold under the furze: studies in folk tradition presented to Caoimhín Ó Danachair*. Dublin: Glendale Press, [1982], 253 p, bibl. 0 907606 06 7.
Includes contributions by B Almqvist, A T Lucas, T Jones-Hughes and E Rynne.

Gillmor, Desmond (ed), *The Irish countryside: landscape, wildlife, history, people*. Dublin: Wolfhound Press, 1989, 240 p, short bibl, index. 0 86327 142 1 hb, 0 86327 159 6 pb.

*Glassie, Henry, *Passing the time: folklore and history of an Ulster community* [Ballymenone]. Dublin: O'Brien, 1982, 852 p, bibl, index. 0 86278 015 2.
Detailed folk life study of a Fermanagh townland; much interesting material which would repay mining out.

Graham, Brian J and Proudfoot, Lindsay J, *An historical geography of Ireland*. London: Academic Press, 1993, xviii, 454 p. 0 12 294881 5 pb.
Textbook, 6th century AD to present.

Jessen, K, on Irish late Quaternary and flora, see under Geology and soils above.

Lynch, A on SW Irish human impact, see Section 6.11.2 Neolithic–Bronze Age.

*MacNeill, Máire, *The festival of Lughnasa: a study of the survival of the Celtic festival of the beginning of harvest*. Oxford: OUP, 1962, x, 697 p.
Important study of the harvest festival as recorded in the last 200 years; first corn, then potatoes. Considers the past histories and ancient myths concealed in the practices, together with religious concepts.

**Mitchell, Frank, *The Shell guide to reading the Irish landscape*. Dublin: Country House, 1990. 0 946172 06 4 hb, 0 946172 19 6 pb.
New edn of the indispensable countryside companion. (Not available to compiler.)

Moloney et al on Co Longford bogs survey, see Section 6.20 Wetlands.

Nolan, William (ed), *The shaping of Ireland: the geographical perspective*. Cork: Mercier Pres, 1986, 203 p, bibl. 0 85342 765 8. (Thomas Davies lecture series.)
Approachable short articles which originated in radio talks by various scholars: early settlement to post-medieval roads etc.

*O'Connell, J W and Korff, A (eds), *The book of the Burren*. Newtownlynch, Kinvara, Co Galway: Tír Eolas, 1991, 228 p. 1 873721 00 X pb.
Sourcebook for an important area.

O'Connell, Michael (ed), *The post-glacial period (10,000–0 BP): fresh perspectives*. Dublin: Ir Ass for Quaternary Studies, 1993, 26 p, map. 0 9479201 3 7 pb.
Extended summaries only, on new palaeoenvironmental evidence.

Ó Danachair, Caoimhín, *Folk and farm: essays in honour of A T Lucas*. Dublin: Roy Soc Antiq Ir, 1976, 277 p, chapter bibls. No ISBN.
Includes about eight papers of interest to archaeologists.

Orme, A R, *The world's landscapes: vol 4, Ireland*.

London: Longman, 1970, xviii, 276 p, bibl, place-name glossary, index. [o] 582 31155 1.
Useful conspectus, to be taken in the light of more recent research.

*Reeves-Smyth, T and Hamond, F (eds), *Landscape archaeology in Ireland. BARBS*, 116, 1983, xi, 389 p, bibls. o 86054 216 5 pb.
Twenty papers on various aspects – techniques, case studies etc.

Rohan, P K, *The climate of Ireland*. Dublin: Meteorological Service, 2 edn 1986, xiv, 146 p, bibl.

*Stephens, Nicholas and Glasscock, R E (eds), *Irish geographical studies in honour of Emyr Estyn Evans*. Belfast: Dept Geogr Queen's University Belfast, 1970, xvi, 403 p, bibls. No ISBN.
Contains 25 papers of which at least eight are useful to archaeologists.

*Waddell, John, O'Connell, J W and Korff, Anne (eds), *The book of Aran: the Aran Islands, Co Galway*. Newtownlynch, Kinvara: Tír Eolas, 1994, 334 p, notes, index. 1 873821 04 2 hb, 1 873821 03 4 pb.
Guide book and source book with long chapters on geology, archaeology and other topics such as maritime history.

Webb, D A, *An Irish flora*. Dundalk: Dundalgan Press, 6 edn 1977, xxi, 277 p.
(Revision of Tempest's 1943 work.)

6.15
Archaeology of Industrial Processes (all periods)

This section owes much to suggestions made by Keith Falconer (for England), Miles Oglethorpe (for Scotland), Brian Malaws (for Wales) and Michael Coulter (for Ireland). None of them are responsible for any remaining errors. The section deals with the history of technology from the earliest metal ages onwards; it also includes the related subject of experimental archaeology, in which attempts are made to replicate early technological developments (see under Coles below).

For the early history of metal technology see below the books by Tylecote, by Craddock (ed) and by Crew, while for the industries of the 18th century and later David Crossley's 'Early industrial landscapes' in B Vyner (ed), *Building on the past* (Roy Archaeol Inst, 1994), pp 244–63 gives a good conspectus of the last three decades of research. Indispensable is Barrie Trinder's encyclopaedia for Blackwell (see below under Bibliographies and reference works). The pioneering series on industrial archaeology from David and Charles covered all the British regions and Ireland in the 1970s, and these works are still useful, especially for their bibliographies; see the portmanteau entry under Green below. David and Charles also published two series on railways ('Regional history of the railways of Great Britain', and 'Forgotten railways'), not listed individually here. Another regional series is listed below under CIVIL ENGINEERING HERITAGE.

The section is divided thus:
Societies and organisations
Periodicals (selected)
Abstracting services
Bibliography and reference works
Books: Britain generally; Wales; Scotland; Isle of Man; Ireland

SOCIETIES AND ORGANISATIONS
(For addresses not shown below see Section 4.2 Organisations)

Airfield Research Group
Arkwright Society
Association for the History of Glass Ltd
Association for Industrial Archaeology
Association of Railway Preservation Societies Ltd
British Brick Society

British Waterways Archive

Business Archives Council (185 Tower Bridge Road, London SE1 2UF – give reference 'IA')

Construction History Society

Dartmoor Tin Working Research Group

Early Mines Research Group [mainly for prehistoric period]

The Historical Metallurgy Society Ltd

Inland Waterways Association

Inland Waterways Protection Society

The International Committee for the Conservation of the Industrial Heritage

IRIS, the Index Record for Industrial Sites (AIA: run by Jane Robson, Project Asst, Lancaster Univ Archaeol Unit, Storey Inst, Meeting House Lane, Lancaster LA1 1TH, tel 01524 848666)

Ironbridge Institute

National Association of Mining History Organisations

National Record of Industrial Monuments (superseded by IRIS, above)

Newcomen Society for the Study of Engineering and Technology

Peak District Mines Historical Society

Railway Heritage Trust

Society for Post-Medieval Archaeology

Tool and Trades History Society

Trevithick Society

Trevithick Trust

Wealden Iron Research Group

(Also myriad local industrial archaeology societies: enquire at local library or museum.)

Selected periodicals

Bulletin: Groupe d'Histoire des Mines et de la Métallurgie. 1983–.

Industrial archaeology. 1, 1964 – 16.4, 1981/2. (Ceased: four successive publishers, and a gap from late 1974–77.)

Industrial archaeology review (0309–0728). 1976–. 2/yr. OUP/AIA. now AIA; may become annual.

Newcomen Society for the Study of Engineering and Technology/ Trans (0372–6187). 1922–. Contains many articles of classic status.

Post-medieval archaeology (0079–4236). 1967–. Annual. Society for Post-Medieval Archaeology.

Technology and culture (0040–165X). 1960–. 4/yr. Chicago: Society for the History of Technology. Contains annual bibliographies (comp. Jack Goodwin and continuer) on the history

of technology; cumulative index for vols 1–10 (1960–9), from 1987 available online.

Abstracting services

***Art and archaeology technical abstracts* (see Section 1.5 Indexing and abstracting services) often contains abstracts on early technological processes.

History of technology index see entry, and Internet address, in Section 1.5 Indexing and abstracting services.

Bibliography and reference works

Baldwin, Mark, 'A bibliography of British canals 1623–1950' in M Baldwin and A Burton (eds), *Canals, a new look: studies in honour of Charles Hadfield* (Phillimore, 1984), pp 130–91.

Benson, John et al (comp), *Bibliography of the British coal industry: secondary literature, Parliamentary and Departmental papers, mineral maps and a guide to sources.* Oxford: OUP for Nat Coal Board, 1981, vii, 760 p, index. 0 19 920120 X.

*Burt, Roger and Waite, Peter, *Bibliography of the history of British metal mining: books, theses and articles published on the history of metal mining in England, Wales, Scotland and the Isle of Man since the Second World War.* Exeter: Exeter Univ Press/Nat Ass of Mining Hist Org, 1988, xi, 177 p. 0 85989 319 7. Regional arrangement, list of periodicals consulted by region, nearly 2,600 items but no index.

**Carding, Janet et al (comp), *Guide to the history of technology in Europe.* London: Science Museum, 1992, 142 p, index. 0 901805 51 3 pb. Lists 800 people in 26 countries with 600 relevant institutions and 130 journals, in ten broad subject areas.

Comité pour la Sidérurgie Ancienne de l'UISPP. Publishes regular bibliographies on ancient ironworking in *Archeologické rozhledy* (Prague, 0323–1267). In its first 50 years nearly 1,800 separate titles (some of them collective volumes) have been listed. The main emphasis remains on the period up to the early Middle Ages, though post-medieval material is also included now.

Corning Museum of Glass Library, *The history and art of glass: index of periodical literature,*

1956–79. Boston: G K Hall Library Catalogs, 1981, 450 p. *See also annual bibliographies on glass provided in* Journal of glass studies *(Corning, NY)*.

***Crossley, D W, Post-medieval archaeology in Britain *(1990) includes an excellent bibliography with a good amount of industrial archaeology.*

Duncan, George S (ed V Dimbleby), *Bibliography of glass (from the earliest records to 1940)*. London: Dawsons of Pall Mall for Soc Glass Technol, 1960, viii, 544 p, index.

Ferguson, Eugene S, *Bibliography of the history of technology*. Cambridge (Mass): *Soc for the Hist of Technol monogr ser*, 5, 1968, xx, 347 p, index. No ISBN.
Introduction to primary and secondary sources.

Fleming, J, *The blacksmith's source book: an annotated bibliography*. Carbondale (Ill): S Illinois Univ Press, 1980, 204 p.

***Forbes, R J, *Studies in ancient technology*. Leiden: Brill, 2 rev edn, ix vols 1964–72.
Classic work: covers various topics, eg vol. ix deals with copper, tin etc.

Greenwood, John, 'Industrial archaeology in western Europe: a bibliography', *Ind archaeol rev*, 6, 1982, pp 125–39.

**— (comp), *The industrial archaeology and industrial history of northern England: a bibliography*. [Cranfield]: privately published, 1985, 300 p, indexes. 0 9510389 0 7.
Classified list of 3,050 books, articles and theses on the six pre-1974 northern counties.

**—, *The industrial archaeology and industrial history of the English Midlands: a bibliography*. [Cranfield]: privately published (Kewdale Pr), 1987, 410 p, index. 0 9510389 1 5.
Classified list of over 4,200 books and articles on the counties of Cheshire, Derbys, Here-Worc, Leics, Lincs, S Humb, Northants, Notts, Shrops, Staffs, Warks and W Midlands.

**—, *The industrial archaeology and industrial history of London: a bibliography*. [Cranfield]: privately published, 1988, 259 p, index. 0 9510389 2 3.
Classified list of 2,900 books and articles for the area of the old Greater London Council.

Jewell, Andrew, *Crafts, trades and industries: a book list for local historians*. London: Nat

Council for Social Service, 1968, 24 p. [o] 7199 0678 4 pb.
Useful once, but now showing its age.

Kay, P, *A guide to railway research and sources for local railway history*. Teignmouth: S G Publns, 1990, 35 p.

Lindsay, C F, *Windmills: a bibliographical guide*. London: the author, 1974, 48 p.
Includes organisations as well as references.

McNeil, Ian (ed), *An encyclopaedia of the history of technology*. London: Routledge, 1990, xv, 1062 p, bibl, indexes. 0 415 01306 2.
The editor is former Secretary of the Newcomen Society: contributions on (eg) non-ferrous metals, ferrous metals, power sources, agriculture, textiles.

Molloy, Peter M, *The history of metal mining and metallurgy: an annotated bibliography*. New York/London: Garland Publishing (= *Bibl of the history of science and technology*, 12), 1986, 350 p. 0 8240 9065 9.

Nicolle, George, *The woodworking trades: a select bibliography*. Plymouth: Twybill Press, 1993, x, 150 p, indexes. 0 9522285 0 5.
Arranged by trade, from brushmakers to wheelwrights, plus rural craftsmen, tools and trades.

Ottley, G (comp), *A bibliography of railway history*. London: HMSO, 2 rev ed 1988, 554 p, index. 0 11 290364 9.
The revision covers material to the end of 1980.

—, *Railway history: a guide to 61 collections in libraries and archives in Great Britain*. London: Lib Ass (= *Subject guide to library resources*, 1, 1973, 80 p, bibl. 0 85365 445 X pb.

Paquie, M M et al, *Bibliographie mines et métallurgie anciennes: 2, le fer*. Besançon, 1991.
Contains over 3,600 unannotated references, from the end of the 19th century onwards, on iron technology, iron ore geology, mining, conservation of iron objects.

Peak District Mines Historical Society, *British mining history* (three-part bibliography: not seen).

Riden, Philip, *A gazetteer of charcoal-fired blast furnaces in Great Britain in use since 1660*. Cardiff: privately, 1987, vi, 48 p, bibl, index. 0 9503299 6 7 pb.

Salaman, R A, *The dictionary of leatherworking tools, c. 1700–1950 and the tools of allied*

trades. London: Allen and Unwin, 1986, xxi, 377 p, bibl, index. 0 04 621030 X.
Over 1,100 tools, with variant names, are presented for the trades of bookbinding, boots and shoes, clogs, gloves, etc.

***Singer, C J et al (eds), *A history of technology*. Oxford: OUP, 5 vols 1954–8.
Classic, monumental work covering in its five volumes the period from early times to c. AD1900. Volume IV (1958) covers the Industrial Revolution.

Tottle, C R, *An encyclopaedia of metallurgy and materials*. Plymouth: Metals Soc/Macdonald and Evans, 1984, ci, 380 p. 0 7121 0571 9.
Less useful for archaeological purposes than it might have been, since obsolete terms have been cut or deleted. Includes ceramics and glass.

***Trinder, Barrie (ed), *The Blackwell encyclopaedia of industrial archaeology*. Oxford: Blackwell, 1992, xxii, 964 p, bibl (pp 873–930), index. 0 631 14216 9.
Over 50 specialist contributors cover the developed world, noting significant sites, manufacturing regions, definitions, significant people from AD 1650, etc. Includes classified finding aid. Indispensable, though the bibliography has too many typographical errors.

Books

BRITAIN GENERALLY

Agricola, see under Hoover below.

Alfrey, Judith and Putnam, Tim, *The industrial heritage: managing resources and uses*. London/New York: Routledge, 1992, xi, 327 p, bibl, index. 0 415 04068 X hb, 0 415 07043 0 pb.
Introduces the assessment, conservation, interpretation, financing and management of the complex heritage of industrial cultures in many countries.

Ashmore, O, *The industrial archaeology of northwest England and where to find it*. Manchester: Manchester Univ Press (= *Chetham Soc*, 3 ser, 29), 1982, 241 p, bibl, index. 0 7190 0820 4.
Gazetteer-style book based on fieldwork up to 1979; intended as a field guide.

Association for Industrial Archaeology. 'Industrial archaeology: working for the future'.
Policy document printed in abridged form in *Brit archaeol news*, 6.4, Jul 1991, pp 44, 48.
Gives objectives, recommends general priorities, and shows where urgent action is needed.

**—, *Recording the industrial heritage*. (Obtainable from address given under IRIS under Organisations above.)
Manual for volunteers recording industrial monuments for entry into sites and monuments records.

—, *see also under* Industrial archaeology review *below*.

Ayris, Ian and Gould, Shane, *Colliery landscapes: an aerial survey of the deep-mined coal industry in England*. London: Engl Heritage, 1994, 140 p. 1 85074 508 0 pb.
Photographic guide to the modern coal industry and its historical context.

Baker, Diane, *Potworks: the industrial architecture of the Staffordshire potteries*. London: RCHME, 1991, xi, 131 p, bibl, glossary, index. 1 873592 01 9 pb.
Traces the evolution of ceramic production from the early cottage-industry kilns of 16th/17th centuries to the purpose-built factories of the 19th.

Baldwin, Mark and Burton, Anthony (eds), *Canals: a new look. Studies in honour of Charles Hadfield*. Chichester: Phillimore, 1984, 195 p. 0 85033 516 7.
See also under Hadfield below.

Biddle, G and Nock, O S, *The railway heritage of Britain*. London: M Joseph, 1983, 270 p. 0 7181 2355 7.
Authoritative general survey.

Blackburn, G on woodworking tools, see Section 6.1 General reference works (under Encyclopaedias).

*Blick, C R (ed), *Early metallurgical sites in Great Britain BC 2000 to AD 1500*. London: Inst of Metals, 1991, 108 p, bibl. 0 901462 84 5.
Treats 15 archaeological sites important to the history of metallurgical development in Britain.

**Bracegirdle, B (ed), *The archaeology of the industrial revolution*. London: Heinemann, 1973, viii, 207 p, chapter bibls, index. 0 435 32990 1.
Collection of essays by eminent authors, profusely illustrated (often in colour).

*Buchanan, R A, *Industrial archaeology in Britain*. London: Allen Lane, 2 edn 1980, 476 p, refs, index. 0 7139 0956 0.
Comprehensive introduction to the subject.

— and Watkins, G, *The industrial archaeology of the stationary steam engine*. London: Allen Lane, 1976, 200 p, gazetteer, bibl. o 7139 0604 9.

Cattell, John and Falconer, Keith, *Swindon: the legacy of a railway town*. London: HMSO/RCHME, 1995, x, 181 p, bibl, index. o 11 300053 7.
On the creation of a large railway engineering works and associated new settlement for the Great Western Railway workers; the buildings were recorded before the reorganisation of BRE.

Cheape, Hugh (ed), *Tools and traditions: studies in European ethnology*. Edinburgh: Nat Mus Scotland, 1993, 256 p, bibls. o 948636 53 X.
Thirty-seven eminent European scholars interpret artefacts and their context.

CIVIL ENGINEERING HERITAGE. Series prepared by Panel for Historical Engineering Works of the Institution of Civil Engineers. London: Thomas Telford Services, 1986 to 1994, each with gazetteer and analysis of selected structures, bibl and index.
Southern England (R A Otter and A G Alnutt, 1994). o 7277 1971 8 pb
Eastern and Central England (E A Labrum, 1994). o 7277 1970 X pb
Wales and Western England (W J Sivewright, 1986). o 7277 0236 X pb
Northern England (under revision for 1996 publication).

***Cleere, H F and Crossley, David (ed Jeremy Hodgkinson), *The iron industry of the Weald*. Cardiff: Merton Priory Press, 2 rev edn 1995, xiv, 425 p, bibl + suppl bibl, index. 1 898937 04 4.
From prehistory to the blast furnace in this important area. The second edition adds some fresh material (additional bloomery sites etc), some corrigenda, bibl supplement, etc.

Coad on royal dockyards, see Section 6.19 Maritime, nautical and underwater archaeology.

**Coles, J M, *Experimental archaeology*. London: Academic Press, 1979, xi, 274 p, bibl, index. o 12 179750 3.
Sets out a number of ways in which archaeological materials, and thus past behaviour, can be better understood by practical experiments such as those involving food production, house and monument building, the manufacture and use of tools and weapons, sailing primitive boats, and so on.

Cossons, Neil (ed), *The BP book of industrial archaeology*. Newton Abbot: David and Charles, 3 edn 1993, 384 p, bibl. o 7153 0134 9 pb.
Good accessible introduction with gazetteer, lists of addresses and of industrial museums, excellent bibliography.

Craddock, P T (ed), *Scientific studies in early mining and extractive metallurgy*. Brit Mus occas pap, 20, 1980, 173 p, bibls. o 86159 019 8 pb.
Part of the proceedings of a 1979 symposium.

—, *on early metal mining and production, see Section 6.11.2 Neolithic–Bronze Age.*

Crew, Peter and Susan (eds), on early mining, see Section 6.11.2 Neolithic–Bronze Age.

Crossley, D W, on Bewl Valley ironworks, see Section 6.11.6 Medieval; and on post-medieval archaeology in Britain, see Section 6.11.7 Post-Medieval.

Crowe, Nigel, *English Heritage book of canal architecture*. London: Batsford/EH, 1994, 144 p, bibl, gazetteer, index. o 7134 6884 X.
General survey.

**Day, Joan and Tylecote, R F (eds), *The industrial revolution in metals*. London: Institute of Metals, 1991, vi, 318 p, bibl, index. o 901462 82 9.
'Concise history of the industrial revolution of metals from the early 17th century through to the mid-19th', treating tin, lead, copper, zinc, brass, iron and steel.

Edlin, H L, *Woodland crafts in Britain: an account of the traditional uses of trees and timber in the British countryside*. Newton Abbot: David and Charles 1973 (reprint of 1949 original), x, 182 p, index. o 7153 5852 9.
Classic account.

Evans, D H and Tomlinson, D G on medieval dyeworks in Beverley, see Section 6.11.6 Medieval.

Falconer, Keith, *Guide to England's industrial heritage*. London: Batsford, 1980, 270 p, index. o 7134 1343 3.
County gazetteer of the most important industrial monuments and sites.

—, (gen ed), *Batsford guide to the industrial*

archaeology of the British Isles. 1976–80. A series of six volumes; Fred Brook on the West Midlands (1977), A J Haselfoot on SE England (1978), David Alderton and John Booker on East Anglia (1980), and C A and R A Buchanan on Central Southern England (1980), plus two by J R Hume which are listed in the Scottish section below.

Fearn, Jacqueline, *Cast iron. Shire album,* 250, 1990, 32 p. 0 7478 0083 9 pb.
Brief introduction to processes and products.

Fitzrandolph, H E and Hay, M D, *The rural industries of England and Wales.* Oxford: OUP, 1926–7, 4 vols.
A survey made for the Agricultural Economy Research Institute, Oxford, which may still be useful.

*Frank, Susan, *Glass and archaeology.* London: Academic Press, 1982, xi, 155 p, bibl, index. 0 12 265620 2.
Includes a chapter on how to search for information on glass history.

**Giles, Colum and Goodall, Ian, *Yorkshire textile mills: the buildings of the Yorkshire textile industry 1770–1930.* London: HMSO for RCHME/WYAS, 1992, 274 p, bibl, index. 0 11 300038 3.
An important contribution to the study of the industrial revolution in England.

*Godfrey, Eleanor S, *The development of English glass-making 1560–1640.* Oxford: Clarendon Press, 1975, 288 p, bibl, index. 0 19 828267 2.
The standard work on an important industry, including techniques, marketing, production costs, specialised glassware, etc.

Goodman, W L, *The history of woodworking tools.* London: Bell and Sons, 1964, 208 p, bibl, index.
Many tools are illustrated and described, and relevant museums listed.

Green, E R R (ed), *Industrial archaeology of the British Isles.* 1965–c. 86. A major series from David and Charles covered the following regions, all with gazetteers of sites and bibliographies: *Cornwall* (A C Todd and P Laws, 1972); *Dartmoor* (Helen Harris, 3 rev edn 1986), *Derbyshire* (F Nixon, 1969); *East Midlands* (D M Smith, 1965); *Hertfordshire* (W Branch Johnson, 1970); *Isle of Man* (T A Bawden et al, 1972); *Lake Counties* (J D Marshall and M Davies-Shiel, 2 edn at Beck-

ermet: Michael Moon, 1977); *Lancashire* (O Ashmore, 1969); *North East England* (Frank Atkinson, 2 vols 1974); *The Peak District* (Helen Harris, 1971); *Southern England* (Kenneth Hudson, 1965); *Staffordshire* (R Sherlock, 1976); *The Tamar Valley* (Frank Booker, rev edn 1971). Associated volume: *The Bristol region* (A Buchanan and N Cossons, 1969). *See also under Wales, Scotland and Ireland below.*

*Hadfield, Charles, *British canals: an illustrated history.* Newton Abbot: David and Charles, 7 edn 1984, 367 p, bibl, index. 0 7153 8568 2.
The doyen of British canal studies also published a regional series with David and Charles (not separately listed here). See also Baldwin and Burton (above).

Hague, D B on lighthouses, see Section 6.19 Maritime, nautical and underwater archaeology.

Harvey, Nigel, *The industrial archaeology of farming in England and Wales.* London: Batsford, 1980, 232 p, bibl, index. 0 7134 1845 1.

Historical Metallurgy Society, *Metallurgical sites in Britain: priorities for research and preservation.* London: HMS, 1991, 12 p.

***Hodges, Henry, *Artifacts: an introduction to early materials and technology.* London: Duckworth, 3 edn 1989, 251 p, bibl, index. 0 7156 2316 8 pb.
The standard work: covers pottery, glazes, metals, glass, stone, wood, organic materials, with bibliography for each.

Holt, Richard, on medieval mills, see Section 6.11.6 Medieval.

Hoover, Herbert C and Hoover, L H, *Georgius Agricola De re metallica: translated from the first Latin edition of 1556.* New York: Dover, 1950 [straight repr of 1912 edn], xxi, 638 p, indexes.
Classic early metallurgical work. *See also Kuhner and Rizzo below.*

Hudson, Kenneth, *Industrial history from the air.* Cambridge: CUP, 1984, xv, 139 p, narrative bibl, index. 0 521 25333 0.
Text with illustrations, mostly of English sites, a few Scottish, with the social and environmental comment this author always provides.

INDUSTRIAL ARCHAEOLOGY OF THE BRITISH ISLES series, see under Green above.

Industrial archaeology review: special numbers have been published as follows: *Metal mining heritage* (as vol 12.1, 1989); *Textile mills* (16.1, 1993); and *the National Trust* (18.1, 1995).

Jenkins, J Geraint (ed), *The woollen textile industry in Great Britain*. London: Routledge and Kegan Paul, 1972, xv, 309 p, bibl, index. The 17 papers include J P Wild on prehistoric and RB textiles, M Ryder on wools, and other contributors on techniques, machinery, etc.

Jones, E, *Industrial architecture in Britain 1750–1939*. London: Batsford, 1985, 240 p, bibl, index. 0 7134 2532 6.

Kelley, D W, *Charcoal and charcoal burning*. Shire album, 159, 1986, 32 p. 0 85263 731 4 pb.

*Kenyon, G H, *The glass industry of the Weald*. Leicester: Leicester Univ Press, 1967, xxii, 231 p, bibl.
Classic work on the medieval industry, to be read now in the context of later works.

Kuhner, D and Rizzo, T, *The Herbert Clark Hoover collection of mining and metallurgy*. Claremont (Calif): Libraries of the Claremont Colleges, 1980, xvii, 219 p. 0 937368 00 8.
Catalogue of 912 items pre-AD 1800.

Lines, C, *Companion to the industrial revolution*. New York: Facts on File, 1990, x, 262 p, bibl. 0 8160 2157 0.

McKnight, H, *The Shell book of inland waterways*. Newton Abbot: David and Charles, 2 edn 1981, 493 p, index. 0 7153 8239 X.

Major, J Kenneth, *Fieldwork in industrial archaeology*. London: Batsford, 1975, 176 p, bibl, index.
Practical guide.

—, *Animal-powered engines*. London: Batsford, 1978, 168 p, bibl, index. 0 7134 0918 5.
Gazetteer and discussion of a formerly important power source. (*See also author's Shire album, 128, 1985, on the same topic.*)

Oddy, W A (ed), *Aspects of early metallurgy*. Brit Mus occas publs, 17, 2 edn 1991, 192 p, bibls. 0 86159 016 3 pb.
Contains the original 15 papers from the 1977 edition plus three new ones on prehistoric topics.

Paget-Tomlinson, E, *The illustrated history of canals and river navigations*. Sheffield: Sheffield

Academic Press, 1994, xv, 400 p, bibl, index. 1 85075 276 1.

Palmer, Marilyn and Neaverson, Peter, *Industrial landscapes of the East Midlands*. Chichester: Phillimore, 1992, xv, 208 p, bibl. 0 85033 829 8.
Covers Leics, Notts, Northants, Derbys.

— and —, *Industry in the landscape 1700–1900*. London: Routledge, 1994, x, 214 p, bibl. 0 415 11206 0.

— (eds), *Managing the industrial heritage*. Leicester: Univ Leicester School of Archaeological Studies (= *Leicester archaeol monogr*, 2), 1995, 150 p. 0 9510377 5 7 pb.
Contributions to a conference: RCHME, English Heritage and AIA staff; sections on establishing what exists; contexts of sites; priorities; protecting important sites.

*Parsons, David (ed), *Stone quarrying and building in England AD 43–1525*. Chichester: Phillimore/RAI, 1990, xii, 244 p, bibl, index. 0 85033 768 2.
Papers from a 1988 conference at Loughborough.

Proudfoot, Christopher and Walker, Philip, *Woodworking tools*. Oxford: Phaidon/Christie's, 1984, 160 p, bibl, index. 0 7148 8005 1.
A survey of types.

READINGS IN GLASS HISTORY. 1973–. Irreg. Jerusalem: Phoenix Publns. Numbers 5, 8, 21 of this occasional series contain topics relevant to European glass making, and number 9 is a cumulative index to numbers 1–8.

*Royal Commission on the Historical Monuments of England (per Anthony Calladine and Jean Fricker), *East Cheshire textile mills*. Swindon: RCHME, 1993, x, 181 p, gazetteer, bibl, index. 1 873592 13 2 pb.
The best introduction to these 18th century silk mills, which were important in the establishment of the factory system in Britain.

Schubert, H R, *History of the British iron and steel industry from c. 450 BC to AD 1775*. London: Routledge and Kegan Paul, 1957, xxi, 445 p, refs, index.
Classic work, to be read now in the light of newer research.

Science Museum guide to the history of technology in Europe, see Carding under Bibliographies earlier in this section.

Scott, B G and Cleere, H F (eds), *The crafts of the blacksmith: essays presented to R F Tylecote . . .* Belfast: Ulster Museum, 1987, 180 p, bibls. o 900761 20 2 pb.
Contains 22 papers, mostly on prehistoric–Roman–AS, with a couple on blast furnaces.

SPAB Wind and Watermill Section, *Mills open.* London: SPAB, 1991, 85 p (new edn in preparation).
Lists c. 300 mills by county, with brief descriptions, locations and opening times.

Straker, Ernest, *Wealden iron.* London: G Bell, 1931, xiv, 487 p. Repr David and Charles 1969, 0 7153 4729 2.
Classic pioneering study (history and topographical survey) of an important medieval and post-medieval industry in Sussex-Surrey-Kent; but see now Cleere and Crossley (above).

Tann, Jennifer, *The development of the factory.* London: Cornmarket, 1970, 175 p. o 7191 2134 5.

Thornes, Robin, *Images of industry: coal.* Swindon: RCHME, 1994, 160 p. 1 873592 23 X pb.
Results of a five-year study of industry, buildings, institutions and communities; includes housing, pithead baths, miners' memorials. Photographs of a vanishing way of life.

Trinder, Barrie, *Industrial archaeology of Shropshire.* Chichester: Phillimore, due late 1995, c. 250 p. 0 85033 989 8.
Brings out many unfamiliar details of this seminal industrial area.

—, *The making of the industrial landscape.* London: Dent, 1982, xii, 278 p, bibl, index. o 460 04427 3.

***Tylecote, R F, *A history of metallurgy.* London: Institute of Metals, 2 edn 1992, xii, 205 p, bibl. o 901462 88 8.
New edition of a standard text with much new material; covers earliest metalworking to 1950. *See also Day and Tylecote above.*

—, *The early history of metallurgy in Europe.* London: Longman, 1987, 352 p, bibl, index. o 582 49195 9.

—, *The prehistory of metallurgy in the British Isles.* London: Inst of Metals, 1986, xiii, 257 p, bibl, index. o 904357 72 4.
Covers the period up to the charcoal blast furnace and fineries.

Wailes, Rex, *The English windmill.* London: Routledge and Kegan Paul, 2 edn 1967, 246 p, bibl, glossary, gazetteer.
Technical and social information.

—, *A source book of windmills and watermills.* London: Ward Lock, 1979, 128 p, index. o 7063 5768 X.
Pocket-sized, basic descriptions, how made and used, many photographs and technical drawings.

Watkins, G, *The steam engine in industry.* Ashbourne: Moorland, 1978, 2 vols. o 903485 65 6.

Williams, M, with Farnie, D A, *Cotton mills in Greater Manchester.* Preston: Carnegie, 1992, xii, 212 p, bibl, index. o 948789 69 7.
The best introduction to the development of the cotton mill.

Williams, Richard, *Limekilns and limeburning. Shire album,* 236, 1989, 32 p. o 7478 0037 5 pb.
Short technological and historical introduction to a long-established trade.

YORKSHIRE TEXTILE MILLS. An index to the RCHME survey archive is held at WYAS (Wakefield).

_____

Wales

SOCIETIES
(addresses in Section 4.2 Organisations)
Welsh Mills Society
Welsh Mines Society

BOOKS
Bennett, J and Vernon, R W, *Mines of the Gwydyr Forest, parts 1–6.* Cheshire: Gwydyr Mines Publns, 1989–, refs, plans.
Traces the history of all known mines in this region NW of Betws-y-coed.

Bick, David, *The old copper mines of Snowdonia.* Newent: The Pound House, 1982, 129 p, refs, index. o 906855 02 7 hb, o 906855 03 5 pb.

—, *The old metal mines of mid-Wales: combined edition.* Newent: The Pound House, 1993, six parts separately paginated in one volume (nearly 400 p), select bibl, indexes. o 906885 12 4.
Also available as separate parts for use in the field. Originally published 1974–8 (parts 1–5), 1991 (part 6). Covers the old counties of

Cardigans and W Montgom, with Aberdovey/ Dinas Mawddwy/Llangynog etc.

Briggs, C S (ed), *Welsh industrial heritage: a review*. CBA res rep, **79, 1992, xii, 168 p, refs, index. 1 872414 13 3 pb.
30 papers (mainly short) from or prompted by a Cadw/CBA conference in Cardiff, 1986. Includes list of scheduled ancient monuments and mine sites.

Gladwin, D D and J M, *The canals of the Welsh valleys and their tramroads*. Oxford: Oakwood Press, 2 edn 1991, 112 p, refs, index. 0 85361 412 1.

Guise, B and Lees, G, *Windmills of Anglesey*. Builth Wells: Attic Books, 1992, 158 p, bibl, index. 0 948083 16 6.
Illustrated historical survey of development and decline of mills and milling on Anglesey, with gazetteer.

Hadfield, Charles, *The canals of South Wales and the Border*. Newton Abbot: David and Charles, 2 edn 1967, 272 p, bibl, index. 0 7153 4027 1.
Includes useful summary of canal facts.

Hague, D B, *A guide to the industrial archaeology of mid-Wales*. ?Telford: Ass for Industrial Archaeol, 1984, 31 p, bibl. (Not available to compiler.)
Description and gazetteer of sites.

See also his lighthouse books in Section 6.19 Maritime, nautical and underwater archaeology.

Hall, G W, *The gold mines of Merioneth*. Gloucester: Griffin, nd, 120 p, index. 0 9502116 3 X.
Traces their development from earliest times to the present.

—, *Metal mines of Southern Wales*. Gloucester: author, 1971, 95 p, index.
Lists and describes every known non-ferrous mine in SW Wales.

Hughes, Stephen, *The Brecon Forest tramroads: the archaeology of an early railway system*. Aberystwyth: RCAHMW, 1990, 367 p, bibl. 1 871184 05 3 pb.
Archaeological and documentary survey of railways in the Swansea Valley; list of significant early railway remains in Wales; recommended walks.

—, *The archaeology of the Montgomeryshire canal: a guide and study in waterways archae-ology*. Aberystwyth: RCAHMW, 1989, 168 p, index. 1 871184 02 9 pb.
Structures and canal of 1794–1821; workers' housing. Gazetteer of selected remains along the Llanymynech branch.

— and Reynolds, Paul, *A guide to the industrial archaeology of the Swansea region*. Telford: Ass Industr Archaeol/RCAHMW, 2 rev edn 1988, 55 p. 0 9508448 2 9 pb.
Lists over 170 sites.

—, Malaws, Brian, Parry, Medwyn and Wakelin, Peter, *Collieries of Wales: engineering and architecture*. Aberystwyth: RCAHMW, [nd but ?1994], 176 p, gazetteer, glossary, index. 1 871184 11 8 pb.

Ince, L, *The South Wales iron industry, 1750–1885*. Cardiff: Merton Priory Press, 1993, 198 p, bibl, index. 0 9518165 1 9.
Detailed historical survey of the rise and fall of the industry.

Jenkins, J Geraint, *The Welsh woollen industry*. Cardiff: Nat Mus Wales, 1969, xviii, 410 p, bibl, index.
Describes techniques and development of mills in each county of Wales.

Lewis, W J, *Lead mining in Wales*. Cardiff; Univ Wales Press, 1967, 415 p, bibl, index.
History and development from earliest times to the present, including techniques.

Lindsay, Jean, *A history of the North Wales slate industry*. Newton Abbot: David and Charles, 1974, 376 p, bibl, index. 0 7153 6264 X.
Comprehensive account of the rise and decline of the industry, with gazetteer of main sites.

Morris, J H and Williams, L J, *The South Wales coal industry 1841–1875*. Cardiff: Univ Wales Press, 1958, xii, 289 p, footnote refs, index.
Traces development of the early industrial period of the industry.

North, F J, *Mining for metals in Wales*. Cardiff: Nat Mus Wales, 1962, viii, 112 p, bibl, index.
Provides a summary of relevant historical and geological literature.

Rees, D Morgan, *Mines, mills and furnaces: an introduction to industrial archaeology in Wales*. London: HMSO, 1969, xiv, 117 p, bibl, index. [o] 11 880083 3.
Introduces the industrial archaeology of Wales through remains of the ferrous works in S Wales and metalliferous mines throughout Wales.

—, *The industrial archaeology of Wales*. Newton Abbot: David and Charles, 1975, 302 p, bibl, index. 0 7153 6819 2.

Richards, Alun John, *A gazetteer of the Welsh slate industry*. Capel Garmon, Llanrwst: Gwasg Carreg Gwalch, 1991, 239 p, bibl. 0 86381 196 5.
Brief archaeological and historical details of over 400 slate quarries and mills.

Sivewright, W J, see under Civil engineering heritage series earlier in this section.

Thomas, W Gerwyn, *Welsh coal mines*. Cardiff: Nat Mus Wales, 1979 and later reprints, 64 p. 0 7200 0059 9 pb.
The North and South Wales coalfields, mainly in pictures.

Scotland

Details of the **Scottish Industrial Heritage Society** will be found in Section 4.2 Organisations (including their guide to selected industrial archaeological sites).

BOOKS
The David and Charles series of the 1960s–70s, with good bibliographies, included works on: *Scotland* (John Butt, 1967); *Galloway* (Ian Donnachie, 1971); and *Canals* (J Lindsay, 1968).

*Bremner, D, *The industries of Scotland: their rise, progress and present condition*. Edinburgh, 1845, republished David and Charles, 1969, [15], viii, 535 p. 0 7153 4385 8.
Classic work with new introduction by Butt and Donnachie.

Calder, Jenni (ed), *The enterprising Scot, Scottish adventure and achievement*. Edinburgh: Roy Mus Scotland, 1986, 172 p, bibl, index. 0 11 492483 x pb.

Douglas, G J et al, *Scottish windmills: a survey*. [Glasgow]: Scott Industrial Archaeol Survey/ RCAHMS, 1984, iii, 124 p. No ISBN.
Lists 62 mills including those on Orkney.

Douglas, Graham and Oglethorpe, Miles, *Brick, tile and fireclay industries in Scotland*. Edinburgh: RCAHMS Scot Industrial Archaeol Survey 1977-83, 1993, 95 p, bibl. 0 7480 0697 4 pb.

***Hay, Geoffrey D and Stell, Geoffrey P, *Monu-

ments of industry: an illustrated historical record*. Edinburgh: RCAHM, 1986, xii, 248 p, footnote refs, glossary, index. 0 11 492457 0.
Fully illustrated account of monuments relating to farming, fishing, whisky distilling, textiles, extractive industries and so on.

Hume, J R, *The industrial archaeology of Scotland*:
   1,*The Lowlands and Borders*. London: Batsford, 1976, 279 p, bibl, index. 0 7134 3234 9
   2, *The Highlands and Islands*. London: Batsford, 1977, 335 p, bibl, index. 0 7134 0809 x
Regional survey and site lists.

*—, *Industrial archaeology of Glasgow*. Glasgow: Blackie, 1974, xviii, 327 p. 0 216 89833 1.
Crucial volume providing the benchmark before huge clearances of industrial heritage in the second city of the former British Empire.

—, *Scotland's industrial past: an introduction to Scotland's industrial history with a catalogue of preserved material*. Edinburgh: Nat Mus Scotl/ Scottish Mus Council, 1990, vii, 72 p, index. 0 948636 22 x pb.
Excellent summary of Scotland's industrial development, with an account of industrial artefacts taken into the care of museums in Scotland.

— and Moss, M, *Workshop of the British Empire: engineering and shipbuilding in the west of Scotland*. London: Heinemann, 1977, xvi, 192 p, bibl, index. 0 435 32590 6.
Heavy industry in and around Glasgow.

*Johnston, I, *Beardmore built: the rise and fall of a Clydeside shipyard*. Clydebank: Clydebank District Lib Mus Dept, 1993, 194 p. 0 906938 08 2 (hb), 0 906938 05 8 (pb)
Excellent account, well illustrated, of one of Scotland's most important engineering and shipbuilding companies.

*Mackay, Sheila, *The Forth Bridge: a picture history*. Edinburgh: HMSO/RCAHMS, 2 edn 1993, 112 p. 0 11 495183 7 pb.
Excellent account of the building of Scotland's most important industrial monument, with contemporary photographs.

Moss, M and Hume, J R *The making of Scotch whisky: a history of the Scotch whisky distilling industry*. Edinburgh: James and James, 1981, 303 p, bibl, index. 0 907383 00 9.

Covers Scotland's largest surviving manufacturing industry.

Munro, R W on Scottish lighthouses, see entry in Section 6.19 Maritime, nautical and underwater archaeology.

Nicolson, M and O'Neill, M, *Glasgow, locomotive builder to the world.* Glasgow: Polygon Books, 1987, 44 p. 0 948275 46 4.
Well illustrated brief guide to an important Glasgwegian industry.

Oglethorpe, Miles (comp), *Catalogue of records compiled by the Scottish Industrial Archaeology Survey, 1977–85.* Edinburgh: RCAHMS, [1990], 0 7480 0305 3 pb.
Over 150 sites recorded and listed by topography, function and thematic surveys.

Sanderson, K W, *The Scottish refractory industry 1830–1980.* Edinburgh: privately published, 1990, 185 p. 0 9515625 0 9.
The author worked in this industry in which Scotland dominated the world.

Shaw, John, *Water power in Scotland: 1550–1870.* Edinburgh: John Donald, 1984, xi, 606 p, bibl, index. 0 85976 072 3.
Mainly historical account.

*Watson, M, *Jute and flax mills in Dundee.* Tayport: Hutton, 1990, 248 p, bibl, index. 0 907033 51 2.
Detailed account of world-dominant industry, with illustrated gazetteer.

Isle of Man

Garrad, L S et al, *The industrial archaeology of the Isle of Man.* Newton Abbot: David and Charles, 1972, 266 p, bibl, index. 0 7153 5440 X.

Ireland

Societies and organisations (addresses given in Section 4.2 Organisations)

Inland Waterways Association of Ireland
Inland Waterways Northern Ireland
Joint Committee on the Industrial Heritage (N Ireland)
Railway Preservation Society of Ireland

BOOKS

Barry, Michael, *Across deep waters: bridges of Ireland.* Rathgar (Dublin): Frankfort Press, 1985, 160 p, bibl, index. 0 9510696 0 8.

Treats railway and suspension bridges, canals, details, road/river/sea.

Beckett, J C et al, *Belfast: the making of the city 1800–1914.* Belfast: Appletree Press, 1982, 187 p. 0 86281 100 7 hb, 0 86281 119 8 pb.

Bielenberg, Andy, *Cork's industrial revolution 1780–1880: development or decline?* Cork: Cork Univ Press, 1991, viii, 171 p, index. 0 902561 58 8 hb, 0 902561 59 6 pb.

Clarke, Peter, *The Royal Canal: the complete story.* Dublin: Elo Publ, 1992, 176 p, bibl, index. 0 9519593 2 8.

Delany, Ruth, *Ireland's Royal Canal 1789–1992.* Dublin: Lilliput, 1993, vii, 216 p, bibl, index. 0 946640 92 0.

—, *A celebration of 250 years of Ireland's inland waterways.* Belfast: Appletree Press, 1986, 200 p, bibl, index. 0 86281 129 5 hb, 0 86281 200 3 pb.

—, *The Grand Canal of Ireland.* Newton Abbot: David and Charles, 1973, 255 p, refs, index. 0 7153 5972 X.
Both of these books, and the next, are mainly historical treatments.

Delany, V T H and Delany, D R, *The canals of the south of Ireland.* Newton Abbot: David and Charles, 1966, 260 pp, refs, index.
Mainly historical treatment of the Grand, Royal, Shannon Navigation and other navigations.

Gailey, R A, *Spade-making in Ireland.* Cultra: Ulster Folk and Transport Museum, 1982. 0 902588 09 5 pb.

***Green, E R R, *The industrial archaeology of County Down.* Belfast: HMSO, 1963, vii, 99 p, bibl, index.
Particular topics include the linen industry, grain milling, brewing, distilling and flax scutching; communications.

Gribbon, H D, *The history of waterpower in Ulster.* Newton Abbot: David and Charles, 1969, 299 p, bibl, index. [0] 7153 4465 X.

**Hamond, Fred, *Antrim coast and glens: industrial heritage.* Belfast: HMSO for DoENI, 1991, 108 p. 0 337 08280 4.
Excellent introduction to this rich area and gazetteer of over 100 sites to visit.

McCaughan, Michael, *Steel and iron, ships and men: shipbuilding in Belfast 1894–1912.* The

Harland and Wolff historic photograph collection at the Ulster Folk and Transport Museum. Belfast: Friar's Bush, 1989, 104 p. 0 946872 23 6.

Contains the best examples of photographs of ships and shipbuilding at Harland and Wolff's shipyards, Belfast, 1894–1912.

**McCutcheon, W A, *The industrial archaeology of northern Ireland*. Belfast: HMSO for DoENI, 1980, xlv, 395 p, bibl, indexes. 0 337 08154 9. Compendium of information on roads and bridges, canals and inland navigations, railways, animal/wind/water/steam power, flax and linen, the Tyrone coalfield, conservation and preservation.

—, *The canals of the north of Ireland*. Dawlish: David and Charles, 1965, 180 p, bibl, refs.

—, *Wheel and spindle: aspects of Irish industrial history*. Belfast: Blackstaff, 1977, viii, 83 p, bibl, index. 0 85640 098 X pb.

The McCutcheon Archive, a 'major source for Irish industrial archaeology', is described by N Cunningham in Ulster Local Studies, *15.1, Summer 1993.*

O'Keeffe, Peter and Simington, Tom, *Irish stone bridges: history and heritage*. Blackrock, Co Dublin: Ir Acad Press, 1991, 352 p, bibl. 0 7165 2465 1.
Well-documented survey.

Rynne, Colin, *The industrial archaeology of Cork City and its environs: a sites and monuments record*. Dublin: Roy Ir Acad, 1991, 28 p.
A framework awaiting full descriptions.

6.16
Garden Archaeology and History

The archaeology of gardens is a relatively new topic, although documentary garden history has been studied for much longer. Relevant organisations, journals and bibliographies are listed first, then follow books. Wales, Scotland and Ireland are treated separately. Note that the county-by-county *Register of historic gardens* produced by English Heritage (1984–8) has now been absorbed into county SMRs. The 1995 edition of it, by David Lambert, can be consulted at English Heritage, the Royal Horticultural Society, Institute of Advanced Architectural Studies and in local authority records. The contact at EH is Krysia Campbell, tel 0171 973 3242. A useful brief history of garden archaeology by Lorna McRobie is in EH's *Conservation bull*, 28, 1996, pp 14–15.

Organisations

(Addresses and other details will be found in Section 4.2 Organisations)

Association of Garden Trusts
Folly Fellowship
Fountain Society
Garden History Society (publishes occasional *Register of research*, both completed and in progress)
Historic Gardens Foundation
Institute of Advanced Architectural Studies' Landscapes and Gardens section (The King's Manor, York YO1 2EP) has replaced the former Centre for Conservation of Historic Parks and Gardens
Northern Ireland Heritage Gardens Committee
Tradescant Trust
Welsh Historic Gardens Trust
National botanical collections are at:
    Royal Botanic Gardens, Kew, Richmond, Surrey TW9 3AB (tel 0181 332 5000)
    Royal Botanic Garden, 20A Inverleith Row, Edinburgh EH3 5LR (tel 0131 552 7171)
    [Irish] **National Botanic Garden**, Glasnevin, Dublin 7 (tel Dublin 837 4388)

Journals

European gardens (awaiting ISSN). 1996–. 2/yr. Historic Gardens Foundation.

Garden history (0307–1243). 1973–. 2/yr. Garden History Society. Indexed from 1966–86, ie includes the early form of this journal as a quarterly newsletter from 1966. (The Newsletter continues to supply much useful information.)

Journal of garden history (0144–5170). 1981–. 4/yr. Taylor and Francis. [Landscape format]. (The volumes for 1982–4 inclusive, plus 1986, contained current bibliographies of garden history.)

Landscape design: journal of the Landscape Institute (0020–2908). 1934–.

Bibliography and reference works

**Desmond, Ray, *A bibliography of British gardens*. Winchester: St Paul's Bibliographies, corr repr 1988, viii, 318 p. 0 906795 15 X.

—, *A bibliography of garden history*. Garden Hist Soc, 1990.

**Lambert, David, Goodchild, Peter and Roberts, Judith, *Researching a garden's history: a guide to documentary and published sources*. Reigate: Landscape Design Trust, [new edn] 1995, 28 p, refs. 0 9518377 0 2 pb.
Invaluable and very practical 'How to' manual which includes lists of publications and resources to consult. (Replaces the edition of 1991 which itself replaced one by J Gallagher 1984.)

*Symes, Michael, *A glossary of garden history*. Princes Risborough: *Shire garden hist*, 6, 1993, 144 p, bibl, index. 0 7478 0223 8 pb.
Over 500 entries, illustrated; includes an appendix on notable garden designers, 17th–20th centuries.

Books

BRITAIN GENERALLY

Anthony, John, *The Renaissance garden in Britain*. *Shire garden hist*, 4, 1991, 96 p. 0 7478 0130 4 pb.

Binney, Marcus and Hills, Anne, *Elysian gardens*. London: SAVE Britain's Heritage, 1979, 72 p. pb.
Mainly consists of aerial views of historic gardens: accompanied a Victoria and Albert Museum exhibition and shows the importance of the formal layout as an element in the history of British gardens. Examines the need for protection of historic gardens.

**Brown, A E (ed), *Garden archaeology: papers presented to a conference . . . 1988. CBA res rep*, 78, 1991, ix, 198 p, bibls, index. 1 872414 17 6 pb.
Contains 15 papers on Romano-British gardens to modern restorations like Painshill; includes air photographic sites. Covers England, Wales and Scotland.

Brown, Jane, *The art and architecture of English gardens: designs for the garden from the collection of the [RIBA], 1609 to the present day*. London: Weidenfeld and Nicolson, 1989, 320 p, bibl, index. 0 297 79638 0.

Elliott, Brent, *Victorian gardens*. London: Batsford, 1986, 285 p, bibl, index. 0 7134 4763 X.

English Heritage (per Carol Colson), *Preparing restoration schemes: a guide for professional advisors: the repair of storm damage to historic parks and gardens*. London: EH, 1988, 10 p leaflet.

Fawcett, E, *Garden statue and ornament survey*. London: ICOMOS UK, 1993, 22p, No ISBN.

Goulty, Sheena, *Heritage gardens: care, conservation, management*. London: Routledge, 1993, xvi, 176 p, bibl, index. 0 415 07474 6 pb.

Hadfield, Miles, *The English landscape garden*. *Shire garden hist*, 3, 2 edn 1988, 72 p. 0 85263 919 8 pb.

Harvey, John, *Restoring period gardens*. Princes Risborough: *Shire garden hist*, 1, 1988, 112 p, bibl. 0 85263 952 X pb.
This author has also published several specialised works on early gardening catalogues, nurserymen and the like. (*See also his book on medieval gardens, listed in Section 6.11.6 Medieval.*)

Hayden, Peter, *Biddulph Grange Staffordshire: a Victorian garden rediscovered*. London: Geo Philip, 1989, 160 p, bibl, index. 0 540 01192 4.
On a garden currently under restoration by the National Trust.

Jacques, D, *Georgian gardens: the reign of Nature*. London: Batsford, 1983, 240 p, bibl, index. 0 7134 3456 2 (not seen).

— and van der Horst, A J, *The gardens of William and Mary*. London: Croom Helm, 1988, xiii, 224 p, bibl, index. 0 7470 1608 9.

Jones, Barbara, *Follies and grottoes*. London: Constable, 2 edn 1974, xx, 459 p, bibl, index. 0 09 459350 7.

Moe, D, Dickson, J H and Jørgensen, P M (eds), *Garden history: garden plants, species, forms and varieties from Pompeii to 1800. PACT, 42,* 1994.
Symposium volume. (Not available to compiler.)

NATIONAL TRUST. Garden surveys have been made to assist management plans at various properties, eg Castle Coole, Stowe, etc: see also Hayden above.

Robinson, John Martin, *Temples of delight: Stowe landscape gardens.* Andover: Pitkin Pictorial/Nat Trust, 1990, 176 p, bibl, index. 0 85372 732 5 hb, 0 85372 733 3 pb.
Seductively illustrated, traces the development of a celebrated landscape garden (currently undergoing restoration by the National Trust).

Strong, Roy, *The Renaissance garden in England.* London: Thames and Hudson, 1979, 240 p, refs, index. 0 500 01209 1.
Historical treatment with many illustrations and contemporary plans from Henry VIII to the outbreak of the Civil War.

Swindells, Philip (ed), *The care and conservation of historic garden landscapes.* London [now Tisbury]: Cathedral Communications Ltd (= *Building conservation directory special rep*, 2), 1994, 36 p. 0 9520080 4 1 pb.
Contains several articles and a long list of useful addresses.

Taigel, Anthea and Williamson, Tom, *Parks and gardens.* London: Batsford (Know the Landscape series), 1993, 160 p, bibl, index. 0 7134 6728 2 pb.
Social and economic history of parks, including urban and suburban green spaces as well as large country estates.

**Taylor, Christopher, *The archaeology of gardens.* Princes Risborough: *Shire archaeol*, 30, 1983, 72 p, bibl, index. 0 85263 625 3 pb.
By an author with a fair claim to be the father of garden archaeology in Britain.

Thacker, Christopher, *England's historic gardens.* London: [Hodder] Headline, 1989, 160 p, bibl, index. 0 7472 0110 2.
Many photographs; book includes about 100 sites (nearly all of Grade I) with visible remains (though not necessarily open to the public).

—, *The genius of gardening: the history of gardens in Britain and Ireland.* London: Dent, 1994, 304 p. 0 460 86149 2.
Covers planning, design, landscaping, planting styles, tools and techniques, socio-economic aspects. From Druid groves through Roman and medieval gardens.

*Thurley, Simon (ed), *The king's privy garden at Hampton Court Palace 1689–1995.* London: Apollo Magazine, [1995], 118 p. 0 95220 816 4 pb.
Several contributors give accounts of the extensive programme of documentary and archaeological research which preceded the reconstruction of William III's garden.

WALES

Cadw, Register of landscapes, parks and gardens of special historic interest in Wales (Cardiff, 1994) – for Gwent and Clwyd (others to appear: Dyfed, late 1996; Gwynedd, early 1997).

Whittle, Elizabeth, *The historic gardens of Wales: an introduction to parks and gardens in the history of Wales.* London: HMSO for Cadw, 1992, 80 p, gazetteer, index. 0 11 701578 4 pb.
Treats Roman and medieval gardens to Edwardian and beyond.

See also Brown, A E under Britain general above.

SCOTLAND

Some references to gardens occur in the *Buildings of Scotland* series (1984–) and in the illustrated architectural guides of the Royal Incorporation of Architects in Scotland (1985–). The **Scottish Record Office Map Collection** and other relevant documents have been indexed for garden history purposes, text available at West Register House, Edinburgh.

**Dingwall, Christopher, *Researching historic gardens in Scotland: a guide to information sources. Scot Natur Herit Rev*, 54, 1955, 57 p, refs.
Excellent guide listing many sources, printed and other: good list of pre-1810 travellers' accounts. A consolidated bibliography would have made for easier use.

**Land Use Consultants (ed E Banks), *An inventory of gardens and designed landscapes in Scotland.* Battleby: Countryside Comm Scotl/

SDD(HBM), 1988, 5 vols [by region], 1917 p, bibl, index. 0 902226 91 6.

Vol 1 gives the methodology and a summary; vols 2–5 describe 275 of the most important historic gardens, arranged alphabetically by region. Bibliography in each volume; raw data deposited at NMRS.

*Tait, A A, *The landscape garden in Scotland 1735–1835.* Edinburgh: EUP, 1980, xi, 282 p, refs, index. 0 85224 372 3.

Important sourcebook which documented all major gardens of this period in the hope of their preservation; detailed footnotes, good index.

See also Brown, A E under Britain general above.

IRELAND

Glin, The Knight of and Bowe, Patrick (eds), *Gardens of outstanding interest in the Republic of Ireland: a preliminary list.* Dublin: [An Taisce], 1980, 16 p.

Howley, James, *The follies and garden buildings of Ireland.* New Haven/London: Yale Univ Press, 1993, 251 p, bibl, index. 0 300 05577 3.
Survey drawings of new and old follies, insights into 18th and 19th century attitudes and so on.

Jupp, Belinda, *[Northern Ireland] Heritage Gardens inventory.* Belfast: Inst of Irish Studies (QUB) for N Ireland Heritage Gardens Committee, 1992, 97 p. 0 853894 18 3.

Lamb, J G D and Bowe, P T P, *A history of gardening in Ireland.* Dublin: Stationery Office, 1995. 0 7076 1666 2. (Not available to compiler.)

Malins, Edward and The Knight of Glin, *Lost demesnes: Irish landscape gardening 1660–1845.* London: Barrie and Jenkins, 1976, 208 p, refs, index. 0 214 20275 5.

N Ireland Heritage Gardens Committee, *Northern gardens: gardens and parks of outstanding historic interest in Northern Ireland.* Belfast: Ulster Archit Herit Soc for ICOMOS, 1982, 23 p.

See also second item under Thacker above; and see archive on historic parks, gardens and demesnes at Environment Service: Historic Monuments and Buildings, 5–33 Hill Street, Belfast BT1 2LA. A proposed inventory of historic gardens in the Republic remains a distant prospect at the time of writing.

6.17
Place-Names and Local History

These topics are treated together as they are so much interlinked. **Place-name studies** have to be treated with great caution, as this is a multi-disciplinary subject involving linguistics, topography and local history, among other topics. There really is no place these days for the 'folk etymology' which crops up in so many popular works. The principal authoritative source for England is the great county series of the English Place-Name Society (EPNS), which began in 1923 and is still issuing yearly volumes. However, there was a considerable revolution in place-name studies during the 1960s and '70s, and even the EPNS volumes issued before that need careful use because so many interpretations have changed. The decade of the 1990s was forecast as likely to be even more productive, and it will also yield the new dictionary of English place-names to replace Ekwall (see below). Readers are advised to study the two books by Margaret Gelling listed below before embarking on any project involving place-names.

For **local history studies** there are enormous numbers of introductory texts, aids, study packs and journals/magazines; only a few titles can be entered here. The *Oxford companion to local and family history* (listed under Hey in Bibliography and Reference below) must now be the best of the reference works, although it is rather light on archaeological aspects. Consult your Local Studies Librarian for assistance on particular topics; and if there is a relevant VCH (Victoria County History) volume, consult that first.

As in other sections of this guide, the most important works are starred. This section is divided as follows:

Societies
Periodicals
Bibliography and reference works
General works and study aids for English local history
Wales
Scotland
Channel Islands
Isle of Man
Ireland

Margaret Gelling kindly made many improvements to an early draft of this section, and the

Scottish entries owe a lot to Simon Taylor, but any remaining errors are the compiler's alone.

Societies

For local history the umbrella body is the **British Association for Local History (BALH)**; for place-names the **Society for Name Studies in Britain and Ireland** (addresses of both will be found in Section 4.2 Organisations). Susanna Guy's resource book (listed below) is very useful on societies and their journals; and the following directory, though greatly in need of revision, may give some hints to follow up:

Pinhorn, M, *Historical, archaeological and kindred societies in the United Kingdom: a list.* Hulverstone Manor, IoW: Pinhorns, 1986, 105 p, pb.
Out of print and out of date in many details. The magazine *Local History* offers regular revisions, or BALH may be consulted.

Periodicals – England (mainly)

Place-names

*Journal of the English Place-Name Society (1351–3095). 1968/9–. Includes bibliography of recent works as well as articles.

Nomina, a journal of name studies relating to Great Britain and Ireland (0141–6340). 1977–. Annual. Society for Name Studies in Britain and Ireland.
A specialised journal, not really for the beginner, but often enjoyable to read.

Local history

Local historian (0024–5585) from the British Association for Local History (address in Section 4.2 Organisations), and the more informal publication *Local history news* (0969–3521, c/o D Hayns, Stoke Cottage, Church Street, Malpas, Cheshire SY14 8PD)

Local history magazine (0266–2698), 3 Devonshire Promenade, Lenton, Nottingham NG7 2DS (contains annual directory of relevant societies, and occasional cumulative indexes of its contents)

Local studies librarian (0263–0273) although primarily for librarians can contain material of general interest (Library Association Local Studies Group, c/o Ian Jamieson, Dept Information and Library Management, University of Northumbria, Lipman Building, Sandyford Road, Newcastle NE1 8ST)

Bibliography and reference works

Bristow, Joy, *The local historian's glossary and vade mecum.* Nottingham: Nottingham Univ (= *Centre for Local History rec ser*, 8), 2 enl edn 1994, 277 p, bibl. 1 85041 069 0 pb.
Gives words and terms, currency, regnal years, Latin words, trades and occupations, weights and measures (etc).

**Early Charters series (from Leicester University): see entries in Section 6.11.5 Migration and early medieval; these help with topography.

***Ekwall, Eilert, *English river names.* Oxford: Clarendon Press, 1928, xcii, 488 p, index.
Classic work not yet superseded.

***—, *Concise Oxford dictionary of English place-names.* Oxford: OUP, 4 edn 1960, l, 546 p.
Also a classic work but now out of date and currently under revision. Even so, A D Mills rates it as 'still indispensable'.

***English Place-Name Society, The University, Nottingham NG7 2RD.
Produces annual volumes, one or more of which deal with a single county. Not yet treated are Cornwall, Co Durham, Hampshire, Herefordshire, Kent, Lancashire, Leicestershire, Northumberland, Somerset and Suffolk. Norfolk, Shropshire and Lincolnshire are in progress at the time of writing. Remember that the 1960s 'revolution' in place-name studies means that earlier volumes have to be used with care. A guide to the various corrigenda and addenda is listed under Hough below; and see A H Smith's volume on place-name elements below. The Society also has a Field Name Project, aiming to prepare booklets on the field names of small, localised areas; two of these were published in 1976 and 1984 respectively, and more are in preparation. Note that a computer database for place-names is under development at Nottingham.

**Fellows Jensen, Gillian, 'Place-names and settlement history: a review with a select bibliography of works mostly published since 1960', *Northern history*, 13, 1977, pp 1–26.
Worth pursuing for its bibliography alone.

**Field, John, *English field-names: a dictionary.*

Newton Abbot: David and Charles, 1972, xxx, 291 p, bibl, index. 0 7153 5710 7.

Field-names are defined as 'names of all pieces of land forming part of the agrarian economy of a town or village', many of which are long-lived and sometimes date to 12th/13th centuries, though the main sources for this volume are 19th century.

Fisher, medieval farming glossary, see Section 6.14 Landscape.

***Guy, Susanna (comp), *English local studies handbook. A guide to resources for each county including libraries, record offices, societies, journals and museums.* Exeter: Univ Exeter Press, 1992, xiv, 343 p. 0 85989 369 3 pb.

Listed here for its indispensable collection of data: a true 'vade mecum'.

***Hey, David (ed), *The Oxford companion to local and family history.* Oxford: OUP, 1996, x, 517 p, article refs. 0 19 211688 6.

The place to start for any local history topic as it rapidly justifies its cost. Over 2,000 entries (some brief, some substantial) from 16 specialist contributors introduce almost every aspect of the subject. For archaeology, however, other sources are better.

Hough, Carole, *The English Place-Name Survey: a finding list to addenda and corrigenda.* Nottingham: Centre for English Name Studies, 1995, vi, 126 p. 0 9525343 1 2 pb.

Marcan, Peter, *London's local history: an annotated catalogue of publications and resources issued by Greater London local authorities, local historical and archaeological societies . . . .* High Wycombe: Peter Marcan, 1983, 62 p, refs. 0 9504211 6 2 pb.

Libraries were enjoined to keep this edition on their shelves as it is not really superseded by the edition produced a decade later.

—, *Greater London local history directory and bibliography: a borough-by-borough guide to local history organisations, their activities, and publications.* London: P Marcan, 2 edn 1993, 111 p. 1 871811 08 2.

Considerably revised and enlarged over previous edition, while not replacing it.

**Martin, Charles Trice, *The record interpreter, see Section 2.1 Record offices . . . .*

Mills, A D, *A dictionary of English place-names.*

Oxford: OUP, 1991, xxvii, 388 p, bibl, glossary. 0 19 869156 4 hb, 0 19 283131 3 pb.

Covers over 12,000 names in handy size, and one reviewer found it indispensable, but its inevitable compression may suggest recourse to the relevant EPNS volume if there is one.

Nicolaisen, W F H et al, *The names of towns and cities in Britain.* London: Batsford, 1970, 215 p, short bibl. [o] 7134 0113 3 (also rev pb 1986). Compilers are M Gelling, Melville Richards and the editor; places are listed in alphabetical order.

Richardson, John, *The local historian's encyclopaedia.* New Barnet: Historical Publications, 2 rev edn 1986, 263 p, index. 0 950365 67 X. A basic work listing useful sources by topic, eg land and agriculture, roads and transport. The archaeological section needs revision.

Rivet, A L F and Smith, C on place-names of Roman Britain, see Section 6.11.4 Romano-British.

Royal Commission on Historical Manuscripts, *Principal family and estate collections: family names A–K.* London: HMSO (= *Guide to sources of British history,* 10), 1996, xv, 118 p, select index. First of two volumes giving summary details of collections known to the National Register of Archives.

*Smith, A H, *English place-name elements.* 2 vols, EPNS 25, 26, 1956. Reprinted CUP 1970 (0 521 04918 0 and 0 521 04919 9). Partly overtaken by events during the 1960s–70s (see introduction to this section).

***Spittal, Jeffrey and Field, John, *A reader's guide to the place-names of the United Kingdom. A bibliography of publications (1920–89) on the place-names of Great Britain and Northern Ireland, the Isle of Man, and the Channel Islands.* Stamford: Paul Watkins, 1990, xxi, 341 pp, indexes. 1 871615 10 0. A valuable and comprehensive reference work, based on counties but ranging from general works down to village level, with some annotations and caveats. (J Freeman's review in *Nomina*, 15, 1991–2 adds some more titles, and a supplement to Spittal and Field is due in 1996.)

Victoria History of the Counties of England (familiarly known as 'VCH'). These are the great red volumes which form such a prominent feature of every local history and archaeology library; the enterprise began, as its name indicates, under Queen Victoria and still continues in some counties today, though currently under financial strain. The emphasis is always on written records and the organisation is by parish. The early volumes treated manorial history in exhausting detail, and their archaeological chapters have to be treated with caution. However, volumes produced in more recent years, say 1960s onwards, may have a good summary of the archaeological knowledge of their time. A complete list of volumes issued may be found in the *General Introduction* (1970) and its supplement (1990), both with somewhat basic indexes. A useful map of progress is in C R Elrington's 'The Victoria County History' in *Local historian*, 22, 1992, pp 128–37; and the *Oxford companion to local and family history* has a good article on it, pp 473–4.

General works and study aids for English local history

Alcock, N W, *Old title deeds: a guide for local and family historians*. Chichester: Phillimore, 1986, 91 p. 0 85033 593 0.
Covers 12th to 20th century and brings out the evidence for buildings and topography that may be found in deeds. *See also Dibben below.*

Barratt, D M and Vaizey, D G, *Oxfordshire: a handbook for students of local history*. Oxford: Blackwell, 1973, 83 p, refs. 0 631 15420 5.
This single example must stand for many excellent county publications which help you to find your way round the rich local sources; check for one covering your own area.

Bettey, J H, *Church and parish: an introduction for local historians*. London: Batsford, 1987, 174 pp, glossary, bibl, index. 0 7134 5101 7 hb, 0 7134 5102 5 pb.
How to find and use the available resources, from Saxon Christianity to 19th century.

***Cameron, Kenneth, *English place-names*. London: Batsford, rev edn 1996, 256 p, refs, index. 0 7134 7378 9 pb.
A standard general work, now completely revised and expanded.

***Currie, C R J and Lewis, C P (eds), *English county histories: a guide. A tribute to C R*

Elrington. Stroud: A Sutton, 1994, xii, 483 p, refs, index.
Discusses the history of county histories, so is more historiography than bibliography though it does provide an introduction to these old works (which have to be interpreted with care but should not be neglected).

Dibben, A A, *Title deeds 13th–19th centuries*. Historical Ass *Helps for students of history*, 72, corrected reprint 1990, 28p. 0 85278 078 8 pb.
A guide to deed-types before the mid-19th century reforms. *See also Alcock above.*

Edwards, Peter, *Farming sources for local historians*. London: Batsford, 1991, 226 p, bibl, index. 0 7134 5116 5.
Mainly documentary evidence, med and post-med, but some material on physical evidence for change.

—, *Rural life: guide to local records*. London: Batsford, 1993, 176 p, bibl, index. 0 7134 6787 8.

Ellis, Mary, *Using manorial records. PRO reader's guide*, 6, 1994, viii, 110 p. 1 873162 12 X.

Evans, Eric J, *Tithes, maps, apportionments and the 1836 Act*. Chichester: Brit Ass for Local Hist, rev edn 1993, 32 p. 0 85033 857 3 pb.

***Field, John, *A history of English field names*. London: Longman, 1993, xviii, 285 p, bibl, index. (Approaches to Local History series.)
Welcomed by one reviewer as 'monumental', and by another as a 'lovely book for the local historian'.

Foxall, H D, *Shropshire field-names*. Shrewsbury: Shrops Archaeol Soc, 1980, xii, 98 p, refs, indexes. 0 9501227 3 4 pb.
This kind of local study can be valuable in locating archaeological sites; see also Herefordshire below.

Friar, Stephen, *The Batsford companion to local history*. London: Batsford, 1991, 432 p. 0 7134 6181 0.
Set out in encyclopaedia style. Reviewers found considerable interest in this work, but tended to prefer other sources.

***Gelling, Margaret, *Signposts to the past: place-names and the history of England*. Chichester: Phillimore, 2 rev edn 1988, 281 p, bibl, index. 0 85033 649 X.
Absolutely indispensable work explaining current theories on how place-names 'work' and

their interrelationship with archaeology, with stress on the need for patient research. See also her updating article in *Local historian*, 22, 1992, pp 114–27 which explains some common place-name elements.

***—, *Place-names in the landscape: the geographical roots of Britain's place-names*. London: Dent, 1984, x, 326 p, bibl, glossarial index. o 460 04380 3; also 1993 paperback, o 460 86086 0.
Illustrates in fascinating detail the landscape value of place-name elements, both those which indicate settlement types and topographical. Indispensable.

**Gooder, Eileen A, *Latin for local history: an introduction*. London: Longman, 2 edn 1978, 171 p. o 582 48728 5 pb.
A very practical and attractive course, using actual records, for 'those whose Latin is weak or non-existent'; complements any basic Latin primer.

Harvey, P D A, *Manorial records*. London: British Records Ass (= *Archives and the user*, 5), 1984, viii, 81 p. o 900222 06 9 pb.
Offers assistance in using these records.

—, *Manorial court rolls and books*. London: Hist Ass, 1993, 8p leaflet.

Hayns, David, 'County local history organisations in England and Wales: a report on the recent BALH survey', in *Local historian*, 22, 1992, pp 89–96.
Includes some reference to archaeological societies.

Herefordshire Field Name Survey (comp Ruth Richardson and Geoff Gwatkin). This award-winning project has now issued 260 parish lists, each with a map of field names taken from tithe maps. The complete set costs over £500, but individual lists are mostly photocopied to order for modest sums. Thematic studies are now in progress using these lists; for instance, looking for kiln fields or deserted villages. Work continues on finding older field names from estate maps etc.

**Hindle, Brian Paul, *Maps for local history*. London: Batsford, 1988, 160 p. o 7134 5584 5.
Practical guide to the history, use and location of historic maps.

**Hoskins, W G, *Fieldwork in local history*.

London: Faber, 2 edn 1982, 202 p, narrative bibl, index. o 571 18050 7.
Classic work which continues to encourage modern workers to 'get their boots dirty' by studying the wealth of information which still lies in our fields and hedges.

**—, *Local history in England*. Harlow: Longman, 3 edn 1984, xviii, 301 p, bibl, index. o 582 49371 4.
Classic, standard introduction to the subject. The new edition has many more illustrations, with captions inviting close study of the photographs.

Jackson, K H on language and history, see Section 6.11.5 Migration and early medieval.

Jamieson, Ian, 'Institutions and societies in local studies', in *Local studies collections: a manual, vol 2* (ed Michael Dewe, 1991), pp 80–101.
Gives information on libraries and on the principal organisations.

Munby, Lionel, *Reading Tudor and Stuart handwriting*. Chichester: Phillimore, 1988, 16 p. o 85033 638 4 pb.
A useful 'decoding' pamphlet for manuscripts of these periods.

Oxford companion to local history, see Hey in Bibliographies above.

Riden, Philip, *Record sources for local history*. London: Batsford, 1987, 253 p, refs, index. o 7134 4726 5 hb, o 7134 5726 0 pb.

—, *Local history: a handbook for beginners*. London: Batsford, 1983, 162 p, index, bibl. o 7134 3871 1 pb.
Riden provides two basic texts on how to find and use the sources.

Phythian-Adams, Charles, *Re-thinking English local history*. Leicester: Leicester Univ Press, 1987, 58 p, notes. o 7185 2041 6.

**Roberts, B K, *The making of the English village: a study in historical geography*. London: Longman Sci and Tech, 1987, xiv, 237 p, bibl, index. o 582 30143 2 pb.
How to use village plans as sources of evidence for past conditions.

*Stephens, W B, *Sources for English local history*. Cambridge: CUP, revised and expanded edn 1981, xv, 342 p, index. o 521 23763 7. (Further reprint from Phillimore, 1994, o 85033 911 1.)
Where to look for research materials.

Stuart, Denis, *Manorial records: an introduction to their transcription and translation*. Chichester: Phillimore, 1992, viii, 120 p, glossary, index. 0 85033 821 2.
Well-recommended tutorial book with exercises, offering a comprehensive guide to the nature and use of these records; includes vocabulary (Latin), reproduces handwriting etc; mid 12th to 18th centuries.

**Tate, W E, *The parish chest: a study of the records of parochial administration in England*. Chichester: Phillimore, 3 edn 1983, xvii, 369 p, bibl, index. 0 85033 507 8.
Another standard work on how to pursue parish history.

**Tiller, Kate, *English local history: an introduction*. Stroud: Sutton, 1992, viii, 247 p, bibl, index. 0 86299 958 8.
Generally well received up-to-date introduction.

*Wainwright, F T, *Archaeology and place-names and history: an essay on problems of coordination*. London: Routledge and Kegan Paul, [1962], xiii, 135 p.
Still worth reading today.

West, John, *Town records*. Chichester: Phillimore, 1983, xviii, 366 p, bibl, index. 0 85033 472 1.
How to find and use these records.

—, *Village records*. Chichester: Phillimore, 2 edn 1982, xxiv, 248 p, bibl, index. 0 85033 444 6.
Much valued by amateur historians but arouses the 'irritation of scholars and purists', says its author. Covers the various types of record from Saxon and early Norman to 19th century. The second edition has a rather muddly presentation and is disappointingly out of date in places.

Wales

An excellent introduction to Welsh local history is in D Huw Owen's contribution to the *Oxford companion to local and family history* (see Hey under Bibliography and Reference above), pp 483–91.

Charles, B G, *The place-names of Pembrokeshire*. Aberystwyth: Nat Lib Wales, 1992 and forthcoming, lxxxvii, 394 p, bibl, index to be in vol 2. 0 907158 58 7.
Organised on the pattern of the English Place-Name Society volumes, but rather out of date in its reference material.

Davies, Elwyn, *A gazetteer of Welsh place-names*. Cardiff: Univ Wales Press, 3 edn 1967 (repr 1975), xxxvii, 119 p.
A standard guide to their orthography; attempts to list all towns and parishes, villages, natural features, even farm names where historically interesting. Four-figure map references given for each.

Ordnance Survey, *Place-names on maps of Scotland and Wales*. Southampton: OS, nd but pre-1971, 23 p.
A glossary of meanings; does not always answer one's question.

Owen, Hywel Wyn, *The place-names of East Flintshire*. Cardiff: Univ Wales Press, 1994, xxxvi, 428 p, glossary/index. 0 7083 1242 X.
Contains the first exhaustive glossary of name elements in Wales.

See also article on county organisations by Hayns listed under England above.

Scotland

The umbrella body here is the **Scottish Local History Forum**, address in Section 4.2 Organisations, which also lists the recently-formed **Scottish Place-Name Society** and the longer-established **Scottish Place-Name Survey** of the School of Scottish Studies, University of Edinburgh. David Moody's article on Scottish local history in the *Oxford companion to local and family history* (see Hey under Bibliography and Reference above, pp 406–12) is an excellent introduction.

PERIODICALS
Scottish archives: the journal of the Scottish Records Association (1353–1964). 1995–. Annual
Scottish local history (0266–2027). 1983–. 2/yr from Scottish Local History Forum
LocScot (0261–7935). 1981–. Scottish branch of the Library Association Local Studies Group

MANUALS AND STUDY AIDS
Moody, David, *Scottish local history: an introductory guide*. London: Batsford, 1986, 178 p, bibl, index. 0 7134 5220 X hb, 0 7134 5221 8 pb.

—, *Scottish towns: a guide for local historians*. London: Batsford, 1992, 190 p, bibl, index. 0 7134 6497 6 pb.

On their history and topography, and how to research them.

Rosie, Alison, for Scot Rec Ass, *Scottish handwriting 1500–1700: a self-help pack*. Scot Rec Office, 1994, portfolio. 1 87087 404 8.

Simpson, G G, *Scottish handwriting 1150–1650: an introduction to the reading of documents*. Edinburgh: Bratton, 1973, 140 p, glossary, bibl. 0 85975 002 7.

Sinclair, Cecil, *Tracing Scottish local history: a guide to local history research in the Scottish Record Office*. Edinburgh: HMSO/SRO, 1994, viii, 167 p, bibl, index. 0 11 495231 0 pb.
Authoritative and highly readable survey of SRO holdings with explanation of how to conduct research on them; includes other sources of information.

GENERAL WORKS
As with other parts of Britain and Ireland, works on Scottish place-names published before the 1960s/70s should be treated with great caution.

Beveridge, E, *The 'Abers' and 'Invers' of Scotland*. Edinburgh: William Brown, 1923, xix, 128 p, bibl, alphabetical arrangement.
More reliable than most of this period!

**Crawford, B (ed), *Scandinavian settlement in northern Britain: thirteen studies of place-names in their historical context*. London: Leicester Univ Press, 1995, 248 p, bibl, index. 0 7185 1923 X.
Studies presented to W F H Nicolaisen, the doyen of Scottish place-name studies. (Includes N English material.)

Dorward, David, *Scotland's place-names*. Edinburgh: Mercat Press, 2 edn 1995, 171 p, reading list, index. 1 873644 50 7 pb.

Jakobsen, Jakob, *The place-names of Shetland*. Lerwick: Shetland Library, 1993 (facsimile reprint of 1936 edition), xxviii, 273 p, bibl, index.

Johnston, J B, *Place-names of Scotland*. Originally 1892: reprint of 3 edn (ed L Murray), 1934 by Scotpress in 1988, xvi, 335 p. 1 559 32191 1.
An A-Z list of c. 3,500 place-names; not reliable, prefer Watson (below).

MacBain, Alex, *Place-names: Highlands and islands of Scotland*. Stirling: E Mackay, 1922, xxxii, 381 p, index.
Notes and foreword are by W J Watson.

MacDonald, Angus, *The place-names of West Lothian*. Edinburgh: Oliver and Boyd, 1941, xi, 179 p, refs, index.
The only Scottish county done on the EPNS pattern.

Mair, Craig, *Mercat cross and tollbooth: understanding Scotland's old burghs*. Edinburgh: John Donald, 1988, vii, 232 p, index. 0 85976 196 7 pb.

Marwick, Hugh, *Orkney farm names*. Kirkwall: Mackintosh, 1952, vi, 266 p, bibl, indexes.

**Nicolaisen, W F, *Scottish place-names: their study and significance*. London: Batsford, 1976, xxviii, 210 p, bibl, index. 0 7134 3253 5 hb, 0 7134 5234 X pb.
Standard work, though somewhat outdated now, especially the maps.

Ordnance Survey, see entry under Wales above.

Stewart, John (ed Brian Smith), *Shetland place-names*. Lerwick: Shetland Lib and Mus, 1987, xii, 353 p, place-name index. No ISBN.

Taylor, Simon, 'Place-names and the early church in Eastern Scotland', in B E Crawford (ed), *Scotland in Dark Age Britain*, 1996, pp 93–110 (Scot Cultural Press).
Discussion of *cill*-element in the area and suggestion that *both* (usually 'shieling') sometimes has strong religious connotations.

Watson, W J, *The history of the Celtic place-names of Scotland*. Edinburgh: Blackwood for Royal Celtic Soc, 1926, xx, 558 p, footnotes, indexes. (Facsimile reprint by Birlinn, 1993, 1 87474 406 8 pb.)
The (expanded) Rhind lectures for 1916. Not very easy to use, but repays the effort, being accounted the best book ever written on Scottish place-names.

See also Hogan under Ireland below.

Channel Islands

Stevens, Charles et al (eds), *Jersey place-names: a corpus of Jersey toponymy. I, The dictionary; II, The maps*. St Helier: Soc Jersiaise, 1986, viii, 555 p.
Said by the *Nomina* reviewer to be 'a delight to hold and work with ... exquisite maps ...' but that the work is marred by its philology.

Isle of Man

Broderick, George, *The place-names of the Isle of Man*. 7 volumes planned. Tübingen: Max Niemeyer. So far issued are volumes for the sheadings of Glenfaba (1994) and Michael (1995).

Kneen, J J, *The place-names of the Isle of Man with their origin and history*. Douglas, IoM: Manx Soc, 6 vols, 1925–8.

Ireland

Relevant organisations are the **Society for Name Studies in Britain and Ireland**, the **Federation of Local History Societies**, and the **Federation for Ulster Local Studies** (addresses in Section 4.2 Organisations). A useful introduction is by Kevin Whelan in *Oxford companion to local and family history* (ed Hey, 1996), pp 240–7. Consult also Section 6.1 Reference works (under Maps, Ireland) for gazetteers and indexes of townlands etc.

PERIODICALS
The Irish local history periodicals are, like the English ones, too numerous to list here; most counties and many towns have them. For place-names nationally, *Dinnseanchas* ran from 1964–77, and occasional articles appear in *Proc Roy Ir Acad*. For Northern Ireland there was also *Bulletin of the Ulster Place-Name Society* (Belfast), Series 1, 1952–7 and Series 2, vols 1–4, 1978–82. *Ainm* (0953-461X, Belfast, 1986–) continues. The Institute of Irish Studies in Belfast publishes a series of volumes on place-names (see under Stockman below). See also *Nomina* listed under England above, which has some Irish material.

Two quarterly magazines can be consulted: *History Ireland* (0791–8224), and *Irish Roots* (0791–6329) which includes some place-name material. *Irish genealogist* contains articles on gravestone inscriptions and associated ecclesiastical buildings.

BOOKS
Canavan, Tony (ed), *Every stoney acre has a name: a celebration of the townland in Ulster*. Belfast: Federation for Ulster Local Studies, 1991, xii, 62 p, bibl. 0 9518279 0 1.
For local historians: the volume's intent was to preserve townland names in the face of a Post Office threat to abandon their use.

Flanagan, Deirdre and Flanagan, Laurence, *Irish place names*. Dublin: Gill and Macmillan, 1994, ix, 271 p, bibl. 0 7171 2066 X pb. Possibly the most complete list.

Hogan, Edmund, *Onomasticon Goedelicum . . . an index . . . to the Gaelic place-names of Ireland and Scotland*. Blackrock, Co Dublin: Four Courts Press, 1993 reissue of original 1910 work, xvi, 695 p, map, bibl. 1 85182 126 0. Spittal and Field note this as a valuable source of early forms, but in need of the revision which it is currently undergoing.

Munn, A M, *Notes on the place-names and the parishes and townlands of the County of Londonderry*. Limited edition reprint 1985 (of the 1925 original) by Ballinascreena Historical Society), 272 p, glossary.
To be used (with caution in view of its age) for incidental information on monuments.

Nolan, W, *Tracing the past: sources for local studies in the Republic of Ireland*. Dublin: Geography Publs, 1982, x, 149 p, bibl. No ISBN, pb.

Power, Patrick (Canon), *Place-names of Decies*. Oxford: Blackwell for Cork Univ Press, 2 edn 1952, 489 p, index, no bibl.

Price, Liam, *The place-names of County Wicklow* (7 parts). Dublin: Inst of Advanced Studies, 1945–67.
Similar to the EPNS series, but the documentation of the early period is much less rich in Ireland.

Room, Adrian, *A dictionary of Irish place-names*. Belfast: Appletree Press, 2 rev edn 1994, 144 p, bibl. 0 86281 460 X.

Stockman, Gerard (general ed), *Place-names of Northern Ireland:*
  vol 1, County Down I: Newry and south-west Down (ed Gregory Toner and M B Ó Mainnín). Belfast: Inst Ir Stud Queen's University Belfast, 1992, xxi, 217 p. 0 85389 449 3 hb, 0 85389 432 9 pb
  vol 2, County Down II: The Ards (ed A J Hughes and R J Hannan), 1992, xxi, 301 p. 0 85389 450 7 hb, 0 85389 433 7 pb
  vol 3, County Down III: The Mournes (ed M B Ó Mainnín), 1993, xxi, 246 p. 0 85389 451 5 hb, 0 85389 448 5 pb

All with glossary, bibliography, index. Forty volumes are planned.

'Townlands index' see Section 6.1 Reference works (under Maps, Ireland).

Walsh, Paul, *The place names of Westmeath.* Dublin: Inst Adv Stud, 1957, 36 + 404 p. (ed Colm Ó Lochlainn from the original 1915 volume transcribing the relevant Ordnance Survey letters.) Part 2 lists place-names by barony.

See also Spittal and Field in the bibliographies under England at the head of this section.

6.18
Vernacular and General Architecture

This section concentrates on traditional buildings rather than 'polite' or architect-designed buildings. The most recent summary of the state of research comes from the Royal Archaeological Institute's *Building on the past* (ed Blaise Vyner, 1994), in which Anthony Quiney provides the chapter on 'Medieval and post-medieval vernacular architecture' (pp 228–43). The other works cited here should be seen in the light of Quiney's paper, which is a valuable critical bibliography in itself.

The following subdivisions will be found:
Societies and their journals
Bibliographies and reference works
Books (England and Britain generally)
Wales
Scotland
Channel Islands
Ireland

My selection has been much improved by Richard Suggett, though any remaining errors are mine alone.

Societies and their periodicals

Numerous societies concern themselves with buildings, some with 'polite' architecture, some with conservation aspects. The three mainly concerned with the small traditional house or farmhouse are:

Historic Farm Buildings Group (and its Newsletter, with regular bibliographies)
Society for the Protection of Ancient Buildings
Vernacular Architecture Group (and its journal *Vernacular Architecture*, 0305–5477, 1970–, annually)
(addresses will be found in Section 4.2 Organisations)
See also the societies listed under Wales, Scotland and Ireland below.

Across the Channel is found:

Centre d'Etudes et de Recherches sur l'Architecture Vernaculaire (CERAV), chez M Christian Lassure, 66 bvd Garibaldi, 75015 Paris; publishes *L'architecture vernaculaire* (title and ISSN vary, currently 0761–7305). 1977–. Annual, with substantial bibliography. *See also Meirion-Jones in next sub-section.*

Bibliography and reference works

Architectural periodicals index (0266–4380). 1973–. 4/yr. British Architectural Library (RIBA), 66 Portland Place, London WIN 4AD. (Formerly RIBA Annual Review of Periodical Articles.)
Indexes selected articles from 300 periodicals worldwide; treats historical as well as modern architecture, but for most purposes the Vernacular Architecture Group bibliographies cited below will be much more useful.

Barley, guide to British topographical collections, see Section 2.2 Guides to . . . prints, drawings (etc).

Buildings of England (ed Nikolaus Pevsner), CD-ROM database for Windows under the title *A compendium of Pevsner's Buildings of England.* Prepared by Michael Good. Oxford: OUP Electronic Publishing, 1994. 0 19 268221 0. (The original printed volumes are fully listed in Section 6.3 Guides to archaeological sites.)

Colvin, H M, *Biographical dictionary of British architects 1600–1840.* New Haven: Yale UP, 3 edn 1995, 1264 p, refs and footnotes, indexes. 0 300 06091 2.
Included for reference purposes, though is 'polite' architecture.

—, *English architectural history: a guide to sources.* London: Pinhorn, 2 edn 1976, iv, 23 pp, refs.
Offers a few main sources for each of the main types of building (royal, public, churches, domestic), and for drawings and topographical views.

Davies, Martin, *Romanesque architecture: a bibliography.* New York: G K Hall (Reference publns in art history), 1993, xxv, 306 p, indexes. 0 8161 1826 4.
The British isles are covered on pp 192–207 of this work, which is unannotated excepted for chapter (country) introductions.

Gee, Eric (comp: ed by Michael McGarvie), *A glossary of building terms used in England from the Conquest to c. 1550.* Frome: Frome Hist Res Group, 1984, 95 p, refs. 0 948014 00 8.
Medieval English, Latin and French terms interleaved with modern English equivalents.

Harvey, John H, *Sources for the history of houses.* London: British Records Assoc (= *Archives and the user,* 3), 1974, 61 p, index. 0 900222 04 2 pb.
Mainly on documentary evidence (where to find it, how to use it), with shorter sections on architectural evidence and on the general historical background.

—, *English mediaeval architects: a biographical dictionary down to 1550.* Stroud: Alan Sutton, rev edn 1984, lxii, 479 p, bibl, indexes. 0 86299 034 3 hb, 0 86299 452 7 pb. Also: 'Supplement to the revised edition of 1984' publ by Pinhorns, 1987, 16 p. 0 901262 24 2 pb.
The indexes allow several different ways into the material.

Harvey, Nigel, *Historic farm buildings study: sources of information.* London: CBA/MAFF, 1985, 83 pp, plastic spiral-bound, no ISBN.
Study commissioned by ADAS, the Agricultural Development and Advisory Service, and supervised by the CBA, to assist officers advising farmers on the conservation of farm buildings; full of useful sources and addresses (but bear in mind its date of publication). Lists published sources, theses, archive and reference sources, farm buildings open to the public, and surveys and studies made of 'HFBs'. (See also entry for HFBG Newsletter at head of this section.)

*Kamen, Ruth, *British and Irish architectural history: a bibliography and guide to sources of information.* London: Architectural Press, 1981, 255 p, refs, index. 0 85139 077 3.
Contains nearly 900 fully annotated entries on organisations, bibliographies and sources, with exemplary index; important for references up to 1980.

Lever, Jill and Harris, John, *Illustrated dictionary of architecture 800–1914.* London: Faber and Faber, 2 edn 1993, 215 p, bibl. 0 571 13765 2.
Expanded and revised from the 1966 edition.

Meirion-Jones, G I, *La maison traditionelle: bibliographie de l'architecture vernaculaire en France.* Paris: CNRS, Centre de Documentation, Sciences humaines, 1978, viii, 153 p, indexes. 2 222 02239 8.
Classified list of works on French vernacular architecture, indexed by location and subject.

Overton, Mark, *Bibliography of British probate inventories.* Newcastle upon Tyne: Geography

Dept Univ Newcastle upon Tyne, 1983, 44 p, index. No ISBN, pb.
Reported by VAG as comprehensive. Useful key to documents that can help in interpreting houses.

*Royal Commission on the Historical Monuments of England/English Heritage, *Thesaurus of monument types: a standard for use in archaeological and architectural records.* Swindon: RCHME, 1995, xxviii, 322 p, looseleaf binder. 1 873592 20 5.
Word list with interrelationships between types set out in formal thesaurus fashion, for use in national and other Sites and Monuments Records.

Russell, T M, *The built environment: a subject index 1800–1960.* Godstone: Gregg, 1989, 4 vols. 0 576 40006 8 set.
The four volumes treat: 1. Town planning and urbanism, architecture, gardens and landscape design; 2. Environmental technology, constructional engineering, building and materials; 3. Decorative art and industrial designs, exhibitions and collections (museums, libraries); 4. Public health, municipal services, community welfare. Good for browsing in (eg for 'Domestic architecture, works before 1900' then same topic by decade up to 1959) but there is no author index, so searchers need familiarity with the classification and some patience.

Smith, J T, *critical bibliography of building conservation, see Section 6.8 Conservation of buildings.*

Society of Architectural Historians of Great Britain Research Register (revision in preparation at 1996).
Classified list of architectural research work in progress or completed.

***Vernacular Architecture Group bibliographies:
Hall, R de Zouche (ed), *A bibliography on vernacular architecture.* Newton Abbot: David and Charles, 1972, 191 p. 0 7153 5653 4
Michelmore, D J H (ed), *A current bibliography of vernacular architecture, 1970–76.* York: VAG, 1979, 40 p. 0 906259 00 2 pb
Pattison, I R and D S and Alcock, N W (eds), *Bibliography of vernacular architecture vol III, 1977–89.* Aberystwyth: VAG, 1992, 144 p. 0 906259 01 0
These VAG bibliographies cover Ireland as well

as the UK, collect from a wide variety of publications, and are classified on a fairly broad scheme with author, place and journal indexes.

Zboiński, A and Tyszyński, L (eds), *Dictionary of architecture and building trades in four languages, English/German/Polish/Russian.* Oxford: Pergamon, 1963, 492 p.

Books (England, and Britain generally)

Alcock, N W (ed), *Cruck construction: an introduction and catalogue. CBA res rep,* 42, 1981, viii, 177 p, bibl, index. 0 906780 11 X pb.
The first full survey of these characteristic buildings of western Britain, with nine papers in addition to the catalogue.

—, *People at home: living in a Warwickshire village, 1500–1800.* Chichester: Phillimore, 1993, xvii, 238 p, glossaries, footnotes, indexes. 0 85033 863 8.
Links architectural and documentary evidence.

***— et al, *Recording timber-framed buildings: an illustrated glossary. CBA practical handbooks in archaeol,* 5, 1989, 52 p. 0 906780 73 X pb.
Essential for the buildings recorder. (New edn due 1996)

**— and Hall, Linda, *Fixtures and fittings in dated houses 1567–1763. CBA practical handbooks in archaeol,* 11, 1994, viii, 75 p. 1 872414 52 4 pb.
Drawings of variants of each type of fitting: balusters, doors, hinges, window catches, etc, all with known dates and locations.

Andrews, David et al, *The survey and recording of historic buildings.* Exeter: AAI&S Techn Pap, 12, 1995, ii, 35 p, bibl. 0 9516721 5 0 pb.
English Heritage staff techniques described in four papers.

Aston and Bond on the landscape of towns, see Section 6.13 Topic surveys.

Barley, M W, *English farmhouses and cottages.* London: Routledge and Kegan Paul, 1961, 297 p, refs, glossary, index.
Classic, seminal work.

—, *Houses and history.* London: Faber and Faber, 1986, 290 p, refs, index. 0 571 13631 1.
From Anglo-Saxon to modern, with discussion of social conditions and physical changes from 1550–1900.

— (ed), *The buildings of the countryside*. CUP, 1990, xxiv, 410 pp, bibl, index. 0 521 36880 4.
This work consists of revised reprints of chapters in Thirsk, J (ed), *The agrarian history of England and Wales, 1500–1750*. Two chapters are by Barley on English buildings and two by Peter Smith on Welsh, both authors adding new introductions updating their 1985 work.

Beacham, Peter (ed), *Devon building. An introduction to local traditions*. Exeter: Devon Co Co, 1990, 160 p, index. 0 86114 852 5.
Good survey of town and country housing and decoration.

Beamon, Sylvia P and Roaf, Susan, *The ice-houses of Britain*. London: Routledge, 1990, xvii, 553 pp, bibl, index. 0 415 03301 2.
Introductory history and county gazetteer of a previously neglected class of buildings.

***Brunskill, R W, *Illustrated handbook of vernacular architecture*. London: Faber and Faber, 3 edn 1987, 256 p, annot. bibl, index. 0 571 13916 7.
Essential work by one of the founding fathers of vernacular architecture studies. Arranges the material by walling methods, roofing methods, plans and sections, architectural details, etc. Includes farm, urban and minor industrial buildings and indicates methods of study.

—, *Brick building in Britain*. London: Gollancz, 1990, 208 p, bibl, index. 0 575 04457 8.
Standard work.

—, *Traditional buildings of Britain: introduction to vernacular architecture*. London: Gollancz, 'new edn of 2 rev edn', 1994, 192 p, bibl, index. 0 575 05299 6 pb.
Classic now available again.

—, *Timber building in Britain*. London: Gollancz/Crawley, 2 rev edn, 1994, 255 p, bibl, index. 0 575 05611 8.
Describes the construction and provides an illustrated glossary of terms and techniques and a chronological survey.

The Builder (1842–1966) see Section 1.2 County bibliographies and pre-20th century sources.

Buildings of England series, see Section 6.3 Guides to archaeological sites; and the CD-ROM version listed near the head of this section.

Chesher, V M and F J, *The Cornishman's house: an introduction to the history of traditional domestic architecture in Cornwall*. Truro: Barton, 1968, 142 p, chapter refs, index. [o] 85153 001 X.

Clifton-Taylor, Alex (ed Jack Simmons), *The pattern of English building*. London: Faber and Faber, 4 edn, 1987, 480 p, bibl, glossary, indexes. 0 571 14890 5 hb, 0 571 13988 4 pb.
Classic work organised by building material (stone, flint, thatch, timber, etc).

Giles, Colum and Wade Martins, Susanna (eds), *Recording historic farm buildings. Proceedings of a one-day conference [York 1994]*. Reading: HFBG, 1994, ii, 44 p, bibls. 0 9517503 1 3 pb.
Several practical articles deal with English, Welsh and Scottish buildings.

Hall, Linda, *The rural houses of North Avon and South Gloucestershire, 1400–1720*. City of Bristol Museum and Art Gallery monogr, 6, xix, 316 p, bibl, index. 0 900199 21 0.
Good, well-illustrated regional study.

Hall, Sir R de Z see Vernacular Architecture Group under Bibliographies and reference works above.

Hansell, Peter and Jean, *A dovecote heritage*. Bath: Millstream Books, 1992, 194 p. 0 948975 32 6.

Harris, Richard, *Discovering timber-framed buildings*. Princes Risborough: Shire, *Discovering*, 242, 3 edn 1993, 96 p, bibl, glossary-index. 0 7478 0215 7 pb.
Accessible introduction.

Harrison, Barry and Hutton, Barbara, *Vernacular houses in North Yorkshire and Cleveland*. Edinburgh: John Donald, 1984, 254 p, refs, index. 0 85976 091 X.
Treats construction and social factors, pays particular attention to plan forms, and constructs a series of village profiles.

Harvey, Nigel, *A history of farm buildings in England and Wales*. Newton Abbot: David and Charles, 2 rev edn 1984, 279 p, bibl, index. 0 7153 8383 3.

Hewett, Cecil A, *The development of carpentry, 1200–1700: an Essex study*. Newton Abbot: David and Charles, 1969, 232 p, refs, index. [o] 7153 4694 6.
Pioneering study on the dating of specific carpentry joints.

—, English historic carpentry. Chichester: Phil-

limore, 1980, xiv, 338 p, bibl, glossary, index. o
85033 354 7.
Mainly on SE English buildings, Saxon to post-
medieval; offers a chronological sequence of
joint types.

Hutton, Barbara, *Recording standing buildings*.
Sheffield: Dept Archaeol and Prehistory/RES-
CUE, 1986, 44 p, bibl, glossary. o 9093789 12 4
pb.
Advice for beginners, based on N Yorkshire
examples.

[ICOMOS], *Guide to recording historic buildings*
[comp Nicholas Cooper]. London: Butterworth
Architecture, 1990, 80 p, bibl. o 7506 1210 X.
Purposes, objectives, occasions for recording;
features to record; approaches and techniques;
initial survey; preserving the record.

**Innocent, C F, *The development of English
building construction*. Cambridge: CUP, 1916,
reprinted David and Charles 1971 (with new
introduction by Sir R de Z Hall), [26], 294 p. o
7153 5299 7.
Classic work, still often cited (as the appearance
of this facsimile edition indicates).

Iredale, David and Barrett, John, *Discovering
your old house*. Princes Risborough: Shire,
3 edn 1991, 112 p. o 7478 0143 6 pb.
Pocket guide, therefore very basic, to tracing
one's house.

*Johnson, Matthew, *Housing culture: traditional
architecture in an English landscape*. London:
UCL Press, 1993, xiv, 220 p, glossary, bibl,
index. 1 85728 111 X.
Interdisciplinary study based on western Suffolk, examining why houses were built, how
built, how used, why they changed in form/
style/technique through time.

Jope, E M (ed), *Studies in building history: essays
in recognition of the work of B H St J O'Neil*.
London: Odhams, 1961, 287 p, bibl of O'Neil
works.
Festschrift containing many useful articles, eg
on Roman timber building, domestic window
glass (Roman to medieval), medieval chimney
pots, 17th century houses in Ireland, etc.

Laxton, R R and Litton, C D, *An East Midlands
master tree-ring chronology and its use for
dating vernacular buildings*. Nottingham: Univ
Nottingham Dept Classical and Archaeol Studies (Archaeol Section), 1988, 82 p, bibl. o
904857 03 4 pb.

London (Corporation of), *London buildings and
sites: a guide for researchers in Guildhall
Library*. Corporation of London, 1976, 20 p.

Machin, R, *Rural housing, an historical approach*.
London: Historical Ass (= *Helps for students of
history*, **96**), 1994, 40 p, bibl. o 85278 381 7 pb.
Useful introduction to problems of interpretation.

***Meirion-Jones, Gwyn and Jones, Michael
(eds), *Manorial domestic buildings in England
and Northern France*. Soc Antiq London occas
pap, **15**, 1994, xvii, 206 p, bibls, index. o 85431
263 3 pb.
Very important volume of papers by J Blair, P W
Dixon, J Munby and others.

Mercer, Eric, *English vernacular houses: a study
of traditional farmhouses and cottages*. London: HMSO, 1975, xxii, 246 p, refs, glossary,
index. o 11 700728 5.
RCHME-inspired work consisting of a general
survey of rural vernacular architecture (much of
it threatened), profusely illustrated by selected
examples.

Michelmore, D see *Vernacular Architecture
Group* under *Bibliographies and reference
works above*.

Parker, Vanessa, *The making of King's Lynn:
secular buildings from the 11th to the 17th
century*. London: Phillimore, 1971 (= *King's
Lynn Archaeological Survey*, 1), 1971, 226 p,
bibl. o 900592 58 3.
Pioneering study of a well-preserved medieval
town.

Parsons, D, on stone quarrying, see *Section 6.15
Archaeology of industrial processes*.

Pattison, I R and D S see *Vernacular Architecture
Group* under *Bibliographies and reference
works above*.

Peters, J E C, *The development of farm buildings
in western lowland Staffordshire up to 1800*.
Manchester: Manchester Univ Press, 1969, xx,
284 p, bibl, index. o 7190 0386 5.
Regional study regularly cited.

Quiney, Anthony, *The traditional buildings of
England*. London: Thames and Hudson, 1990,
224 p, glossary, bibl, index of places. o 500
34110 9 hb, o 500 27661 7 pb.
Good introduction.

Royal Commission on the Historical Monuments

of England, thesaurus, see under Bibliographies and reference works above.

—, on shielings and bastles, see Section 6.11.6 Medieval.

—, per Sarah Pearson, *Rural houses of the Lancashire Pennines, 1560–1760. RCHME suppl ser,* 10, 1985, x, 202 p, refs, index. o 11 701192 4 pb.
This and the following volumes represent the new RCHME policy of pursuing themes across particular areas, more selectively than in the old Inventories.

—, per Colum Giles, *Rural houses of West Yorkshire, 1400–1830. RCHME suppl ser,* 8, 1986, xx, 240 p, bibl, index. o 11 701194 0 pb.

—, per Lucy Caffyn, *Workers' housing in West Yorkshire 1750–1920. RCHME suppl ser,* 9, 1986, 160 p, bibl, index. o 11 300002 2 pb.

—, per D W Black et al, *Houses of the North York Moors.* London: HMSO, 1987, xi, 256 p, bibl, index. o 11 300014 6 pb.

—, *Houses of the North York Moors: a selective inventory.* London: RCHME, 1989, 109 p, bibl, index. o 9507236 8 1.
Companion volume to the previous entry.

—, per J T Smith, *English houses 1200–1800: the Hertfordshire evidence.* London: HMSO for RCHME, 1992, xx, 215 p, gazetteer, bibl, index. o 11 300037 5 pb.
Though centred on Hertfordshire, a county selected for its richness in pre-19th century buildings and its good documentary evidence, 'the conclusions reach far beyond the limits of a single county'. Synoptic companion to the next entry.

—, per J T Smith, *Hertfordshire houses: selective inventory.* London: RCHME, 1993, xviii, 248 p, bibl, indexes. 1 873592 10 8 pb.
Companion volume to the previous title: each house described and plans of many.

—, per Sarah Pearson, *The medieval houses of Kent: an historical analysis.* London: HMSO for RCHME, 1994, x, 196 p, bibl, index. o 11 300047 2 pb.
Discusses evolution, differences in type and distribution across the county, historical reasons for such patterns, etc.

—, per Sarah Pearson et al, *A gazetteer of medieval houses in Kent.* London: HMSO for RCHME,

1994, xii, 145 p, refs, index of houses. o 11 300049 9 pb.
Detailed record of the 414 buildings surveyed.

—, per P S Barnwell and A T Adams, *The house within: interpreting medieval houses in Kent.* London: HMSO for RCHME, 1994, xii, 163 p, refs, index. o 11 300048 0 pb.
Non-specialist guide to principal features, which may lie under later guises.

—, per Hermione Hobhouse, *London survey'd: the work of the Survey of London 1894–1994.* London: RCHME, 1994, x, 85 p, notes, index. 1 873592 19 1 pb.
Illustrated history of the organisation set up by C R Ashbee to record ancient buildings threatened by London's rapid growth. Contains complete list of Survey volumes published from 1900 onwards, and the monograph series (for single buildings) 1896 onwards.

—/SAHGB [eds Kirsty Cook and Jan Cornell], *Recording historic buildings: a symposium, London, May 1991, organised jointly by RCHME and Society of Architectural Historians of Great Britain.* London: RCHME, 1991, 71 leaves. 1 873592 03 5 pb.
Papers on the national view, with some case studies; the thrust is analysis rather than collection, and against attempting the 'total record'.

Salzman, L F, *Building in England down to 1540: a documentary history.* Oxford: Clarendon Press, 1952, revised 1967, reissued 1992, xvi, 637 p, bibl, indexes. o 19 817158 7.
Classic work, almost entirely non-vernacular but indispensable for its range of sources.

Samson, Ross (ed), *The social archaeology of houses.* Edinburgh: EUP, 1990, v, 282 p. o 7486 0290 9.
Includes papers on the feudal village, tower houses, and the morphological analysis of small building plans.

Saunders, Matthew, *The historic home owner's companion.* London: Batsford, 1987, 171 p, bibl, index. o 7134 4230 1.
Treats the legal, aesthetic and structural problems of ownership, from terraced cottages to country houses.

Slocombe, Pamela M, *Medieval houses of Wiltshire.* Stroud: Alan Sutton (= *Wiltshire Buildings Record monogr,* 3), 1992, 110 p. o 7509 0285 x pb.
The same author has also published Wiltshire

farmhouses and cottages 1500–1850; Wiltshire farm buildings 1500–1900; two more volumes in preparation.

Smith, Lance, *Investigating old buildings*. London: Batsford Academic and Educational, 1985, 160 p, glossary, bibl, index. 0 7134 3633 6 hb, 0 7134 3634 4 pb.
Covers research and rescue; materials and construction; fieldwork; research background.

Stell, Christopher (ed), on recording chapels and meeting houses, see Section 6.11.7 under Non-Conformist Working Party.

Suddards, Roger W on listed buildings legislation, see Section 6.6 Planning and legislation (under Standing Buildings).

Survey of London see under Royal Commission (Hobhouse) above.

Taylor, Richard S, *Drawing traditional buildings*. London: Robert Hale, 1987, 192 p, bibl, index. 0 7090 2969 1 hb, 0 7090 4665 0 pb (1991).

Vernacular architecture (journal), see under Societies and journals above.

Wade Martins, Susanna, *Historic farm buildings, including a Norfolk survey*. London: Batsford, 1991, 256 p, bibl, index. 0 7134 6507 7.
History, present state, future prospects.
(*See also Giles and Wade Martins above*).

—, *Old farm buildings in a new countryside, see Section 6.8 Conservation of buildings.*

Ward, R G W (ed), *Applications of tree-ring studies: current research in dendrochronology and related subjects. BAR int ser*, 333, 1987, 232 p. 0 86054 428 1 pb.
One of several books providing master chronologies.

***Wood, Jason (ed), *Buildings archaeology: applications in practice. Oxbow monogr*, 43, 1994, vii, 263 p. 0 946897 75 1.
Papers covering various aspects of intensive and extensive survey: a seminal work.

***Wood, Margaret, *The English medieval house*. London: Phoenix House, 1965, xxxi, 448 p, bibl, index.
Absolutely indispensable classic work, often reprinted (eg Studio 1994).

Yeomans, David T, *The trussed roof: its history and development*. Aldershot: Scolar Press, 1992, xv, 221 p, bibl, index. 0 85967 874 1.
Covers the period 17th–19th century, ie be-

tween medieval methods of construction and 19th century ironwork. Includes study of the behaviour of the truss and assesses the contribution of Wren and Inigo Jones.

Wales

Buildings of Wales, see Section 6.3 Guides to archaeological sites (under Wales).

Davies, Martin, *Save the last of the magic. Traditional qualities of the West Wales cottage*. Llandysul: [privately?], 2 rev edn 1993, iv, 50 p. 0 9527704 0 4 pb.
Survey of the vulnerable vernacular of West Wales.

*Fox, Cyril and Raglan, Lord, *Monmouthshire houses: a study of building techniques and smaller house-plans in the 15th to 17th centuries*. Cardiff; originally published by Nat Mus Wales/Welsh Folk Mus, but all produced by Merton Priory Publications (Cardiff) in 2 rev edn with Peter Smith introduction, 1994. 0 9520009 9 7 (set):
Vol I. *Medieval*, 1951, xxviii, 114 p, indexes
Vol II. *Sub-medieval c. 1550–1610*, 1953, 135 p, indexes
Vol III. *Renaissance c. 1540–1714*, 1954, 178 p, indexes
Classic studies, now supplemented by the Peter Smith volume (below).

Lowe, J B, *Welsh industrial workers' housing 1775–1875*. Cardiff: Nat Mus Wales, 1977 (later reprints with postscript), 64 p. 0 7200 0099 8 pb.
Each house type is illustrated and a simple classification presented.

—, *Welsh country workers' housing 1775–1875*. Cardiff: Nat Mus Wales, 1985, 49 p, bibl. 0 7200 0298 2 pb.

Nash, Gerallt, *Timber-framed buildings in Wales*. Cardiff: Nat Mus Wales, 1995, 46 p, short bibl. 0 7200 0420 9 pb.
Based on the buildings in the Museum of Welsh Life, St Fagans.

Peate, Iorwerth C, *The Welsh house: a study in folk culture*. Liverpool: H Evans, 3 edn 1946, xviii, 204 p, bibl.

**Royal Commission on the Ancient and Historical Monuments of Wales, *An inventory of the ancient monuments in Glamorgan. Vol IV: Domestic architecture from the Reformation

to the Industrial Revolution. Part 1, The greater houses. Cardiff: HMSO, 1981, xl, 379 p, footnotes, glossary, index. 0 11 700754 4.
and Part 2, Farmhouses and cottages. London: HMSO, 1988, xviii, 661 p, footnotes, glossary, index. 0 11 300020 0.

**Smith, Peter, Houses of the Welsh countryside: a study in historical geography. [s l]: HMSO for RCAHMW, 2 enlarged edn 1988, xl, 723 p, refs, glossary, index. 0 11 300012 X.
Historical survey of vernacular architecture with many distribution maps. Basically the same text as the 1975 edition with many new illustrations, addenda/corrigenda, new introduction.
See also under Barley in 'Britain' section above.

Wiliam, Eurwyn, The historical farm buildings of Wales. Edinburgh: John Donald, 1986, x, 202 p, bibl, index. 0 85976 136 3.
Pioneering study based on examination of over 900 farmsteads, mainly of 19th century: seeks to answer the question 'what did a farm need to function before mechanisation?'

—, Home-made homes: dwellings of the rural poor in Wales. Cardiff: Nat Mus Wales, 1988, 36 p, bibl. 0 7200 0320 2 pb.
Agricultural labourers' cottages c. 1750–1900; building techniques and plans.

—, Welsh long-houses: four centuries of farming at Cilewent. Cardiff: Nat Mus Wales, 1992, 44 p. 0 7083 1164 4 pb.
First comprehensive review of the topic since the 1940s: includes previously unpublished photographs from the 1890s. Cilewent itself has now been re-erected at the Museum of Welsh Life, St Fagans.

—, Traditional farm buildings in north-east Wales, 1550–1900. Cardiff: Nat Mus Wales, 1982, xx, 334 p, bibl, index. 0 85485 049 X.
Based on author's thesis; practical details and statistics.

Scotland

ORGANISATIONS
(Addresses will be found in Section 4.2 Organisations)
Architectural Heritage Society of Scotland
Cairdean nan Taighean Tugha/Friends of Thatched Houses
Glasgow West Conservation Trust

Royal Incorporation of Architects in Scotland
Scottish Civic Trust
Scottish Historic Buildings Trust
Scottish Vernacular Buildings Working Group

PERIODICALS
Architectural heritage: the journal of the Architectural Heritage Society of Scotland. (ISBNs only.) Annual.

Vernacular building (former title Scottish vernacular building newsletter) (0267–3088). 1975–. Annual publication of Scottish Vernacular Buildings Working Group.

BOOKS
Buildings of Scotland series see Section 6.3 Guides to archaeological sites (under Scotland).

Buxbaum, Tim, Scottish doocots. Princes Risborough: Shire, 1987, 32 p, 0 85263 848 5 pb.
Introduction to dovecotes in Scotland.

Dunbar, J G, The architecture of Scotland. London: Batsford, 2 rev edn 1978, 209 p, bibl, index. 0 7134 1142 2 (first edn was entitled The historic architecture of Scotland).

Fawcett, Richard, Scottish architecture 1371–1560. Edinburgh: EUP, 1995, xxi, 386 p, bibl, index. (The architectural history of Scotland series.)

Fenton, Alexander and Walker, Bruce, The rural architecture of Scotland. Edinburgh: John Donald, 1981, xii, 242 p, bibl, index. 0 85976 020 0.

—, — and Stell, Geoffrey (eds), Building construction in Scotland: some historical and regional aspects. Edinburgh/Dundee: Scot Vernacular Buildings Working Group, 1976, 71 p. Papers from a 1974 conference.

Fraser, L J W et al (eds), Scottish vernacular building. Bibliography 2. Edinburgh: Scot Vernacular Buildings Working Group/Scottish Country Life Museums Trust, 1987, 67 p. 0 9505084 7 0 pb.
Covers publications 1964–86. See also under Stell below.

Howard, Deborah, Scottish architecture: reformation to Restoration 1560–1660. Edinburgh: EUP, 1995, xvi, 270 p, bibl, index. 0 7486 0530 4.

Naismith, R J (for Countryside Commission Scotland), Buildings of the Scottish countryside.

London: Gollancz/Crawley, 1985, 224 p, bibl, glossary, index. 0 575 03383 5. (Not seen.) Selection from a survey of some 23,000 buildings.

Pride, Glen L, *Glossary of Scottish building.* Glasgow: Scott Civic Trust, rev edn 1989.

—, *Dictionary of Scottish building terms.* Edinburgh: Rutland Press, forthcoming.

Riches, Anne and Stell, Geoffrey, *Materials and traditions in Scottish building: essays in memory of Sonia Hackett.* Edinburgh: Scot Vernacular Buildings Working Group regional and thematic studies, 2, 1992, 102 p, bibls. Includes essays on various house types, thatching techniques etc, and a glossary of technical terms.

Stell, G and Walker, B, *Scottish Vernacular Buildings Working Group bibliography 1.* Dundee/Edinburgh: [the Group?], 1984, 21 p. *See also Fraser above.*

Channel Islands

McCormack, John, *The Guernsey house.* Chichester: Phillimore, 1987 edn, 418 p. 0 85033 380 6. (Not seen.) Study of many houses shown on a late 18th-century map.

Stevens, Joan, *Old Jersey houses Vol I: before 1700. Vol II: from 1700 onward.* Chichester: Phillimore, 1977 and 1980, 264 p and 272 p. 0 85033 269 9 and 0 85033 389 X. (Not seen.)

Ireland

SOCIETY
Ulster Architectural Heritage Society (address at end of this sub-section)

BOOKS AND REFERENCE WORKS
Buildings of Ireland, see Section 6.3 Guides to archaeological sites (under Ireland).

Craig, Maurice, *The architecture of Ireland from the earliest times to 1880.* London: Batsford, 1982, 358 p, bibl, index. 0 7134 2586 5.

Curl, James Stevens, *The Londonderry plantation: 1609–1914. The history, architecture and planning of the estates of the City of London and its livery companies in Ulster.* Chichester: Phillimore, 1986, 503 p, bibl, index. 0 85033 577 9.

Thorough study of a formative period in Ulster's history.

Dixon, H, *An introduction to Ulster architecture.* Belfast: Ulster Archit Herit Soc, 1975, 93 p, bibl, index. No ISBN. From prehistoric times to the 20th century; comprises a selection of fine b/w photographs with extended captions.

Evans, E Estyn, *Irish folk ways.* London: Routledge and Kegan Paul, 1957, xvi, 324 p. 0 7100 1344 2. Chapters on the thatched house, hearth and home, furniture and fittings, farmyards and fences, etc; lively text and many (rather small) illustrations.

Gailey, Alan, *Rural houses of the north of Ireland.* Edinburgh: John Donald, 1984, x, 289 p, bibl, glossary, index. 0 85976 098 7.

Kamen, on British and Irish architectural sources, see above under Bibliography and reference works.

Loeber, Rolf, *A biographical dictionary of architects in Ireland 1600–1720.* London: John Murray, 1981, 127 p. 'Polite' architecture.

McKinstry, Robert et al, *The buildings of Armagh.* Belfast: Ulster Archit Heritage Soc, 1992, xviii, 217 p, bibl, index. 0 900457 42 2 pb. Street-by-street gazetteer of a historic city.

Ní Fhloinn, Bairbre and Dennison, Gabriel (eds), *Traditional architecture in Ireland and its role in rural development and tourism.* Dublin: Univ Coll Dublin Envir Inst, 1994, 94 p, bibls. 1 898473 09 9 pb. Papers from a 1993 conference on how to understand these buildings and preserve them within a living landscape.

Shaffrey, Patrick and Maura, *Irish countryside buildings: everyday architecture in the rural landscape.* Dublin: O'Brien Press, 1985, 128 p, bibl, index. 0 86278 049 7.

—, *Buildings of Irish towns: treasures of everyday architecture.* Dublin: O'Brien, 1983, 128 p. 0 86278 045 4. (Also London: Architectural Press and New York: Templegate Press.)

Simms, Anngret and Andrews, J H (eds), *Irish county towns.* Cork: Mercier Press, 1994, 192 p, bibls. 1 85635 088 6 pb.

This and the next both originate in The Thomas Davis Lecture Series.

—, *More Irish county towns*. Cork: Mercier, 1995, 206 p, bibls. 1 85635 121 1 pb.

Ulster Architectural Heritage Society has published a long series *The architectural heritage of . . .* for individual towns. There are also some thematic volumes, eg mausolea, courthouses, estate gates, etc. (For full list apply to Society at 181 Stranmillis Road, Belfast BT9 5DU)

The Vernacular Architecture Group bibliographies (see above in English sub-section) also contain some Irish material.

6.19
Maritime, Nautical and Underwater Archaeology

The section is divided as follows:
    Legislation etc
    Societies and institutions
    Periodicals
    Bibliography and reference works
    Books – England and Britain generally
    Scotland
    Ireland

Internet: The (unmoderated) discussion list for underwater archaeology SUB-ARCH includes news such as book and conference announcements as well as discussion of current issues. To subscribe, send message to
    listserv@asuvm.inre.asu.edu with the command SUBSCRIBE SUB-ARCH.

Many improvements in this section are due to Dr Ben Ferrari, but any errors are the compiler's alone.

See also Section 6.20 Wetlands (for underwater settlements).

Legislation etc

Advisory Committee on Historic Wreck Sites, 'Runciman Committee', formerly Dept of Trade, now under Dept of National Heritage (Rm 306, 2–4 Cockspur Street, London SW1Y 5DH, tel 0171 211 6368/9), which can supply *The Protection of Wrecks Act 1973: notes for the guidance of finders of historic wreck*. (Redraft under consideration at time of writing)

***Archaeological Diving Unit, *Guide to historic wreck sites designated under the Protection of Wrecks Act (1973)*. (Last printed edition 1995; tel ADU, 01334 462919 to check its availability on Internet.)

Dromgoole, S, 'Protection of historic wreck: the UK approach part I: the present legal framework' [and] 'Part II: towards reform'. *Int j estuarine and coastal law*, 4, 1989, pp 26–51 and 95–116.

Detailed, important review of one piece of legislation.

—, 'Underwater cultural property: UK law and European harmonization', in Susan Pearce (ed), *Museums and Europe 1992* (London: Athlone Press, 1992), pp 66–86, refs.
Outlines the present state of UK law and assesses the extent to which it may need to be amended in future. Also discusses the Council of Europe draft convention on the protection of the underwater heritage (1985, now lapsed).

***Joint Nautical Archaeology Policy Committee, *Code of practice for seabed developers* (endorsed by Dept of National Heritage).
Sets out recommended procedures for consultation and cooperation between seabed developers and archaeologists. The JNAPC can be contacted via the Maritime Section, RCHME, National Monuments Record Centre, Swindon SN2 2GZ (tel 01793 414713).

—, *Heritage at sea: proposals for the better protection of archaeological sites underwater.* London: National Maritime Museum, 1989, 39 p. 0 948065 07 9 pb.
Recommended a central record of historic wrecks to be compiled by RCHME, which responded by commissioning a report on the creation of a national record (*Testing the water: report on the task of creating a National Archaeological Record – Maritime Sites*) and setting up a pilot study.

National Monuments Record – Maritime Sites. A basic national record of the archaeology of the territorial sea. Contact the Maritime Section, RCHME, National Monuments Record Centre, Swindon SN2 2GZ (tel 01793 414713).

Societies and institutions

(Addresses in Section 4.2 Organisations)

International Institute of Maritime Studies (Alderney, CI, due to open 1997)
MARE (Marine Archaeological Research and Excavation)
Maritime Trust [incorporated Cutty Sark Soc]
Mary Rose Trust
National Historic Ships Committee
Nautical Archaeology Society
Shipwreck and Heritage Centre, Charlestown, Cornwall
Society for Nautical Research

Southampton Oceanographic Centre, Empress Dock, Dockgate 4, European Way, Southampton SO14 3ZH (tel 01703 595000)
see also under Scotland and Ireland below.

Periodicals

International journal of nautical archaeology and underwater exploration (1057–2414). 1972–. 4/yr. London: Academic Press. Contains regular bibliographies of recent works.

Mariner's mirror (0025–3359). 1911–. 4/yr. London: Society for Nautical Research. Mainly concerned with documentary research, eg ship histories; publishes annual bibliography.

Bibliography and reference works

Bryon, R V and Bryon, T N (eds), *Maritime information: a guide to libraries and sources of information in the United Kingdom.* London: Witherby for Maritime Info Ass, 3 edn 1993, vi, 222 p, index. 1 85609 069 8 pb.
Lists c. 500 institutions with notes on their holdings.

Greenhill, Basil, *The development of the boat: a select bibliography.* Greenwich: National Maritime Museum, [1971], vii, 120 p, index. 0 9501764 3 5 pb.

Illsley, John (comp), *An indexed bibliography of underwater archaeology and related topics.* Oswestry: Nelson (= *Internat marit archaeol ser* 3), 1996, 360 p, au and keyword indexes. 0 904614 57 3 pb.
Includes over 12,000 references; sadly the index is in ASCII (ie non-standard) sequence, so use with care.

See also Mariner's mirror *above under Periodicals.*

Books – England and Britain generally

Bound, Mensun (ed), *Archaeology of ships of war.* Oxford: Anthony Nelson (= *Int maritime archaeol ser*, 1), 1995, 192 p. 0 904614 52 2 pb. Proceedings of a 1992 conference, the sections being: excavation and interpretation; ordnance; construction, reconstruction and preservation. Includes material on the *Mary Rose* and wrecks from Alderney, Out Skerries and Duart Point.

Cederlund, C O (ed), *Post-medieval boat and ship*

archaeology: papers based on those presented to an International Symposium on Boat and Ship Archaeology in Stockholm in 1982. BAR int ser, S256, 1985, 440 p, bibl. 0 86054 327 7 pb.

Champion, T and Fulford, M (eds), England's coastal heritage. EH Archaeol rep, 15, forthcoming 1996. 0 85074 630 3 pb.

*Coad, J G, The Royal Dockyards 1690–1850: architecture and engineering works of the sailing Navy. Aldershot: Scolar, 1989, 425 p, refs, index. 0 85967 803 2.
Covers buildings, docks and ships, chapels and schools, cordage manufacture, introduction of steam power, ordnance, victualling yards, hospitals.

***Dean, Martin et al (eds), Archaeology underwater: the NAS guide to principles and practice. London: NAS/Archetype, corr reprint 1995, 332 p, bibl, index. 1 873132 25 5 pb.
Also serves as a textbook for the NAS Certification Scheme. Contributions deal with how to get involved, practical advice, safety and responsible conduct to the archaeological record; five appendices of useful information.

Firth, Antony, 'The management of archaeology underwater', in J Hunter and I Ralston (eds), Archaeological resource management in the United Kingdom (1993), pp 65–76.

Friel, Ian, The good ship: ships, shipbuilding and technology in England 1200–1520. London: Brit Mus Press, 1995, 208 p, bibl, index. 0 7141 0574 0.
More historical and documentary analysis than archaeology.

*Green, Jeremy, Maritime archaeology: a technical handbook. London: Academic Press, 1990, xx, 282 p, bibl, index. 0 12 298630 X.
Guide to prospecting for sites, recording, excavation, collections management, post-excavation.

Hague, D B (ed Stephen Hughes), Lighthouses of Wales: their architecture and archaeology. Aberystwyth: RCAHMW, 1994, 104 p, refs, index. 1 871184 08 8 pb.

— and Christie, Rosemary, Lighthouses: their architecture, history and archaeology. Llandysul: Gomer Press, 1975, xv, 307 p, bibl, index. 0 85088 324 5 pb.

Heal, Veryan, Britain's maritime heritage. London: Conway Maritime Press, 1988, 126 p. 0 85177 474 1 pb.
Guide to historic vessels, museums, maritime collections.

International Symposia on Boat and Ship Archaeology, see Section 4.10 Recurrent conferences.

Johnstone, Paul, The sea-craft of prehistory. London: Routledge, 2 edn 1988, xxiv, 260 p, bibl, index. 0 415 02635 0 pb.
The new edition was seen through the press by Sean McGrail. It covers skin boats, dugouts, planked boats, and Roman and Celtic river craft.

Larn, Richard and Larn, Bridget, Shipwreck index to the British Isles. London: Lloyd's Register of Shipping, up to 10 vols planned, 1995–.
The volumes will list 120,000 wrecks, of which only 10% are said to be accurately located. Vol 1 (1995, 0 900528 88 5) includes over 7,100 ships lost since AD 877 around the southwestern peninsula. Vol 2 (1995, 0 900528 99 0) deals with the coasts from Hampshire round to the Thames Estuary, including the Goodwin Sands.

McGrail, S (ed), Sources and techniques in boat archaeology . . . symposium in Greenwich in September 1976. BAR int ser, S29, 1977, xii, 315 p, bibls. 0 904531 82 1 pb.
Includes glossary of boat archaeology terms, papers on wood conservation, quantitative methods for logboat study, recording, reconstruction, experimental, ancient boatbuilding.

—, Ancient boats in NW Europe: the archaeology of water transport to AD 1500. London: Longman, 1987, xxi, 321 p, bibl, index. 0 582 49267 x.

— (ed), Maritime Celts, Frisians and Saxons: papers presented to a conference at Oxford in November 1988. CBA res rep, 71, 1990, x, 140 p, bibls, index. 0 906780 93 4 pb.
Maritime and riverine studies of the southern North Sea and the Channel region from c. 300 BC to c. AD 800.

Marsden, P R V, The wreck of the Amsterdam. London: Hutchinson, 2 rev edn 1985, 207 p, bibl, index. 0 09 160811 2.
On the 18th century wreck trapped in Hastings sands and its excavation, conservation and reconstruction in Amsterdam.

—, 'A comparative look at records of 20 years of

wreck archaeology', in *Int j naut archaeol*, 23.2, 1994, pp 155–8.

Compendium book review noting an unsatisfactory situation: many investigated sites remain unpublished and underwater archaeology is still a Cinderella subject.

—, *Ships of the port of London: first to eleventh centuries*. Engl Heritage archaeol rep, new ser 3, 1994, 237 p, bibl, glossary index. 1 85074 470 x pb.

On the port itself as it developed, plus individual ship discoveries.

Martin, C J M and Parker, G, *The Spanish Armada*. London: Penguin, 1989, 296 p, index. o 14 012268 o pb.

***Muckelroy, Keith, *Maritime archaeology*. Cambridge: CUP, 1978, x, 270 p, bibl, index. o 521 22079 3 hb, o 521 29348 o pb.

Not a 'how to do it' book but a statement of proper concerns, scope and potential, theory, the archaeology of ships and of maritime cultures.

Parker, A J, *Ancient shipwrecks of the Mediterranean and the Roman provinces*. BAR int ser, S580, 1992, 547 p, bibl, index. o 86054 736 1 pb.

Includes 10 British finds, 11 from Germany/ Netherlands, and over 280 from France. From computer database.

Redknap, Mark, *The Cattewater wreck. The investigation of an armed vessel of the early sixteenth century*. BARBS, 131, 1984, 145 p, bibl. o 86054 285 8 pb.

Remains one of the fullest publications of a designated site.

Ritchie, L A (ed), *The shipbuilding industry: a guide to historical records*. Manchester: Manchester Univ Press, 1992, 206 p. o 7190 3805 7.

Succinct list and description of the records of some 200 businesses, 1800–1990.

*Robinson, Wendy, *First aid for marine finds*. London: Nat Maritime Mus, 1981, ix, 40p. o 905555 52 x. (New edn due 1996.)

Describes short-term conservation measures.

Rule, Margaret H, *The Mary Rose: the excavation and raising of Henry VIII's flagship*. London: Conway Maritime Press, 2 edn 1983, 240 p, bibl, index. o 85177 289 7 hb, o 85177 382 6 pb.

— *and Monaghan on Guernsey wreck, see Section 6.11.4 Romano-British.*

Taylor, J du Plat and Cleere, H F (eds) on Roman shipping and trade, see Section 6.11.4 Romano-British.

Westerdahl, C, 'The maritime cultural landscape', *Int j naut archaeol*, 21, 1992, pp 5–14.

Important discussion of the approach to the study of maritime culture and space.

— (ed), *Crossroads in ancient shipbuilding: proceedings of the sixth international symposium on boat and ship archaeology, Roskilde 1991*. Oxbow monogr, 40, 1994, vii, 290 p, bibl. o 946897 70 o pb.

Mostly Scandinavian, Mediterranean and Netherlands material, but also includes boats from Caldicot and N Ferriby (both BA), London (AS), plus technical papers on nails, tree-ring dating, etc.

Scotland

ORGANISATIONS AND INSTITUTIONS

Maritime Fife Project: Director Ian Oxley, Scottish Institute of Maritime Studies, University of St Andrews, Fife KY16 9AJ (tel 01334 462916). To survey, record and research the maritime history and archaeological resource preserved in the coastal, foreshore and seabed areas of Fife, including the establishment of an inventory of sites and submerged landscapes.

RCAHMS Maritime Record: being compiled from 1995 as an extension to the terrestrial database.

Scottish Institute of Maritime Studies, University of St Andrews, Fife KY16 9AJ (tel 01334 476161): teaching and research institute which also houses the Archaeological Diving Unit.

PUBLICATIONS

Dixon, Nicholas, 'The history of crannog survey and excavation in Scotland', *Int j naut archaeol*, 20, 1991, pp 1–8.

Munro, R W, *Scottish lighthouses*. Stornoway: Thule, 1979, 307 p. o 906191 32 7.

Ireland

For advice and relevant material in N Ireland consult Brian Williams, Senior Inspector, Environment and Heritage Service: Historic Monuments and Buildings, 5–33 Hill Street,

Belfast BT1 2LA. The Maritime Archaeological Project is housed at the Queen's University Belfast: see Colin Breen, 'Maritime archaeology in Northern Ireland: an interim statement', *Int j naut archaeol*, 25, 1996, pp 55–65.

See Section 4.2 Organisations for details of both the following:

Irish Underwater Archaeological Research Team (IUART)

Maritime Institute of Ireland, Dun Laoghaire

BOOKS

Bourke, Edward J, *Shipwrecks of the Irish coast 1105–1993*. Dublin: the author, 1994, 240 p, bibl, index. pb.
More than 2,000 wrecks from Louth to Donegal are detailed.

*Flanagan, Laurence, *Ireland's Armada legacy*. Dublin: Gill and Macmillan, 1988, 210 p, index. 0 7171 1593 3 pb.
Based on the material in the Ulster Museum which has over 95% of the world's authenticated Spanish Armada material, including that from the *Girona, La Trinidad Valencera* and *Santa Maria de la Rosa*.

—, *Irish shipwrecks of the Spanish Armada*. Dublin: Town House and Country House, 1995, 46 p. 0 946172 47 1 pb.
Introductory booklet.

McCaughan, Michael and Appleby, John (eds), *The Irish Sea: aspects of maritime history....* Belfast: Queen's Univ Belfast IIS and Ulster Folk and Transport Museum Cultra, 1989, viii, 177 p, bibl. 0 85389 327 6.
Covers the geographic context, Vikings, early Irish maritime trade and ships, the later middle ages, the *Trinidad Valencera* as case study, Belfast shipbuilding, etc.

McGrail, Sean, *Medieval boat and ship timbers from Dublin*. Dublin: Roy Ir Acad (= *Medieval Dublin excavations 1962–81*, series **B.3**, 1993, xi, 178 p, bibl. 1 874045 05 4 pb.
Study of the timbers recovered from Dublin's wet sites.

Martin and Parker on Armada wrecks, see earlier in this section.

O'Neill, T on merchants and mariners in medieval Ireland, see Section 6.11.6 Medieval.

Sténuit, R, *Treasures of the Armada*. London: Sphere (Cardinal), 1972, 271 p, no refs, index. 0 351 18326 4 pb.

Wilson, Ian, *Shipwrecks of the Ulster coast, from Carlingford Lough to Inishowen Head*. Coleraine: Impact Printing, 2 edn 1985, 188 p, bibl. 0 948154 0 5.

Section 6.20 Wetlands gives details of publications from IUART.

6.20
Wetlands Research

England, Wales, Scotland and Ireland are given in a single sequence for this relatively small (but burgeoning) topic. See also Section 6.19 Maritime, nautical and underwater archaeology. Listed here are organisations, journals and series, and books.

Organisations

(See Section 4.2 Organisations for addresses and other details where not given below)

Fenland Project, Cambridgeshire County Council
Humber Wetlands Survey, School of Geography and Earth Resources, University of Hull
Irish Archaeological Wetland Unit
Irish Underwater Archaeological Research Team
Irish Underwater Council (coordinates sport and research divers), 78A Patrick Street, Dun Laoghaire
North-West Wetlands Survey, Lancaster University Archaeological Unit, Storey Institute, Meeting House Lane, Lancaster LA1 1TH
Scottish Trust for Underwater Archaeology
Severn Estuary Levels Research Committee (listed under Wales in Section 4.2)
Wetland Archaeological Research Project (WARP)

Periodicals and series

Fenland research (0268–263X). 1983–. (Cambridge Archaeological Unit)
Irish Underwater Archaeology Research Team/ transactions (0791–8186). 1993–. Irregular. Dublin: Crannog Publications, Univ College Dublin
NewsWARP, newsletter of the Wetland Archaeological Research Project (0950–8244). Dec 1986–. (NB: contents of nos 1–16 and of WARP occas pap 1–8 are listed in NewsWARP 16, Oct 1994)
Severn Estuary Levels Research Committee annual reports (1354–7089)
Somerset Levels papers (0307–8582). 1975–89
WARP occasional papers (0950–8244). 1986– (various co-publishers)

Books

Coles, Bryony (ed), *The wetland revolution in prehistory: proceedings of a conference . . . Exeter 1991.* Exeter: WARP occas pap, 6, 1992, iv, 153 p, bibls. 0 9519117 0 8 pb.
Mostly overseas material, but includes papers on English and Irish topics.

— (ed), *Organic archaeological remains in south-west Britain: a survey of the available evidence.* Exeter: WARP occas pap, 4, 1990, 92 p, bibl.
Covers material from Cornwall, Devon, Somerset, Dorset and Wilts.

—, *Wetland management: a survey for English Heritage.* Exeter: WARP occas pap, 9, 1995, 126 p, bibl, index. 0 9519117 2 4 pb.
Nature conservation agencies were surveyed to see what practices could be adapted to wet (inland) archaeological sites to ensure their survival.

Coles, J M, *Precision, purpose and priorities in wetland archaeology.* Reprinted from Antiq j, 66, 1986 as WARP occas pap, 1, 1986

Coles, J M and B J (eds), *The archaeology of rural wetlands in England: proceedings of a conference . . . 1989.* Exeter/London: WARP/English Heritage, 1989 (= WARP occas pap, 2), iv, 54 p, bibl.
A dozen papers on different themes and areas.

***— and —, *Enlarging the past: the contribution of wetland archaeology.* Soc Antiq Scot monogr, 11, 1996, xx, 172 p, bibl. 0 903903 11 3 pb.
The 1995 Rhind Lectures cover the topic from the earliest bog discoveries to wetland finds made with the help of modern advanced technology; world-wide survey of the richness of information emerging and discussion of measures needed to preserve such productive wetlands.

— and — (eds), *People of the wetlands: bogs, bodies and lake-dwellers.* London: Thames and Hudson, 1989, 215 p, bibl, index. 0 500 02112 0.
Europe and further afield; includes Scottish and Irish crannogs, Glastonbury, Late Mesolithic coastal sites, Flag Fen; brief guide to sites and museums.

— and Goodburn, D M (eds), *Wet site excavation and survey: proceedings of a conference at the Museum of London, October 1990.* Exeter/London: WARP/Mus of London/NAS (= WARP occas pap, 5), 53 p, bibls. Paperback in plastic binder.

—, Fenwick, V and Hutchinson, G (eds), *A spirit of enquiry: essays for Ted Wright*. Exeter: WARP occas pap, 7, 1993, 96 p, bibls. o 9519117 1 6.
Papers in honour of the discoverer of the Brigg boats.

— et al (eds), *Waterlogged wood: the recording, sampling, conservation and curation of structural wood*. Exeter/London: WARP/English Heritage (= WARP occas pap, 3), 1990, 49 p, bibl.
More papers from a conference, including guidelines on the recording and treatment of structural wood.

See also Coles and Coles, Sweet Track to Glastonbury, in Section 6.11.2 Neolithic-Bronze Age; and J M Coles on Meare and on Glastonbury in Section 6.11.3 Iron Age.

Cowell, R W and Innes, J B, *The wetlands of Merseyside*. Lancaster: *Lancaster imprint*, 2, 1994, 288 p, bibl, index. o 901800 40 6 pb.
First of the North West Wetlands Surveys: contribution to methodology and new evidence from Mesolithic to post-medieval times. Further volumes will appear.

Cox, Margaret, Straker, Vanessa and Taylor, D (eds), *Wetlands: archaeology and nature conservation. Case studies and action plans*. London: HMSO, forthcoming 1996, xx, 284 p, bibls, index. o 11 300004 9 pb.
Papers from the Bristol international conference 1994: 22 papers, nearly all UK-based.

Earwood, Caroline, on domestic wooden artefacts (many from wet sites), see Section 6.13 Topic surveys.

Howard-Davies, Christine, Stocks, C and Innes, J, *Peat and the past: a survey and assessment of the lowland wetlands of NW England*. Lancaster: Lancaster Univ, 1988, 47 p, bibl, glossary. o 901272 50 7 pb.
Site list for Cumbria, Lancs, Merseyside, Greater Manchester and Cheshire.

Moloney, A and Jennings, David, *Excavations at Clonfinlough, Co Offaly*. Ir Archaeol Wetland Unit/ trans, 2, 1994, x, 131 p, refs.
Report on an LBA palisaded settlement.

— et al (eds), *Survey of the raised bogs of County Longford*. Ir Archaeol Wetland Unit/ trans, 1, 1993, 120 p, bibl.

Catalogue of over 650 sites discussing excavations, methodology and analysis.

— et al, *Blackwater survey and excavations*. Ir Archaeol Wetland Unit/ trans, 4, 1995, 205 p. (ISSN 0791-8186).
Includes parts of counties Galway, Offaly, Westmeath, Roscommon; excavations were undertaken at Bofeenaun (Co Mayo), Annaghcorrib (Co Galway) and Ballynahownwood (Co Westmeath). Emphasis on crannogs; also an important survey of artefact deterioration in peatlands.

Morrison, Ian, on Scottish crannogs, see entry in Section 6.11.3 Iron Age, under Scotland; similarly for Munro (1882).

Murphy, Peter and French, Charles (eds), *The exploitation of wetlands*. BARBS, 186 / Symposia Ass Envir Archaeol, 7, 1988, x, 371 p, chapter bibls. o 86054 535 0 pb.
Papers treat insects, mollusca, fish, woodland management, buried soils etc.

Nayling, Nigel T, *The archaeological wood survey: a review of the problems and potential of waterlogged structural wood*. London: Engl Heritage (= AML rep, 61/89) 1989, 61 p, plastic binder.
Treats 1968–87 material from England, Scotland and Wales, which is placed in a wider context by contributions from J M Coles and Jacqui Watson.

Noort, Robert Van de and Davies, Paul (ed Stephen Ellis), *Wetland heritage: an archaeological assessment of the Humber wetlands*. Kingston-upon-Hull: Humber Wetlands Project/ Engl Herit, 1993, 181 p, bibl.
List of sites with comments on their potential for preservation, threats to them, recommendations.

Raftery, B, *Mountdillon excavations 1985–91*. Ir Archaeol Wetland Unit/ trans, 3 (forthcoming 1996).
Trackway of Neolithic to Early Christian date and associated environmental evidence.

Spriggs, James A (ed), *A celebration of wood: proceedings of a conference held . . . in York, June 1993*. WARP occas pap, 8, [1994], 74 p. 1 874454 03 5 pb.

Turner and Scaife, on bog bodies, see Section 6.10 Science-based archaeology (under Environmental and biological examination).

Index of Authors and Subjects

Page numbers in **bold** indicate a main reference to a subject; for a society, bold within a sequence of numbers indicates the page number of the address. Within an entry, chronological references occur after general ones. A subject or author can occur on a page more than once.

British Association of Nature
Conservationists 69
British Association of Numismatic
Societies 69
British Association of Picture
Libraries and Agencies (BAPLA)
165
British Aviation Archaeological
Council 70
British Borehole Catalogue, CD-
ROM 29
British Brick Society 54, 70, 345
British Cave Research
Association 70
British Dovecote Society 70
British Gas Grassroots Action
Scheme 149
British Geological Survey 35, 70,
335, 336, 337
Scottish Office 117
British humanities index 28
British Library 34
Legal Deposit (copyright)
Office 10, 32, 34
map collections 34, 182
reference works 10, 23, 29,
31, 43, 44, 52, 163
British Library Document Supply
Centre (Boston Spa) 10, 34, 51,
234
British Museum 10, 44, 156, 266,
275, 279, 290
catalogues 13, 160
Department of Scientific
Research 237
maps 182
Object Name Working
Party 157
radiocarbon lab 241
reference collections of
pottery 159–60
Research Register 155
T D Kendrick Archive (stone
crosses) 48
British national bibliography 10,
29
British Numismatic Society 54, 70
British Photographers' Liaison
Committee 165
British Properties Federation 69
British Record Society 71
British Records Association 41,
70–1
British Sub-Aqua Club 71
British Tourist Authority 71
British Trust for Conservation
Volunteers 71
British Universities Film and Video
Council (BUFVC) 168
British Waterways Archive 71,
166, 346
British Waterways, Scottish
Region 117
Britnell, W J and Savory, H N 262
Brittany 28, 111, 178, 190, 257
Britton, F 160

Britton, J *see* Brayley, E W
Broderick, G 366
Brodribb, G 276
Bronze Age *see* Neolithic and Bronze
Age
bronzes, prehistoric 256, 257,
258–9, 260
brooches 268, 282, 293
Brooke, C J 220, 228
Brooke, D 300
Brooking Collection 219
Brooks, A *see* Pewsey, S
Brooks, Catherine M *see* McCarthy,
M
Brooks, Chris et al 322
Brooks, M M *see* O'Connor, S A
Brothwell, D R 244, 266; *see also*
Baker, J R; Stead, I M
Brothwell, D R and Higgs, E S 238
Brough of Birsay 300
Brown: Allen Brown Memorial
Lectures 164
Brown: Audrey Barrie Brown
Memorial fund 100, 146
Brown, A E 228, 276, 357
Brown, D *see* Strong, D
Brown, E H and Clayton, K 336
Brown, G J *see* Harris, E C
Brown, I W *see* Berry, A
Brown, J 357
Brown, L M and Christie, I R 20
Brown, M 290
Brown, M R (III) *see* Harris, E C
Brown, R A 310–11
Brown, S A 308
Browne, D M 285
Bruce, A P C 20
Bruce, J C 276–7
Bruce, J R 205
Bruce-Mitford, R L S 290
BRUFF Aerial Photographic
Survey 172
Brunaux, J-L 272
Brunsden, D *see* Goudie, A
Brunskill, R W 370
Bryon, R V and T N (eds) 32
Buchanan, R A 348–9
Buchanan, R A and Watkins, G 349
Buchanan, T 220–1
Büchsenschütz, O *see* Audouze, F
Buckinghamshire 139, 200, 202
Buckland, P C and Coope, G R 243
Buckley, D G (ed) 199
Buckley, V M 204, 256
Buckley, V M and Sweetman, P D
204
Budd, P et al 238
Bugsworth Basin, Derbys 86
Buikstra, J E and Ubelaker, D H
244–5
The Builder 13
building conservation 65, 67, 71,
74, 75, 79, 88–9, 101, 149,
219–23, 225
organisations 219–20, 223
and see also Association of

Conservation Officers;
Pembrokeshire Coast
National Park Authority
Building Conservation Trust *see*
UPKEEP
building materials 64, 221, 275;
see also bricks and brickwork;
stone; thatch *see* Cairdean
nanTaighean Tugha
Building Preservation Trusts 64,
67, 222
Building Research Establishment 71,
219
buildings
conservation *see* building
conservation
ecclesiastical *see* abbeys and
priories; cathedrals; churches
and chapels; monasteries
historic, listed and vernacular
see architecture
thatched *see* Cairdean nan
Taighean Tugha
Buildings at Risk Trust 71
Buildings of England Office 71
Buildings of England series 47, 71,
190, 368
Buildings of Ireland series 194
Buildings of Scotland series 122,
192–3, 358
Buildings of Scotland Trust 193
Buildings of Wales series 192
*Bulletin: Groupe d'Histoire des
Mines et de la Métallurgie* 346
Bulletin of primitive technology 249
Burgess, C et al 256–7; *see also*
Colquohoun, I; Lynch, F; Miket,
R; Schmidt, P K
Burgess, C and Gerloff, S 257
Burgess, C and Miket, R (eds) 257
Burgess, F K 322
burghs, Scottish 123, 127, 365
burial grounds *see* cemeteries
burials
and the law 227
located by forensic
archaeology 230, 246
by period 256, 265, 281, 288,
291, 292, 298, 324
post-excavation 232
see also barrows; Cave Burial
Research Project; cemeteries;
human skeletal remains;
London, Spitalfields; Sutton
Hoo; tombs
Burl, H A W 190, 257
Burman, P (ed) 221
Burman, P, Feilden, B and Kennet,
Lord (eds) 215
Burman, P and Stapleton, H 215
Burnell, S *see* Hooke, D
Burnett, C J and Tabraham, C J
325
Burnham, B C and Davies, J L
(eds) 285
Burnham, D K 174

Geological Association 336
Geological Society 53, 83, 335
Geological Survey of Ireland 131, 172
Geological Survey of Northern Ireland 131
Geologists' Association 83, 335
geology 24, 29, 35, 53, 131, 183, 250, 335–8, 344; see also preceding entries and British Geological Survey
geophysics and geophysical prospection 19, 47, 70, 170, 228, 229, 239, 240, 241
GEOREF 29
Georgian Group 83–4, 89, 219
Georgian period 182, 184, 357; see also Georgian Group; Irish Georgian Society
Gerlach, G and Hachmann, R 16
Gerloff, S 258; see also Burgess, C
German Archaeological Institute, Rome 105
German language 224, 232, 239–40, 273
dictionaries etc 174, 175, 176
Germany 54, 279, 303, 312, 369
abstracting services 26, 27, 28
Gerrard, C see Darvill, T
Getty Art History Information Program 175
Getty Conservation Institute 222
Getty: J Paul Getty Jr General Charitable Trust 147
Getty thesaurus 159
Gibbard, P L 250; see also Ehlers, J
Gibson, A M 201, 258
Gibson, A M and Woods, A 334
Gibson, D B see Arnold, B
Gibson, J S W and Peskett, P 42
Gilchrist, R and Mytum, H (eds) 312
'Gildas' 328
Giles, C and Goodall, I 350
Giles, C and Wade Martins, S (eds) 370
Gilg, A W 217
Gillespie, R 241
Gillingham, J see Falkus, M
Gillmor, D 344; see also Fenton, A
GIS see Geographical Information Systems
Gladfelter, B G see Singer, R
Gladwin, D D and J M 353
Glamorgan 192, 198, 262, 270, 299, 317
Glamorgan-Gwent Archaeological Trust 115, 142, 171
Glasgow 180, 193, 354, 355
Mitchell Library 37
radiocarbon lab 241
University 50, 52, 116, 152, and see also CTICH
Glasgow archaeol j 164
Glasgow West Conservation Trust 119, 223, 374

glass 27, 159, 240, 333, 346, 347, 350, 351
beads 267
conference 163
Roman 277
medieval 309
stained see window glass
see also Association for the History of Glass Ltd; Glass Circle; Society of Glass Technology; window glass
Glass Circle 84
Glasscock, R E 320; see Stephens, N
Glassie, H 344
Glastonbury 266, 381
Glencolmcille, summer school 226
Glenfiddich Living Scotland Awards 150
Glenveagh National Park 144
Glin, The Knight of and Bowe, P (eds) 359
Glin, The Knight of see also Malins, E
Global Positioning System (GPS) 183
glossaries 173–7
Gloucester 180
Gloucestershire 140, 200, 201, 202, 370
GMPCA 237, 239
Goad, C E, fire insurance plans 182, 184
Goddard, S 19
Godfrey, A 186
Godfrey, E S 350
Gododdin (poem) 299, 301
Godwin, H 245
gold and gold-working 162, 240, 258, 261, 265, 301, 353
Goldberg, P see Courty, M
Goldsmiths' Company's Charities 147
Gomme, G L 13, 14, 16–17
Goodall, I see Giles, C
Goodburn, D M see Coles, J M and B J
Goodchild, P see Lambert, D
Gooder, E 363
Goodman, W L 350
Gordon, J E and Sutherland, D G (eds) 337
Gosling, P 194, 204, 320–1
gospel-books, Insular 289
Goudie, A 245, 336
Goudie, A and Brunsden, D 180
Gould, S see Ayris, I
Goulty, G A 336
Goulty, S 357
Govan 302
Gower database 47
Gowers, Sir E 209
Gowlett, J A J and Hedges, R E M 241
GPS see Global Positioning System
Graham, B J 321

Graham, B J and Proudfoot, L J 344
Graham, J J 177
Graham-Campbell, J 297, 301
Grant, A see Astill, G G
Grant, E 11
Grant, Eric see Dolphin, P
Grant, E G see Bintliff, J
Grant, S A V see Booth, B K W
grants and grant-making bodies 145–51, 220
Grants disk 145
Graphic archaeology 65, 230
Graveney boat 291
Graves, C see Heizer, R F
Graves, E B (ed) 20
Graves-Brown, P, Jones, S and Gamble, C 330
gravestones and grave memorials 56, 83, 167, 220, 325, 336
graveyards see cemeteries
Gray, I 44
Gray, J M and Lowe, J J (eds) 337
Greater London 73, 140, 361
Greater London Record Office and History Library 34
Greater Manchester 140, 199, 352, 382
Green, E R R 350, 355
Green, H S and Walker, E 251
Green, J 378
Green, M J 175, 267; see also Barrett, J C
Green, S 328
Green, S H 251
Green, S W and Zvelebil, M 254
Greene, J P 312
Greene, K 188, 224–5, 278
Greenfield, J 155, 211
Greenhill, B 377
Greenland 28
Greeno, P see Blackaby, J R
Greenwell, W and Rolleston, G 258
Greenwood, J 347
Greig, J et al 245
Greig, M K see Shepherd, I A G
Gresham, C 317
Grew, F and de Neergaard, M 312
Grierson, P 312
Griffin, D J and Lincoln, S 45
Griffith, F 170
Griffith, J E 262
Griffiths, A and Williams, R 44
Griffiths, D M see Charleston, R J
Griffiths, N et al 231; see also Cowgill, J
Grigson, C see Wilson, B
Grimes, W F 161, 258, 278, 312
Grinsell, L V 160, 258
Grinsell, L V, Rahtz, P and Williams, D P 234
Groam House lecture series 164, 301
Grogan, E and Hillery, T 194